Fourth Edition

Research Methods in Psychology

John J. Shaughnessy
Hope College

Eugene B. Zechmeister
Loyola University of Chicago

The McGraw-Hill Companies, Inc.
New York   St. Louis   San Francisco   Auckland   Bogotá   Caracas
Lisbon   London   Madrid   Mexico City   Milan   Montreal   New Delhi
Paris   San Juan   Singapore   Sydney   Tokyo   Toronto

McGraw-Hill

A Division of The McGraw·Hill Companies

RESEARCH METHODS IN PSYCHOLOGY
International Editions 1997

Acknowledgements appear on pages 509–513 and on this page by reference.

1 2 3 4 5 6 7 8 9 0 KKP UPE 9 8 7

This book was set in Palatino by Ruttle, Shaw & Wetherill, Inc.
The editors were Brian McKean and Peggy Rehberger;
the production supervisor was Louise Karam.
The design manager was Anne Manning.
Original drawings by Fran Hughes.
New figures were done by Fine Line Illustrations, Inc.
Project supervision was done by Ruttle, Shaw & Wetherill, Inc.

Library of Congress Cataloging-in-Publication Data

Shaughnessy, John J., (date)
    Research methods in psychology / John J. Shaughnessy, Eugene B.
Zechmeister. – 4th ed.
      p.   cm.
    Includes bibliographical references and indexes.
    ISBN 0-07-057272-0
    1. Psychology–Research–Methodology.   2. Psychology,
Experimental.   I. Zechmeister, Eugene B., (date).   II. Title.
BF76.5.S46 1997
150'.72–dc20
                              96-22572

When ordering this title, use ISBN 0-07-114710-1

Printed in Singapore

About the Authors

JOHN J. SHAUGHNESSY is Professor of Psychology at Hope College, a relatively small, select, undergraduate liberal arts college in Holland, Michigan. After completing the B.S. degree at Loyola University of Chicago in 1969, he received the Ph.D. in 1972 from Northwestern University. He is a Fellow of the American Psychological Society, and he has been a frequent contributor of research on human memory, a reviewer for several journals, and coauthor, with Benton J. Underwood, of *Experimentation in Psychology* (Wiley, 1975). He was selected by students in 1992 as the Hope Outstanding Professor Educator, and his teaching expertise has been recognized by his colleagues' selection of him as a campus teaching consultant.

EUGENE B. ZECHMEISTER is Professor of Psychology at Loyola University of Chicago, a large metropolitan university where he has taught both undergraduate and graduate courses since 1970. Professor Zechmeister completed his B.A. in 1966 at the University of New Mexico. He later received both the M.S. (1968) and Ph.D. (1970) from Northwestern University. A specialist in the field of human cognition, Professor Zechmeister authored, with S. E. Nyberg, *Human Memory: An Introduction to Research and Theory* (Brooks/Cole, 1982), and with J. E. Johnson, *Critical Thinking: A Functional Approach* (Brooks/Cole, 1992). He is a Fellow of both of the American Psychological Association (Divisions 1, 2, and 3) and the American Psychological Society. In 1994, he was awarded the Loyola University Sujack Award for Teaching Excellence in the College of Arts and Sciences. Professor Zechmeister currently is the Undergraduate Program Director for the Loyola University of Chicago Psychology Department.

To Paula (J.J.S.)

To Ruth O'Keane and to the Memory of James O'Keane,
Kathleen O'Keane Zechmeister, and My Mother (E.B.Z.)

Contents

PART IV

APPLIED RESEACH

9 Single-Case Research Designs

10 Quasi-Experimental Designs and Program Evaluation

Preface

We have written a broad-based introduction to research methods in psychology that emphasizes a multimethod approach to hypothesis testing. Various methodological approaches in psychology (e.g., naturalistic observation, survey research, and experimentation) are viewed as complementary. We hope students will recognize that all methodologies have limitations as well as strengths. Because of this, we will reach our goal of understanding behavior and mental processes only when we combine evidence gathered using many different approaches.

We continue in this edition to draw from the rich world of psychological research for our examples. Students will find that we introduce a wide array of contemporary research issues while discussing research methods. Among the many topics highlighted are social loafing, people's perception of pain, relationship between temperature and aggression, cognitive theories of depression, racial interactions, discrimination in the workplace, and behavioral treatments of maladaptive behavior. As they progress in their understanding of psychological research methods, students will find that they have learned much about psychology in general. Of course, we also hope that by using a variety of research examples we have made this task of learning about psychological research an interesting one.

Students will find the necessary background to help them do research as part of their undergraduate or postgraduate careers. Nevertheless, many students who study research methodology will only be research consumers rather than research producers. With this in mind, we have attempted to help all students become discerning research consumers by developing their critical thinking skills. We emphasize that research is a form of problem solving that begins with the selection of an appropriate method to answer a research question, and continues through the process of critically analyzing the strengths and weaknesses of the evidence obtained. We include Challenge Questions at the end of each chapter to permit students to test their critical thinking skills. Many of these questions are based on reports of research found in popular news outlets. We urge instructors to provide students with additional opportunities to develop their analytical abilities by encouraging them to examine critically other reports of psychology-related research findings that appear in newspapers and other media.

As experienced instructors of research methods, we are aware that many students approach a research methods course with apprehension. Their concern sometimes arises from anxiety about the perceived difficulty of the material. To address this concern we have tried in this edition to increase the clarity of our presentation to help students more easily gain the knowledge they need. At times, though, students' concerns arise because they fail to see a relationship between their interests in studying and applying psychology and the requirement to study research methods. A familiar lament is, "I did not become a psychology major because I wanted to do research!" We continue to work in this edition to find ways to show the skeptical student that psychology, in all its manifestations, has a scientific foundation.

CHANGES IN THE FOURTH EDITION

Previous users of this book will find that the major organization of earlier editions is still present. However, we also have made some changes based on suggestions of those who have used or reviewed the previous edition. We highlight these changes roughly in the order that they appear in the text.

We have made a significant change in nomenclature. The fourth edition of the APA *Publication Manual* (1994) recommends that the term *subjects* be changed to a more descriptive term, such as students, children, or older adults, or to participants if no more specific term is appropriate. We also decided to replace the term *subject variable* (see Chapter 1) by identifying this type of variable as an *individual differences variable* or, sometimes, a *natural groups variable*. We have continued to use the term *subjects* when referring to animals in research or to terms in generic statistical analyses (e.g., the *subjects* term in analyses of variance). We also made a change in the term we use for the designs discussed in Chapter 7. We now refer to them as Repeated Measures designs, because we think this term is stylistically preferable and because it is consistent with the terminology in many statistics books.

To make Chapter 1 more manageable for both the instructor and the student, we reduced the number of new concepts introduced in Chapter 1. We moved much of the discussion of correlation to Chapter 4 (Correlational Research: Surveys), and we moved some of the discussion of control techniques to Chapter 6 (Independent Groups Designs). Even with these changes, we still view Chapter 1 as the first of many lessons students will have emphasizing the vocabulary of the research enterprise. Students need to become familiar with the concepts introduced in Chapter 1; this familiarity will enable them to appreciate the concepts more fully as they progress through the course.

We continue in this edition to treat ethical issues early in the book, in Chapter 2. Although instructors will find that they can introduce this material in Chapter 2 at any point in the course without too much difficulty, we want to point out another change in this edition. We have attempted to distribute the discussion of ethical issues more evenly throughout the book by discussing them in the context of particular methodologies. Deception, for example, is covered at length in Chapter 2, but is also raised as an issue when a study using deception is discussed in Chapter 6. Also new to this edition is a series of "What Do You Think?" sections in Chapter 2. In these sections we ask students (and instructors) to respond to difficult ethical research dilemmas (e.g., the use of animals in psychological research). We hope these changes better inform students about the important role ethics plays in psychological research.

One major change reflects our continuing journey to find the best way to help integrate research designs and statistics. In the third edition we tried to concentrate material on statistics in a single chapter, Analysis of Experiments. Many users of the third edition pointed out problems with this approach. Thus, having been detoured, we return in this edition to an approach resembling the one we used in the first two editions. Material on statistical analysis is presented in sections of the chapters in which the corresponding research designs are covered. We also discuss effect sizes, as we did in the third edition, as well as alternatives to traditional hypothesis testing techniques, such as the use of confidence intervals. We have retained a statistics appendix (Appendix A), but in this edition the emphasis is on interpretation of output from statistical software packages.

Finally, we have changed the title of what we had called the "writing appendix." Appendix C is now titled Communication in Psychology. Given the explosion in electronic communication, it seemed appropriate to broaden our presentation in this section to include use of the Internet. We have illustrated for students some of the many ways in which scientists are making use of electronic communication (e.g., e-mail) as a research tool. We have retained our presentation of guidelines for effective writing and a sample manuscript in APA format. The material on writing is based on the most recent edition of the APA *Publication Manual*. We also changed the way the comments on the APA-style sample paper are presented. We replaced the previous edition's typed notes in the paper's margins with handwritten notes on the paper itself. Our hope is that students will be more likely to make use of the information in this format.

By the way, because the authors, too, have found the electronic highway an indispensable route to take, we both have e-mail addresses to which comments may be sent:

John J. Shaughnessy: shaughnessy@hope.edu
Eugene B. Zechmeister: ezechme@orion.it.luc.edu

Or, if you wish, we may be contacted through the World Wide Web page that is associated with this book: HTTP://www./uc.edu/depts/psychology/research_methods.html. We urge both instructors and students to visit the page, because it contains not only information about the book and suppplementary material but also links with the American Psychological Association and American Psychological Society, as well as information and suggestions for using the World Wide Web for psychological research. Whatever means you choose to use, we do welcome comments about the book, including suggestions for future editions.

We believe that the present edition retains a structure that permits instructors considerable flexibility in the organization of their courses. Even the authors do not always require students to read every chapter in a particular semester. We sometimes make changes, for example, depending on the nature of the research project assigned for a given class. Nevertheless, we consider Chapters 1, 3, 6, 7, 8, and 10 to be an essential core for most research methods courses. The remaining chapters and appendixes can be used to expand on this core material according to the instructor's preferences.

WORDS OF THANKS

We would like to thank the following reviewers for their many helpful comments and suggestions. If we didn't make every change suggested, be assured that we gave every suggestion serious consideration. This most recent edition benefited greatly from the reviews of the previous edition provided by: Bernard Beins, Ithaca College; Dennis Cogan, Texas Tech University; Steven L. Cohen, Bloomsburg University of Pennsylvania; Wendy Domjan, University of Texas at Austin; Dana S. Dunn, Moravian College; Rosemary T. Hornak, Meredith College; John C. Jahnke, Miami University of Ohio; Rosanne Lorden, Eastern Kentucky University; Catherine S. Murray, St. Joseph's University; and Jeanne Zechmeister, Loyola University.

As usual, we didn't do this alone. Many people contributed in significant ways to the preparation of this edition, some more than they will ever know. Unfortunately, space doesn't permit us to name them all. We do wish, however, to highlight the contributions made by Kathy Adamski, Mark Cook, and Paula Shaughnessy, especially, but not solely, for their help with Appendix C. As she has done with previous editions, Liz Zechmeister did a great job preparing the indexes. With this edition she also took over the time-intensive job of securing permissions for authors' works. Of special importance were the contributions of Jeanne S. Zechmeister, who brought particular expertise, patience, insight, and wonderful writing skills to this project. Jeanne was reviewer, sounding board, and steadfast supporter throughout this edition's preparation, but, most importantly to EBZ, his "bestest friend."

We also want to acknowledge the much appreciated support of colleagues in our respective psychology departments. Staff members at both Hope College and Loyola University of Chicago also played a critical role in this edition, as they have in previous editions. Many individuals associated with McGraw-Hill, Inc. made this book happen. We'd like to single out Jane Vaicunas for her continued support of this project, Brian McKean for his supervisory skills, Susan Elia and Peggy Rehberger for coordinating so much that needed coordinating, and Anne Manning for finding some great photos. Peg Markow of Ruttle, Shaw & Wetherill, Inc., oversaw production and kept us on schedule. Finally, Fran Hughes provided us with beautiful drawings to help humanize our presentation of research methods.

John J. Shaughnessy
Eugene B. Zechmeister

I

General
Issues

Chapter 1

Introduction

PSYCHOLOGY AS A SCIENCE

There is no record of who first observed behavior carefully and systematically, who conducted the first public opinion survey, or even of who performed the first psychology experiment. We don't really know exactly when psychology first became an independent discipline. It emerged gradually, with its roots in the thinking of Aristotle (the "father" of all psychology; Keller, 1937), in the writings of later philosophers such as Descartes and Locke, and, even later, in the work of early 19th-century physiologists and physicists.

The date usually taken to mark psychology's official beginning is 1879. In that year Wilhelm Wundt established a formal psychology laboratory in Leipzig, Germany. Wundt, like many scientists of his time, had a doctoral degree in medicine. He even published for a while in the fields of anatomy and physiology. These experiences gave Wundt a basis for his ideas about a "physiological psychology" that led to his scientific approach to psychology. Dozens of researchers from around the world came to his psychology laboratory to learn about the "new" discipline. As a consequence, from Wundt's laboratory a scientific psychology spread quickly to the intellectual centers of the world. According to one noted historian, Wilhelm Wundt was the first person "who without reservation is properly called a psychologist" (Boring, 1950, p. 316).

Whatever exact date one accepts for the beginning of a scientific psychology, we can see that the enterprise is little more than 100 years old. Near the end of the 19th century, in 1892, the American Psychological Association (APA) was formed, with G. Stanley Hall as its first president. Hall had been a student at

Wilhelm Wundt
(1832–1920)

William James
(1842–1910)

Harvard of the well-known American philosopher and psychologist William James. In 1878, James awarded Hall the first Ph.D. in psychology given in the United States. After receiving his degree, Hall left the United States to study with Wundt in Germany (Boring, 1950). Still later, in 1887, Hall founded the first psychology journal in the United States, the *American Journal of Psychology*. The APA had only a few dozen members in its first year; 100 years later, in 1992, when the APA celebrated its 100th birthday, there were approximately 70,000 members (see American Psychological Association, 1991).

Psychology has changed significantly since its beginnings. Wundt and his colleagues were primarily interested in questions of sensation and perception—for instance, visual illusions and imagery. Experiments on reaction time also were conducted with the goal of measuring the time necessary for various cognitive processes, such as those involved in making choices (Boring, 1950). Psychologists continue to be interested in sensation and perception, and Wundt's procedures form the basis of some of the experimental methods in use today. However, research on sensation and perception represents but a fraction of the research undertaken in contemporary psychology. Today psychologists are interested in a myriad of topics, including those in such general areas as clinical, social, industrial, counseling, physiological, cognitive, educational, and developmental psychology.

Psychology has also not developed strictly as a laboratory science. Although laboratory investigation remains at the heart of psychological inquiry, psychologists and other behavioral scientists do research in schools, clinics, businesses, hospitals, and other nonlaboratory settings. Many research psychologists, for instance, are engaged in program evaluation, a type of research in which the impact of large-scale interventions on groups or institutions is evaluated. Program evaluators confront questions such as whether a new management–labor relations program will lead to increased employee morale and company productivity, or whether the nationwide Head Start program has significantly raised the IQ of hundreds of thousands of preschoolers (see Chapter 10).

Promotion of psychological research is a concern of the APA as well as the more recently founded American Psychological Society (APS). Formed in 1988 to emphasize mainly scientific issues in psychology, APS has grown at a phenomenal rate. In just its first two years, membership increased to over 10,000 (McGaugh, 1990). While many psychologists choose to join either APA or APS, many join both. APA and APS both sponsor annual conventions, which psychologists attend to learn about the most recent developments in their fields; each organization also publishes scientific journals in order to communicate the latest research findings to its members and to society in general; and both organizations encourage student affiliation, which provides educational and research opportunities for both undergraduate and graduate psychology students. By affiliating with APA and APS, students can subscribe to major psychology journals at a relatively low cost as well as become involved at an early stage in a career in psychology. Information about joining APA and APS as a regular member or as a student affiliate can be obtained by writing to the respective head offices, or by consulting their World Wide Web pages on the Internet. (APA: http: //www.apa.org APS: http://psych.hanover.edu/APS).

THE SCIENTIFIC METHOD

There is one way in which psychology has not changed in the 100 years or so of its existence: The scientific method is still emphasized as the basis for investigation. The founding of Wundt's laboratory marked the beginning of the formal application of the scientific method to problems in psychology. This method is not identified with particular kinds of equipment, nor is it associated exclusively with specific research procedures. The scientific method is something abstract. It is an approach to knowledge that is best described by distinguishing it from what might be called *nonscientific* or "everyday" approaches to knowledge.

SCIENTIFIC AND NONSCIENTIFIC APPROACHES TO KNOWLEDGE

Several major differences between a scientific and a nonscientific approach to knowledge are outlined in Table 1.1. Collectively, the characteristics listed under "Scientific" define what is called the **scientific method.** The distinctions made in Table 1.1 between a scientific and a nonscientific approach highlight differences that frequently exist between an informal and casual approach, which often characterizes our everyday thinking, and thinking characteristic of the scientist's approach to knowledge.

General Approach   Many everyday judgments are made intuitively. This usually means that we act on the basis of what "feels right" or what "seems

TABLE 1.1   CHARACTERISTICS OF SCIENTIFIC AND NONSCIENTIFIC (EVERYDAY) APPROACHES
TO KNOWLEDGE*

	Nonscientific (everyday)	Scientific
General Approach:	Intuitive	Empirical
Observation:	Casual, uncontrolled	Systematic, controlled
Reporting:	Biased, subjective	Unbiased, objective
Concepts:	Ambiguous, with surplus meanings	Clear definitions, operational specificity
Instruments:	Inaccurate, imprecise	Accurate, precise
Measurement:	Not valid or reliable	Valid and reliable
Hypotheses:	Untestable	Testable
Attitude:	Uncritical, accepting	Critical, skeptical

*Based in part on distinctions suggested by Marx (1963).

reasonable." Intuition is not based on a formal decision process, such as that of deductive logic, nor is it based on information that was taught to us or we acquired through direct experience. The many everyday inferences and conclusions reached intuitively are the product of insight and of what we quickly perceive as true.

Intuition is a valuable cognitive process. We frequently have little to go on other than what intuition suggests is the right answer or the proper course to follow. Intuition can also help us make decisions in situations that we have not encountered before. Consider, for example, what intuition might suggest as the answer to a question based on the following situation:

> Assume that on two different occasions you are the victim of a street crime. Let us say you are walking down the street and someone tries to grab your wallet or purse. The thief begins to wrestle with you in order to get it. You find yourself in need of assistance. On one occasion there is a crowd of bystanders who witness the attempted robbery. On the other occasion there is only one person who sees the event.
> The question is, in which situation would you be more likely to receive help, when many people are present or when only one person is present?

Intuition would suggest that the more people present, the greater the chances that at least one person would help. Surprisingly, social psychologists have determined that just the opposite is true. A bystander is more likely to act in an emergency when alone than when a group of people is present (Latané & Darley, 1970; see also Chapter 3 in this book).

Our intuition about what is true does not always agree with what is actually true because we fail to recognize that our perceptions may be distorted by what are called cognitive biases or because we neglect to weigh available evidence appropriately (Kahneman & Tversky, 1973; Tversky & Kahneman, 1974). One such cognitive bias, for instance, is called *illusory correlation*. This is our tendency to perceive a relationship between events when none exists. To illustrate this bias, Ward and Jenkins (1965) showed people the results of a hypothetical 50-day cloud-seeding experiment. For each of the 50 days, the research participants were told whether cloud seeding had been done and whether it had rained on that day. Ward and Jenkins constructed the results so there was actually no relationship between cloud seeding and the likelihood of rain—rain was equally likely on days when seeding had and had not been done. Nonetheless, people were convinced the evidence supported their intuitive supposition that cloud seeding and rain varied together. One possible basis for the illusory-correlation bias is that we are more likely to notice events consistent with our beliefs than events that violate our beliefs. Thus, in Ward and Jenkins's study, people may have been more likely to notice and remember the days on which cloud seeding was followed by rain than the days on which clouds were seeded in vain because they believe cloud seeding produces rain.

The scientific approach to knowledge is empirical rather than intuitive. An **empirical approach** emphasizes direct observation and experimentation as a way of answering questions. This does not mean that intuition plays no role in science. Any scientist can probably recount tales of obtaining empirical results that intuition had suggested would emerge. On the other hand, the same scientist is also likely to have come up with just as many findings that were counterintuitive. Research at first may be guided by what the scientist's intuition suggests is the proper direction to take. Eventually, however, the scientist strives to be guided by what direct observation and experimentation reveal to be true.

Observation   We can learn a great deal about behavior by simply observing the actions of others. However, everyday observations are not always made carefully or systematically. Most people do not attempt to control or eliminate factors that might influence the events they are observing. As a consequence, erroneous conclusions are often drawn. Consider, for instance, the classic case of Clever Hans. Hans was a horse that was said by his owner, a German mathematics teacher, to have amazing talents. Hans could count, do simple addition and subtraction (even involving fractions), read German, answer simple questions ("What is the lady holding in her hands?"), give the date, and tell time (Watson, 1914/1967). Hans answered questions by tapping with his forefoot or by pointing with his nose at different alternatives shown to him. His owner considered Hans to be truly intelligent and denied using any tricks to guide his horse's behavior. And, in fact, Clever Hans was clever even when the questioner was someone other than his owner.

Newspapers carried accounts of Hans's performances, and hundreds of people came to view this amazing horse (see Figure 1.1). In 1904, a scientific commission was established with the goal of discovering the basis for Hans's abilities. The scientists found that Hans was no longer clever if either of two circumstances existed. First, Hans did not know the answers to questions if the questioner also did not know the answers. Second, Hans was not very clever if he could not see his questioner. It was discovered that Hans was responding to very slight movements of the questioner. A slight bending forward by the ques-

FIGURE 1.1   Top: Clever Hans performing before onlookers. Bottom: Hans being tested under more controlled conditions when Hans cound not see the questioner.

tioner would start Hans tapping, and any movement upward or backward would cause Hans to stop tapping. The commission demonstrated that questioners were unintentionally cueing Hans in this way.

This famous account of Clever Hans illustrates the fact that scientific observation (unlike casual observation) is systematic and controlled. Indeed, it has been suggested that **control** is the essential ingredient of science, distinguishing it from nonscientific procedures (Boring, 1954; Marx, 1963). In the case of Clever Hans, investigators exercised control by manipulating, *one at a time*, conditions such as whether the questioner knew the answer to the questions asked and whether Hans could see the questioner (see Figure 1.1). By exercising control, taking care to investigate the effect of various factors one by one, the scientist seeks to gain a clearer picture of the factors that actually produce a phenomenon.

The factors that the researcher controls or manipulates in order to determine their effect on behavior are called the **independent variables.** In the simplest of studies, the independent variable has two levels. These two levels often represent the presence and the absence of some treatment, respectively. The condition in which the treatment is present is commonly called the *experimental condition*; the condition in which the treatment is absent is called the *control condition.* If we wanted to study the effect of drinking alcohol on the ability to process complex information quickly and accurately, for example, the independent variable would be the presence or absence of alcohol in a drink that participants were given. Participants in the experimental condition would receive alcohol; participants in the control condition would receive the same drink without alcohol. The levels of the independent variable do not always represent the presence and the absence of some treatment; moreover, an independent variable may have more than two levels. What is critical is that the levels differ with respect to the variable of interest. For example, Heath and Davidson (1988) recruited female college students to participate in a study designed to aid in the development of a rape-prevention pamphlet. When volunteers appeared in the laboratory, they were asked to review one of three packages of materials that they were told was being considered for possible inclusion in the pamphlet. The three packages of materials varied in the manner in which rape was described. Specifically, the materials to be reviewed presented rape as being very controllable, somewhat controllable, or not at all controllable. After reviewing the materials, the women were asked a series of questions regarding their own perceptions of the risk of rape. The independent variable in this study was the degree of control emphasized in the pamphlet materials; it had three levels (high, medium, low).

Sometimes the levels of the independent variable are selected by a researcher rather than manipulated. This is typically the case when an individual differences variable serves as the independent variable. An **individual differences variable** is a characteristic or trait that varies consistently across individuals. For example, a researcher may be interested in how depression affects perceptions of other people (Albright & Henderson, 1995). Do depressed individuals, for instance, perceive others more or less accurately than individuals who are not depressed? Level of depression would be the independent variable in this study. Level of depression is an individual differences variable and typically is not manipulated by a researcher; rather, the researcher controls this independent variable by systematically selecting individuals who exhibit varying levels of naturally occurring depression. Intelligence, age, aggressiveness, gender, and fraternity or sorority membership are other examples of individual differences variables. Because individuals are selected from preexisting groups, such as those who are depressed, female, aggressive, and so forth, these variables are also sometimes referred to as *natural groups variables.*

The term *independent variable* is used both for individual differences variables when levels of the variable are selected (e.g., level of depression) and for manipulated variables when the levels are implemented by the researcher (e.g., type of booklet describing rape). Nevertheless, as you will see later in Chapter 6, there are important differences between these two kinds of independent variables.

The measures of behavior that are used to assess the effect (if any) of the independent variables are called **dependent variables.** In our example of a study that investigates the effects of alcohol on processing complex information, the researcher might measure the number of errors made by control and experimental participants when playing a difficult video game. Errors, then, would be the dependent variable. Most studies in psychology are done in order to discover the nature of the relationship between particular independent and dependent variables. In the Heath and Davidson (1988) rape study, there were several dependent variables, which represented the women's responses to questions on the rape-perception questionnaire. The results showed that women who read materials emphasizing rape as an uncontrollable event reported higher anxiety when outside on the street or inside their homes, and a greater intention to take precautionary steps, than did women who reviewed the materials describing rape as more controllable. Interestingly, results of additional experiments carried out by Heath and Davidson (1988) indicated that although uncontrollable rape is definitely viewed as anxiety producing, the "intent" to be more cautious reported by their research participants may not always be followed by actual changes in behaviors. Unfortunately, when rape is perceived as an uncontrollable event some women may view attempts to reduce their vulnerability to attacks as futile.

If changes in the dependent variable are to be interpreted unambiguously as a result of the effect of the independent variable, proper control techniques must be used. The story of Clever Hans was used to show how scientists use control to eliminate alternative explanations for a phenomenon (e.g., that Clever Hans was, in fact, clever). Throughout this text, we describe specific control procedures used by psychologists when carrying out research (see especially Chapters 6 and 7).

Reporting   If we ask someone to *report* to us about events that occurred in our absence, we probably want the report to be unbiased and objective. Otherwise we will be unable to determine exactly what happened. As you might imagine, personal biases and subjective impressions often enter into everyday reports that we receive. Ask anyone to describe an event to you and you are likely to receive not merely details of the event but also personal impressions.

You may also find that the details reported to you are not the ones you would have reported. We often report events in terms of our own interests and attitudes. Obviously, these interests and attitudes do not always coincide with those of others. The next time you take a class examination, poll several classmates on their impressions of the test. Their reports are likely to vary dramatically, depending on such factors as how well prepared they were, what they concentrated on when they studied, and their expectations about what the instructor was going to emphasize on the test.

When scientists report their findings, they seek to separate what they have observed from what they conclude or infer on the basis of these observations. For example, consider the photograph in Figure 1.2. How would you describe to someone what you see there? One way to describe this scene is to say that two people are running along a path with one person in front of the other. You might also describe this scene as two people *racing* each other. If you use this second description, you are reporting an inference drawn from what you have seen and not just reporting what you have observed. The description of two people running would be preferred in a scientific report.

This distinction between description and inference in reporting can be carried to extremes. For example, describing what is shown in Figure 1.2 as running could be considered an inference, the actual observation being that two people are moving their legs up and down and forward in rapid, long strides.

FIGURE 1.2   How would you describe this scene?

Such a literal description also would not be appropriate. The point is that, in scientific reporting, observers must guard against a tendency to draw inferences too quickly. Further, events should be described in sufficient detail without including trivial and unnecessary minutiae. Proper methods for making observations and reporting them are discussed in Chapter 3.

Scientific reporting seeks to be unbiased and objective. One accepted check on whether a report is unbiased is whether it can be verified by more than one independent observer. A measure of interobserver agreement, for example, is usually found in observational studies (see Chapter 3). Unfortunately, many biases are subtle and not always detected even in scientific reporting. Consider the fact that there is a species of fish in which the eggs are incubated in the mouth of the male parent until they hatch. The first scientist to observe the eggs disappear into their father's mouth could certainly be forgiven for assuming, momentarily, that he was eating them. That's simply what we expect organisms to do with their mouths! But the careful observer waits, watches for unexpected results, and takes nothing for granted.

Concepts We use the term *concepts* to refer to things (both living and inanimate), to events (things in action), and to relationships among things or events, as well as to their characteristics (Marx, 1963). "Dog" is a concept, as is "barking," and so is "obedience." Concepts are the symbols by which we ordinarily communicate. Clear, unambiguous communication of ideas requires us to use concepts that are explicitly defined and free of unwarranted or surplus meaning. That is, a concept should not convey more meaning than we intended.

In everyday conversation we often get by without having to worry too much about how we define a concept. Many words, for instance, are commonly used and apparently understood even though neither party to the communication knows *exactly* what the words mean. We are suggesting that people frequently communicate with one another without being fully aware of what they are talking about. This may sound ridiculous but, to prove our point, try the following.

Ask a few people whether they believe that intelligence is mostly inherited or mostly acquired. You might try arguing a point of view opposite to theirs just for the fun of it. After having engaged them in a discussion about the roots of intelligence, ask them what they mean by "intelligence." You will probably find that most people have a difficult time defining this concept. Yet people are frequently willing to debate an important point regarding intelligence, and even take a definite stand on the issue, without being able to say exactly what "intelligence" is. When someone does provide a definition, it is unlikely to be exactly the same as that given by another person. That is, "intelligence" means one thing to one person and something else to another. Clearly, in order to attempt to answer the question of whether intelligence is mainly inherited or mainly acquired, we must provide an exact definition that all parties involved can accept. On the other hand, we can talk about it, even argue about it, on an everyday basis without knowing exactly what it is we are talking about!

One way in which a scientist gives meaning to a concept is by defining it operationally. An **operational definition** explains a concept solely in terms of the operations used to produce and measure it. Intelligence, for instance, can be defined operationally by specifying a paper-and-pencil test emphasizing understanding of logical relationships, short-term memory, and familiarity with the meaning of words. Some may not like this operational definition of intelligence, but once a particular test has been identified, there can at least be no argument about what intelligence means *according to this definition*. Operational definitions facilitate communication, at least among those who know how and why they are used.

Although exact meaning is conveyed via operational definitions, this approach to communication has not escaped criticism. One problem has been alluded to already. That is, if we don't like one operational definition of intelligence, there is nothing to prevent us from giving intelligence another operational definition. Does this mean there are as many kinds of intelligence as there are operational definitions? Each time a new set of questions is added to a paper-and-pencil test of intelligence do we have a new definition of intelligence? The answer, unfortunately, is that we don't really know. To determine whether a different procedure yields a new definition of intelligence, we would have to seek additional evidence. For example, do people who score high on one test also score high on the second test? If they do, the new test may be measuring the same thing as the old one.

Another criticism of using operational definitions is that the definitions are not always meaningful. For example, defining intelligence in terms of how long one can balance a ball on one's nose is an operational definition that most people would not find very meaningful. How do we decide whether a concept has been meaningfully defined? Once again, the solution is to appeal to other forms of evidence. How does performance on a balancing task compare to performance on other tasks that are commonly accepted as measures of intelligence? We must also be willing to apply common sense to the situation. Do people usually consider balancing a ball evidence of intelligence? Scientists are generally aware of the limitations of operational definitions; however, the clarity of communication that derives from this approach is assumed to outweigh the problems it raises.

Instruments   You depend on instruments to measure events more than you probably realize. The speedometer in the car, the clock in the bedroom, and the thermometer used to measure body temperature are all instruments that we would find it difficult to do without. And you can appreciate the problems that arise if one of these instruments is inaccurate. *Accuracy* refers to the difference between what an instrument says is true and what is known to be true. A clock that is consistently 5 minutes slow is not very accurate. Inaccurate clocks can make us late, inaccurate speedometers can earn us traffic tickets, and inaccurate thermometers can lead us to believe we are ill when we are not. The accuracy of an instrument is determined by *calibrating* it, or checking it with another instrument known to be true. Thus, we periodically call the telephone company to check the accuracy of our clocks based on the recorded messages telling us the "time at the tone," which we assume represent the true time. The accuracy of speedometers can be checked using a combination of observations of roadside distance markers and the seconds ticking off on an accurate watch.

Measurements can be made at varying levels of *precision.* A measure of time in tenths of a second is not as precise as one that is in hundredths of a second. One instrument that yields imprecise measures is the gas gauge in most cars. Although reasonably accurate, gas gauges do not give very precise readings. Most of us have wished at one time or another that the gas gauge would permit us to determine whether we had that extra half gallon of gas to get us to the next service station.

We also need instruments to measure behavior. Wundt used a reaction-time apparatus to measure the time required for cognitive processing. You can be assured that the precision, and even the accuracy, of instruments of this kind have improved significantly in the last 100 years. Today electronic counters provide precise measures of reaction time in milliseconds (thousandths of a second). Many other instruments are employed in contemporary psychology. To perform a biofeedback experiment requires instruments that give accurate feedback to a participant regarding such internal states as heart rate and blood pressure. Tests of anxiety sometimes employ instruments to measure galvanic skin response (GSR). Other behavioral instruments are of the paper-and-pencil variety. Questionnaires and tests are popular instruments used by psychologists to measure behavior (see especially Chapter 4). So, too, are the rating scales used by human observers (see Chapter 3). For instance, rating aggression in children on a 7-point scale ranging from not at all aggressive (1) to very aggressive (7) can yield relatively accurate (although perhaps not too precise) measures of aggression. It is the responsibility of the behavioral scientist to use instruments that are as accurate and as precise as possible.

Measurement   Psychologists must deal with two types of measurement. The first type, *physical measurement,* involves dimensions for which there is an agreed-on standard and an instrument for doing the measuring. Length is a dimension that can be scaled with physical measurement, and there are agreed-on standards for units of length. For instance, 1 meter was at one time defined as 1/10,000,000 of the distance between the North Pole and the equator. This proved impossible to measure precisely, so the definition of 1 meter was changed to the distance between two points on a platinum-iridium bar kept under controlled conditions near Paris, France. Although this provided accuracy to one part in a million, greater precision was sought. In 1960 the meter was defined as 1,650,763.73 wavelengths of the red-orange radiation of the inert gas krypton-86. But even this proved not precise enough for scientists. (When using the krypton measure to determine the distance from the earth to the moon, scientists found themselves in error by more than 1.5 meters.) Recently, the definition of the meter was changed to the length of the path traveled by light in a vacuum in 1/299,792,458 of a second.

In most research in psychology, however, the dimensions to be measured do not involve physical measurement. Rulers do not exist for measuring beauty, aggression, or intelligence. For these dimensions we must use a second type of measurement: *psychological measurement*. Agreement among a certain number of observers provides the basis for psychological measurement. If several independent observers agree that a certain action warrants a rating of 3 on a 7-point rating scale of aggression, we can say that we have a psychological measurement of the aggressiveness of the action. When Albright and Henderson (1995) asked individuals who were depressed and who were not depressed to evaluate other people, the researchers provided participants with an 8-point scale to judge the degree to which various statements about people were true. The rather counterintuitive finding was that depressed individuals provided more accurate ratings of other people than did those who were not depressed.

Of course, many dimensions that can be scaled physically can also be measured using psychological measurement. Observers can be asked to judge which of two lines is longer, and, if they consistently select the longer one, we know the observers can "measure" length. This type of measurement is called psychophysical measurement and it represents one of the earliest areas of experimental investigation in psychology.

It is important that measurement be both valid and reliable. In general, **validity** refers to the "truthfulness" of a measure. A valid measure of a concept is one that measures what it claims to measure. We discussed this aspect of measurement when we mentioned possible operational definitions of intelligence. Intelligence, it was suggested, could be defined in terms of performance on a task requiring one to balance a ball on one's nose. According to the principle of "operationalism," this is a perfectly permissible operational definition. However, most of us would question whether such a balancing act is really a measure of intelligence. In other words, we would want to know if this is a valid measure of intelligence. Can intelligence actually be measured by how long we can keep a ball twirling on our nose? As we indicated earlier, evidence bearing on the validity of this definition would have to come from other sources. The validity of a measure is supported to the extent that people do as well on it as they do on independent measures that are presumed to measure the same concept. For example, if time spent balancing a ball is a valid measure of intelligence, then a person who does well on the balancing task should also do well on such measures as size of vocabulary, reasoning ability, and other accepted measures of intelligence.

The **reliability** of a measurement is indicated by its consistency. Several different kinds of reliability can be distinguished. When we speak of instrument reliability, we are discussing whether an instrument works consistently. The car that sometimes starts and sometimes doesn't when we engage the ignition is not very reliable. Observations made by two or more independent observers are said to be reliable if they show agreement—that is, if the observations are consistent from one observer to another. In the context of psychological testing, researchers need to be concerned with test reliability. Are the results obtained on a test consistent from one administration of the test to another? In subsequent chapters of this book we discuss various kinds of validity and reliability and introduce you to various methods for measuring them.

Hypotheses   A **hypothesis** is a tentative explanation for something. It frequently attempts to answer the questions "How?" and "Why?" At one level, a hypothesis may simply suggest how particular variables are related. For example, consider the phenomenon of "depressive realism," which we alluded to previously. This refers to the fact that in many situations depressed individuals make more accurate (or realistic) judgments than do individuals who are not depressed. This led Albright and Henderson (1995) to hypothesize that depressed individuals would judge other people more accurately than would those who were not depressed. That is, they hypothesized that level of depression and accuracy of judgments were *related.* You may remember that when these researchers asked participants to rate the degree to which various statements about people were true, the results supported their hypothesis: Depressed individuals gave more accurate ratings of other people than did those who were not depressed.

At a more theoretical level, a hypothesis may offer a reason (the "why") for the way that particular variables are related. For example, Albright and Henderson (1995) suggested that many of us avoid symptoms of depression by perceiving other people less favorably than is actually true. (This way we always look good!) Such a strategy may help us to feel good about ourselves. These researchers further hypothesized that depressed individuals, in contrast, may lose this ability to view people unfavorably. That is, "why" depressed individuals make more accurate (realistic) judgments is *because* they have lost the ability to view others unfavorably. Moreover, consistent with their reasoning, *non*-depressed individuals rated others *inaccurately* in the predicted direction. That is, individuals who were not depressed (unlike depressed individuals) rated others less favorably than was objectively true.

Nearly everyone has proposed hypotheses to explain some human behavior at one time or another. Why do people commit apparently senseless acts of violence? What causes people to start smoking cigarettes? Why are some students academically more successful than others? One characteristic often distinguishes the hypotheses proposed by the nonscientist from those offered by the scientist: testability. As attractive as it might be, if a hypothesis cannot be tested, it is of no immediate use to science (Marx, 1963).

Hypotheses are not testable *if the concepts to which they refer are not adequately defined.* To say that a would-be assassin shot a U.S. president or other prominent figure because he was mentally disturbed is not a testable hypothesis unless a definition of mentally disturbed can be agreed upon. Unfortunately, psychologists and psychiatrists cannot always agree on what terms such as "mentally disturbed" mean. Often this occurs because an accepted operational definition is not available for these concepts. You may have learned in a psychology class that many of Freud's hypotheses are not testable. One reason has to do with the lack of operational definition for such concepts as *id*. As one prominent researcher has commented, "a criterion of whether or not a so-called empirical concept is a scientific concept is whether or not it has been operationally defined" (Underwood, 1957, p. 52). Therefore, in addition to facilitating clarity in communication, operational definitions offer a means of evaluating whether our hypotheses contain scientifically acceptable concepts.

Hypotheses are also untestable if they are *circular*, in which case the event itself becomes an explanation for the event. One scientist has pointed out that using a definition of an event as an explanation for the event, that is, a *circular hypothesis*, is something you can "catch the late-night talk show hosts doing" all the time (Kimble, 1989). Consider these examples:

> "Your eight-year-old son is distractable in school and having trouble reading because he has an attention deficiency disorder." "The stock market crash of October 19, 1987, was caused by widespread economic panic" (Kimble, 1989, p. 495).

Do you see that by saying a boy is "distractable . . . *because* he has an attention deficiency disorder" doesn't explain anything? An attention deficiency disorder is defined by the inability to pay attention. Thus, such a statement simply says that he doesn't pay attention because he doesn't pay attention! Or that by saying a "stock market crash . . . was *caused* by widespread economic panic" simply suggests that economic panic (as defined by the stock market crash) is due to economic panic?

This scientist goes on to say that "If [he] could make just one change in what the general public (and some psychologists) understand about psychology, it would be to give them an immunity to such misuses of definitions" (Kimble, 1989, p. 495).

A hypothesis also may be untestable if it *appeals to ideas or forces that are not recognized by science.* As we have shown, science deals with the observable, the demonstrable, the empirical. To suggest that people who commit horrendous acts of violence are under orders from the Devil is not testable because it invokes a principle (the Devil) that is not in the province of science. Such hypotheses might be of value to philosophers or theologians but not to the scientist.

Hypotheses in scientific research are often derived from a theory. We discuss the nature of scientific theories, their function, and how they are constructed and tested later in this chapter. But now, let us complete this description of a scientific approach by discussing the attitude you must have as a scientist.

Attitude More than anything else, scientists are skeptical. Not only do they want to "see it before believing it," but they are likely to want to see it again, and again, perhaps under conditions of their own choosing. Behavioral scientists come to this skepticism by recognizing two important facts. First, behavior is complex, and often many factors interact to give rise to a psychological phenomenon. Discovering these factors is often a difficult task. The explanations proposed are sometimes premature, not enough factors having been considered or the existence of one or more factors having gone unnoticed. Second, the behavioral scientist recognizes that science is a human endeavor. People make mistakes. Human inference, as we have suggested, is not always to be trusted. Therefore, scientists are often skeptical about "new discoveries" and extraordinary claims. The skepticism of scientists produces a cautiousness that is often lacking in those without scientific training. Too many people are apparently all too ready to accept explanations that are based on insufficient or inadequate evidence. This is illustrated by the widespread belief in the occult. Rather than approach cautiously the claims of those who promote belief in the paranormal, many people are uncritical in their acceptance. According to public opinion surveys, a large majority of Americans believe in ESP (extrasensory perception), and many people apparently are convinced that beings from outer space have visited Earth. About 2 in 5 Americans give some credibility to astrology reports, and as many as 12 million adults report changing their behavior after reading astrology reports (Miller, 1986). Such beliefs are held despite minimal and often contradictory evidence of the validity of horoscopes. This human tendency to ignore certain kinds of evidence is not new. When scientists successfully demonstrated the means by which Clever Hans was so clever, many people continued to believe in his superior reasoning ability (Watson, 1914/1967).

What is responsible for this tendency to propose explanations based on the occult and to resist obvious evidence to the contrary? Singer and Benassi (1981) suggest that an uncritical attitude toward such events has several sources. First, there are many distortions in the media. The public is constantly exposed to television shows, newspaper accounts, and other reports of events presumably caused by supernatural forces. These reports are often presented with little critical evaluation, and scientific evidence for alternative explanations is frequently ignored. The sheer pervasiveness of such reports may lend credibility to them.

Another reason for the widespread acceptance of the occult may be deficiencies in human reasoning. As we emphasized earlier in this chapter, everyday inferences are susceptible to many biases, including the tendency to seek only confirmatory evidence, to jump to conclusions, and to perceive causality in events when none is actually present (Zechmeister & Johnson, 1992). Finally, Singer and Benassi find fault with science education. Too often, they suggest, science is taught as a set of facts rather than as a way of approaching knowledge critically and systematically. Thus, people are often impatient with the scientific process and even confused when scientists appear to change their minds or when they attempt to clarify earlier findings. Singer and Benassi also find that the general public exhibits woefully little general scientific knowledge. Many people believe that islands float on the ocean surface, for instance, and that the moon is fixed in the sky but only visible at night. Belief in astrology reports and "lucky numbers," for example, is stronger among people with little formal education than it is among college-educated individuals (Miller, 1986).

Scientists do not, of course, automatically assume that unconventional interpretations of unexplained phenomena could not possibly be true. They simply insist on being allowed to test all claims and to reject those that are inherently untestable. Scientific skepticism is a gullible public's defense against charlatans and others who would sell them ineffective medicines and cures, impossible schemes to get rich, and supernatural explanations for natural phenomena.

GOALS OF THE SCIENTIFIC METHOD

The scientific method is intended to meet three goals: description, prediction, and understanding.

Description   Description refers to the procedures by which events and their relationships are defined, classified, catalogued, or categorized. Clinical research, for instance, has provided practitioners with many different sets of criteria for classifying mental disorders. Many of these are found in the American Psychiatric Association's *Diagnostic and Statistical Manual of Mental Disorders* (4th ed., 1994), also known as *DSM-IV.* Consider, as one example, the criteria used to define the disorder labeled *Dissociative Fugue* (formerly Psychogenic Fugue).

Diagnostic Criteria

A. The predominant disturbance is sudden, unexpected travel away from home or one's customary place of daily activities, with inability to recall one's past.
B. Confusion about personal identity or assumption of a new identity (partial or complete).
C. The disturbance does not occur exclusively during the course of Dissociative Identity Disorder and is not due to the direct physiological effects of a substance (e.g., a drug of abuse, medication) or a general medical condition (e.g., temporal lobe epilepsy).
D. The symptoms cause clinically significant stress or impairment in social, occupational, or other important areas of functioning. (*DSM-IV,* 1994, p. 481)

The diagnostic criteria used to define dissociative fugue provide an operational definition for this disorder. Like many other unusual mental disorders, dissociative fugues are relatively rare; thus, we typically learn about these kinds of disorders based on individual descriptions of people exhibiting them. These descriptions are called *case studies.* Clinical research frequently makes use of case studies, a procedure we discuss in detail in Chapter 9. Research also seeks to provide clinicians with descriptions of the prevalence of a mental disorder and their relationship to variables including, but not restricted to, gender and age. According to the *DSM-IV* (1994), for instance, dissociative fugue is seen primarily in adults, and although it is relatively rare, it is more frequent "during times of extremely stressful events such as wartime or natural disaster" (p. 482).

Another example of description in psychological research is the work of Levine (1990), who described the "pace of life" in various cultures and countries of the world. Measures of a country's tempo were made by noting the accuracy of outdoor bank clocks in a country's cities, by timing the walking speed of pedestrians over a distance of 100 feet, and by measuring the speed with which postal clerks processed a standard request for stamps. The investigator frequently enlisted the help of students to make observations while they traveled during summer vacations or semester breaks. The results of this study are shown in Figure 1.3. The citizens of Japan exhibited, overall, the fastest pace of life; the citizens of Indonesia were the slowest. U.S. citizens were second overall.

Psychology (like science in general) develops descriptions of phenomena using the *nomothetic approach*. The objective of the nomothetic approach is to establish broad generalizations and "universal laws" that apply to a wide population of organisms. As a consequence, psychological research frequently consists of studies involving large numbers of participants with the purpose of determining the "average," or typical, performance of a group. This average may or may not represent the performance of any one individual in the group. Not all citizens of Japan or the United States, for example, are on the fast track. In fact, Levine (1990) and his colleagues found wide differences in the pace of life among various cities within a country. Inhabitants of large cities walked faster than did those of medium-sized cities in the various countries that were

FIGURE 1.3   Measures of accuracy of a country's bank clocks, pedestrian walking speed, and the speed of postal clerks performing a routine task served to describe the pace of life in a country. In the graph a longer bar represents greater accuracy of clocks or greater speed of walking and performing a task (from Levine, 1990).

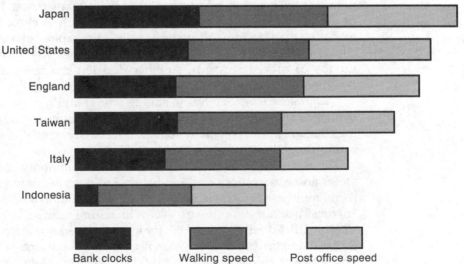

visited. In the United States, differences in a city's tempo were found depending on the region of the country. Cities in the Northeast (e.g., Boston, New York) had a faster tempo than did cities on the West Coast (e.g., Sacramento, Los Angeles). Of course, there will be individual variations within cities as well. Not all citizens of Los Angeles are going to be slow paced, nor are all New Yorkers going to be fast paced. Nevertheless, the Japanese move *in general* at a faster pace than do Indonesians, and Americans on the West Coast exhibit, *on the average,* a slower pace of life than do residents of the Northeast.

The nomothetic approach does not deny there are important differences *among* individuals; it simply seeks to identify the similarities that exist among these differences. For example, a person's individuality is not threatened by our knowledge that that person's heart, like the hearts of other human beings, is located in the upper left chest cavity. Similarly, we do not deny a person's individuality when we state that that person's behavior is influenced by patterns of reinforcement. Researchers merely seek to describe what organisms are like in general on the basis of the average performance of a group of different organisms.

Although the nomothetic approach predominates in psychological research, there is an alternative. Some psychologists, notably Allport (1961), argue that the nomothetic approach is inadequate—the individual cannot be represented by an average value. Allport claims that the individual both is unique and exhibits behavior which conforms to general laws, or principles. He maintains that study of the individual, called *idiographic research,* is important. A major form of idiographic research is the case study method, which we describe in detail in Chapter 9.

Whether a researcher seeks to make generalizations about groups of individuals or is looking for the lawfulness found in one individual's behavior is based on a choice made by the researcher. This choice is largely dictated by the nature of the question being asked. And while many researchers do mainly one or the other kind of research, others may do both. A clinical psychologist, for instance, may decide to pursue mainly idiographic investigations of a few clients in therapy but consider nomothetic issues when doing research with groups of college students. Another decision the researcher must make is whether to do quantitative or qualitative research.

Quantitative research refers to studies whose findings are mainly the product of statistical summary and analysis. *Qualitative research* produces research findings that are not arrived at by statistical summary or analysis and lack quantification altogether (Strauss & Corbin, 1990).

The data of qualitative research are most commonly obtained from interviews and observations and can be used to describe individuals, groups, and social movements (Strauss & Corbin, 1990). Qualitative research is often about "naturally occurring, ordinary events in natural settings" (Miles & Huberman, 1994, p. 10). Powell-Cope (1995), for instance, used qualitative methods to "describe the experiences of gay couples when at least one was diagnosed with symptomatic HIV infection or AIDS" (p. 36). Van Meter, Yokoi, and Pressley

(1994) used a qualitative research approach to develop a theory of student note taking. The researchers met with university undergraduates in small discussion groups, conducted both directed and undirected interviews, and then developed and administered formal questionnaires. According to the authors, this qualitative approach to research on student note taking yielded "many insights into note-taking dynamics that have not been identified in previous research" (p. 323). Other examples of qualitative research are found in Chapter 3 when we discuss narrative records of observed behavior; case studies described in Chapter 9 also are a form of qualitative research. Just as psychological research is more frequently nomothetic than idiographic, it is also more typically quantitative than qualitative. And while both kinds of research can be usefully employed to describe behavior, our emphasis in this book is mainly on quantitative research.

Prediction Description of events and their relationships often provides a basis for *prediction*, the second goal of the scientific method. There are important questions in psychology that call for predictions. For example: Does the early loss of a parent make a child especially vulnerable to depression? Are children who are overly aggressive likely to have emotional problems as adults? Do stressful life events lead to increased physical illness? Research findings suggest an affirmative answer to all of these questions. This information not only adds valuable knowledge to the discipline of psychology but is also helpful in both the treatment and the prevention of emotional disorders.

An important occupation of many psychologists is the prediction of later performance (for example, on the job, in school, or in specific vocations) on the basis of earlier performance on various standardized tests. For instance, a student's scores on the Graduate Record Examination (GRE), as well as undergraduate grade-point average (GPA), can be used to predict how well the student will do in graduate school. Interestingly, research has shown that faculty recommendations, which are usually required for graduate school admittance, are a rather poor predictor of whether a student will successfully complete a doctorate degree (Willingham, 1974). On the other hand, there is research showing that the amount of undergraduate research activity and ratings by peers of a student's commitment to psychology are better predictors of later success in psychology (as measured, for example, by number of scientific publications) than are the more traditional measures, such as GRE scores and GPA (Hirschberg & Itkin, 1978).

When scores on one variable can be used to predict scores on a second variable, we say the two variables are correlated. A **correlation** exists when two different measures of the same people, events, or things vary together, that is, when particular scores on one variable tend to be associated with particular scores on another variable. When this occurs, the scores are said to "covary." Levine (1990) found a positive correlation between a city's pace of life and its deaths from heart disease. This indicates that the faster the pace in a city, the more likely its inhabitants are to die from heart disease. Death rates from heart disease, in other words, can be predicted by simply measuring how fast its inhabitants typically walk 100 feet or even by checking the accuracy of the city's clocks!

We are concerned with issues of correlation at various points in this text and discuss the more general topic of correlational research in Chapter 4. (Computational procedures for the more common correlation coefficients are found in Appendix A.) Correlational research, which seeks to describe predictive relationships among variables, such as scores on a paper-and-pencil personality test and frequency of hospitalization for depression, is a major area of psychological research.

It is important to point out that successful prediction doesn't always depend on knowing why a relationship exists between two variables. Consider the report that the Chinese rely on observing animal behavior to help them predict earthquakes. Certain animals apparently behave in an unusual manner just before an earthquake. The dog that barks and runs in circles and the snake seen fleeing its hole, therefore, may be reliable predictors of earthquakes. If so, they could be used to warn people of forthcoming disasters. We might even imagine that in areas where earthquakes are likely, residents would be asked to keep certain animals under observation (as miners once kept canaries) to warn them of conditions of which they are as yet unaware. This would not require that we understand why certain animals behave strangely before an earthquake, or even why earthquakes occur.

You may remember that Levine (1990) showed that measures of the pace of a city can be used to predict death rates from heart disease. However, we can only speculate about why these measures are related. One possible explanation for this correlation suggested by the researchers is that people living in time-urgent environments engage in unhealthy behaviors, for example, cigarette smoking and poor eating habits, which increase their risk of heart disease (Levine, 1990).

Understanding   Although they are important goals in themselves, description and prediction are only the first steps in understanding a phenomenon. Understanding is the third and most important goal of the scientific method. It is achieved when the cause or causes of a phenomenon are identified. The scientist sets three important conditions for making a **causal inference** and, hence, of understanding: *covariation of events; a time-order relationship; and the elimination of plausible alternative causes.* If one event is the cause of another, the two events must vary together; that is, when one changes, the other must also change. This is the principle of covariation that we noted was the basis of the goal of prediction. Further, the presumed cause must occur before the presumed effect. This is the second condition, a time-order relationship. Finally, causal explanations are accepted only when other possible causes of the effect have been ruled out—when plausible alternative causes have been eliminated.

Unfortunately, people have a tendency to conclude that all three conditions for a causal inference have been met when really only the first condition is satisfied. For example, research has suggested that parents who are stern disciplinarians and who use physical punishment are more likely to have aggressive children than are parents who are less stern and use other forms of discipline. Parental discipline and children's aggressiveness obviously covary. Moreover, the fact that parents are typically assumed to influence how their children behave might lead us to think that the time-order condition has been met—parents use physical discipline and children's aggressiveness results. More recent research has shown, however, that infants vary in how active and aggressive they are and that the infant's behavior has a strong influence on the *parents'* responses in trying to exercise control. In other words, some children may be naturally aggressive and require stern discipline rather than stern discipline's producing aggressive children. Therefore, the direction of the causal relationship may be opposite to what we thought at first.

It is important to recognize, however, that the causes of events cannot be identified unless covariation has been demonstrated. The first objective of the scientific method, description, can be met by describing events under a single set of circumstances. The goal of understanding, however, requires more than this. For example, suppose a teacher wished to demonstrate that so-called active learning strategies help students learn. She could teach students using this approach and then describe the performance of the students who received instruction in this particular way. But at this point what would she know? How do we know that another group of students taught using an approach that did not use active learning strategies might not learn the same amount? Before the teacher could claim the performance she observed was caused by the use of active learning strategies, she would have to compare this method with some other reasonable approach that did not employ active learning strategies. She would look for a difference in learning between the group using active learning strategies and a group not using this method. Such a finding would show that teaching strategy and performance covary. As you will see in Chapter 6, this is one reason why manipulation is such an important method of control for scientists. By manipulating independent variables, such as type of learning strategy, the investigator can determine whether any subsequent covariation occurs in the dependent variable. If it does, a bonus results from using manipulation: the time-order condition has also been met because the researcher changes the independent variable (e.g., teaching method) and *subsequently* measures the changes, if any, in the dependent variable (e.g., a measure of student learning).

By far the most challenging condition to be met in making a causal inference is eliminating other plausible alternative causes. For example, consider a study in which the effect of two different teaching approaches (active and passive) is to be assessed. You can see that one way not to assign students to teaching conditions in this study would be to have all men in one group and all women in the other. If this were done, the independent variable of teaching method would be "confounded" with the independent variable of gender. **Confounding** occurs when two potentially effective variables are allowed to covary simultaneously. When research is confounded, it is impossible to determine what variable is responsible for any obtained difference in performance. If males were assigned to one condition of our hypothetical teaching experiment and females to another, then we would not know whether any difference we observed was due to gender of the participant or to the independent variable of type of teaching. When no confoundings are present, a research study is said to have **internal validity.** Much of the discussion in this book focuses on developing skills in performing internally valid research by learning to identify and eliminate confoundings.

The internal validity of a study, which relates to our ability to make causal inferences based on it, must be distinguished from the study's external validity. **External validity** involves the extent to which the research results can be generalized to different populations, settings, and conditions. A research finding may be internally valid and have little external validity. Although free of confoundings, the study may not be able to be generalized. Questions of external validity in science often arise when results obtained with animal subjects are claimed to apply to human participants as well. Researchers frequently depend on experiments with animals to obtain information about human psychopathology. In one series of experiments, uncontrollable electric shock was used in an attempt to investigate in animal subjects the kinds of stressful experiences that are thought to contribute to ulcers and depression in humans (Weiss, 1977). Animal models have also been used to study drug addiction, minimal brain dysfunction, and various forms of mild to severe psychopathology (Maser & Seligman, 1977). While these studies yield valuable information about the effects of uncontrollable stress in animals, it is not clear whether these findings can be easily generalized to situations involving human responses to uncontrollable stress.

Because laboratory research, in general, is often conducted under more controlled conditions than are found in natural settings, an important task of the scientist is to determine whether laboratory findings generalize to the real world. This is often the goal of what is called *field research*. By performing an experiment in the "field" (outside the laboratory) similar to one carried out in the laboratory, a researcher can provide evidence bearing on the external validity of laboratory results. Research conducted outside the laboratory often requires methods and procedures that are specifically designed for this less well-controlled environment. Later in this book we introduce some of the methods used by psychologists to conduct field research (see especially Chapters 3 and 10).

SCIENTIFIC THEORY CONSTRUCTION AND TESTING

Theories are "ideas" about how nature works. Psychologists propose ideas about why behavior occurs the way it does (e.g., what causes schizophrenia), about the nature of cognition (e.g., how people solve problems), and so on. A psychological theory can be developed on different levels: for example, it can be developed on a physiological or on a symbolic level (Anderson, 1990; Simon, 1992). A theory of schizophrenia may, in other words, propose biological causes (e.g., specific genetic carriers), psychological causes (e.g., patterns of emotional conflict, stress), or both. The propositions contained in theories may be expressed as verbal statements, as mathematical equations, or even as computer programs.

An important dimension on which theories differ is scope. The *scope* of a theory refers to the range of phenomena that it seeks to explain. A theory of "flashbulb memory," for instance, attempts to explain why the personal circumstances surrounding particularly surprising and emotional events, such as the explosion of the space shuttle *Challenger* (Figure 1.4), are remembered better than are details associated with everyday events (Brown & Kulik, 1977; McCloskey, Wible, & Cohen, 1988).

Many older adults, for instance, can apparently remember precisely what they were doing when they heard about the assassination of President Kennedy. The scope of a theory of flashbulb memory is relatively restricted, proposing as it does an explanation of the nature and cause of an interesting but very specific memory phenomenon. A theory of human love, such as that proposed by Sternberg (1986), is an example of a psychological theory of much greater scope. Sternberg shows how the amount and kind of love one experiences is a function of three critical behavioral components: intimacy, passion, and decision/commitment. Even broader in scope is Anderson's (1990, 1993; Anderson & Milson, 1989) theory of human cognition, which offers an account

FIGURE 1.4   A theory of "flashbulb memory" seeks to explain why personal circumstances surrounding vivid, emotional events, such as the explosion of the space shuttle *Challenger*, are seemingly remembered so much better than are details of everyday events.

of how cognition works in general, including ideas about learning, memory, problem solving, and so on.

Clearly, the scope of a theory can be quite large. In general, the greater the scope of a theory the more complex it is likely to be. Complexity sometimes may be a necessary characteristic of psychological theories given the nature and range of phenomena psychologists try to understand. Complexity also can be a serious obstacle, however, to testing a theory. Most theories in contemporary psychology tend to be relatively modest in scope, attempting to account only for a limited range of phenomena. The source of a scientific theory is a mixture of intuition, personal observation, and discovered knowledge (known facts and ideas). The famous philosopher of science, Karl Popper (1976, p. 268–269), suggested that truly creative theories spring from a combination of "intense interest in a problem (and thus a readiness to try again and again)" and "critical imagination." *Critical imagination* is the ability to think critically, but there is more. It includes a readiness to challenge accepted ideas and an "imaginative freedom that allows us to see so far unsuspected sources of error" in previous thinking about a problem. Critical imagination, in other words, means traveling beyond what others have said are the boundaries (limits) of thinking about a problem. Assuming we have that important burning interest in a problem, one way we might approach constructing a scientific theory is by critically examining what is known, looking for flaws or unseen sources of error in that knowledge.

Whatever the nature and scope of a theory, whether it be expressed mathematically or verbally or developed at a physiological level or at some higher-order level, the theory includes certain assumptions and concepts that must be explained in order for it to be understood and tested. A theory of flashbulb memory, for instance, needs to state exactly what a flashbulb memory *is*, showing, for example, how flashbulb memory differs from other, more typical memory. To be complete, therefore, a theory must include definitions of various events or concepts (e.g., emotional events, test accuracy), information about relationships between these events (e.g., the relationship between degree of emotional involvement and amount remembered), and so forth. Thus, we can offer the following formal definition of a scientific **theory:** a logically organized set of propositions (claims, statements, assertions) that serves to define events (concepts), describe relationships among these events, and explain the occurrence of these events.

The major functions of a theory are to *guide* research and to *organize* empirical knowledge (Marx, 1963). In the early 1960s, Rotter (1966) developed a theory of internal versus external locus of control. In this theory, Rotter differentiates individuals who perceive a contingency between their behavior and what happens to them (internal locus of control) and those who perceive that their behavior has little consequence for what happens to them (external locus of control). Rotter developed a questionnaire to define this concept on the basis of the idea that individuals differ in locus of control because of the way they have been rewarded during their development. The theory suggests a relationship between perceived locus of control and anxiety, with greater anxiety associated with greater perceived external locus of control. The theory has guided researchers for many years and has served to organize a body of empirical literature regarding self-efficacy, or the feeling of being able to cope with the environment (Tedeschi, Lindskold, & Rosenfeld, 1985). The success of a psychological theory such as the locus-of-control theory can be measured by the degree to which it achieves the two important goals of guiding research and organizing empirical findings.

A scientific theory guides research by suggesting testable hypotheses. You may remember that hypotheses, like theories, are explanations for behavior; however, a hypothesis typically is simpler and more tentative than a scientific theory (Marx, 1963). We reviewed previously several factors affecting the testability of hypotheses, including the important criterion of operational specificity of concepts. It is important that hypotheses derived from a theory attempt to meet these criteria. Theories frequently require that we postulate intervening processes to account for observed behavior (Underwood, 1975). An intervening process is one that "mediates" between certain antecedent conditions and behavior. We have been discussing one such intervening process, memory. We can safely say that we have never "seen" memory. It is something we infer based on observations of our own behavior and that of others when asked about a previous experience. We assume there is some record of experiences somewhere inside us to which we refer when queried about a previous experience. The concept "memory" is proposed as an intervening process to explain the behavior we have observed. Mediating processes such as memory are called *intervening variables*. To be useful to the scientist, it is important that these concepts have a clear relationship to behavior (Kimble, 1989). That is, while we might infer many kinds of unseen processes to help explain behavior, unless we tie down intervening processes to observed relationships between specific antecedents (independent variables) and behavior (dependent variables), our theories are scientifically weak. For example, a theory that proposes a "free-floating" process to explain behavior cannot be shown to be wrong. Because free-floating processes (e.g., "the little person inside me") are not tied to specific empirical relationships, they can be called into play in any and every situation to "explain" behavior.

How scientific theories should be evaluated and tested is one of the most complex and difficult issues in psychology and philosophy (Meehl, 1978, 1990a, 1990b; Popper, 1959). At least one scientist, however, suggests a rather straightforward procedure. Kimble (1989, p. 498) says quite simply, "The best theory is the one that survives the fires of logical and empirical testing." While somewhat simplistic, this is a good starting point. A theory can be evaluated first on the basis of its organization, its logical consistency. Are its propositions arranged in a meaningful way? Is the theory free of contradictions? Can specific deductions about expected behavior be made from it easily? Theories are tested logically by exposing their internal structure to the critical eye of members of the scientific community. A particular theory's propositions, assumptions, and definitions are frequently the topic of debate in scientific journals.

Ideas about the exact definition of flashbulb memories, for example, have been debated at length in the psychology literature (Cohen, McCloskey, & Wible, 1990; Pillemer, 1990).

Kimble (1989) suggests that a theory is strengthened or weakened according to the outcomes of empirical tests of hypotheses derived from it. Successful tests of a hypothesis serve to increase the acceptability of a theory; unsuccessful tests serve to decrease the theory's acceptability. The best theory, in this view, is the one that passes these tests successfully. But there are serious obstacles to testing hypotheses and, as a consequence, confirming or disconfirming scientific theories. For example, a theory, especially a complex one, may produce many specific testable hypotheses. Therefore, a theory is not likely to fail on the basis of a single test (Lakatos, 1978). Moreover, theories may include propositions and concepts that have not been adequately defined or suggest intervening processes that are related to behavior and to each other in complex and even mysterious ways. Such theories may have a long life, but their value to science is questionable (Meehl, 1978).

When constructing and evaluating a theory, scientists place a premium on parsimony (Marx, 1963). The *rule of parsimony* is followed when the simplest of alternative explanations is accepted. When choosing among theoretical propositions, scientists tend to favor the simplest of them. *Precision of prediction* is another criterion by which a theory can be evaluated. Theories that make precise predictions about behavior are preferred to those that make only general predictions (Meehl, 1990a). For instance, a theory of flashbulb memory that predicts the precise nature and duration of a "forgetting function" for such a memory is clearly a better theory than one that simply states that these memories will be remembered "longer" than other memories. Stated another way, some tests are easier for theories to pass than are others. A good scientific theory is one that is able to pass the most rigorous tests. *Rigorous testing* includes more tests that seek to falsify a theory's propositions than ones that seek to confirm them (Cook & Campbell, 1979). While confirming a particular theory's propositions provides support for the specific theory being tested, confirmation logically does not rule out other, alternative theories of the same phenomenon.

Although theories can be difficult and challenging to work with, the process of constructing and evaluating them is at the core of the scientific enterprise and absolutely essential for the continuation of the science of psychology.

SCIENTIFIC INTEGRITY

Science is a search for truth. Fraud, lies, and misrepresentations should play no part in a scientific investigation. But science is also a human endeavor, and frequently much more is at stake than truth. Both scientists and the institutions that hire them compete for rewards in a game with jobs, money, and reputations on the line. The number of scientific publications authored by a university faculty member, for instance, is usually a major factor influencing decisions regarding promotion and tenure. Under these circumstances, there are unfortunate, but seemingly inevitable, cases of scientific misconduct.

A variety of activities constitute violations of scientific integrity. They include data fabrication, plagiarism, selective reporting of research findings, failure to acknowledge individuals who made significant contributions to the research, misuse of research funds, and unethical treatment of humans or animals (Adler, 1991). Some transgressions are easier to detect than others. Out-and-out fabrication of data, for instance, can be revealed when, in the normal course of science, results are not able to be reproduced by independent researchers, or when logical inconsistencies appear in published reports. However, more subtle transgressions, such as reporting only data that meet expectations or misleading reports of results, are difficult to detect. The dividing line between intentional misconduct and simply bad science is also not always clear. To educate researchers about the proper conduct of science, and to help guide them around the many ethical pitfalls that are present, most scientific organizations have adopted formal codes of ethics. In Chapter 2 we introduce you to the APA ethical principles governing research with humans and animals. As you will see, ethical dilemmas often arise. Consider the research by Heath and Davidson (1988) mentioned earlier in this chapter. You may remember that they asked groups of university women to help prepare a new rape-prevention pamphlet. Their participants reviewed materials that presented rape as very controllable, somewhat controllable, or not at all controllable. Women who read the uncontrollable version reported greater levels of anxiety about rape than did women who read the other versions. However, the researchers did not actually intend to produce a new rape-prevention pamphlet. Participants in this research were deceived regarding the true purpose of the study: to investigate how perceived controllability of rape influences women's perceptions of vulnerability to rape. Under what conditions should researchers be allowed to deceive research participants?

Deception is just one of many ethical issues that researchers must confront. As yet another illustration of ethical problems, we mentioned that animal subjects sometimes are used to help understand human psychopathology. This may mean exposing animal subjects to stressful and even painful conditions. Again, we must ask about the ethical issues involved with this type of research. Under what conditions should research with animal subjects be permitted? The list of ethical questions raised by psychological research is a lengthy one. Thus, it is of the utmost importance that you become familiar with the APA ethical principles and their application at an early stage in your research career, and that you participate (as research participant, assistant, or principal investigator) only in research that meets the highest standards of scientific integrity.

THE GOALS OF THIS BOOK AND GETTING STARTED DOING RESEARCH

This book provides an introduction to the way in which the scientific method is applied in psychology. As you are probably aware, the scope of psychology is quite large, encompassing many areas of study. Moreover, no single research methodology can be said to answer all the questions raised in a particular area. Thus, the best approach to answering a question about behavior or mental processes is frequently a multimethod one, that is, searching for an answer using different research methodologies. The organization of the book follows loosely the goals for the scientific method. Following a discussion of ethical issues in research (Chapter 2), we introduce you to what are called *descriptive methods*. Naturalistic observation, for instance, is an important tool of psychologists who want to describe behavior in a natural context (see Chapter 3). Questionnaires are among the most commonly used instruments in psychology and frequently are the basis for making *predictions* about behavior. The nature of questionnaires and their use in survey research are discussed in Chapter 4. Several less commonly used measures of behavior—those based on the examination of archival records and those derived from the study of physical traces—are treated in Chapter 5. In the third part of the book we deal with *experimental approaches* to the study of behavior. The emphasis is on experiments done with groups of participants (see Chapters 6–8). Experimental approaches are aimed chiefly at discovering cause-and-effect relationships. However, experimental methods used in the laboratory are not necessarily the same as those used outside the laboratory.

Finally, in the fourth part of the book we introduce you to the methods employed in *applied research*. In Chapter 9 we discuss experiments conducted with small numbers of research participants, in fact, with single individuals ($N = 1$). We also describe the important case study method. The last chapter deals with quasi-experimental designs and with the important topic of program evaluation, which is concerned with assessing the effects of "treatments" applied in natural settings (see Chapter 10).

Many decisions must be made before beginning a research study. The first one, of course, is, what to study. In what area of psychology do I wish to do research? Many students approach the field of psychology with interests in psychopathology and issues associated with mental illness. Others are intrigued with the puzzles surrounding human cognition, such as learning, memory, and problem solving. Still others are interested in problems of developmental and social psychology. Psychology provides a smorgasbord of research possibilities to explore, as illustrated by the literally hundreds of scientific journals that publish the results of psychological research. Our own experience suggests that research ideas spring from one or more of the following:

> simple curiosity;
> observation of people and events;
> reading or hearing about research findings.

No matter how or where you begin to develop a topic for research, at some point you will find yourself needing to peruse the published literature of psychological research. There are several reasons why you must search the psychology literature before beginning to do research. One obvious reason is that the answer to your research question may already be there. Someone else may have entertained the same question and provided an answer, or at least a partial one. It is highly unlikely that you will not find some research finding related to the topic you have chosen. This should not discourage you; in fact, it should be a source of satisfaction. Finding that other people have done research on the same or similar idea will give you the "in" that is necessary to build the science of psychology. Doing research without a careful examination of what is already known may be interesting or fun (it certainly may be easy); perhaps you could call it a "hobby," but we can't call it science. Science is a cumulative affair: Current research builds on previous research. Once you have identified a body of literature related to your research idea, your reading may lead you to discover whether:

there are still things we don't know;

inconsistencies or contradictions are present in the published research;

the research findings are limited in terms of the nature of the participants studied or the circumstances under which the research was done;

a psychological theory is in need of testing;

the results can be applied to societal problems.

Having made such a discovery, you have found a solid research lead, a path to follow.

Searching the psychology literature is not the tedious task it once was; computer-aided literature searches, including use of the Internet, have made identifying related research a relatively easy, even exciting task. In Appendix C of this book we outline how to search the psychology literature, including ways to use computer-based guides.

Of course, identifying a research problem doesn't necessarily tell you *how* to do the research. Once you have a topic in mind, you must begin to formulate a research question. What is it exactly that you want to know? Answering this question will mean that you must make other decisions as well. Should I do a qualitative or quantitative research study? What is the nature of the variables I wish to investigate? How do I find reliable and valid measures of behavior? What is the research method best suited to my research question? What kinds of statistical analyses will be needed? Do the methods I choose meet accepted moral and ethical standards?

One of our major goals is to provide you with the information to make these decisions and many others associated with the research process. But this book is not just about research methods in psychology. We have attempted to incorporate many of the interesting facts and ideas in psychology that have been associated with particular research methods. We have avoided hypothetical examples describing situations that no one is likely to encounter. Instead, we have drawn on the rich field of psychology for examples. Accordingly, reading this book will increase your general knowledge of psychology. In this chapter you have already learned something about the historical basis for a scientific psychology, research on the "pace of life," flashbulb memory, and about scientists' concern regarding the public's uncritical acceptance of the occult. It is now time to get on with the study of specific research methods so that you can learn more about what psychologists have discovered, how they have gone about making these discoveries, and, most importantly, how *you* can do research in psychology.

SUMMARY

Psychology's official beginning is marked by the establishment, in 1879, of a formal psychology laboratory in Leipzig, Germany, under the direction of Wilhelm Wundt. With this beginning came the first applications of the scientific method to problems of psychology. As an approach to knowledge, the scientific method is characterized by a reliance on empirical procedures, rather than intuition, and by an attempt to control the investigation of those factors believed responsible for a phenomenon. Those factors that are systematically controlled in an attempt to determine their effect on behavior are called independent variables. The measures of behavior used to assess the effect (if any) of the independent variable are called dependent variables. Scientists seek to report results in an unbiased and objective manner. This goal is enhanced by giving operational meaning to concepts. Scientists also seek to measure phenomena as accurately and precisely as possible. Measurement involves both physical and psychological measurement. Scientists seek both validity and reliability of these measures.

Hypotheses are tentative explanations of events. To be useful to the scientist, however, hypotheses must be testable. Hypotheses that lack adequate definition, that are circular, or that appeal to ideas or forces outside the province of science are not testable. Hypotheses are often derived from theories. More than anything else, scientists are skeptical. A skeptical attitude is not always found among nonscientists, who may rush to accept "new discoveries" and extraordinary claims.

The goals of the scientific method are description, prediction, and understanding. Both quantitative and qualitative research are used to describe behavior. Observation is the principal basis of scientific description. When two measures correlate, we can predict the value of one measure by knowing the value of the other. Understanding is achieved when the causes of a phenomenon are discovered. This requires that evidence be provided for covariation of events, that a time-order relationship exist, and that alternative causes be eliminated. When two potentially effective variables covary such that the independent effect of each variable on behavior cannot be determined, we say our research is confounded. Confounding must be avoided if we wish to produce a study with internal validity. The external validity of a study involves the extent to which research results can be generalized to different populations, settings, and conditions. Scientific theory construction and testing provide the bases for a scientific approach to psychology. Theories have the important function of guiding research and organizing empirical knowledge. Finally, many ethical questions are raised by psychological research; it is important that the science of psychology be carried out according to the highest standards of scientific integrity.

KEY CONCEPTS

scientific method
empirical approach

reliability
hypothesis

control	correlation
independent variable	causal inference
individual differences variable	confounding
dependent variable	internal validity
operational definition	external validity
validity	theory

REVIEW QUESTIONS

1 For each of the following characteristics, indicate briefly how the scientific approach differs from nonscientific (everyday) approaches to knowledge: general approach, observation, reporting, concepts, instruments, measurement, hypotheses, and attitudes.
2 What is the major advantage of using operational definitions in psychology? What disadvantages are there in using operational definitions?
3 Distinguish between the accuracy of a measuring instrument and its precision.
4 What distinguishes physical measurement from psychological measurement?
5 What three shortcomings often keep hypotheses from being testable?
6 Why do behavioral scientists always seek to maintain a skeptical attitude?
7 What are the three goals of the scientific method?
8 What do we mean when we say the nomothetic approach is used in science? How is the nomothetic approach different from the idiographic approach?
9 Provide an example both of quantitative research and of qualitative research?
10 What three conditions must be met if one event is to be considered the cause of another?
11 Distinguish between the internal validity and the external validity of a research study.
12 Describe how a scientific theory can be used to guide and organize empirical research.
13 Identify at least three characteristics used to evaluate a theory.
14 Explain the use of intervening variables in theory construction. What important quality should an intervening variable have?

CHALLENGE QUESTIONS

1 In each of the following descriptions of research studies, you are to identify the independent variable(s) (IV). You should also be able to identify at least one dependent variable (DV) in each study.
  A A psychologist was interested in the effect of food deprivation on motor activity. She assigned each of 60 rats to one of four conditions differing in the length of time for which the animals were deprived of food: 0 hours, 8 hours, 16 hours, 24 hours. She then measured the amount of time the animals spent in the activity wheel in their cages.
  B A physical education instructor was interested in specifying the changes in motor coordination with increasing age in young children. He selected six groups of children and gave each child a test of motor coordination. The groups of children differed in age; that is, one group was made up of all 5-year-olds, the next group was all 6-year-olds, and so on, up to the sixth group, which was all 10-year-olds.
  C A developmental psychologist was interested in the amount of verbal behavior very young children displayed depending on who else was present. The study he

did involved selecting children who were either 2, 3, or 4 years old. These children were observed in a laboratory setting for a 30-minute period. Half of the children of each age were assigned to a condition in which an adult was present with the child during the session. The other half of the children were assigned to a condition in which another young child was present during the session with the child being observed. The psychologist measured the number, duration, and complexity of the verbal utterances of each observed child.

2 In the following description the independent variable of interest is confounded with a potentially relevant independent variable. Identify the confounding variable and explain clearly how the confounding occurred. Also state exactly what conclusion can be supported on the basis of the evidence presented. Finally, suggest ways in which the study could be done so that it would be internally valid.

A physiological psychologist developed a drug that she thought would revolutionize the world of horse racing. She named the drug Speedo, and it was her contention that this drug would lead horses to run much faster than they do now. (Forget, for the sake of this problem, that it is illegal to give drugs to racehorses.) She selected two groups of horses and gave one of the groups injections of Speedo once a week for 4 weeks. Because Speedo was known to have some negative effects on the horses' digestive systems, those horses given the Speedo had to be placed on a special high-protein diet. Those horses not given the Speedo were maintained on their regular diet. After the 4-week period, all the horses were timed in a 2-mile race and the mean times for the horses given Speedo were significantly faster than the mean times for those not given Speedo. The psychologist concluded that her drug was effective.

3 Two physicians did a study to try to determine why people who are allergic to cats still keep them as pets. They asked 67 patients (22 male and 45 female) with an average age of 40 years to complete a questionnaire concerning the nature of their attachment to their cat. Even though 11 people had a history of emergency room visits following exposure to cats, 38 said they would definitely replace their cat if it died, and an additional 16 reported they would have difficulty avoiding a new acquisition. Having someone to love and companionship were the most commonly selected reasons for having cats. The physicians concluded that cat ownership meets strong psychological needs in allergic patients. What comparison information is needed before reaching the conclusion that the psychological reasons for owning a cat are peculiar to allergic patients?

4 When presented with only correlational evidence, the investigator can only hypothesize about possible causal factors underlying a relationship between variables. A stage wherein the investigator thinks about possible causal factors and "tries them out" as explanations, perhaps during discussions with other researchers, is often a preliminary step to doing research which may provide evidence for the factors responsible for the reported relationship. For each of the following reports of covariation, identify a possible causal factor; that is, speculate on *why* these events are correlated.

A A study of nearly 5,000 Swedish women (20 to 44 years old) revealed that couples who live together before marriage have an 80% higher probability of getting divorced than do married couples who do not live together before marriage.

B Dual-income couples now outnumber those with single incomes, and questions have been raised about how career demands affect relationships. One study reported that among dual-income couples the greater the amount of togetherness, the more satisfactory was the relationship.

C Married women are found to suffer from depression more than men. However, the greater the marital compatibility is, the less the risk of depression among women.

D In 12 countries, including the United States, married men consistently earn more than single men. Marriage has a particularly powerful effect on men's earnings in the United States, Norway, Sweden, and Switzerland, but the general pattern holds true for most nations. The average earnings of married men were consistently higher than the earnings of their unmarried counterparts in all the countries studied. The effect persisted even when education, age or experience, and race were taken into account. Married men in the United States, for example, earned an average of 30.6 percent more income than unmarried men.

ANSWER TO CHALLENGE QUESTION 1

A IV: hours of food deprivation with four levels; DV: time (in minutes) animals spent in activity wheel.

B IV: age of children with six levels (distinguish selection of levels from manipulation in part A); DV: scores on test of motor coordination.

C IV: age at three levels and additional person present with two levels (again, distinguish selection and manipulation); DV: number, duration, and complexity of child's verbal utterances.

Chapter 2

Ethical Issues in the Conduct of Psychological Research

INTRODUCTION

A scientist has an ethical responsibility to do the following:

- seek knowledge;
- carry out research in a competent manner;
- report results accurately;
- manage available resources honestly;
- fairly acknowledge, in scientific communications, the individuals who have contributed their ideas or their time and effort;
- consider the consequences to society of any research endeavor;
- speak out publicly on societal concerns related to a scientist's knowledge and expertise (Diener & Crandall, 1978).

In order to meet these obligations, the scientist must consider the numerous ethical issues and questions of proper scientific conduct that we introduced briefly in Chapter 1. These issues are complex and may arise at any point in the research process. To help guide the ethical behavior of psychologists, the American Psychological Association (APA) has formulated an Ethics Code to aid ethical decision making in the context of doing research, as well as in other contexts, for example, when teaching, doing therapy, or serving as administrators (see American Psychological Association, 1992a). The Ethics Code deals with such diverse issues as sexual harassment, fees for psychological services, test construction, classroom teaching, and expert witnesses.

As stated in the Preamble to the Ethics Code, psychologists are expected to make "a personal commitment to a lifelong effort to act ethically; to encourage ethical behavior by students, supervisees, employees, and colleagues, as appropriate; and to consult with others, as needed, concerning ethical problems" (p. 39). It is important for students of psychology also to make this commitment. They should familiarize themselves with the Ethics Code and make every effort to live up to its stated ideals and standards of behavior. A copy of the complete APA Ethics Code can be obtained from the APA Order Department, American Psychological Association, 750 First Street, N.E., Washington, DC 20002-4242.

Many of the ethical standards in the APA's Ethics Code deal directly with psychological research (see especially Sections 6.06–6.26 of the code). These standards deal with the treatment of both humans and animals in psychological research. As with most ethical codes, the standards tend to be general in nature and require specific definition in particular contexts. Often more than one ethical standard applies to a research situation, and at times the standards may even appear to contradict one another. For instance, ethical research requires that human participants be protected from physical injury. Some research, however, that involves drugs or other invasive treatments may place participants at risk of physical harm. The welfare of animal subjects should be protected; however, as we saw in Chapter 1, certain kinds of research may involve inflicting pain or other suffering on an animal. Solving these ethical dilemmas is not always easy. Thus, you must not only become familiar with the ethical standards, but also practice applying them to real research situations. As you will see, application requires a problem-solving approach to ethical decision making.

Ethical decisions are best made after consultation with others, including one's peers but also those who are more experienced or knowledgeable in a particular area. (In fact, review of a research plan by persons not involved in the research is legally required in some situations.) In the remaining sections of this chapter, we identify those standards from the Ethics Code that deal specifically with psychological research. We also offer a brief commentary on some aspects of these standards and present several hypothetical research plans that raise ethical questions. By putting yourself in the position of having to make judgments about the ethical issues raised in these proposals, you will begin to learn to grapple with applying particular ethical standards and with the difficulties of ethical decision making in general. We urge you to discuss these research proposals with peers, teachers, and others who have had prior experience doing psychological research.

THINGS YOU NEED TO KNOW BEFORE YOU BEGIN TO DO RESEARCH

Because research psychologists must consider a host of ethical issues, problems can be avoided only by planning carefully and consulting with appropriate individuals and groups *prior to doing the research*. Not only does the failure to conduct research in an ethical manner undermine the entire scientific process, retard the advancement of knowledge, and erode the public's respect for the scientific and academic communities, but it can also bring significant legal and financial penalties down on individuals and institutions. The following ethical standards spell out some things researchers must keep in mind as they begin to do psychological research.

APA ETHICAL STANDARDS

6.06 Planning Research

1 (a) Psychologists design, conduct, and report research in accordance with recognized standards of scientific competence and ethical research.

(b) Psychologists plan their research so as to minimize the possibility that results will be misleading.

(c) In planning research, psychologists consider its ethical acceptability under the Ethics Code. If an ethical issue is unclear, psychologists seek to resolve the issue through consultation with institutional review boards, animal care and use committees, peer consultations, or other proper mechanisms.

(d) Psychologists take reasonable steps to implement appropriate protections for the rights and welfare of human participants, other persons affected by the research, and animal subjects.

6.07 Responsibility

1 (a) Psychologists conduct research competently and with due concern for the dignity and welfare of the participants.

(b) Psychologists are responsible for the ethical conduct of research conducted by them or by others under their supervision or control.

(c) Researchers and assistants are permitted to perform only those tasks for which they are appropriately trained and prepared.

(d) As part of the process of development and implementation of research projects, psychologists consult those with expertise concerning any special population under investigation or most likely to be affected.

6.08 Compliance With Law and Standards

Psychologists plan and conduct research in a manner consistent with federal and state law and regulations, as well as professional standards governing the conduct of research, and particularly those standards governing research with human participants and animal subjects.

6.09 Institutional Approval

Psychologists obtain from host institutions or organizations appropriate approval prior to conducting research, and they provide accurate information about their research proposals. They conduct the research in accordance with the approved research protocol.

COMMENTARY

As you can see, the importance of consulting with others about ethical issues prior to doing research cannot be overemphasized. It is particularly critical that a researcher obtain prior approval from the proper institutional committee before doing research.

FIGURE 2.1
Many ethical questions are raised when research is
performed with humans and animals.

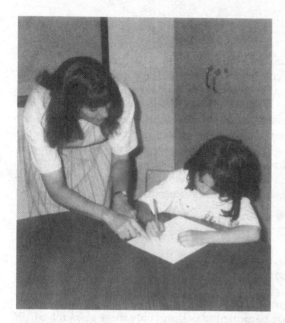

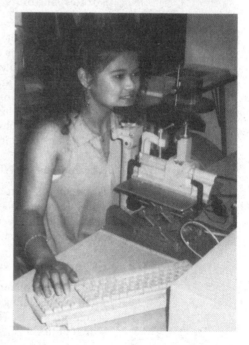

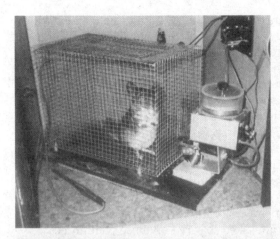

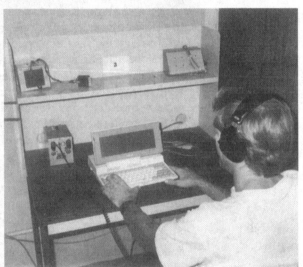

The National Research Act, signed into law in 1974, resulted in the creation of the National Commission for the Protection of Human Subjects of Biomedical and Behavioral Research. This act requires that institutions, such as colleges and universities that seek research funds from specific federal agencies, establish committees to review research sponsored by the institution. These committees, referred to as Institutional Review Boards (IRBs), are frequently called on to review psychological research in order to safeguard the right and welfare of human participants. Federal regulations impose very specific requirements on the makeup and duties of these committees (see *Federal Register*, June 18, 1991). For example, an IRB must be composed of at least five members with varying backgrounds and fields of expertise. Both scientists and nonscientists must be represented, and there must be at least one IRB member who is not affiliated with the institution. Responsible members of the community, such as members of the clergy, lawyers, and nurses, are asked to serve on these committees.

A psychology student seeking to do research with human participants is apt to be asked first to satisfy the regulations of a department committee charged with reviewing research conducted in the psychology department. Depending on the association of this departmental committee with an IRB, research falling into various well-defined categories is either reviewed at the departmental level or referred to the IRB, which has the authority to approve, disapprove, or require modifications prior to the approval of the research.

In a similar vein, in 1985 the Department of Agriculture, as well as the Public Health Service, formulated new guidelines for the care of laboratory animals (Holden, 1987). As a result, every institution doing research with animal subjects is now required to have an Institutional Animal Care and Use Committee (IACUC), whose members minimally must include a scientist, a veterinarian, and at least one person not affiliated with the institution. Review of animal research by IACUCs extends to more than simply overseeing the research procedures. Federal regulations governing the conduct of animal research extend to specifications of animal living quarters and the proper training of personnel who work directly with the animals (Holden, 1987).

Nearly every college and university requires that all research conducted at the institution be reviewed at some stage by an independent committee. Violation of federal regulations regarding the review of research involving humans or animals can bring a halt to research at an institution, spell the loss of federal funds, and result in substantial fines (Holden, 1987; Smith, 1977). Given the complex nature of federal regulations, and the policies of most institutions requiring review of research with humans and animals, *any individual who wants to do research should inquire of the proper authorities, prior to starting research, about the appropriate procedure for institutional review.*

THE RISK/BENEFIT RATIO

In addition to checking if appropriate ethical principles are being followed, a major function of an IRB is to arrive at a consensus regarding what is sometimes called the *risk/benefit ratio*. Despite use of the term *ratio*, the risk/benefit ratio is nothing like a mathematical ratio with easily calculable components. The decision to do research must rest on a subjective evaluation of the costs and benefits both to the individual and to society. Failure to do research may cost society the benefits of the knowledge gained from the research and, ultimately, an opportunity to improve the human condition. To do research may at times exact a cost from individual participants—for example, research participants risk injury when exposed to potentially harmful circumstances. The principal investigator must, of course, be the first one to consider these potential risks and benefits; however, determining the ratio, and hence the decision to do research, is most appropriately made by knowledgeable individuals who do not have a personal interest in the research. As we have indicated, this is often the role played by an IRB.

In its simplest form, the **risk/benefit ratio** asks the question, Is it worth it? When the inconvenience and possible risks to participants are considered, is there sufficient potential benefit to the individual and to society to carry out this research? Many factors affect a decision regarding the proper balance of risks and benefits of a particular research activity. The most basic are the nature of the risk and the magnitude of the probable benefit to the participant as well as the potential scientific and social value of the research (Fisher & Fryberg, 1994). When the benefits to an individual are clear and immediate, or when there is obvious scientific and social value associated with the research, a greater risk can be tolerated than when the benefits are less clear or their application is less immediate. For instance, in the context of research investigating the antecedents of psychotic behavior, the possible benefits to both the participants and society may be substantial if a proposed treatment has a good possibility of having a beneficial effect. Society will also benefit as psychologists come to understand more completely such behaviors as aggression, altruism, bystander intervention, deviance, and suicide. The benefits to be gained by investigating these behaviors, however, must be continually weighed against the risks to the participants.

In determining the risk/benefit ratio, a researcher must also take into account the probability that valid and interpretable results will be produced. An established scientist with a history of successful research in her field, for instance, would reasonably be judged to have a greater chance of obtaining important results than would an undergraduate psychology major. Rosenthal (1994) makes a clear point in this regard: "Everything else being equal, research that is of a higher scientific quality is more ethically defensible" (p. 127). More specifically, "If because of the poor quality of the science no good can come of a research study, how are we to justify the use of participants' time, attention, and effort and the money, space, supplies, and other resources that have been expended on the research project?" (Rosenthal, 1994, p. 128). Thus, *an investigator is obliged to seek only to do research that meets the highest standards of scientific excellence.*

In addition to making sure the research has been planned competently, when risk is present, a researcher must confirm there are no alternative, low-risk procedures that might be substituted or that previous research has not already successfully addressed the research question being asked. Without careful prior review of the psychological literature, for instance, a researcher might carry out research that has already been done, thus exposing individuals to needless risk.

DETERMINATION OF RISK

Determining whether research participants are "at risk" illustrates the difficulties involved in ethical decision making. Life itself is a risky affair. Commuting to work or school, crossing streets, and riding on elevators are all activities that have an element of risk. Simply showing up for an appointment to serve in a psychology experiment must be judged to entail some degree of risk. To say that human participants in psychological research can never risk injury would bring all research to a halt. Decisions about what constitutes risk must take into consideration those risks that are part of everyday life.

Any determination of risk must also consider the nature of the participants. Certain activities can reasonably be judged to pose a serious risk for some individuals but not for others. Running up a flight of stairs may substantially increase an elderly person's chance of suffering a heart attack; the same task would not be a serious risk for most young adults. Individuals who are exceptionally depressed or anxious might be expected to show more severe reactions to certain psychological tasks than would other people. Statements about what constitutes risk cannot be easily generalized to all individuals or populations.

Risk is often associated with the possibility of physical injury as when bodily harm is threatened. More often, however, participants in social science research risk social or psychological injury. The potential for social risk exists when information gained about an individual through her or his participation in psychological research is revealed to others. Simply knowing that someone completed a questionnaire inquiring about deviant sexual practices could cause social injury if those who knew reacted differently to that individual as a consequence of their knowledge. Information collected during the conduct of research may include important personal facts about intelligence, personality traits, and political, social, or religious beliefs. A research participant is not likely to want this information divulged to teachers, employers, or peers. Failure to protect the confidentiality of a participant's responses may significantly increase the possibility of social injury.

The potential for psychological injury exists whenever the procedures associated with a research activity are likely to induce serious mental or emotional stress in the participants. A participant in a social psychology experiment involving a simulated emergency, as when smoke enters a room where she is waiting, may experience a substantial amount of emotional stress until the true simulated character of the event is revealed. Merely participating in a psychology experiment is anxiety provoking for some individuals. After learning a list of nonsense syllables, a student participant once volunteered that he was sure the researcher now knew a great deal about him! The student assumed the psychologist was interested in his mental state as revealed by the associations he used when learning the list. In reality, this person was participating in a simple memory experiment designed to measure forgetting. Even here, the researcher is responsible for putting the participant's mind at ease. Thus, *a researcher is under an obligation to protect participants from emotional or mental stress, including, when possible, that which might arise due to a participant's misconceptions about the nature of a psychological task.*

MINIMAL RISK

A distinction is sometimes made between a participant "at risk" and one who is "at minimal risk." One definition of minimal risk is that followed by IRBs in their review of biomedical and behavioral research (*Federal Register*, January 26, 1981; amended *Federal Register*, June 18, 1991).

Minimal risk means that the probability and magnitude of harm or discomfort anticipated in the research are not greater in and of themselves than are those ordinarily encountered in daily life or during the performance of routine physical or psychological examinations or tests.

As an example of minimal risk, consider the fact that many psychology laboratory experiments involve lengthy paper-and-pencil tests intended to assess various mental abilities. Participants are frequently under time pressure to complete the tests and may receive specific feedback regarding their performance. No doubt some degree of mental or even emotional stress is associated with participation in these kinds of activities. Within limits, however, the risk of psychological injury in this situation would generally be assumed to be no greater than that of being a student. Therefore, college students would be judged to incur only minimal risk in such experiments. Nevertheless, when the possibility of injury is judged to be more than minimal, individuals are considered to be "at risk." When this occurs, more serious obligations fall on the researcher to protect the welfare of such participants.

DEALING WITH RISK

Even when only a slight potential for injury exists, the researcher should try to minimize the risk and provide safeguards for the participants. For instance, stating at the beginning of a memory experiment that the tasks are not intended to measure intelligence or personality reduces the level of stress that some participants experience. When substances are to be taken internally, individuals should be screened prior to participation in order to identify and excuse any who might show unusual physical reactions. In situations where the possibility of harm is judged to be significantly greater than that occurring in daily life, the researcher's obligation to protect participants increases correspondingly. It is not unheard of for an IRB to require that a clinical psychologist be available to counsel individuals when, by participating in a psychology experiment, they are exposed to the possibility of serious emotional stress.

No research activity involving serious risk to participants should be carried out unless alternative, low-risk methods of data collection have been explored. In some cases, descriptive approaches involving observation or questionnaires should be substituted for experimental treatments. It is also possible to take advantage of naturally occurring "treatments." For example, Anderson (1976) interviewed owner-managers of small businesses that had been damaged by hurricane floods. He found that the likelihood of problem-solving coping behaviors by the participants showed an inverted U-shaped function when related on a graph to perceived stress, indicating there is an optimal level of stress and that, when stress is higher or lower than this optimal level, performance decreases. A similar relationship has been demonstrated in a number of experimental laboratory tasks using experimenter-induced stress.

In order to protect research participants from social injury, the method of data collection used should preserve the anonymity of participants or, when this is not possible, ensure the confidentiality of responses. Thus, *if at all possible, a researcher should obtain information about participants in a manner that does not require individuals to be identified.*

Simply not having participants sign their names to the test instruments is obviously one way to keep participation anonymous. When the researcher must test people on more than one occasion or otherwise track specific individuals, numbers can be randomly assigned to participants at the beginning of a study. Only these numbers need appear on participants' response sheets.

When anonymity cannot be preserved, confidentiality should be protected through some type of code system. If the information supplied by participants is particularly sensitive, such a scheme is necessary to minimize the risk of social injury. One procedure is to assign code numbers to participants. Names are linked with the code numbers on a master list. Access to this list is restricted by keeping it under lock and key. Even this system may not adequately protect participants if information about them is related to criminal activity. The master list could be legally subpoenaed. In at least one case, in order to safeguard the rights of his participants, a researcher went so far as to place the master list with the information that linked coded data to specific individuals in the vault of a foreign bank (Diener & Crandall, 1978).

Assuring participants of their anonymity or the confidentiality of their responses can also benefit the researcher if such assurances lead the participant to be more honest and open when responding (Blanck, Bellack, Rosnow, Rotheram-Borus, & Schooler, 1992). It can be assumed that participants will be less likely to fabricate or withhold information if they do not have to worry about who will have access to their responses.

WHAT DO YOU THINK?

For each of the following research situations, do you think only "minimal risk" is present or more than minimal risk is present and participants would be considered "at risk"? If participants are judged to be "at risk," you might think of what safeguards could be employed to reduce that risk. As you do so, you will undoubtedly begin to anticipate some of the ethical issues yet to be discussed in this chapter.

1 College students are asked to complete an adjective checklist describing their current mood. The researcher is seeking to identify students who are depressed so that they can be included in a study examining cognitive deficits associated with depression.

2 Elderly adults in a nursing home are given a battery of achievement tests in the dayroom at their home. A psychologist seeks to determine if there is a decline in mental functioning with advancing age.

3 Students in a psychology research methods class see another student enter their classroom in the middle of the class period, talk loudly with the instructor, and then leave. As part of a study of eyewitness behavior, the students are then asked to describe the intruder.

4 A researcher recruits students from introductory psychology classes to participate in a study of the effects of alcohol on cognitive functioning. The experiment requires that some students drink 2 ounces of alcohol (mixed with orange juice) before performing a computer game.

OBTAINING INFORMED CONSENT

The success of most human psychological research depends on the willingness of students, patients, clients, and other members of the community to take part in a scientific investigation. At times, participants in psychological research are given money or other compensation for their time and effort. At other times, people simply respond to requests by researchers for volunteers to participate in a research endeavor and expect no compensation. Researchers obtain the **informed consent** of participants to ensure that the participants explicitly express a willingness to take part in the research after having been informed about the nature of the research, the consequences of not participating, and the factors that might be expected to influence their willingness to participate. Researcher and participant enter into a social contract. This contract is sometimes an informal one; however, in other circumstances, the contract includes statements signed by both researcher and participant, as well as by witnesses. As part of this contract, *a researcher has an ethical responsibility to make clear to the participant what the research entails, including any possible risk to the participant, and to respect the dignity and rights of the individual during the research experience.*

Although not often discussed, we wish to emphasize that the research participant also has an ethical responsibility to behave in an appropriate manner, for example, by paying attention to instructions and by performing tasks in the manner requested by the researcher. In other words, *lying, cheating, or otherwise fraudulent behavior on the part of someone who has agreed to participate in a scientific investigation is as much of a violation of the scientific integrity of the research situation as is the failure of a researcher to fully explain to the participant the risks inherent in the research task.*

APA ETHICAL STANDARDS

6.10 Research Responsibilities

Prior to conducting research (except research involving only anonymous surveys, naturalistic observations, or similar research), psychologists enter into an agreement with participants that clarifies the nature of the research and the responsibilities of each party.

6.11 Informed Consent to Research

(a) Psychologists use language that is reasonably understandable to research participants in obtaining their appropriate informed consent (except as provided in Standard 6.12, Dispensing With Informed Consent). Such informed consent is appropriately documented.

(b) Psychologists inform participants of the nature of the research; they inform participants that they are free to participate or to decline to participate or to withdraw from the research; they explain the foreseeable consequences of declining or withdrawing; they inform participants of significant factors that may be expected to influence their willingness to participate (such as risks, discomfort, adverse effects, or limitations on confidentiality, except as provided in Standard 6.15, Deception in Research); and they explain other aspects about which the prospective participants inquire.

FIGURE 2.2   When college students are asked to participate in psychological research as part of a course they are taking, equitable alternative activities should be provided for those who do not wish to participate.

(c) When psychologists conduct research with individuals such as students or subordinates, psychologists take special care to protect the prospective participants from adverse consequences of declining or withdrawing from participation.

(d) When research participation is a course requirement or opportunity for extra credit, the prospective participant is given the choice of equitable alternative activities.

(e) For persons who are legally incapable of giving informed consent, psychologists nevertheless (1) provide an appropriate explanation, (2) obtain the participant's assent, and (3) obtain appropriate permission from a legally authorized person, if such substitute consent is permitted by law.

6.12 Dispensing With Informed Consent

Before determining that planned research (such as research involving only anonymous questionnaires, naturalistic observations, or certain kinds of archival research) does not require the informed consent of research participants, psychologists consider applicable regulations and institutional review board requirements, and they consult with colleagues as appropriate.

6.13 Informed Consent in Research Filming or Recording

Psychologists obtain informed consent from research participants prior to filming or recording them in any form, unless the research involves simply naturalistic observations in public places and it is not anticipated that the recording will be used in a manner that could cause personal identification or harm.

6.14 Offering Inducements for Research Participants

(a) In offering professional services as an inducement to obtain research participants, psychologists make clear the nature of the services, as well as the risks, obligations, and limitations. (See also Standard 1.18, Barter [With Patients or Clients].)

(b) Psychologists do not offer excessive or inappropriate financial or other inducements to obtain research participants, particularly when it might tend to coerce participation.

COMMENTARY

Ethical research practice requires that research participants be informed of all features of the research that reasonably might be expected to influence their willingness to participate. The researcher is obligated to respond to any inquiries that individuals might make about the research. By doing this, the researcher assures that participants can make an informed decision about their participation. Participants should also be informed that they are free to withdraw their consent at any time without penalty or prejudice. Consent must be given freely, without undue inducement or pressure. *Informed consent should always be obtained and is absolutely essential when participants are exposed to the possibility of serious injury.*

True informed consent cannot be obtained from certain individuals, such as the mentally impaired or emotionally disturbed, young children, and others who are recognized as having limited ability to understand the nature of research and the possible risks. In these cases, consent must be obtained from the participants' parents or legal guardians. Developmental psychologists who want to test schoolchildren are often faced with the task of contacting dozens (if not hundreds) of parents in order to secure permission for the children to participate in psychological research. Ethical restrictions such as those involving informed consent also raise methodological issues (Adair, Dushenko, & Lindsay, 1985). Results of one study revealed that children of parents who did not provide parental consent for a research project were academically less successful and less popular with their peers than were children of parents who did provide consent (Frame & Strauss, 1987).

Consider, for example, the dilemma faced by one graduate student who was seeking to interview adolescents receiving services from a family planning clinic (Landers, 1988). Parental permission was not required for the teens to attend the clinic; thus, if the investigator asked the parents for permission for their children to participate in the study, she would be revealing to the parents the teens' use of the clinic's services. Yet obtaining permission of parents before conducting research with minors is standard ethical practice and also is mandated by federal laws. To help make a decision regarding proper ethical procedures in this difficult case, the graduate student correctly sought advice from experts, specifically, from members of APA's Committee for the Protection of Human Participants in Research. In 1990, this committee was renamed Committee on Standards in Research, and the scope of its ethical concerns was enlarged (Grisso et al., 1991). The student used the information obtained from the experts to formulate the procedures that she proposed to use as part of her dissertation research. Although advice should be sought from knowledgeable others whenever ethical dilemmas arise, *final responsibility for conducting research ethically always rests with the investigator.*

It is not always easy to decide what constitutes undue inducement or pressure to participate. Paying college students $5 an hour to take part in a psychology experiment would not generally be considered improper coercion. Recruiting very poor or disadvantaged persons from the streets with a $5 offer may be more coercive and less acceptable (Kelman, 1972). Prisoners may believe that any refusal on their part to participate in a psychology experiment will be viewed by the authorities as evidence of uncooperativeness and will therefore make it more difficult for them to be paroled. Parents of schoolchildren may fear that their children will be less well treated by teachers if they refuse to give permission for their children to participate in research. When college students are asked to fulfill a class requirement by serving as participants in psychology experiments (an experience that presumably has some educational value), an alternative method of earning class credit should be made available to those who do not wish to participate in psychological research. Such options should be equivalent, in terms of time and effort, with the requirements of research participation.

Serious ethical problems can arise when a researcher withholds certain information about a psychological treatment from a research participant. The reason for withholding information may be a legitimate concern on the part of the researcher that informing participants of all the details of the experiment will negate the effect of a particular treatment. For example, research on conformity behavior often requires participants to believe that responses of other persons in the situation represent those individuals' own opinions. Telling individuals before the experiment that responses made by other people will be purposely misleading would appear to make this type of research impossible. (We discuss the use of deception in psychological research later in this chapter.)

WHAT DO YOU THINK?

Failure to obtain informed consent was at the center of a controversy surrounding a researcher who submitted copies of a fake article to a number of academic journals in the field of social work (Coughlin, 1988). It is standard practice for journal editors to ask relevant experts to critique papers submitted for possible publication. On the basis of these evaluations, editors make decisions regarding the suitability of prospective articles. The researcher in question wanted to investigate the possibility that social work journals exhibit a confirmational bias, namely, editors tend to accept articles for publication that confirm the value of social work interventions and reject articles that do not. Using fictitious names, he submitted two different versions of a bogus research study to various journals. One version showed a positive outcome from a social work intervention; the other version revealed no positive outcome. Only when the journal editors accepted or rejected his article did he notify them that they had been participants in an experiment.

When the researcher submitted his findings as part of a legitimate article to a scholarly journal, the article was rejected by the editors and a complaint lodged against the researcher with the National Association of Social Workers. The complaint said that the researcher practiced deception and failed to obtain informed consent from the journal editors and expert reviewers. Critics of the research pointed out that the evaluation and processing of the manuscript cost time and money, which, in the view of at least some editors, was not justified by the potential benefits of the findings. The researcher argued that the editorial policies of journals have a significant influence on the practice of science and thus warrant investigation. Many journal editors would undoubtedly agree. However, the question raised is whether the methods used by the researcher in this investigation were ethical.

Do you believe the investigator's methods were ethical?

IRBs require investigators to document that the proper informed consent procedure has been followed for any research involving human participants. A sample informed consent form for use with a normal adult population is shown in Box 2.1. This form may be submitted to an IRB for approval when deception is not present and when no more than minimal risk is anticipated. *If the research involves more than minimal risk or if deception is used, the investigator has*

BOX 2.1

SAMPLE INFORMED CONSENT FORM

[DATE]

I, [NAME OF PARTICIPANT], state that I am over 18 years of age and that I voluntarily agree to participate in a research project conducted by [NAME OF PRINCIPAL INVESTIGATOR, TITLE, INSTITUTIONAL AFFILIATION].

The research is being conducted in order to [BRIEF DESCRIPTION OF THE GOALS OF THE RESEARCH]. The specific task I will perform requires [DETAILS OF THE RESEARCH TASK, INCLUDING INFORMATION ABOUT THE DURATION OF PARTICIPANT'S INVOLVEMENT. ANY POSSIBLE DISCOMFORT TO PARTICIPANT MUST ALSO BE DESCRIBED.]

I acknowledge that [NAME OF PRINCIPAL INVESTIGATOR OR RESEARCH ASSISTANT] has explained the task to me fully; has informed me that I may withdraw from participation at any time without prejudice or penalty; has offered to answer any questions that I might have concerning the research procedure; has assured me that any information that I give will be used for research purposes only and will be kept confidential. [PROCEDURE FOR PROTECTING CONFIDENTIALITY OF RESPONSES SHOULD BE EXPLAINED.]

I also acknowledge that the benefits derived from, or rewards given for, my participation have been fully explained to me—as well as alternative methods, if available, for earning these rewards—and that I have been promised, upon completion of the research task, a brief description of the role my specific performance plays in this project. [THE EXACT NATURE OF ANY COMMITMENTS MADE BY THE RESEARCHER, SUCH AS THE AMOUNT OF MONEY TO BE PAID TO INDIVIDUALS FOR PARTICIPATION, SHOULD BE SPECIFIED HERE.]

_____ [SIGNATURE OF RESEARCHER]

_____ [SIGNATURE OF PARTICIPANT]

---

the responsibility to seek advice from those with experience in the particular problem area under investigation. Others should also be consulted, such as the chairperson of an IRB, in order to prepare a consent procedure that protects the rights of the participants. (General requirements of IRBs for informed consent, including a description of those conditions under which a consent procedure may be modified, have been published in the *Federal Register*, June 18, 1991.)

In some situations it may not be necessary to obtain informed consent. The most obvious example would be when researchers are observing individuals' behavior in public places without any intervention. An investigator, for instance, who wishes to gather evidence about race relations on a college campus by observing the frequency of mixed-race versus unmixed-race groups sitting at tables in the college cafeteria or walking across campus would not ordinarily need to obtain students' permission before making the observations. (We assume the identity of specific individuals will not be recorded.) Such student behavior can be considered public, and the method is naturalistic observation (see Chapter 3). However, deciding what is public or what is private behavior is not always easy.

Diener and Crandall (1978) identify three major dimensions to consider when deciding what information is private and what safeguards should be employed: sensitivity of the information, setting, and degree of dissemination of the information. Clearly, some kinds of information are more sensitive than others. Individuals interviewed about their sexual practices, religious beliefs, or criminal activities are likely to be more concerned about the dissemination of this information than those interviewed about who they believe will win the World Series. Similarly, organizations and businesses are likely to perceive some types of information about them as more sensitive than other types.

The setting in which behavior is observed is also a factor in defining what constitutes private activity. Individuals engaged in what reasonably might be considered public behaviors, such as attending a baseball game or other outdoor event, give up a certain degree of privacy. What is public behavior is not always easy to decide. Such behaviors as riding inside one's own car, using public bathrooms, or picnicking in a park are not easily classified. Decisions about ethical practice in these situations sometimes depend on the sensitivity of the data and the manner in which the information will be disseminated.

Dissemination of information in terms of group averages or proportions is unlikely to reflect on specific individuals. In other situations, code systems can be used to protect participants' confidentiality. *Dissemination of sensitive information about individuals or groups without their permission is a serious breach of ethics.* When information about individuals has been collected unobtrusively (for example, by a concealed observer), one approach that has been suggested is to contact the individuals after the observations have been made and ask whether this information can be used by the researcher.

FIGURE 2.3   Deciding what is public or what is private behavior is not always easy.

As Diener and Crandall indicate, the most difficult decisions regarding privacy involve situations in which there is an obvious ethical problem on one dimension but not on others and situations in which there is a slight problem on all three dimensions. For instance, the behavior of individuals in the darkened setting of a movie theater would appear to have the potential of yielding sensitive information about the individual, but the setting could be reasonably classified as public. **Privacy** refers to the rights of individuals to decide how information about them is to be communicated to others. Whenever possible, the manner in which information about participants will be kept confidential should be explained to participants in psychological research so they may judge for themselves whether the safeguards taken to ensure their confidentiality are reasonable. Implementing the principle of informed consent requires that the investigator seek to balance the need to investigate human behavior on the one hand with the rights of human participants on the other.

During the 1980s, the APA Committee for the Protection of Human Participants in Research became involved in a number of controversies over the ethical issues related to psychosocial research on acquired immune deficiency syndrome (AIDS) (Melton, Levine, Koocher, Rosenthal, & Thompson, 1988). Particularly salient among the ethical dilemmas posed by this research is that related to privacy. Control over knowledge about oneself and one's body is basic to respect for persons and is even constitutionally protected; on the other hand, the courts have supported the government's police power to curb threats to public health (Melton & Gray, 1988). The transmission of AIDS is known to take place via the sharing of body fluids, such as sexual contact or sharing of needles for intravenous injections. Thus, to understand fully the spread of AIDS requires gathering data regarding individuals' sexual practices, drug use, medical history, travel, and acquaintances. Unfortunately, confidentiality cannot always be guaranteed to participants in AIDS research because of laws requiring the reporting of AIDS cases and the fact that records can sometimes be legally subpoenaed (Gray & Melton, 1985). New federal and state laws may be needed to protect the privacy of participants in research involving diseases of this nature (Melton & Gray, 1988).

As in other areas when ethical dilemmas arise, the investigator is obligated to seek advice from knowledgeable others regarding the appropriateness of a research procedure. For example, consultation with members of IRBs, experienced researchers, members of ethics committees, and representatives of the population at risk (Melton et al., 1988) will help ensure that the rights of participants are protected when the psychosocial aspects of communicable diseases are investigated.

DECEPTION IN PSYCHOLOGICAL RESEARCH

No ethical issue related to research is more controversial than that of deception. There are those who would argue that participants should *never* be deceived in the context of psychological research. Deception runs counter to the principle of openness and honesty that ethical practice says should characterize the relationship between experimenter and participant. **Deception** can occur either through *omission*, the withholding of information, or *commission*, the presentation of misinformation to participants about an aspect of the research. Either kind of deception contradicts the principle of informed consent. To some, deception is morally repugnant; it is no different from lying. Nevertheless, despite the increased attention given to deceptive methodological practices over the last couple of decades, the use of deception in psychological research has not declined (Adair, Dushenka, & Lindsay, 1985).

APA ETHICAL STANDARDS

6.15 Deception in Research

(a) Psychologists do not conduct a study involving deception unless they have determined that the use of deceptive techniques is justified by the study's prospective scientific, educational, or applied value and that equally effective alternative procedures that do not use deception are not feasible.

(b) Psychologists never deceive research participants about significant aspects that would affect their willingness to participate, such as physical risks, discomfort, or unpleasant emotional experiences.

(c) Any other deception that is an integral feature of the design and conduct of an experiment must be explained to participants as early as is feasible, preferably at the conclusion of their participation, but no later than at the conclusion of the research. (See also Standard 6.18, Providing Participants With Information About the Study.)

COMMENTARY

It is simply impossible to carry out certain kinds of research without withholding information from participants about some aspects of the research. In other situations, it may be necessary to misinform participants in order to have them adopt certain attitudes or behaviors. As we explain in Chapter 3, participant observers may find it necessary to give false information in order to gain access to a particular group or setting.

Rosenthal's (1966) research investigating experimenter bias was based on the assumption that the participants believed they were experimenters working for a principal investigator. The "experimenters" were actually the participants. The data collected by these participant-experimenters sometimes differed because of the expectations they had about the research outcome. Although deception is sometimes justified on methodological grounds, deceiving participants for the purpose of getting them to participate in research in which they would not normally take part, or research that involves serious risk, is always unethical.

Milgram (1977) has questioned whether the term *deception* is a fair description of the procedures used by psychologists. He suggests that more neutral terms, such as *masking* or *technical illusions*, would be more appropriate. After

all, illusions are sometimes created in real-life situations in order to make people believe something. When listening to a radio program, people are not generally bothered by the fact that the thunder they hear or the sound of a horse
galloping are merely technical illusions created by a sound effects specialist.
Milgram argues that technical illusions should be permitted in the case of scientific inquiry. We deceive children into believing in Santa Claus. Why cannot
scientists create illusions in order to help them understand human behavior?

Just as illusions are often created in real-life situations, in other situations,
Milgram points out, there can be a suspension of a general moral principle. If
we learn of a crime, we are ethically bound to report it to the authorities. On
the other hand, a lawyer who is given information by a client must consider
this information privileged even if it reveals that the client is guilty. Physicians
perform very personal examinations of our bodies. Although it is morally permissible in a physician's office, the same type of behavior would not be con-
doned outside the office. Milgram argues that, in the interest of science, psychologists should occasionally be allowed to suspend the moral principle of
truthfulness and honesty.

A basic assumption underlying the use of deception is that it is necessary to
conceal the true nature of an experiment so that participants will behave as
they normally would or so that they will act in accordance with the stated instructions and cues provided by the experimenter. If people come to realize
(and perhaps many already have) that psychologists often present misinformation and serving in a psychology experiment means they are likely to be deceived, then the very assumption on which the use of deception is based will
be lost. Participants will no longer act in accordance with the instructions of the
experimenter because they will no longer believe the experimenter is telling
the truth. Frequent and casual use of deception undermines the usefulness of
deception as a methodological tool (Kelman, 1967).

The fact that psychologists are often identified with deceptive practices, and
the fact that deception may be the basis for experimental manipulations in natural settings, also may affect the way people react to emergencies or other
events they witness. On one college campus a student was attacked and shot
by another student. Witnesses did not try to help, and the assailant was not
pursued. When bystanders were asked why they did not intervene, some said
they thought it was just a psychology experiment (Diener & Crandall, 1978).

Kelman (1972) suggests that, *before using deception, a researcher must give very
serious consideration to (1) the importance of the study to our scientific knowledge, (2)
the availability of alternative, deception-free methods, and (3) the "noxiousness" of the
deception.* This last consideration refers to the degree of deception involved and
to the possibility of injury to the participants. In Kelman's (p. 997) view: "Only
if a study is very important and no alternative methods are available can anything more than the mildest form of deception be justified." *When deception is
used, the researcher must inform participants after the experiment of the reasons for the
deception, discuss any misconceptions they may have, and remove any harmful effects
of the deception.* One goal of this debriefing is educating the participant about
the need for deception. For example, after female participants were deceived

FIGURE 2.4   Deception is sometimes the basis for experimental manipulations in natural settings; for example, to investigate helping behavior, psychologists may create a situation involving what appears to be a person in distress.

about the true purpose of a study investigating women's perceptions of vulnerability to rape (see Chapter 1, Heath & Davidson, 1988), the researchers explained the reasons for the deception and corrected any misperceptions that had been created.

One final note regarding what is or is not deception should be made. Those who are just beginning to do research sometimes believe that unless they tell participants exactly what they expect to find, that is, the hypothesis being tested, they are deceiving participants. This is not necessarily the case. Information about the specific hypothesis being tested is often withheld from participants in order not to bias them to behave in a certain way. For example, simply telling a group of control participants that comparisons will be made between their responses and those of a group receiving a particular treatment may introduce an unwanted spirit of competition. In most situations, not telling participants exactly what the researcher is testing is simply considered good experimental procedure. Of course, the researcher can never ethically withhold information that might seriously influence a participant's willingness to participate (APA Ethical Standard 6.15). Debriefing provides an opportunity to inform participants about the specific goals of a study and to educate them about the need to do psychological research.

WHAT DO YOU THINK?

The use of deception in psychological research continues unabated, and perhaps has even increased over the past several decades; however, debate in the scientific community concerning its use also has not abated (Fisher & Fryberg, 1994). This debate can be summarized as follows: "Ethical arguments have focused on whether deceptive research practices are justified on the basis of their potential societal benefit or violate moral principles of beneficence and respect for individuals and the fiduciary obligations of psychologists to research participants" (Fisher & Fryberg, 1994, p. 417). A moral principle of beneficence refers to the idea that research activities should be beneficent (bring benefits) for individuals and society. The moral principle of respect for individuals is just that: People should be treated as "persons" and not "objects" for study, for example. This principle would suggest that people have a right to make their own judgments about the procedures and purpose of the research in which they are participating (Fisher & Fryberg, 1994). "Fiduciary obligations of psychologists" refer to the responsibilities of individuals who are given trust over others, even if only temporarily. In the case of psychological research, the researcher is considered to have responsibility for the welfare of participants during the study and for the consequences of their participation.

These ideas and principles can perhaps be illustrated through the arguments of Baumrind (1985), who argues persuasively that "the use of intentional deception in the research setting is unethical, imprudent, and unwarranted scientifically" (p. 165). Specifically, she argues that the costs to the participants, to the profession, and to society of the use of deception are too great to warrant its continued use. Although these arguments are lengthy and complex, let us attempt a brief summary. First, according to Baumrind, deception exacts a cost to participants because it undermines the participants' trust in their own judgment and in a "fiduciary" (someone who is holding something in trust for another person). When research participants find they have been duped or tricked, Baumrind believes this may lead the participants to question what they have learned about themselves and to lead them to distrust individuals (e.g., social scientists) who they might have previously trusted to provide valid information and advice. A cost to the profession is exacted because participants (and society at large) soon come to realize that psychologists are "tricksters" and not to be believed when giving instructions about research participation. If participants tend to suspect psychologists of lying then one may question whether deception will work as it is intended by the researcher. Moreover, Baumrind argues that the use of deception reveals psychologists are willing to lie, which seemingly contradicts their supposed dedication to seeking truth. Finally, there is harm done to society because deception undermines people's trust in experts and makes them suspicious in general about all contrived events.

Of course, these are not the views of all psychologists (Christensen, 1988). For example, earlier in this chapter we discussed briefly Milgram's

(1977) views on deception. You may remember that Milgram suggested that deceptive practices of psychologists are really a kind of "technical illusion" and should be permitted in the interests of scientific inquiry. What do you think about the use of deception in psychological research?

ADDITIONAL RESPONSIBILITIES TO RESEARCH PARTICIPANTS

Over the years, many researchers have fallen into the trap of viewing human participants in research chiefly as means to an end, as "objects" used to obtain data in order to meet the goals of a research study. While perhaps conscientiously giving participants the opportunity to give their informed consent and carefully safeguarding them from serious injury, researchers sometimes have considered their responsibility to participants to end when the last response was made or the final piece of data collected. A handshake or "thank you" was frequently all that marked the end of the research session. This meant the research participants likely left with unanswered questions about specific aspects of the situation and with only the vaguest idea of the role they played in the scientific endeavor. It is important both in the planning and in the conduct of research to consider how the experience may affect the research participant and the participant's environment after the research is completed and to seek ways in which the participant will benefit from participation. As we have just seen, these concerns follow directly from the moral principles of beneficence and respect of individuals.

APA ETHICAL STANDARDS

6.16 Sharing and Utilizing Data

Psychologists inform research participants of their anticipated sharing or further use of personally identifiable research data and of the possibility of unanticipated future uses.

6.17 Minimizing Invasiveness

In conducting research, psychologists interfere with the participants or milieu from which data are collected only in a manner that is warranted by an appropriate research design and that is consistent with psychologists' roles as scientific investigators.

6.18 Providing Participants With Information About the Study

(a) Psychologists provide a prompt opportunity for participants to obtain appropriate information about the nature, results, and conclusions of the research, and psychologists attempt to correct any misconceptions that participants may have.

(b) If scientific or humane values justify delaying or withholding this information, psychologists take reasonable measures to reduce the risk of harm.

6.19 Honoring Commitments

Psychologists take reasonable measures to honor all commitments they have made to research participants.

COMMENTARY

Earlier we mentioned that protecting the confidentiality of a participant's responses brought benefits both to the participant (safeguarding from social injury) and to the researcher (increasing the probability of honest responding). **Debriefing** participants at the end of a research session also carries benefits both to participant and researcher (Blanck et al., 1992). As we saw when discussing the use of deception, *debriefing is necessary to remove any harmful effects or misconceptions about participation (although see Baumrind, 1985), as well as to explain to participants the need for deception; however, debriefing also has the important goals of educating participants about the research (rationale, method, results) and of leaving them with positive feelings about their participation.* Whenever possible, a researcher should take the time to explain the nature of the participant's specific performance and to show how it relates to group or normative data. If this is not feasible, participants should be given the opportunity at some future time to learn about the general outcome of the research. Some researchers take it upon themselves to mail a written report of a study's results to the participants; others, especially when testing captive populations such as college students, invite participants to come back later (for instance, at the end of a semester) to obtain a report summarizing the study's findings. In this way, participants can learn more about their particular contribution to the research study and, in doing so, feel more personally involved in the scientific process.

Debriefing is an opportunity for participants to learn more about research in general—by having the study's methodology explained to them, for instance, or by being introduced to various tests or instruments used in psychological research. Because the "educational value" of participation in psychological research is one reason given to justify the use of large numbers of volunteers from college introductory psychology classes, researchers testing the students have an important obligation to attempt to educate participants about psychological research. In addition to being debriefed, student participants have sometimes been asked by classroom instructors to write brief reports about their research experience, including details about the study's purpose, the techniques used, and the significance of the research to understanding behavior. One evaluation of such a procedure revealed that students who wrote reports were more satisfied with the research experience and experienced a significantly greater overall educational benefit from it than did students who did not write reports (Richardson, Pegalis, & Britton, 1992).

Debriefing can help a researcher by providing an opportunity to find out how the participant viewed the situation and any treatments that were administered. For example, a researcher may wish to know whether a particular experimental procedure was perceived by the participant in the way the investigator intended (Blanck et al., 1992). Studies of what is called incidental learning involve exposing participants to certain kinds of critical material (e.g., the contents of a room, another person, a list of words, and so on) and then later asking them what they can remember of this material. It is important that participants, when exposed to the critical material, be unaware that a memory test will later be given (otherwise, intentional, not incidental, learning will take place). Debriefing enables the investigator to find out how participants perceived the tasks given to them and whether they were aware that their memory would be tested.

Debriefing which seeks to discover how participants perceive a specific task or situation must be done in a manner that avoids pressing them to reveal information they believe they are not supposed to possess. Research participants generally want to help with the scientific process, and many realize that in any valid psychological study information may be purposely withheld from them (Orne, 1962). To tell the researcher that they really *did* know about these details may seem to participants to threaten the study's validity and hence "ruin" it. Thus, if questioned directly, participants may withhold information about their perceptions in a misguided, albeit well-intentioned, attempt to protect the scientific integrity of the study. Debriefing should thus be carried out in an informal manner, with the participant carefully led by the investigator to respond honestly and openly. This is often best accomplished by using general questions in an open-ended format (e.g., What do you think this study was about?) and following up with more specific questions which, as much as possible, do not cue the participant about what responses are expected (Orne, 1962). Debriefing provides yet another benefit to researchers. It can provide them with "leads for future research and help identify problems in their current protocols" (Blanck et al., 1992, p. 962). Debriefing, in other words, can provide clues as to the reasons for a participant's performance, which may help when discussing the overall results or may set the stage for another study. Errors in experimental materials—for instance, missing information or ambiguous instructions—are sometimes detected through postexperimental interviews with participants. As we said, *debriefing is good for both the participant and the scientist.*

RESEARCH WITH ANIMALS

Each year millions of animals are tested in laboratory investigations aimed at answering a wide range of important questions. New drugs are tested on animals before they are used with humans. Substances introduced into the environment must first be given to animals to test their effects. Animals are exposed to diseases in order that investigators may observe symptoms and test various cures. New surgical procedures—especially those involving the brain—are often first tried out on animals. Many animals are also used for behavioral research, for example by ethologists and experimental psychologists. These investigations yield much information that contributes to human welfare (Miller, 1985). In the process, however, many animals are subjected to pain and discomfort, stress and sickness, and death. Although rodents, particularly rats and mice, are the largest group of laboratory animals, researchers use a wide variety of species in their investigations, including monkeys, fish, dogs, and cats. Specific animals are frequently chosen because they are good models of human responses. For example, psychologists interested in audition some-times use chinchillas as subjects because their auditory processes are very simi-lar to those of humans.

Apparently, chimpanzees are the only nonhuman primates that can harbor the virus linked to AIDS (Landers, 1988). As a result, concern over the dwin-dling numbers of these animals has been expressed, not only by animal conser-vationists, who worry about the extinction of the species, but by biomedical re-searchers, who may have to depend on these animals for laboratory research aimed at finding a vaccine for AIDS (Booth, 1988; Goodall, 1987).

APA ETHICAL STANDARDS

6.20 Care and Use of Animals in Research

(a) Psychologists who conduct research involving animals treat them humanely.

(b) Psychologists acquire, care for, use, and dispose of animals in compliance with current federal, state, and local laws and regulations, and with professional stan-dards.

(c) Psychologists trained in research methods and experienced in the care of labora-tory animals supervise all procedures involving animals and are responsible for ensuring appropriate consideration of their comfort, health, and humane treat-ment.

(d) Psychologists ensure that all individuals using animals under their supervision have received instruction in research methods and in the care, maintenance, and handling of the species being used, to the extent appropriate to their role.

(e) Responsibilities and activities of individuals assisting in a research project are consistent with their respective competencies.

(f) Psychologists make reasonable efforts to minimize the discomfort, infection, ill-ness, and pain of animal subjects.

(g) A procedure subjecting animals to pain, stress, or privation is used only when an alternative procedure is unavailable and the goal is justified by its prospective scientific, educational, or applied value.

(h) Surgical procedures are performed under appropriate anesthesia; techniques to avoid infection and minimize pain are followed during and after surgery.

(i) When it is appropriate that the animal's life be terminated, it is done rapidly, with an effort to minimize pain, and in accordance with accepted procedures.

COMMENTARY

The use of animals as laboratory subjects has often been taken for granted. In fact, the biblical reference to humankind's "dominion" over all lesser creatures is sometimes invoked to justify the use of animals as laboratory subjects (John-son, 1990; Rollin, 1985). More often, however, research with animal subjects is justified by the need to gain knowledge *without putting humans in jeopardy* about aspects of nature that directly affect the human condition. Few cures, drugs, vaccines, or therapies have come about without experimentation on animals (Rosenfeld, 1981). It would be difficult to contemplate the consequences of doing research on such diseases as cancer or muscular dystrophy without the opportunity first to examine the course of the disease or try out a new cure on animal subjects. Feeney (1987), for example, has called attention to the contributions that basic research with animal subjects has made to the treatment of patients recovering from brain and spinal cord injury. He also points out that our understanding of the relationship between brain and behavior was advanced significantly by the now classic work in the 1960s of Roger Sperry, who won a Nobel Prize for his work on the "split brain" (the functioning of the brain after the corpus callosum has been cut). Early investigations by Sperry and others, using cats and monkeys as subjects, demonstrated that the two hemispheres of the brain can function independently in learning and memory.

Many questions, however, have been raised about the role of animal subjects in laboratory studies (Novak, 1991; Shapiro, 1991; Ulrich, 1991). These questions include the most basic one, whether animals should be used at all in scientific investigations, as well as important questions about the care and protection of animal subjects. Clearly, according to the APA principles, *the researcher who uses animal subjects in an investigation has an ethical obligation to look out for their welfare and to treat them humanely.* Only individuals qualified to do research and to manage and care for the particular species being used should be allowed to participate. When the research exposes the animals to pain or discomfort, it must be justified by the potential scientific, educational, or applied goals. As we noted earlier when institutional review was discussed, animal review boards (IACUCs) are now in place at research facilities receiving funds from the Public Health Service. These committees are charged with determining the adequacy of the procedures for controlling pain, carrying out euthanasia, housing animals, and training personnel, as well as determining whether the experimental design is sufficient to gain important new information and whether the animal model is appropriate or whether nonanimal models could be used (Holden, 1987).

Partly in response to calls from members of animal rights groups during the 1980s, investigators must now meet a host of federal and state requirements, including inspection of animal facilities by veterinarians from the U.S. Department of Agriculture (Landers, 1987a, 1987b). These regulations are often welcomed by members of the scientific community, and many animal researchers belong to groups such as the APA Committee on Animal Research and Experimentation (CARE) that seek to protect laboratory animals. (CARE has developed a list of specific guidelines to be followed when animal subjects are used in psychological research. A copy of these guidelines may be obtained by writing CARE, c/o Science Directorate, American Psychological Association, 750 First Street, N.E., Washington, DC 20002-4242.) As with any ethically sensitive issue, however, it is clear that compromises must be made. For example, until alternatives to animal research can be found, the need to conduct research using animal subjects in order to battle human disease and suffering must be balanced against the need for adequate control over the way animals are treated in laboratory research (Goodall, 1987). Hovering above this discussion is the need for a balanced treatment of the issues (Kelly, 1986). As APA's chief executive officer, Raymond Fowler, pointed out, it is important that the use of animal subjects not be restricted because the application of the research is not readily apparent (Fowler, 1992). "The charges that animal research is of no value because it cannot always be linked to potential applications is a charge that can be made against all basic research." Such an indictment "threatens the intellectual and scientific foundation" of all psychology, including both "scientists and practitioners" (p. 2).

While few scientists would disagree that restrictions are necessary to prevent needless suffering in animals, most want to avoid a quagmire of bureaucratic restrictions and high costs that will undermine research. Feeney (1987) suggests that severe restrictions and high costs, as well as the negative publicity (and occasional terrorist acts) directed toward individuals and institutions by extremists within the animal activist groups, may deter young scientists from entering the field of animal research (see also Azar, 1994a). If such is the case, the result possibly could be to deprive the (presently) incurably ill or permanently paralyzed of the hope that comes through scientific research.

Clearly, the issues surrounding the debate over the relevance of animal research to the human situation are many and complex. As Ulrich (1992) has commented, discussion of these issues must be approached with "wisdom and balance" (p. 386).

WHAT DO YOU THINK?

Ethical decision making often pits opposing philosophical positions against one another. This is clearly seen in the debate over the use of animals in research. At the center of this debate is the question of the "moral status" of humans and nonhuman animals. As the Australian philosopher Peter Singer (1990, p. 9) points out, two generally accepted moral principles are:

1 All humans are equal in moral status.
2 All humans are of superior moral status to nonhuman animals.

Thus, Singer continues, "On the basis of these principles, it is commonly held that we should put human welfare ahead of the suffering of nonhuman animals; this assumption is reflected in our treatment of animals in many areas, including farming, hunting, experimentation, and entertainment" (p. 9).

Singer, however, does not agree with these commonly held views. He argues that "there is no rational ethical justification for always putting human suffering ahead of that of nonhuman animals" (p. 9). Unless we appeal to religious viewpoints (which Singer rejects as the basis of decisions in a pluralistic society), there is, according to Singer, no special moral status to "being human." This position has roots in the philosophical tradition known as *utilitarianism*, which began with the writings of

David Hume (1711–1776) and Jeremy Bentham (1748-1832), as well as John Stuart Mill (1806–1873) (Rachels, 1986). Basically, this viewpoint holds that whenever we have choices between alternative actions we should choose the one that has the best overall consequences (produces the most "happiness") for everyone involved. What matters in this view is whether the individual in question is capable of experiencing happiness-unhappiness, pleasure-pain; whether the individual is human or nonhuman is not relevant (Rachels, 1986).

What do you think about the moral status of humans and animals and its relation to psychological research?

REPORTING OF PSYCHOLOGICAL RESEARCH

Generally, once a psychological investigation is completed, the principal investigator prepares a manuscript for submission to one of the dozens of psychology-related scientific periodicals. Publication in a psychology journal not only achieves the goal of communicating the results of a study to members of the scientific community and to society in general but, as we have seen, may also enhance the researcher's reputation and even the reputation of the institution that sponsored the research. But getting the results of a scientific investigation published is not always an easy process, especially if the researcher wishes to publish in one of the more prestigious scientific journals. Journals sponsored by APA, such as the *Journal of Abnormal Psychology, Journal of Educational Psychology, Journal of Experimental Psychology: Learning, Memory, and Cognition,* and *Psychological Review,* can have rejection rates as high as 90% (American Psychological Association, 1995). Manuscripts submitted for publication must be prepared according to strict stylistic guidelines (see Appendix C), meet rigorous methodological and substantive criteria, and be appropriate for the particular journal to which the manuscript is submitted.

Problems in any of these three areas may be sufficient to deny publication; however, manuscripts are more commonly rejected because of problems in the methodology of the study, problems in the statistical treatment of the results, or because the results do not make a significant enough contribution to scientific progress in the field. Decisions about the acceptability of a scientific manuscript are made by the journal's editors, usually on the basis of comments made by the experts in the field who have been asked by the editors for their opinions about the manuscript's scientific worth. This process is known as *peer review,* and many scientists have had their hopes of being published dashed along this difficult path. Despite the many pressures to publish in order to earn promotion or tenure at a university, it is imperative that all scientists adhere strictly to the code of ethics governing the reporting of results.

APA ETHICAL STANDARDS

6.21 Reporting of Results

(a) Psychologists do not fabricate data or falsify results in their publications.

(b) If psychologists discover significant errors in their published data, they take reasonable steps to correct such errors in a correction, retraction, erratum, or other appropriate publication means.

6.22 Plagiarism

Psychologists do not present substantial portions or elements of another's work or data as their own, even if the other work or data source is cited occasionally.

6.23 Publication Credit

(a) Psychologists take responsibility and credit, including authorship credit, only for work they have actually performed or to which they have contributed.
(b) Principal authorship and other publication credits accurately reflect the relative scientific or professional contributions of the individuals involved, regardless of their relative status. Mere possession of an institutional position, such as Department Chair, does not justify authorship credit. Minor contributions to the research or to the writing for publications are appropriately acknowledged, such as in footnotes or in an introductory statement.
(c) A student is usually listed as principal author on any multiple-authored article that is substantially based on the student's dissertation or thesis.

6.24 Duplicate Publication of Data

Psychologists do not publish, as original data, data that have been previously published. This does not preclude republishing data when accompanied by proper acknowledgment.

6.25 Sharing Data

After research results are published, psychologists do not withhold the data on which their conclusions are based from other competent professionals who seek to verify the substantive claims through reanalysis and who intend to use such data only for that purpose, provided that the confidentiality of the participants can be protected and unless legal rights concerning proprietary data preclude their release.

6.26 Professional Reviewers

Psychologists who review material submitted for publication, grant, or other research proposal review respect the confidentiality of and the proprietary rights in such information of those who submitted it.

COMMENTARY

The ethical standards governing the reporting of the results of a scientific investigation seem more straightforward than in other areas of ethical concern. There are areas of ethical decision making, however, in which the lines cannot always be drawn clearly. Consider, for example, ethical issues related to assigning *publication credit* to those who make contributions to a research project. Research is often a collaborative effort, involving, for instance, colleagues who offer suggestions about a study's design, graduate or undergraduate students who assist a principal investigator by testing participants and organizing data, technicians who construct specialized equipment, and expert consultants who give advice about computer programs needed for statistical analyses. Because authorship of a published scientific study frequently is used to measure an individual's motivation and competence in a scientific field, *it is important to acknowledge fairly those who have contributed to a project.* However, deciding whether an individual should be credited by being an "author" of a scientific paper or whether that individual's contribution should be acknowledged in a less visible way, such as in a footnote, is not always easy. If authorship is granted, then the order of authors' names must also be decided. "First author" of a multiple-authored article generally signifies a greater contribution than does "second author" (which is greater than third, etc.). There is a general consensus that contributions leading to authorship should be based mainly in terms of their scholarly importance (e.g., aiding the conceptual aspects of a study) and not by the time and energy invested in the study (Bridgewater, Bornstein, & Walkenbach, 1981; Fine & Kurdek, 1993).

A rather troublesome area of concern, not only for some professionals but frequently for students, is that of **plagiarism.** Again, the ethical standard seems clear enough: Don't present substantial portions or elements of another's work as your own. But what constitutes "substantial portions or elements," and how does one avoid giving the impression that another's work is one's own? This can be like walking a tightrope. On one side is the goal of achieving recognition for contributing to the solution of a problem; on the other side is the goal of recognizing others who have previously contributed to its solution. The fact that both professionals and students are too often caught in the act of plagiarizing suggests that many veer from the tightrope by seeking their own recognition at the expense of giving due credit to the work of others. Sometimes acts of plagiarism result from sloppiness (failing to double-check a source to verify that an idea which is presented did not originate with someone else, for example). Errors of this kind are still plagiarism; *ignorance is not a legitimate excuse.* On other occasions, especially among students, plagiarism can result from failure to identify literal passages through the use of quotation marks or to acknowledge the use of secondary sources. A *secondary source* is one that discusses other (original) work. Most textbooks can be considered secondary sources. Again, ignorance concerning the proper form of citation is not an acceptable excuse, and on unfortunate occasions researchers—professors as well as students—have seen their careers ruined by accusations of plagiarism.

Mistakes can be made all too easily. For example, what constitutes a "substantial" element of another's thinking is not always determined by quantity, as is sometimes assumed. That is, researchers occasionally ask "how much" of a passage can be used without putting it in quotation marks or otherwise identifying its source. However, a substantial element can be a single word or short phrase if that element serves to identify a key idea or concept which is the result of another's thinking. Students and other novices in an academic discipline, who may not yet be cognizant of important concepts and ideas in an area of knowledge, must be particularly careful when referring to the work of others. *Whenever material is taken directly from a source it should be placed in quotation marks and the source properly identified.*

Because students and others new to a scientific field frequently rely on secondary sources, it is very important that they understand how to use and cite such sources, which include not only textbooks, but published reviews of research such as appear in scientific journals like the *Psychological Bulletin,* and any other sources whose authors refer to another's findings and ideas. It is always unethical to present an idea or result from an article or publication found in a secondary source *in a manner that suggests you consulted the original work* when your only source of information about the critical material comes from the secondary source. For example, suppose you wish to discuss the interesting work done by Levine (1990) on pace of life that we discussed in Chapter 1 of this text. Unless you are able to locate and peruse the original article, it is unethical for you simply to acknowledge Levine when citing his work; you must also cite the authors of the textbook who discussed his work. It is also bad scholarship because if your readers rely on your report, they will be relying on your interpretation of the textbook authors' interpretation of the original (Levine's) work. It isn't difficult to see how building a base of scientific knowledge on interpretations of interpretations (and so on, when others interpret *your* work) would quickly produce inconsistencies and contradictions.

Citing work mentioned in a secondary source should be avoided whenever possible (for example, by taking the time to locate and consult the original), but when it is necessary to do so, proper citation means informing your reader that you did *not* consult the original work (for example, by using the phrase "as cited in . . ." when referring to the original work). This gives your reader fair warning that the identification and interpretation of the critical material did not originate with you. (Students of psychology are expected to be familiar with the stylistic rules and guidelines for manuscript preparation found in the *Publication Manual of the American Psychological Association,* 4th ed., 1994. See also Appendix C in this textbook.) As with other areas of ethical decision making, when in doubt get advice from others with experience in the area in which you have questions.

WHAT DO YOU THINK?

Ethical concerns associated with the assigning of authorship can take many forms. For example, not only is it unethical for a faculty member to take credit for a student's work, it is also unethical for students to be given undeserved author credit. This latter situation may arise, for instance, in a misguided attempt by a faculty mentor to give a student an edge when competing for a position in a competitive graduate program. According to Fine and Kurdek (1993), awarding students undeserved author credit may falsely represent the student's expertise, give the student an unfair advantage over peers, and, perhaps, lead others to create impossible expectations for the student. These authors recommend that faculty and students collaborate in the process of determining authorship credit and discuss early on in the project what level of participation warrants author credit.

As with many ethical issues, the process of making a good decision is not always easy. Consider the following scenario presented by Fine and Kurdek (1993) as part of their discussion of this important issue:

An undergraduate student asked a psychology member to supervise an honors thesis. The student proposed a topic, the faculty member primarily developed the research methodology, the student collected and entered the data, the faculty member conducted the statistical analyses, and the student used part of the analyses for the thesis. The student wrote the thesis under very close supervision by the faculty member. After the honors thesis was completed, the faculty member decided that data from the entire project were sufficiently interesting to warrant publication as a unit. Because the student did not have the skills necessary to write the entire study for a scientific journal, the faculty member did so. The student's thesis contained approximately one third of the material presented in the article. (pp. 1141–1142)

What do you think? Should the student be an author on any publication resulting from this work? Or, perhaps, should the student's work only be acknowledged in a footnote to the article? If you think the student should be given author credit, do you think the student should be first author or second author?

STEPS FOR ETHICAL DECISION MAKING

Should research participants be placed at risk of serious injury to gain information about bystander apathy? Should psychologists use deception to learn about the causes of date rape? Is it acceptable to make animals suffer in order to learn about human drug addiction? These questions require answers; however, you no doubt realize by now that the answers do not come easily. Moreover, it is often unclear what the "right" answer is or even if there *is* a right answer. More often than not, at least in the context of doing psychological research, the answer is based on the reflective judgment of a group of individuals with varying backgrounds and experiences who are asked to review the study. The people who comprise a university IRB or IACUC, for instance, are one such group. Recommendations can be made regarding the steps to be taken in this review process (Keith-Spiegel & Koocher, 1985). We have prepared one set of recommendations based on our readings and on discussions with philosophers involved in ethical decision making.*

1 Find out all the facts of the situation. In other words, determine exactly what is involved in terms of procedure, nature of participants, and so on.
2 Identify the relevant ethical issues. An important part of this inquiry will be consulting ethical guidelines that are available, such as the APA Ethics Code

*We wish to acknowledge the contributions in this section of various members of the Loyola University of Chicago Center for Ethics, especially David Ozar, Mark Waymack, and Patricia Werhane.

we have excerpted in this chapter, as well as policy statements from various professional organizations. Also, make sure you are aware of state and federal regulations or laws in this area.

3 Decide what is at stake for all parties involved (participants, researchers, institutions). This will mean taking different viewpoints, for example, by asking what is at stake from a scientific point of view, from society's viewpoint, from the view of participants, and from an overall moral viewpoint.

4 Identify alternative methods or procedures, discussing the consequences of each alternative, including their ethical implications. As part of this discussion, consider the consequences of *not* doing the proposed research. Examine the practical constraints of each alternative.

5 Decide on the action to be taken. Judge the "correctness" of your decision not in terms of whether it makes you feel happy (you may not), but, rather, in terms of the process that was followed. Is it the best that can be done given the circumstances?

SUMMARY

Psychological research raises many ethical questions. Thus, before beginning a research project, you must consider the specific ethical issues, as well as the various federal and state laws, relevant to your project. In most cases formal institutional approval—for example, from an IRB or IACUC—must be obtained before beginning to do research. One function of an IRB is to reach a consensus regarding the risk/benefit ratio of the proposed research. Risk can involve physical, psychological, or social injury. Informed consent must be obtained from human participants in most psychological research. Researchers must take special safeguards to protect human participants when more than minimal risk is present and to provide appropriate debriefing following their participation. Debriefing can also help human participants feel more fully involved in the research situation as well as help the researcher learn how the participants perceived the treatment or task. Serious ethical questions arise when researchers withhold information from participants. When deception is used, debriefing should include providing information concerning the reasons for having used deception.

Psychologists testing animal subjects must obey a variety of federal and state guidelines and, in general, must treat the animals humanely. Animals may be subjected to pain or discomfort only when alternative procedures are not available and when the goals of the research are judged to justify such procedures. Reporting of psychological findings should be done in a manner that gives appropriate credit to the individuals who helped with the project. Appropriate acknowledgment must also be made of those individuals whose ideas or findings have previously been reported in the published literature and who therefore contributed to the investigator's planning or thinking about the study.

KEY CONCEPTS

risk/benefit ratio   deception
minimal risk   debriefing
informed consent   plagiarism
privacy

REVIEW QUESTIONS

1 Briefly summarize the role of Institutional Review Boards (IRBs) and Institutional Animal Care and Use Committees (IACUCs) in overseeing psychological research.
2 How is the risk/benefit ratio used in ethical decision making?
3 Differentiate among the following possible types of injury in psychological research: physical, psychological, social.
4 How is the possibility of social risk typically safeguarded against?
5 Under what conditions do the APA ethical standards indicate that informed consent may not be necessary?
6 What do Diener and Crandall (1978) say are three important dimensions to consider when making decisions about what information is private?
7 When is it unethical to deceive human participants?
8 What are the major benefits of debriefing, both to the participant and to the researcher?
9 What kinds of special knowledge are required by the APA standards for those working with animal subjects?
10 According to the APA standards, what circumstances must be present before animals may be subjected to stress or pain?
11 What allows an individual to claim "authorship" of a published scientific report?
12 What specific ethical procedure should be followed when it is necessary to cite information from a secondary source?

CHALLENGE QUESTIONS

NOTE: Each of the challenge questions for Chapter 2 includes a hypothetical research proposal involving a rationale and method similar to that of actual published research. To answer these questions, you will need to be familiar with the APA ethical principles and other material on ethical decision making presented in this chapter, including the recommended steps for ethical decision making that were outlined at the end of this chapter. As you will see, your task is to decide whether specific ethical standards have been violated and to make recommendations regarding the proposed research, including the most basic recommendation of whether the investigator should be allowed to proceed. Unlike other chapters, no answers to the questions are provided. To resolve the ethical dilemmas, you must be able not only to apply the appropriate ethical standards but also to reach an agreement regarding the proposed research after discussion with others whose backgrounds and knowledge differ from your own. You will therefore have to consider points of view different from your own. We urge you to approach these problems as part of a group discussion of these important issues.

I. Assume you are a member of an Institutional Review Board (IRB). Besides yourself, the committee includes a clinical psychologist, a social psychologist, a social worker, a philosopher, a Protestant minister, a history professor, and a respected business executive in the community. The following is a summary of a research proposal that has been submitted to the IRB for review. You are asked to consider what questions you might want to ask the investigator and whether you would approve carrying out the study at your institution in its present form, whether modification should be made before approval, or whether the proposal should not be approved. (An actual research proposal submitted to an IRB would include more details than we present here.)

PROPOSAL 1
RATIONALE

Psychological conformity occurs when people accept the opinions or judgments of others in the absence of significant reasons to do so or in the face of evidence to the contrary. Previous research has investigated the conditions under which conformity is likely to occur and has shown, for example, that conformity increases when people anticipate unpleasant events (e.g., shock) and when the pressure to conform comes from individuals with whom the individuals identify. The proposed research examines psychological conformity in the context of discussions about alcohol consumption among teenage students. The goal of the research is to identify factors that contribute to students' willingness to attend social events where alcohol is served to minors and to allow obviously intoxicated persons to drive an automobile. This research seeks to investigate conformity in a natural setting and in circumstances where unpleasant events (e.g., legal penalties, school suspension, injury, or even death) can be avoided by not conforming to peer pressure.

METHOD

The research will involve 36 high school students between the ages of 16 and 18 who have volunteered to participate in a research project investigating "beliefs and attitudes of today's high school students." Participants will be assigned to four-person discussion groups. Each person in the group will be given the same 20 questions to answer; however, they will be asked to discuss each question with members of the group before writing down their answers. Four of the 20 questions deal with alcohol consumption by teenagers and with possible actions that might be taken to reduce teenage drinking and driving. One member of the group will be appointed discussion leader by the principal investigator. Unknown to the participants, they will be assigned randomly to three different groups. In each group, there will be either 0, 1, or 2 students who are actually working for the principal investigator. Each of these "confederates" has received prior instructions from the investigator regarding what to say during the group discussion of the critical questions about teenage drinking. (The use of confederates in psychological research is discussed in Chapter 3.) Specifically, confederates have been asked to follow a script which presents the argument that the majority of people who reach the legal driving age (16), and all individuals who are old enough (18) to vote in national elections and serve in the armed forces, are old enough to make their own decisions about drinking alcohol; moreover, because it is up to each individual to make this decision, other individuals do not have the right to intervene if someone under the legal age chooses to drink alcohol. Each of the confederates "admits" to drinking alcohol on at least two previous occasions. Thus, the experimental manipulation involves either 0, 1, or 2 persons in the four-person groups suggesting they do not believe students have a responsibility to avoid situations where alcohol is served to minors or to intervene when someone chooses to drink and drive. The effect of this argument on the written answers given by the actual participants in this experiment will be evaluated. Moreover, audiotapes of the sessions will be made without participants' knowledge, and the contents of these audiotapes will be analyzed. Following the experiment, the nature of the deception and the reasons for making audiotapes of the discussions will be explained to the participants.

II. Assume you are a member of an Institutional Animal Care and Use Committee (IACUC). Besides yourself, the committee includes a veterinarian, a biologist, a philosopher, and a respected business executive in the community. The following is a summary of a research proposal that has been submitted to the IACUC for review. You are asked to consider what questions you might want to ask the investigator and whether you would approve carrying out this study at your institution in its present form, whether modification should be made before approval, or whether the proposal should not be approved. (An actual research proposal submitted to an IACUC would include more details than we present here.)

PROPOSAL 2
RATIONALE

The investigators seek to investigate the role of subcortical structures in the limbic system in moderating emotion and aggression. This proposal is based on previous research from this laboratory which has shown a significant relationship between damage in various subcortical brain areas of monkey subjects and changes in eating, aggression, and other social behaviors (e.g., courtship). The areas under investigation are those that sometimes have been excised in psychosurgery with humans when attempting to control hyperaggressive and assaultive behaviors. Moreover, the particular subcortical area which is the focus of the present proposal has been hypothesized to be involved in controlling certain sexual activities that are sometimes the subject of psychological treatment (e.g., hypersexuality). Previous studies have been unable to pinpoint the exact areas thought to be involved in controlling certain behaviors; the proposed research seeks to improve on this knowledge.

METHOD

Two groups of rhesus monkeys will be the subjects. One group ($N = 4$) will be a control group. These animals will undergo a sham operation, which involves anesthetizing the animals and drilling a hole in the skull. These animals then will be tested and evaluated in the same manner as the experimental animals. The experimental group will undergo an operation to lesion a small part of a subcortical structure known as the amygdala. Two of the animals will have lesions in one site; the remaining two will receive lesions in another site of this structure. After recovery, all animals will be tested on a variety of tasks measuring their food preferences, social behaviors with same and opposite-sex monkeys (normals), and emotional responsiveness (e.g., reactions to a novel fear stimulus: an experimenter in a clown face).

The animals will be housed in a modern animal laboratory; the operations will be performed and recovery monitored by a licensed veterinarian. After testing, the experimental animals will be sacrificed and the brains prepared for histological examination. (Histology is necessary to confirm the locus and extent of lesions.) The control animals will not be killed; they will be returned to the colony for use in future experiments.

Part

II

Descriptive
Methods

Observation

As we mentioned in Chapter 1, scientists and nonscientists alike rely on observation to learn about behavior. What distinguishes scientific observation from nonscientific observation is the manner in which observations are made. Nonscientists are likely to observe casually and are often unaware of personal and situational biases that may influence their observations. Nonscientists rarely keep formal records of what they observe and consequently depend on memory for information about an event. Unfortunately, what one remembers about an event is not likely to be a literal record of what one experienced, and memory can be affected by information added after an event is observed (Bartlett, 1932; Lepore & Sesco, 1994; Loftus, 1979b, 1993).

Scientific observation, on the other hand, is made under precisely defined conditions, in a systematic and objective manner, and with careful record keeping. When observations are made in this manner, valuable information about behavior and its antecedents can be obtained. And, while observation is basic to all of psychology, we can distinguish among several types of observational studies.

An important task of the psychologist is to describe behavior in its natural context and to identify relationships among variables that are present. Changes in behavior are frequently observed to result from the context in which behavior occurs. For example, Schaller (1963) observed that mountain gorillas regularly eat meat when in captivity, but he found no evidence of meat eating by gorillas in the wild. Moderately obese people eating in a cafeteria were observed to purchase less food and to consume fewer calories when eating with others than when eating alone (Krantz, 1979). By describing behavior in natural settings, the psychologist seeks to establish a basis for predicting future behavior.

Often, observation is also the first step in discovering the reasons why organisms behave the way they do. Observation, in other words, is an important step in hypothesis generation. For example, both animals and humans are known to display distinctive reactions to novel or unfamiliar situations. Observing a group of 2- and 3-year-old children in the presence of an unfamiliar person or object, Kagan, Reznick, and Snidman (1988) identified those children who were consistently shy, quiet, and timid and those who were consistently sociable, talkative, and affectively spontaneous. When the same children were observed at 7 years of age, a majority of the children in each group exhibited similar behaviors. The researchers hypothesized that shyness in childhood as well as extreme social anxiety in adulthood are the result of temperamental differences present at birth.

Systematic observation is an important tool not only of psychologists but of anthropologists, sociologists, and ethologists. In this chapter we examine observational methods used to investigate behavior—especially, but not exclusively, in natural settings. As you will see, the scientist-observer is not always passive, present merely to record behavior. Researchers sometimes intervene in the situation in which they are observing behavior. We take a look at scientists' reasons for intervening in natural settings. Methods for recording data and techniques for analyzing data are also illustrated, and we explain some limitations and problems associated with the observation of behavior.

CLASSIFICATION OF OBSERVATIONAL METHODS

Observational methods can be classified according to the degree to which an observer intervenes in an observational setting as well as according to the way in which that behavior is recorded (Willems, 1969). Hence we make an important distinction between observation with intervention and observation without intervention. Methods of recording behavior also generally differ in terms of whether all (or nearly all) of the behavior exhibited in a given setting is recorded or only particular units of behavior are recorded. In some situations an observer may seek a comprehensive description of behavior. This may be accomplished by the use of film, tapes, or lengthy verbal descriptions. More often, a researcher records specific units of behavior that are related to the goals of a particular study. An investigator, for instance, who is interested in prosocial behavior likely will concentrate on specific behaviors that define this type of behavior. For example, Chambers and Ascione (1987) observed children while they played either an aggressive video game or a video game with prosocial content. Children who played the aggressive game were later observed to put less money in a donation box and to volunteer to help sharpen pencils significantly less than did those who played the prosocial game. We discuss observational methods first in terms of the extent of observer intervention and then in terms of methods of recording behavior.

OBSERVATION WITHOUT INTERVENTION

Observation of behavior in a more or less natural setting, without any attempt by the observer to intervene, is frequently called **naturalistic observation.** An observer using this method of observation acts as a passive recorder of what occurs. The events witnessed are those that occur naturally and have not been manipulated or in any way controlled by the observer. What exactly constitutes a natural setting is not easily identified (Bickman, 1976; Willems & Raush, 1969). In general, we can consider a natural setting one in which behavior occurs ordinarily and one that has not been arranged specifically for the purpose of recording behavior. Observing people in a psychology laboratory would not, for instance, be considered naturalistic observation. The laboratory situation has been created specifically to study behavior and, in a manner of speaking, is an artificial rather than a natural setting. In fact, an important reason for doing naturalistic observation is to verify relationships between variables that have been identified in the psychology laboratory. Observation in natural settings serves, among other functions, as a way to establish the external validity of laboratory findings.

The major goals of observation in natural settings are to describe behavior as it ordinarily occurs and to investigate the relationship among variables that are present. Hartup (1974), for instance, chose naturalistic observation to investigate the frequency and types of aggression exhibited by preschoolers in a St. Paul, Minnesota, children's center. He distinguished hostile aggression (person-oriented) from instrumental aggression (aimed at the retrieval of an object, territory, or privilege). Although he observed boys to be more aggressive over-

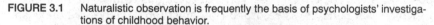

FIGURE 3.1   Naturalistic observation is frequently the basis of psychologists' investigations of childhood behavior.

all than girls, his observations provided no evidence that the types of aggression differed between the sexes. Thus, Hartup was able to conclude that, with respect to hostile aggression, there was no evidence that boys and girls were "wired" differently.

Hartup's study of children's aggression illustrates why a researcher may choose to use naturalistic observation rather than to manipulate conditions related to behavior. There are certain aspects of human behavior that moral or ethical considerations prevent us from controlling. Researchers may be interested in the relationship between early childhood isolation and later emotional and psychological development. However, we would object strenuously if they tried to take children from their parents in order to raise them in isolation. Alternative methods of data collection must be considered if this problem is to be investigated. For example, the effect of early isolation on later development has been studied through experimentation on animal subjects (Harlow & Harlow, 1966), case studies of children subjected to unusual conditions of isolation by their parents (Curtiss, 1977), and systematic observation of institutionalized children (Spitz, 1965). The nature of children's aggression is another aspect of behavior the investigation of which is subject to moral and ethical limitations. We would not want to see children intentionally harassed and picked on simply to record their reactions. However, as anyone knows who has observed children, there is plenty of naturally occurring aggression. Hartup's study shows how observation without intervention can be a useful alternative to methods of data collection that attempt to manipulate the behavior of interest.

Psychologists are not the only researchers who observe behavior in natural settings. Observation is a fundamental method of ethologists. Although related to psychology, **ethology** is generally considered a branch of biology (Eibl-Eibesfeldt, 1975). Ethologists study the behavior of organisms in relation to their natural environment. A major question they seek to answer is how natural selection has worked to produce particular behavior patterns in an animal species. The focus of an ethological investigation is often the development of an **ethogram,** a complete catalog of all the behavior patterns of an organism, including information on frequency, duration, and context of occurrence for each behavior.

Ethologists adopt a comparative approach to understanding behavior and often seek to explain behavior in one animal species on the basis of innate patterns of behavior observed in species lower on the evolutionary scale. Speculations about the role of innate mechanisms in determining human behavior are not uncommon among ethologists. For instance, Barash (1977) observed whether male and female human pedestrians visually scanned both directions before crossing a dangerous intersection in Seattle, Washington. When a male adult and a female adult were together, adult males scanned more than females. This was true regardless of whether children were also present. The ethologist-observer suggested an evolutionary explanation: Adult male monkeys and baboons in the wild generally function as lookouts to warn the rest of the group of approaching danger. An ethological perspective has proved important for the understanding of both normal and abnormal human behavior.

An interesting example is the ethological analysis of psychiatric problems based on comprehensive descriptions of facial behavior of schizophrenic patients (Pitman et al., 1987).

OBSERVATION WITH INTERVENTION

It is characteristic of the scientist to tamper with nature, to intervene, in order to make a point or to test a theory. Intervention rather than nonintervention characterizes most psychological research. Kinds of intervention vary widely in psychological studies, depending on such things as the purpose for investigating behavior, the nature of the behavior under observation, and the ingenuity of the researcher.

Although the types of intervention employed by psychologists are too numerous and diverse to classify, their reasons for intervening are generally one or more of the following:

1 To precipitate or cause an event that occurs infrequently in nature or normally occurs under conditions that make it difficult to observe.

2 To investigate the limits of an organism's response by varying systematically the qualities of a stimulus event.

3 To gain access to a situation or event that is generally not open to scientific observation.

4 To arrange conditions so that important antecedent events are controlled and consequent behaviors can be readily observed.

5 To establish a comparison by manipulating one or more independent variables to determine their effect on behavior.

These reasons for intervening are illustrated in three methods of observation: participant observation, structured observation, and the field experiment. As we review these major observational techniques, the investigator's reasons for intervening will become clear.

PARTICIPANT OBSERVATION

Observation of behavior by someone who also plays an active and significant role in the situation or context in which behavior is recorded is called **participant observation.** In *undisguised* participant observation, the individuals who are being observed know the observer is present for the purpose of collecting information about their behavior. This method is frequently used by anthropologists who seek to understand the culture and behavior of groups by living and working with members of the group.

When the observer's role is not known to those who are being observed, we speak of *disguised* participant observation. As you might imagine, people do not always behave in the way they ordinarily would when they know their behavior is being recorded. Politicians, for instance, often make different statement when speaking to the press, depending on whether their comments are "for" or "off" the record. Our own behavior is likely to be affected by knowing we are being watched. This problem associated with observational methods is discussed more fully later in the chapter. For now, let us simply say that researchers may decide to disguise their role as observers if they believe that people being observed will not act as they ordinarily would if they know their activities are being recorded.

Disguised participant observation was used by Rosenhan (1973) to investigate the basis of psychiatric diagnosis in the context of a mental institution. Eight individuals (including psychologists, a pediatrician, and a housewife) misrepresented their names and occupations and sought admission to 12 different mental hospitals. Each complained of the same general symptom: He or she was hearing voices. Rosenhan (p. 251) described these symptoms and the rationale for their selection by the observers as follows:

> Asked what the voices said, he replied that they were often unclear, but as far as he could tell they said "empty," "hollow," and "thud." The voices were unfamiliar and were of the same sex as the pseudopatient. The choice of these symptoms was occasioned by their apparent similarity to existential symptoms. Such symptoms are alleged to arise from painful concerns about the perceived meaninglessness of one's life. It is as if the hallucinating person were saying, "My life is empty and hollow." The choice of these symptoms was also determined by the *absence* of a single report of existential psychoses in the literature. Beyond alleging the symptoms and falsifying name, vocation, and employment, no further alterations of person, history, or circumstances were made.

Immediately after being put in the mental ward, the researchers stopped complaining of any symptoms and refrained from acting abnormally. In addition to observing patient-staff interactions, the observers were interested in how long it took for a "sane" person to be released from the hospital. Length of hospitalization ranged from 7 to 52 days. The researchers were never detected as sane and, when they were discharged, their schizophrenia was said only to be "in remission." Apparently, once the pseudopatients were labeled schizophrenic, they were stuck with that label no matter what the nature of their subsequent behavior.

Participant observation allows an observer to gain access to a situation that is not usually open to scientific observation. In addition, the participant observer is often in a position to have the same experiences as the people under study. This may provide important insights and understanding of individuals or groups. The pseudopatients in the Rosenhan study, for instance, felt what it was like to be labeled schizophrenic and not to know how long it would be before they could return to society. In the fall of 1959, John Howard Griffin set out to research "what it was like to be a Negro in a land where we keep the Negro down." Griffin, a white man, darkened his skin using medication and stain in order to pass himself off as black. For more than a month he traveled (walking, hitchhiking, riding buses) through Mississippi, Alabama, and Georgia. He described his experiences as a participant observer in his book *Black Like Me*

(1960), which was an important precursor of the civil rights movement of the 1960s.

A participant observer's role in a situation can produce certain methodological problems. By identifying with the individuals under study, it is possible for an observer to lose the scientific objectivity that accurate and valid observation requires. Changes in a participant observer are sometimes dramatic and not easily anticipated. Witness the experiences of a criminologist who used undisguised participant observation to study police officers at work. Kirkham (1975) went through police academy training like any recruit and became a uniformed patrol officer assigned to a high-crime area in a city of about half a million. His immersion in the daily activities of an officer on the beat led to marked changes in his attitudes and personality. As Kirkham (p. 19) himself noted:

> As the weeks and months of my new career as a slum policeman went by, I slowly but inexorably began to become indistinguishable in attitudes and behavior from the policemen with whom I worked. . . . According to the accounts of my family, colleagues and friends, I began to increasingly display attitudinal and behavioral elements that were entirely foreign to my previous personality—punitiveness, pervasive cynicism and mistrust of others, chronic irritability and free-floating hostility, racism, a diffuse personal anxiety over the menace of crime and criminals that seemed at times to border on the obsessive. A former opponent of capital punishment, I became its vociferous advocate in cases involving felony murder, kidnapping and the homicide of police officers—even though as a criminologist I continued to recognize its ineffectiveness as a deterrent to crime. Participant observers must be aware of the threat to objective reporting that arises due to their involvement in the situation wherein they are recording behavior. This threat necessarily increases as degree of involvement increases.

Another problem with observer involvement is the effect the observer has on the behavior of those being studied. It is more than likely that the participant observer will have to interact with other people, make decisions, initiate activities, assume responsibilities, and otherwise act like everyone else in that situation. Whenever observers intervene in a natural setting, they must ask to what degree participants and events are affected by the intervention. Is what is being observed the same as it would have been if the observer had never appeared? It is difficult to generalize results to other situations if intervention produces behavior specific to the conditions and events created by the observer.

In the case of participant observation, the extent of an observer's influence on the behavior under observation is not easily assessed. Several factors must be considered, such as whether participation is disguised or undisguised, the size of the group entered, and the role of the observer in the group. Griffin, for example, was not known to be a white man even by most of the blacks he associated with, and his entry into a subculture of literally thousands of disadvantaged blacks could not reasonably be expected to influence the nature of black-white interactions that he observed. Similarly, it does not appear that Rosenhan and his associates significantly affected the natural environment of the mental ward by assuming the role of mental patients. (However, some of the patients—although none of the staff—apparently detected the sanity of the pseudopatients, suggesting to the observers that they were there to check up on the hospital.)

When the group under observation is small or the activities of the participant observer are prominent, the observer is more likely to have a significant effect on participants' behavior. This problem confronted several social psychologists who infiltrated a group of people who claimed to be in contact with beings from outer space (Festinger, Riecken, & Schachter, 1956). A leader of the group said he had received a message from the aliens predicting a cataclysmic flood on a specific date. The flood was to stretch from the Arctic Circle to the Gulf of Mexico. The prophecy was reported in the newspapers, and certain psychologists who read the account saw an opportunity to test a theory of group cohesion and reaction in the face of unfulfilled prophecy. (The psychologists assumed the flood was not going to occur.) Because of the attitudes of members of the group toward "nonbelievers," the researchers were forced to make up bizarre stories in order to gain access to the group. This tactic worked too well. Not only were the disguised participant observers welcomed into the group, which never consisted of more than a dozen hard-core believers, but their stories were taken as signs from the extraterrestrial beings. One of the observers was even thought to be a spaceman bringing a message. The researchers had inadvertently reinforced the group's beliefs and influenced in an undetermined way the course of events that followed. By the way, the flood never occurred, but at least some of the group members came to use this disconfirmation as a means of strengthening their initial belief. They began to seek new members by arguing that their faith had prevented the prophesied flood.

Thus, although participant observation may permit an observer to gain access to situations not usually open to scientific investigation, the observer using this technique must seek ways to deal with the possible loss of objectivity and the potential effects that a participant observer may have on the behavior under study.

STRUCTURED OBSERVATION

A variety of observational methods using intervention are not easily categorized. Because researchers exert some control over the events, these procedures differ from naturalistic observation without intervention. However, the degree of control in these instances is often less than that seen in field experiments, which we consider later. We have labeled these procedures **structured observation.** Often the observer intervenes in order to cause an event to occur or to "set up" a situation so that events can be more easily recorded than they would be without intervention. In other cases the observer may create quite elaborate procedures to investigate a particular behavior more fully.

Structured observations may occur in a natural setting or in a laboratory setting. Structured laboratory observations are often used by clinical psychologists when making behavioral assessments of parent-child interactions (Hughes & Haynes, 1978). A parent and child who are seeking some sort of help come to a diagnostic clinic or laboratory and are asked to engage in specific tasks while being observed (often from behind a one-way window). Observations are made of various specific behaviors (for instance, tantrums or other emotional outbursts by the child) and of the general nature of the parent-child interactions. Partly on the basis of the results of this structured observation, the therapist plans a strategy to address the behavioral problems that exist. In another context, a group of educational psychologists observed elementary and junior high school students while they worked on class assignments. Observations were made in a private room containing various kinds of furniture, as well as a television set and radio (Patton, Routh, & Stinard, 1986). Results confirmed what had been reported previously for descriptions of study at home: A majority of the children preferred to study with the television set or radio turned on.

Structured observations are also frequently used by developmental psychologists. Perhaps most notable are the methods of Jean Piaget (1896–1980). In many of Piaget's studies a child is first given a problem to solve and then given several variations on the problem to test the limits of the child's understanding. The observer acquaints the child with the nature of the problem and then usually asks questions to probe the child's reasoning processes. These structured observations have provided a wealth of information regarding children's cognition and are the basis for Piaget's stage theory of intellectual development.

Structured observation is a compromise between the passive nonintervention of naturalistic observation and the systematic manipulation of independent variables and precise control that characterize laboratory methods. Such a compromise permits observations to be made under conditions that are more natural than those imposed in a laboratory. Nevertheless, there may be a price to pay. The failure to follow similar procedures each time an observation is made may make it difficult for other observers to obtain the same results when investigating a problem. Uncontrolled, and perhaps unknown, variables may play an important part in producing the behavior under observation. For example, the fact that structured observations like those used by Piaget do not always follow the same procedure from one observation to another can be viewed as a problem with these techniques (Brainerd, 1978).

To reinforce this point regarding the possible influence of uncontrolled variables in structured observation, let us relate a historical anecdote about two well-known psychologists in the first half of the twentieth century (Cohen, 1979).

In 1913, the same year he launched psychology on a new course with his remarks entitled, "Psychology as the Behaviorist Views It," John B. Watson set sail for the Tortugas islands off the coast of Florida. On a previous visit to the islands, he had begun observations of noddy and sooty terns in their natural habitat. Accompanying him was Karl Lashley, a student of Watson's who later did important physiological studies of brain function. Lashley went with Watson to help him make his observations and to help test the homing abilities of terns. At one point during the summer, Lashley removed 30 birds from their nests and took them with him on a boat trip to Mobile, Alabama, where he released 15 of them. Traveling more than 100 miles farther to Galveston, Texas, Lashley set free the remaining 15 birds. Watson waited on the island to record the arrival of the birds if, indeed, they were able to make it back as popular stories of the time suggested. Four days after Lashley released them, the birds began returning to the island. Watson and Lashley had demonstrated that terns could safely navigate across an open sea with no obvious landmarks from a distance of 1,000 miles. They were at a loss to explain how the birds managed their remarkable feat, and, as events transpired, Watson did not have the opportunity to carry out any more tests of the birds' homing abilities.

Suppose, however, that the procedure of taking the terns on board a ship caused some of the birds to become ill (something that had actually happened on a previous occasion, when the birds died in transit), and their illness affected their homing behavior. When no birds returned to their nests after being released, the observers might have wrongly concluded that the animals had no homing instinct. This possibility does not seem that farfetched when you consider that more recent observations of bird navigation have revealed that homing pigeons make use of airborne odors to recognize the location of their lofts (Wallraff & Sinsch, 1988). Birds who were allowed to smell only filtered air before being released did not show any tendency to return home.

Structured observations are often important for gathering information about behavior, and even for testing specific hypotheses. Researchers must be aware of the limitations they impose when they allow some variables to remain uncontrolled and when procedures differ with the circumstances or the behavior of the subject under observation.

Ethologists frequently use structured observation to study the limits of an organism's response by varying systematically the characteristics of a stimulus event. For example, observations by Nobel Prize-winning ethologist Konrad Lorenz led to the discovery of imprinting (Eibl-Eibesfeldt, 1975). Imprinting is a process by which certain animal species form an attachment to an object encountered during a critical or sensitive period in their lives. Immediately after hatching, for example, the young graylag gosling imprints on almost any moving object in its environment and follows that object for some time afterward. Under ordinary conditions, the object of the bird's imprinting is its parent, and the innately triggered response is important for the young bird's survival. To understand the imprinting response better, ethologists have sometimes created models of both male and female parents and tested the young animal's response when the models were moving, when they made a noise, or when the imprinting response was punished (Eibl-Eibesfeldt, 1975). Lorenz himself served as a model; many students of psychology have been introduced to ethology by scenes of the famous ethologist being energetically pursued over land and water by the young birds who attached themselves (imprinted) to him.

FIELD EXPERIMENTS

When an observer manipulates one or more independent variables in a natural setting in order to determine their effect on behavior, the procedure is called a **field experiment.** Although we discuss experimental methods extensively in later chapters, we mention the field experiment here because it represents one end of the nonintervention-intervention dimension that characterizes observational methods. In conducting a field experiment, the observer (now usually called the experimenter) seeks to control the antecedents of an event in order to measure systematically the effect of a variable on behavior. Control or comparison groups are used, and the experimenter usually dictates the assignment of participants to conditions. The field experiment is probably the most frequently used field observation technique in social psychology (Bickman, 1976). In most cases individuals are unaware that they are participating in an experiment. In a field experiment a researcher also typically makes use of confederates. A **confederate** is someone in the research situation who is instructed to behave in a certain way in order to produce an experimental situation. Confederates, for example, have been employed by social psychologists to pose as robbers when bystander reaction to a crime has been investigated (Latané & Darley, 1970) and to mimic the behavior of individuals cutting into a waiting line in order to study the reactions of those in line (Milgram, Liberty, Toledo, & Wackenhut, 1986).

Field experiments sometimes yield valuable practical knowledge. For example, research by Latané and Darley and others has helped us understand the variables that affect a bystander's willingness to come to the aid of a victim. Interestingly, many studies show that a bystander is more likely to aid a victim when the bystander is alone than when other bystanders are present. In a less serious, but also in a potentially practical vein, Crusco and Wetzel (1984) investigated the effect of touching on diners in a restaurant. Waitresses working as confederates touched restaurant customers on either the hand or the shoulder while returning change. The researchers speculated that a touch on the hand would produce positive affect toward the waitress whereas a touch on the shoulder, which may be seen as a sign of dominance, would not be viewed positively, especially by male diners. The participants were 114 diners from two restaurants who were randomly assigned to three levels of the independent variable: Fleeting Touch, when the waitress twice touched the diner's palm for 1/2 second when returning change; Shoulder Touch, when she placed her hand for from 1 to 1 1/2 seconds on the diner's shoulder as she gave back change; and No Touch, when no physical contact was made with the customers. The major dependent variable was the size of the tip. Results showed that males tipped overall more than females but that both male and female diners gave a significantly larger tip after being touched than when not touched. The results did not show, as the researchers had expected, that the nature of the touch made a difference; male and female diners were affected equally by both kinds of touches.

RECORDING BEHAVIOR

We have mentioned two important characteristics of observational methods. One is the degree of observer intervention, the other the method of recording behavior. As we have tried to show, intervention is a dimension anchored at one end by the absence of any intervention (as is associated with passive observation in a natural setting) and at the other end by the active and systematic manipulation of antecedent events that characterizes field experiments. Observational methods also differ in the manner in which behavior is recorded, particularly the degree to which behavior is abstracted from the situation in which it is observed (see Willems, 1969, for a thorough discussion of this aspect of observational methods).

In general, methods of recording behavior can be classified as those that seek a comprehensive description of behavior and the situation in which it occurs and those that focus on only certain kinds of behavior or events. Whether all behavior in a given setting or only selected aspects are to be observed depends on the purposes or goals of an observational study. Decisions regarding the manner in which behavior is recorded also depend on whether the investigator is doing qualitative or quantitative research. As we saw in Chapter 1, the results of a qualitative study are presented chiefly in the form of verbal description and logical argument, whereas quantitative research emphasizes statistical description and analysis of data to support a study's conclusions. The important point for you to remember is that how the results of a study are eventually summarized, analyzed, and reported hinges on the way in which the behavior is initially recorded.

NARRATIVE RECORDS

Narrative records are intended to provide a more or less faithful reproduction of behavior as it originally occurred. Written descriptions of behavior made by an observer are one major type of narrative record. So are the spoken records produced by using a tape recorder and the visual records obtained with videotape or movie cameras. Ethologists are often interested in every detail of a behavioral event, so motion picture film turns out to be one of their most important means of recording behavior (Eibl-Eibesfeldt, 1975). For example, to study the function of the "eyebrow flash" in social interactions, ethologists made use of 67 hours of film showing individuals in naturally occurring social situations (Grammer, Schiefenhovel, Schleidt, Lorenz, & Eibl-Eibesfeldt, 1988). Across three different cultures, the eyebrow flash, usually accomplished by a smile, was found to be a universal social signal, for example, as a sign of factual "yes."

Once narrative records are obtained, the observer can study, classify, and organize the records at leisure. Particular hypotheses or expectations about the behaviors under observation can be tested by examining the data. This constitutes an important difference between narrative records and other forms of behavior measurement wherein the classification or coding of behaviors is done at the time of observation. Thus, narrative records must capture the particular information that is critical for evaluating a study's goals or hypotheses.

We have already mentioned how Piaget used structured observation to study the cognitive development of children. Having selected a problem to present to the child, Piaget then made a rather literal record of the child's attempts to solve the problem. The following narrative record was obtained by Piaget when investigating a 4-year-old child's understanding of quantity: The child is given two containers A and L of equal height, A being wide and L narrow. A is filled to a certain height (one-quarter or one-fifth), and the child is asked to pour the same quantity of liquid into L. The dimensions are such that the level will be four times as high in L as in A for the same amount of liquid. In spite of this striking difference in the proportions, the child at this stage proves incapable of grasping that the smaller diameter of L will require a higher level of liquid. Those children who are clearly still at this stage are satisfied there is "the same amount to drink" in L when they have filled it to the same level as A.

> Blas (4.0): "Look, your mummy has poured out a glass of lemonade for herself (A) and she gives you this glass (L). We want you to pour into your glass as much lemonade as your mummy has in hers.—(She poured rather quickly and exceeded the level equal to that in A that she was trying to achieve.)—Will you both have the same like that?—*No.* —Who will have more?—*Me.* —Show me where you must pour to so that you both have the same.—(She poured up to the same level.) —Will you and mummy have the same amount to drink like that? —*Yes.* —Are you sure? —*Yes.*" (Piaget, [1965]. *The child's conception of number* [pp. 11–12]. New York: Norton. First published in French in 1941 under the title *La Genèse du nombre chez l'enfant.*)

The narrative begins with the observer's comments to the child, Blas. The observer says, "Look, your mummy has poured out a glass of lemonade . . ." After that follows an exact reproduction of what the observer said, what the child said, and what happened in this situation. The narrative contains little observer inference, and the exact sequence of behaviors is recorded. His many observations of children's behavior led Piaget to a number of important conclusions about human cognitive development. As you can see, Piaget used the narrative record to illustrate that the 4-year-old has not yet mastered the principle of "conservation of volume." The two containers, which were of equal height but different width, were perceived by the child to hold the same amount of liquid when the level of the liquid was the same.

Hartup (1974) obtained narrative records as part of his naturalistic study of children's aggression. He investigated a number of different aspects of children's aggression, including the relationship between particular kinds of antecedent events and the nature of the aggressive episodes that followed. Consider this sample narrative record from Hartup's study (p. 339):

Marian [a 7-year-old] . . . is complaining to all that David [who is also present] had squirted her on the pants she has to wear tonight. She says, "I'm gonna do it to him to see how he likes it." She fills a can with water and David runs to the teacher and tells of her threat. The teacher takes the can from Marian. Marian attacks David and pulls his hair very hard. He cries and swings at Marian as the teacher tries to restrain him; then she takes him upstairs. . . . Later, Marian and Elaine go upstairs and into the room where David is seated with a teacher. He throws a book at Marian. The teacher asks Marian to leave. Marian kicks David, then leaves. David cries and screams, "Get out of here, they're just gonna tease me."

Hartup (1974) instructed his observers to avoid making inferences about the intentions, motives, or feelings of the participants and to use precise language in describing behavior. Note that we are not told why David might want to throw a book at Marian or how Marian feels about being attacked. Hartup believed that certain antecedent behaviors are related to specific types of aggression. Because any inferences or impressions of the observers were strictly excluded, the content of the narrative records could be classified and coded in a more objective manner. Thus, individuals coding the narrative would not be influenced by what the observer inferred was going on.

Not all narrative records are as focused as those obtained by Piaget or Hartup, nor do narrative records always avoid inferences and impressions of the observer. An important goal of **ecological psychology** is the comprehensive description of individuals in everyday contexts. One example of this type of research is a study of "a day in the life" of a midwestern schoolgirl (Barker, Wright, Schoggen, & Barker, 1978, pp. 56–58). Eight different observers took turns observing an 8-year-old girl from the time she awoke in the morning until she went to sleep at night. Because the researchers wanted to include information about the girl's motives, feelings, and perceptions, they required that the observers make a number of inferences. Generally, only the inferences that two or more observers agreed on were included. For example, people can often agree as to when someone is sad or happy or excited or calm. The narrative record of this little girl's day was about 100,000 words in length and was later determined to contain 969 different behavior episodes.

Narrative records also are not always meant to be comprehensive descriptions of behavior as we have seen illustrated in the context of structured observations used by Piaget or in the study of the day in the life of a young schoolgirl. Often the narrative records of an observer are merely running descriptions of the participants, events, settings, and behaviors. These records are generally called **field notes.** Field notes are nothing more than the verbal records of a trained observer. Used by journalists, social workers, anthropologists, ethologists, and others, they do not always contain an exact record of everything that occurred. Events and behaviors that especially interest the observer are recorded and are likely to be interpreted in terms of the observer's specialized knowledge or expertise. For example, in making notes about a particular patient, a psychiatrist might compare the client's symptoms with those of other patients or with a textbook definition. An ethologist might record how the behavior of one species appears to parallel that of another.

Field notes tend to be highly personalized (Brandt, 1972), but they are probably used more frequently than any other kind of narrative record. Field notes have generated numerous revelations about behavior; they are the basis of Darwin's theory of evolution as well as Rosenhan's description of being sane in insane places. Their usefulness as scientific records depends on the accuracy and precision of their content. These characteristics will be related to the training of the observer and the extent to which the observations that are recorded can be verified by independent observers and through other means of investigation.

Practical, as well as methodological, considerations dictate the manner in which narrative records are made. As a general rule, records should be made during or as soon as possible after behavior is observed. The passage of time blurs details and makes it harder to reproduce the original sequence of actions. Adjang (1986) used a portable cassette recorder to make narrative records of his spoken observations of the teasing behavior of young chimpanzees; however, he then transcribed these spoken reports onto paper "as soon as possible" (p. 139). This rule is sometimes not easy to follow when observations are made in natural settings. An ethologist who is trying to record the behavior of animals in the wild is sometimes hampered by bad weather, animal migration, dwindling daylight, and so forth. Notes may have to be made quickly—even while the observer is quite literally on the run. At other times observers may have to wait until they return to camp to make written records of behavior. When Festinger et al. (1956) infiltrated the group of people waiting for spacemen to rescue them from a cataclysmic flood, the participant observers sometimes found it difficult to take notes without being seen by members of the group. Excuses had to be made to leave the group (to go to the bathroom, for example) in order to make written records of the group's activities.

Decisions regarding the content of a narrative record must be made prior to observing behavior. We have seen, for example, that verbal narratives may differ according to the degree of observer inference or the completeness of the behavioral record. Thus, these aspects of a narrative record, as well as others, must be decided on prior to beginning a study (Brandt, 1972). Once the content of narrative records is decided, observers must be trained to record behavior according to the criteria that have been set up. Practice observations may have to be conducted and records critiqued by more than one investigator before "real" data are collected.

OBTAINING QUANTITATIVE MEASURES OF BEHAVIOR

When only certain behaviors or specific aspects of individuals and settings are of interest, the behaviors need to be defined prior to beginning an observational study. Decisions also should be made as to exactly how characteristics of their occurrence should be measured, that is, how the behavior can be *quantified*. For example, assume that you wish to observe reactions to individuals with obvious physical disabilities by those who do not have such disabilities. In order to conduct your study, it would be necessary to define what constitutes a "reaction" to a physically disabled individual. Are you interested, for example, in helping behaviors, approach/avoidance behaviors, eye contact, length of conversation, or in some other behavioral reaction? As you consider what behaviors you will use to define people's "reactions," you will also have to decide how you will measure these behaviors. Assume, for instance, that you are planning a study using naturalistic observation and that you have chosen to measure people's reactions by observing eye contact between individuals who do not have obvious physical disabilities and those who do. Exactly how should you measure eye contact? Should you simply measure whether a passerby does or does not make eye contact, or do you want to measure the *duration* of any eye contact? The decisions you make will depend on the particular hypotheses or goals of your study, but they will also be influenced by information gained by examining previous studies that have used the same or similar behavioral measures. (Unfortunately, previous research indicates that reactions to physically disabled individuals frequently can be classified as unfavorable. See, for example, Thompson, 1982.) Of course, you may wish to make multiple measures, a research strategy that is recommended whenever it is feasible.

Measurement Scales   Defining a behavioral measure involves deciding what scale of measurement to use. Thus, it is important for you to be familiar with the types of measurement scales used in behavioral research. Four levels of measurement, or **measurement scales**, apply to both physical and psychological measurement. The lowest level, or scale, is called a *nominal scale*; it involves simply categorizing the stimulus to be measured into one of a number of discrete categories. For instance, we could measure the color of people's eyes by categorizing them as "brown eyed" or "blue eyed." When studying people's reactions to individuals with obvious physical disabilities, a researcher might use a nominal scale by measuring whether persons make eye contact or do not make eye contact with someone who has an obvious physical disability. This type of category system is called a **checklist.** Age, race, and sex are examples of participant characteristics that are often noted. Features of the setting—such as time of day, location, and whether other people are present—also may be part of a checklist. A checklist can also be used to record the presence or absence of specific behaviors. Whether or not individuals make contact with a physically disabled person is one example. A classroom observer may note whether children are talking or are quiet. An environmental psychologist may be interested in whether people use seat belts or do not use seat belts, or in whether people dispose of litter or do not dispose of litter.

Specific characteristics of people as well as their behavior are likely to be of interest. For example, it is often informative to observe behavior as a function of certain static characteristics. Do males use seat belts more than females? Are people who drive inexpensive automobiles more likely to share a ride than people who drive expensive automobiles? These questions can be answered by observing the presence or absence of certain behaviors (seat-belt use or car pooling) for different categories of participants and events (male and female, expensive and inexpensive automobiles).

Jenni (1976; also Jenni & Jenni, 1976) used a checklist to study the book-carrying behavior of male and female college students. Three types of book-carrying behaviors were defined: two major types and an "other" category. Figure 3.2 illustrates the two major types of carrying behavior. Students using Type I wrap one or both arms around the books, with the short edges of the books resting on the hip or in front of the body. Students using Type II support the books by one arm and hand at the side of the body, with the long edges of the books approximately horizontal to the ground. The "other" category includes a variety of book-carrying methods that do not fit either Type I or Type II. For example, students occasionally hold books by the edges with both hands in front of the body (for instance, when reading while walking).

Observations of 2,626 individuals were made on six college campuses (three in the United States, one in Canada, and two in Central America). Individuals were observed as they passed a certain point on campus. Type of carrying behavior and sex of the student were noted. In terms of the arithmetic operations that we can perform on data recorded on a nominal scale, we can use only the relationships "equal" and "not equal." A common way of summarizing nominal data is to report the frequency, proportion, or percentage of instances in each of the several categories. Across the six college campuses, 82% of the females were observed to use the Type I method, whereas only 3% of the males used this method. On the other hand, the observers found that 96% of the males used the Type II carrying method compared with 16% of the females.

FIGURE 3.2   Two methods that students were observed to use to carry books. In the Type I method, the short edges of the book rest on the hip or in front of the body. In the Type II method, the books are either pinched from above or supported from below by the hand or by both the hand and the arm (from Jenni & Jenni, 1976).

Type I   Type II

The "other" methods were used 2% of the time or less by both male and female students. It appears that book-carrying behavior among college students is almost totally gender specific. Take a look around a college campus and see whether you observe these same sex-specific patterns.

The second level, or scale, called an *ordinal scale*, involves ordering or ranking stimuli to be measured. Ordinal scales add the arithmetic relationships "greater than" and "less than" to the measurement process. One common example of an ordinal scale is class rank. We can order students in a class from highest to lowest, but if we know only their ranks we have no information about how far apart the students are in academic performance. When we know an Olympic distance runner won a silver medal, we do not know whether she finished second in a photo finish or trailed 200 meters behind the gold-medal winner.

The third level, or scale, called an *interval scale*, involves specifying how far apart two stimuli are on a given dimension. On an ordinal scale, the difference between the stimulus ranked first and the stimulus ranked third does not necessarily equal the distance between the stimuli ranked third and fifth. For example, the difference in grade-point averages (GPAs) between the first and third students in a class may not be the same as the difference in GPAs between the third and fifth ranked students. On an interval scale, however, differences of the same numerical size in scale values are equal. For example, the difference between 50 and 70 correct answers on an aptitude test is equal to the difference between 70 and 90 correct answers, and the ratio of these scale intervals is also meaningful.. What is missing from an interval scale is a meaningful zero point. For instance, if your score were zero on a verbal aptitude test, you would not necessarily have absolutely zero verbal ability. On the other hand, the standard arithmetic operations of addition, multiplication, subtraction, and division can be performed on data that are measured on an interval scale. Whenever possible, therefore, psychologists try to measure psychological dimensions using interval scales.

In the context of an observational study, observers are sometimes called on to make ratings of behaviors and events. This usually involves making subjective judgments about the degree or quantity of some trait or condition (Brandt, 1972). Generally a rating system requires an observer to evaluate some characteristic of an individual or situation on a psychological dimension. For example, Dickie (1987) asked observers to rate parent-infant interactions in the context of a study designed to assess the effects of a parent training program. The observers visited the home and rated both the mother and the father while the parents interacted with their infant child. During most of the observation period, the observers sat in the room with the infant and asked the parents to "act as normal as possible—just as if we [the observers] weren't here." Structured observations involving assigned play with each parent were also used. Parent-infant interactions were rated on 13 different dimensions, including degree of verbal, physical, and emotional interaction. For each dimension a continuum was defined that represented different degrees of this variable. A 7-point scale

TABLE 3.1   EXAMPLE OF RATING SCALE USED TO MEASURE A PARENT'S WARMTH AND AFFECTION
TOWARD AN INFANT CHILD*

Scale Value	Description
1	There is an absence of warmth, affection, and pleasure. Excessive hostility, coldness, distance, and isolation from the child are predominant. Relationship is on an attacking level.
2	
3	There is occasional warmth and pleasure in interaction. Parent shows little evidence of pride in the child, or pride is shown in relation to deviant or bizarre behavior by the child. Parent's manner of relating is contrived, intellectual, not genuine.
4	
5	There is moderate pleasure and warmth in the interaction. Parent shows pleasure in some areas but not in others.
6	
7	Warmth and pleasure are characteristic of the interaction with the child. There is evidence of pleasure and pride in the child. Pleasure response is appropriate to the child's behavior.

*From materials provided by Jane Dickie.

was used; 1 represented the absence or very little of the characteristic and larger numbers represented increasingly more of the trait. Table 3.1 outlines one of the dimensions used by the observers in this study: warmth and affection directed toward the child. Note that precise verbal descriptions are given with the four odd-numbered scale values to help observers define different degrees of this trait. The even-numbered values (2, 4, 6) are used by observers to rate events that they judge fall between the more clearly defined values. The investigators found that parents who had taken part in a program aimed at developing competency in dealing with an infant were rated higher than were untrained parents on many of the variables.

At first glance, a rating scale such as that used by Dickie would appear to represent an interval scale of measurement. There is no true zero, and the intervals seem to be equal. And, in fact, many researchers treat such rating systems *as if* they represented interval scales of measurement. Closer examination, however, reveals that most of the rating scales used by observers to evaluate people or events on a psychological dimension really yield only ordinal information. For a rating system to be truly an interval level of measurement, a rating of 2, for instance, would have to be the same distance from a rating of 3 as a rating of 4 is from 5 or a rating of 6 is from 7. It is highly unlikely that human observers can make subjective judgments of traits such as warmth, pleasure, aggressiveness, anxiety, and so forth, in a manner that yields precise interval distances between ratings. Classification of measures according to level of measurement is not always easy, and advice should be sought from knowledgeable experts when in doubt. In this way you will be prepared to make the correct choices regarding the statistical description and analysis of your data.

The fourth level of measurement is a *ratio scale*. A ratio scale has all the properties of an interval scale with the important additional quality of an absolute zero point. In terms of arithmetic operations, a zero point makes the ratio of scale values meaningful. For example, temperature as expressed on the Celsius scale represents an interval scale of measurement. A reading of 0 degrees Celsius does not really mean absolutely no temperature. Therefore it is not meaningful to say that 100 degrees Celsius is twice as hot as 50 degrees, or that 60 degrees is three times as warm as 20 degrees. On the other hand, the Kelvin scale of temperature does have an absolute zero, and the ratio of scale values can be meaningfully calculated. Physical scales measuring time, weight, and distance can usually be treated as ratio scales.

As an example of ratio measurement, consider an interesting study by LaFrance and Mayo (1976). They investigated racial differences in amount of eye contact between individuals of the same race engaged in conversation. Pairs of black individuals and pairs of white individuals were observed in natural settings. The amount of time each member of the pair spent looking into the face of the other member was recorded. Duration of eye contact represents a ratio level of measurement. The researchers found that blacks gazed less at another person while listening to conversation than did whites. LaFrance and Mayo suggest that subtle differences in eye contact may be a source of social misunderstandings. White speakers may feel that lack of eye contact by a black listener indicates untrustworthiness or lack of interest when it may merely be a manifestation of a cultural difference between the races.

Another important measure of behavior is *frequency* of occurrence. This measure sometimes produces confusion when attempting to identify the level of measurement. For example, in observing book-carrying behavior, Jenni (1976) made only one observation of each individual. As we noted, this represents a nominal level of measurement: Behaviors were recorded as falling in one of several mutually exclusive categories. Frequency of book-carrying behavior, therefore, was described in terms of the number (or percentage) of *different* individuals who used one method or another.

Checklists also can be used to obtain information about the frequency of particular behaviors in the same individual or group of individuals. In this case, repeated observations of the same individual or group are made over a period of time. The presence or absence of specific behaviors is noted at the time of each observation. In these situations, frequency of responding can be assumed to represent a ratio level of measurement. That is, if "units" of some behavior (e.g., occasions when a child leaves classroom seat) are being counted, then zero represents an absence of that specific behavior. Ratios of scale values would be meaningful as long as, for instance, an individual with 20 units had twice as many units as someone with 10.

Consider, for instance, the Schedule for Classroom Activity Norms (SCAN), which is a checklist that divides classroom behavior into 27 discrete categories (McKinney, Mason, Perkerson, & Clifford, 1975). At repeated intervals of time, an observer records what each child in the classroom is doing. Many observations of the same child show which categories of behavior are most frequent for that child. In one study using the SCAN checklist, researchers looked for relationships between the frequency of certain classroom behaviors and performance on standard tests of academic achievement. Combining information obtained from observing the children's behavior with information obtained from IQ tests yielded a more accurate prediction of school achievement than could be obtained by using either observation or IQ information alone.

Table 3.2 summarizes the characteristics of levels of measurement we have discussed. You will need to keep these four types of scales in mind as you select statistical procedures for analyzing the results of the research you will be doing (see Appendix A).

Electronic Recording   Recording behavior is sometimes aided by the use of hand-held microcomputers and various electronic tracking devices. For example, in an observational study of family interactions of depressed women, the observers used microcomputers to record both static and active categories of relevant behavior (see Hops et al., 1987). Family members were given codes, as were various behaviors and characteristics of the family interaction, and these were recorded using hand-held high-technology devices. Kirmeyer and Biggers (1988) used a similar electronic recording device to record the duration and characteristics of activities of 72 police radio dispatchers as part of an observational study investigating Type A behavior (that is, "behavior characterized by ambitiousness, hostility, impatience, and competitiveness," p. 997). As in the previously mentioned study, codes were developed for both static and active aspects of behavior and observers were rehearsed prior to actual data collection in the use of the microcomputer recording system. In the study of radio dispatchers, Type A individuals were observed to place demands on themselves by initiating work tasks and by attending to multiple tasks.

As part of a study investigating the relationship between cognitive coping strategies and blood pressure among college students, participants were outfit-

TABLE 3.2   CHARACTERISTICS OF MEASUREMENT SCALES

Type of Scale	Operations	Objective
Nominal	Equal/not equal	Sort stimuli into discrete categories
Ordinal	Greater than/less than	Rank-order stimuli on a single dimension
Interval	Addition/multiplication/subtraction/ division	Specify the distance between stimuli in a given dimension
Ratio	Addition/multiplication/subtraction/ division/formation of ratios of values	Specify the distance between stimuli in a given dimension and express ratios of scale values

ted with an ambulatory blood pressure monitor (Dolan, Sherwood, & Light, 1992). College students wore the electronic recording device during two "typical" school days, one of which, however, included an exam. Participants also completed a questionnaire assessing coping strategies and kept detailed logs of their daily activities. The researchers compared blood pressure readings for different times of the day and as a function of coping style. Students classified as exhibiting "high self-focused coping," that is, who showed tendencies "to keep to themselves and/or blame themselves in stressful situations" (p. 233), had higher blood pressure responses during and after an exam than did those who were classified as low in self-focused coping strategies.

SAMPLING TECHNIQUES

Before conducting an observational study, a researcher must make a number of important decisions about "when" and "where" observations will be made. In some cases, it might be possible to observe all the behavior of interest—for instance, the behavior patterns of certain short-lived organisms. In most cases, however, something considerably less than "all" of behavior will be observed. Imagine the task, if you will, that Barker et al. (1978) would have faced had they tried to record the behavior exhibited by an 8-year-old every day of her life. If she exhibited 969 behavioral episodes in a single day, imagine the number of episodes in her lifetime!

Needless to say, in the vast majority of observational studies, however, the investigator must be satisfied with something considerably less than a complete record of behavior. Only certain behaviors occurring at particular times and in specific settings can generally be observed. In other words, behavior and settings must be sampled. The nature of these samples determines the extent to which generalizations are possible. Observations made of classroom behavior at the beginning of a school year, for instance, may not yield results that are typical of behavior seen at the end of the school year. Nor, for that matter, do observations made in the morning necessarily reveal the same pattern of classroom behavior as observations made in the afternoon. The frequency and type of aggression observed in children who are required to wear school uniforms may not be representative of the aggression found in children who do not wear school uniforms. As we saw in Chapter 1, our ability to generalize research findings depends on the study's external validity. Results can reasonably be generalized only to participants, conditions, and situations similar to those in the study in which the results were actually observed. Time sampling, event sampling, and situation sampling are used to lend external validity to observational findings.

TIME AND EVENT SAMPLING

Hartup (1974) used a combination of time and event sampling when studying children's aggression. In **time sampling,** the intervals at which observations are made are chosen either systematically or randomly with the goal of obtaining a representative sample of behavior. As examples, we might consider the application of these techniques in the context of observing a child's classroom behavior.

Suppose that observations are to be made for a total of 2 hours each day. As we indicated, restricting observations to certain times of the day (say, mornings only) would not necessarily permit us to generalize our findings to the rest of the school day. One approach to obtaining a representative sample is to schedule observation periods *systematically* throughout the school day. Observations might be made during four 30-minute periods beginning every 2 hours. The first observation period could begin at 9 a.m., the second at 11 a.m., and so forth. Another possibility would be to schedule 10-minute observation periods every half hour during the school day. A *random* time-sampling technique could be used in the same situation by distributing four 30-minute periods (or twelve 10-minute periods) randomly over the course of the day. A different random schedule would be determined each day on which observations are made. Times would vary from day to day but, over the long run, behavior would be sampled equally from all times of the school day.

Systematic and random time-sampling procedures are often combined, as when observation intervals are scheduled systematically but observations within an interval are made at random times. For example, having scheduled four 30-minute observation periods at the same time each day (e.g., 9:00 a.m., 11:00 a.m., etc.), an observer might then decide to observe only during 20-second intervals that are randomly distributed within each 30-minute period. Or observation periods might be scheduled randomly during certain weeks of the school year but with weeks selected systematically from the early, middle, and late parts of the year. Whatever method is used, the observer must carefully scrutinize the schedule, noting both its limitations and its advantages in terms of yielding a representative record of behavior. Sampling plays a central role in conducting surveys. We discuss many issues related to the topic of sampling in Chapter 4 when survey methods are introduced.

Event sampling may be a more efficient method of sampling behavior than time sampling when the event of interest occurs infrequently. In this case researchers want to maximize their opportunities to observe an event in order to get enough information about its occurrence to make investigating it worthwhile. Not only may time sampling cause precious instances of an event to be missed, but if the event is of significant duration, time sampling may not permit an observer to be present at the beginning of an event or to witness an event in its entirety. In event sampling the observer records each event that meets a predetermined definition. Researchers interested in children's reactions to special events in school, such as a Christmas play, would want to use event sampling. The special event defines when the observations are to be made. Researchers would certainly not want to use time sampling in this situation in the hope that a special event might occur during one of their randomly selected observation periods.

In many situations in which event sampling is used, a formally scheduled event like a school play is not the event of interest. Instead, researchers are often interested in events that occur unpredictably, such as natural or technical disasters. Researchers, for example, who are interested in victims' reactions to violent crimes depend on event sampling in selecting the occasions for making their observations. Whenever possible, observers try to be present in those situations and at those times when an event of interest has occurred or is likely to occur. Thus, in an ethological study of children's "rough-and-tumble" play, an observer positioned herself in the corner of a playground to observe members of a nursery school class (Smith & Lewis, 1985). Event sampling was the method of choice due to the relatively low frequency of this behavior, and the researcher made observations whenever rough play began. However, this manner of observing behavior can easily introduce biases into the behavioral record—as when, for instance, an observer samples at the times that are most "convenient" or only when an event is certain to occur. Characterization of events at these times may not be the same as at other times. In most situations, only through some form of time sampling is an observer likely to guarantee a representative sample of behavior.

SITUATION SAMPLING

The external validity of observational findings can be significantly increased through **situation sampling.** Whenever possible—and when it is in keeping with the goals of a study—behavior should be observed under many different circumstances, locations, and conditions. By sampling different situations researchers reduce the chance that their results will be peculiar to a certain set of circumstances or conditions. It is clear that behavior often changes as a function of the context in which it is observed. Animals do not behave the same way in zoos as they do in the wild. Children do not always behave the same way with one parent as they do with the other parent. By sampling different situations, a researcher can also increase the diversity of the subject sample and hence achieve greater generality than could be claimed if only particular types of individuals were observed. As part of a naturalistic observation of beer drinking among college students, investigators purposely sampled behavior in various settings where beer was served, including five town bars, a student center, and a fraternity party (Geller, Russ, & Altomari, 1986). When LaFrance and Mayo (1976) investigated racial differences in eye contact, they sampled many different situations. Pairs of individuals were observed in college cafeterias, business district fast-food outlets, hospital and airport waiting rooms, and restaurants. By using situation sampling the investigators were able to include in their sample people who differed in age, socioeconomic class, sex, and race. Their observations of an apparent cultural difference in eye-contact behavior have considerably greater external validity than if only certain types of participants, or behavior in only a specific situation, had been studied.

ANALYSIS OF OBSERVATIONAL DATA

DATA REDUCTION

Analysis of Narrative Records   Once they have been collected, narrative records can provide a wealth of information about behavior in natural settings. However, for meaningful information to emerge, data relevant to the goals of an observational study must be abstracted from the lengthy behavioral descriptions included in most narrative records. Results must be organized, and statements summarizing important findings must be prepared. This process of abstracting and summarizing behavioral data is called **data reduction.** The first step in quantitative analysis of the content of narrative records often consists of identifying units of behavior, or particular events. This stage of data reduction involves **coding** behavioral records according to specific criteria. For instance, we previously noted that a narrative record describing a day in the life of a schoolgirl was found to contain 969 different behavior episodes (Barker et al., 1978, pp. 56–58). Hartup's (1974) 10-week observation of children's aggression yielded information about 758 units of aggression. As part of an ethological study of preschool children, McGrew (1972) identified 115 different behavior patterns. He classified patterns of behavior according to the body part involved, ranging from facial expressions such as bared teeth, grin face, and pucker face, to locomotion behaviors such as gallop, crawl, run, skip, and step. Coders classified these behavioral patterns while watching videotape records showing interactions of children attending nursery school.

Relevant units of behavior or events are often classified in terms of their apparent function or their particular antecedents. For instance, Hartup used 9 categories to classify the nature of aggressive episodes. Antecedents of aggression were described using 18 different categories. Relationships between antecedent events and types of aggression were then summarized, and comparisons were made between different age groups. When derogation ("put-down") elicited aggression, more younger children than older children retaliated via some form of physical aggression (such as hitting). McGrew (1972) found that children exhibit a "pout face" after losing a fight over a toy. This ethologist-observer noted that young chimpanzees show a similar expression when seeking reunion with their mother. A "pucker face" was observed in children particularly after being frustrated (and often just prior to weeping). Interestingly, there seems to be no record of a pucker face in nonhuman primates.

Descriptive Measures   When events are classified into mutually exclusive categories, the most common descriptive measure is one of relative frequency. The proportion or percentage of times that various behaviors occur is expressed in terms of the total frequency of events observed. We have already seen several examples of this type of descriptive measure. Jenni (1976), for instance, reported the percentage of times that male and female students were observed to use three different book-carrying methods. Barash (1977) summarized his observations of pedestrian behavior in terms of the percentage of people in various social groupings who looked both ways.

When behavior is recorded on at least an interval scale of measurement, as when measures of time (duration, latency) are used and frequently when ratings are made, one or more measures of central tendency are generally reported. The most common measure is the *arithmetic mean,* or *average.* The mean describes the "typical" score in a group of scores and is an important summary measure of group performance. Measures of variability or dispersion of scores around the mean are necessary to describe group performance completely. The *standard deviation* approximates the average distance of a score from the mean. (For computational procedures for measures of central tendency and variability, as well as confidence intervals for the mean, see Appendix A.)

The mean and standard deviation as descriptive measures are illustrated in the results of the study by LaFrance and Mayo (1976). You may remember that these investigators observed other-directed looking behavior in pairs of black and white conversants. The number of seconds that each listener in a pair spent looking into the speaker's face was recorded. Table 3.3 gives the means and standard deviations that summarize the results of this study. As we noted previously, white listeners spent more time looking into the faces of white speakers than black listeners spent looking into the faces of black speakers. This was found for same-sex pairs as well as mixed-sex pairs.

OBSERVER RELIABILITY

In assessing the results of an observational study, we need to inquire about reliability of an observer. Would another observer viewing the same events obtain the same results?

Interobserver Reliability   The degree to which two independent observers are in agreement is referred to as **interobserver reliability.** Lack of agreement

TABLE 3.3   MEANS AND STANDARD DEVIATIONS DESCRIBING THE TIME (IN SECONDS) THAT LISTENERS SPENT LOOKING INTO THE FACE OF A SPEAKER PER 1-MINUTE OBSERVATION UNIT*

Group	Mean	Standard Deviation
Black conversants		
Male pairs	19.3	6.9
Female pairs	28.4	10.2
Male-female pairs	24.9	11.6
White conversants		
Male pairs	35.8	8.6
Female pairs	39.9	10.7
Male-female pairs	29.9	11.2

*From LaFrance and Mayo (1976).

from one observer to another leaves us uncertain about what is being measured and prevents us from generalizing research results. Low interobserver reliability can be due to characteristics of the observers or to the procedures and methods of observing. In the context of a behavioral study, differences between observers in terms of experience, attitude, fatigue, boredom, and outcome expectancies are possible reasons for low interobserver reliability. Observer reliability is generally increased by training observers and giving them specific feedback regarding any discrepancies between their observations and those of other observers (Judd, Smith, & Kidder, 1991).

Low interobserver reliability may also result when the event to be recorded is not clearly defined. Imagine Hartup (1974) asking his observers to record aggressive episodes among children without giving them an exact definition of aggression. What exactly is aggression? Some observers might decide to define aggression as one child's physical attack on another; other observers might include verbal assaults in their definition of aggression. What is a playful push and what is an angry shove? Without a clear definition of behavior or of the events to be recorded, observers do not always agree—and hence show low interobserver reliability. In addition to providing precise verbal definitions, giving concrete examples of a phenomenon generally helps increase reliability among observers. Showing observers the pictures of book-carrying methods in Figure 3.1, for example, could be assumed to improve their ability to classify behavior according to this characteristic.

High observer reliability is not necessarily sufficient evidence that observations are accurate. We can imagine two observers of behavior who are both "in error" to the same degree. For instance, both might be influenced in a similar way by what they expect the outcome of the observational study to be. It is conceivable that the two observers would agree about what they saw but neither observer would provide a valid (accurate) record of behavior. Instances are occasionally reported in the media of several observers claiming to see the same thing (for instance, an unidentified flying object, or UFO), only to have the event or object turn out to be something other than what observers claimed it to be (for instance, a weather balloon). Nevertheless, when two independent observers agree, we are generally more inclined to believe their observations are valid than when data are based on the observations of a single observer. In order for observers to be independent, each must be unaware of what the other has recorded. The chance of both observers being influenced to the same degree by outcome expectancies, fatigue, or boredom is generally so small that we can feel confident that what was reported actually occurred. Of course, the more independent observers who agree, the more confident we become.

Measures of Reliability How observer reliability is measured depends on the way in which behavior is measured. When events are classified according to mutually exclusive categories, such as when individuals are classified in terms of whether they show a certain behavior, observer reliability is generally assessed via a percentage agreement measure.

Here is a formula for calculating percentage agreement between observers:

$$\frac{\text{Number of times two observers agree}}{\text{Number of opportunities to agree}} \times 100$$

Barash (1977) reported that observers were 100% reliable when classifying pedestrians as to the type of social group that was present (adult male and female, female with children, and so on) and in agreement 97% of the time when deciding whether pedestrians scanned both directions before crossing the street. Hartup (1974) reported measures of reliability that ranged from 83% to 94% for judges who coded narrative records according to type of aggression and nature of antecedent events. Although there is no hard-and-fast percentage of agreement that defines low interobserver reliability, a perusal of the literature reveals that researchers generally report estimates of reliability that exceed 85%, suggesting that agreement much lower than that is unacceptable.

Because in many observational studies most of the data are collected by one observer, or by several observers who collect data at different times, measures of reliability are often based only on a sample of observations for any one observer. For example, two observers might be asked to record behavior according to some time-sampling procedure and there might be only a subset of times during which both observers are present. Amount of agreement for the times when both observers were present can be used to indicate the degree of reliability for the study as a whole. For example, when studying beer drinking among college students, investigators reported the percentage agreement for two independent observers who were present at slightly fewer than half of the 243 total observation periods; during the remaining periods only one observer was present (Geller et al., 1986). Observer reliability for home observations of family interactions involving depressed women was based on 86 (17%) of the 520 sessions (Hops et al., 1987).

When observational data are of at least an interval nature, as is often assumed when subjective ratings are made or when some variable such as time is measured, observer reliability can be measured using what is called the Pearson Product-Moment Correlation Coefficient r. (The formula for the Pearson r is found in Appendix A.) LaFrance and Mayo (1976) obtained measures of reliability when observers recorded how much of the time a listener gazed into the speaker's face during a conversation. The average correlation for observer reliability between pairs of observers was .92 in their study.

PROBLEMS IN THE CONDUCT OF OBSERVATIONAL RESEARCH

INFLUENCE OF THE OBSERVER

Reactivity The influence that an observer has on the behavior under observation is referred to as **reactivity.** Generally, we can think of reactive research situations as situations in which individuals "react" to the presence of an observer. Behavior in these situations may not be representative of behavior when an observer is not present. Underwood and Shaughnessy (1975) relate how a student, as part of a class assignment, set out to observe whether drivers

FIGURE 3.3   Reactivity refers to the influence that an observer has on the behavior under observation; for example, motorists are more likely to stop at a stop sign if an observer is visibly present.

came to a complete stop at an intersection with a stop sign. The student had hypothesized that drivers of high-priced cars would be less likely than drivers of low-priced cars to stop at the sign. The observer located himself on the street corner with clipboard in hand. However, he soon observed that all cars were stopping at the stop sign. He then realized that his presence was influencing the driver's behavior. When he concealed himself near the intersection, he found that drivers' behavior changed and he was able to gather data regarding his hypothesis.

Although human research participants may not exhibit innate reactions to an observer, as is the case with certain animals (Moore & Stuttard, 1979), they can respond in very subtle ways when they are aware that their behavior is being observed. For instance, participants are sometimes apprehensive and more than a little anxious about participating in psychological research. Measures of arousal, such as heart rate and galvanic skin response (GSR), may show changes simply as a function of an observer's being present.

Social psychologists have long been aware that behavior is affected by the presence of another person. Research has shown that performance on simple tasks can be facilitated by the presence of another person, a so-called facilitation effect, whereas performance on more complex tasks is often inhibited, a so-called social-impairment effect (Bond & Titus, 1983). As you might suspect, whether social facilitation and impairment effects are found depends not only on the complexity of the task but on who is present. For example, if the other person present is someone whose job it is to evaluate performance, as would be the case if an experimenter or observer were present, then effects due to another's presence are rather robust (Guerin, 1986). In this case, social facilitation is usually attributed to increased arousal brought about by anticipation of being evaluated or to an increased desire on the part of the participant to gain approval and do what is socially acceptable. Social impairment would be produced if increased arousal interfered with performance, as sometimes happens when an individual facing tough competition "chokes," or if the presence of an observer distracts an individual and brings about poorer performance than that found when the person is alone. Although of interest as social psychological phenomena, these effects, of course, also help to define reactivity in a research situation and must be guarded against by the researcher.

Research participants may also attempt to behave in the way they think the researcher wants them to behave. Knowing they are part of a scientific investigation, individuals usually want to cooperate and be "good" participants. Being a good participant may be seen as doing what is expected by the observer. Orne (1962) has referred to the cues and other information used by research participants to guide their behavior in a psychological study as the **demand characteristics** of the research situation. Orne suggests that individuals generally ask themselves the question, "What am I supposed to be doing here?" By paying attention to cues present in the setting, including those that are part of the research procedure itself, or even by attending to implicit cues given by the researcher, the research participants can perhaps figure out what is "expected" of them and attempt to modify their behavior accordingly. An individual's reactions to the demand characteristics of a research situation pose threats to both the external and the internal validity of psychological research. When research participants behave in a manner that is not representative of their behavior outside the psychological research setting, our ability to generalize the results is restricted. Also, by behaving in a manner they think is expected of them, participants may unintentionally make a research variable look more effective than it actually is or even nullify the effects of an otherwise significant variable. The problem of demand characteristics is often cited as a reason for limiting individuals' knowledge about their role in a study or about the study's hypothesis. By keeping participants unaware of important details regarding the study, the investigator hopes to obtain more representative behavior. However, limiting an individual's information about a study raises ethical concerns, which we discussed in Chapter 2, and about which we have more to say later in this chapter.

Controlling Reactivity   Problems of reactivity can be approached in several ways. Reactivity can be eliminated if observations are made in such a way that the presence of the observer is not detected by research participants. Measures of behavior in such circumstances are referred to as **unobtrusive (nonreactive) measures.** Obtaining unobtrusive measures may involve concealing the observer or hiding mechanical recording devices such as tape recorders and videotape cameras. LaFrance and Mayo (1976) observed people in conversation without their knowledge. Observations were made in a variety of natural settings, such as restaurants and waiting rooms, so we can imagine that observers had to keep their stopwatches and data sheets hidden behind menus and potted plants in order to obtain unobtrusive measures of behavior. Yet another approach is for a researcher to adopt a role in the situation other than that of observer. Participants do not know that an observer is present, so we assume that they act as they ordinarily would. To investigate honesty, Hays (1980) worked as a clerk in a college student union. When patrons asked for change for a dollar bill, he gave them a nickel extra. Only 45% of those patrons who were judged by the observer to be aware of the extra nickel returned the extra money.

Another way of dealing with reactivity is to adapt participants to the presence of an observer. It can be assumed that, as participants get used to an observer being present, they will come to behave normally in that person's presence. Adaptation can be accomplished through either habituation or desensitization. In a *habituation* procedure observers simply introduce themselves into a situation on many different occasions until the participants cease to react to their presence. In order to film a documentary entitled *An American Family*, which was shown on public television in the early 1970s, observers (with their cameras) literally moved into a California home and recorded the activities of a family over a 7-month period. Although it is impossible to tell how much of their behavior was influenced by the observers' presence, the events that unfolded and remarks made by family members gave evidence of a habituation process having taken place. During filming the family broke up, the mother asking the father to move out of the house. When interviewed later about having the divorce announced to millions of television viewers, the father admitted that they could have asked the camera crew to get out but that, by this time, "we had gotten used to it" ("Divorce of the Year," *Newsweek*, 1973, p. 49).

Habituation may result when undisguised participant observers spend a great deal of time with the participants they are observing. Although they are still aware that an observer is present, participants may begin to behave as though the observer were not present. As part of a study of aggressive behavior in preschool children, Addison (1986) reported that before actual data were collected, a 5-day period was used to adapt the children to the presence of both the observer and the videotape equipment. Because the children often experienced classroom observers in the form of student teachers and other adults, there appeared to be no effect due to the presence of the researcher. Moreover, Addison (1986) stated that the children's interest in the videotape equipment diminished after a few days.

Hart and Risley (1995) recorded children's vocabulary growth in their homes for more than 2 years. They began, however, "when the children were 7–9 months old so we would have time for the families to adapt to observation before the children actually began talking" (p. 28). Later, they were able to report that, "Although no parent was unaware that the observer was there, over time the observer tended to fade into the furniture" (p. 35).

Desensitization as a means of dealing with reactivity is similar to the desensitization used in the behavioral treatment of phobias. In a therapy situation, an individual with a specific fear (say, an irrational fear of spiders) is first exposed to the feared stimulus at a very low intensity. The patient may be asked to think of things that are related to spiders, such as dusty rooms and cobwebs. At the same time the therapist helps the patient practice relaxing. Gradually the intensity of the stimulus is increased until the patient can tolerate the actual stimulus itself.

Desensitization is often used by ethologists to adapt animal subjects to the presence of an observer. Prior to a violent death in the land of her beloved subjects, Fossey (1981, 1983) conducted fascinating observational studies of the mountain gorilla in Africa. Over a period of time she moved closer and closer to the gorillas so that they would get used to her presence. She found that by imitating their movements—for instance, by munching the foliage they ate and by scratching herself—she could put the gorillas at ease. Eventually she was able to sit among the gorillas and observe them as they touched her and explored the research equipment she was using.

Finally, nonreactive measures of behavior can be obtained by observing behavior indirectly (Webb, Campbell, Schwartz, Sechrest, & Grove, 1981). This may involve examining physical traces left behind or examining archival information, which are records kept by society about individuals and events. One researcher investigated the drinking behavior of people living in a town that was officially "dry" by counting empty liquor bottles in their trash cans. Another researcher used the records kept by a library to assess the effect on a community of the introduction of television. Withdrawals of fiction titles dropped, but the demand for nonfiction was not affected (Webb et al., 1981). Physical traces and archival data are important unobtrusive measures that can be valuable sources of information about behavior. In Chapter 5 we discuss more fully these indirect methods of observation.

Ethical Issues   Whenever individuals are observed without their knowledge, as we saw may occur when an investigator seeks to control for reactivity, important ethical issues arise. For instance, in many circumstances, observing people without their consent can represent a serious invasion of privacy. As you saw in Chapter 2, deciding what constitutes an invasion of privacy is not always easy, and must include a consideration of the sensitivity of the information, the setting where observation takes place, and the degree of dissemination of the information obtained (Deiner & Crandall, 1978).

When individuals are involved in situations that are deliberately arranged by an investigator, as might happen in a field experiment, ethical problems associated with placing participants at risk may arise. Consider, for instance, a field experiment designed to investigate how college students' attitudes toward racial harassment are affected by hearing other students either condone or condemn racism (Blanchard, Crandall, Brigham, & Vaughn, 1994). More than 200 white undergraduate women attending various universities were "naive participants." The women were approached by a white interviewer as they walked across campus and were invited to answer a short series of questions about "how their college should respond to acts of racism" (p. 994). A female confederate, posing as a student, approached the interviewer so that she arrived at the same time as the naive participant. The interviewers asked both "students" the same five questions; however, the interviewer always questioned the confederate student first. At this point, the confederate responded by either condemning or condoning racists' acts. Of interest was the effect of these statements on the naive participants' responses to the same questions. The results were clear: Hearing another student condemn racism produced more condemning responses relative to a no-influence control group, and hearing another student condone racism produced more condoning reactions to racism than hearing no one else express an opinion. Thus, as the authors suggest, the findings "imply that a few outspoken people can influence the normative climate of interracial social settings in either direction" (p. 997).

Were the naive participants "at risk"? If you think the participants were at risk, what degree of risk was present? Did the goals of the study, and the knowledge potentially obtained, outweigh any risk? Although participants were "debriefed immediately" in this study, is that sufficient to address any concerns the naive students might have about how they behaved when confronted with racist opinions, or even to restore confidence in a science that seeks knowledge through deception? Attempting to provide answers to these kinds of questions highlights the difficulty of ethical decision making. (Recommended steps in the process of ethical decision making are outlined in Chapter 2.)

OBSERVER BIAS

You may remember that when Rosenhan (1973) and his colleagues observed the interaction between staff members and patients in mental hospitals, they found a serious bias on the part of the staff. Once patients were labeled schizophrenic, their behavior was interpreted solely in light of this label. Behaviors that might have been considered normal when performed by sane individuals were interpreted by the staff as evidence of the patients' insanity. For instance, note taking by the participant observers, which was done openly, was later discovered to have been cited by members of the staff as an example of the pseudopatients' pathological state. As a result of the staff's tendency to interpret patients' behavior in terms of the label that had been given them, the sanity of the pseudopatients was not detected. This example clearly illustrates the danger of **observer bias**, the systematic errors in observation that result from the observer's expectations.

Expectancy Effects   Although we might hope that scientific observations are free from the kind of observer bias documented by Rosenhan, we know this is not always the case. In many scientific studies the observer has some expectancy about what behavior should be like in a particular situation or should result from a specific psychological treatment. This expectancy may be created by knowledge of the results of past investigations or perhaps by the observer's own hypothesis about behavior in this situation. Expectancies can be a source of observer bias—*expectancy effects*—if they lead to systematic errors in observation (Rosenthal, 1966, 1976).

An example of a study designed to document observer bias illustrates this problem (Cordaro & Ison, 1963). The study required college student observers to record the number of head turns and body contractions made by two groups of flatworms. The observers were led to expect different rates of turning and contracting in the two groups. The worms in the groups were, however, essentially identical. What differed was the observers' expectations about what they would see. Results showed that the observers reported twice as many head turns and three times as many body contractions when a high rate of movement was expected than when a low rate was expected. Apparently, the students interpreted the actions of the worms differently depending on what they expected to observe.

Other Biases   An observer's expectancies regarding the outcome of a study may not be the only source of observer bias. You might think that using automated equipment such as movie cameras would eliminate observer bias. Although automation reduces the opportunity for observer bias, it does not necessarily eliminate it. Consider the fact that, in order to record behavior on film, the observer must determine the angle, location, and time of filming. To the extent that these aspects of the study are influenced by personal biases of the observer, such decisions can introduce systematic errors into the results. Altmann (1974) describes an observational study of animal behavior in which the observers biased the results by taking a midday break whenever the animals were inactive. Observations of the animals during this period of inactivity were conspicuously absent from the observational records. Furthermore, using automated equipment generally only postpones the process of classification and interpretation, and it is perfectly possible for the effects of observer bias to be introduced when narrative records are coded and analyzed.

Controlling Observer Bias   Observer bias cannot be eliminated, but it can be controlled in several ways. As we mentioned, the use of automatic recording equipment can help, although the potential for bias is still present. *Probably the most important control over observer bias is the awareness that it might be present.*

Observer bias also can be reduced by limiting the information provided to observers. When Hartup (1974) analyzed the results of his observational study of children's aggression, the individuals who performed the analysis were not permitted to see all the narrative records. When the nature of the aggressive act was classified, the antecedent events were blacked out; and when antecedent events were coded, the nature of the aggressive act was blacked out. Therefore, in making their classifications, the coders could not be influenced by information related to the event they were coding. In a manner of speaking the coders were blind to certain aspects of the study. Observers are *blind* when they do not know why the observations are being made or the goals of a study. When Burns, Haywood, and Delclos (1987) observed the problem-solving strategies of children from two different socioeconomic groups, they first videotaped the children while they worked on five tasks selected from standardized intelligence tests. When task strategies were observed and coded from the videotape records, however, the observer-coder was blind to which group the child was from. When LaFrance and Mayo (1976) investigated eye contact between individuals conversing in natural settings, their observers did not know that possible differences along racial lines were being probed. Using "blind" observers greatly reduces the possibility of introducing systematic errors due to observer expectancies.

SUMMARY

Observational methods can be characterized in terms of both the degree of observer intervention and the manner in which behavior is recorded. Observation in a natural setting without observer intervention is called naturalistic observation. On the other hand, both structured observation (frequently used by the developmental psychologist Piaget) and field experiments (often used by social psychologists) depend on some degree of observer intervention. The manner of record keeping in an observational study varies according to whether a comprehensive description of behavior is sought or the observer seeks only to describe certain predefined units of behavior. Whereas narrative records, including field notes, are used to provide comprehensive descriptions of behavior, checklists (action and static) are typically used when it is simply of interest whether a specific behavior has occurred. The frequency and duration of behaviors also may be recorded, and observers are sometimes called on to make subjective judgments, in the form of ratings, about the quality or degree of a characteristic of the subject or situation.

How quantitative data are described and analyzed depends on the scale of measurement used. The four levels of measurement used by psychologists are nominal, ordinal, interval, and ratio.

Observations can rarely be made of all behavior that occurs. Consequently, some form of behavior sampling (time and event) or situation sampling must be used. An important goal of sampling is to achieve a representative sample of behavior. When narrative records are made, some type of coding system is generally used as one step in the process of data reduction. Measures of frequency and duration, as well as ratings, are typically summarized, using descriptive statistics such as the mean and standard deviation.

It is essential to provide measures of observer reliability when reporting the results of an observational study. Depending on the level of measurement that has been used, either a percentage agreement measure or a correlation coefficient can be used to assess reliability. Finally, it is important to control for the possible influence of both reactivity and observer bias in any observational study.

KEY CONCEPTS

naturalistic observation	checklist
ethology	time sampling
ethogram	event sampling
participant observation	situation sampling
structured observation	data reduction
field experiment	coding
confederate	interobserver reliability
narrative records	reactivity
ecological psychology	demand characteristics
field notes	unobtrusive (nonreactive) measures
measurement scale	observer bias

REVIEW QUESTIONS

1 What three characteristics distinguish scientific observation from nonscientific observation?
2 What critical characteristics distinguish among naturalistic observation, participant observation, structured observation, and a field experiment?
3 What two dimensions can be used to classify observational methods?
4 There are five general reasons for intervening in conducting an observational study. Identify a study illustrating each reason—either from the studies cited in this chapter or from research you have read about in other psychology courses.
5 What two methodological problems arise in participant observation?
6 What factors in participant observation can be expected to influence the extent of the observer's influence on the behavior being observed?
7 What is the principal advantage of the structured observation method?
8 Describe the role of a confederate in a field experiment.
9 In what ways does the narrative record from the study of a day in the life of a midwestern schoolgirl differ from that taken from Hartup's study of children's aggression?
10 What factors determine the usefulness of field notes as scientific records, and what determines the likelihood that these factors will be present?
11 Name the four scales of measurement, and give an example of each.
12 What aspect of an observational study is the proper use of time sampling and situation sampling intended to ensure?

13 What are the most common descriptive measures (a) when events are classified into mutually exclusive categories, and (b) when behavior is recorded on at least an interval scale?

14 What factors contribute to low interobserver reliability, and how can interobserver reliability be increased?

15 Does high interobserver reliability ensure the validity of observations? Why or why not?

16 Why are participants' reactions to demand characteristics a threat to both the internal and the external validity of psychological research?

17 What ethical issues must one address when using unobtrusive measures?

18 Give an example of each of the two ways in which investigators attempt to mitigate reactivity by adapting individuals to the presence of the observer?

19 What is the best procedure to control observer bias?

CHALLENGE QUESTIONS

1 Students in a developmental psychology lab course conducted an observational study of parent-infant interactions in the home. When they first entered the home on each of the 4 days they observed a given family, they greeted both the parents and the infant (and any other children at home). They instructed the family to follow its daily routine and they asked a series of questions about the activities of that day to determine whether it was a "normal" day or something unusual had happened. The students tried to make the family feel comfortable, but they also tried to minimize their interactions with the family and with each other. For any given 2-hour observation period there were always two student observers present in the home, and the two observers recorded their notes independently of each other. There were six pairs of students who were randomly assigned to carry out the 8 hours of observation on each of the 12 families that volunteered to serve in the study. The same pair of observers always observed a given family, and two families were assigned to each pair of observers. The observers used checklists to record behaviors on a number of different dimensions, such as mutual warmth and affection of the parent-infant interaction.

A Cite two specific procedures used by the students to ensure the reliability of their findings.

B Cite one possible threat to the external validity of the findings of this study; once again, cite a specific example from the description provided.

C Cite one specific aspect of their procedure that indicated the students were sensitive to the possibility that their measurements might be reactive. What other methods might they have used to deal with this problem of reactivity?

2 A naturalistic observation study was done to assess the effects of environmental influences on drinking by college students in a university-sponsored pub. Eighty-two students between the ages of 18 and 22 were observed. Observations were differentiated on the basis of whether the person being observed was with one other person or was in a group of two or more other people. The observations were made over a 3-month period; sessions were always from 3 p.m. to 1 a.m., and observations were made Monday through Saturday. Each participant was observed for up to 1 hour from the time he or she ordered the first beer. Two observers were always present during any observation session. The results showed that in terms of number of beers drunk per hour, men drank more and faster than did women. Men drank faster when with other men, and women also drank faster with men present. Both men and women drank

more in groups than when with one other person. These results do indicate that the environment within which drinking occurs plays an important role in the nature and extent of that drinking.

A Identify the independent and dependent variables in this study.

B What is the operational definition of a group in this study?

C Identify one specific aspect of this study that increases the external validity of the findings.

3 A friend of yours is absolutely convinced that he has a positive influence on the friendliness of conversations in which he is a participant. He has reached this conclusion on the basis of his everyday observations. You convince him that a systematic study is needed to confirm his hypothesis. Your friend (still smiling) carefully develops an operational definition of the friendliness of a conversation and records a rating for each of the next 50 conversations in which he is a participant. His results show that 75% of these conversations are rated "very friendly," 20% are rated "friendly," and 5% are rated neutral. Your friend returns to you—now convinced beyond a shadow of a doubt that he has a positive effect on the friendliness of a conversation. Although your friend won't be pleased with you, explain to him why the results of his study are essentially useless as a means of confirming his hypothesis. While you have this chance to teach your friend about research methods, explain to him why it would be better for you or someone else to rate the friendliness of the conversations in a proper study testing your friend's hypothesis.

4 A recent carefully controlled observational study was undertaken to determine whether differences in student-teacher ratings correspond to genuine instructional differences among teachers. The participants were 48 full-time social science faculty (39 males and 9 females) at a major university. Ten were full professors, 18 were associate professors, and 20 were assistant professors. A number of undergraduate students were carefully trained as observers. They used a checklist including 100 specific observable classroom behaviors, and their visits to the classrooms were unnoticed by the professors. Six to eight observers visited three separate 1-hour class periods taught by these instructors over a 3-month period. The results of the study showed that teachers who receive high ratings from students do in fact teach differently from instructors who receive average or poor ratings.

Use the preceding description to answer the following questions:

A What specific procedure was used in this study to avoid reactivity?

B What factor in this study is likely to have affected the reliability of the results?

C What factor in this study affected the external validity of the findings?

D Given the final conclusion, which goal of the scientific method (description, prediction, understanding) was the basis for this study?

ANSWER TO CHALLENGE QUESTION 1

1 **A** The students' procedures that enhanced reliability were as follows: observing each family for 8 hours, using two independent observers, and using checklists to provide operational definitions.

B One possible threat to the external validity of the findings was that the 12 families volunteered for the study and such families may differ from typical families.

C The students' efforts to minimize interactions with the family and with each other suggested they were sensitive to the problem of reactivity. Two other methods they might have used are habituation and desensitization.

Chapter 4

Correlational Research: Surveys

Campaigns for political offices frequently are accompanied by media reports revealing the results of the latest poll. A poll supposedly tells us which candidate is ahead at any particular time. Media analysts spend a lot of time interpreting poll results, giving us their opinions about what the latest figures mean for the candidates. You may even have seen debates about whether polls have an undue influence on the political process; for example, analysts have argued that some people switch sides to support a front-runner in the poll in order to be on the winning side. Although the polls are intended to describe people's voting preferences at the time the poll is taken, they are also used to predict how people will vote at the time of the actual election. Candidates use poll results to help orchestrate their campaigns, for example, by identifying places they should visit and issues on which they should focus. Political polls involve the use of survey-research methods. As you will see in this chapter, however, surveys have a much broader application than their use in political polling; they are an important research tool of psychologists.

Survey research represents a more general approach to psychological research called correlational research. Correlational research, unlike experimental research (see Chapter 6), does not involve the manipulation of independent variables. Instead, **correlational research** assesses the relationships among naturally occurring variables with the goal of identifying predictive relationships. The predictive relationships found in correlational research have implications for decisions such as identifying emotional disorders and selecting among job applicants. A decision to admit you to college was likely made with the help of correlational research showing the relationship between various predictors (e.g., high school rank, academic test scores) and a measure of success in college (e.g., first-year college GPA).

Larose and Roy (1995) gave a questionnaire to students who were beginning their college studies. The questionnaire measured nonintellectual aspects of the students' personal approach to learning. For example, the questionnaire included items asking about students' attitudes toward teachers and the students' priorities regarding their use of time. Larose and Roy found that using their instrument they could predict students' academic success in the first year of college better than when only high school grade-point average was used as a predictor of college success. Their instrument was also useful in predicting which students were likely to be at risk academically in their first year of college. Clearly, correlational research can play an important role in decision making.

In this chapter we also introduce the basic logic and techniques of *sampling*—the process of selecting a subset of a population to represent the population as a whole—which is so often critical to successful prediction. You will then learn about the advantages and disadvantages of various survey-research methods and survey-research designs. We conclude the chapter with a brief discussion of the correspondence between people's reported behavior and their actual behavior. Do people really do what they say they do?

CORRELATIONAL RESEARCH

THE NATURE OF CORRELATIONS

Prediction, as you saw in Chapter 1, is an important goal of the scientific method. Correlational research frequently provides the basis for this prediction. A **correlation** exists when two different measures of the same people, events, or things vary together, that is, when scores on one variable covary with scores on another variable. For example, typically we find a correlation between first and last test scores in a large introductory psychology class. Students with high scores on the first test tend to have high scores on the last test; students with low scores on the first test tend to score low on the last test. The presence of this correlation allows us to make predictions about students' test scores. For example, if we know students' scores on the first test we can predict (to some degree) students' scores on the final test. The nature of these predictions and the confidence we have in making them depends on the direction and the strength of the correlation.

It is possible to determine quantitatively the nature and strength of a correlation by computing a **correlation coefficient.** We can use the correlation coefficient as a quantitative index of how well we are able to predict one set of scores (for example, final test scores) based on another set of scores (for example, first test scores). A correlation coefficient expresses the relationship between two variables in terms of both the *direction* and the *magnitude* of that relationship.

The direction of a correlation coefficient can be either positive or negative. A positive correlation indicates that, as the value of one measure increases, the value of the other measure also increases. Scores on the first and final tests in a large psychology class should be positively correlated. Similarly, Scholastic Aptitude Test (SAT) scores and the first-semester GPAs of college students are positively correlated. Thus, we would predict that students with higher SAT scores would have higher first-semester GPAs. In a negative correlation, as the value of one measure increases, the value of the other measure decreases. A national survey of high school seniors showed a negative correlation between the amount of time spent watching TV and the number of correct answers on an academic achievement test (Keith, Reimers, Fehrmann, Pottebaum, & Aubrey, 1986). Based on this finding, if you knew that a student scored very high on the achievement test, would you predict the student had spent "a lot" of time or "a little" time watching TV?

The magnitude (degree) of a correlation coefficient can range in absolute values from 0.0 to 1.00. A value of 0 indicates there is no correlation and we have no ability to predict one measure on the basis of knowing a value on another measure. The relationship between intelligence and mental illness, for example, exhibits a zero correlation; we cannot predict the likelihood that a person will become mentally ill by knowing the person's IQ. A value of +1.00 indicates a perfect positive correlation, and a value of –1.00 indicates a perfect negative correlation. When a correlation coefficient is either +1.00 or –1.00, we can make predictions with absolute confidence. Values between 0 and 1.00 indicate predictive relationships of intermediate strength and, therefore, we have less ability to predict confidently. Remember, the sign of the correlation signifies only its direction; a correlation coefficient of –.46 indicates a stronger relationship than one of +.20. (Note: In practice, only the sign of negative correlation coefficients is indicated; a coefficient without a plus or minus sign is treated as positive, that is, .20 = +.20.)

The nature of a correlation can be represented graphically in the form of a scatterplot. A scatterplot shows the intersecting points for each pair of scores in a data set. Hypothetical examples of scatterplots showing strong positive, practically zero, and moderate negative correlations are shown in Figure 4.1. The magnitude or degree of correlation is seen in a scatterplot by determining how well the points correspond to a straight line. Thus, the correlation is stronger in the first example (a) than in the other two examples; however, the correlation represented in the third example (c) would be stronger than the second example (b). The direction of a correlation can be seen in the scatterplot by noting how the points are arranged. When the pattern of points is from lower left to upper right (a), then the correlation is positive (low scores go with low scores and high scores go with high scores). When the pattern of points is from upper left to lower right (c), the correlation is negative (low scores go with high scores and high scores go with low scores). Whether represented in a scatterplot or in a correlation coefficient, the purpose of a correlation is to determine how well we predict one measure based on its covariation with another measure.

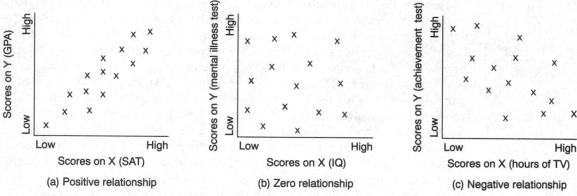

FIGURE 4.1   Three scatterplots illustrating a strong positive (a), a zero (b), and a moderate negative (c), correlation between scores on two variables: X and Y.

CORRELATIONAL STUDIES

A study by Lubin and his colleagues (1988) illustrates how useful correlational studies can be in psychological research. They investigated correlations among measures of physical and psychological health in their survey of 1,543 adults living in the United States. Respondents provided self-ratings of physical health and information about such health-related factors as frequency of visits to a physician and the nature and frequency of any medications they were taking. The interviewers also collected data regarding the respondent's occupation and religious affiliation, frequency of volunteer and social activities, and so forth. Each of the respondents also completed a paper-and-pencil test measuring both positive affect (for example, happiness) and negative affect (for example, depression). Measures of psychological health and measures of physical health were found to be correlated. For instance, positive affect was positively correlated with self-ratings of physical health; happier people were more healthy. Additionally, frequency of volunteer activities correlated negatively with a measure of depression; people who were more active in volunteer activities experienced less depression. Correlations like these can prove useful in predicting physical and psychological health-related problems.

Correlational studies are the method of choice when the goal of the research is prediction. There are serious limitations, however, on using results of correlational studies to infer causal relationships. For instance, there is a reliable correlation between being outgoing and being satisfied with one's life (Myers & Diener, 1995). Based on this correlation alone, however, we could not argue convincingly that being more outgoing causes people to be more satisfied with their lives. Outgoing people may be more satisfied with their lives because they have more active social lives. Or, people may be more outgoing and have more active social lives because they are more satisfied with their lives. The causal relationship could go both ways—being more outgoing leads to greater life satisfaction *or* being more satisfied with life leads to being more outgoing.

Another possibility is that a third variable, having more friends, leads people to be more outgoing *and* more satisfied with their lives. A correlation that can be explained away by a third variable is called a *spurious relationship* (Kenny, 1979). In this particular example, "number of friends" is a possible third variable that could account for the relationship between being outgoing and being satisfied with one's life. These problems with understanding the nature of causal relationships based on correlations should make it clear that *more than mere correlational evidence is necessary to make causal statements.*

Nevertheless, sophisticated statistical techniques can be used to help with causal interpretations of correlational studies (Baron & Kenny, 1986). One technique involves the identification of moderator variables. A *moderator variable* is a variable that affects the direction or strength of the correlation between two variables. We can use a study by Stern, McCants, and Pettine (1982) to illustrate this concept. The researchers carried out a correlational study in which they measured the number of significant life changes (e.g., divorce, death of a spouse, job change) and the severity of illness over the previous 3 years for 197 young adults. They found a positive correlation (.40) between the total number of significant changes people experienced in their lives and the severity of their subsequent illness: As the number of life changes increased, the severity of illness also increased.

More importantly for our purposes here, Stern et al. (1982) identified a moderator variable that affected the obtained relationship between life changes and illness. The moderator variable was how controllable the participants thought the life changing events were. Life changes such as the death of a close friend were perceived to be uncontrollable events and changes such as marriage were perceived to be controllable events. The correlation for life changing events and severity of illness was stronger for uncontrollable events (.43) than for controllable events (.27). The identification of this moderator variable indicates that we should consider the perceived controllability of life changes when we try to predict how these changes will affect our health, since uncontrollable events may have more adverse health effects than controllable events. More generally, although we still can't make definite causal statements based on an analysis of moderator variables, the use of sophisticated statistical techniques like those involved in identifying moderator variables can greatly enhance our ability to interpret the results of correlational studies.

MEASURES IN CORRELATIONAL RESEARCH

QUESTIONNAIRES AS INSTRUMENTS

The value of correlational research (and of any other type of research) ultimately depends on the quality of the measurements that researchers make. The quality of these measurements, in turn, depends on the quality of the instruments used to make the measurements. The primary research instrument in survey research is the questionnaire. On the surface, a questionnaire may not look like the high-tech instruments used in much modern scientific research;

but, when constructed and used properly, a questionnaire is a powerful scientific instrument.

Demographic variables, one important type of variable frequently measured in survey research, are used to describe the characteristics of the people who are surveyed. Religious affiliation and occupation, which Lubin and his colleagues (1988) measured in their study of psychological and physical health, are demographic variables. Measures such as race, ethnicity, age, and socioeconomic status are also examples of demographic variables. Whether we decide to measure these variables depends on the goals of our study, as well as on other considerations. Entwisle and Astone (1994), for example, provide a practical reason for including race and ethnicity as demographic variables in survey research. This practical reason is the ever increasing diversity of the U.S. population. Approximately 12% of the U.S. population is African American and about 9% is Latino. Entwisle and Astone point out that "The ethnic and racial diversity of the U.S. population is now projected to increase through the middle of the next century, so that by then the majority of the U.S. population will be persons whose ethnicity would now be classified as 'nonwhite'" (p. 1522). By asking respondents to identify their race we are able to document the racial mix of our sample and, perhaps, compare racial groups in our analyses.

Measuring a demographic variable such as race may at first seem very easy. One straightforward method is simply to ask respondents to identify their race in a fill-in-the-blank question: What is your race? _____ Such an approach may be straightforward, but the resulting measurement of race may not be all that satisfactory. For example, some respondents may mistakenly confuse "race" and "ethnicity." Important distinctions in identifying ethnic groups may go unrecognized by respondents and researchers. For instance, Hispanic does not identify a race; Hispanic designates all those whose country of origin is Spanish speaking. So, a person born in Spain would be classified as Hispanic. *Latino* is a term sometimes used interchangeably with Hispanic, but Latino designates people whose origin is from the countries of North and South America, excluding Canada and the United States. Distinctions like these can be confused. For example, a person known to the authors is of European Spanish heritage and correctly considers himself a Caucasian, and not Hispanic. He could be classified as Hispanic, however, especially since his surname is one many people identify as Hispanic.

In general, so-called quick and dirty approaches to measurement in survey research tend to yield messy data that are hard to analyze and interpret. Entwisle and Astone (1994) recommend a more deliberate—and effective—approach when measuring race. They outline a series of nine questions to measure a person's race. One of these questions is, What race do you consider yourself to be? Other questions seek information such as what countries the person's ancestors came from, and whether Latino respondents were Mexican, Puerto Rican, Cuban, or something else. This more detailed series of questions allows researchers to measure race less ambiguously, more accurately, and more precisely. We use this example of measuring race to illustrate a more general principle: *The accuracy and precision of questionnaires as survey-research in-*

struments depends on the expertise and care that go into their construction. (For important information on questionnaire construction, see Appendix B.)

MARGIN OF ERROR

Survey-research results are often reported in terms of the percentage of respondents who prefer a certain candidate or who agree or disagree with a certain position. We must be careful, however, when we translate this numerical information into a verbal description of the results. For example, a major metropolitan newspaper reported on the National Collegiate Athletic Association's (NCAA) 1995 Division I Graduation-Rates Report. The graduation data in the NCAA report were for students entering college in 1988 because the students are given 6 years to graduate. The overall graduation rate for all students entering in 1988 (both athletes and nonathletes) was 57%. The graduation rate for football players entering in 1987 was 55% and the newspaper indicated this rate had risen in 1988. That sounds like good news. But it turns out that the percentage increase in the graduation rate for football players was not particularly impressive. It was 1%, that is, a 56% overall graduation rate for 1988. The graduation rates for 1987 and 1988 were included in the newspaper article so there was no effort to mislead the reader about the size of the increase. Nonetheless, survey researchers need some way to translate absolute differences in percentages into appropriate verbal statements. Is a change from 55% to 56% a "meaningful" or "significant" increase? When it comes to describing survey results, a difference is not always a difference.

As we describe more fully later in this chapter, survey research relies heavily on sampling. The results obtained with the sample are used to describe the population from which the sample was drawn. Well-selected samples provide good estimates of the population, but it is unlikely the results for a given sample are going to be exactly equal to the corresponding values for the population as a whole. If the average age in a classroom of 33 college students is 26.4, it is not necessarily the case that a sample of 10 students will have a mean of exactly 26.4, even if the sample was selected randomly. If 65% of a city's population favor the present mayor and 35% favor a new mayor, we wouldn't necessarily expect an exact 65:35 split in a poll of 100 voters sampled randomly from the city population. We expect some slippage due to random sampling, some error between the actual population value and the estimate from our sample.

It is possible to estimate the **margin of error** between the sample results and the true population values. That is, we can estimate how large a difference between the sample results and the population values we might expect simply on the basis of chance. Because of sampling error, absolute differences in percentages (for example, between 55% and 56%) are not directly interpretable; differences in percentages must be evaluated in terms of their margin of error. Let's consider a specific example using the hypothetical mayoral election we just referred to. Assume that in a random sample of 100 voters, 63 people said they favor the present mayor and 37 said they want her replaced. (Let us assume we know that in the population 65% of the people favor the incumbent and 35%

want a new mayor.) The question we must ask is, Is the difference between 63 and 65 (the sample estimate and population value, respectively) a *real* difference? Another way of stating this is, Is the sample value of 63 within the margin of error that is expected when random samples of this size are taken? If it is, then the difference may not be a real difference but one due to sampling error.

The margin of error gives us the range of values we can expect based on sampling error. In the mayoral election example, let us assume that a poll is taken and a media spokesperson gives the following report: "Results indicate that 63% of those sampled favor the incumbent. We can say with 95% confidence that the poll has a margin of error of 5%." The reported margin of error with the specified level of confidence (usually 95%) indicates that the percentage of the actual population who favor the incumbent is estimated to fall in a range between 58% and 68% (plus or minus the margin of error around the sample value of 63%). It is reasonable, therefore, to assume that 65% of the population do favor the present mayor even though results of the poll "say" only 63% favor her.

The margin of error is primarily determined by the size of the sample—the larger the sample size, the smaller the margin of error. Thus, in order to reduce the margin of error an obvious decision would appear to be to increase the size of the sample. While this may make sense in some situations, we must be aware that increasing sample sizes can make the cost of doing a survey too high. For example, if our margin of error is 5% with a sample size of 100, we would have to quadruple the sample size to 400 to decrease the margin of error by half.

Another factor that influences the margin of error is the confidence we want to have in the accuracy of our estimate. Given a sample of specific size, we can be more confident about estimating a population value when we have a larger margin of error to work with. As an illustration, think of what your weight is right now. Can you confidently estimate your weight within 5 pounds (a margin of error)? Would you be more confident of your estimate if you were allowed to be within 10 pounds? We could express the differences in the sizes of the intervals in terms of confidence. A person might say, "I am 99% confident that my weight is between 160 and 170, but I'm only 90% confident that my weight is within 165 and 170." When survey results are considered, therefore, a 99% confidence level results in a larger margin of error than does a 90% confidence level (assuming the same sample size for the two different confidence levels).

The margin of error for a given sample can be computed using the sample size and a specified confidence level. In practice, however, a desired margin of error (e.g., 3%) and confidence level (e.g., 95%) are selected and the sample size necessary to achieve these two objectives is then calculated.

Margins of error are routinely included when national surveys are reported in the media. This is useful information for those who know how to interpret margins of error. At this point, you should be able to interpret the following statements reflecting hypothetical survey results. (It is *not* necessary to know what the real population value of voters favoring the present mayor is in order to understand these results. The survey tells you "with a margin of error" what the population value is.)

(a) "A survey of voters recently showed that 62% of those sampled would vote for the present mayor if the election were held today. The poll has a margin of error of 5% with a 99% confidence level."

(b) "A survey of voters recently showed that 62% of those sampled would vote for the present mayor if the election were held today. The poll has a margin of error of 3% with a 95% confidence level."

Knowing the margin of error for a survey is not sufficient to assure the interpretability of the survey's results. Interpretable results also depend on factors such as how the survey sample was selected, how many of those selected for the sample actually responded to the survey, how the questions on the questionnaire are worded, and how well trained the interviewers who administer the questionnaire are (Converse & Traugott, 1986). Unfortunately, these important aspects of survey research are unlikely to be reported in the media. Thus, we should be cautious in accepting interpretations of survey-research results found in the media unless we are well informed about critical characteristics of the survey. As you will soon see, problems can arise even in a carefully conducted survey.

RELIABILITY AND VALIDITY

Reliability and validity are vital characteristics of all psychological measurement. Thus, it makes sense that measurements in survey research must be reliable and valid. In this section we describe some procedures researchers use to determine whether measures are reliable and valid.

Our examples involve assessing the reliability and validity of tests. Tests, like surveys, are commonly used instruments in correlational research. We chose to use tests for our examples because you already know a great deal about tests. Taking tests is a routine part of a student's life. You may even prefer a particular type of test because you believe you perform better on that type of test. Most of us experience emotional reactions when taking tests, ranging from exhilaration to terror! There are good reasons for these emotional reactions. Important decisions frequently are based in part on test results—admission to college, passing or failing courses, admission to graduate or professional schools. Although you have considerable experiential knowledge about taking tests, what else do you know about the tests you take? For example, have you ever wondered whether all the tests you have taken have been reliable and valid? Consider that question for a moment. How would you be able to tell whether a test was reliable and valid? Asked a different way, what are the fundamental characteristics of a reliable and valid test?

Reliable tests, like reliable observers or any other reliable measurements, are characterized by consistency. A reliable test is one that yields similar (consistent) results each time it is taken. Tests must be reliable if they are to be used to make predictions about who will be selected for a scholarship, who will be hired for a competitive job, or who should be fired from a job. For example, Powell and Whitla (1994) have developed a test they call MicroCog to measure normal cognitive aging. As part of the natural aging process, older adults experience some problems with memory and other cognitive functions. They may find they have more trouble than they used to remembering people's names. Problems such as these lead some older adults to wonder if they are "losing it." This question is also pertinent in the workplace. In 1994, it became illegal in the United States for an employer to compel a worker to retire because of age. Tests like MicroCog are likely to be useful to older adults to help allay their fears about memory loss and to employers to help them make difficult decisions about whether an older employee is able to continue working. When test results are used as part of the process of making such important personal decisions it is essential that the tests be as reliable as possible—reliability is no longer just a measurement issue.

There are several ways to measure a test's reliability. One common method is to compute a *test-retest reliability*. Usually, test-retest reliability involves administering the same test to a large sample of people at each of two different times. For a test to be reliable, people do not have to obtain identical scores on the two administrations of the test, but a person's relative position in the distribution of scores should be similar at the two test times. The consistency of this relative positioning is determined by computing a correlation coefficient using the two test scores for each person in the sample. A desirable value for test-retest reliability coefficients is in the range of .80 or above, but the size of the coefficient does depend on factors such as the types of items and the number of items.

As we just mentioned, one of the most important factors affecting the reliability of a test is the number of items on the test; in this case, more is better. We are likely to have unreliable measures if we try to measure a student's mastery of material based on a single item on a test, or a baseball player's hitting ability based on a single time at bat, or a person's attitude toward the death penalty based on a single question in a survey. The reliability of our measures will increase greatly if we average the behavior in question across a large number of observations—many test items, many at bats, and many survey questions (Epstein, 1979).

In general, measurements will also be more reliable when there is greater variability on the factor being measured among those individuals being tested. Individuals who vary a great deal from one another are easier to differentiate reliably than are individuals who differ by only a small amount. For example, differentiating among the academic ability of a group drawn from the general student population would be easier than differentiating the ability levels of a more homogeneous group of honor students. Thus, a test would be more reliable when administered to the general population of students than when given to only honor students.

A third and final factor affecting reliability is related to actual test administration. Tests will be more reliable when the testing situation is free of distractions and when clear instructions are provided for completing the test. These three factors affecting the reliability of tests (number and type of items, variability in the sample, and testing procedures) apply equally to the measurements made using questionnaires in survey research.

The reliability of a test is easier to determine and to achieve than is the validity of a test. The definition of validity is straightforward—a valid test measures what it is intended to measure. For example, a valid test of research methods knowledge might ask you about the terms *reliability* and *validity;* we suspect that you would question the validity of such a test if asked about the classical counterpoint in the fugue of Mozart's Symphony No. 4 in C Major (finale).

At this point, we focus on construct validity, which is just one of the many ways in which the validity of a test is assessed. The *construct validity* of a test represents the extent to which the test measures the theoretical construct it is intended to measure. Quantitative reasoning, self-esteem, anxiety, and depression represent examples of theoretical constructs that have been measured using tests. One approach to determining the construct validity of a test relies on two other kinds of validity: convergent validity and discriminant validity. These concepts can best be understood by considering an example.

Table 4.1 presents hypothetical data showing how we might assess the construct validity of a quantitative reasoning test. Look first at the values in parentheses that appear on the diagonal. These parenthesized correlation coefficients represent the test reliabilities of the three measures appearing in the table (quantitative reasoning, classroom math test, and verbal reasoning, respectively). Let us assume that each reliability coefficient was obtained from giving two equivalent forms of a test to the same students. As you can see, the three measures show good test-retest reliability (each is above .80). Our focus, however, is on measuring the construct validity of the quantitative reasoning test; so let's look at what else is in Table 4.1.

It is reasonable to expect that scores on the quantitative reasoning test should correlate with students' scores on a math test in class. That is, if the quantitative test is indeed measuring the ability to reason quantitatively, then students who score high on this test would be expected to get good scores on a math test in class, and those who score low on the test would be expected to earn lower scores. The correlation of .60 between the quantitative reasoning

TABLE 4.1 HYPOTHETICAL EXAMPLE ILLUSTRATING CONSTRUCT VALIDITY

Test Form A	Test Form B		
	Quantitative reasoning	Math test	Verbal reasoning
Quantitative reasoning	(.90)	.60	.15
Math test		(.80)	.10
Verbal reasoning			(.85)

test and math test scores indicates that the two measures do correlate as expected. This finding provides evidence for *convergent validity;* the two tests converge (or "go together") as measures of quantitative reasoning.

The case for the construct validity of a test can be made even more strongly when the test is shown to have discriminant validity. As you can see in Table 4.1, the correlations between quantitative reasoning and verbal reasoning (.15) and between math test scores and verbal reasoning (.10) are low. These findings show that the quantitative test does not correlate with a test designed to measure another theoretical construct, namely, verbal reasoning. The low correlation between the quantitative reasoning test and the verbal reasoning test indicates that the two tests are measuring different constructs. Thus, there is evidence for *discriminant validity* of the quantitative reasoning test because it seems to "discriminate" quantitative reasoning from verbal reasoning. The construct validity of the quantitative reasoning test gains strong initial support in our example because there is evidence for both convergent validity and discriminant validity.

PREDICTIONS AND DECISIONS

The results of correlational research have implications for decision making. Predictive relationships that have been established in research studies can be used in making such diverse decisions as who should pursue a career as a salesperson or who should be admitted to a psychiatric hospital. As we described in the previous section, predictive relationships must be reliable if they are to be the basis for making good decisions. Based on highly reliable predictive relationships we can accurately predict what people's average behavior will be. This type of prediction is called **actuarial prediction.** For example, students who score in the highest 20% on an academic aptitude test are on average more likely to succeed in college than are students who score in the lowest 20%. Actuarial predictions do not necessarily tell us what an individual person will do in a particular situation. Thus, knowing a student's score on an academic aptitude test does not allow us to predict with certainty whether *that* student will graduate from college even if the academic aptitude test is a reliable predictor of success in college. We can only predict what students "like this student" will typically (on the average) do. Nonetheless, actuarial prediction can still be extremely useful.

Important decisions that involve correlational research are rarely based on a single source of information. When more than one measure has been shown to have some predictive value, we can make use of several measures to aid in prediction. The use of several different predictors in developing an effective decision-making process follows a logic similar to that of the multimethod approach to research. Just as the use of several different research methods to investigate a problem increases the likelihood of converging on a valid conclusion, so, too, does the use of several different predictors in a decision-making process increase the likelihood of making good decisions.

In the graduate application process, for instance, GRE test scores, undergraduate GPA, letters of recommendation, and a personal essay all contribute to the admission committee's decisions. Similarly, decisions involving selections among applicants in more applied settings rely on the use of multiple predictors. Broach (1992) reported that predictions of performance by air traffic controllers in radar-based training after 1 or 2 years in that occupation were better when biographical data (such as age and prior experience) were included than when the predictions were based only on a civil service test.

Statistical prediction based on correlational research is sometimes contrasted with clinical prediction. Meehl (1954) studied the task that clinical psychologists routinely face when they must diagnose the emotional disorders experienced by their clients. Meehl compared the accuracy of two different approaches to making these challenging diagnostic decisions: clinical prediction and statistical prediction. These two approaches represent different ways of combining information to make a decision. Clinical prediction occurs when a clinician reviews the available evidence pertinent to a case, including the clinician's impressions from interviewing the client, and then makes a diagnosis (prediction) of the client's disorder. Clinical prediction relies heavily on the personal and professional *judgment* of the clinician.

Statistical prediction is essentially the same as actuarial prediction. Correlational research is used to identify predictive relationships that are the basis for statistical prediction. For example, a large amount of research has shown that the occurrence of "depression" is correlated with low energy, difficulty sleeping, and crying; the occurrence of "schizophrenia" is correlated with withdrawal and disordered thinking. Information about a given client is then entered into this predictive (correlational) system, and a statistical prediction is made about which emotional disorder is most likely for the client. The distinguishing characteristic of statistical prediction is that it is based on empirical evidence (for example, results of paper-and-pencil tests) rather than on the individual judgment of a clinician. Which of these two approaches yields more accurate predictions of emotional disorders?

Meehl (1954) found that, in an absolute sense, neither clinical prediction nor statistical prediction was very accurate—a not surprising finding given the complexity involved in diagnosing psychological disorders. Meehl did find, however, that statistical prediction was more accurate than clinical prediction. In fact, research has shown that statistical prediction is superior to clinical prediction across a wide variety of areas, including predictions about who to admit to graduate school, who is a good risk for a bank loan, who is at risk for a heart attack, and who should be paroled from prison (Dawes, Faust, & Meehl, 1993). We should generally trust, therefore, what the data "say" more than what one person says when we need to make important decisions.

Although evidence like this suggests that we should rely on statistical prediction whenever possible, it is not always practical to do so. As Meehl (1993) emphasizes, "You could not choose a graduate school, buy a car, get married (or divorced), let alone invest money or vote for president, if you required all your choices to be derived rigorously from scientific proof" (p. 727). Empirical evidence simply is not available for many important decisions. When we have no basis for making a statistical prediction, then we must make the best decision we can based on our own judgment. When we do have evidence to serve as the basis for a statistical prediction, we face a different situation. Meehl argues that we are making an ethically questionable choice if we ignore this evidence and rely on clinical prediction. Our hope is that the knowledge you have gained about correlational research as a basis for predictions will allow you to make more informed decisions.

USES OF SURVEYS

We discussed in Chapter 3 how psychologists use observational methods to infer what people must have been thinking or feeling to have behaved in a certain way. Survey research is designed to deal more directly with the nature of people's thoughts, opinions, and feelings. On the surface, survey research is deceptively simple. If you want to know what people are thinking, ask them! In a similar vein one could suggest that, if you want to know what people are doing, observe them! As we have seen, however, when we hope to infer general principles of behavior, our observations must be more sophisticated. So, too, the proper use of the survey-research method requires more than simply asking people questions.

The deceptive ease of conducting a survey is illustrated in a report by a young girl named Bridgette that was published in a suburban grammar school's newsletter. The report read, "I surveyed 50 people on which candy bar they liked best. Here are my results in order of preference: Hershey bar—35, Snickers—10, Whachamacallit—5." These results may please the manufacturers of Hershey bars, but the operator of the school's vending machine should be wary of stocking it on the basis of these findings. Who were the "50 people" surveyed and how were they selected? How was the survey conducted? Was each child interviewed separately? If other children were present during the interview, were they eating candy bars? If so, what brands? Do the children who claim to like Hershey bars best really eat them most often? These and many other questions must be answered before we can confidently interpret the results of this survey.

You may be thinking at this point that we are taking Bridgette's survey more seriously than she intended, and you are probably right. Nonetheless, these questions are typical of those that should be asked when we read or hear a report of a nationwide survey indicating that, for example, a majority of Americans oppose gun control. A goal of this chapter is to help guide you to ask the right questions about surveys and to aid you in evaluating the soundness of answers to these questions.

Surveys are used in research by social scientists such as political scientists, psychologists, and sociologists for a variety of reasons. For example, Cherlin et al. (1991) conducted national surveys in Great Britain and the United States to investigate the effects of divorce on children. Myers and Diener (1995) reported the results of many studies that used surveys to study factors affecting people's personal sense of well-being.

Surveys are also used to meet the more pragmatic needs of political candidates, public health officials, professional organizations, and advertising and marketing directors. The scope and purpose of such surveys can be limited and specific, or they can be global. The Practice Directorate of APA conducted a survey with a more limited and specific purpose (Peterson, 1995). The directorate focuses primarily on the concerns of clinical psychologists. They participated with other groups in a national survey of 1,087 adults that was designed to help the directorate understand better what the public thinks that psychologists do, what kind of education psychologists have, and in what settings psychologists practice. Findings of the survey included that 46% of respondents reported having seen a mental health professional or having someone in their family who had, and that 80% said that psychologists usually work in private practice. More than half of psychologists do work in the mental health field, but fewer than half of those work in private practice. Clearly, the public's estimate of 80% is high. Nonetheless, results from this survey will be useful to the directorate in focusing their public education strategies.

Myers and Diener (1995), on the other hand, reported the results of a survey sampling people from 24 countries representing every continent but Antarctica. One of the questions addressed in this survey was whether people in rich countries have a greater sense of well-being than those in not-so-rich countries. The results of the survey showed that national wealth, as indexed, by gross national product per capita, is positively correlated with well-being (.67). But this relationship is not a simple one because national wealth is confounded with other variables that are highly correlated with well-being such as number of continuous years of democracy (.85). This research illustrates that survey research can be truly a global enterprise.

One of the ways that surveys can be used is noteworthy because it raises a serious ethical question. The ethical dilemma arises when sponsors of survey research have vested interests in how the results turn out. Crossen (1994) has highlighted this issue, ". . . more and more of the information we use to buy, elect, advise, acquit, and heal has been created not to expand our knowledge but to sell a product or advance a cause" (p. 14). Crossen provides examples such as a national survey sponsored by the zinc industry showing that 62% of respondents wanted to keep the penny (which is zinc based), and a survey sponsored by a manufacturer of cellular phones showing that 70% of respondents (all of whom used cellular phones) agreed that people who use cellular telephones are more successful in business.

So, should we conclude that any time the outcome of a study is favorable for the sponsoring agency, the results are biased? Answers to ethical questions are rarely simple and the answer to this one certainly is not. High quality and ethical research can certainly be done when the sponsor has an interest in the outcome. Knowing the sponsor of the research can be important in evaluating the results, but knowing the sponsor is far from sufficient to judge whether the study is biased. It is much more important to know whether a biased sample has been used, or whether the wording of questions has been slanted, or whether the data have been selectively analyzed or reported. Any of these aspects of survey research can bias the results. And, unethical researchers can use these techniques to make the results "turn out right." The best protection against unethical researchers and poor quality research is to examine carefully the procedures and analyses used in the survey.

CHARACTERISTICS OF SURVEYS

Although they differ in how they can be used, all surveys have some characteristics in common. These shared characteristics make properly conducted surveys an excellent basis for describing people's attitudes and opinions. Surveys generally involve sampling, a concept we introduced in our discussion of observational methods (Chapter 3) and say more about in the next section of this chapter. Surveys are also characterized by their use of a set of predetermined questions for all respondents. Oral or written responses to these questions constitute the principal data obtained in a survey. By using the same phrasing and ordering of questions, it is possible to summarize the views of all respondents succinctly.

A series of national surveys asked respondents the same questions about their attitudes toward premarital sex (Gallup, 1988). In 1969, 68% of the respondents condemned premarital sex as wrong. The corresponding percentages were 48% in 1973, 50% in 1978, 39% in 1985, and 40% in 1991. These findings indicate that attitudes toward premarital sex have changed since the late 1960s, but then remained fairly stable with half or fewer than half of respondents disapproving from the 1970s to the early 1990s. As this example illustrates, the study of trends in people's attitudes over time is possible when the same survey question has been asked of comparable samples in successive surveys.

SAMPLING TECHNIQUES

Assume you have decided on a research question to answer using the survey method and you have determined the population of interest for your survey. The next step is to decide who to interview. This involves selecting a sample of respondents to represent the population. The power and efficiency of sampling are aptly summarized by survey researcher Angus Campbell (1981, p. 17):

> The method of choice for portraying all the variety of a large heterogeneous population is clearly that of the sample survey. Ever since statisticians and social scientists learned how to draw a sample from a large universe in such a way that every member of the universe has an equal chance of being chosen, it has been possible to describe the national population accurately by obtaining information from a few thousand carefully selected individuals.

Whether we are describing a national population or a much smaller one, such as the students of a certain university, the procedures are the same. We explain in this section how to make that careful selection of individuals which Campbell describes.

BASIC TERMS OF SAMPLING

As we begin to talk about sampling techniques, we need to define four terms: *population, sampling frame, sample,* and *element.* The relationships among the four critical sampling terms are summarized in Figure 4.2. A **population** is the set of all the cases of interest. If you were interested in the attitudes of students on your campus toward the services provided by the library, your population would be all students on your campus. In a survey, we select a subset of the population to represent the population as a whole.

Next, we need to develop a specific list of the members of the population. This specific list is called a **sampling frame** and is, in a sense, an operational definition of the population of interest. In a survey assessing the attitudes of students toward library services, the sampling frame might be a list obtained from the registrar's office of all currently enrolled students. The extent to which the sampling frame reflects the population of interest determines the adequacy of the subset we ultimately select. The list provided by the registrar

FIGURE 4.2   Illustration of relationships among four basic terms in sampling.

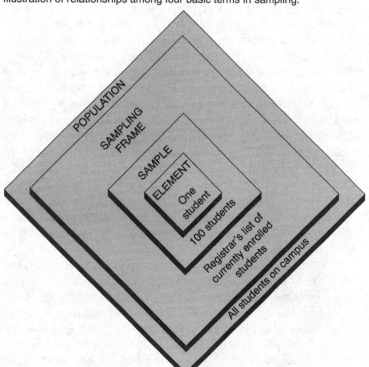

should provide a good sampling frame, but some students might be excluded, such as students who registered late.

An inadequate sampling frame can pose a serious problem, as pollsters in the 1936 presidential election found out. In 1936, a *Literary Digest* poll involving a mail survey of almost 2 million voters predicted incorrectly that Alfred M. Landon would beat Franklin D. Roosevelt by a landslide. The sample of voters was drawn from telephone directories, magazine subscription lists, and automobile registration lists. Using this sampling frame, pollsters had correctly predicted the outcome of the previous four elections. Spurred by the Depression, however, increasing numbers of the poor voted in 1936 and were not adequately represented on such lists. The underrepresentation of poor voters in the polls was responsible for the incorrect prediction that Landon would become president.

The subset of the population actually drawn from the sampling frame is called the **sample.** We might select 100 students from the registrar's list to serve as the sample in our library survey. How closely the attitudes of this sample of students will represent those of all the students depends critically on how the sample is chosen. Each member of the population is called an **element.** The identification and selection of elements that make up the sample are the basis of all sampling techniques.

It is important to emphasize that samples are of little or no interest in themselves. Library policy would not be changed solely for the 100 students surveyed. Similarly, the social psychologist is not interested solely in the racial attitudes of the 50 people he surveyed, nor is the marketing director interested only in the preferences of the 200 consumers she surveyed. The power of descriptions derived from an analysis of the sample is based on the assumption that these descriptions are applicable to the population from which the sample was drawn. Populations, not samples, are of primary interest.

The ability to generalize from a sample to the population depends critically on the **representativeness** of the sample. Clearly, individuals in a population differ in many ways and the relative frequencies with which these characteristics appear in the population vary. For example, in one population there might be 40% males and 60% females, whereas in another the distribution might be 75% female and 25% male. *A sample is representative of the population to the extent that it exhibits the same distribution of characteristics as the population.* If it is to be representative, approximately how many sophomores should there be in your library survey sample of 100 students if 30% of the students on your campus are sophomores?

The major threat to representativeness is bias. A **biased sample** is one in which the distribution of characteristics in the sample is *systematically* different from the target population. A sample that included 80% females and 20% males would be biased if the population the sample was intended to represent was 40% female and 60% male. There are two sources of bias: selection bias and response bias. (We discuss selection bias now and deal with response bias in the Survey Methods section.) **Selection bias** occurs when the procedures used to select the sample result in the overrepresentation of some segment of the popu-

• Breakdown by sex was where the electorate looked most like the general public.

SEX

U.S. POPULATION
Male, 48.8%
Female, 51.2%

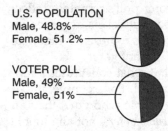

VOTER POLL
Male, 49%
Female, 51%

• Middle-aged people voted in greater numbers than the young or elderly people.

AGE

U.S. POPULATION
18-29: 18%
30-44: 24.3%
45-59: 14.8%
60+: 16.7%

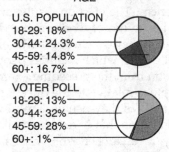

VOTER POLL
18-29: 13%
30-44: 32%
45-59: 28%
60+: 1%

• Working women played a smaller role in the election.

WORKING WOMEN

U.S. POPULATION
Employed, 45.8%

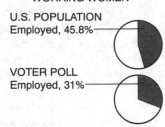

VOTER POLL
Employed, 31%

• Compared to their percentage in the population, black turnout in 1994 was low and white turnout high.

RACE

U.S. POPULATION
White, 74.8%
Black, 11.8%
Hispanic, 9.4%
Asian, 3%
Other, less than 1%

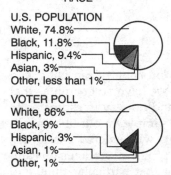

VOTER POLL
White, 86%
Black, 9%
Hispanic, 3%
Asian, 1%
Other, 1%

• Compared to the general population, those with some college, a college degree or a graduate degree played more of a role.

EDUCATION*

U.S. POPULATION
Not H.S. graduate, 19.8%
H.S. graduate, 35.4%
Some college, 16.6%
College graduate, 20.8%
Postgraduate, 7.4%

*1993, for persons 25 years old and over.

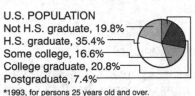

VOTER POLL
No H.S., 6%
H.S. graduate, 23%
Some college, 28%
College graduate, 26%
Postgraduate, 17%

• The wealthy played a bigger role, and the poor a smaller role, in the 1994 election, with wealthy voters leaning heavily toward Republicans.

INCOME

U.S. POPULATION
Less than $14,999, 37.4%
15-34,999, 20.7%
35-49,999, 29.1%
50-74,999, 8.2%
75 and over, 4.6%

Source: U. S. Bureau of the Census, Voter Service

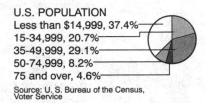

VOTER POLL
Less than $15,000, 10%
15-30,000, 22%
30-50,000, 30%
50-75,000, 22%
75-100,000, 9%
Over $100,000, 7%

FIGURE 4.3 Selection bias in 1994 Election Exit Polls. (*Source:* Madigan, C. M. [March 19, 1995]. Hearing it right: Small turnout spoke. *Chicago Tribune, 4,* 1–2.)

lation or, conversely, in the exclusion or underrepresentation of a significant segment.

Charles Madigan, a senior writer for the *Chicago Tribune,* documented a selection bias in the 1994 national election. He identified the selection bias by comparing the demographic characteristics of the voters interviewed in exit polls to characteristics of the population drawn from U.S. census data. Figure 4.3 shows the comparisons for several characteristics between the sample of voters and the U.S. population. The gender breakdown for the sample and for the population was the most similar of any of the characteristics (see Figure 4.3). The sample differed from the population on the characteristics of age, race, education, income, and the proportion of working women. The systematic differences in these characteristics between the voter sample and the general population indicates that the sample is not representative of the population due to a selection bias. Basing conclusions on such biased samples can lead to unfortunate consequences. The election results and the voter poll accurately reflect the interests and attitudes of those people who voted. Politicians may face resistance, however, if they conclude that the election results represent a mandate from the general public, which includes people who did not vote.

A general lesson from the preceding example is that what constitutes a representative sample is relative to the question being asked. For example, if exit polls are concerned (as they usually are) only with people who vote, then an unbiased sample is one that is representative of *probable voters*, not all eligible voters. Similarly, a researcher who wishes to survey single college students concerning the characteristics of the person they would like to marry ("the ideal mate"), then the target population is unmarried college students, not college students in general. An unbiased sample would, in this case, be representative of that subset of students who are single.

Survey researchers must be constantly alert to the threat of selection bias in sampling. Fortunately, as we will see, they have developed techniques that can minimize the risk.

APPROACHES TO SAMPLING

There are two basic approaches to sampling: nonprobability sampling and probability sampling. In **nonprobability sampling** we have no guarantee that each element has some chance of being included and no way to estimate the probability of each element's being included in the sample. In our library survey, if a researcher interviewed the first 10 students who entered the library, she would be using nonprobability sampling. Clearly, not all students on campus would be equally likely to be at the library at that particular time, and some students would have essentially no chance of being included in the sample.

By contrast, if the researcher were to select 10 students randomly from the registrar's list of enrolled students, she would be using probability sampling. In **probability sampling** all students (elements) have an equal chance of being included in the sample. We determine that this researcher used probability sampling by examining the way she carried out her sampling procedure (i.e., selecting randomly from a predetermined list). Probability sampling is preferred because it allows researchers to estimate how likely it is that their sample findings differ from the findings they would have obtained by studying the whole population. Probability sampling is far superior to nonprobability sampling in ensuring that selected samples will be representative samples. Thus, the researcher who selects 10 students randomly from the registrar's list of students is more likely to have a representative sample than the researcher who bases her survey results on the first 10 students who show up at the library as it opens its doors in the morning.

Nonprobability Sampling   Two types of nonprobability sampling are accidental sampling and purposive sampling. **Accidental sampling** involves selecting respondents primarily on the basis of their availability and willingness to respond. Newspapers commonly interview "the person on the street" and publish their comments. Their comments may make interesting reading, but their opinions are unlikely to represent those of the wider community because accidental sampling was used. Accidental sampling also is involved when people respond to surveys in *Cosmopolitan* or other magazines because the magazine has to be available (and purchased), and people must be willing to send in their responses.

Crossen (1994) describes the drawbacks of another variation of accidental sampling, call-in surveys. Call-in surveys are used by TV and radio shows to poll the views of their audience. Those who happen to be in the audience and who are willing to call (and sometimes to pay the charge for calling a 900 number) make up the sample for these call-in surveys. Keep in mind that people who make calls in response to a call-in request differ from the general population not only because they happen to be people who are characteristic of this particular audience but are people who are motivated enough to make a call.

Crossen discusses a prime-time TV-news show that conducted a call-in survey with a question concerning the location of the United Nations. It turns out that another survey-research study involving about 500 randomly selected respondents also asked the same question. The question was whether the United Nations (UN) headquarters should remain in the United States. Of the 186,000 callers who responded, a solid majority (67%) wanted the UN *out of the United States.* Of the respondents to the survey research study (i.e., using a random sample of individuals), a clear majority (72%) wanted the UN *to stay in the United States.* How could these two surveys yield such different—even opposite—results? Should we put more confidence in the results of the call-in survey because of the massive size of the sample? Absolutely not! A large accidental sample is just as likely to be an unrepresentative sample as is any other accidental sample. As a general rule, you should consider that accidental sampling will result in a biased sample unless you have strong evidence confirming the representativeness of the sample.

A second type of nonprobability sampling is **purposive sampling,** in which the investigator selects the elements to be included in the sample on the basis of their special characteristics. The individuals selected are commonly those who have an expertise or experiences related to the purpose of the study.

Goleman (1981) describes a study in which purposive sampling was used. In developing new tests for use in personnel selection, psychologist David C. McClelland asked top management people to nominate "water walkers"—people who were so outstanding they could do no wrong. The managers were also asked to nominate employees who simply did their jobs well enough not to get fired. McClelland and his colleagues then conducted intensive interviews of the nominees from both groups and, from these interviews, developed a list of competencies that set the water walkers apart from the more typical employees. Job applicants were then screened on the basis of these competency-based tests to try to detect potential water walkers. McClelland was not primarily interested in the characteristics of workers in general. So, purposive sampling was ideally suited to the purpose of his study.

Probability Sampling The distinguishing characteristic of probability sampling is that the researcher can specify, for each element of the population, the probability that it will be included in the sample. Two common types of probability sampling are simple random sampling and stratified sampling. **Simple random sampling** is the basic technique of probability sampling. The most common definition of random sampling is that every element has an equal chance of being included in the sample. The procedures for simple random sampling are outlined in Box 4.1.

One critical decision that must be made in selecting a random sample is how large it should be. Earlier in this chapter we described the relationship between margin of error and sample size; the smaller the desired margin of error, the larger the sample size needs to be. For now, we simply note that the size of a random sample needed to represent a population depends on the homogeneity (variability) of the population. College students in Ivy League schools represent a more homogeneous population than college students in all U.S. colleges in terms of their academic abilities. At one extreme, the most homogeneous population would be one in which all members of the population are identical. A sample of 1 would be representative of this population regardless of the size of the population. At the other extreme, the most heterogeneous population would be one in which each member was completely different from all other members on all characteristics. No sample, regardless of its size, could be representative of this population. Every individual would have to be included to describe such a heterogeneous population. Fortunately, the populations with which survey researchers work fall somewhere between these two extremes. Thus, the representativeness of samples, like the joy of eating a piece of chocolate cake, increases with increasing size—up to a point.

The representativeness of a sample can often be increased by using stratified random sampling. In **stratified random sampling,** the population is divided into subpopulations called *strata* (singular, *stratum*), and random samples are drawn from each of these strata. There are two general ways to determine how many elements should be drawn from each stratum. One way (illustrated in the last example of Box 4.1) is to draw equal-sized samples from each stratum. The second way is to draw elements for the sample on a proportional basis. Consider a population divided into three strata representing 40%, 40%, and 20% of the population, respectively. A stratified random sample of 200 drawn from this population would include 80 individuals from each of the first two strata. How many would be drawn from the third stratum?

In addition to its potential for increasing the representativeness of samples, stratified random sampling is useful when you want to make statements about portions of the population you have sampled. For example, a simple random sample of 100 students would be sufficient to survey students' attitudes on a campus of 2,000 students. Suppose, however, your sample included only 2 of

40 chemistry majors on campus. It would be risky to use the views of two chemistry students to represent those of all 40 chemistry majors. If you knew in advance that you wanted to describe the views of students majoring in various departments, you could use stratified random sampling according to students' majors without drastically increasing the overall sample size.

SURVEY METHODS

Selecting the sample is only one of several important decisions to be made in survey research. You also need to decide how you will interview the respondents among three general methods: mail surveys, personal interviews, and telephone interviews. As was true of sampling techniques, there is no one best method for all circumstances; each survey method has its own advantages and disadvantages. The challenge you face is to select the method that best fits the problem you are studying.

MAIL SURVEYS

Mail surveys are used to distribute self-administered questionnaires that respondents fill out on their own. One advantage of mail surveys is that they usually can be completed relatively quickly. Because they are self-administered, mail surveys also avoid the problems due to interviewer bias (which we define more completely in the next section). And among the three survey methods, mail surveys are the best for dealing with highly personal or embarrassing topics, especially when anonymity of respondents is preserved.

Unfortunately, there are many disadvantages to mail surveys, some less serious than others. For instance, because the respondent will not be able to ask questions, the questionnaire must be completely self-explanatory. A second less serious disadvantage is that the researcher has little control over the order in which the respondent proceeds through the questionnaire. Responding to questions in different orders may affect the way respondents answer certain questions. A serious problem with mail surveys, however, is one of bias—namely, response bias.

Response bias is a threat to the representativeness of a sample because not all respondents complete the survey. There are many reasons why individuals may not complete the questionnaire used in a mail survey. Mail surveys tend to exclude respondents with literacy problems and are generally intimidating to those of limited educational background. Those with problems with their vision, such as many of the elderly, may also fail to complete the questionnaire. The major factor leading to response bias in mail surveys is the generally low response rate. Quite often people included in a sample are too busy or not interested enough in the study to return a completed questionnaire.

Low response rates necessarily produce smaller samples. Generally, however, the size of the sample is not the most serious concern. The problem is that

BOX 4.1

SAMPLES OF RANDOM SAMPLES

The following names represent a scaled-down version of a sampling frame obtained from the registrar's office of a small college campus. Pro-

cedures for drawing both a simple random sample and a stratified random sample from this list are described below.

Adamski	F	Jr	Hedlund	F	So
Alderink	F	Sr	Johnson	F	Fr
Baxter	M	Sr	Klaaren	F	Jr
Bowen	F	Sr	Ludwig	M	Fr
Broder	M	So	Nadeau	F	Sr
Brown	M	Jr	Nowaczyk	M	Jr
Bufford	M	So	O'Keane	F	Sr
Campbell	F	Fr	Osgood	M	So
Carnahan	F	So	Owens	F	So
Cowan	F	Fr	Penzien	M	Jr
Cushman	M	Sr	Powers	M	Sr
Dawes	M	Jr	Ryan	M	Fr
Dennis	M	Sr	Sawyer	M	Jr
Douglas	F	Fr	Shaw	M	Sr
Dunne	M	So	Sonders	F	Sr
Fahey	M	Fr	Suffolk	F	So
Fedder	M	Fr	Taylor	F	Fr
Foley	F	So	Thompson	M	Fr
Grossman	F	Jr	Watterson	F	Jr
Harris	F	Jr	Zimmerman	M	So

Drawing a simple random sample

Step 1. Number each element in the sampling frame: Adamski would be number 1, Harris number 20, and Zimmerman number 40.
Step 2. Decide on the sample size you want to use. This is just an illustration, so we will use a sample size of 5.
Step 3. Choose a starting point in the Table of Random Numbers in Appendix A (a finger stab with your eyes closed works just fine—our stab came down at column 8, row 22 at the entry 26384). Because our sampling frame ranges only from 1 to 40, we had decided *prior* to entering the table to use the left two numbers in each set of five and to go across the table from left to right. We could just as easily have decided to go up,

down, or from right to left. We could also have used the middle two or the last two digits of each set of five, but one should make these decisions before entering the table.
Step 4. Identify the numbers to be included in your sample by moving across the table. We got the numbers 26, 06, 21, 15, and 32. Notice that numbers over 40 are ignored. The same would be true if we had come across a repetition of a number we had already selected.
Step 5. List the names corresponding to the selected numbers. In our case the sample will include Nowaczyk, Brown, Hedlund, Dunne, and Ryan.

An even easier system, called *systematic sam-*

pling, can be used to obtain a random sample. In this procedure you divide the sample size you want into the size of the sampling frame to obtain the value *k*. Then you select every *k*th element after choosing the first one randomly. In our example we want a sample size of 5 from a sampling frame of 40, so *k* would be 8. Thus we would choose one of the first eight people randomly and then take every eighth person thereafter. If Alderink were chosen from among the first 8, the remaining members of the sample would be Cowan, Foley, Nowaczyk, and Shaw. Note: This system should *not* be used if the sampling frame has a periodic organization—if, for example, you had a list of dormitory residents arranged by room and every tenth pair listed occupied a corner room. You can readily see that, in such a list, if your sampling interval was 10 you could end up with all people from corner rooms or no people from corner rooms.

Drawing a stratified random sample

Step 1. Arrange the sampling frame in strata. For our example we will stratify by class standing, so our sampling frame now looks like this:

Freshmen	Sophomores	Juniors	Seniors
1 Campbell	1 Broder	1 Adamski	1 Alderink
2 Cowan	2 Bufford	2 Brown	2 Baxter
3 Douglas	3 Carnahan	3 Dawes	3 Bowen
4 Fahey	4 Dunne	4 Grossman	4 Cushman
5 Fedder	5 Foley	5 Harris	5 Dennis
6 Johnson	6 Hedlund	6 Klaaren	6 Nadeau
7 Ludwig	7 Osgood	7 Nowaczyk	7 O'Keane
8 Ryan	8 Owens	8 Penzien	8 Powers
9 Taylor	9 Suffolk	9 Sawyer	9 Shaw
10 Thompson	10 Zimmerman	10 Watterson	10 Sonders

In our example the strata are equal in size, but this need not be the case.

Step 2. Number each element within each stratum, as has been done in the foregoing list.

Step 3. Decide on the overall sample size you want to use. For our example we will draw a sample of 8.

Step 4. Draw an equal-sized sample from each stratum such that you obtain the desired overall sample size. For our example this would mean drawing 2 from each stratum.

Step 5. Follow the steps for drawing a random sample and repeat for each stratum. We used the previously determined starting point (column 8, line 22) in the Table of Random Numbers, but this time we used the last digit in each set of five. The numbers identified for each stratum were: Freshmen (4 and 1), Sophomores (6 and 4), Juniors (7 and 9), and Seniors (2 and 9).

Step 6. List the names corresponding to the selected numbers. Our stratified random sample would include Fahey, Campbell, Hedlund, Dunne, Nowaczyk, Sawyer, Baxter, and Shaw.

low response rates typically suggest response bias. Because of response bias, a carefully selected probability sample may become a nonprobability sample—an accidental sample in which individuals' availability and willingness determine whether they will complete the survey. For example, if 200 store managers are included in a survey about store security, but only 50 respond, the results may be affected by response bias if only those stores that are the least busy are represented or if only those who have experienced security problems reply. Unless the return rate is 100%, the potential for response bias exists regardless of how carefully the initial sample was selected. Demonstrating the absence of response bias is much more crucial for ensuring the representativeness of a sample than is the absolute level of the response rate.

The typical return rate for mail surveys is only around 30%. But certain strategies may increase the return rate. Return rates will be highest when the questionnaire has a personal touch, when it requires a minimum of effort for the respondent, when the topic of the survey is of intrinsic interest to the respondent, and when the respondent identifies in some way with the organization or researcher sponsoring the survey. Warwick and Lininger (1975) describe a survey that met these requirements. About 100,000 members of women's religious congregations in the United States were surveyed. The study was sponsored by, and had the support of, the religious congregations. It was done by a visible and respected member of one of the religious orders, and the subject matter was of great interest to the respondents. The result was an almost perfect response rate.

PERSONAL INTERVIEWS

When personal interviews are used to collect survey data, respondents are usually contacted in their homes or in a shopping mall, and trained interviewers administer the questionnaire. The personal interview allows greater flexibility in asking questions than does the mail survey. In a personal interview the respondent can obtain clarification when questions are unclear and the trained interviewer can follow up incomplete or ambiguous answers to open-ended questions. The interviewer controls the sequencing of questions and can ensure that all respondents complete the questionnaire in the same order. Traditionally, the response rate to personal interviews has been higher than for mail surveys.

The advantages of using personal interviews are impressive, but there are also a few disadvantages. Growing fear of urban crime and an increasing number of households with no one home during the day have reduced the attractiveness of conducting personal interviews in the home. A significant disadvantage of personal interviews is that it is costly. The use of trained interviewers is expensive in terms of both money and time. Perhaps the most critical disadvantage of personal interviews involves the potential for interviewer bias. The interviewer should be a neutral medium through which questions and answers are transmitted. **Interviewer bias** occurs when the interviewer tries to adjust the wording of a question to fit the respondent or records only selected portions of the respondent's answers. For example, if a respondent in a survey of television viewing said that the major problem with current TV programming was excessive violence, the interviewer could ask, "Could you elaborate on what you mean by violence?" This more neutral probe would be better than asking, "By violence do you mean murders, muggings, and rapes?"

The best protection against interviewer bias is to employ highly motivated, well-paid interviewers who are trained to follow question wording exactly, to record responses accurately, and to use follow-up questions judiciously. Interviewers should also be given a detailed list of specifications—that is, instructions about how difficult or confusing situations are to be handled. Finally, interviewers should be closely supervised by the director of the survey project. The decision to use personal interviews is not one survey researchers take lightly.

So far we have been describing the personal interview as a way of administering a highly structured questionnaire to an individual respondent. A frequently used variation of the personal interview is the *focused interview* (also called *focus group*). The focused interview is done in a group setting, and the researcher tries to learn from the respondents more about the reasons for the attitudes or opinions that they hold. Focused interviews are used extensively in market research to determine consumers' reactions to current or new products or services. Focused interviews are increasingly being used as part of the strategic planning process by civic organizations, colleges and universities, and churches. There is less of an emphasis in this approach on obtaining a quantitative summary of the views across all respondents. Instead, the goal is to obtain a qualitative description of the ideas that emerge from a guided group discussion.

TELEPHONE INTERVIEWS

The prohibitive cost of personal interviews and difficulties supervising interviewers have led survey researchers to turn to telephone interviews. Phone interviewing met with considerable criticism when it was first used because of serious limitations on the sampling frame of potential respondents. Many people had unlisted numbers, and the poor and those in rural areas were unlikely to have a phone. By 1979, however, more than 95% of all households had telephones, and households with unlisted numbers could be reached using random-digit dialing. Telephone interviewing also provides better access to dangerous neighborhoods, locked buildings, and respondents available only during evening hours. Interviews can be completed more quickly when contacts are made by phone, and interviewers can be better supervised when all interviews are conducted from one location.

The telephone survey, like the other two survey methods, is not without its drawbacks. A possible selection bias exists when respondents are limited to those who have telephones, and the problem of interviewer bias remains.

There is a limit to how long respondents are willing to stay on the phone, and respondents may respond differently when they are talking to a faceless voice. Moreover, extensive use of phone solicitation for selling products and requesting contributions has led many people to be less willing to be interviewed. And many people who are working two jobs are rarely at home to answer the phone. In spite of these limitations and perhaps others you can think of, the telephone interview is the method of choice for nearly all brief surveys.

SURVEY-RESEARCH DESIGNS

You are no doubt developing a sense that doing survey research, like doing all types of research, requires making a series of choices and decisions. For example, survey researchers decide who to survey when they choose a sampling plan, and they decide how to administer the survey when they choose a survey method. In this section we describe one of the most important decisions survey researchers must make—the choice of a research design. A survey-research design is the overall plan or structure according to which the entire study is carried out. There are three general types of survey-research designs: the cross-sectional design, the successive independent samples design, and the longitudinal design. As you probably already suspect, no all-purpose research design meets every survey need; the choice of design must be tailored to the objectives of the study.

CROSS-SECTIONAL DESIGN

One of the most commonly used survey-research designs is the cross-sectional design. In a **cross-sectional design,** one or more samples are drawn from the

FIGURE 4.4   The three general methods for conducting interviews (telephone interviews, personal interviews, and mail surveys) have both advantages and disadvantages.

population *at one time.* Information collected from the sample(s) is used to describe the population at that point in time. A researcher who gave questionnaires to samples of 20-year-olds, 30-year-olds, and 40-year-olds, asking about solutions to the homeless problem in the United States, would be using a cross-sectional design. So, too, would a researcher who sampled male and female college students and asked their opinions about various career possibilities following graduation.

Jessor, Chase, and Donovan (1980) used the cross-sectional design in their nationwide survey of drinking and marijuana use among teenagers. Their survey took each respondent 45 minutes to complete, but the overall testing of 16,000 respondents took over a month. In some studies it can take even longer. (Thus, you can see that even cross-sectional designs are not necessarily simple or quick.) The focus in a cross-sectional survey is on description—describing the characteristics of a population or the differences among two or more populations. Jessor et al. made many comparisons among different samples defined by age, gender, and ethnic group.

Cross-sectional designs also can be used to assess interrelationships among variables within a population. Jessor et al. explored interrelationships among variables when they tried to determine what personality, social, and behavioral characteristics were most strongly related to marijuana use. They found that increased marijuana use was associated with several factors, such as lower expectations for academic achievement, greater tolerance of deviance, less compatibility between friends and parents, and a greater value placed on independence than on academic achievement. The three strongest predictors of marijuana use, however, were friends as models of marijuana use, the number of times drunk in the past year, and involvement in general deviant behavior. Thus, marijuana use can be understood as a component of a larger behavior pattern and not as an isolated issue.

Cross-sectional designs are ideally suited to the descriptive and predictive functions associated with correlational research. Surveys are also used to assess changes in attitudes or behaviors over time and to determine the effect of some naturally occurring event, such as the passage of a law to raise the drinking age. For these purposes the cross-sectional design is not the method of choice. Rather, research designs are needed that systematically sample respondents over time. We discuss two such designs in the next two sections.

SUCCESSIVE INDEPENDENT SAMPLES DESIGN

The **successive independent samples design** can be understood as a series of cross-sectional surveys in which the same questions are asked of each succeeding sample of different respondents. This design is most appropriate when the major aim of the study is to describe changes over time in the attitudes or behaviors of members of a population. A researcher might, for instance, ask samples of male and female college seniors about their career goals at a particular point in time (e.g., 1990), then 10 years later (i.e., in 2000) ask *different samples* of college seniors the same questions.

The successive independent samples design is useful in epidemiology, the study of the incidence and prevalence of diseases in a population. In an epidemiological study, the presence of disease in a particular sample is identified. In successive independent samples, the presence of disease is assessed in samples taken at different times. Seligman (1988) used successive independent samples for those born in 1960, 1945, 1925, and 1910 to make a provocative argument about factors contributing to an increase in the occurrence of depression. The first step in his investigation was to determine whether there had, in fact, been a change in the occurrence of depression. Seligman used the lifetime prevalence of depression—the percentage of individuals in the population that has had the disorder at least once in their lifetime. In general, this is a cumulative statistic; if you look at the prevalence of broken legs, you find it increases with age. As expected, the prevalence of depression increased from about 5% for those born around 1960 to about 9% for those born around 1945. For those born around 1925, however, the lifetime prevalence went down (4%), and for those born around 1910 it went down even further (1%).

After carefully tracking through possible artifacts in these results, Seligman concluded that there had been a genuine tenfold increase in the prevalence of depression since World War II. He went on to argue that the increase was attributable to an increasing emphasis on individualism and a decreasing emphasis on commitment to common values such as family and religion. Seligman's interpretation is one well worth considering, but the methodological point his study illustrates is that the successive independent samples design can play a critical role in epidemiological studies in psychology. Such studies can not only be used to test theoretical explanations of disorders such as depression but can also be helpful in identifying individuals or groups at risk for certain disorders.

Studies using the successive independent samples design are invaluable when discussion turns to the topics of the "good old days" or the "wonders of modern times." For instance, you may have heard someone say that people are not as happy as they used to be. Myers and Diener (1995) report the results of surveys done by the National Research Center studying people's perceived happiness. The results of their successive independent samples over the period from 1957 through 1993 are presented in Figure 4.5. The dependent variable plotted on the right ordinate in the figure is the percentage of respondents who reported being "very happy." There is some fluctuation across years, but the general pattern is that Americans today are neither more nor less happy than they were over 30 years ago.

This lack of change is remarkable, given the many changes in American society that occurred during this period. Consider, for example, the changes in personal income in the United States during this period. In Figure 4.5 the average per-person income in 1990 dollars is plotted. The average income doubled from $8,000 in 1957 to $16,000 in 1993. Sufficient income to provide life's necessities is essential to our well-being. Beyond that minimum, increasing wealth is not a guarantee to happiness. Myers and Diener (1995) summarize the relationship between wealth and happiness well. "Satisfaction is less a matter of getting

FIGURE 4.5 Perceived happiness and personal income in successive independent samples (*Source:* Figure 10-9 [p. 348] of Myers, D. G., *Exploring Psychology* [1996]. Worth Publishers.)

what you want than wanting what you have" (p. 13). Findings like those reported by Myers and Diener are typical of the provocative information that becomes available when the successive independent samples design is used.

The successive independent samples design does have limitations. As way of illustration, the data presented in Table 4.2 represent the results of a successive independent samples design measuring people's trust in government in 1972 and 1978. Clearly, more Americans were cynical in 1978 than in 1972.

TABLE 4.2 TRUST IN GOVERNMENT, 1972–1978*

	1972	1978
Cynical	36%	52%
Mixed	24%	26%
Trusting	38%	19%
Not answered	2%	3%
Number of cases	(2285)	(2304)

*Data taken from Campbell (1981), Appendix Table 8.

These findings also illustrate, however, one of the limitations of successive in-dependent samples designs. Consider the change from 36% to 52% in the "cyn-ical" category from 1972 to 1978. We might be tempted to conclude that 16% of the population was added in 1978 to the original 36% of Americans who were already cynical about government in 1972. We might even try to say that, of the 19% who were no longer "trusting" (the drop from 38% in 1972 to 19% in 1978), 16% were now cynical, 2% had mixed feelings, and 1% failed to answer. What we must remember, however, is that the people surveyed in 1978 were not the same people surveyed in 1972! The extent to which individuals change their views over time can be determined only by testing the same individuals on both occasions. We cannot determine in the successive independent samples design who has changed or by how much. Accordingly, the successive inde-pendent samples design is not very helpful in ferreting out the reasons for ob-served changes like those shown in Table 4.2. (As you will soon see, another survey design, the longitudinal design, is more appropriate in these situa-tions.)

A second potential problem with the successive independent samples de-sign arises when the successive samples are not representative of the same population. Imagine that the researchers who did the surveys reported in Table 4.2 had sampled affluent Americans in 1972 and poor Americans in 1978. Their comparisons of Americans' attitudes toward government over this time period would be meaningless. The affluent and poor samples illustrate the problem of *noncomparable successive samples.* Changes in the population across time can be described accurately only when the successive independent samples represent the same population. You must check carefully to assure that the successive in-dependent samples are comparable. Sophisticated statistical procedures can be used to try to unravel the problems of interpretation that arise because of non-comparable successive samples. But the best solution to the problem of non-comparable successive samples is to avoid the problem by carefully selecting successive samples that represent one population.

LONGITUDINAL DESIGN

The distinguishing characteristic of the **longitudinal design** is that the same sample of respondents is interviewed more than once. A researcher interested in people's opinions about ways to administer welfare programs, for instance, might give a questionnaire to a sample of individuals at the beginning of a na-tional election campaign, and then give *the same questionnaire to the same individ-uals* following the election.

There are two principal advantages of the longitudinal design. First, the in-vestigator can determine the direction and extent of change for individual re-spondents. This advantage makes it easier to answer questions about the rea-sons for attitude or behavior changes. Second, the longitudinal design is the best available survey-research design when the effect of some naturally occur-ring event needs to be assessed. Measuring people's attitudes before and after a national election is an example of assessing the effect of a naturally occurring event. (For further discussion of assessing the effects of naturally occurring events, see Chapter 10.)

Cherlin et al. (1991) used the longitudinal design to investigate the effects of divorce on children in Great Britain and the United States. Over 17,000 British mothers who had had a child in the first week of March were interviewed in 1958. Almost 15,000 of these women were interviewed in 1965 when their children were 7 and again in 1969 when the children were 11. The original sample for the U.S. survey was done in 1976 and included 2,279 children aged 7 to 11 from 1,747 families. Follow-up interviews were done in 1981 in all families from the 1976 U.S. sample that had experienced a separation or divorce and in a randomly selected subsample of intact families. The distinguishing characteristic of the longitudinal design in both the British and the U.S. studies is the fact that the same individuals were surveyed in each successive phase of the study.

Longitudinal designs like the one used in the Cherlin et al. (1991) study involve a massive effort. The potential power of such an undertaking, however, can be illustrated by describing just one aspect of Cherlin et al.'s findings. They differentiated three distinct sources of problems that could contribute to differences in adjustment between children from families in which the parents have separated or divorced and children from intact families. The first source is growing up in a home with serious problems that can make normal development difficult; the second source is growing up in the midst of severe marital conflict; and the third source is making the difficult transition that occurs after the couple separate.

Cherlin et al. (1991) argued that most research has focused only on the period after the separation has occurred. By using a longitudinal design that allowed them to gather data prior to the separation or divorce, Cherlin et al. were able to show that "Overall, the evidence suggests that much of the effect of divorce on children can be predicted by conditions that existed well before the separation occurred. These predivorce effects were stronger for boys than for girls" (p. 1388). One important implication of these findings is that children in troubled intact families may require at least as much attention as those children who suffer the trauma of separation or divorce. More generally, the Cherlin et al. study illustrates how crucial the longitudinal design is in studying changes over time due to naturally occurring events.

One potential problem with longitudinal designs is that it can be difficult to obtain a sample of respondents who will agree to participate in a longitudinal study, which more often than not means a long-term study. In many studies the respondents may be asked to complete several lengthy surveys at regular intervals over a number of years. People are often hesitant to make the commitment of time necessary to complete such an extensive project.

Even when the respondents do agree to participate, there can be further problems. You might think this design solves the problem of noncomparable samples that can occur when successive independent samples are used. After all, how much more comparable can a sample be than one that is identical to the original sample (because the sample people participate over and over)? Unfortunately, successive samples in a longitudinal design are identical only if all members of the original sample participate throughout the study. This is not likely to be the case. For example, in the Cherlin et al. (1991) study there were 17,414 mothers interviewed in the original 1958 sample. In 1965, 14,746 parents (usually mothers) were reinterviewed. Unless all the respondents in the original sample complete all phases of a longitudinal design, there is a possible problem due to *respondent mortality* (sometimes literal, but most often figurative). Respondent mortality is probably the most serious disadvantage of the longitudinal design. It is usually possible, however, to determine whether the final sample is comparable to the original sample in a longitudinal design. The characteristics of nonrespondents in the follow-up phase are known because they were included in the original sample. Therefore, we can look again at their original responses to see how these individuals may have differed from those who continued their participation.

Paradoxically, problems can also arise in longitudinal designs because the same respondents are interviewed more than once. One possible problem is that respondents may strive heroically to be consistent across interviews. This can be particularly troublesome if the study is designed to assess changes in respondents' attitudes. Although their attitudes have actually changed, people may report their original attitudes in an effort to appear consistent. Another potential problem is that the initial interview may sensitize respondents to the issue under investigation. For example, consider a longitudinal design used to test the effectiveness of TV political ads. People interviewed prior to the broadcast of the ads may pay more attention to the ads after the interview because the interview piqued their interest in election issues. You might recognize that this is another illustration of reactive measurement—people reacting differently because they know they are being observed (see Chapter 3).

CORRESPONDENCE BETWEEN REPORTED AND ACTUAL BEHAVIOR

Regardless of how carefully survey data are collected and analyzed, the value of these data depends on the truthfulness of the respondents' answers to the survey questions. How willing should we be to believe that the survey responses reflect people's true thoughts, opinions, feelings, and behavior? The question of the truthfulness of verbal reports has been debated extensively, and no clear-cut conclusion has emerged. Judd, Smith, and Kidder (1991) note, however, that in everyday life we regularly accept the verbal reports of others as valid. If a friend tells you that he enjoyed reading a certain novel, you may ask why, but you do not usually question whether the statement accurately reflects your friend's feelings. This is not to say that in everyday life we don't ever come across situations in which we *do* have reason to suspect the truthfulness of someone's statements. When shopping for a used car, for instance, we might not always want to trust the sales pitch we receive. Generally, however, we accept people's remarks at their face value unless we have reason to do otherwise. We should apply the same standards to the information we obtain from survey responses.

By its very nature, survey research involves reactive measurement. Respondents not only know that their responses are being recorded, but they may also suspect their responses may serve as the basis for some social, political, or commercial action. Hence the pressures are strong for people to respond as they think they "should" and not as they actually do believe. The term often used to describe these pressures is **social desirability.** For example, if respondents are asked whether they favor giving help to the needy, they may respond affirmatively because they believe this is the most socially acceptable attitude to have. As we suggested in Chapter 3, the best protection against reactive measurement is to be aware of its existence.

Sometimes researchers can examine the accuracy of verbal reports directly by using archival data or unobtrusive measures (topics discussed more fully in Chapter 5). Judd et al. (1991) describe research by Parry and Crossley (1950) wherein responses obtained by experienced interviewers were subsequently compared with archival records of respondents kept by various agencies. Forty percent of respondents gave inaccurate reports to a question concerning contributions to United Fund (a charitable organization), 25% erred when reporting whether they had registered and voted in a recent election, and 17% misrepresented their age. A pessimist might find these figures disturbingly high, but an optimist would note that a majority of respondents' reports were accurate even when social desirability pressures were high, as in the question pertaining to charitable contributions.

Another source of evidence researchers use to assess the accuracy of verbal reports is direct observation of the respondents' behavior. The field experiment done by Latané and Darley (1970) illustrates the problem. They found that bystanders are more likely to help a victim when the bystander is alone than when other witnesses are present. Subsequently, a second group of participants was asked whether the presence of others would influence the likelihood that they would help a victim. They uniformly said it would not. Milgram (1974) conducted a series of experiments on factors affecting people's obedience to authority. In one of his experiments Milgram found that 63% of the men he tested (ages 20-50) complied fully with the instructions they were given. The men were instructed to administer increasing levels of shock to a learner each time the learner made a mistake. The 63% who complied fully continued to apply shocks to the highest level specified in the experiment. Prior to doing this experiment Milgram asked a different group of people what they would do in this situation. Most said they would certainly stop before reaching the highest level of shock. Research findings such as these should make us extremely cautious of reaching conclusions about people's behavior solely on the basis of verbal reports. Of course, we should be equally cautious of reaching conclusions about what people think solely on the basis of direct observation of their behavior.

We want to make one final point about the usefulness of survey results. The process of doing a survey has much in common with the process of writing an essay. You often begin with a grand topic that must be focused so it can be covered manageably. As you narrow your focus, you may sometimes have the feeling that your original topic has been lost or at least made trivial. No essay can capture all aspects of a given topic, and no 20-item or even 200-item questionnaire can do so, either. Survey research, like the rest of the scientific enterprise, is built on faith that compiling reliable findings in a series of limited studies will eventually lead to increased understanding of the important broader issues we face.

SUMMARY

Correlational research focuses on assessing the covariation among naturally occurring variables. Its goal is to identify predictive relationships by using correlations or more sophisticated statistical techniques. The results of correlational research also have implications for decision making as reflected in the appropriate use of actuarial prediction. The greatest limitation of correlational research is the problem of interpreting causal relationships.

Survey research illustrates the principles of correlational research and provides an accurate and efficient means of describing people's thoughts, opinions, and feelings. Surveys differ in purpose and scope, but they generally involve sampling, the procedure whereby results obtained with a carefully selected sample are used as a basis for describing the entire population of interest. Surveys also involve the use of a predetermined set of questions, generally in the form of a questionnaire.

In sampling, a specified number of elements are drawn from a sampling frame that represents an actual list of the possible elements in the population. Our ability to generalize from the sample to the population depends critically on the representativeness of the sample, the extent to which the sample has the same characteristics as the population. Representativeness is best achieved by using probability sampling rather than nonprobability sampling. In simple random sampling, the most common type of probability sampling, every element is equally likely to be included in the sample. Stratified random sampling is used when analysis of subsamples is of interest.

There are three general survey methods: mail surveys, personal interviews, and telephone interviews. Mail surveys avoid problems of interviewer bias and are especially well suited for examining personal or embarrassing topics. The problem of response bias is a serious limitation of mail surveys. Personal interviews and phone surveys usually have higher response rates and provide greater flexibility. The phone survey is the method of choice for most brief surveys.

Survey research is carried out according to an overall plan called a research design. There are three survey-research designs: the cross-sectional design, the successive independent samples design, and the longitudinal design. Cross-sectional designs focus on describing the characteristics of a population or the differences between two or more populations at one point in time. Describing changes in attitudes or opinions over time requires the use of successive independent samples or longitudinal designs. The longitudinal design is generally preferred because it allows the assessment of changes for specific individuals and avoids the problem of noncomparable successive samples.

Survey results, like those of other verbal reports, can be accepted at face value unless there is reason to do otherwise. One such reason is the pressure on respondents to give socially desirable responses. People's behavior does not always conform to what they say they would do, so survey research will never replace direct observation. However, survey research does provide an excellent way to examine people's attitudes and opinions.

KEY CONCEPTS

correlational research	nonprobability sampling
correlation	probability sampling
correlation coefficient	accidental sampling
margin of error	simple random sampling
actuarial prediction	stratified random sampling
population	response bias
sampling frame	interviewer bias
sample	cross-sectional design
element	successive independent samples
representativeness	longitudinal design
biased sample	social desirability
selection bias	

REVIEW QUESTIONS

1 Describe the major goal of correlational research, and briefly explain how correlational research is different from experimental research.
2 What two types of information do you gain by knowing the sign and the numerical value of a correlation coefficient?
3 Identify at least two factors beyond the margin of error of the sample that you would need to know to be sure a survey's results are interpretable.
4 Describe briefly one way you could measure a test's reliability and one way you could measure a test's validity.
5 Explain how clinical and actuarial prediction could be used in deciding which students to admit to your college or university. What is the relative predictive accuracy of these two approaches?
6 What information is needed to address the ethical issue that arises when the sponsoring agency of a survey has a vested interest in how the results turn out?
7 What two characteristics do surveys have in common regardless of the purpose for which the survey has been done?
8 What is the greatest threat to the interpretability of the results of a survey when an accidental sample is used?
9 Explain the relationship between the homogeneity of the population from which a sample is to be drawn and the size of a sample needed to ensure representativeness.
10 What factors would you consider in deciding whether to use a mail survey, personal interviews, or telephone interviews for your survey-research project?

11 What aspect of a survey-research project is threatened by response bias and what factor contributes most to the potential for response bias?

12 What would you need to be assured of before interpreting group changes in attitudes over time that were found in using a successive independent samples design?

13 Which survey-research design would you choose if you want to assess the direction and extent of change over time in the opinions of individual respondents?

14 How would you respond if someone told you that survey results were useless because people did not respond truthfully to questions on surveys?

CHALLENGE QUESTIONS

1 A survey researcher selected a random sample of households for a survey of consumer attitudes. In conducting the personal interviews for the survey he often found that no one was home at the households he had selected. His solution to this problem was a simple one. He interviewed whichever next-door neighbor of the selected household happened to be home. Comment critically on the researcher's solution to his problem.

2 Dual-income couples now outnumber those with single incomes, which has led researchers to examine how dual-career demands affect relationships. A survey-research study on this topic was described in *Psychology Today* (1988). The researchers found that among dual-career couples there was a positive correlation such that couples who spent greater amounts of time together found their relationship more satisfactory.

A Presume this finding is a reliable one. What two alternative explanations would you propose for why this correlation exists?

B What moderator variables could you use to explore possible causal relationships underlying this correlation? Be sure to specify how you think the size or direction of the original correlation will change as you change the values of the moderator variable.

3 Survey research is difficult to do well, especially when the topic is people's sexual attitudes and practices. For a book focusing in part on women's sexuality, an author mailed 100,000 questionnaires to women who belonged to a variety of women's groups in 43 states. These groups ranged from feminist organizations to church groups to garden clubs. The author's questionnaire included 127 essay questions. The author received responses from 4,500 women. Findings in this survey included that 70% of respondents married 5 years or more reported having extramarital affairs and that 95% of respondents felt emotionally harassed by the men they love.

A The final sample in this study is large (4,500). Is this sufficient to assure the representativeness of the sample? If not, what survey-research problem lessens the sample's representativeness?

B Is it possible on the basis of your response to Part A of this question to argue that any conclusions drawn by the author from her data are incorrect? What could you do to determine whether the results were correct?

4 Two student researchers have been asked to do a survey to determine the attitudes of other students toward fraternities and sororities on campus. There are 2,000 students in the school. About 25% of the students belong to the Greek organizations and 75% do not. The two student researchers agree they should use a cross-sectional design for their study. But they disagree about what sampling plan is best for the study. One researcher thinks they should draw a stratified random sample of 200 students: 100

from among those students who belong to Greek organizations and 100 from among the independent students. The second researcher thinks they should draw one simple random sample of 100 students from the campus as a whole. Comment critically on these two sampling plans. Finally, develop your own sampling plan if you decide that neither of the ones proposed so far is optimal.

ANSWER TO CHALLENGE QUESTION 1

1 The interviewer's solution is likely to introduce a bias, thereby threatening the representativeness of the sample and the subsequent generality of any findings. Factors such as employment or socioeconomic status might make those who happen to be home systematically different from those who were originally selected for the sample who happened not to be available to be interviewed.

Unobtrusive Measures of Behavior

Thus far, we have emphasized how the behavioral scientist learns about behavior through some form of direct observation (Chapter 3) or from data obtained through survey research (Chapter 4). In this chapter we consider some alternatives to major approaches to the study of behavior. These alternatives receive the name **unobtrusive measures** because they tell us about behavior indirectly. Although these alternative methods are often important in themselves, they also frequently provide a means of confirming the validity of conclusions reached on the basis of direct observation or surveys.

One type of unobtrusive measure is the examination of **physical traces** produced by individuals' behavior. Consider, for example, the possibility that Latin Americans differ from North Americans in their concern for punctuality. Possible cultural differences in the importance of punctuality could be investigated by surveying people in both North American and Latin American countries about how they feel about concerts or sporting events that begin later than the scheduled starting time. However, an alternative, unobtrusive, method would be to examine clocks in cities of North America and South America. It seems reasonable to assume that people's concern for time will be reflected in how accurately they set their clocks. In fact, researchers have found that public clocks (those located in banks) in a Brazilian city were less accurate than those in a similar-sized city in the United States (Levine, West, & Reis, 1980). Although there may be alternative explanations for this finding, differences in this physical-trace measure support the notion that cultural differences in concern for being on time do exist. You may remember from the discussion in

Chapter 1 that Levine (1990) also used accuracy of public clocks to help define the pace of life in cities and countries around the world. Direct observation revealed that the walking speed of a country's citizens was positively correlated with the accuracy of the country's public clocks.

Archives constitute another important unobtrusive source of information about behavior. **Archival data** are obtained by inspecting the records and documents produced by society, as well as by analyzing reports in the media. For example, researchers have claimed that analyses of mortality data reveal a lower than expected frequency of deaths before important events, such as birthdays and religious holidays, and a higher than expected frequency of deaths after these important events. The general procedure for investigating the relationship between death and important occasions is to examine archival data revealing the death dates of individuals in relation to certain important events. Three major positive events have been examined by researchers: birthdays, national elections, and religious holidays.

One of the early studies to offer data supporting a "death-dip hypothesis" used birthdates and death dates of persons listed in the book *Four Hundred Notable Americans* (Schulz & Bazerman, 1980). Based on chance alone, one would expect that an individual's death is equally likely in any of the 12 months. However, the number of deaths during the month prior to the month of an individual's birth was found to be lower than the death rate for other months. This supported the death-dip hypothesis. According to Schulz and Bazerman, a general explanation for this type of finding is that people are somehow able to prolong their lives or delay death until a special event, such as a birthday, has been experienced. Exactly how one might do this is not particularly clear. One suggestion is that looking forward to a positive event creates a state of positive anticipation that precipitates beneficial neurochemical changes. Another possible explanation is that elderly persons are more likely to follow their health and medical regimens closely as an important date nears, so as to reduce the chances of dying before the event arrives.

In this chapter we present the rationale for using physical traces and archival data. Particular kinds of physical traces are identified and examples of their use in psychological studies are offered. We also review types of archives and the kinds of data that can be drawn from archival sources. Several important advantages of the use of physical traces or archival data are highlighted. Some limitations and problems with these unobtrusive measures are also discussed.

PHYSICAL TRACES

RATIONALE

As everyone who has heard a few detective stories knows, examining physical evidence of past behavior can provide important clues to the characteristics (or even identity) of individuals, as well as information about the conditions under which an event occurred. The size of footprints in the ground says something about the size and age of the person who stepped there. The distance between footprints can indicate whether the person was walking or running. And so on. As we have already seen, physical evidence (in the form of clock settings) can be of value to behavioral scientists. Physical traces (like the archival data we discuss later in this chapter) are especially valuable because they provide non-reactive measures of behavior (Webb et al., 1981).

Recall from Chapter 3 that a behavioral measure is reactive when the participants' awareness of an observer affects the measurement process. This is often the case when direct observations are made, and it is nearly always the case when surveys are conducted. Reactivity introduces the problem of response bias. Aware that their responses are being recorded, participants may behave in a way that does not correspond to their normal behavior. Survey data are particularly susceptible to reactive effects because respondents may give answers they feel the researcher wants to hear or may answer in a way that makes them (the respondents) look good.

Physical-trace measures are unobtrusive (because they are obtained indirectly, in the absence of the subject), so they are valuable alternatives to the reactive measures obtained via direct observation or surveys. Although a physical-trace measure might be the only measure of behavior in some studies, physical traces are more commonly used in combination with other measures. As we emphasized previously, a research study can be strengthened considerably by including several different measures of behavior. A **multimethod approach** to hypothesis testing is recommended because it reduces the likelihood that research findings are due to some artifact of a single measurement process (Webb et al., 1981). There are few (if any) perfect measures in the social sciences. Therefore, the results of a study must be carefully scrutinized to determine whether some characteristic of the measurement instrument (such as its reactivity) has contributed to the results. Even then, it is possible that some artifact has been overlooked. *The most persuasive argument supporting the validity of a particular research hypothesis is one based on evidence obtained by applying a combination of measures.*

Researchers investigating cultural differences in time perception used such a multimethod approach. They surveyed individuals living in Latin America and in the United States to find out how frequently the respondents were late for appointments and to discover their attitudes toward being late (Levine et al., 1980). Citizens of Brazil reported themselves more often late for appointments and expressed less regret at being late than did citizens of the United States. However, a bias in these responses could be present if people described themselves in a way that fit their cultural "image," rather than as they actually behaved. As we already noted, however, the researchers also found that public clocks were less accurate in Brazil than in the United States. Further, the researchers observed that watches worn by people in the United States deviated less from the correct time than watches worn by people in Brazil. The data obtained by examining public clocks and the watches worn by citizens of each country tended to confirm the validity of the survey responses and, in combination with the survey results, provided impressive evidence for the research hypothesis.

TYPES OF PHYSICAL TRACES

Physical traces are the remnants, fragments, and products of past behavior. Two broad categories of physical traces are use traces and products. *Use traces* are what the label implies—the physical evidence that results from use (or nonuse) of an item. Clock settings are an example of a physical-use trace. So are the remains of cigarettes in ashtrays and the marks made in textbooks. *Products* are the creations, constructions, or other artifacts of earlier behavior. Anthropologists are often interested in the surviving products of ancient cultures. By examining the types of vessels, paintings, and other artifacts that remain, the anthropologist can often describe precisely the pattern of behavior exhibited in a setting that is thousands of years old. Psychologists may also examine physical products in order to describe behavior or to test hypotheses. Psychologists who study animal behavior, for instance, may learn about the behavior of different species by examining the types of nests that are constructed.

Use Traces   An examination of physical evidence provides measures of both accretion and erosion (Webb et al., 1981). *Accretion measures* are based on the accumulation of material. Measuring the amount of litter found on a college campus, for example, would be taking an accretion measure. *Erosion measures* are obtained when the physical evidence is the result of selective wear and tear. The degree to which a young child's dolls show signs of wear is an erosion measure that might indicate which dolls the child likes best. The distinction between accretion measures and erosion measures is not always so obvious. Settings of clocks, for instance, resist easy classification. Nevertheless, classifying physical-use traces in terms of accretion or erosion is often a meaningful description of physical traces, and the distinction calls our attention to two important dimensions of use traces.

Physical-use traces are also classified as either natural or controlled (planned). *Natural* use traces are produced without any intervention by the investigator. Their appearance is the result of naturally occurring events. *Controlled,* or planned, measures result to some degree from the intervention or manipulation of an investigator. A study by Friedman and Wilson (1975) illustrates the distinction between these two types of measures.

The investigators employed both controlled and natural accretion measures to investigate college students' use of textbooks. They affixed tiny glue seals between adjacent pages of textbooks before the students purchased the books for a course. At the end of the semester the investigators obtained the books from the students and recorded how many seals in the textbooks had been broken and where the broken seals were located. Because the researchers controlled the presence of glue seals in the books this constituted a controlled (accretion) measure. The investigators also analyzed the frequency and nature of underlining by students in the textbooks, something, of course, typically associated with textbook use. This constituted a natural accretion measure. Analysis of these physical-use measures indicated that students more often read (and presumably studied) the chapters that appeared early in the book than those appearing later in the book.

Table 5.1 contains examples of physical-use traces and the variables being measured. These measures either were used as part of an actual scientific study or represent suggestions by researchers of possible novel and nonreactive measures of behavior (Webb et al., 1981). The examples given in Table 5.1 have been organized according to whether they are accretion or erosion measures and

TABLE 5.1   EXAMPLES OF PHYSICAL-USE TRACES AND VARIABLES BEING MEASURED*

Trace	Variable
Natural accretion	
Inscriptions (graffiti) on walls of public rest rooms	Sexual preoccupation
Radio dial settings	Popularity of radio stations
Fingerprints or smudges on pages of books	Book usage
Liquor bottles in trash cans	Alcohol consumption of households
Odometer readings in cars	Conservation of gasoline
Litter	Effectiveness of antilitter posters
Dust on books	Frequency or recency of use
Garbage	Food use and lifestyle
Locked/unlocked cars	Concern for property
Lengths of cigarette butts	Cultural differences in death rate due to cancer
Controlled accretion	
Glue seals broken (seals inserted prior to distribution)	Index of specific pages read
Nose prints on windows of museum exhibit (windows wiped clean each night)	Popularity (frequency) and age (height of prints) of viewers
Natural erosion	
Wear on floor or steps	Amount of foot traffic
Wear on library books	Frequency of use
Food consumed	Eating behavior
Spots (produced by rubbing) on statues or religious objects	Level of religious belief
Controlled erosion	
Wear on children's shoes (measured at two points in time)	Activity level of children
Removal of "tear-away" tags on ads or notices	Interest in notice
Wear on mats or other floor coverings placed in specific areas	Amount of foot traffic
Change in statues or objects coated with substances sensitive to touching	Superstitious behavior

*From Webb et al. (1981).

whether their use is natural or controlled. As you examine the contents of Table 5.1, can you think of other possible physical traces that could serve as measures of the variables listed?

Products   Physical products have been examined less frequently in psychological studies than have physical-use traces. Nevertheless, this category of physical traces has been used in interesting and meaningful ways to test hypotheses about behavior. A particularly good example of the use of physical products is found in a study by Coren and Porac (1977). They investigated the extent of human right-handedness in various cultures since ancient times. To determine manual preference, they examined more than 12,000 works of art, including paintings, sculpture, and other products that spanned more than 50 centuries of human endeavor. The researchers recorded instances of unambiguous tool or weapon use depicted in the artworks. They looked for any differential trend in the depiction of right- or left-handers in different cultures and at different times in human history. No differences were evident. Rather, across many cultures and in every epoch, 93% of the artworks examined showed persons using their right hand. The results provide evidence for a physiological rather than a sociocultural theory of handedness.

Brandt (1972) points out that the products people own provide important clues to their lifestyle and behavior patterns. What personality differences, for instance, are reflected in the purchase of different models of cars or in the extras and options ordered with a car? Besides serving as a measure of social status or personality, the products a person owns can be used to assess the validity of certain kinds of verbal reports. Are individuals' statements about their attitude toward energy conservation, for instance, related to the kinds of products they own and use?

Mooney and Brabant (1987) reported that various kinds of greeting cards—for example, those celebrating birthdays or holidays, as well as those conveying sympathy—represent over half of all the personal mail moved annually by the U.S. Postal Service. It is not surprising, therefore, that this particular product of society has proved to be a veritable treasure trove for researchers investigating attitudes toward such social phenomena as drinking, aging, and death. Mooney and Brabant, for instance, randomly sampled birthday cards from 14 retail outlets in a metropolitan area as part of a study of the deviant messages in interpersonal communications. The cards were classified according to various categories of deviant behavior (for example, making reference to obesity, violence, marital infidelity, or mental illness) as well as to a category of nondeviant behavior. Approximately 16% of the cards sampled contained some form of deviant message. Among the many differences noted between deviant and nondeviant cards was that deviant cards were more likely to present stereotypes, particularly of males, than were nondeviant cards. According to Mooney and Brabant, because cards containing deviant messages are the "moral opposite" of traditional birthday greetings, they likely signal a "unique moral order" between those involved, and, according to the authors, are perhaps appropriate when "you care enough to send the very worst" (p. 386).

PROBLEMS AND LIMITATIONS

Physical measures offer a researcher valuable and sometimes novel means to study behavior. And the measures available are limited only by the ingenuity of the investigator. However, the validity of physical traces must be carefully examined and verified through independent sources of evidence. Bias can be introduced in the way physical-use traces are laid down and in the manner in which traces survive over time. Does a well-worn path to the right indicate people's interest in objects in that direction or simply a natural human tendency to turn right? Is the setting of clocks a good measure of people's regard for punctuality, or do inaccurate clock settings indicate poor artisanship, inadequate maintenance, or irregular electrical service?

Problems associated with the analysis of physical traces are illustrated in a classic study of honesty carried out using the "lost-letter technique" (Merritt & Fowler, 1948). We can consider the method as controlled accretion. The investigators "accidentally" dropped postcards and envelopes at various locations in cities of the East and Midwest. Two types of envelopes were "lost." One contained a written message, and the other contained a lead slug the size of a 50-cent piece. All the letters were addressed and bore proper postage, but no return address was shown. Although 85% of the "empty" envelopes were returned, only 54% of the envelopes with a slug found their way to a mailbox. Further, more than 10% of the envelopes with a slug were returned after having been opened.

Before the researchers could conclude that the return rates represented a valid measure of the public's honesty (or dishonesty), several possible biases associated with this physical trace had to be considered. Postcards, for instance, were less likely than sealed envelopes to be returned, but the fact that

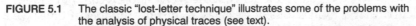

FIGURE 5.1   The classic "lost-letter technique" illustrates some of the problems with the analysis of physical traces (see text).

postcards may be more easily disturbed by natural conditions than are larger envelopes may have contributed to this difference. On the other hand, envelopes with a slug are heavier and less likely to be blown away—and these were still less likely to be returned. Letters that were dropped in certain locations (for example, where many children are present) or at certain times of the day (for example, just before nightfall) are also likely to be "lost" for reasons other than the public's dishonesty or apathy.

Some of these possible biases associated with the lost-letter technique were avoided by the methods of dispersal used by the researchers, whereas others were checked via direct observation of a letter's fate. Observation of a sample of dropped letters revealed that a letter was picked up 90% of the time by the first person who saw it, suggesting that dropped letters were soon in the hands of unknowing participants.

Whenever possible, supplementary evidence for the validity of physical traces should be obtained (Webb et al., 1981). Alternative hypotheses for changes in physical traces must be considered, and data must be collected that allow different interpretations to be dismissed.

ARCHIVAL DATA

RATIONALE

When we were born, a record was made of our birth. Information on the birth record probably included the city and state in which we were born, the date and time of our birth, our parents' names, and our name. When we die, another record will be made. It will include such details as probable cause of death, date and time of death, and our age. In between these two events, innumerable records are made of our behavior. Physicians record visits. Hospitals keep a record of when we enter and when we leave. Schools record our grades and extracurricular activities. Businesses may record the number of times we are late or how often we fail to show up for work. Newspapers describe notable successes and failures. Local governments record when we get married and to whom, as well as when we buy a house and how much it costs. The federal government records, among other things, what we pay in income taxes.

Records are kept not only of individuals but also of countries, institutions, cities, and businesses. The gross national product of a country, its major exports and imports, the size of its defense budget, the distribution of its population, and the number of television sets owned by its populace are but a few of the facts that are frequently recorded. How much profit a company makes is part of its report to stockholders. Voting behaviors of state and federal legislators are recorded, as is the amount of money a city spends on social services. Analysis and interpretation of local and world events flood the media. The contents of the media and of documents and books (published and unpublished) are a source of information about current fads and prejudices, changing patterns of belief, and the ideas of important (and not so important) members of society.

Archives are records or documents recounting the activities of individuals or of institutions, governments, and other groups. As measures of behavior, archival data share some of the same advantages as physical traces. Archival measures are nonreactive and therefore provide an alternative to data collection via surveys. Like physical-trace measures, archival data can be used to check the validity of other measures as part of a multimethod approach to hypothesis testing. A nice illustration of the use of archival data in the context of a multimethod approach to hypothesis testing is Frank and Gilovich's (1988) investigation of the strong cultural association that exists between the color black and "badness," or evil.

As Frank and Gilovich point out, in vintage American western movies you could always tell the good guys from the bad guys. The good guys, of course, wore white hats and the bad guys wore black hats. There is a strong cultural association between black and badness. We speak of people being "blackballed," "blacklisted," "blackmailed," and a person's reputation's being "blackened." When terrible things happen it is a "black day." Black is seen in many cultures as the color of death. The good and bad sides of human nature are also contrasted using black-and-white images, as was illustrated by the characters of the famous *Star Wars* movie. Viewers of this classic movie likely will remember the confrontation between the villain, Darth Vader (dressed completely in black), and the young hero, Luke Skywalker (dressed in white or light colors). Vader, unfortunately, had gone over to the dark side.

Frank and Gilovich wanted to find out if this strong cultural association between black and evil would affect the way people behave. Specifically, they asked whether professional sports teams that wear black uniforms are more aggressive than those that wear nonblack uniforms. Using archival data obtained from the central offices of the National Football League (NFL) and the National Hockey League (NHL), Frank and Gilovich analyzed penalty records of each major professional team in these sports between 1970 and 1986. Yards penalized were analyzed in the NFL, and minutes that a player was assigned to the penalty box were calculated in the NHL. These particular measures were deemed more appropriate given the study's hypothesis than was number of infractions. Penalties for overaggressiveness are generally more severe (in yards or minutes) than are those for simple rule violations. The operational definition of a "black uniform" was that the colored version of the team's uniform (the one used typically for away games in the NHL and for home games in the NFL) was more than 50% black. (An exception was made for the Chicago Bears of the NFL, who wear dark blue uniforms but whose uniforms many people mistakenly remember as black; thus, they were included among the black-uniform teams.) According to the authors' hypothesis, teams wearing black should be penalized more than would be expected simply by chance. And they were. Thus, teams with black uniforms, such as Oakland, Chicago, and Cincinnati in the NFL, and Philadelphia, Pittsburgh, and Vancouver in the NHL, were reliably more aggressive than were many other teams.

What psychological processes might account for these effects? Frank and Gilovich suggest that both social perception and self-perception processes are at work. They argue that others (specifically, referees) "see" players in black as more aggressive than players not wearing black (and therefore award more penalties to players in black), and that players themselves behave more aggressively when they put on black uniforms. As part of their multimethod approach to this issue, they provided support for these explanations by collecting data from laboratory experiments. In one experiment, both college students and referees watched staged football games between teams wearing black or white uniforms and rated their aggressiveness. In a second study, students donned either black or white uniforms in anticipation of an athletic competition before choosing a game from a list of aggressive and nonaggressive games. In the first experiment, both referees and college students were more likely to rate a team wearing black as aggressive. The second experiment showed that students who donned black uniforms chose more aggressive games. By combining data obtained from archival analyses and laboratory experiments, the investigators provide an unusually strong case for their explanations of this interesting cultural phenomenon.

An examination of archival information may also provide a way to test the external validity of laboratory findings. Lau and Russell (1980) analyzed the contents of the sports pages in eight daily newspapers in order to test whether results obtained from laboratory-based experiments investigating *causal attributions* (the reasons people give for a certain outcome, or the cause they attribute the outcome to) were relevant to real-world settings. A major finding from laboratory studies of attributions is that people tend to make internal attributions (assuming the outcome is due to some characteristic within themselves) for success and to make external attributions (assuming the outcome is due to something beyond their control) for failure. Lau and Russell's analysis of explanations given by sportswriters or team members for the outcome of baseball and football games supported this conclusion. Specifically, they identified 594 explanations for success and failure involving 33 major sporting events. From the perspective of the winning team, 75% of the attributions were internal, whereas only 55% of the attributions of the losing team were internal.

Support for this laboratory-based attribution theory has also been obtained by analyzing letters and replies published in two widely syndicated newspaper advice columns: Ann Landers and Dear Abby (Fischer, Shoeneman, & Rubanowitz, 1987; Schoeneman & Rubanowitz, 1985). The investigation was based on 15 randomly selected columns of each adviser from 1980. The researchers, along with two-person teams of undergraduates trained for this task, first identified explanatory statements in the published letters. The explanations were then coded according to whether the locus of the explanation was internal, that is, inherent to the writer, or external, implicating situations and circumstances. For one analysis, explanations were also coded in terms of temporal stability and controllability (Fischer et al., 1987). A stable cause is unchanging over time; an unstable cause is changeable. Attributions reflected controllable causes only when a person was deemed capable of exercising control over them. One major finding of this archival study was that people view their own problems as the result of others' (external) invariable (stable) willful (controllable) tendencies. One letter writer illustrated this attribution bias when she identified the source of her problematic vacations as follows: "Sydney is a drag on a trip [because] he has no interest in seeing new places or meeting new people" (Fischer et al., 1987, p. 461).

Other reasons for using archival data are to test hypotheses about previous behavior and to assess the effect of a natural treatment. It is possible, for instance, to obtain a measure of television-viewing habits by studying the water pressure records of a city (Webb et al., 1981)! When a television show is watched by many of a city's residents, water pressure levels are found to fluctuate in accordance with the show. For example, in one city a "30-million-gallon effect" was found for half-time and end-of-game breaks in a Super Bowl game, whereas only a "15-million-gallon effect" was found at the end of a presidential debate. Changes in level of water pressure presumably reflect trips that viewers make to get a drink of water or to use the toilet when a convenient break appears in the television show they are watching. Archival records also have played a central role in studies of the "home advantage" in sports competitions (Courneya & Carron, 1992). The *home advantage* refers to the fact that in many sports competitions a team wins consistently more games played at home than it does games played away.

FIGURE 5.2
Archival records permit psychologists to study the "home advantage" in sports competitions.

Natural treatments are naturally occurring events that have significant impact on society at large or on particular members. Because it is not always possible to anticipate these events, the investigator who wishes to assess their impact must be prepared to use a variety of behavioral measures, including archival data. School records of absenteeism have been used as an indirect measure of health in a study investigating the effect of aircraft noise on children (Cohen, Evans, Krantz, & Stokols, 1980). Assassinations of world leaders, drastic changes in the stock market, and the passage of new laws are examples of the kinds of events that may have important effects on behavior and might be investigated using archival data.

Another reason for considering archival data as a behavioral measure is simply because archival data are so plentiful. We noted earlier the extensive records that society keeps on individuals, groups, and institutions. Through careful analysis of archival information, the industrious researcher can seek evidence to support numerous hypotheses. There are practical advantages as well. Archival data represent data that have already been collected; at times, initial summary descriptions may also be provided in archival records. Thus, an extensive data collection stage may be circumvented. Because archival information is frequently part of the public record and usually reported in a manner that does not identify individuals, ethical concerns are less worrisome. One goal of this chapter is to alert you to the possible rich rewards of analyzing archival data in the context of psychological studies of behavior. As more and more archival sources become available through the Internet, researchers will find it even easier to examine behavior in this way.

TYPES OF ARCHIVAL DATA

The sheer diversity and extent of archival sources make their classification rather arbitrary. Records that are continuously kept and updated are frequently referred to as *running records.* Tax records and records of various government agencies are good examples, as are the myriad records of sports teams. Because of their continuous nature, running records are particularly useful in longitudinal studies or in the documentation of trends. Other records, such as personal documents, are more likely to be discontinuous or episodic (Webb et al., 1981). Archival records can also be distinguished by the degree to which they are available for public inspection. Many records kept by government agencies are easily obtainable. Most records of private institutions and businesses, however, are not open to public scrutiny or can be obtained only after many requests and considerable patience on the part of the researcher.

The news media are yet another important source of archival information. Various records, ranging from stock market reports to crime statistics, are published in newspapers and reported on television. The content of media reports is also a form of archival record and subject to analysis. Earlier we described how the contents of sports pages were used to test a theory of causal attribution. The placement of "found" advertisements in the lost and found section of a newspaper can be used to measure public altruism (Goldstein, Minkin, Minkin, & Baer, 1978).

Phillips (1977) used running records of motor vehicle fatalities kept by the California Highway Patrol and a measure of suicide publicity derived from California newspapers to determine whether there is a significant suicidal component to motor vehicle fatalities. He hypothesized that a substantial number of deaths arising from motor vehicle accidents are actually the result of individuals using their cars to commit suicide. To test this hypothesis, Phillips investigated whether motor vehicle fatalities would, like suicides in general, increase after a well-publicized suicide story. Components of the publicity measure included the daily circulation of each newspaper and the number of days the newspaper carried the suicide story. This measure correlated significantly with changes in motor vehicle fatalities after each story. The number of motor vehicle fatalities increased significantly during the few days after a well-publicized suicide story, reaching a peak on Day 3. This result is shown in Figure 5.3. Changes in frequency were determined by comparing experimental periods (the week right after the story) with control periods that were free from suicide stories and were matched with the experimental periods in terms of day of the week, presence or absence of holidays, and time of the year. Phillips concluded that suicide stories stimulate a wave of imitative suicides, some of which are disguised as motor vehicle accidents " (p. 1464).

Table 5.2 contains a list of selected sources of archival information and the nature of the data that might be obtained from them. The types of archival data shown in Table 5.2 have been rather arbitrarily classified as running records, those pertaining to the media, and "other records," including records of businesses, schools, and other private institutions. An examination of the sources described in Table 5.2 will introduce you to the variety of possible measures that can be obtained from archival sources. Then, following a brief discussion

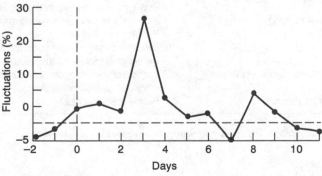

FIGURE 5.3   Daily fluctuation in motor vehicle accident fatalities for a 2-week period before, during (Day 0), and after publication of suicide stories. (From Phillips, 1977.)

TABLE 5.2 SELECTED SOURCES OF ARCHIVAL INFORMATION AND ILLUSTRATIVE DATA FOR THREE TYPES OF ARCHIVES*

Source	Illustrative data
Running records	
Congressional Record	Statements of position on particular issues
Telephone directories	Community ethnic group membership
Salaries of teachers or government employees	Community support
Government agency records (labor, commerce, agriculture departments)	Living trends
Judicial record	Uniformity in sentencing for antisocial behavior
Moody's Handbook	Corporate financial structure
Who's Who in America	Nature of cited accomplishments of successful people
Tax records	Regional differences in patterns of living
City budgets	Perceived value or extent of support of various activities
Media	
Society section of metropolitan newspaper	Upper-middle-class and lower-upper-class activities
Children's books on sale	Qualities of models (heroes and heroines)
Movie announcements in newspapers	Changing taboos and enticements
Want ads	Employer inducements
Obituary columns	Charity preferences
Published speeches	Political, social, economic attitudes
Newspaper headlines	Press bias
Other records†	
Absentee and tardiness records	Work habits or motivation
Military reenlistment and longevity figures	Morale indicator
Pay increase and promotion lists	Perceived value of individuals to an organization
Number of people one supervises	Measure of management responsibility
Production and other output figures	Performance of individuals, departments, and so on
Sales contest records	Selling effectiveness, effectiveness of incentive plans
Sales slips at Delegates' Lounge bar in UN	Tension indicator
Peanut sales at ball games	Excitement indicator (greater after than before seventh inning)
Sales level of consumer goods	Effectiveness of display location, advertisement, or style of packaging
Air trip insurance figures	Public concern before and after air crashes
Sales of layettes by color (blue or pink)	Sex preference in different social classes
Sale price of autographs	Popularity indicator
Club membership list	Indicator of segment of society involved
Committee reports	Institutional modification attempts
Actuarial records: birth, baptismal, death records; marriage licenses	Comparative demographic data (occupation, religion, time of day, cause of death, and so on)
Cemetery documents, burial-lot records	Family membership

*Adapted from Brandt (1972).
†Institutions, businesses, hospitals, schools, and so on; may or may not be opened to public inspection.

of content analysis of archival sources, we review several specific illustrations of the use of archival data in the context of hypothesis testing.

CONTENT ANALYSIS

Although many sources of archival data can be identified, the usefulness of these sources depends ultimately on how their content is analyzed. In the simplest case, the analysis required may be minimal. Recording the votes of state legislators may be as simple as transcribing vote tallies found in legislative documents. Similarly, determining the win-loss record of sports teams playing at home or away is simply a matter of working with data found in one of the myriad sports digests on the market. In many cases, however, extracting relevant data from an archival source requires careful procedures and relatively complex analysis of the source's content. Furthermore, problems of sampling, reliability, and validity of measures must be addressed, just as these problems are addressed in situations where behavior is observed directly.

Content analysis is generally defined as any technique for making inferences by objectively identifying specific characteristics of messages (Holsti, 1969). Although it is associated primarily with written communications, content analysis may be used with any form of message, including television and radio programs, speeches, films, and interviews. Weigel, Loomis, and Soja (1980) used content analysis to study race relations as they are depicted on prime-time television. They analyzed the frequency of appearances of blacks and whites on evening television shows carried by all three major networks. In addition, they rated the quality of black-white and white-white interactions. Appearances by blacks involved less than 9% of human appearance time in programs and commercials, and, compared with white-white interactions, black-white interactions were relatively infrequent and more formalized when they did occur.

There are several discernible steps in conducting research using content analysis. First is the identification of a relevant archival source. What is relevant, of course, depends on the goals of the study and the questions the researcher is asking. In some cases merely a statement of the purpose of the study is sufficient to pinpoint an appropriate archival source. A researcher who sets out to study humor in tombstone messages, the manifest content of suicide notes, or race relations on television has already identified the general source for content analysis. In other situations the identification of relevant sources depends on the ingenuity of the researcher. Lau and Russell's (1980) choice of the sports page represented an appropriate and clever use of archival sources as a test of the external validity of laboratory findings related to attribution.

Having identified an archival source, the researcher must sample selections from this source appropriately. Sampling procedures similar to those described in previous chapters can be used. As is the case when behavior or events are sampled, the goal of sampling is to obtain a sample that is representative of all the data of interest. To investigate race relations on television, Weigel et al. (1980) videotaped a full week's broadcasts by the three major networks in the spring of 1978. Only programs with a story line, but all product commercials, were included in the sample. The decision not to use documentaries, news broadcasts, and sports shows reduced the sample of viewing time by about 20%. As always, the extent to which the results of an archival study can be generalized depends on the nature of the sample used.

The next step in performing a content analysis is *coding*. This step is similar to the scoring of narrative records (see Chapter 3) and requires that relevant descriptive categories and appropriate units of measure be defined (Holsti, 1969). As with the choice of the archival source itself, what determines a relevant descriptive category is related to the goals of the study. This aspect of a content-analysis task can be illustrated by examining the categories used by Weigel et al. (1980) in their study of race relations. Four major categories were defined: (1) human appearance time, (2) black appearance time, (3) cross-racial appearance time, and (4) cross-racial interaction time. Each category was operationally defined. For instance, cross-racial interaction was defined as "the time during which black and white characters were engaged in active, on-screen interactions (talking, touching, or clear nonverbal communication)" (p. 886). The use of precise operational definitions permitted coders viewing the sample broadcasts to make reliable judgments of events.

In many content-analysis studies, the communication is written. The units of classification for quantitative analysis generally include single words, characters, sentences or paragraphs, themes, or particular items (Holsti, 1969). Lau and Russell (1980), for instance, determined the frequency of attribution statements that were categorized as either internal or external and were made by members of the winning or losing team. Another unit of measure often used when newspaper content is analyzed is that of space—for instance, number of column inches devoted to a particular topic. When television or radio broadcasts are studied, the unit of measure may be time. Such was the case for the study by Weigel et al. (1980). Both black appearances and black-white appearances were expressed in terms of the percentage of total human appearance time.

Qualitative measures are also used as part of content analysis. These qualitative assessments are frequently in the form of ratings. For example, in addition to measuring time of cross-racial interactions on prime-time television, Weigel et al. sought to determine the "degree to which cross-racial interactions on television were characterized by the conditions that promote friendliness and mutual respect in face-to-face encounters" (pp. 886–887). To do this, they developed a series of rating scales that emphasized the interpersonal dimensions found to be important in previous race-related research. Broadcasts videotaped a year earlier were used to define levels of the scales, and coders were trained in the use of the scales before real data were collected. As we mentioned, the quality of black-white interactions, relative to white-white interactions, differed on several dimensions.

Satterfield and Seligman (1994) used the CAVE technique to investigate the explanatory styles of George Bush and Saddam Hussein during several historical periods of conflict, including the Persian Gulf crisis. The acronym CAVE stands for "content analysis of verbatim explanations" (Schulman, Castellon, & Seligman, 1989). The CAVE guidelines help researchers identify causal statements in written or spoken verbatim messages. The statements can then be rated on dimensions of explanatory style, similar to those used by Lau and Russell in their study of causal attributions in sports. The content analysis of verbatim explanations by Bush and Hussein for periods preceding military actions or political conflicts produced an interesting result:

> When the leaders were pessimistic (relative to themselves), their subsequent actions were more cautious and passive. When the leaders were relatively optimistic, their subsequent actions were more aggressive and risky. (Satterfield & Seligman, 1994, p. 79)

The authors noted the many limitations of their study (for example, a relatively small sample of verbatim messages and world events was analyzed). They also appropriately acknowledged that the correlational nature of their study means they must "leave open the large class of third-variable accounts before concluding that explanatory style itself causes cautious versus risky actions" (p. 79). For example, before a definitive conclusion regarding the relationship between explanatory style and political action can be reached, such issues as political demands on the leaders or cultural differences in rhetorical style need to be investigated further. Nevertheless, the data suggest that "shifts in explanatory style seem at least to signal corresponding shifts in aggressivity and risk taking" (p. 80). Archival research of this kind may help us better understand the psychological nature of political decision making and perhaps even help predict the course of world events.

Whenever possible, coders should be blind to important aspects of the study, such as the main hypotheses, the source of the messages, and the immediate surrounding context. Coders in the Satterfield and Seligman (1994) study of explanatory style, for example, rated the world leaders' statements only after "all potentially biasing date information was removed" (p. 78) and after source material had been assigned random number codes.

ILLUSTRATIVE USES OF ARCHIVAL DATA

Analysis of Communications   Satterfield and Seligman's (1994) analysis of the explanations by George Bush and Saddam Hussein for world events is a good example of the use of archival data to analyze communications. So, too, is an interesting study by Osgood and Walker (1959) who compared the content of real suicide notes, simulated suicide notes (notes deliberately faked), and ordinary letters. Working under the assumption that language behavior changes as a function of heightened motivation, they suggested that suicide notes should differ from ordinary letters and faked notes in several ways. Specifically, the researchers hypothesized that, relative to other messages, suicide notes would show (a) greater stereotypy (more repetitions, fewer modifiers, more familiar words and phrases); (2) greater disorganization of language (more grammatical errors, shorter units); (3) more frequent use of self-destructive motives (greater use of self-critical statements); and (4) more evidence of conflict (greater qualification of statements, more frequent use of constructions with "however," "but," and "if").

The investigators chose 16 different measures to test their hypotheses regarding the content of these messages (for example, number of syllables per word and number of distress-expressing phrases). Many of these measures revealed significant differences between suicide notes and ordinary letters, lending support to three of the four major hypotheses. Interestingly, suicide notes did not show greater disorganization. When quantitative measures that were successful in distinguishing between suicide notes and ordinary letters were used to differentiate between faked and real suicide notes, the analysis correctly predicted the real suicide note in 10 of 13 matched pairs.

Analysis of Trends Over the years, women have frequently been underrepresented in businesses and professions. In the last few decades, however, significant attempts have been made to reduce any sex bias affecting hiring and promotion as well as entry into various professions. Scientific organizations, such as those in psychology, have taken steps to reduce discriminatory practices. The *APA Publication Manual* (American Psychological Association, 1994), for instance, includes specific guidelines for using inclusive language in APA journals (see also Appendix C). The APA Ethics Code, which we discussed in Chapter 2, clearly promotes respect for people's rights and for the dignity of all individuals without regard to gender (as well as to other cultural, social, or physical factors). According to General Principle D of the Ethics Code, "Psychologists try to eliminate the effect on their work of biases based on these factors, and they do not knowingly participate in nor condone unfair discriminatory practices" (American Psychological Association, 1992, p. 1600).

To what extent have psychologists been successful in reducing sex bias in their research activities? To attempt to answer this question, researchers reviewed nearly 5,000 scientific articles from eight psychology journals published between 1970 and 1990 (Gannon, Luchetta, Rhodes, Pardie, & Segrist, 1992). The journals were selected to represent various topic areas (developmental, abnormal, and so on) within psychology. With the exception of one journal that did not begin publication until 1978, the contents of all articles published in these journals in 1970, 1975, 1980, 1985, and 1990 were examined. Eight different variables were identified, and the contents of the articles were coded according to these variables. Among them were the sex of the first author, sex of the participants, the type of language (i.e., sexist or nonsexist) used, and the existence of generalizations based on gender (e.g., generalizations of results obtained from participants of one sex to both sexes).

The results of this trend analysis of sex bias in published psychology articles revealed that while "sexism has clearly diminished in the past two decades," there is "continued evidence of discriminatory practices" (p. 389). For example, on the positive side, significant increases between 1970 and 1990 in the percentages of articles with female first authors were found in nearly every journal;

the percentages of studies that had male-only participants declined significantly in most journals. In addition, sexist language in these psychology journals was all but totally eliminated by 1990. On the negative side, a substantial
percentage of articles showing sex bias were still being published in 1990. An
article was considered sex biased "if participants included only one gender for
no obvious reason or with no reason explicitly stated, if sexist language was
used, or if the discussion section contained inappropriate generalizations" (p.
393). Under this definition, sex-biased studies averaged about 85% in 1970 and
about 30% in 1990. As the authors indicated, the archival analysis revealed an
obvious reduction in sex bias in psychological studies, but it is evident from the
data that there is still room for improvement.

An analysis of APA journals by Graham (1992) revealed room for improvement also in the way psychologists approach the study of African Americans.
Archival data obtained from six major APA journals indicated that the presence
of empirical articles on African Americans decreased during the period 1970 to
1989. The bottom line was highlighted in the title of her article: "Most of the
Subjects Were White and Middle Class." This trend seems unfortunate when,
as the author notes, "social concerns demand increased understanding of the
psychological functioning of Black Americans, and pedagogical needs call for
cultural diversity in our academic curricula" (p. 629). These analyses of trends
in APA journals illustrate how archival information can be a source of important information about the practice of the science of psychology.

Assessing the Effect of a Natural Treatment   A study investigating the
effect of a natural treatment (one we mentioned previously) is that of Phillips
(1977). In this study, the "treatment" was the publicity given by major newspapers to suicides, and the effect of this publicity on motor vehicle fatalities was
assessed. In a subsequent study, Phillips (1978) used records of the U.S. National Transportation Safety Board (*Briefs of Accidents: U.S. Civil Aviation*) to
show a relationship between well-publicized murder-suicides and changes in
fatal aircraft accidents. This archival study revealed a sharp increase in multifa-
tality crashes (implying both a murder and a suicide component) in the period
following the widespread publicizing of a murder-suicide story. Interestingly,
the peak increase in aircraft fatalities occurred on Day 3 following the story, just
as Phillips found when suicide stories were related to motor vehicle fatalities
(see Figure 5.1).

Yet another finding by Phillips (1983) is that homicides increased significantly following heavyweight championship prizefights during the period
1973 to 1978. At the time this study was conducted, daily counts of homicides
in the United States for this 6-year period were publicly available from the National Center for Health Statistics. Particularly intriguing is the fact that deaths
due to homicides peaked 3 days following the prizefight, as had been found in
previous analyses of motor vehicle and airplane fatalities following well-publicized suicide stories. According to Phillips, the heavyweight prizefights pro-
voked a brief, sharp increase in homicides. As evidence that this effect is due to
some type of modeling of aggression, Phillips carried out additional analyses

showing that homicides increased with an increase in the level of publicity surrounding the event. He operationally defined level of publicity in terms of whether the fight was discussed on television network news. He found that the increase in homicides was significantly greater when the fight was given more publicity on the network news.

This series of studies by Phillips and his colleagues is an impressive demonstration of the use of archival data to provide external validity to the results of laboratory findings. Phillips noted that laboratory studies have shown that exposure to violent films and television produces brief increases in aggression by laboratory subjects. Often, however, neither the setting nor the nature of the violence studied (for example, hitting inflatable toys) is similar to that found in the real world. In contrast, studies using archival data, although lacking the rigorous control possible in the laboratory, provide evidence of what happens to people who are exposed to real media instances of aggression.

PROBLEMS AND LIMITATIONS

When discussing the validity of physical traces, we mentioned that biases may result from the way physical traces are established and from the manner in which they survive over time. These biases are referred to as selective deposit and selective survival, respectively, and they are no less a problem for archival records (Webb et al., 1981). Either of these biases can impose severe limitations on the generality of research findings.

Problems of **selective deposit** arise when biases exist in the production of archival sources. An interesting example of selective deposit is that associated with suicide notes. We mentioned earlier the research of Osgood and Walker (1959), who performed a content analysis of suicide notes and compared real suicide notes to ordinary letters and to faked suicide notes. We might ask whether the thoughts and feelings expressed in suicide notes are representative of all suicides. It happens that fewer than a fourth of all individuals who commit suicide leave notes, so it is possible that those who do leave notes are not representative of no-note individuals (Webb et al., 1981).

Problems of selective deposit may also arise when individuals associated with archival sources have the opportunity to edit and alter records before they are permanently recorded. This is illustrated by legislators' use of the *Congressional Record*. Although the *Congressional Record* is ostensibly a spontaneous record of speeches and remarks made before the Congress, legislators actually have the opportunity to edit their remarks before they are published (Webb et al., 1981) and even to enter into the record documents and accounts that were never really read aloud. No doubt remarks that are, in hindsight, viewed as less than politically expedient are changed prior to publication in the *Congressional Record*. Researchers who use archival data must be aware of the biases that may enter in when an archive is produced. Consider, for example, what types of biases might cause selective recording of crime statistics, income expense accounts, or sales figures.

Problems associated with **selective survival** arise when records are missing or incomplete (something an investigator may or may not even be aware of). It is important to consider whether there are reasons to suspect systematic biases in the survival of certain records. Are documents missing that are particularly damaging to certain individuals or groups? Following a change of presidential administrations, are some types of archives destroyed or misplaced? Are published letters to the editor representative of all letters that were received? Schoeneman and Rubanowitz (1985) cautioned that when analyzing the contents of advice columns, they could not avoid the possibility of a preselection bias, since advice columnists print only a fraction of the letters they receive. As one prominent group of researchers has commented, when one examines archival data, "the gnawing reality remains that archives have been produced for someone else and by someone else" (Webb et al., 1981, p. 140).

In addition to problems arising from selective deposit and survival, the researcher using archival sources must be aware of possible errors in the record keeping and changes over time in the manner in which the records were kept. It is important to demonstrate that the record keeping was relatively constant and stable over the period of the study. When running records are kept, there is always the possibility that the definitions of categories have been changed midstream. For example, had the U.S. National Transportation Safety Board made important changes in the definition of "noncommercial" aircraft during the period of Phillips's (1978) study, it would have seriously affected the statistics he used to implicate murder-suicides in aircraft fatalities.

Although archives represent nonreactive measures of behavior, their classification as such applies only to archival analysis; it does not imply that reactivity was not a problem when the archive was produced. Statements made by public figures and printed in newspapers or reported by other media must be evaluated for their reactive components. Politicians and others who are constantly exposed to media publicity no doubt learn how to use the media, and their public stance may not match their private views. Lau and Russell (1980) had to consider whether the public statements made by players and coaches about a team's performance were really the same as those they made in private. They concluded that differences between public and private statements of attribution no doubt existed but these differences do not invalidate their generalization of laboratory findings to real-world settings. The only way to control for reactive effects in archival data is to be aware that they may exist and, when possible, to seek other forms of corroborative evidence.

Yet another problem in the analysis of archival data is identifying spurious relationships. A **spurious relationship** exists when evidence falsely indicates that two or more variables are associated. Such evidence may be the result of inadequate or improper statistical treatment. This problem may exist in studies showing a relationship between frequency of deaths and important occasions. Although many people appear to endorse the view that individuals can somehow prolong their life in order to experience certain important events, such as birthdays, Schulz and Bazerman (1980) reanalyzed data from several studies to show that supportive evidence may be the result of statistical artifacts—for example, the way in which the period of time before and after a death was measured. This reanalysis of the data eliminated any evidence for the death-dip hypothesis. These researchers also reanalyzed data from other studies supporting the death-dip and death-rise hypotheses and showed how statistical artifacts could account for the results. Nevertheless, Schulz and Bazerman suggested that data supporting the death-dip hypothesis "may well be within reach if we use the proper methodologies and carefully select important events" (p. 261).

Spurious relationships can also exist when variables are accidentally or coincidentally related. This is sometimes the case when changes in two variables are the result of another, usually unknown, third variable. For instance, it has been noted that ice cream sales and the crime rate are positively correlated. However, before concluding that eating ice cream prompts people to commit crimes, it is important to consider the fact that both variables are affected by increases in temperature; neither eating ice cream nor committing a crime directly affects the other.

Several studies (e.g., Baron & Reiss, 1985) have been done to determine whether Phillips's (1983) finding of a relationship between heavyweight prizefights and homicides in the United States is a spurious one. Critics have suggested that statistical artifacts are present; others have questioned whether important variables were controlled. Baron and Reiss, for instance, suggested that the third-day peak, which Phillips (1983) admitted he could not readily interpret, was quite possibly due to the occurrence of holidays or weekends near prizefight dates or even to fluctuations in the unemployment rate. Nevertheless, extensive reanalysis of Phillips's original data has tended to reaffirm a link between violence portrayed in the media and violence acted out in society (Miller, Heath, Molcan, & Dugoni, 1991; Phillips & Bollen, 1985).

There is no easy way to deal with spurious relationships except to gather, from independent sources, additional data that will help confirm a relationship and to subject the available archival data to more than one kind of analysis. This often is no easy task and explains why, as we have noted on more than one occasion, that researchers are appropriately cautious when giving their final conclusions about the outcome of an archival study. As one last example, consider the problems associated with interpreting the outcome of archival studies examining the relationship between temperature and aggression (Anderson, 1989).

Psychologists frequently have used archival records of temperatures and of frequencies of aggressive or violent acts—such as assaults, rapes, and homicides—in order to test the hypothesis that aggression increases with increases in temperature. Data supporting the temperature-aggression hypothesis have been around for years. Nevertheless, researchers have also been aware of possible artifacts of tests of this hypothesis. For example, is aggression more likely when people are outdoors, interacting in groups (shopping, playing sports, taking vacations)? If this is the case, and if we assume people are more likely to be outside in the warmer months, then a relation between temperature and aggression may be a spurious one. Temperature and violence would not be directly related but accounted for by some third variable such as opportunity for outdoor activities (Anderson, 1989). You may recognize this argument as a variation on the ice cream sales–crime rate relationship we mentioned earlier. Researchers have responded to this criticism by looking at a wide variety of measures, collected during different historical periods and across cultures. The relationship between temperature and aggression was similar in these studies, making an alternative explanation less plausible (Anderson, 1989).

The manner in which spurious relationships appear can be illustrated with another set of data collected to test the temperature-aggression hypothesis. One way to test this hypothesis is to examine frequency of violent acts as a

FIGURE 5.4   Summaries of data relevant to tests of the temperature-aggression hypothesis. Data on the bottom show monthly distribution of assaults; data on the top describe monthly distribution of homicides. (From Anderson, 1989.)

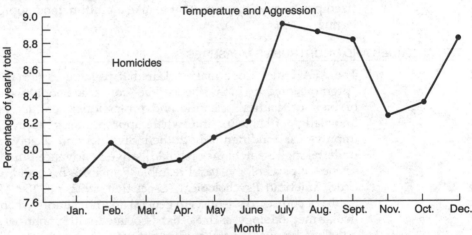

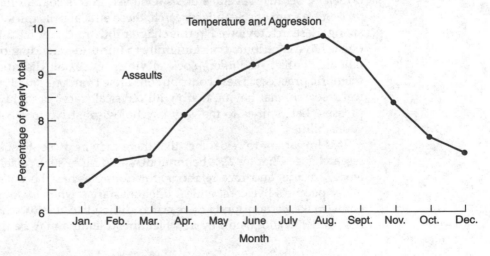

function of month of the year, the expectation being that violent acts will be most frequent during the hottest months of the year, such as July and August. Anderson (1989) summarized the results of several studies that looked at this relationship. On the bottom of Figure 5.4, you can see data revealing the frequency of assaults across the 12 months of the year. The data in this figure appear to support the temperature-aggression hypothesis: Frequency of assaults is least during the cold months and peaks during July and August. Now look at the data on the top of Figure 5.4. In this graph the monthly frequencies of homicides are graphed. The frequencies of homicides and assaults are similar for the first few months of the year and, in fact, July and August reveal peak periods for both kinds of violent acts. However, the frequency of homicides is also very high in the cold month of December. Is the temperature-aggression hypothesis invalidated? Or is there an artifact in these data? One artifact has been mentioned, namely, that homicides increase in December due to an increase in family disputes during the holidays (Anderson, 1989). Researchers must be constantly alert to possible artifacts in a data set. As we have emphasized previously, it is important to take a multimethod approach to hypothesis testing.

ETHICAL ISSUES AND UNOBTRUSIVE MEASURES

The APA Ethics Code makes clear that psychologists have an obligation to "promote integrity in the science," be "concerned about the ethical compliance of their colleagues' scientific and professional conduct," seek to "broaden knowledge of behavior and, where appropriate, to apply it pragmatically to improve the condition of both the individual and society." Moreover, "when undertaking research, they [should] strive to advance human welfare and the science of psychology" (see Preamble, Principles B, C, and F, of the *APA Ethics Code*; American Psychological Association, 1992, pp. 1599–1600). These goals apply, of course, to scientists in general and not simply when they use one particular methodology, such as that associated with unobtrusive measures. Nevertheless, because several studies reviewed in this chapter highlight nicely the *proactive* nature of scientific research, these ethical principles are worth emphasizing. Research reviewed in this chapter illustrates, for instance, how psychologists have contributed meaningfully to our understanding of suicide, race relations, conflict resolution, societal violence, sexual discrimination, and fair scientific practices. These contributions arise from one small part of psychological research, that having to do with physical traces or archival data. This impressive list testifies to the way psychologists strive to meet their ethical responsibilities.

It is important to remember that there may be a cost to society of *not* doing research (see Chapter 2). A better understanding of such social problems as violence, suicide, and race relations, for example, has the potential to improve many people's lives. Yet ethical dilemmas arise when serious risks to participants make certain kinds of research difficult to justify when considering a risk/benefit ratio. One way in which this dilemma may be resolved is to seek alternative, low-risk methods of data collection (see Chapter 2). In the present chapter, you have seen how research can be carried out on important psychological problems under conditions where ethical issues are often minimal relative to more intrusive methods. Thus, in some situations, unobtrusive measures may represent an important low-risk methodology for research on important social issues.

SUMMARY

Unobtrusive measures such as physical traces and archival data are important alternatives to direct observation and surveys. Physical traces are the remnants, fragments, and products of past behavior. Physical-use traces are based on the accumulation of evidence (accretion measures) or are the result of selective wear (erosion measures). Furthermore, use traces can either result naturally, without any intervention by the investigator, or be planned by the investigator. Physical traces may provide important nonreactive (unobtrusive) measures of behavior and can be used as the sole dependent variable or in combination with other measures of behavior. Multimethod approaches to the study of behavior are particularly recommended because they reduce the chance that results are due to some artifact of the measurement process. In obtaining physical traces, an investigator must be aware of possible biases in the way in which traces accumulate or survive over time.

Archival data are found in records and documents that recount the activities of individuals, institutions, governments, and other groups. These sources of information are valuable because they provide a way of investigating the external validity of laboratory findings, assessing the effect of a "natural treatment" (such as a political assassination), analyzing the content of communications, and describing trends. Archival records are nonreactive measures of behavior and, like physical traces, can be used in multimethod approaches to hypothesis testing. The analysis of archival data typically requires some form of content analysis, a process that can involve problems of sampling and coding not unlike those that arise in the analysis of narrative records (see Chapter 3). Problems of selective deposit and selective survival must be investigated when archival data are used, and evidence should be presented showing that observed relationships are not spurious.

Unobtrusive measures can be an important alternative to more intrusive methodologies, permitting psychologists to do research on important issues with minimal risk to the participants.

KEY CONCEPTS

unobtrusive measures
physical traces
archival data
multimethod approach

content analysis
selective deposit
selective survival
spurious relationship

REVIEW QUESTIONS

1 What characteristic of physical traces and archival data makes them especially attractive alternatives to the direct observation and survey method of measuring?

2 Why are multimethod approaches to hypothesis testing recommended?

3 What are the different kinds of physical-trace measures used by psychologists, and in what ways do they differ?

4 What possible sources of bias exist when physical-use traces are the dependent variable in a research study, and how can the validity of these measures be verified?

5 Identify and give an example of one of the four reasons for using archival data.

6 What dimensions distinguish the various types of archival sources used by psychologists?

7 What three basic steps must be taken in any research in which content analysis is done?

8 Explain the role of precise operational definitions in content analysis, and give one example of a quantitative unit and one example of a qualitative unit of measurement in content analysis.

9 Identify and give an example of the problems that researchers must be aware of when they make use of archival sources.

10 Explain the two ways in which evidence indicating spurious relationships most often arises.

CHALLENGE QUESTIONS

1 Suggest two sources of archival data for each of the following variables. Be sure to specify an operational definition of each variable.
A Public's interest in cultural events
B Students' political attitudes
C Community concern about crime
D Amount of mobility in a corporation
E Citizens' attitudes toward their schools
F Ethnic grouping of neighborhoods
G Current fads in dress

2 For each of the following archival sources, specify two kinds of data that might be useful in a psychological study. Once again, be sure to specify the operational definition that could be used for the variable you have identified.
A Weekly newsmagazine
B Television soap operas
C Classified section of newspaper
D Annual city budgets
E Student yearbooks
F List of donors to a university
G Television commercials

3 A bright female graduate student in psychology has been offered a job with both *Newsweek* and *Time*. The salary offers of the two companies are basically the same, and it appears that both the working conditions and the job responsibilities are similar. To help her decide which job to accept, she resolves to determine whether one magazine has a better attitude toward women than the other. She appeals to you to

help her with a content analysis of these two newsmagazines. What specific advice would you give her regarding each of the following steps of her content analysis?

A Sampling

B Coding

C Reliability

D Quantitative and qualitative measures

4 An educational specialist was convinced that schoolyard fights among young boys were more violent than those among young girls. To gather evidence relevant to her hypothesis, she checked the records at the nurse's office of her school. She found that, of the 100 injuries resulting from fights reported to the school nurse, 75% involved boys and only 25% involved girls. The investigator was convinced on the basis of these findings that her hypothesis was correct. Criticize this conclusion by showing how these very same findings could result if exactly the opposite of the investigator's hypothesis were true—namely, that fights among young girls are more violent. (Be sure to confine your answer to the adequacy of the data that the investigator has presented to support her conclusion.)

5 A researcher wishes to test the hypothesis that children attending private grade schools are not as "dirty-minded" as students attending public grade schools. He chooses two schools (one a parochial school and one public) that are located in the same neighborhood, approximately a mile apart. Both schools include grades 1 through 8. To test the hypothesis, the investigator decides to use measures both of natural accretion and of controlled accretion. Specifically, he operationally defines "dirty-mindedness" as the number of obscene words (from a predetermined list) found in the rest rooms of each school. The natural accretion measure is simply the number of new target words appearing on the walls of the rest rooms at the end of each week. As a measure of controlled accretion, the investigator obtains permission from the school authorities to place pads of paper and pencils in the toilet stalls of the rest rooms at each school. On each pad of paper is written "Leave me a note." At the end of each week the investigator replaces the pad with a fresh one and examines the pages that have been written on for the appearance of obscene words.

A Comment on possible problems of selective deposit and survival for the physical-trace measures proposed in this study.

B Frame questions that might be asked concerning the external validity of this study.

C Suggest ways in which the investigator might use a multimethod approach to this problem.

ANSWER TO CHALLENGE QUESTION 1

The sources of archival data listed here for each of the variables represent only illustrations and not definitive answers. Operational definitions are only sketched here; they should be developed more fully through discussion in class.

A Public's interest in cultural events—attendance figures for theater and concerts in the past calendar year; membership lists of organizations that support cultural events.

B Students' political attitudes—records of participation by students at local, state, and national conventions; membership lists of organizations that advocate political positions.

C Community concern about crime—police records of all calls reporting "suspicious" activities in the community; sales records for locks, burglar alarms, and firearms.

D Amount of mobility in a corporation—company records of average time spent by employees in various positions; company records with annual lists of promotions within the company.

E Citizens' attitudes toward their schools—records of the election results for tax increase requests for schools, including number of tax votes that passed and number of times each had to come up for a vote; membership lists for parent-teacher organizations with the implication that active participation suggests positive attitudes.

F Ethnic grouping of neighborhoods—analysis of the ethnic origins of the names in neighborhood phone directories; city licensing records for restaurants and food stores in the neighborhoods.

G Current fads in dress—sales records for selected articles of clothing that typify a particular fad; magazine, newspaper, and television advertisements for clothing.

Part

III

Experimental Methods

Independent Groups Designs

Outline

Psychologists use the experimental method to construct artificial situations (usually in the laboratory) to isolate the process they want to investigate. For instance, imagine you are observing adults while they are reading. Would you be able to tell whether the people were saying the words to themselves as they read silently? Most adult readers don't move their lips when reading and thus it is unlikely you could tell if they were saying words silently to themselves. The process you are interested in is literally unobservable. Haber and Haber (1982) constructed a situation in which they were able to study this unobservable process. The term they used for the unobservable process of talking to oneself while reading was *subvocal articulation*. They gave college students two types of sentences to read, tongue twisters (Francis Forbes's father fries five flounders) and control sentences that were not tongue twisters (Mary Wright's uncle cooks red lobsters). Haber and Haber reasoned that, if the students did say the words to themselves as they read silently, the tongue-twister sentences would be harder to read and thus take longer to read than the control sentences. This is exactly what they found, so they concluded that we do "talk to ourselves" as we read.

Haber and Haber never did observe subvocal articulation directly. They constructed a situation in which a difference in behavior occurred as a result of a process that they presumed was occurring. The situation the researchers created allowed this process to show itself. Much of the experimental research in psychology is like that of the Haber and Haber study. Theoretical processes are proposed [*we talk to ourselves when we read*], experiments are done in which outcomes are predicted on the basis of these explanatory processes [*tongue-twister sentences should take longer to read than control sentences*], and the outcomes of the experiments are used to make decisions about the existence of these unobservable theoretical processes [*since the tongue-twister sentences did take longer to read, we conclude that we do talk to ourselves when we read*]. The role of theories in psychological research was discussed in Chapter 1. In the next few chapters we explore how the experimental method is used to test psychological theories.

In the present chapter we discuss the most commonly used experimental design—the random groups design. We introduce you to the underlying logic of this design, the procedures for forming random groups, the ways in which the external validity of experiments can be established, and the challenges to internal validity that apply specifically to the random groups design. Two alternative experimental designs involving independent groups also are considered: the matched groups design and the natural groups design. We conclude this chapter by describing how the results of experiments are analyzed. Statistical analysis gives us the evidence we need to decide if our experiment worked to reveal the process we are investigating.

CHARACTERISTICS OF EXPERIMENTS

In previous chapters we discussed research methods that serve primarily to fulfill the descriptive and predictive functions of the science of psychology. Psychologists use observational methods to develop detailed descriptions of behavior, often in natural settings. Survey-research methods allow psychologists to describe people's attitudes and opinions. Successful prediction is achieved when we discover that measures of behavior covary reliably; for instance, people who have many significant changes in their lives are also more stressed. The analysis of archival data provides a nonreactive means of obtaining converging evidence to enhance the validity of descriptions of behavior based on observation and survey research. As essential as they are to the scientific study of behavior, description and prediction are not sufficient. Psychologists also seek understanding—the "why" behind the "what" of behavior. Scientific understanding is achieved when the causes of a phenomenon have been identified. Chapters 6, 7, and 8 focus on the best available research method for specifying causal relationships—the experimental method.

The distinction between experimental methods and descriptive research methods should not be drawn too sharply. Observation, survey research, and archival data can certainly contribute to our understanding of the causes of behavior. In a real sense, experiments are a kind of structured observation. Field experiments and longitudinal designs in survey research also embody the principles of the experimental methods, although we have discussed them in the context of descriptive research methods. Similarly, experimental methods can be used effectively to develop accurate descriptions of behavior, especially when the methods are applied to practical research problems such as those involving the effectiveness of a behavior modification program (see Chapter 9).

As we have emphasized repeatedly, the best overall approach to research is the multimethod approach (see Chapters 1 and 5). If we obtain comparable answers to a research question after using different methods to study it, our confidence in our conclusions increases. Our conclusions are then said to have *convergent validity*. Each method has different shortcomings, but the methods have complementary strengths that overcome these shortcomings. The experimental method, however, is especially effective in establishing cause-and-effect relationships.

An experiment involves the *manipulation* of one or more factors and *measurement* of the effects of this manipulation on behavior. The factors that the researcher controls or manipulates are called the **independent variables**. The measures used to assess the effect (if any) of the independent variables are called **dependent variables**. When Haber and Haber (1982) investigated subvocal articulation, they manipulated the independent variable of the type of sentence students read (tongue twister or control). The dependent variable was the length of time it took students to read each sentence.

There are many ways to distinguish experiments done properly from those done improperly. We have chosen to emphasize four characteristics to evaluate whether an experiment has been done properly: internal validity, reliability, sensitivity, and external validity. An experiment that has *internal validity* is one in which cause and effect is interpretable—that is, one can conclude that manipulating the independent variable caused a change in the dependent variable and other plausible causes for the outcome have been ruled out. The purpose of an experiment is to produce a difference in behavior; thus, a *reliable experiment* is one in which the obtained difference is likely to be found again if the experiment is repeated. Independent variables differ in terms of how large an effect they have on behavior. For example, when students read tongue twisters there may be an increase in reading time over that when reading control sentences, as Haber and Haber found; however, an even larger mean difference in reading time might have been found had the experimenters compared students' reading sentences forward and backward. A *sensitive experiment* is one likely to detect the effect of an independent variable even when that effect is a small one. The findings of an experiment that has *external validity* can be generalized to individuals, settings, and conditions beyond the scope of the specific experiment. That is, questions of external validity ask whether the findings observed in an experiment would be observed when other individuals participate, when other settings and conditions are used.

You will want to learn ways to enhance each of these characteristics in the experiments you do. However, there are many challenges because these four important characteristics of a good experiment cannot always be maximized simultaneously. For instance, the procedures that increase the sensitivity of an experiment can reduce its external validity. Thus, planning an experiment is something of a juggling act. In what follows you'll find directions for managing this complex task.

WHY PSYCHOLOGISTS CONDUCT EXPERIMENTS

A major purpose of conducting experiments is to provide an empirical test of hypotheses derived from psychological theories (see Chapter 1). If the results of the experiment are consistent with what is expected from the hypothesis, then the proposed explanation receives support. If the results are not what had been expected, then the proposed explanation may need to be modified and a new hypothesis developed and tested in the next experiment. The process of conducting experiments to test even a single hypothesis can be a long and painstaking one. Hypothesis testing is also not a process that provides definitive conclusions. It can thus be frustrating for a person who wants to know all the answers right away. The self-correcting nature of the interplay between experiments and proposed explanations, however, does provide a challenging and satisfying approach to understanding the causes of the way we think, feel, and behave.

The relationship between experiments and proposed explanations can be illustrated using research by social psychologists on the topic of social loafing. Latané, Williams, and Harkin (1979) defined social loafing as "a decrease in individual effort due to the social presence of others" (p. 823). Social loafing has been studied using simple, but physically exerting, tasks such as rope pulling (see Figure 6.1 for a real-life illustration of this task), hand clapping, or shouting. Latané et al. used shouting in their experiments on social loafing. The participants were told that the purpose of the study was to investigate how much noise people make in social settings. The participants were told that their task throughout the experiment was to shout as loudly as they could. If you were participating in this experiment, you would be one of six participants sitting in a semicircle. The researchers would tell you that you would be blindfolded and would wear headphones over which recordings of people shouting would be played throughout the experiment. The researchers would explain that they were doing this because they want to study how loudly people shout when their sensory feedback is reduced. Another reason for using blindfolds was so that participants could not see whether other participants were shouting. Moreover, the headphones with the recorded shouting being played over them prevented participants from hearing themselves shout or from hearing the other participants shouting.

The independent variable in the experiment involved the instructions participants were given. They were instructed either that they were shouting alone or they were shouting together with the others in the semicircle. The dependent variable in the experiment was a measure of how loudly the participants shouted. The participants who thought they were shouting alone shouted louder than the participants who thought the other five were shouting with them. Individual effort was less in the group than when alone, thus demonstrating social loafing.

One proposed explanation of social loafing is based on the idea of individual accountability. Many of us make less of an effort when our work cannot be

FIGURE 6.1   What effect does working in a group have on the individual efforts of these students who are participating in the annual Hope College "Pull"?

individually evaluated. Social loafing is presumed to occur because working in a group makes the individual's work less identifiable. To test this proposed explanation, Williams, Harkin, and Latané (1981) did another shouting experiment in which the independent variable was whether or not the participants wore a microphone. The participants were told that with the individual microphones the researchers could monitor each person's contribution to the group output when they were shouting together. Thus, the participants were aware that their individual performances were identifiable.

The experimenters compared the performance of participants who were wearing individual microphones while they were shouting with those who were not wearing microphones. The dependent variable was the measured loudness of shouting. The hypothesis tested was that participants who wore microphones (and believed they were being overheard) would shout as loudly in a group as when alone—they would not show social loafing. Those who did not wear microphones (and who did not believe their shouting was being recorded), however, were expected to show social loafing. The results were consistent with the hypothesis. Social loafing did occur when participants did not wear microphones, and social loafing did not occur when participants did wear individual microphones. This finding supports the proposed explanation that individual accountability (or lack thereof) contributes to the phenomenon of social loafing.

Besides providing empirical tests of proposed explanations derived from theories, experiments can be used to test the effectiveness of a treatment or program. As Thomas (1992) reminds us, this role of experiments has a long history. He describes, for instance, how experiments were used to determine the effectiveness of some early medical treatments. Near the beginning of the nineteenth century, typhoid fever and delirium tremens were often fatal. The standard medical practice at that time was to treat these two conditions by bleeding, purging, and the administration of other, similar "therapies." An experiment was performed to test the effectiveness of these supposedly beneficial treatments. One group was randomly assigned to receive the standard treatment of the day, and a second group was randomly assigned to receive nothing but bed rest, good nutrition, and close observation. Thomas describes the results of this experiment as "unequivocal and appalling" (p. 9): The group given the standard medical treatment of the time did *worse* than the group left untreated. Treating such conditions in the way they were treated in the early nineteenth century was worse than not treating them at all. Experiments such as these contributed to the insight that many medical conditions are self-limited; the illness runs its course, and patients recover on their own. Many psychological disorders also will disappear when left untreated, a process known as spontaneous remission. As you will see in Chapters 9 and 10, well-conducted experiments can provide vital information about the effectiveness of treatments and programs in a wide variety of areas. Experiments serve a useful purpose not only when we are testing theories but also when we are making decisions in practical situations.

EXPERIMENTAL CONTROL

The primary reason that experiments are so effective for testing hypotheses is that they allow us to exercise a relatively high degree of control. Control is used in experiments primarily to meet the conditions necessary for a causal inference, that is, to be able to state with confidence that the independent variable caused the observed changes in the dependent variable. These three conditions are covariation, time order, and elimination of plausible alternative causes. The internal validity of an experiment is established when the conditions for a causal inference are met. The covariation condition is met when we observe systematic changes in the dependent variable as a function of the manipulated independent variable. For example, when Haber and Haber (1982) manipulated the tongue-twister and control sentences, the time it took students to read the sentences differed. When we manipulate an independent variable in an experiment we change it *before* we measure the changes in the dependent variable. Thus, the time-order condition will be met when manipulation is used and a subsequent change in behavior is observed.

Manipulation, holding conditions constant, and *balancing* are the three types of control used in experiments. As we have just seen, psychologists use the control technique of manipulation when they vary systematically the independent variable prior to measuring changes in behavior (dependent variable). Nevertheless, the most challenging condition necessary for a causal inference is eliminating plausible alternative causes. Holding conditions constant and balancing are two control techniques we can use to assure that this critical condition for a causal inference is met. These control techniques can be illustrated using another social loafing experiment done by Williams et al. (1981).

The purpose of their experiment was to make an additional test of the individual accountability explanation of social loafing. The dependent variable in this experiment was again how loudly the participants shouted. By manipulating the instructions they gave their participants, they varied the accountability of the participants. Three different sets of instructions were used; each set of instructions was used with a different group of participants. Thus, their independent variable had three levels. The first set of instructions indicated that the experimenters could monitor each participant's shouting when the participant shouted alone but not when others were shouting (the "identifiable-only-when-alone" group). The second group was told that the experimenters were able to monitor each participant's shouting both when the participant shouted alone and in a group (the "always-identifiable" group). Instructions given to the third group indicated that the experimenters could not monitor each participant's shouting either when the participant shouted alone or in a group (the "never-identifiable" group).

Results of the experiment showed, first, that social loafing occurred in the identifiable-only-when-alone group. When participants believed their shouting with the group was not being evaluated they exhibited less effort in the task. In the always-identifiable group, there was no social loafing. As expected, when people knew they were being evaluated they did not slack off. Finally, in the never-identifiable group, there was a low and equal level of shouting whether the participants shouted alone or in groups. That is, participants "loafed" even when alone. Can you see how these results (along with the microphone experiment) support the individual accountability explanation of social loafing?

The results of an experiment involving a manipulated independent variable permit a causal inference only if the independent variable is the only factor that makes the groups different. Williams et al. (1981) used the technique of *holding conditions constant* to make sure the independent variable of instructions was the only factor that systematically varied across groups. For example, participants in all three groups were tested in the same soundproof room. All of the participants were blindfolded so they could not see each other, and they wore headsets over which the experimenters played loud shouting such that the participants could not hear themselves shout. The instructions for all three groups included the same statement that the experimenters wanted the participants to make as "much noise as you can." Only males participated in this experiment, thereby holding the gender of the participants constant.

If the three groups had differed on a factor other than the instructional manipulation, then the results of the experiment would have been uninterpretable. For example, if the participants in the always-identifiable group had not worn headphones while the participants in the other two groups had worn them, then the groups would have differed not just in terms of the instructions they received but also in terms of whether they wore headphones. Thus, participants without headphones would have been able to hear if other participants were shouting; those wearing headphones could not have heard the other participants because they would have heard only the recorded shouting through their headphones. When the independent variable of interest and a different, potential independent variable are allowed to covary, a **confounding** is present. Control techniques are used to avoid confoundings. By holding wearing of the headphones constant across conditions of their experiment, Williams et al. avoided a confounding. A factor that is held constant (i.e., does not change) cannot possibly covary with the intended independent variable.

It is important to recognize, however, that we choose to control only those factors we think might influence the behavior we are studying—what we consider *plausible* alternative causes. For instance, Williams et al. (1981) controlled what participants could see by blindfolding them and what participants could hear by having them wear headphones. The researchers held these conditions constant because they thought these conditions could influence social loafing. They also held the setting constant by testing all their participants in the same room, but it is unlikely that they monitored the room temperature to be sure it stayed constant because room temperature probably would not affect social loafing (at least when varying only a few degrees). The point of this brief discussion is to emphasize that we control only those factors we believe are potentially relevant. Nevertheless, we should constantly remain alert to the possibility that there may be confounding factors in our experiments whose influence we had not anticipated or considered.

The control technique of *balancing* is required because not all the factors we want to control can be held constant. The most important factor in psychological research that cannot be held constant is the characteristics of the participants who are tested. Individual differences among participants cannot be eliminated. Therefore, an experimenter must find a way to make sure these subject characteristics do not confound the independent variable being investigated. In an **independent groups design,** each group represents a different condition as defined by the level of the independent variable. The experiments on social loafing we have been discussing are examples of independent groups designs: The independent variable of type of instructions varied across groups of participants. It is important in the independent groups design to balance individual differences among the participants in the different groups of the experiment. That is, we must make sure one group is not smarter, more motivated, more conscientious, contains more females, has fewer psychology majors, and so forth, than another group. Exactly how this is done is the major topic of the next section where we examine the most commonly used design involving independent groups of subjects: the random groups design.

Before turning to the next topic, however, consider one other characteristic of the methodology used in this series of social loafing experiments: The experimental manipulations involved deception because the experimenters could actually monitor shouting in all conditions even when participants were told they could not be monitored. That is, the participants in some conditions of the experiments were purposely misled to have them believe no one was evaluating their behavior. Of course, the researchers did record their performance to compare it with that of participants in other conditions of the experiment. We can assume that the researchers would argue deception was necessary in order for the phenomenon of social loafing to be investigated in this manner. If participants knew they were being evaluated, then, by definition, they would know they were individually accountable. Thus, their lack of individual accountability could no longer be the basis for an important comparison group. Whether the use of deception was justified in this case was a decision left up to an ethics committee that reviewed a proposal of this research before it was conducted. As you learned in Chapter 2, debriefing of participants is always necessary when deception is used in order to help the participants understand the reasons why they were deceived and to clear up any misunderstandings that might arise from their role in the experiment. How do you feel about the use of deception in psychology experiments? Does the experimenters' use of deception in these social loafing experiments seem justified?

RANDOM GROUPS DESIGN

RANDOM ASSIGNMENT

The simplest experiments involve two conditions. That is, individuals participate in two levels of one independent variable. The effect of the independent variable is assessed by observing the difference in the dependent variable between these two levels. As we have seen, in the independent groups design, a different group of subjects participates in each level. In an experiment done by Loftus and Burns (1982), for example, one group of participants was assigned to view a violent version of a film while a second group of participants viewed a nonviolent version of the same film. Both groups were then tested for their memory of details included in the films. The logic of the design is straightforward. *If* the two groups are comparable on all important characteristics at the start of the experiment *and if*, in the experiment itself, the two groups are treated the same *except* for the level of the independent variable (e.g., violent or nonviolent film), *then*, any difference in the performance (e.g., memory for details) of the two groups must be due to the independent variable.

Clearly, one key to this logic behind the experimental method is forming comparable groups. In the **random groups design,** comparable groups are formed prior to the introduction of the independent variable. This is accomplished by sampling subjects in a way that ensures that each subject has an equal likelihood of being included in each group of the experiment. One possible procedure for accomplishing this goal is random selection, as, for example, when we sample randomly from a registrar's list of students to obtain a representative sample of students for a survey (see Chapter 4). Actually, random selection is rarely used to establish comparable groups in a psychology experiment. Random selection requires well-defined populations (e.g., a registrar's list of students), but psychology experiments usually involve accidental samples from ill-defined populations. For example, human adult participants are often students from introductory psychology courses who volunteer for experiments as part of the course. Individuals enrolled in a general psychology course just happen to be those students who are taking this course in a given quarter or semester on a particular day at some specified time. Similarly, animal subjects typically are those that happen to be shipped to the researcher by a supplier. The animal researcher may not be aware of the precise nature of the population from which the animals were obtained or how they were selected.

The most common solution to the problem of forming comparable groups when ill-defined populations are involved is to use **random assignment** to place subjects in the conditions of the experiment. A closer look at the details of the Loftus and Burns experiment illustrates both the procedures of random assignment and the power of the random groups design. Their experiment concerned the effect of viewing a violent scene on a person's memory for information in the film that was presented seconds before the individual witnessed the mentally shocking event. The experiment was done at the University of Washington, and 226 students volunteered to participate in order to fulfill a course requirement. The students participated in small groups, and each small group was randomly assigned to view one of two films. Approximately half of the students (115) were assigned to view a violent version of a film. Near the end of the film, these students saw a robber, while running to a getaway car, turn and fire a shot toward two men who were pursuing him. The shot hit a boy in the face, and the boy fell bleeding to the ground. The other half of the students viewed a nonviolent version of the film that was identical to the violent version until just before the shooting. At this point in the film, the camera switched back to inside the bank, where the students saw the bank manager telling the customers and employees what happened and asking them to remain calm. The two versions of the film (violent and nonviolent) represent the levels of the independent variable in the experiment.

After viewing the film, students in both groups were asked to answer 25 questions about events in the film. One question was critical: It asked for the number on the football jersey worn by a boy playing in the parking lot outside the bank. The boy wearing the jersey (see Figure 6.2) was visible for 2 seconds during the film—the 2 seconds before the shooting (violent version) or the 2 seconds before the scenes back in the bank (nonviolent version). The dependent

FIGURE 6.2   Black-and-white representation of scene viewed by subjects, showing boy with the number 17 on his football jersey. (From Loftus and Burns, 1982.)

variable was the percentage of students who correctly recalled the jersey number. The results were clear-cut: Just over 4% of the students correctly recalled the number in the violent condition, whereas nearly 28% did so in the nonviolent condition. Thus, Loftus and Burns concluded that an emotionally shocking event can impair memory for details immediately preceding the event.

The major benefit of randomly assigning subjects to groups is to balance or average out the characteristics of the subjects in the two groups. For example, if the groups of participants viewing the two versions of the film differed in memory ability, then we could reasonably argue that the difference found in the experiment was simply due to this characteristic of the participants and not due to the type of film that was viewed. However, because the two samples of over 100 students in the Loftus and Burns experiment were randomly assigned to conditions, they are unlikely to differ (on the average) in memory ability, in attentiveness, or in any other way that might influence their performance on the memory test.

The balancing accomplished through random assignment was not the only control technique that Loftus and Burns used in their experiment. For instance, the equipment used to present the films, the quality of the films, the instructions given prior to showing the films, the tone of voice used by the experimenter in giving these instructions, and any other factors that could be controlled by being held constant were identical in the two conditions of the experiment. And, of course, Loftus and Burns controlled the independent variable of type of film by manipulating the violent and nonviolent versions of the film. Because other potential causal factors were controlled by holding them constant and because individual differences among the students in the two groups were controlled by balancing them using random assignment, we can conclude that the different versions of the film caused the difference in students' performance.

A common procedure for carrying out random assignment is block randomization. First we describe exactly how block randomization is carried out and then look at what it accomplishes. A "block" is made up of a random order of all of the conditions of the experiment. In block randomization, a subject is assigned to *each* group before a second subject is assigned to *any* one group. That is, we assign subjects to conditions one block at a time. For example, if we want to have 20 subjects in each of five groups, then there would be 20 blocks in the block-randomized schedule. Each block would consist of a random arrangement of the five conditions. You might think of this procedure as one where you take the first five people who show up for an experiment and assign each one randomly to one of the five conditions, then take the next five people and assign each to one of the five conditions, and so on, until you have done this 20 times.

Block randomization is an important technique for randomly assigning subjects to groups because it produces groups that are of equal size while controlling for time-related variables. The number of observations in each group influences the reliability of the descriptive statistics for each group. Because you will be comparing descriptive statistics across groups in your experiment, you want these measures to be of comparable reliability. So, each group should be of equal size. As we have just seen, block randomization accomplishes this. Also, because subjects are assigned to conditions one block at a time, events that occur during the time when the experiment is being done are likely to be experienced by equal numbers of subjects in all conditions of the experiment. This is important because experiments often take a substantial amount of time to complete, and events affecting the behavior of participants can occur during the conduct of the experiment.

For example, suppose you are doing a Loftus-and-Burns-type experiment that requires 100 participants assigned randomly to four conditions. Assume further you are drawing participants from introductory psychology classes. Given the availability of participants and your own personal schedule, such an experiment may take several weeks to complete. What if, after beginning the experiment, an instructor in one of the introductory psychology classes happens to describe the Loftus and Burns experiment? An experiment just like yours! Some students participating in your experiment may now recognize the film of the bank robbery and be prepared for a memory test, which could affect their performance. If all those with prior knowledge ended up in one particular experimental condition, this would produce a serious confounding. Although this is not a desirable situation, the beauty of block randomization is that it will balance any effect of participants' prior knowledge across the conditions of your experiment. That is, participants from that particular introductory psychology class will be randomly assigned to all of the conditions of your experiment in approximately equal numbers. Thus, although there may be more variability in the groups' performances (which, you will see, is not a good thing), you will avoid a confounding. Block randomization works to balance other time-related variables, such as changes in experimenters or even changes in the populations from which subjects are drawn. An experiment conducted across two semesters of a school year, drawing participants from both fall and spring semester classes, would be perfectly acceptable if a block randomization schedule was used.

The procedure of block randomization, like many procedures, is best learned by doing it. You can get an idea of what using block randomization is like by doing Challenge Question 1A at the end of the chapter.

ESTABLISHING EXTERNAL VALIDITY

Although random assignment is the most commonly used procedure for carrying out a random groups design, it does not provide representative samples that can serve as the basis for generalizing the results of an experiment beyond the particular subjects who happened to participate in the experiment. For example, we previously pointed out that participants in many psychology experiments form an accidental sample from an ill-defined population. Random assignment of subjects to conditions of an experiment *within* this accidental sample will establish comparable groups and, thus, help assure the internal validity of the experiment. But how do we establish the external validity of experiments that involve random assignment?

One answer to this question is a bit unsettling, at least initially. For some experiments we do not establish external validity. Mook (1983) has argued that, when the purpose of an experiment is to test a specific hypothesis derived from a psychological theory, the question of external validity of the findings is irrelevant. An experiment is often done to determine whether subjects *can* be induced to behave in a certain way. The question whether subjects *do* behave that way in their natural environment is secondary to the question raised in the experiment. The issue of the external validity of experiments is not a new one, as reflected in the following statement by Riley (1962, p. 413): "In general, laboratory experiments are not set up to imitate the most typical case found in nature. Instead, they are intended to answer some specific question of interest to the experimenter."

There are circumstances, however, in which it is critical to obtain results that can be generalized beyond the boundaries of the experiment itself. Ceci (1993) described a research program that he and his colleagues conducted on children's testimony. He described how their research program was motivated in part because previous studies on this topic did not capture all the dimensions of an *actual* eyewitness situation. He stated, "We have come to believe that the majority of cases of children's suggestibility in actual criminal investigations and acrimonious custody adjudications bear little resemblance to the research studies that have tested suggestibility for a single leading question, posed for the first time during a single interview" (p. 18). Ceci described how their research program included factors such as multiple suggestive interviews, very long retention intervals, and recollections of stressful experiences. Including these factors made the experiments more representative of situations that are actually involved in taking children's testimony.

Ceci (1993) also pointed out, however, that important differences remained between the experiments and real-life situations:

> High levels of stress, assaults to a victim's body, and the loss of control are characteristics of events that motivate forensic investigations. Although these factors are at play in some of our other studies, we will never mimic experimentally the assaultive nature of acts perpetrated on child victims, because even those studies that come closest, such as the medical studies, are socially and parentally sanctioned, unlike sexual assaults against children. (pp. 41–42)

As Ceci's comments reveal, in some situations, such as those involving eyewitness testimony about despicable acts, there may be important ethical constraints on establishing the external validity of experiments.

When the external validity of an experiment can be established within appropriate ethical boundaries and when external validity is a high priority for the research, a simple general rule should be followed: Include a representative sample on any dimension in your experiment to which you want to generalize your results. When that dimension is the subjects in your experiment, then random selection is preferable to random assignment.

Replication also plays a role in establishing external validity. **Replication** means repeating all of the procedures used in a particular experiment in order to determine whether the same results will be obtained a second time with different participants. Most replications are done when an initial finding is unexpected or judged to be especially important. Typically, replication is said to occur if the effect of the independent variable is present in both the original study and in the replication study. *Replication serves the important goal of providing evidence for the reliability of an experimental finding.* As you might imagine, an exact replication is almost impossible to carry out. The subjects tested in the replication necessarily will be different from those tested in the original study; the testing rooms, experimenters, and even apparatus also may be different. Thus, when attempting to replicate an experimental result, in nearly every instance the replication will be only a partial replication. *Partial replications,* however, are commonly done as a routine part of the process of investigating the conditions under which a phenomenon reliably occurs.

A partial replication can help to establish both experimental reliability (by demonstrating that a similar experimental result occurs when the same basic experimental procedures are repeated) and external validity (by showing that a similar experimental result occurs when slightly different experimental procedures are used). By repeating some but not all of the conditions of the original experiment, a researcher can provide evidence for the external validity of a finding across many critical dimensions. That is, those aspects that are changed from the original experiment represent factors that help demonstrate the external validity of the finding. For example, when the same basic experiment is done in both a large metropolitan public university and in a small rural private college, the participants and the settings in the experiments are very different, and so the two experiments represent partial replications. If the same results are obtained in these partial replications of the experiment, we can be confident that the findings are not peculiar to the particular type of participant tested or to the particular setting in which the experiment took place. The dimensions that are *not* replicated across the two experiments provide the basis for increased external validity. Notice that neither experiment alone has external validity; it is the findings that occur in both experiments that have external validity.

A frequently asked question concerning external validity of psychological research findings is related to the nature of the "subjects." As you are aware, many studies in psychology involve college students who participate in experiments as part of their introductory psychology course. Dawes (1991), among others, has argued that college students are a select group who may not always provide a good basis for building general conclusions about human behavior and mental processes. For example, Dawes argues that the college environment tends to protect students from external problems, thereby enhancing their feeling of control over their lives. People living outside the college environment may not have the same sense of control that college students do. Thus, research

FIGURE 6.3   Questions of external validity include those related to the nature of the participants in psychological research; for example, we might ask whether results of studies done with college students will generalize to people not in a college.

on "locus of control" done with college students may not generalize to people living outside the college environment. In general, the arguments raised by Dawes and others should lead us to exercise care in generalizing conclusions from studies in which college students are participants.

It would be virtually impossible to establish the external validity of each finding in psychology by performing partial replications across each of the dimensions over which we would want to generalize (e.g., subjects, settings, tasks, and so on). But if we take arguments like those of Dawes seriously, as indeed we should, it would appear that we have an impossible task in front of us. How, for instance, do we show that an experimental finding obtained with a group of college students will generalize to groups of older adults, working professionals, less educated individuals, and so forth? Underwood and Shaughnessy (1975) provide an answer, or at least an approach worth considering. Their notion is that we should assume behavior is relatively continuous across time, subjects, and settings unless we have reason to assume otherwise. For instance, most experiments are carried out in individual laboratory rooms, but we would not be likely to argue that the results of the experiment therefore apply only to those particular rooms. Similarly, the particular subjects tested in an experiment are considered, according to this reasoning, to be generally representative of other, similar individuals who might have been tested.

Underwood and Shaughnessy's (1975) assumption is not a call to blind faith in any experimental finding. The boundaries for generalizing experimental findings are set by consensus of the research community. The research community may agree, for example, that introductory psychology students who volunteer for experiments are representative of college students in general but not of young children or of the elderly. Or, agreement may be reached for some phenomena and not others. For instance, generalizing results of a memory experiment based on a college student sample may be safer than generalizing results of a locus of control experiment. Underwood and Shaughnessy have argued that the burden of proof regarding questions of external validity rests with the person claiming we should *not* generalize. Thus, in response to criticisms such as those by Dawes questioning the generalizability of results based on college students, the burden of proof rests on an empirical demonstration that results based on college students are, in fact, limited.

One way to respond to challenges of external validity is to carry out a partial replication including as an independent variable the dimension on which the generalization has been challenged. For example, Singer (1982) noted that most studies conducted on reading comprehension in the previous decade had been based on reading in a laboratory situation. He was concerned that laboratory reading might involve goals or techniques different from those used in natural reading. So, he conducted an experiment in which he asked participants who had not read a particular newspaper article to read it in the laboratory. These participants were then given a memory test that was also given to individuals who had read the article *outside* the laboratory. The two groups performed similarly on the tests, leading to Singer's conclusion: "These effects, coupled with the similarity of the natural and laboratory readers, provide reassurance that it is reasonable to treat laboratory reading as an approximation of natural reading" (p. 331). Such direct tests using partial replications represent perhaps the best way to establish the external validity of experimental findings.

CHALLENGES TO INTERNAL VALIDITY

Testing Intact Groups   Random assignment is used to assure comparable groups in the random groups design. There are times, however, when noncomparable groups are formed even when random assignment appears to have been used. This problem occurs when intact groups (and not individual subjects) are randomly assigned to the conditions of an experiment. *Intact groups* are those that were formed prior to the start of the experiment. For example, the different sections of an introductory psychology class are intact groups. The introductory psychology classes were not formed randomly. They probably meet at different times of the day, have different instructors, and differ on any number of other factors that influenced the students' choices to be in one section rather than another. Random assignment of such intact groups to experimental conditions is simply not sufficient to balance the systematic differences among the intact groups that are almost guaranteed to confound the independent variable under investigation. The solution to this problem is simple: Do not use intact groups in a random groups design. (As you will see in Chapter 10, there are situations when researchers use intact groups because random assignment of participants to conditions is not possible; however, this means the problem of confounding must be dealt with, and is always a less desirable alternative to a random groups design.)

Balancing Extraneous Variables   A number of factors in an experiment may vary as a result of practical considerations in carrying out the study. For example, in order to complete an experiment more quickly, a researcher might decide to have several different experimenters test small groups of participants. The sizes of the groups and the experimenters themselves become potentially relevant variables that could confound the experiment if their effects are not somehow balanced across conditions. If all the individuals in the experimental group are tested by one experimenter and all those in the control group are tested by another experimenter, for example, differences between the experimenters would confound the intended independent variable. One would not be able to determine whether an observed difference between the control group and experimental group on the dependent variable was due to the experimental manipulation or to the fact that different experimenters implemented the study.

Potential independent variables that are not directly of interest to the researcher but serve only as vexing sources of confounding are called **extraneous variables**. But don't let the term fool you! An experiment confounded by an extraneous variable is no less confounded than if the confounding variable were of considerable inherent interest. Evans and Donnerstein (1974) studied one such extraneous variable—the differences between participants who volunteer early in the term and those who volunteer late in the term. Their results indicated that those who volunteer early are more academically oriented and more likely to have an internal locus of control (to emphasize their own responsibility for their actions rather than to emphasize external factors). Their findings suggest it would not be wise to test a control group at the end of the term if the participants in the other conditions of the completed experiment had been tested in the first half of the term. As we have seen, block randomization should be used to balance characteristics of participants, such as those associated with "early" and "late" volunteers, across the conditions of an experiment.

Block randomization provides an easy and effective way to control numerous extraneous variables by balancing them across groups. All that is required is that entire blocks be tested at each level of the extraneous variable. For example, if there were four different experimenters, entire blocks of the block-randomized schedule would be assigned to each experimenter. Because each block contains all the conditions of the experiment, this strategy guarantees that each condition will be tested by each experimenter. Usually, we would assign the same number of blocks to each experimenter, but this is not essential. What is essential is that entire blocks be tested at each level of the extraneous variable, which, in this case, is the experimenter. The balancing act can become a bit tricky when there are several extraneous variables, but careful advance planning can avoid confounding by such factors.

Even when their potential effects have been controlled through balancing, extraneous variables affect the sensitivity and external validity of an experiment. For example, if five different experimenters test an equal number of participants in each of two conditions, the experiment will be free of confounding due to any differences across experimenters. The performance of the participants within each condition, however, is likely to vary more than if one experimenter had tested all the participants. Participants are likely, after all, to respond differently to the different experimenters, even when the experimenters try to treat all participants within a condition the same way. This increased variation within each group makes it harder to detect differences between the groups, thus reducing the sensitivity of the experiment. If a difference is obtained between the two conditions, however, this finding has greater external validity than it would have had if only one experimenter had done the testing.

This is the general principle that emerges: *Controlling extraneous variables by holding them constant leads to more sensitive experiments with less external validity, whereas controlling extraneous variables by balancing them leads to lower sensitivity but increased external validity*. Both balancing and holding extraneous variables constant are equally effective control techniques, however, in ensuring that an experiment is internally valid.

Subject Loss Internally valid experiments involving the random groups design need to have comparable groups not only at the beginning of an experiment but, except for the addition of the independent variable, also at the end.

When subjects begin an experiment but fail to complete it successfully, the internal validity of the experiment can be threatened. There are two types of subject loss: mechanical and selective. It is important to distinguish between these two ways by which subjects are lost because selective subject loss poses a threat to internal validity (Underwood & Shaughnessy, 1975).

Mechanical subject loss occurs when a subject fails to complete the experiment because of an equipment failure (in this case, the experimenter is considered part of the equipment). If a light bulb burns out, or if someone inadvertently interrupts an experimental session, or if the experimenter reads the wrong set of instructions, the subject who was being tested represents a mechanical subject loss. Mechanical loss is unrelated to any characteristic of the subject, so it should not lead to systematic differences between the characteristics of the subjects who successfully complete the experiment in the various conditions of the experiment. In a real sense, mechanical subject loss represents the effect of chance events (e.g., a projector bulb happens to burn out) and, thus, should be expected to occur equally across conditions of an experiment. Hence, internal validity is not typically threatened when data from such subjects are excluded from the experiment. When mechanical subject loss occurs, the name of the dropped subject and the reason for the loss need to be recorded. The lost subject is then replaced by the next subject tested.

Selective subject loss is a far more serious matter. **Selective subject loss** occurs when subjects are lost differentially across the conditions of the experiment and when some characteristic of the subject related to the outcome of the study is responsible for the loss. Selective subject loss destroys the comparable groups that are essential to the random groups design and can thus render the experiment uninterpretable. This problem can arise in a variety of experimental situations, for example, physiological studies involving surgical or drug treatments, memory experiments testing retention over days or weeks, and longitudinal designs in survey research (see Chapter 4).

The problems associated with selective subject loss can be illustrated by considering a fictitious but realistic example. Assume the directors of a local fitness center decide to do an experiment to test the effectiveness of a one-month fitness program they have developed. They identify 80 people who are willing to volunteer for the experiment, and they randomly assign 40 to each of two groups. Members of the control group are simply asked to come to the center at the end of the month. When they arrive, they are given a fitness test. Those in the experimental group participate in a vigorous fitness program for 1 month prior to the test at the end of the month. All 40 control subjects are given the fitness test. Only 25 of the experimental subjects stay with the rigorous fitness program for the full month, and only these 25 people are given the test. The average fitness score is significantly higher for the experimental group, leading the directors of the fitness center to make the claim that "A scientifically based research study has shown that our program leads to better fitness."

Do you think the fitness center's claim is justified? It's not. At least not on the basis of the study we have described. This hypothetical study represents a classic example of selective subject loss. The loss occurred differentially across conditions; subjects were lost only from the experimental group. The problem is not that the groups ended up different in size. The results would have been interpretable if 25 people had been randomly assigned to the experimental group and 40 to the control group and all the individuals had completed the experiment. The problem is that the 25 experimental participants who completed the fitness program are not likely to be comparable to the 40 control participants. It is likely that only the more naturally fit experimental participants could complete the rigorous program; it is the less fit individuals who likely dropped out. Thus, the loss is traceable to a characteristic of the subjects—their original level of fitness—and this characteristic is relevant to the outcome of the study. The final fitness scores of the experimental participants might have been higher even if they had not participated in the fitness program!

If selective subject loss is not identified until after the experiment is completed, little can be done except to chalk up the experience of having conducted an uninterpretable experiment. You can take some preventive steps, however, if you realize in advance that selective loss may be a problem. One alternative is to administer a pretest and screen out subjects who are likely to be lost. In our example, an initial test of fitness could have been given, and only those subjects who scored above some minimal level allowed into the experimental and the control groups. The cost associated with this alternative is decreased external validity because the results could be generalized only to people above the minimal fitness level. This cost may be well worth paying because an interpretable study of limited external validity is still preferable to an uninterpretable study.

The second way to minimize the risk of selective subject loss also involves a pretest. Here all subjects are given the pretest but are then simply randomly assigned to one of the conditions. Then, if a subject is lost from the experimental group, a subject with a comparable pretest score is dropped from the control group. In a sense, this approach tries to restore the comparability of the groups. This approach also entails a cost of decreased external validity, since those subjects who finally end up in the study may differ from those in the original sample. The advantage of this approach is that external validity is lost *only if* selective subject loss *does* occur. When a pretest is used to check for selective subject loss, it is essential that the pretest measure the dimension responsible for the loss. In our example, a fitness pretest would be preferable to a pretest of visual acuity. Thus, the researcher must be ready to anticipate possible reasons for selective subject loss and measure these factors prior to beginning the study.

Placebo Control and Double-Blind Experiments   The final challenge to internal validity we describe arises because of expectations held by both participants and experimenters. In our discussion of the problem of reactivity in observational research (Chapter 3), we introduced the concept of demand characteristics (Orne, 1962). **Demand characteristics** refer to the cues and other information used by individuals to guide their behavior in a psychological study. For example, if participants know they have been given alcohol, they may expect certain effects, such as relaxation or giddiness, and behave accordingly. In addition to potential problems due to demand characteristics, there are also potential biases traceable to the expectations of the experimenters. The general term used to describe these biases is **experimenter effects** (Rosenthal, 1963). Experimenter effects may lead the experimenters to treat subjects differently in the different groups of the experiment in ways other than those required to implement the independent variable. In the context of our example experiment involving alcohol, experimenter effects could occur if the experimenters treated people in the different groups differently by, for example, reading the instructions more slowly to individuals who had been given alcohol. Experimenter effects also include biased observations by experimenters when they know which treatment the subject has received. Biased observations due to experimenter effects would arise in the alcohol study, for example, if the experimenters were more likely to notice unusual motor movements or slurred speech among the "drinkers" (because they "expect" drinkers to behave this way).

The problems of demand characteristics and experimenter effects can never be eliminated, but there are special research designs that control for both demand characteristics and experimenter effects. The first research design involves the use of **placebo control** groups. A *placebo* (from the Latin word meaning "I shall please") is a substance that looks like a drug or other active substance but is actually an *inert*, or inactive, substance. Pishkin and Shurley (1983) used a placebo control group to demonstrate the effectiveness of two drugs (doxepin and hydroxyzine). The drugs were tested to determine if they reduced arousal levels of psychiatric patients in response to the stress of failure on a cognitive task. The placebo participants were given capsules identical to the two drugs, but the placebo capsules contained only lactose, a sugar found in milk. None of the participants in the placebo control group realized the pill they took contained no medicine, so all the groups had the same "awareness" of taking a drug. Thus, any differences between the experimental groups and the placebo control group could legitimately be attributed to an effect of the drug taken by the experimental participants, and not the participants' expectations about receiving a drug.

Placebo control groups can be used in combination with a technique that even more effectively controls for demand characteristics and experimenter effects. The technique is called a **double-blind** procedure because both the participant and the observer are blind to (unaware of) what treatment is being administered. In an experiment such as the Pishkin and Shurley (1983) study, two researchers would be needed to accomplish the double-blind procedure. The first researcher would prepare the drug capsules and code each capsule in some way; the second researcher would distribute the drugs to the participants, recording the code for each drug as it was given to an individual. This procedure ensures that there is a record of which drug each person received, but neither the participant nor the experimenter who actually administers the drugs knows which treatment the participant received.

ALTERNATIVE INDEPENDENT GROUPS DESIGNS

MATCHED GROUPS DESIGN

The random groups design is by far the most common type of independent groups design. To work effectively, however, the random groups design requires samples of sufficient size to guarantee that individual differences among subjects will be balanced through random assignment. Specifically, the assumption behind the random groups design is that individual differences average out across groups. But how many subjects are required to ensure that this averaging process works as it should? The answer is, "It depends." More subjects will be needed to average out individual differences when sampling from a heterogeneous population than from a more homogeneous one. As you will learn in Chapter 7, power analysis is a statistical procedure used to estimate the number of subjects needed in your sample to observe the effect of the independent variable.

We can be relatively confident that random assignment will *not* be effective in balancing the differences among subjects when small numbers of subjects are tested from heterogeneous populations. This is exactly the situation researchers face in several areas of psychology. For example, some developmental psychologists study newborn infants; others study elderly people. These psychologists often have available only limited numbers of participants, and both newborns and the elderly certainly represent diverse populations.

One alternative that researchers have in this situation is to administer all the treatments to all the subjects, using a repeated measures design (discussed in Chapter 7). Nevertheless, some independent variables require separate groups of subjects for each level. For instance, consider that you are trying to assess the effects of participation in a special program for senior citizens. You will need to have a separate control group that does not participate in the program. Or suppose you wish to administer two types of postnatal care to different groups of premature infants. In these situations a repeated measures design is of no use.

The matched groups design is a good alternative when neither the random groups design nor repeated measures design can be used effectively. The logic of the **matched groups design** is simple and compelling. Instead of trusting random assignment to form comparable groups, the researcher makes the groups equivalent by matching subjects. In most uses of the matched groups design a pretest task is used to match subjects. The challenge is to select a pretest task (also called a matching task) that equates the groups on a dimension relevant to the outcome of the experiment. *The matched groups design is useful only when a good matching task is available.*

Researchers have several options when selecting a matching task. The most preferred option is to match subjects on the same task that will be used in the experiment itself. For example, if the dependent variable in the experiment is blood pressure, participants should be matched on blood pressure prior to the start of the experiment. The matching is accomplished by measuring the blood pressure of all subjects and then forming pairs, triples, or quadruples of subjects (depending on the number of conditions in the experiment) who have identical or similar blood pressures. After these matched sets are formed, the investigator must assign subjects randomly to the conditions of the experiment in order to balance individual differences other than those included in the matching task.

In some experiments, the experimental task cannot be used as the matching task. For example, consider an experiment involving different approaches to solving a puzzle. If a pretest was given to see how long it took individuals to solve this puzzle, the participants would likely learn the solution to the puzzle during the pretest. If they did learn the solution during the pretest, then it would be impossible to observe differences in the speed with which different groups of participants solved the puzzle in the experiment itself. After having experience with the puzzle in the pretest, all subjects would likely solve the puzzle very quickly. In this situation the next best alternative to using the experimental task as the matching task is to use a task from the same class or category as the experimental task. In our problem-solving experiment, participants could be matched on their performance solving a different puzzle from the experimental puzzle. However, it is important that performance on the experimental puzzle correlates with performance on the matching puzzle. The least preferred alternative is to use a task from a class different from the experimental task. For our problem-solving experiment, participants could be matched on some test of general ability, such as an intelligence test. As is true for all effective matching tasks, this general matching task must correlate with performance on the experimental task. Keep in mind that as the correlation between the matching task and the dependent variable decreases, the advantage of the matched groups design, relative to the random groups design, also decreases.

An additional important issue arises with the matched groups design even when a good matching task is available. Consider an experiment comparing two different methods of caring for premature infants. The matched groups design would work well for this type of experiment. Six pairs of premature infants could be matched on their body weight and on measures such as their scores on an infant motor coordination test. This experiment illustrates the conditions when a matched groups design is most helpful—the need to test separate groups with only small numbers of participants available and good matching tasks. You may remember we began our discussion of the matched groups design by saying it is useful when we have too few participants to allow randomization to form comparable groups. Nevertheless, a matching task like the body weights of the premature infants ensures comparable groups *only* on the dimension measured by the matching task. Although the matched groups design serves a very important purpose by allowing us to form comparable groups on the significant dimensions reflected in good matching tasks (e.g., body weights of premature infants), there remain potentially relevant characteristics of the participants in addition to those assessed by the matching task. For example, we may not know if the two groups of premature infants are comparable in their general health or in their degree of parental attachment. It is important, therefore, to use random assignment in the matched groups design to balance other potential factors beyond the matching task. For instance, after matching the infants on body weight and motor coordination, the pairs of infants would be randomly assigned to one of the two groups. In conclusion, the matched groups design is a better alternative than the random groups design when a good matching task is available and when only a small number of (heterogeneous) subjects is available for an experiment that requires separate groups for each condition.

NATURAL GROUPS DESIGN

Researchers in many areas of psychology are interested in independent variables called *individual differences variables* or *subject variables*. Individual differences variables such as gender, introversion-extraversion, or aggressiveness are important independent variables in personality psychology, abnormal psychology, developmental psychology, and social psychology. These variables cannot be manipulated. We cannot assign someone to be 20 years old or to be an introverted or aggressive person, or to be male or female. Instead, we *select* the levels of these independent variables.

It is important to differentiate experiments involving independent variables whose levels are selected from those involving independent variables whose levels are manipulated. Experiments involving independent variables whose levels are selected—like individual differences variables—are called **natural groups designs.** The natural groups design is frequently used in situations in which ethical and practical constraints prevent us from directly manipulating independent variables. No matter how interested we might be in the effects of traumatic events such as major surgery on subsequent depression, we could not ethically perform major surgery on a randomly selected group of introductory psychology students and then compare their performance with that of another group who did not receive surgery! Similarly, if we were interested in the relationship between divorce and emotional disorders, we could not randomly assign some people to get divorced. By using the natural groups design, however, we can compare people who have had surgery with those who have not. Similarly, people who have chosen to divorce can be compared with those who have chosen to stay married.

The intent of studies using the natural groups design is to determine whether these natural "treatments" result in systematic differences in behavior. For example, studies have shown that people who are separated or divorced are much more likely to receive psychiatric care than those who are married, widowed, or have remained single (Bloom, Asher, & White, 1978). In general, the natural groups design involves looking for correlations between subjects' characteristics and their performance. Because of this, the natural groups design represents a type of correlational research (see also Chapter 4).

Natural groups designs are highly effective in meeting the first two objectives of the scientific method—description and prediction. Serious problems can arise, though, when the results of natural groups designs are used as a basis for causal inference. For instance, the finding that divorced persons are more likely than married persons to receive psychiatric care shows that these two factors covary. This result could be taken to mean that divorce causes emotional disorders that lead to the need for psychiatric care. Before reaching this conclusion, however, we must assure ourselves that the time-order condition for a causal inference has been met—namely, that divorce preceded the emotional disorder. Demonstrating covariation does nothing to specify the direction of the causal relationship. Perhaps those who suffer from emotional disorders are more likely to get divorced because the disorder placed strain on the relationship or because the emotional disorder contributed to marrying unwisely in the first place.

The most critical problem in drawing causal inferences based on the natural groups design is meeting the third condition for demonstrating causality: eliminating plausible alternative causes. Do you see how this problem is especially troublesome with the natural groups design? Eliminating plausible alternative causes requires a high degree of control, and the experimenter has far less control in the natural groups design. The individual differences being studied in the natural groups design are usually confounded. This is because groups of individuals are likely to differ in many ways beside the variable used to classify them. For example, introverts and extraverts differ with respect to a number of characteristics other than their degree of introversion. For instance, extraverts are apt to prefer excitement and practical jokes but not like quiet reading; introverts generally show the opposite pattern. The manipulation done by "nature" is rarely the controlled type we have come to expect in establishing the internal validity of an experiment.

In Chapter 8 we discuss an effective approach to drawing causal inferences in the natural groups design. The approach requires that *individual differences be studied in combination with independent variables that can be manipulated.* This combination of more than one independent variable in one experiment requires the use of a complex design that we cover in Chapter 8. For now, just recognize that drawing causal inferences based on the natural groups design can be a treacherous enterprise.

ANALYSIS OF EXPERIMENTS

The purpose of an experiment is to determine whether an independent variable has had an effect on behavior as indicated by changes in the dependent variable. The foundation of the analysis of an experiment is the description of the results. Descriptive statistics are the core of this foundation, the best way for you to answer the question, "What happened in your experiment?" Some researchers (e.g., Loftus, 1993) argue that descriptive statistics, when reported properly, are sufficient for the analysis and interpretation of the results of an experiment. Let's take a look at this approach to the analysis of experiments.

Figure 6.4 is an example used by Loftus (1993). The figure illustrates graphically the results of an experiment involving human perception. The purpose of the experiment was to examine how people process visual information over brief time intervals. Understanding visual information processing can be useful in analyzing the work done by air traffic controllers. The participants in the experiment saw four dots that were randomly presented in a large matrix of cells on the computer screen. The participants' task was to reproduce the pattern of four dots after viewing the pattern briefly. One independent variable in this experiment was the duration of exposure of the dot pattern. There were eight levels of exposure duration ranging from 25 to 250 milliseconds (ms). A second independent variable was how certain participants could be about what they saw. For example, if the participants saw the dots on a clear screen, their uncertainty would be low. If, on the other hand, they saw the dots on a "fuzzy" screen, their uncertainty would be high. The researcher expected that participants would be better able to reproduce the dot pattern as exposure duration of the presentation of the dots increased. The researcher also expected that performance in the experiment would be better under conditions of low uncertainty than under conditions of high uncertainty. The analysis technique we now describe allows the researcher to test these two hypotheses.

FIGURE 6.4   Ilustration of plot-plus-error-bar procedure. Adapted from Figure 1 of Loftus (1993).

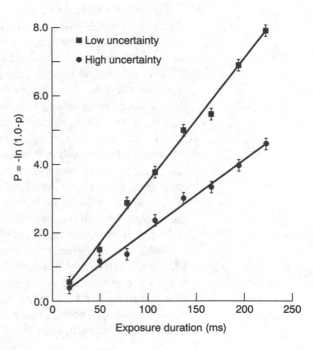

In Figure 6.4, one independent variable, exposure duration, appears on the abscissa (X-axis). The dependent variable (how accurately the participants reproduced the dot patterns) appears on the ordinate (Y-axis). It is not critical for this illustration that you understand the mathematical equation which describes the dependent variable. What you need to pay attention to is the fact that as the value of the independent variable increases, performance increases. A second independent variable, uncertainty, distinguishes the two lines in the body of the graph. As you can see in the graph, as exposure duration increases, performance increases—just as the researcher had expected. Also, the points for the low uncertainty conditions are generally higher than those for the high uncertainty conditions. This finding is also consistent with what the researcher expected. Perhaps the most useful information in the figure are the bars that surround each data point. We can use these bars to make decisions about whether the effects of each of the two independent variables were reliable.

Figure 6.4 represents what is called the *plot-plus-error-bar* procedure. Each circle near the lower line represents the mean performance across eight exposure durations under high uncertainty. Similarly, each square represents the mean performance across eight exposure durations under low uncertainty. These means indicate how well the participants did on the average in each of the conditions. (Note there are 16 conditions in this experiment.) The "bars" surrounding each mean reflect the standard error of the mean for each mean. The *standard error of the mean* indicates how much sampling error there is in estimating the population mean based on a sample mean. The smaller the error (i.e., the smaller the difference between bars), the better is our estimate of the population mean.

The standard error of the mean is described in Appendix A. We describe here only a brief example of how the standard error of the mean is interpreted. Suppose the mean performance at an exposure duration of 50 ms was 1.2. Assume further that the standard error of the mean for an average performance of 1.2 was 0.1. Knowing both the mean and the standard error of the mean, we would be able to draw an error bar around 1.2 that would be .4 wide (2 times the standard error of the mean above *and* below the mean). The error bar tells us that with 95% confidence the population mean falls between 1.0 and 1.4. Saying this slightly differently, if a mean falls outside this confidence interval marked by the error bar, it is likely to be different from the mean of 1.2. In general, smaller error bars indicate smaller standard errors of the mean, and larger error bars indicate larger standard errors of the mean. It is noteworthy that in Figure 6.4 all of the error bars around the 16 means are similar in size, and they are all small. More typically in psychology experiments the error bars are larger and vary from each other more.

We can learn a great deal from Figure 6.4 about the results of the experiment. The small error bars indicate that the means in the experiment are good estimates of the corresponding population means; there is relatively little "error" in estimating the true or population mean. This increases our confidence in using the sample means to describe the results of the experiment. We can begin to use the information in the figure to describe the effect of the independent variable of exposure duration. As you can see, the two lines in Figure 6.4 are a good fit for the data points—the data points fall close to a straight line for both high and low uncertainty. The good fit of these lines, the fact that both lines increase with increasing exposure duration, and our confidence in the estimates of the means for each condition lead us to the reasonable conclusion that performance on the dot reproduction task improved with increasing exposure duration. This conclusion is consistent with what the researcher expected the effect of exposure duration would be.

Describing the effect of the independent variable of uncertainty illustrates another important aspect of interpreting graphs like Figure 6.4. With the plot-plus-error-bar procedure we assume we can be confident that means which differ by more than the span of the error bar are likely to be really different. For example, for the 75 ms exposure duration the error bars for the low uncertainty and high uncertainty conditions do not overlap. The same is true for all the exposure durations above 75 ms. One key to interpreting figures that use the plot-plus-error-bar procedure is to remember that differences are "small" or "large" only in relation to the size of the error bars. The large mean differences between performance in the low and high uncertainty condition at 75 ms duration and the absence of overlap between the error bars between these two conditions gives us confidence that performance in the two uncertainty conditions did differ reliably. The mean performance indicates clearly that performance was better under low uncertainty than under high uncertainty. This finding is again consistent with what the researcher expected the effect of uncertainty would be. The use of the plot-plus-error bar procedure illustrates that a picture can tell us a lot *if we know how to look at it*!

The analysis of nearly every psychology experiment involves descriptive statistics, and some involve the use of analysis techniques like the plot-plus-error-bar procedure. However, inferential statistics are most commonly used in conjunction with descriptive statistics to analyze and interpret the results of experiments. We introduce the idea of inferential statistics with the results from a classic series of studies by Asch (1951, 1955) on conformity to group pressure.

NULL-HYPOTHESIS TESTING

The task in Asch's experiments was a simple one. Male participants were shown two cards. The first card contained one line, called the standard. The second card contained three lines of different lengths, only one of which matched the standard. The participant's task was to select the line that was the same length as the standard. Eighteen tests of this kind were given to each participant. During a test session varying numbers of other men were present. These men were introduced to the participant as fellow participants in the experiment, but they were actually working as confederates of the experimenter (see Chapter 3 for a discussion of the ethics of using confederates). These confederates responded with incorrect responses on 12 of the 18 trials. When more than one confederate was present, each confederate gave the same incorrect response. Thus, the independent variable was the number of confederates present, and there were seven levels of this variable (0, 1, 2, 3, 4, 8, and 16). Participants were randomly assigned to a group representing one of these seven levels. The dependent variable was the number of trials (out of the 12 possible on which the confederates gave incorrect responses) on which the participant conformed to group pressure by choosing the incorrect response instead of what was obviously the correct choice.

Two questions were addressed in Asch's experiment. First, would participants conform? That is, would they chose the incorrect line more in the conditions when others were present than when they were alone? Second, would conformity increase with increasing size of the incorrect majority? Asch conducted a properly controlled experiment, so it is possible to use the results of the study to answer these two questions.

The first and most important step in analyzing an experiment is to summarize the results using an appropriate descriptive statistic. The most commonly used descriptive statistic in psychology experiments is the mean. The mean number and the range of errors for the participants who had been randomly assigned to each of the seven groups in the Asch experiment are presented in Table 6.1. The results seem clear. Fewer errors, on the average, were made when the participants were alone than when they were confronted with the incorrect responses of other "participants." And mean errors increased with increasing size of the dissenting majority, at least up to groups of four.

Descriptive statistics alone are not sufficient, however, to answer the two questions that Asch's experiment addressed. The problem rests with the nature of the control provided by balancing through random assignment. Random assignment does not eliminate the differences among subjects. Random assignment simply distributes the differences among subjects equally across the groups in the experiment. That is, the differences among subjects are not allowed to vary systematically across groups.

The nonsystematic variation due to differences among subjects within each group is called *error variation*. The individual differences within each group are reflected in the range of errors presented in the second row of Table 6.1. Even with a dissenting majority of 16 (last column), at least one participant made no errors while another participant made 10 errors. The presence of error variation

TABLE 6.1   MEAN NUMBERS OF ERRORS AS A FUNCTION OF THE SIZE OF THE DISSENTING MAJORITY

	Size of dissenting majority						
	0	1	2	3	4	8	16
Mean number of errors	0.08	0.33	1.53	4.00	4.20	3.84	3.75
Range of errors	0–2	0–1	0–5	1–12	0–11	0–11	0–10

Adapted from Asch (1951).

in experiments poses a problem. The problem is that the means of the groups in the experiment may differ due to error variation even if the independent variable has had no effect. Thus, by themselves, the mean results of the best controlled random-groups design experiment do not permit a definite conclusion about the effectiveness of the independent variable.

The best way to determine whether the differences obtained in an experiment are reliable would be to replicate the experiment and see if the same outcome is obtained. Partial replications do occur in the natural course of research on a topic. For example, subsequent experiments that were done to locate the basis of conformity in the Asch experiment included at least some conditions from the original study. Nevertheless, replication would be a cumbersome and inefficient way to establish the reliability of experimental findings if it were required for each experiment done in psychology. Participants for experiments are a scarce resource, and each replication costs us a study that could be done to ask new and different questions about behavior. We need some alternative to replication for determining whether the differences obtained in a single experiment are larger than would be expected on the basis of error variation alone.

Inferential statistics provide a way to test whether the differences in a dependent variable associated with various conditions of an experiment can be attributed to an effect of the independent variable. Statistical inference is inductive and indirect. It is inductive because we draw general conclusions about populations on the basis of the specific samples we test in our experiments. Statistical inference is indirect because it begins by assuming the null hypothesis. As the name implies, the **null hypothesis** is the assumption that the independent variable has had *no* effect. Once we make this assumption, we can use probability theory to determine the likelihood of obtaining the difference that we did obtain in our experiment if the null hypothesis were true (if the independent variable had no effect). If this likelihood is small, we reject the null hypothesis and conclude that the independent variable did have an effect. Outcomes that lead us to reject the null hypothesis are said to be **statistically significant.** A statistically significant outcome means only that the difference we have obtained in our experiment is larger than would be expected if error variation alone (i.e., chance) were responsible for the outcome.

Perhaps you can appreciate the process of statistical inference by considering the following dilemma. A friend offers to toss a coin with you to see who pays for the meal you just enjoyed at a restaurant. Your friend happens to have a coin ready to toss. Now it would be convenient if you could directly test whether your friend's coin were biased. The best you can do, however, is to test your friend's coin indirectly by assuming it is not biased and seeing if you consistently get outcomes that differ from the expected 50-50 split of heads and tails. If the coin does not exhibit the ordinary 50-50 split, you might surmise your friend is trying, by slightly underhanded means, to get you to pay for the meal. Similarly, we would like to make a direct test of statistical significance for an obtained difference in our experiments. The best we can do, however, is to compare our obtained outcome with the expected outcome of no difference. *The key to understanding null-hypothesis testing is to recognize that we can use the laws of probability to estimate the likelihood of an outcome only when we assume chance factors are the sole cause of that outcome.*

A statistically significant outcome is one that has only a small likelihood of occurring if the null hypothesis is true. But just how small is small enough? Although there is no definitive answer to this important question, the consensus among members of the scientific community is that outcomes associated with probabilities of less than 5 times out of 100 (or .05) if the null hypothesis were true are judged to be statistically significant. The probability that we elect to use to indicate an outcome is statistically significant is called the *level of significance.* The level of significance is indicated by the Greek letter alpha (α). Thus, we speak of the .05 level of significance, the .10 level, or the .01 level, which we report as $\alpha = .05$, $\alpha = .10$, $\alpha = .01$.

You must choose the level of significance *before* you begin your experiment, not after you have done the statistical analysis. Choosing the level of significance before doing the analysis allows you to avoid the temptation of using the probability of your obtained outcome as the level of significance you *would have chosen.* Strictly speaking, only two conclusions are possible when you do an inferential statistics test: You either reject the null hypothesis or you fail to reject the null hypothesis. There are, however, alternatives to tests of statistical significance that can be used to determine the amount of impact an independent variable has had.

When we take a strict approach to null-hypothesis (H_0) testing, we are essentially acknowledging that it is impossible to prove something does not exist. For example, if we were to propose there was a monster in Lake Michigan, you would be unable to prove to us this was not so. Putting ecological considerations aside for the moment, you might drain Lake Michigan to show no monster is there, but we could simply assert the monster dug into the bed of the lake. You might then begin to dredge the lake, and if you still came up with no monster we could argue our monster is digging faster than you are dredging. Becoming more desperate, you might fill the lake with explosives and if after detonating them, you found no remains of the monster, we could calmly propose our monster is impervious to explosives. So long as we were free to add characteristics to our monster, there is no test you could perform that would convincingly show the monster does not exist. Practically speaking, however, if we continued to believe in our monster after reasonable efforts had failed to yield evidence of its existence, we would be judged unreasonable and would lose credibility with other members of the community.

A similar practical problem faces the community of researchers in psychology. Although we recognize the logical impossibility of proving H_0 is true, we also must have some method of deciding which independent variables are not worth pursuing. Most often, experiments are done to show that an independent variable causes a change in behavior. We should not get too discouraged, however, if the particular independent variable we are studying does not produce a statistically significant difference in our experiment. The discipline of psychology also progresses by identifying factors that do not influence behavior.

Somewhat ironically, the standards for experiments that show an independent variable is irrelevant are even higher than the standards for those that show the independent variable is relevant. This is understandable when you recognize that experiments showing differences are likely to be subject to replication, whereas experiments finding no effects may discourage investigators from pursuing those areas of investigation any further. All too often, however, after failing to reject H_0, researchers do a small (and insensitive) "replication" to confirm their original conclusion. If anything, the second experiment should be more sensitive than the first if it is to strengthen the conclusion that the independent variable has had no effect (Tversky & Kahneman, 1971).

Yeaton and Sechrest (1986, pp. 836–837) argue persuasively that findings of no difference (those that would lead us to accept the null hypothesis) are especially critical in applied research. They cite several questions to illustrate their point:

> Does Agent Orange increase the risk of health problems? Are the pollutants in Love Canal associated with an increased risk of genetic defects? Are children who are placed in day-care centers as intellectually, socially, and emotionally advanced as children who remain in the home? Is a new, cheaper drug with fewer side effects as effective as the existing standard in preventing heart attacks? Does saccharin increase one's risk of developing bladder cancer?

These important questions clearly illustrate situations in which accepting the null hypothesis involves more than a theoretical issue—life and death consequences rest on making the correct decision. Frick (1995) argues that never accepting the null hypothesis is neither desirable nor practical for psychology. As a community, we need some way to assure ourselves that some monsters are just not worth searching for.

There is a troublesome aspect to the process of statistical inference. No matter what decision you reach and no matter how carefully you reach it, there is always some chance you are making an error. The two possible "states of the world" and the two possible decisions an experimenter can reach are listed in Table 6.2. The independent variable either does or does not have an effect on behavior. The two possible correct decisions the researcher can make are represented by the upper-left and lower-right cells of the table. If the independent variable does have an effect, the researcher should reject the null hypothesis; if it does not, the researcher should fail to reject the null hypothesis.

TABLE 6.2   POSSIBLE OUTCOMES OF DECISION MAKING WITH INFERENTIAL STATISTICS

	States of the world	
	Null hypothesis is false	Null hypothesis is true
Reject null hypothesis	Correct decision	Type I error
Fail to reject null hypothesis	Type II error	Correct decision

The two potential errors are represented by the other two cells of Table 6.2, and these two types of errors have the highly descriptive names of Type I error and Type II error. These errors arise because of the probabilistic nature of statistical inference. When we decide an outcome is statistically significant because the outcome's probability of occurring under the null hypothesis is less than .05, we acknowledge that in 5 of every 100 tests, the outcome *could* occur even if the null hypothesis were true. The level of significance, therefore, represents the probability of making a *Type I error*: rejecting the null hypothesis when it is true. The probability of making a Type I error can be reduced simply by making the level of significance more stringent, perhaps .001. The problem with this approach is that it increases the likelihood of making a *Type II error*: failing to reject the null hypothesis when it is false.

The problem of Type I errors and Type II errors should not immobilize us. But it should help us understand why researchers rarely use the word *prove* when they describe the results of an experiment that involved inferential statistics. Instead, they describe the results as "consistent with the hypothesis," or "confirming the hypothesis," or "supporting the hypothesis." These more tentative statements are a way of indirectly acknowledging that the possibility of making a Type I error or a Type II error always exists. The .05 level of significance represents a compromise position that allows us to strike a balance and avoid making too many of either type of error. The problem of Type I errors and Type II errors also reminds us that statistical inference can never replace replication as the ultimate test of the reliability of an experimental outcome.

LIMITATIONS OF NULL-HYPOTHESIS TESTING

One common misuse of statistical inference occurs when we confuse the statistical significance of a finding with the significance of the conclusion based on that finding. The statistical significance of a finding does nothing to enhance the internal validity of the experiment. Although we might be tempted to accept an interpretation if it is based on a "statistically significant" finding, we must remember that our ability to draw appropriate conclusions depends, most of all, on the internal validity of the study. And internal validity, as we have seen, depends mainly on whether the investigator has been able to exert enough control to eliminate alternative explanations. In other words, confounded experiments can easily produce statistically significant outcomes! These "significant outcomes" should, of course, never be interpreted as valid when an experiment lacks internal validity.

J. Cohen (1995) provides a cogent critique of null-hypothesis testing. He points out two common misunderstandings of what a null-hypothesis test tells us. The first misunderstanding is that a statistically significant finding tells us the probability that the null hypothesis is true. This misunderstanding is illustrated by a conclusion such as, "Our statistically significant finding proves that the probability of obtaining our results by chance is less than .05." What a statistically significant finding *does* tell us is the probability of our obtained difference *given that the null hypothesis is true*. We assume the null hypothesis; we do not determine the probability that the null hypothesis is true or the probability that our obtained results are due to chance. An appropriate conclusion could be phrased, "Our statistical significant finding would occur with a probability less than 0.05 if the null hypothesis were assumed to be true."

A second misunderstanding involves the replicability of a finding associated with a certain probability such as $p = .01$ under the null hypothesis. This probability *does not* indicate that the outcome would be replicated 99% of the time if the experiment were repeated. Or, stated slightly differently, we *can not say* with 99% confidence that the outcome is reliable—that is, it would be replicated. What we can say is that the finding we obtained in our experiment is an unlikely one if the independent variable had no effect. The only way to find out for sure if a finding will replicate is to replicate it!

Another limitation of null-hypothesis testing is that the likelihood of obtaining a statistically significant finding is directly related to the sample size tested in the experiment. If we do an experiment with a very large number of subjects, almost any finding will be statistically significant. Cohen (1995) describes a slightly different aspect of this problem. He argues that the null hypothesis is almost never literally true in terms of an absolute difference of zero. If there is any sampling error at all (and it's almost guaranteed there will be), then the means in each of the two groups of an experiment will not be identical. Practically speaking, then, researchers do not expect the difference between means to be zero. Yet the null hypothesis literally says that we are testing for a difference of zero. Cohen goes on to argue that, "If it [null hypothesis] is false, even to a tiny degree, it must be the case that a large enough sample will produce a significant result and lead to its [null hypothesis] rejection" (p. 1000). This problem can be lessened by testing hypotheses that specify intervals of values under the null hypothesis rather than single values (e.g., exactly 0). For example, a researcher could test whether performance in a memory experiment was better or worse than an interval between 40% and 60%. An even better way to deal with the problem of the influence of sample size on statistical significance is to report measures of effect size (discussed later in this chapter) that are independent of the number of subjects in the experiment.

You may be wondering at this point how null-hypothesis testing continues to be used when it has so many limitations. As Cohen (1995) says, "don't look for a magic alternative to NHST [null hypothesis significance testing], [or] some other objective mechanical ritual to replace it. It doesn't exist" (p. 1001). He advocates that researchers seeking to generalize from their data should use a variety of analysis techniques such as graphic data analysis (like the plot-plus-error-bar procedure). He also argues that improved statistical analysis in psychology requires improvements in psychological measurement and theory construction so the hypotheses psychologists test will be more specific. Cohen concludes his critique of null-hypothesis testing with some sage advice, ". . . we have a body of statistical techniques, that, used intelligently, can facilitate our efforts. But given the problems of statistical induction, we must finally rely, as have the older sciences, on replication" (p. 1002). The most prevalent alternative to replication currently used in psychological research is statistical inference. We have introduced you to the strengths and weaknesses of this statistical technique. We hope you now recognize how critical it is that this important research tool be used properly.

ANALYSIS OF VARIANCE (ANOVA)

Statistical inference requires a test that can be used to determine whether or not the outcome of an experiment was statistically significant. The most commonly used inferential statistics test in the analysis of experiments is the *analysis of variance* (or ANOVA). As its name implies, the analysis of variance is based on analyzing different sources of variation in an experiment. In this section we briefly introduce the use of the analysis of variance in analyzing experiments that involve the random groups design.

There are two sources of variation in any random groups experiment. First, variation within each group can be expected because of the individual differences among the subjects who have been randomly assigned to that group. The variation due to individual differences can not be eliminated, but it is presumed to be balanced across groups because of random assignment. In a properly conducted experiment the differences among subjects within each group should represent only error variation because all the subjects in the group have been treated in the same way according to the level of the independent variable.

The second source of variation in the random groups design is variation between the groups. If the null hypothesis is true, the nonsystematic variation among the means of the groups can also be attributed to error variation. When the null hypothesis is true, the performance in each group reflects the same underlying population, and thus the average performance in each group should be the same as the average performance in every other group. If several random samples are drawn from the same population, however, we cannot expect the means of these samples to be identical. Fluctuations produced by sampling error make it likely that the means for the different random samples will vary somewhat. Thus, the variation among the group means, under the condition that the null hypothesis is true, provides a second estimate of error variation. If the null hypothesis is true, this estimate of error variation between groups should be comparable to the earlier estimate we described of error variation within groups. Thus, the random groups design provides two independent estimates of error variation, one within the groups and one between the groups.

Now suppose the null hypothesis is false. That is, suppose the independent variable has had an effect. If the independent variable has had an effect, should the means for the different groups be the same or different? An independent variable that has an effect should produce *systematic differences* in the means across the different groups of the experiment. This systematic variation will be added to the differences in the group means that always result from error variation.

The F-Test   We are now in a position to develop a statistic that will allow us to tell whether the variation due to our independent variable is larger than would be expected on the basis of error variation alone. This statistic is called F; it is named after Ronald Fisher, the statistician who developed the test. The conceptual definition of the **F-test** is the following ratio:

$$F = \text{variation between groups} / \text{variation within groups}$$
$$= \text{error variation} + \text{systematic variation} / \text{error variation}$$

If the null hypothesis is true, there is no systematic variation and the resulting F ratio has an expected value of 1.00 (since error variation divided by error variation would equal 1.00). As the amount of systematic variation increases, however, the expected value from the F-test becomes greater than 1.00.

The analysis of experiments would be easier if we could isolate the systematic variation produced by the independent variable. Unfortunately, the systematic variation between groups comes in a "package" along with error variation. Consequently, the value of the F ratio may sometimes be larger than 1.00 simply because our estimate of error variation between groups happens to be larger than our estimate of error variation within groups. This problem becomes less and less likely with increasingly larger F values, but we are still faced with a nagging question. How much greater than 1.00 does the F statistic have to be before we can be relatively sure it reflects systematic variation? Our earlier discussion of statistical significance provides an answer to this question. To be statistically significant, the F value needs to be large enough so its probability of occurring if the null hypothesis were true is less than our chosen level of significance, usually .05.

We are now ready to apply the principles of null-hypothesis testing and the procedures of the analysis of variance to analyze a specific experiment. We use the Asch experiment we described earlier. The first step in doing an inferential statistics test like the F-test is to state the research question the analysis is intended to answer. Typically, this takes the form of "Did the independent variable have any overall effect on performance?" In the Asch experiment this question would be, "Did varying the size of the dissenting majority have any effect on the number of errors participants made?" Once the research question is clear, the next step is to develop a null hypothesis for the analysis.

The initial overall analysis of the experiment is called an *omnibus F-test*. The null hypothesis for such omnibus tests is that all the group means are equal. The formal statement of a null hypothesis (H_0) is always made in terms of population characteristics. These population characteristics are indicated by Greek letters, and the population mean is symbolized as μ(mu). We can use a subscript for each mean in the Asch experiment to reflect the size of the dissenting majority. Our null hypothesis then becomes:

$$H_0: \mu_0 = \mu_1 = \mu_2 = \mu_3 = \mu_4 = \mu_8 = \mu_{16}$$

The alternative to the null hypothesis is that one or more of the means of the groups are not equal. In other words, the alternative hypothesis states that H_0 is wrong, there is a difference somewhere. If the size of the dissenting majority does have an effect (i.e., if the independent variable produces systematic variation), we will be led to reject the null hypothesis.

Analysis of Variance Summary Table   The next step in an analysis of variance is to do the computations to obtain the estimates of variation that make up the numerator and denominator of the F-test. Computing F-tests is best done using a computer; the procedures for doing computer analyses are described in Appendix A. Our focus now is on interpreting the results of the computations. The results of an analysis of variance are presented in an Analysis of Variance Summary Table. The summary table for the Asch experiment is presented in the top half of Table 6.3.

The means for each group that were presented earlier in Table 6.1 are repeated at the bottom of the table. We examine the components of the summary table before looking at the outcome of the F-test for the experiment.

The left column of a summary table lists the sources of variation. In this case the independent variable of the dissenting majority is a source of variation between the groups and the within-groups differences provide an estimate of error variation alone. The total variation in the experiment is the sum of the variation between and within the groups. The next column is the degrees of freedom (df). In general, the statistical concept of degrees of freedom is defined as the number of entries of interest minus one. Since there are 7 sizes of the dissenting majority, there are 6 df between groups ($7-1=6$). There are 10 participants within each group and so there are 9 df within each group. Because all 7 groups are the same size we can determine the within-groups df by multiplying the df within each group by the number of groups (9×7) for 63 df. The total df is the number of subjects minus one (and also the sum of df between groups plus df within groups).

TABLE 6.3   ANALYSIS OF VARIANCE SUMMARY TABLE

Source of Variation	df	SS	MS	F	p
Between Groups (Majority Size)	6	198.98	33.16	27.2	.0001
Within Groups (Error)	63	77.13	1.22		
Total	69	276.11			

	Size of dissenting majority						
	0	1	2	3	4	8	16
Mean Number of Errors	.08	.33	1.53	4.00	4.20	3.84	3.75

The sums of squares (SS) and the mean square (MS) are computational steps in obtaining the *F* statistic (see Appendix A). The MS between groups (row 1) is the numerator of the *F*-test that is an estimate of both systematic and error variation. The MS within groups (row 2) is the denominator of the *F*-test that is an estimate of error variation only. The *F*-ratio is obtained by dividing the MS between groups by the MS within groups. We are now ready to use the information in the summary table to test for the statistical significance of the outcome in the Asch experiment.

The obtained *F* value in this analysis appears in the second to last column of the summary table and it is $F(6,63) = 27.18$. An *F* is identified by its degrees of freedom. In this case there are 6 *df* between groups and 63 *df* within groups. That is why the result of the *F*-test for the Asch experiment is reported above as $F(6,63) = 27.18$. The probability of obtaining an *F* as large as 27.18 if the null hypothesis were true is shown in the last column of the summary table (.0001). The obtained probability of .0001 is less than the level of significance ($\alpha = .05$), so we reject the null hypothesis and conclude that the overall effect of the size of the dissenting majority is statistically significant.

Just what have we learned when we find a statistically significant outcome in an analysis of variance testing an omnibus null hypothesis? In one sense, we have learned something very important. We are now in a position to state that manipulation of the independent variable produced a change in performance (i.e., participants' errors). In another sense, merely knowing our outcome is statistically significant tells us nothing about the *nature* of the effect of the independent variable. The descriptive statistics (in our example, the mean number of errors in Table 6.3) are the basis for our description of the nature of the effect. For example, if participants had made the most errors when they were alone, the results could also have been statistically significant but in the opposite direction. This finding would lead us to draw a very different conclusion from the one we would reach based on the means in Table 6.3. The point is, *never try to interpret a statistically significant outcome without referring to the corresponding descriptive statistics.*

Knowing the omnibus test is statistically significant also does not tell us the *source* of the effect. All we know is that there is systematic variation *somewhere* in our experiment. On the basis of the omnibus test, we can only respond to a person who asked, "What happened in your experiment?" by saying, "Something." This response is not very satisfying and would almost surely prompt the exasperated reply, "Yes, but what?" But based on the omnibus *F*-test alone, we are unable to state which groups' means differed from which other group means. Fortunately, there are analysis techniques that allow us to locate more specifically the sources of systematic variation in our experiments. These techniques are called analytical comparisons, and they are linked directly to the hypotheses that led the researcher to do the experiment in the first place.

Analytical Comparisons Asch did not do his experiment simply to find out whether something would happen when he manipulated the size of the dissenting majority. Instead, he had at least two specific questions to address in the experiment. Would participants choose the incorrect line more in the conditions when others were present than when they were alone? And would conformity increase with increasing size of the dissenting majority? **Analytical comparisons** are a way to translate these research questions into a form that allows us to locate a specific source of systematic variation in our experiment (see Appendix A for more information about analytical comparisons). We illustrate this process with the first of Asch's two research questions.

The first step in doing an analytical comparison, like the first step in doing an omnibus analysis, is to state the null hypothesis for the analysis. The verbal statement of the null hypothesis for Asch's first research question is: The mean for the group when participants are alone is equal to the mean of all the groups in which other participants were present. More formally, the null hypothesis is as follows:

$$H_0: \mu_0 = (\mu_1 + \mu_2 + \mu_3 + \mu_4 + \mu_8 + \mu_{16})/6$$

We can compute a mean square for this particular comparison. The mean square for the comparison reflects a combination of error variation and systematic variation due to this specific comparison. An F-ratio can then be formed with the comparison mean square in the numerator and the mean square within groups in the denominator (estimate of error variation alone). Because this analytical comparison essentially involves the contrast between two means (participants alone and participants in groups), it has only 1 degree of freedom. We then determine the probability of the resulting F-ratio by using the same procedures we described earlier for omnibus F-tests.

The computations for the first analytical comparison in the Asch experiment result in $F(1,63) = 57.53$ with a $p = .0001$. The obtained p is less than the conventional .05 level of significance, and so the analytical comparison is statistically significant. This outcome allows us to state that one source of systematic variation in the Asch experiment was that participants in groups performed differently from participants who were alone. Because the mean number of errors for participants in groups (2.94) was higher than that for participants alone (0.08), we can conclude that Asch's first hypothesis was confirmed. Think again about your friend's question about "what happened" in your experiment. Can you see why you would be glad you know about analytical comparisons when you try to answer your friend's question?

EFFECT SIZE

When we do an inferential statistics test we are interested in determining whether the independent variable had an effect. One limitation of inferential statistics tests, however, is that the outcome of such tests is influenced by the sample size used in the experiment. That is, if an independent variable has an effect of a certain size, then the value from the F-test used to test the effect of that independent variable will increase as sample size increases. In other words, the F ratio can increase even when the effect size does not. This means we need something other than an inferential statistics test to measure the size of the effect of an independent variable. What is needed to measure **effect size** is an indicator that reflects the strength of the relationship between the independent and the dependent variables and is independent of sample size. Several measures of effect size meet these criteria (Keppel, 1991). We do not describe here how these different measures of effect size are computed. What we will do is use one of these measures to describe the nature of an effect size and the way an effect size generally is interpreted.

One commonly used measure of effect size in experimental research is called *d*. It is a ratio that measures the difference between the means for the levels of the independent variable relative to the within-group standard deviation. The standard deviation tells us approximately how far, on the average, scores vary from a group mean (see Appendix A). It is a measure of the "dispersal" of scores around a mean and, in the case of the within-group standard deviation, tells us about the degree of "error" due to individual differences (i.e., how individuals vary in their responses). The standard deviation serves as a useful metric by which we can assess a difference between means. The "size" of the effect of the independent variable, in other words, is always in terms of the average dispersal of scores occurring in an experiment. If there is lots of within-group variability (i.e., the within-group standard deviation is large) then the difference between, for instance, two means must be greater to produce the same effect size than when there is little within-group variability (i.e., the standard deviation is small). Because effect sizes are presented in standard deviation units, they can be used to make meaningful comparisons of effect sizes across experiments using different dependent variables.

Fortunately, there are some guidelines to help us interpret *d* ratios. J. Cohen (1992) has provided a useful classification of effect sizes with three values—small, medium, and large. Cohen describes the rationale for his classification of effect size (ES) as follows:

> My intent was that medium ES represent an effect likely to be visible to the naked eye of a careful observer. (It has since been noted in effect-size surveys that it approximates the average size of observed effects in various fields.) I set small ES to be noticeably smaller than medium but not so small as to be trivial, and I set large ES to be the same distance above medium as small was below it. Although the definitions were made subjectively, with some minor adjustments, these conventions . . . have come into general use." (p. 156)

Each of the classes of effect size can be expressed in quantitative terms; for example, a medium effect for a two-group experiment is a *d* of .50; a small and large effect are *d*s of .20 and .80, respectively.

There are several advantages of using measures of effect size (see, for example, Chow, 1988):

1 Measures of effect size provide information about the *amount* of impact an independent variable has had. Thus, they complement tests of statistical significance which give only an indication of the presence or absence of an effect of an independent variable. In this way, we can use measures of effect size to rank several independent variables within the same experiment as one indication of the relative importance of the independent variables.

2 Measures of effect size can be used to summarize a series of experiments that have included the same independent variable or dependent variable. This allows for a quantitative comparison of the outcomes across the series of experiments. For example, effect size can be used to find out whether a particular independent variable consistently had about the same amount of impact across the experiments.

3 Effect sizes can be averaged to provide an estimate of the overall effect size of an independent variable across a series of experiments. This comparison is especially important in applied research examining the effectiveness of treatments like an educational innovation or a new approach to psychotherapy.

None of the important questions addressed using effect size can be answered using the *F* ratios or *p* values obtained when inferential statistics tests are done. Nonetheless, measures of effect size and inferential statistics tests are complementary (Chow, 1988). For example, measures of effect size are more informative than are "*p* values" in helping researchers determine the substantive importance of experimental outcomes. At times, we want to know just how much of an "effect" our treatment had. Knowing the answer may help us decide whether to actually implement this treatment in an applied setting. When an experiment is being done to test predictions derived from a theory, however, the size of the effect of an independent variable is less critical. In this case, we are usually content with knowing that the independent variable "worked" as a theory said it should. In fact, as tests of a theory become more sophisticated, it is likely that small effects will be more critical. Inferential statistics tests are useful when experiments are done to test theories by confirming that an effect is present.

There is another reason not to discount small effect sizes. Consider the fact that studies have indicated there is a small positive effect of taking aspirin to try to prevent heart attacks. Considering the large number of people who are at risk for heart attacks, the small positive effect of taking aspirin could still have an impact on thousands of people. In terms of the potential numbers of people who could benefit, the small beneficial effect of taking aspirin would not be a small effect at all.

Abelson (1985) has identified another subtle aspect of interpreting small effect sizes. Abelson argues there are processes that can have tiny individual influences that can cumulate to produce meaningful outcomes. He uses a sports analogy to make his point. Abelson calculated how much of the variation in whether or not a batter got a hit in a single time at bat could be predicted on the basis of skill differences in major league batters. The skill differences were measured using the major league players' batting averages over 5 years. Abelson found that less than 1% of the variation in a single at bat could be predicted by the batters' skill. If we interpreted the small value of this effect size at face value we would come to the very improbable conclusion that batting skill has almost nothing to do with batting success! When averages over 5 years are used to predict a subsequent season's batting average, however, batting skill is a much stronger predictor of batting success.

The problem here is a familiar one; Abelson is illustrating what happens if we try to predict the outcome of single observations—in this case, single at-bats. Abelson draws an apt analogy to the situation researchers face when interpreting an effect size based on a single experiment. A small effect size need not indicate that an independent variable is unimportant. Effect sizes can be used more effectively when they are based on a series of experiments. We conclude this chapter by describing a procedure for just this purpose, meta-analysis.

META-ANALYSIS

Each strand contributes to the strength of a rope. But the rope is stronger than any strand. Similarly, each properly done experiment strengthens our confidence in a principle of psychology. But the principles of psychology are stronger than the results of any individual experiment. This is because principles of psychology (laws, if you will) emerge only after looking at the relationships among the results of many individual experiments. When a particular finding is found again and again under many different experimental situations, we are in a position to state with confidence a general law of behavior.

Meta-analysis is a valuable tool that makes it easier to summarize the results of experiments investigating the same independent variable or dependent variable. **Meta-analysis** is the analysis of the results of several independent experiments. In any experiment, the unit of analysis is the responses of individual subjects. In a meta-analysis, the unit of analysis is the results of individual experiments. These results are summarized using measures of effect size like those we described in the previous section. Meta-analyses are used to answer questions like these: Are there gender differences in conformity? What are the effects of class size on academic achievement? Is cognitive therapy effective in the treatment of depression? The results of individual experiments, no matter how well done, are not likely to be sufficient to provide answers to questions about such important general issues. We need to consider a body of literature (i.e., many experiments) pertaining to each issue.

Prior to the use of meta-analysis, the results of previous research on a particular topic were summarized using some form of narrative review. These reviews were typically published in the *Psychological Bulletin*. The reviewers were often experts in the area of research under investigation. After reading and thinking about the relevant studies, the reviewers would draw conclusions that they thought were supported by the evidence. Meta-analysis is not intended to replace these narrative reviews; instead, it is meant to strengthen the evidence used to reach conclusions. For example, reviewers previously would tally the number of experiments that did or did not show a statistically significant effect of an independent variable. This "voting method" was a crude measure of the effect of the independent variable. Meta-analysis allows for the direct measurement of the average effect size for a given independent variable across experiments.

Rosenthal used meta-analysis to summarize the results of 345 experiments on experimenter effects. Experimenter effects occur when the participants in an experiment respond in ways that correspond to the expectancies of the experimenter (see earlier section in this chapter on placebo control and double-blind experiments, as well as Chapter 3). Experimenter effects represent a specific instance of the more general category of interpersonal expectancy effects. Table 6.4 presents the mean effect sizes for each of eight domains in which interpersonal expectancy effects have been studied. The table also includes a brief description of an example of a type of study done in each domain. The mean effect size across all 345 studies is .70, a medium effect using J. Cohen's (1992) scale. For four of the eight domains the mean effect size is greater than .80, indicating a large effect. Table 6.4 also shows that the interpersonal expectancy finding has considerable external validity, since there is at least a medium size effect in six of the eight domains. Thus, we are in a position to state with confidence a general principle: Interpersonal expectancies can influence people's behavior.

Meta-analyses like the one summarized in Table 6.4 provide an efficient and effective way to summarize the results of large numbers of experiments. Nevertheless, the sophisticated statistical techniques used in meta-analyses are powerful only when the data from the studies being analyzed have been gathered in appropriate ways. For example, just which experiments are going to be included in the meta-analysis? Will only experiments reported in journals with high editorial standards be included, or will the meta-analysis include research reports that have not undergone editorial review? In general, the methodologi-

TABLE 6.4   ILLUSTRATION OF USE OF MEAN EFFECT SIZE IN META-ANALYSIS

Domain	d	Example of type of study
Laboratory interviews	.14	Effects of sensory restriction on reports of hallucinatory experiences
Reaction time	.17	Latency of word associations to certain stimulus words
Learning and ability	.54	IQ test scores, verbal conditioning (learning)
Person perception	.55	Perception of other people's success
Inkblot tests	.84	Ratio of animal to human Rorschach responses
Everyday situations	.88	Symbol learning, athletic performance
Psychophysical judgments	1.05	Ability to discriminate tones
Animal learning	1.73	Learning in mazes and Skinner boxes
Overall mean	.70	

Adapted from Rosenthal, R. (1994). Interpersonal expectancy effects: A 30-year perspective. *Current Directions in Psychological Science, 3*, 176–179.

cal quality of the experiments included in the meta-analysis will determine its ultimate value (Judd et al., 1991).

Our hope is that this brief introduction to the analysis of experiments gives you an appreciation of the variety of ways statistical analysis can be done. One theme emerges from our discussion of statistical analysis. There is no one best approach to analyzing an experiment just as there is no one best research method. Analysis techniques, like any tools, are best used when we know their strengths and weaknesses. We need to recognize that statistical analysis does not determine the conclusions we draw from our experiment—we do that! Statistical analysis does help us constrain the conclusions we reach. Most of all, statistical analysis is not a necessary evil in experimental research; it is a critical step on the path from asking a research question to answering it.

SUMMARY

Experimental research allows us to observe the unobservable. Predictions based on proposed explanatory processes can be either confirmed or refuted by experimental outcomes. Properly done experiments are internally valid, reliable, sensitive, and externally valid. A major purpose of experiments is to test hypotheses derived from theories, but experiments can also be useful in testing the effectiveness of treatments or programs in applied settings. The experimental method is ideally suited to identifying cause-and-effect relationships when the control techniques of manipulation, holding conditions constant, and balancing are properly implemented.

In this chapter we have focused on the application of these control techniques in experiments in which different groups of subjects are given different treatments represented by the levels of the independent variable. In the most common design of this type, the random groups design, the groups are formed using randomization procedures such that the groups are comparable at the start of the experiment. If the groups perform differently, it is presumed the independent variable is responsible. Random assignment is the most common method of forming comparable groups. By distributing subjects' characteristics equally across the conditions of the experiment, random assignment is an attempt to ensure that the differences among subjects are balanced. The most common technique for carrying out random assignment is block randomization.

Random assignment contributes to the internal validity of an experiment, but external validity must be established in some other way. One approach to enhancing external validity is to select representative samples of all dimensions on which you wish to generalize. Replication serves primarily as a check on the reliability of experimental findings, but replication also plays a key role in establishing external validity. When we obtain the same outcomes in two partial replications of the same experiment done in two widely different settings with different subjects, our confidence in the external validity of that finding increases. A partial replication, including the dimension on which you want to generalize as an independent variable, is perhaps the best way to establish external validity.

Testing intact groups even when the groups are randomly assigned to conditions should be avoided because the use of intact groups is highly likely to result in a confounding. Extraneous variables, such as different rooms or different experimenters, must not be allowed to confound the independent variable of interest. Even when such extraneous variables are controlled, however, they can contribute to the sensitivity and external validity of an experiment. Holding extraneous variables constant increases sensitivity and decreases external validity, whereas balancing extraneous variables decreases sensitivity and increases external validity.

A more serious threat to the internal validity of the random-groups design is involved when subjects fail to complete the experiment successfully. Selective subject loss occurs when subjects are lost differentially across the conditions and some characteristic of the subject that is related to the outcome of the experiment is responsible for the loss. We can help prevent selective loss by restricting subjects to those likely to complete the experiment successfully, or we can compensate for it by selectively dropping comparable subjects from the group that did not experience the loss. Demand characteristics and experimenter effects can be minimized through the use of proper experimental procedures, but they can best be controlled by using placebo control and double-blind procedures.

The matched groups design is an alternative to the random groups design when only a small number of subjects is available along with a good matching task and when the experiment requires separate groups for each treatment. The biggest problem with the matched groups design is that the groups are equated only on the characteristic measured by the matching task. In the natural groups design, researchers select the levels of independent variables (usually individual differences or subject variables) and look for systematic relationships between these independent variables and other aspects of behavior. Essentially, the natural groups design involves looking for correlations between subjects' characteristics and their performance. Such correlational research designs pose problems in drawing causal inferences.

The purpose of analyzing an experiment is to determine whether an independent variable has had an effect on behavior as reflected by differences in the dependent variable across the levels of the independent variable. The identification of such differences begins with descriptive statistics such as the plot-plus-error-bars procedure. Inferential statistics are used because differences in the dependent variable can arise because of error variation alone. The inductive and indirect process of null-hypothesis testing provides a set of guidelines for deciding on the statistical significance of a finding. There are important limitations of null-hypothesis testing that prevent it from ever replacing replication; replication remains the ultimate test of the reliability of a research finding. The most commonly used inferential statistics test in the analysis of experiments is the analysis of variance (ANOVA).

Measures of effect size provide important information that cannot be obtained from inferential statistics tests. One strength of effect size is that it is a measure which is independent of the sample size in an experiment. Measures of effect size do have limitations, but effect size can be especially useful in meta-analysis. Meta-analysis provides a quantitative summary of the results of a large number of experiments on an important research problem.

KEY CONCEPTS

independent variables	experimenter effects
dependent variables	placebo control
confounding	double-blind
independent groups designs	matched groups design
random groups design	natural groups designs
random assignment	inferential statistics
block randomization	null hypothesis
replication	statistically significant
extraneous variables	*F*-test (analysis of variance)
mechanical subject loss	analytical comparison
selective subject loss	effect size
demand characteristics	meta-analysis

REVIEW QUESTIONS

1 Briefly outline the logic of the random groups design.
2 What issues would you consider if you wanted to establish the external validity of an experiment you were planning to do that involved random assignment?
3 Describe the role of partial replications in establishing the external validity of a research finding.
4 What impact do extraneous variables have on the sensitivity and external validity of an experiment?
5 What preventive steps could you take if you anticipate that selective subject loss may pose a problem in your experiment?
6 Explain the logic of the two techniques used to control demand characteristics and experimenter effects.
7 Describe the conditions under which you would recommend that the matched groups design be used.
8 How do individual differences differ from manipulated independent variables and why does this difference make it difficult to draw causal inferences on the basis of the natural groups design?
9 How do you determine whether there is an effect of an independent variable when using the plot-plus-error-bar procedure?
10 How would you explain to a friend that statistical inference is inductive and indirect?
11 Explain what you have learned about the effect of an independent variable when you find out it has produced a statistically significant outcome. Is a statistically significant finding necessarily an important finding?

12 Distinguish between the information you gain from an omnibus *F*-test and from an analytical comparison.

13 Describe one advantage and one limitation of using measures of effect size.

14 What is the major difference between meta-analysis and narrative review in summarizing the results of previous research on a particular topic?

CHALLENGE QUESTIONS

1 An experimenter is planning to do a random groups design experiment to study the effect of the rate of presenting stimuli on people's ability to recognize the stimuli. The independent variable is the presentation rate and it will be manipulated at four levels: Very Fast, Fast, Slow, and Very Slow. The experimenter is seeking your help and advice with the following aspects of the experiment.

A The experimenter asks you to prepare a block randomized schedule such that there will be four participants in each of the four conditions. To do this you can use the following random numbers that were taken from the random number table in Appendix A.

1-5-6-6-4-1-0-4-9-3-2-0-4-9-2-3-8-3-9-1-9-1-1-3-2-2-1-9-9-9
5-9-5-1-6-8-1-6-5-2-2-7-1-9-5-4-8-2-2-3-4-6-7-5-1-2-2-9-2-3

B The experimenter is considering restricting participants to those who pass a stringent reaction time test so as to be sure they will be able to perform the task successfully with the Very Fast presentation rate. Explain what factors the experimenter should consider in making this decision, being sure to describe clearly what risks, if any, are taken if only this restricted set of participants is tested.

C The experimenter discovers it will be necessary to test participants in two different rooms. How should the experimenter arrange the testing of the conditions in these two rooms so as to avoid possible confounding by this extraneous variable?

2 A researcher was conducting a series of experiments on the effects of external factors on people's persistence in exercise programs. In one of these experiments, the researcher manipulated three types of distraction while subjects walked on a treadmill. The three types of distraction were concentrating on one's own thoughts, listening to a tape of music, and watching a video of people engaging in outdoor recreation. The dependent variable was how strenuous the treadmill exercise was at the time the subject decided to end the session (the incline of the treadmill was regularly increased as the person went through the session, thereby making the exercise increasingly strenuous). In an introductory psychology course, 120 students volunteered to participate in the experiment, and the researcher randomly assigned 40 students to each of the three levels of the distraction variable.

After only 2 minutes on the treadmill each subject was given the option to stop the experiment (this option came before any of the subjects could reasonably be expected to be experiencing fatigue). Data for the subjects who decided to stop after only 2 minutes were not included in the analysis of the final data. Twenty-five subjects who were concentrating on their own thoughts completed the experiment; 30 subjects in the music condition completed the experiment; and 40 subjects in the video group completed the experiment. The mean strenuousness score was highest for the concentration group ($n = 25$), next highest for the music group ($n = 30$), and lowest for the video group ($n = 40$). These results did not support the researcher's prediction that the mean strenuousness score would be highest in the video group.

    A What methodological problem may threaten the internal validity of this experiment? What factors indicate this problem occurred?

    B Assume a pretest measure was available for each of the 120 subjects and that the pretest measured the degree to which each subject was likely to persist at exercise. Describe how you could use these pretest scores to confirm that the problem you identified in Part A had occurred.

3 The newspaper headline summarizing research that had been reported in a medical journal read, "Study: Exercise Helps at Any Age." The research described in the article involved a 10-year study of nearly 10,000 men—and only men. The men were given a treadmill test between 1970 and 1989. Then they were given a second treadmill test 5 years after the first test and their health was monitored for another 5 years. Men who were judged unfit on both treadmill tests had a death rate over the next 5 years of 122 per 10,000. Men judged fit on both treadmill tests had a 5-year death rate of only 40 per 10,000. Most interestingly, men judged unfit on the first treadmill test but fit on the second had a death rate of 68 of 10,000. The benefits of exercise were even greater when only deaths from heart attacks were examined. The benefits from exercise were present across a wide range of ages—thus, the headline.

    A Why is the newspaper headline for this article potentially misleading?

    B Why do you think the researchers tested only men?

    C Identify two different ways of obtaining evidence that you could use to decide whether the results of this study could be applied to women. One of the ways would make use of already published research and the other way would require doing a new study.

4 An experiment was done to test the effectiveness of a drug being considered for possible use in the treatment of people who experience chronic anxiety. Fifty people who are chronically anxious are identified through a local health clinic and all 50 give their informed consent to participate in the experiment. Twenty-five people are randomly assigned to the experimental group and they receive the drug. The other 25 people are randomly assigned to the control group and they receive a placebo. The participants in both groups are monitored by a physician and a clinical psychologist during the 6-week treatment period. After the treatment period, the participants provide a self-rating on a reliable and valid 20-point scale indicating the level of anxiety they are experiencing (higher scores indicate greater anxiety). The mean self-rating in the experimental group was 10.2 and the mean rating in the control group was 13.5. The F-test for the mean difference between the two groups was $F(1,48) = 7.50, p = .01$.

    A Explain why a double-blind procedure would be useful in this experiment and describe how the double-blind procedure could be carried out in this experiment.

    B What information would you use to describe "what happened" in this experiment? What additional information do you need to use the plot-plus-error-bar procedure to describe the results of this experiment?

    C Is the F-test for this experiment statistically significant? Be sure to provide the evidence on which you base your decision.

    D The effect size for this experiment is $d = .37$. What does this effect size tell you about the effectiveness of the drug beyond what you know from the test of statistical significance?

ANSWERS TO CHALLENGE QUESTION 1

    A The first step is to assign a number from 1 to 4 to the respective conditions: 1 = Very Fast; 2 = Fast; 3 = Slow; and 4 = Very Slow. Then, using the random numbers, select four sequences of the numbers from 1 to 4. In doing this you skip any numbers greater than 4 and any number that is a repetition of a number already selected in the sequence. For example, if the first number you select is a 1, you skip all repetitions of 1 until you have selected all the numbers for the sequence of 1 to 4. Following this procedure and working across the rows of random numbers from left to right we obtained the following four sequences for the four blocks of the randomized block schedule. The order of the conditions for each block is also presented. The block randomized schedule specifies the order of testing the conditions for the first 16 participants in the experiment.

Block 1: 1-4-3-2   Very Fast, Very Slow, Slow, Fast
Block 2: 4-2-3-1   Very Slow, Fast, Slow, Very Fast
Block 3: 1-3-2-4   Very Fast, Slow, Fast, Very Slow
Block 4: 2-3-4-1   Fast, Slow, Very Slow, Very Fast

B The investigator is taking a reasonable step to avoid selective subject loss, but restricting participants to those who pass a stringent reaction time test entails the risk of decreased external validity of the obtained findings.

C The rooms can be balanced by assigning entire blocks from the block randomized schedule to be tested in each room. Usually, the number of blocks assigned to each room is equal, but this is not essential. For effective balancing, however, several blocks should be tested in each room.

Repeated Measures Designs

As we have emphasized, the experimental method involves at least two conditions (often a "treatment" condition and a "control" condition) in order to determine the differential influence of these conditions, if any, on behavior. Thus far we have considered experimental designs in which each condition is represented by a separate group of subjects. These independent groups designs (random groups, matched groups, and natural groups) are powerful tools for studying the effects of a wide range of independent variables. There are times, however, when it is inefficient to have conditions represented by different groups of participants. In such circumstances, it is still possible to do an interpretable experiment by having each participant experience all the conditions of an experiment. These designs are called **repeated measures designs** (or *within-subjects designs*). In an independent groups design, a separate group serves as a control for the group given the experimental treatment. In a repeated measures design, subjects *serve as their own controls* because they participate in both the experimental and control conditions.

We begin this chapter by exploring the reasons why a researcher might choose a repeated measures design. We next examine practice effects in the repeated measures designs. Practice effects arise because participants undergo changes as they are repeatedly tested. Participants may improve with practice, for example, because they learn more about the task or because they become more relaxed in the experimental situation. They also may get worse with practice—for example, because of fatigue or reduced motivation.

We described in Chapter 6 that individual differences among participants cannot be eliminated in the random groups design, but they can be balanced by using random assignment. Similarly, temporary changes participants experience due to repeated testing in the repeated measures designs (i.e., practice effects) cannot be eliminated. Like individual differences in the random groups design, however, practice effects can be balanced across the conditions of a repeated measures design experiment. When practice effects are balanced, the effect of an independent variable in a repeated measures design experiment is interpretable. Balancing *does not eliminate* practice effects from repeated measures designs. Balancing works by *averaging out* the practice effects across conditions. By doing this, we avoid confounding practice effects with the conditions of the experiment. This chapter discusses various techniques for accomplishing this balancing. We also describe potential limitations of repeated measures designs. We conclude the chapter with an introduction to procedures for analyzing the results of repeated measures designs.

REASONS FOR USING REPEATED MEASURES DESIGNS

There are at least four reasons why a researcher might choose a repeated measures design. First, repeated measures designs require fewer participants, so they are ideal for situations in which only a small number of participants is available.

The second reason for choosing a repeated measures design applies even when sufficient numbers of participants are available for an independent-groups design. A researcher might choose to use a repeated measures design for the sake of convenience or efficiency. For example, Posner (1973) describes a series of experiments dealing with the cognitive processes required to identify individual letters while reading. In one of these experiments, the investigators measured how long it took participants to decide whether two briefly presented letters had the same name. There were two conditions in the experiment: Either the two presented letters were physically identical (AA) or they had the same name but were physically different (Aa). Even though the participants' task was the same in the two conditions (to decide whether the two letters had the same name), the researchers found that participants could respond 80 milliseconds (ms) faster when the letters were physically identical than they could when the letters had only their name in common. Each trial in this experiment required only a few seconds to complete. Posner could have tested separate groups of participants for each of the two conditions, but this approach would have been horribly inefficient. It would have taken more time to instruct participants regarding the nature of the task than it would to do the task itself! A repeated measures design in which each participant was tested on both types of pairs of letters provided the experimenters with a far more efficient way to answer their research question.

The third reason to choose a repeated measures design for an experiment is that the experiment will generally be more sensitive than one that uses an independent groups design. As we noted in Chapter 6, sensitivity refers to the extent that an experiment is able to detect differences in the dependent variable as a function of the independent variable. In repeated measures designs, the investigator is trying to detect differences in the performance of the same participants under different conditions. In independent groups designs, researchers are trying to detect differences in the performance of different participants under different conditions. Repeated measures designs are generally more sensitive than independent groups designs because the two types of designs differ in the amount of error variation present. Simply speaking, there is usually more variation between people than there is within people. That is, participants will vary within themselves over time (in a repeated measures design) less than participants will vary from other participants (in an independent groups design), and, thus, error variation is less in a repeated measures design. The less error variation, the easier it is to see the effect of an independent variable. The increased sensitivity of repeated measures designs is especially attractive to researchers who are studying independent variables that have small (hard-to-see) effects on behavior.

The fourth reason for choosing a repeated measures design is that some areas of psychological research require its use. When the research question involves studying changes in participants' behavior over time, such as in a learning experiment or in a longitudinal design (see Chapter 4), a repeated measures design is needed. Further, whenever the experimental procedure requires that participants compare two or more stimuli relative to one another, a repeated measures design must be used. For example, a repeated measures design would have to be used if a researcher wanted to measure the minimum amount of light that must be added before participants could detect a spot of light had become brighter. It would also be called for if a researcher wanted participants to rate the relative attractiveness of a series of photographs. In general, the research areas of psychophysics (illustrated by the light-detection experiment) and scaling (illustrated by the ratings of attractiveness) rely heavily on repeated measures designs. Journals such as *Perception & Psychophysics* and *Journal of Experimental Psychology: Human Perception and Performance* frequently publish results of experiments using repeated measures designs.

Before continuing our discussion of repeated measures designs, let's make a distinction between this type of design and other designs that also test subjects repeatedly, but are not, strictly speaking, repeated measures designs. Psychologists frequently measure subjects on more than one occasion. There are important reasons for doing this that usually have to do with reliability. First, as you saw in earlier chapters, a researcher may obtain two (or more) measures of the same individual in order to establish the reliability (consistency) of a measure. For example, a group of participants may be given the same aptitude test on two different occasions in order to assess the test-retest reliability of such an instrument. A correlation coefficient would likely be used to measure reliability in this situation. Another reason for testing subjects repeatedly is to obtain a more stable and, hence, reliable measure of behavior. For example, consider a study of individuals' current level of depression based on a self-report inventory. An investigator who measures depression would probably not want to use a questionnaire that has only one item asking about depression. Rather, such a measure will be more reliable if it is based on people's responses to many different items asking about their current mood. These situations, in which we test subjects repeatedly in order either to measure reliability or to increase the reliability of our measurement should be differentiated from repeated measures designs in which we contrast subjects' behavior in two or more conditions of an experiment.

PRACTICE EFFECTS

At first glance, repeated measures designs might appear far superior to independent groups designs. The repeated measures designs require fewer participants, and experiments can usually be completed more quickly. In addition to their greater efficiency, the repeated measures designs offer another advantage: The problem of confounding the conditions of the experiment with the characteristics of the participants within each condition is avoided. That is, in an independent groups design, participants in different conditions of the experiment must be essentially equivalent in terms of important characteristics (e.g., motivation, aptitude, etc.). An experiment is confounded if participants in various groups differ in ways other than the levels of the independent variable. In a repeated measures design, the same participants are tested in all conditions, so it is impossible to end up with brighter, more aggressive, or more anxious participants in one condition than in another condition. Stated formally, there can be no confounding by individual difference variables in the repeated measures designs.

The apparent superiority of repeated measures designs diminishes, however, when we realize these designs require the same participant to be tested more than once. Participants may change across repeated testings even if all tests are done under the same conditions. That is, participants may get better and better at doing a task if a skill is being developed, or they may get worse and worse at the task because of such factors as fatigue and boredom. The repeated testing of each participant in the repeated measures designs gives the participants practice with the experimental task. The changes participants undergo with repeated testing are called **practice effects.**

Kahneman, Frederickson, Schreiber, and Redelmeier (1993) used a repeated measures design in a series of experiments investigating people's perception of pain. They argued that the duration of an aversive experience plays a much smaller role in our perception of pain than do two other factors. They demonstrated that our evaluations of pain are influenced most by the worst moments and the final moments of the experience. In other words, we judge how painful an experience was by judging how painful it was at the point of most intense pain and by how painful it was at the end of the experience. These two factors were shown to be more important in the perception of pain than the amount of time the pain lasted. We illustrate the balancing of practice effects using one of the experiments that Kahneman et al. did to determine the influence of the intensity of the pain in the final moments of the experience. Other experiments in the series addressed how the most intense moments of pain in an experience affected the evaluation of pain.

There were two conditions in the experiment. In the first condition (short trial) students immersed one hand in cold water (14° C) for 60 seconds. In the second condition (long trial) the students also immersed their hand in 14° water for 60 seconds, but they then kept their hand immersed 30 seconds longer while the temperature of the water was gradually raised (warmed) to 15°. Each participant experienced both the short trial and the long trial only once. There was a 7-minute interval filled with another activity after each trial. One dependent variable was people's ratings of their degree of pain after each trial. The most important measure in the experiment, however, was the choice students made when they were asked to choose which trial they preferred to repeat.

The researchers found that the students' ratings of pain indicated that the 15° water was painful, but noticeably less painful than the 14° water. Overall, the long trial was rated by students as more painful than the short trial. Nonetheless, when students were asked which trial they preferred to repeat, 69% chose the more painful long trial. Kahneman et al. (1993) argued that the students chose the long trial because it was less painful in the final moments of the experience. The overall duration of the long trial was less critical in determining students' choice than was the fact that it was less painful at the end of their experience. To reach this intriguing insight the researchers had to make sure that practice effects were balanced in the experiment.

Suppose that Kahneman et al. (1993) had tested all the students by giving them the short trial first and then the long trial. In this case, practice effects would not have been balanced. The problem with using only one testing order is that differences between the two types of trials would be confounded with the order in which they occurred: The short trial would always be the first trial and the long trial would always be the second trial. Students might become more familiar with the sensations resulting from having their hand immersed in cold water as they move from one trial to the other. Or maybe they would be less apprehensive about possible pain after they had experience with one trial. There are many important ways in which the students could change over the two trials. We call the summation of these changes *practice effects*. If only one order had been used, practice effects and the conditions of the experiment would be confounded. Thus, if people rated the two conditions differently, we wouldn't know if the difference in ratings was due to the type of trial (short or long) or the temporal order (first or second) in which the conditions appeared.

Kahneman et al. (1993) balanced practice effects by administering the conditions in two different orders. Half of the students received the short trial followed by the long trial, and half received the long trial followed by the short trial. Since both orders were used equally often, the students' preference to repeat the long trial rather than the short trial cannot be attributed to the long trial always having been presented last. The changes due to practice effects that occurred for the students from the first trial to the second trial are likely to fall equally on each of the two conditions because half the students experienced practice effects during a long trial, and half on a short trial. Practice effects should average out across conditions. Any difference in performance, therefore, between the two conditions is the result of the nature of the short and long trials and not the result of practice effects.

BALANCING PRACTICE EFFECTS

There are two types of repeated measures designs. In the *complete design*, practice effects are balanced for each participant. Balancing practice effects for each participant is accomplished by administering the conditions to each participant several times, using different orders each time. Each participant can thus be considered a "complete" experiment. In the *incomplete design*, each condition is administered to each participant *only once*. The order of administering the conditions is varied across participants rather than for each participant as is the case in the complete design. Practice effects in the incomplete design average out when the results are combined for all participants. This may seem a bit confusing at this point, but it should become clearer as we discuss these types of designs. The techniques for balancing practice effects—called **counterbalancing**—are different in the two repeated measures designs, so we discuss the two designs separately. Just keep in mind that a major goal when using a repeated measures design is to control for practice effects; exactly how we do that depends on the specific repeated measures design used.

COMPLETE DESIGN

Does one side of your face express emotion more intensely than the other side? Sackheim, Gur, and Saucy (1978) used a repeated measures design to attempt to answer this question. Earlier research had shown that participants given photographs depicting posed facial expressions of six basic human emotions (happiness, surprise, fear, sadness, anger, and disgust) could readily and accurately identify the expressed emotion. Sackheim and coworkers took advantage of a technique developed in earlier work on facial recognition whereby a full photograph of a face can be constructed using only one side of a person's face. The technique involves developing both a photograph of a full face and a photograph of its mirror image. These two photographs are then split down the middle and two composite photographs are made—one from the two versions of the left side of the face and one from the two versions of the right side. Illustrative photographs are presented in Figure 7.1. In the center is a photograph of a person expressing disgust. The two composite photographs made from the center photograph are presented on either side of the original. Does one of the two composites in Figure 7.1 look more disgusted than the other?

Participants were shown slides of photographs like those in Figure 7.1 and asked to rate each slide on a 7-point scale indicating the intensity of the expressed emotion. The slides were presented individually for 10 seconds, and participants were then given 35 seconds to make their rating. To increase the external validity of their experiment, the investigators had photographs of 14 different people depicting the 6 identifiable emotions and one neutral expression.

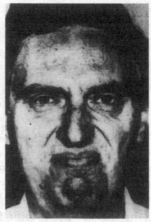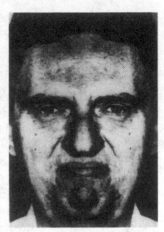

FIGURE 7.1   (a) Left-side composite, (b) original, and (c) right-side composite of the same face. The face is expressing disgust. (From Sackheim et al., 1978.)

The critical independent variable in the experiment, however, was the *version* of the photograph (left composite, original, or right composite). Each participant rated 54 slides: 18 left composites, 18 originals, and 18 right composites.

Participants' ratings of emotional intensity were consistently higher for the left composite than for the right composite. Sackheim et al. interpreted these findings in terms of hemispheric specialization of the brain. In general, the left hemisphere controls the right side of the body and the right hemisphere controls the left side of the body. Thus, the left composite reflects control by the right hemisphere, and the right composite reflects control by the left hemisphere. The higher ratings of emotional intensity for the left composite photographs suggest the right hemisphere may be more heavily involved than the left hemisphere in the production of emotional expression.

The interpretation of the differences in the ratings depended critically on the order in which the slides were presented to participants. If all the original versions were presented first, followed by all the right composites, then by all the left composites, higher ratings for the slides shown at the end of this long sequence may reflect the intensity of the participants' boredom and fatigue rather than the intensity of the emotions actually depicted in the photographs. If you imagine yourself in this experiment making a rating for each of the slides in this long sequence (over 40 minutes), you will get a sense of what we mean by practice effects. Surely your attention, motivation, and experience in rating the emotionality of photographs will change as you work through the sequence of slides. Sackheim et al. used balancing techniques specifically developed for use with the complete design in repeated measures experiments to ensure that each of the three versions of the photographs was equally likely to appear at any point in the long series of slides.

In the complete design, participants are given each treatment enough times to balance practice effects for each participant. Of course, this is possible only when each treatment can be administered more than once. When the task is simple enough and not too time-consuming (such as judging the emotional intensity of photographs), it is possible to give one participant several experiences with each treatment. In fact, in some complete designs, only one or two participants are tested and each participant experiences literally hundreds of trials. More commonly, however, researchers use procedures like those used by Sackheim et al. That is, several participants are tested, and each participant is given each treatment only a relatively small number of times. Researchers have two choices in deciding how to arrange the order in which the treatments in a complete design are administered: block randomization and ABBA counterbalancing.

Block Randomization   We introduced block randomization in Chapter 6 as an effective technique for assigning participants to conditions in the random-groups design. *Block randomization* can also be used to order the conditions for each participant in a complete design. For instance, Sackheim et al. administered each of the three versions of their photographs (left composite, original, and right composite) 18 times to each participant. The sequence of trials shown in Table 7.1 illustrates how block randomization could be used to arrange the order of the three conditions in their experiment. The sequence of 54 trials is broken up into 18 blocks of 3 trials. Each block of trials contains the three conditions of the experiment in random order. In general, the number of blocks in a block-randomized schedule is equal to the number of times each condition is administered, and the size of each block is equal to the number of conditions in the experiment.

If a participant rated the photographs following the sequence in the block-randomized schedule shown in Table 7.1, it is unlikely that changes in the participant's attention, motivation, or experience with rating photographs would affect any one of the conditions more than any other. The practice effects can reasonably be expected to average out over the three experimental conditions. Determining the average position of each of the three conditions in the block-randomized sequence gives a rough indication of the balancing of practice effects. This can be done by summing the trial numbers on which each condition appears and dividing by 18. For instance, the original version of the photographs appeared on trials 1, 5, 8, 11, 13, 18, 21, 24, 27, 28, 33, 34, 39, 40, 44, 48, 49, and 53. The average position of the original photographs, therefore, was 27.6. The corresponding values for the left and right composite photographs are 27.7 and 27.2, respectively. That these average values are so similar tells us that any one version of the photographs was not more likely to appear at the beginning, middle, or end of the sequence of 54 trials.

Block randomization is effective in balancing practice effects, but each condition must be repeated several times before we can expect practice effects to average out. We should not expect practice effects to be balanced after two or

TABLE 7.1   BLOCK-RANDOMIZED SEQUENCE OF TRIALS IN AN EXPERIMENT WITH THREE CONDITIONS ADMINISTERED 18 TIMES EACH

Trial	Conditions	Trial	Conditions
1	O	28	O
2	L	29	L
3	R	30	R
4	R	31	R
5	O	32	L
6	L	33	O
7	R	34	O
8	O	35	R
9	L	36	L
10	L	37	L
11	O	38	R
12	R	39	O
13	O	40	O
14	L	41	R
15	R	42	L
16	R	43	R
17	L	44	O
18	O	45	L
19	R	46	R
20	L	47	L
21	O	48	O
22	L	49	O
23	R	50	R
24	O	51	L
25	R	52	R
26	L	53	O
27	O	54	L

Note: The conditions are the three versions of the photographs used by Sackheim et al. (1978): L = left composite, O = original, R = right composite.

three blocks—any more than we would expect sample sizes of two or three in the random groups design to result in comparable groups. Fortunately, a technique is available to balance practice effects when it is not possible to administer each condition often enough for the averaging process of block randomization to work effectively.

ABBA Counterbalancing   In its simplest form, ABBA counterbalancing can be used to balance practice effects in the complete design with as few as two administrations of each condition. **ABBA counterbalancing** involves presenting the conditions in one sequence (i.e., A then B) followed by the opposite of that same sequence (i.e., B then A). Its name describes the sequences when there are only two conditions (A and B) in the experiment, but ABBA counterbalancing is not limited to experiments with just two conditions. Sackheim et al. could have presented the versions of their photographs according to the sequence outlined in the row of Table 7.2 labeled "Condition."

Note that the order of the three conditions on the first three trials is simply reversed for trials 4 to 6. The row of Table 7.2 labeled "Practice effect (linear)" illustrates how ABBA counterbalancing can balance practice effects. When practice effects are linear, the same amount of practice effects is added to or subtracted from performance on each successive trial. In our example, suppose one "unit" of hypothetical practice effects is added to performance on each trial. Because there would be no practice effect associated with the first trial, the amount of practice added to Trial 1 in the table is zero. Trial 2 has one unit of hypothetical effects added because of participants' experience with the first trial; in Trial 3 there are two units added because of participants' experience with two trials, and so on. If you add up these hypothetical practice effects for each condition, you will see that all the totals are the same, namely 5. The left composite condition gets the least and the greatest influence from practice effects; the right composite condition gets two intermediate amounts. The ABBA cycle can be applied with any number of conditions and repeated any number of times. It balances practice effects even more effectively with larger numbers of repetitions of the cycle. Usually, however ABBA counterbalancing is used when the number of conditions and the number of repetitions of each condition are relatively small. Whenever ABBA counterbalancing is used there must be an even number of repetitions of each condition.

Although ABBA counterbalancing provides a simple and elegant means to balance practice effects, it is not without limitations. For example, when practice effects for a task are not linear but involve abrupt initial changes followed by relatively little change thereafter, ABBA counterbalancing is ineffective. This is illustrated in the last row of Table 7.2. The left composite receives a total of

TABLE 7.2   ABBA COUNTERBALANCED SEQUENCE OF TRIALS IN AN EXPERIMENT WITH THREE CONDITIONS (LEFT COMPOSITE, ORIGINAL, AND RIGHT COMPOSITE)

	Condition:	Trial 1 Left	Trial 2 Original	Trial 3 Right	Trial 4 Right	Trial 5 Original	Trial 6 Left
Practice effect (linear)		+0	+1	+2	+3	+4	+5
Practice effect (nonlinear)		0	+6	+6	+6	+6	+6

only 6 hypothetical units of practice effects, and the other two conditions receive a total of 12 units each. When practice effects of this type are anticipated, researchers often ignore performance on the early trials and wait until the practice effects reach a steady state. Reaching a steady state is likely to take several repetitions of each condition, so researchers tend to use block randomization to balance practice effects in these situations. This problem should alert you to the fact that there are situations when you should not choose a repeated measures design, for example, if nonlinear changes cannot easily be eliminated from your analysis.

A second limitation of ABBA counterbalancing is the problem of anticipation effects. *Anticipation effects* occur when a participant develops expectations about which condition should occur next in the sequence. The participant's response to that condition may then be influenced more by this expectation than by the actual experience of the condition itself. For example, consider a time-perception experiment in which the participant's task is to estimate the length of time that has passed between when the experimenter said "Start" and when the experimenter said "Stop." (Of course, participants have to be prevented somehow from marking off time during the interval by counting or rhythmically tapping.) If the time intervals in such an experiment are 12, 24, and 36 seconds, then one possible ABBA sequence of conditions could be 12-24-36-36-24-12. If this cycle were repeated several times, participants probably would recognize the pattern and expect a series of increasing and then decreasing intervals. Their time estimates might soon begin to reflect this pattern rather than their perception of each independent interval. In general, block randomization should be used if anticipation effects are likely.

INCOMPLETE DESIGN

In the incomplete design, each participant is given each treatment *only once.* The results for any one participant, therefore, are uninterpretable because the levels of the independent variable for each participant are perfectly confounded with the order in which those levels were presented. For instance, the first participant in an incomplete design experiment might be tested first in the experimental condition (E) and second in the control condition (C). Any differences in the participant's performance between the experimental and control conditions could be due to the effect of the independent variable *or* to the practice effects resulting from the EC order. To break this confounding of the order of conditions and the independent variable, we can administer different orders of the conditions to different participants. For example, we could administer the conditions of our incomplete design experiment to a second participant in the CE order, testing the control condition first and the experimental condition second. In this way, we could balance the effects of order across the two conditions using two participants instead of one.

To illustrate the techniques for balancing practice effects in the incomplete design, we use an experiment by Erber (1991) on the effects of people's moods on their perceptions of other people. There were two stages in this experiment. In the first stage, participants were asked to read one of three stories about events in the life of a young female artist. These stories were previously shown to be effective in inducing positive, neutral, or negative moods in people. The story for the positive-mood condition included several events culminating in the artist receiving a scholarship to college. The neutral-mood story described how the artist decided which college to attend. The negative-mood story described how the artist was overcome by a rare disabling illness at the end of her first year in college. (In the first stage, the independent variable of mood was manipulated using independent groups, that is, each participant was in only one mood group.)

After reading one of these stories, the second stage of the experiment began. The participants believed the second stage was a separate experiment, one in which they were asked to rate the likelihood of a person engaging in a particular behavior (welcoming a friend with a hug, getting depressed over the weather, and so on). Four individuals were described to the participants, and then the participants were asked to rate the likelihood that these individuals would demonstrate various behaviors. Four brief descriptions were provided to each participant, one for each "target" individual they would rate. For reasons that will become apparent, the descriptions were based on somewhat contradictory traits. Each of the four "target people" was described as (1) moody and warm; (2) pessimistic and understanding; (3) unselfish and unsociable; or (4) trustworthy and possessive. A repeated measures design was used to implement the independent variable of the target person, which, of course, had four levels. Specifically, an incomplete design was used in which each participant rated all four target people once.

Before describing the techniques that can be used to balance practice effects for an independent variable in the incomplete design, let's take a brief look at the results of the Erber study. The dependent variable in this study was the participants' ratings of the likelihood that the target people would engage in certain behaviors. The researcher hypothesized that these ratings would be influenced by *participants'* mood (positive, neutral, or negative) as manipulated in the first stage of the experiment. Because the target people were described using both a positive (e.g., warm) and a negative (e.g., moody) trait, the researchers wanted to see if the participants' mood would determine which of the two traits most influenced their ratings. For example, the participant's task was to rate how likely it was for someone described as "warm and moody" to engage in positive behavior, such as "welcoming a friend with a hug," or in negative behavior, such as "getting depressed over the weather." Welcoming someone with a hug is something a "warm" person might do; getting depressed is something a "moody" person is more likely to do. Perhaps you can anticipate what happened in this experiment.

Erber found that if a participant was in a positive mood, then a "warm and moody" person was rated as more likely to engage in positive behavior (e.g., welcoming with a hug) than in negative behavior (e.g., getting depressed over the weather). If the participant was in a negative mood, the same "warm and moody" individual was rated more likely to engage in negative behavior than in positive behavior. The effect of mood on ratings of negative behaviors was larger than was the effect of mood on ratings of positive behaviors. These findings (along with other findings reported in the study) indicate that mood can influence the way we perceive other people in important ways. One such influence, Erber argues, is that negative mood may facilitate the accessibility of negative information about others. In other words, if you're in a bad mood, you're more likely to accentuate someone's negative traits!

The repeated measures independent variable in the Erber (1991) experiment was the four types of target people. In order to rule out practice effects as an alternative explanation for the findings it is essential that the order in which the targets are rated is balanced. We turn now to the balancing techniques used in the incomplete design. The general rule for balancing practice effects in the incomplete design is a simple one: *Each condition of the experiment must appear in each ordinal position equally often.* Several techniques are available for satisfying this general rule. These techniques differ in what additional balancing they accomplish, but so long as the techniques are properly used, the basic rule will be met and the experiment will be interpretable. That is, if appropriate balancing is carried out, then we will be in a position to determine whether the independent variable, and not practice effects, influenced the participants' behavior.

All Possible Orders   The preferred technique for balancing practice effects in the incomplete design is to use all possible orders of the conditions. Each participant is randomly assigned to one of the orders. With only two conditions there are only two possible orders (AB and BA); with three conditions there are six possible orders (ABC, ACB, BAC, BCA, CAB, CBA). In general, there are N! (which is read "N factorial") possible orders with N conditions, where N! equals $N(N - 1) (N - 2) \ldots (N - [N - 1])$. As we just saw, there are six possible orders with three conditions, which is 3! ($3 \times 2 \times 1 = 6$). The number of required orders increases dramatically with increasing numbers of conditions. For instance, for only five conditions there are 120 possible orders of the conditions, and for six conditions there are 720 possible orders. Because of this, the use of all possible orders is usually limited to experiments involving four or fewer conditions. With four conditions, how many possible orders are there?

Because there were four target people in the Erber (1991) experiment, 24 sequences would be required to obtain all possible orders of the conditions. These sequences are presented in the left column of Table 7.3. Using all possible orders certainly meets the general rule of ensuring that all conditions appear in each ordinal position equally often. The first ordinal position shows this balancing most clearly: The first six sequences begin with the Moody-Warm (M) target, and each succeeding set of six sequences begins with one of the other three targets. The same pattern applies at each of the four ordinal positions. For example, the "M" target also appears six times in the second ordinal position, six times in the third ordinal position, and six times in the fourth ordinal position. The use of all possible orders also provides two other potentially useful

TABLE 7.3   ALTERNATIVE TECHNIQUES TO BALANCE PRACTICE EFFECTS IN AN INCOMPLETE REPEATED MEASURES DESIGN EXPERIMENT WITH FOUR CONDITIONS

All possible orders								Selected orders							
								Latin Square				Random starting order with rotation			
Ordinal position				Ordinal position				Ordinal position				Ordinal position			
1st	2d	3d	4th	1st	2d	3d	4th	1st	2d	3d	4th	1st	2d	3d	4th
M	P	U	T	U	M	P	T	M	P	U	T	P	U	T	M
M	P	T	U	U	M	T	P	P	T	M	U	U	T	M	P
M	U	P	T	U	P	M	T	T	U	P	M	T	M	P	U
M	U	T	P	U	P	T	M	U	M	T	P	M	P	U	T
M	T	P	U	U	T	M	P								
M	T	U	P	U	T	P	M								
P	M	U	T	T	M	P	U								
P	M	T	U	T	M	U	P								
P	U	M	T	T	P	M	U								
P	U	T	M	T	P	U	M								
P	T	M	U	T	U	M	P								
P	T	U	M	T	U	P	M								

Note: The four conditions are identified by the first letter of the first adjective describing each of the four target people in the Erber (1991) experiment: Moody-Warm (M), Pessimistic-Understanding (P), Unselfish-Unsociable (U), and Trustworthy-Possessive (T).

types of balancing. First, careful examination of the 24 sequences reveals that each condition precedes and follows every other condition equally often. For instance, the Unselfish-Unsociable target (U) precedes the Trustworthy-Possessive target (T) six times, and the reverse order (TU) also appears six times. Note how this occurs for every pair of conditions (e.g., MP and PM, PT and TP, etc.) Second, each condition precedes and follows every other condition equally often at each ordinal position. That is, the orders UT and TU appear exactly twice in ordinal positions 1 and 2, 2 and 3, and 3 and 4.

One other issue must be addressed in deciding to use all possible orders. For this technique to be effective, it is essential that at least one participant be tested with each of the possible orders of the conditions. That is, at least one participant should receive the MPUT order, at least one should receive the MPTU order, and so on. Therefore, the use of all possible orders requires at least as many participants as there are possible orders. That is, if there are four conditions in the experiment, you must test 24 participants (or 48 or 72 or some other multiple of 24). This restriction makes it very important that you have a good idea of the number of potential participants available to you before testing the first participant.

Selected Orders   We have just described the preferred method for balancing practice effects in the incomplete design, all possible orders. There are times, however, when the use of all possible orders is not practical. For example, if we wanted to use the incomplete design to study an independent variable with seven levels, we would need to test 5,040 participants if we used all possible orders—one participant for each of the possible orders of the seven conditions (7! orders). We obviously need some alternative to using all possible orders if we are to use the incomplete design for experiments with five or more conditions.

Practice effects can be balanced by using just some of all the possible orders. The number of selected orders will always be equal to some multiple of the number of conditions in the experiment. For example, to do an experiment with one independent variable with seven levels, we need to select 7, 14, 21, 28, or some other multiple of seven orders to balance practice effects. The two basic variations of using selected orders are illustrated in Table 7.3. To allow you to compare the types of balancing more directly, we have illustrated the techniques for selected orders with the four-level independent variable from Erber's (1991) experiment that we described in the previous section.

The first type of balancing using selected orders is called the Latin Square. In a **Latin Square**, the general rule for balancing practice effects is met. That is, each condition appears at each ordinal position once. For example, in Table 7.3, we can see that in the Latin Square, condition "M" appears exactly once in the first, second, third, and fourth ordinal positions. This is true for each condition. Additionally, in a Latin Square each condition precedes and follows each other condition exactly once. Examination of the Latin Square in Table 7.3 shows that the order "MP" appears once, as does the order "PM." The order "PV" appears once, as does the order "VP," and so on, for every combination of conditions. Latin Squares are limited to experiments with an even number of conditions. Procedures for selecting or constructing Latin Squares are described in Winer, Brown, and Michels (1991, pp. 674-679) should you need to use a Latin Square for an experiment you are doing.

The second balancing technique using selected orders requires you to begin with a random order of the conditions and to rotate this sequence systematically with each condition moving one position to the left each time (see the example in Table 7.3). Using a random starting order with rotation effectively balances practice effects because, like the Latin Square, each condition appears in each ordinal position. However, the systematic rotation of the sequences means that each condition always follows and always precedes the *same* other conditions, which is not like the Latin Square technique. The simplicity of the random starting order with rotation technique and its applicability to experiments with more than four conditions are its primary advantages.

The use of all possible orders, Latin Squares, and random starting orders with rotation are equally effective in balancing practice effects because all three techniques ensure that each condition appears in each ordinal position equally often. Regardless of which technique one uses to balance practice effects, the sequences of conditions should be fully prepared prior to testing the first participant, and participants should be randomly assigned to these sequences.

LIMITATIONS OF REPEATED MEASURES DESIGNS

The first obvious limitation of the repeated measures designs is that they cannot be used to study individual differences variables such as age and gender. A 40-year-old person cannot be 20 years old, then 60 years old, and then 40 years old again (although we've all known people who act that way!). Second, repeated measures designs also are not appropriate when the levels of the independent variable represent an unfolding sequence of successive events. For example, a study of brain lesions would require controls such as Anesthesia Only and a Sham-Operated condition, and the sequential nature of these treatments seems to demand separate groups. That is, an animal could not be tested in the Anesthesia Only group once the animal was lesioned. Third, experiments in which each condition takes a great deal of time to implement are not likely to be suitable for repeated measures designs. For example, if the treatment involved participation in a year-long program, one ABBA sequence in a repeated measures design would take 4 years to implement! It is unlikely that the random groups design will be completely replaced by the repeated measures designs.

IRREVERSIBLE TASKS

An experiment by Sharma and Moskowitz (1972), looking at the effects of marijuana use, illustrates how one problem sometimes encountered in a repeated measures design, that of irreversible tasks, must be dealt with. They asked participants to come to their laboratory on four different days. Each day the participants were given 20 minutes to smoke two cigarettes that contained one of four dose levels of marijuana—a placebo control (0) and doses of 50, 100, and 200 units (1 unit = 1 µg/kg of body weight). The doses reflected the amount of tetrahydrocannabinol (THC; the active agent in marijuana) in the two cigarettes combined. Sharma and Moskowitz did a repeated measures experiment using an incomplete design, so each participant was given each dose once. The order of the doses across participants was determined using a Latin Square. Immediately after the participants smoked the two cigarettes, they were tested on an autokinetic illusion task. In this task the participant is placed in a darkened room and asked to focus on a pinpoint of light. The illusion that participants often experience in this situation is that the pinpoint of light appears to move, even though it is really stationary. Sharma and Moskowitz found that the degree of the autokinetic illusion—that is, the degree of apparent movement—increased with increasing doses of marijuana. Such an outcome indicates that there may be hazards associated with driving a car or flying an airplane at night under the influence of marijuana, especially at relatively high doses.

The task designed to measure the autokinetic illusion can be given repeatedly to participants without their mastering it. Participants will continue to experience the illusion even after being tested several times. Therefore, Sharma and Moskowitz needed to balance practice effects only for the marijuana variable. That is, they needed only to balance the order of marijuana doses (0, 50, 100, 200) given to their participants, which, we have seen, they did through the use of a Latin Square.

Consider, however, how the situation would change if Sharma and Moskowitz had been interested in the effects of marijuana on people's ability to learn and remember new information. One way to carry out an experiment like this would be to give each participant a different list of words to learn under each dose of marijuana. A different list of words would be needed each time because a memory task of this type is an *irreversible task*, one that cannot be administered more than once without risking that the participant will master the task. Once participants master the task, their performance under subsequent conditions is not likely to vary. In a sense, irreversible tasks result in a "ceiling effect" for all conditions after the first one under which the task has been performed. When performance hits a "ceiling" there is no way to measure any further improvement in performance in the other conditions (see Chapter 8).

Suppose in this example that the researchers had given the same list of words to participants on each of the four days. Consider the performance of a participant who received the following sequence of doses: 0, 50, 200, and 100. Performance may not be all that good on the first day (0 dose) as the participant is learning the list of words for the first time. However, on the second, and following days, his or her performance is likely to be better because the list had been learned on Day 1. Note that this improvement would be seen just when the participant is receiving doses (50, 200, 100) of marijuana. This may make marijuana look like a drug that enhances memory! Of course, it would not be a valid finding because of the problem with irreversible tasks. Because the list was mastered early in the experiment, it would be impossible to know if marijuana had any effects on memory.

The solution to the problem of irreversible tasks, which requires two steps, is outlined in Table 7.4. The first step is to balance practice effects for the primary independent variable (in our case, the marijuana variable). A random starting order with rotation has been used to accomplish the balancing of the four dose levels (0, 50, 100, and 200 units). The sequences for the first four participants appear in the upper-left quadrant of the table. Because each dose appears with each of four lists exactly once, the marijuana variable is also balanced for the possible effects of the list variable. Thus, if any list happens to be easier for a participant to learn, any one dosage level would not have an advantage due to the easier list.

A problem would arise, however, if the researcher were to try to assess differences among the four lists. The lists for the first four participants are perfectly confounded by the ordinal position. That is, list A is always learned first, list B is learned on day 2, list C on the third day, and list D is always last. The confound-

TABLE 7.4   BALANCING EXPERIMENTS WITH IRREVERSIBLE TASKS IN REPEATED MEASURES DESIGNS

	Ordinal position					Ordinal position			
	1st	2d	3d	4th		1st	2d	3d	4th
		List					List		
Subject	A	B	C	D	Subject	B	C	D	A
1	050	200	000	100	5	050	200	000	100
2	200	000	100	050	6	200	000	100	050
3	000	100	050	200	7	000	100	050	200
4	100	050	200	000	8	100	050	200	000
	Ordinal position					Ordinal position			
	1st	2d	3d	4th		1st	2d	3d	4th
		List					List		
Subject	C	D	A	B	Subject	D	A	B	C
9	050	200	000	100	13	050	200	000	100
10	200	000	100	050	14	200	000	100	050
11	000	100	050	200	15	000	100	050	200
12	100	050	200	000	16	100	050	200	000

Note: The numbers 000, 050, 100, and 200 refer to dose levels.

ing of lists and ordinal position can be overcome by taking the second step in dealing with the problem of irreversible tasks. In general, this second step requires testing additional participants so the list variable and ordinal position are also balanced. In our example, 12 additional participants need to be tested, with the order of the lists systematically rotated for each successive set of four participants. This is illustrated in Table 7.4. Each quadrant of the table includes the same order of the marijuana doses. The list order for each group of four participants is different, however. The order of the lists has been determined using a random starting order with rotation, such that four different orders of the lists are used: ABCD, BCDA, CDAB, DABC. The two-step process of balancing in experiments involving irreversible tasks ensures that each of three variables (the independent variable of interest, stage of practice, and task) are balanced for the other two. Thus, the effects of all three variables are interpretable.

DIFFERENTIAL TRANSFER

The most consistent and vocal critic of repeated measures designs has been E. C. Poulton (1973, 1975, 1982; Poulton & Freeman, 1966). While conceding that balancing techniques control practice effects, Poulton has argued that they do not eliminate a more serious problem. This problem arises when performance in one condition differs depending on the condition that precedes it. We call this **differential transfer.**

Consider a problem-solving experiment in which two types of instructions are being compared in a repeated measures design. One set of instructions (A) is expected to enhance problem solving, whereas the other set of instructions (B) serves as the neutral control condition. It is reasonable to expect that participants tested in the order AB will be unable or unwilling to abandon the approach outlined in the A instructions when they are supposed to be following the B instructions. Giving up the "good thing" participants had under instruction A would be the counterpart of successfully following the admonition "Don't think of pink elephants!" When participants fail to give up the instruction from the first condition (A) when they are supposed to be following instruction B, any difference between the two conditions is reduced. For those participants, after all, condition B was not really tried, and it becomes similar to a situation in which they participated in an "AA" condition, not an "AB" condition.

In general, the presence of differential transfer threatens internal validity because it becomes impossible to determine if there are true differences between the conditions. It also tends to underestimate differences between the conditions and thereby reduces the external validity of the findings. Thus, repeated measures designs should not be used when differential transfer may arise. Differential transfer is sufficiently common with instructional variables to advise against the use of repeated measures designs for these variables (Underwood & Shaughnessy, 1975). Unfortunately, differential transfer can arise in any repeated measures design. For instance, the effect of 50 units of marijuana may be different if administered after the participant has received 200 units than if administered after the participant has received the placebo (e.g., if the participant has an increased tolerance for marijuana after receiving the 200 dose). There are ways, however, to determine whether differential transfer is likely to have occurred.

Poulton (1982) maintains that the best way to determine whether differential transfer is a problem is to do two separate experiments. The same independent variable would be studied in both experiments, but a repeated measures design would be used in one experiment and a random groups design in the other. The random groups design cannot possibly involve differential transfer because each participant is tested in only one condition. Poulton argues that differential transfer is not a problem if the repeated measures design shows the same effect of the independent variable as that shown in the random groups design. If the two designs show different effects for the same independent variable, however, differential transfer is likely to be responsible for producing the different outcome in the repeated measures design. When differential transfer does occur, the results of the random groups design should be used to provide the best description of the effect of the independent variable.

Perhaps the most efficient way to follow Poulton's advice is to do experiments involving a relatively large repeated measures experiment using the incomplete design. For example, if 48 participants were tested in a four-condition experiment with all possible orders of the conditions (i.e., 24 different orders), there would be 12 participants tested in each of the four conditions at the first stage of practice. That is, with 24 possible orders, each of four conditions (A,B,C,D) would appear six times in the first ordinal position, and since there are 2 participants tested in each sequence, there would be 12 receiving A first, 12 B first, and so on. So long as participants have been randomly assigned to sequences, the repeated measures design contains a random groups design for the first condition given to each participant. In other words, at this point, you have 12 participants assigned randomly to each of four conditions. The results for this first stage can then be compared with the overall results to achieve the comparison Poulton recommends between the random groups design and the repeated measures design for the same independent variable.

ANALYSIS OF REPEATED MEASURES DESIGNS

SENSITIVITY AND POWER

Before we discuss the use of the *F*-test in the analysis of repeated measures designs, we describe the concept of power in statistical analyses. The **sensitivity** of an experiment is the likelihood that it will detect an effect of the independent variable if the independent variable does, indeed, have an effect. As we have mentioned, repeated measures designs are generally more sensitive than independent groups designs. An experiment is said to have sensitivity; a statistical test is said to have power. The **power** of a statistical test is the probability that the null hypothesis will be rejected when it is false. The null hypothesis is the hypothesis of "no difference," and, thus, is false and should be rejected when the independent variable has made a difference. You may remember that in our discussion of Type I and Type II errors (see Chapter 6), we defined a Type II error as the probability of failing to reject the null hypothesis when it is false. The probability of a Type II error was called ß. Power can also be defined as 1-ß. (J. Cohen [1992] provides a brief introduction to power, and, in another article, J. Cohen [1988] provides a more thorough introduction.) It is important to be aware of the factors in an experiment that affect the power of the statistical test which will be used to analyze the data *before* beginning to collect the data.

Keppel (1991) provides an excellent description of the factors affecting the power of a statistical test such as the analysis of variance. The power of a statistical test is determined by the interplay of three factors: the level of statistical significance, the size of the treatment effect, and the sample size. Keppel goes on to argue, however, that for all practical purposes sample size is the primary factor that researchers can use to control power. He describes how to use power charts to select an appropriate sample size for a given level of power with a certain level of significance and with an expected treatment effect that is either small, medium, or large. (We described the nature of small, medium, and large effects when we described the measurement of effect sizes in Chapter 6.) The differences in sample size needed to detect effects of different sizes can be dramatic. For example, J. Cohen (1988) reports the sample sizes needed for an independent groups design experiment with one independent variable manipulated at three levels. It takes a sample size of 30 to detect a large treatment effect; it takes a sample size of 76 to detect a medium treatment effect; and it takes a sample size of 464 to detect a small treatment effect. It thus takes over 15 times more participants to detect a small effect than it does to detect a large effect!

Sample size is the major factor researchers can control to affect the power of the statistical analyses they use to analyze their experiments. Using repeated measures experiments can also affect the power of the statistical analyses researchers use. Repeated measures experiments are generally more sensitive than independent groups experiments. This is because, as we mentioned earlier, the estimates of error variation are generally smaller in repeated measures experiments (see also next section). The smaller error variation leads to an increased ability to detect small treatment effects in an experiment. And that is just what the power of a statistical analysis is—the ability to detect small treatment effects when they are present.

REPEATED MEASURES ANALYSIS OF VARIANCE

The analysis of experiments using repeated measures designs involves the same general procedures used in the analysis of independent groups design experiments. The principles of null-hypothesis testing are applied to determine whether the differences obtained in the experiment are larger than would be expected on the basis of error variation alone. The analysis begins with an omnibus analysis of variance to determine whether the independent variable has produced any systematic variation among the levels of the independent variable. Should this omnibus analysis prove statistically significant, analytical comparisons can be made to find the specific source of the systematic variation, that is, to determine which specific levels differed from each other. Because we have already described the logic and procedures for this general analysis plan in Chapter 6, we focus in this section on the analysis procedures specific to repeated measures designs.

The first step in analyzing an experiment is preparing a matrix summarizing participants' performance in each condition of the experiment. In random groups designs, this means simply listing the scores of the participants tested in each of the conditions of the experiment and then summarizing these scores with some descriptive statistic such as the mean. Similarly, in repeated measures designs, we prepare a matrix in which the scores for each participant in each condition of the experiment are listed. An example of such a matrix appears in the upper portion of Table 7.5. The data represent performance of the five participants tested in a time perception experiment done as a classroom demonstration of a repeated measures design. The purpose of the experiment was not to test the accuracy of participants' time estimates compared with the actual interval lengths. Instead, its purpose was to determine whether participants' estimates of time increased systematically with increasing lengths. In other words, could participants discriminate between intervals of different lengths? Each participant was tested using all four interval lengths (12, 24, 36, and 48 seconds).

Each of the four interval lengths was tested six times in the experiment, and block randomization was used to determine the order in which the intervals were presented. Thus, each participant provided 24 time estimates, 6 estimates for each of the four interval lengths. Any one of the 6 estimates for a given time interval is contaminated by practice effects, so some measure that combines information across the 6 estimates is needed. Typically, the mean across the 6 estimates for each interval would be calculated for each participant to provide a single estimate of performance in each condition. As you may remember, however, the mean is influenced by extreme scores; it is quite possible that participants gave extreme estimates of the time intervals for at least one of the six tests of each interval. Thus, for this particular set of data, the median of the 6 estimates probably provides the best measure to reflect the participants' estimates of the time intervals. These median estimates (rounded to the nearest whole number) are listed in Table 7.5. The point of this illustration is that you must compute a score for each participant in each condition before you begin to do an analysis of variance.

TABLE 7.5   DATA MATRIX AND ANALYSIS OF VARIANCE SUMMARY TABLE FOR A REPEATED MEASURES DESIGN EXPERIMENT

	Data matrix			
	Interval length			
Participant	12	24	36	48
1	13	21	30	38
2	10	15	38	35
3	12	23	31	32
4	12	15	22	32
5	16	36	69	60
Mean	12.6	22.0	38.0	39.4

Note: Each value in the table represents the median of the participants' six responses at each level of the internal length variable.

Source of Variation	df	SS	MS	F	p
Subjects	4	1553.5	—	—	—
Interval Length	3	2515.6	838.5	15.6	.0004
Residual (error variation)	12	646.9	53.9		
Total	19	4716.0			

Once an individual score for each participant in each condition has been obtained, the next step is to summarize the results across participants, using an appropriate descriptive statistic. The mean estimates across participants for each of the four intervals are listed in the row labeled Mean in Table 7.5. Even though the data for only five participants are included in the table, these mean estimates are reasonably accurate reflections of the actual interval lengths, at least for intervals up to 36 seconds.

The focus of the analysis was on whether the participants could discriminate intervals of different lengths. As you have probably already realized, we cannot confirm the participants' ability to discriminate intervals of varying lengths until we know that the mean differences in Table 7.5 are greater than would be expected on the basis of error variation alone. That is, even though it may *appear* that participants were able to discriminate between the different intervals, we do not know if their performance was different from what would occur by chance. The null hypothesis for an omnibus analysis of variance for the data in Table 7.5 is that the mean estimates for each interval are the same. To perform an F-test of this null hypothesis, we need an estimate of error variation plus systematic variation (the numerator of an F-ratio). The variation among the mean estimates across participants for the four intervals provides the information we need for the numerator. Even if these five participants had been tested on only one interval length several times, we would not expect their mean estimates to be identical. Thus, we know the mean estimates we have for each level of the interval variable reflect error variation as well. We also know, however, that if the different interval lengths did systematically affect the participants' judgments, then the mean estimates for the intervals would reflect this systematic variation. To complete the F-ratio, we also need an estimate of error variation alone (the denominator of the F-ratio).

One distinctive characteristic of the analysis of repeated measures designs is the way in which error variation is estimated. You may remember that for the random groups design individual differences among subjects, which are balanced across groups, provide the estimate of error variation that becomes the denominator of the F-ratio. Because individuals participate in only one condition in these designs, differences among subjects cannot be eliminated—they can only be balanced. In repeated measures designs, on the other hand, there is systematic variation among subjects. Some subjects consistently perform better across conditions, and some subjects consistently perform worse. Because each subject participates in each condition of repeated measures designs, however, differences among subjects contribute equally to the mean performance in each condition. Accordingly, any differences among the means for each condition in repeated measures designs cannot be the result of systematic differences among subjects. In repeated measures designs, however, differences among subjects are not just balanced, they are actually eliminated from the analysis. The ability to eliminate systematic variation due to subjects in repeated measures designs makes these designs generally more sensitive than random groups designs.

If differences among subjects cannot be the basis of estimating error variation in repeated measures designs, how do we get an estimate that involves only error variation in these designs? The source of error variation in the repeated measures designs is the differences in the ways the conditions affect different subjects. Perhaps the best way to describe the way we get these estimates is to say that we do it "by default." We first determine how much total variation there is in our experiment. Then we subtract the two potential sources of systematic variation: the independent variable and subjects. The remainder is called *residual variation*, and it represents our estimate of error variation alone. (For a more complete discussion of residual variation and why it is an estimate of error variation alone, see Keppel [1991].) As was the case in the random groups design when we used variation within groups as our estimate of error variation alone, residual variation serves as the denominator for the F-ratio in repeated measures designs (i.e., as an estimate of error variation alone).

The analysis of variance summary table for this analysis is presented in the lower portion of Table 7.5. As described in Appendix A, the computations of a repeated measures analysis of variance would be done using a statistical software package on a computer. Our focus now is on interpreting the values in the summary table and not on how these values are computed. Table 7.5 lists the four sources of variation in the analysis of a repeated measures design with one manipulated independent variable. Reading from the bottom of the summary table up, these sources are (1) total variation, (2) residual variation, (3) variation due to interval length (the independent variable), and (4) variation due to subjects.

As in any summary table, the most critical pieces of information are the F-test for the effect of the independent variable of interest and the probability associated with that F-test under the null hypothesis. The important F-test in Table 7.5 is the one for interval length. The numerator for this F-test is the mean square (MS) for interval length; the denominator is the residual MS. There are four interval lengths, so there are 3 degrees of freedom (df) for the numerator. There are 12 df for the residual variation. We can obtain the df for the residual variation by subtracting the df for subjects and for interval length from the total df ($19 - 4 - 3 = 12$). The obtained F of 15.6 has a probability under the null hypothesis of .0004, which is less than the .05 level of significance we have chosen as our criterion for statistical significance. So we reject the null hypothesis and conclude the interval length was a source of systematic variation. This means we can conclude that the participants' estimates did differ systematically as a function of interval length.

This omnibus analysis of variance would almost certainly be followed by analytical comparisons (such as comparing the mean for each interval to the mean for the succeeding interval) to determine more exactly that mean estimates increased with increasing interval lengths. Once again, the logic of these analytical comparisons corresponds to the logic we discussed in Chapter 6 when we considered analytical comparisons in the random groups design. In most instances, the residual MS can be used as an estimate of error variation alone in computing the *F*-tests for the analytical comparisons. (See Keppel [1991], however, for a discussion of the complications that can arise in doing analytical comparisons in repeated measures designs.)

SUMMARY

Repeated measures designs provide an effective and efficient way to conduct an experiment by administering all the conditions in the experiment to each participant. Repeated measures designs are useful when only very few participants are available or when an independent variable can be studied most efficiently by testing fewer participants several times. The area of psychological research (e.g., psychophysics) may also require the use of repeated measures designs. Finally, repeated measures designs may be used when a more sensitive experiment is required.

For any repeated measures design experiment to be interpretable, however, practice effects must be balanced. Practice effects are changes that participants undergo because of repeated testing. In a complete repeated measures design, practice effects are balanced for each participant. In an incomplete repeated measures design, each participant receives each treatment only once, and the balancing of practice effects is accomplished across participants.

Block randomization and ABBA counterbalancing can be used to balance practice effects in a complete repeated measures design. ABBA counterbalancing should not be used, however, if practice effects are expected to be nonlinear (and cannot be eliminated from the analysis) or if anticipation effects are likely. Techniques for balancing practice effects in an incomplete repeated measures design involve either the use of all possible orders or selected orders (the Latin Square and rotation of a random starting order). When irreversible tasks are used, three independent variables must be balanced (the independent variable of interest, stage of practice, and the task variable). The most serious problem in any repeated measures design is differential transfer—when performance in one condition differs depending on which of two other conditions it follows. Procedures for detecting the presence of differential transfer are available, but little can be done to salvage a repeated measures study in which it occurs.

The analysis of the results of repeated measures designs follows the same principles of null-hypothesis testing used to analyze independent groups designs. Estimates of error variation are determined differently, however, in the analyses of variance for repeated measures designs. The generally smaller estimates of error variation in repeated measures designs increases the sensitivity of these designs. The greater sensitivity of the experiments generally increases the power of the resulting statistical analyses in repeated measures experiments.

KEY CONCEPTS

repeated measures designs	Latin Square
practice effects	differential transfer
counterbalancing	sensitivity
ABBA counterbalancing	power

REVIEW QUESTIONS

1 Researchers choose to use a repeated measures design for several different reasons. What are four of those reasons?

2 Distinguish between a complete design and an incomplete design for repeated measures designs.

3 What options do researchers have in balancing practice effects in a repeated measures experiment using a complete design?

4 Under what two circumstances would you recommend against the use of ABBA counterbalancing to balance practice effects in a repeated measures experiment using a complete design?

5 State the general rule for balancing practice effects in repeated measures experiments using an incomplete design.

6 What techniques can be used to balance practice effects in the repeated measures experiments using an incomplete design? Which technique is preferred?

7 For which types of independent variables are repeated measures designs unlikely to prove useful?

8 Describe how researchers can determine if differential transfer has occurred in a repeated measures experiment using an incomplete design.

9 Explain the different roles played by systematic differences across participants in the analysis of random-groups designs and repeated measures designs.

10 What three factors determine the power of a statistical test? Which factor is the primary one that researchers can use to control power?

CHALLENGE QUESTIONS

1 The following problems represent different situations in the repeated measures designs in which practice effects need to be balanced.

   A Consider a repeated measures experiment using a complete design involving one independent variable. The independent variable has three levels (Low, Medium, and High). Prepare an order for administering the conditions of this experiment so the independent variable is balanced for practice effects. First use block randomization to balance the variable and then use ABBA counterbalancing to balance the variable. Each condition should appear twice in the order you prepare. Use the first row of the random number table in Appendix A to determine your two random orders for block randomization.

   B Consider a repeated measures experiment using an incomplete design. One independent variable is to be manipulated at six levels (A, B, C, D, E, and F). Present a table showing how you would determine the order of administering the conditions to the first six participants of the experiment. Be sure that practice effects are balanced for these participants.

2 Consider a repeated measures experiment using an incomplete design to manipulate an environmental variable, room temperature. There are three levels of the variable (60°, 65°, and 70°). The dependent variable of interest is the amount of time taken to solve a list of word problems. Thus, three different word problem lists are required (designated as Lists A, B, and C). Present a table showing how you could administer the conditions of the experiment in order to determine the effect of the three independent variables: room temperature, stage of practice, and list. You have only 9 people available for participants, but previous research indicates that you need not be concerned with problems of differential transfer.

3 The pursuit rotor is a test of perceptual-motor coordination. It involves a turntable with a disk about the size of a dime embedded in it. The participant is given a pointer and asked to keep the pointer on the disk while the turntable is rotating. The dependent variable is the percentage of time on each trial that the participant keeps the pointer on the disk. Learning on this task is linearly related to trials over many periods of practice, and the task generally takes a long time to master. A researcher wants to study the influence of time of day on the performance on this task with four different times (10 a.m., 2 p.m., 6 p.m., and 10 p.m.). The participants will receive a constant number of trials under each of the four conditions, and participants will be tested in one condition per day over four consecutive days. The researcher has 96 participants available.

A   What design is being used for the time-of-day variable in this experiment?

B   What research design is included in the first stage of practice of this experiment? How could the researcher use the results of the design in the first stage of practice as an indication of whether differential transfer had occurred?

4 The following table represents the order of administering the conditions to participants in a repeated measures experiment using an incomplete design in which the independent variable was the difficulty of the task given to the participant (High, Medium, or Low Difficulty). The values in parentheses represent the number correct for each participant in each condition. Use this table, when necessary, to answer the questions that follow.

Participant	Order of Conditions		
1	High (2)	Medium (9)	Low (9)
2	Medium (3)	Low (5)	High (7)
3	Low (4)	High (3)	Medium (5)
4	High (6)	Low (10)	Medium (8)
5	Medium (7)	High (8)	Low (6)
6	Low (8)	Medium (4)	High (4)

A   What method was used to balance practice effects?

B   Present the values you would use to describe the overall effect of the task difficulty variable. Include a verbal description of the effect along with the descriptive statistics that you use as a basis of your description.

C   What would you conclude if the F-test for the effect of task difficulty was $F(2, 10) = 4.25$, $p < .05$?

ANSWER TO CHALLENGE QUESTION 1

A   Assigning the values 1, 2, and 3 to the Low, Medium, and High conditions, respectively, and using the first row of the random number table in Appendix A beginning with the first number in the row, the block-randomized sequence is Low-High-Medium-Low-Medium-High. One possible ABBA counterbalanced sequence is Low-Medium-High-High-Medium-Low.

B   Because there are six conditions, all possible orders are not feasible. Therefore, either a Latin Square or a random-starting order with rotation is needed to balance practice effects. A possible set of sequences using rotation is as follows:

	Position					
Participant	1st	2nd	3rd	4th	5th	6th
1	B	D	E	C	A	F
2	D	E	C	A	F	B
3	E	C	A	F	B	D
4	C	A	F	B	D	E
5	A	F	B	D	E	C
6	F	B	D	E	C	A

Complex Designs

Outline

In the last two chapters we described the basic experimental designs that psychologists use to study the effect of an independent variable. We discussed how an independent variable could be implemented with a separate group of participants in each condition (Chapter 6) or with each participant experiencing all the conditions (Chapter 7). We limited our discussion in these two chapters to experiments involving only one independent variable because we wanted you to concentrate on the characteristics of each research design. Experiments involving only one independent variable are not, however, the most common type of experiment in current psychological research. Instead, researchers most often use **complex designs** in which two or more independent variables are studied simultaneously in one experiment.

Consider, for example, a study by May, Hasher, and Stoltzfus (1993). These researchers used a complex design to study the effects of time of day on memory performance of younger and older people. In a preliminary study they determined that most younger adults (ages 18–22) were classified as "evening types" and most older adults (ages 66–78) were classified as "morning types." They reasoned on the basis of these results that the optimal time of day for doing a memory task would be in the afternoon for younger adults and in the morning for older adults. In their experiment they tested 11 older adults in the morning and 11 in the afternoon. Similarly, they tested 10 younger adults in the morning and 10 in the afternoon. All the participants first read 10 short stories. Immediately after reading the last story they were tested for their recognition of sentences that either were included in the story (old sentences) or were not included in the story (new sentences).

As indicated in the following diagram, this experiment involved four conditions: (1) older adults tested in the morning; (2) older adults tested in the afternoon; (3) younger adults tested in the morning; and (4) younger adults tested in the afternoon.

Age Group	Time of Testing	
	Morning	Afternoon
Older Adults	1	2
Younger Adults	3	4

In this complex design, one independent variable is an individual differences variable (age), with two levels, older adults and younger adults. The second independent variable is a manipulated independent groups variable, the time of testing, which also has two levels, morning or afternoon. In a complex design such as this one, the levels of each of the two independent variables are combined *factorially*. Factorial combination involves pairing each level of one independent variable with each level of a second independent variable. For example, older and younger adults are tested both in the morning and in the afternoon. The number of conditions in a complex design is always equal to the product of the number of levels for each independent variable included in the experiment. In the May et al. (1993) experiment there are two levels of age and two levels of time of testing so there are four conditions ($2 \times 2 = 4$). If these two age groups had been tested at three times of day there would have been six conditions ($2 \times 3 = 6$).

Factorial combination in complex designs makes it possible to assess the effect of each independent variable alone (*main effect*) and the effect of the independent variables in combination (*interaction*). For example, May et al. found, as expected, that younger adults performed better overall on the recognition memory test than did older adults. This represents a main effect of the age variable. That is, "collapsed" across time of testing, younger adults performed better on the dependent variable than did older adults. More importantly, they found that recognition performance did not differ for younger and older adults in the morning (older adults' optimal time); but younger adults did much better than older adults in the afternoon (younger adults' optimal time). In other words, being tested at their nonoptimal time hurt older adults more than it did younger adults. This type of effect, called an *interaction effect,* can be discovered only when two or more independent variables are included in the same experiment. In general, an **interaction** occurs when the effect of one independent variable differs depending on the level of a second independent variable. Complex designs may seem a bit complicated at this point, but the concepts will become clearer as you progress through this chapter. In what follows, we describe the procedures for producing, analyzing, and interpreting main effects and interactions.

We begin with a review of guidelines for identifying or selecting an experimental design. We then describe the basic concepts of main effects and interactions in complex designs. The analysis plans for complex designs are introduced along with the application of analysis of variance to complex designs. We give special attention to the interpretation of interactions in complex designs.

GUIDELINES FOR IDENTIFYING AN EXPERIMENTAL DESIGN

An experiment with a complex design has, by definition, more than one independent variable. Each independent variable in a complex design must be implemented using either an independent groups design or a repeated measures design according to the procedures we described in Chapters 6 and 7. Before examining complex designs themselves, we need to review briefly the characteristics of the various experimental designs that can be used to study a single independent variable. You will be better able to understand descriptions of complex designs if you can quickly and accurately identify the independent variables, their levels, and the design used to implement each independent variable. Similarly, your ability to carry out your own experiments using complex designs will be enhanced if you can confidently select the most appropriate design for each independent variable in which you are interested.

The flowchart in Figure 8.1 summarizes the distinctions among experimental designs by taking you through a series of questions. The diagram will probably prove most useful to you when you are reading about a particular experiment in either your text or a journal article. As you identify each independent variable in an experiment, you can track the variable through Figure 8.1 to determine what design has been used to implement the independent variable. The first question at the top of the diagram is the most critical one. The answer to the question, How many levels of the independent variable were administered to each participant?, determines whether the independent groups or the repeated measures design has been used. Answering the subsequent questions for the independent groups designs will allow you to identify the particular type of design by examining the procedures used to form the groups. For the repeated measures designs, we have included questions to help you distinguish complete and incomplete repeated measures designs and to identify the appropriate balancing techniques for each type.

Complex designs require that you go through the diagram as many times as necessary to identify the design for each independent variable in the experiment. In a complex design, the two or more independent variables need not be implemented in the same way. For example, in the May et al. (1993) study, the age group independent variable (younger adults or older adults) represented a natural groups design. The time of day independent variable (morning or afternoon) was manipulated using the random groups design.

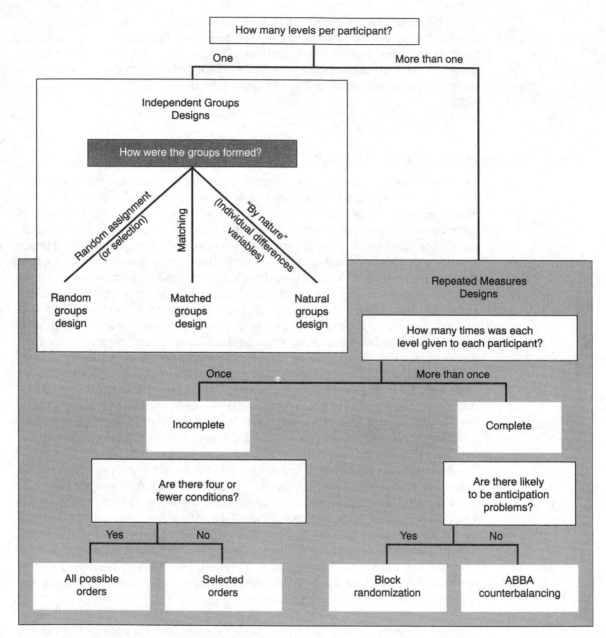

FIGURE 8.1   Flowchart for identifying experimental designs.

THE NATURE OF MAIN EFFECTS AND INTERACTIONS

The simplest possible experiment involves one independent variable manipulated at two levels. Similarly, the simplest possible complex design involves two independent variables, each of which is manipulated at two levels. Complex designs are identified by specifying the number of levels of each of the independent variables in the experiment. A 2×2 (which is read "2 by 2") design, then, identifies the most basic complex design. Conceptually, there is an unlimited number of complex designs because any number of independent variables can be studied and each independent variable can have any number of levels. In practice, however, it is unusual to find experiments involving more than four or five independent variables. Regardless of the number of independent variables, the number of conditions in a complex design can be determined by multiplying the number of levels of the independent variables. For instance, as we saw in the May et al. study of age and time of day, there are two independent variables with each having two levels in a 2×2 design; thus, there are four conditions in a 2×2 design. In a 3×3 design there are two independent variables with 3 levels each so there are nine conditions. In a $3 \times 4 \times 2$ design there are three independent variables with 3, 4, and 2 levels, respectively, and a total of 24 conditions. The primary advantage of all complex designs is the opportunity they provide for identifying interactions between independent variables.

The nature of main effects and interactions is essentially the same in all complex designs, but they can be seen most easily in a 2×2 design. Consider an experiment by Haas, Katz, Rizzo, Bailey, and Eisenstadt (1991). They used a 2×2 design to investigate cross-racial evaluations of performance, an important research topic both theoretically and practically. When given comparable information about a white and a black applicant for a job, for instance, do evaluators rate the candidate of their own race (in-group) more favorably than the candidate of the other race (out-group)?

The students in the Haas et al. (1991) experiment (all of whom were white) were told by a white female experimenter that the researchers were developing a new quiz game for college students called Trivia Challenge. The participants were tested in small groups, but one member of the group was always a confederate of the experimenter. The race of the group captain was the first independent variable. The two levels were Black and White captains. The experimenter made sure that an election among the group members always resulted in the confederate being selected as the captain of the group. The captain selected the questions that the group had to answer in the quiz game. The nature of these questions defined the second independent variable in the experiment, outcome, which also had two levels. In the success outcome conditions, the captain selected easy questions and the group easily reached the criterion for correct answers in the allotted time. In the failure outcome condition, the captain selected questions of such difficulty that the group failed to meet the criterion. Groups of participants were randomly assigned to the four groups

TABLE 8.1   EXAMPLE OF A 2 × 2 DESIGN WITH AN INTERACTION
Mean Evaluation Scores for Captains in Each Group

	Race of captain	
Outcome	Black	White
Success	309.6	280.9
Failure	155.3	196.1

Adapted from Haas et al. (1991).

formed by the factorial combination of the race of the captain (Black, White) and the outcome (success, failure).

After the quiz game, participants completed a questionnaire that included several items requiring them to evaluate the captain of their group. The responses to these questions were combined into an overall evaluation score, with higher scores indicating more favorable evaluations of the captain. The mean evaluation scores for the four conditions of the experiment are presented in Table 8.1. We use the data in this table to illustrate two critical concepts in complex designs: *main effects* and *interactions*.

In any complex factorial design it is possible to test predictions regarding the overall effect of each independent variable in the experiment while ignoring the effect of the other independent variable(s). The overall effect of an independent variable in a complex design is called a **main effect.** For example, the overall mean for success outcomes (295.2) can be obtained by averaging the two values for the Black and White captains in the two success conditions: (309.6 + 280.9)/2 = 295.2. Similarly, the mean of the failure outcomes can be computed to be 175.7.[1] The means for a main effect represent the overall performance at each level of a particular independent variable collapsed across (averaged over) the levels of the other independent variable. In this case we collapsed over the race of the captain variable to obtain the means for the main effect of the outcome variable. The main effect of the outcome variable is the *difference between the means for the two levels of the outcome variable*—(295.2 – 175.7). In the Haas et al. (1991) experiment, the main effect of the outcome variable indicates that, overall, the evaluation scores for captains were higher for success outcomes (295.2) than for failure outcomes (175.7).

Similarly, we can also determine whether there is a main effect of the second independent variable, race of captain. The procedure is exactly like that out-

[1]The simple averaging of the values within each row and column to obtain the means for the main effects is possible *only* when there are equal numbers of participants contributing to each mean in the table. For procedures to use when the cells of the table involve different sample sizes, see Keppel (1991).

lined for determining the effect of the outcome variable, but, of course, this time we must average across the success and failure conditions. The main effect for captain is the difference between the mean evaluation ratings for the two types of captains. You should be able to determine for yourself that these means were 232.4 and 238.5 for Black and White captains, respectively. Thus, it appears that in the Haas et al. experiment, White captains were rated overall more favorably than Black captains. However, the difference was not great, and one would have to test whether the difference is statistically significant.

Analysis procedures for determining the statistical significance of main effects are described in the next section. For now, we need only note that the interpretation of main effects critically depends on whether an interaction is or is not present. In general, main effects should be interpreted with caution whenever an interaction is present in the experiment. When no interaction occurs, the main effects of each independent variable can be interpreted as though they had been manipulated in two separate experiments, each of which involved only one independent variable.

The most important aspect of Table 8.1 is that it reflects an interaction between the two independent variables, race of the captain and outcome. If only successful outcomes had been tested in the experiment (first row of Table 8.1), we would have concluded that Black captains are evaluated more favorably than White captains. On the other hand, if only outcomes involving failure had been tested (second row of Table 8.1), we would have concluded that White captains are evaluated more favorably than Black captains. These results indicate that whether Black or White captains are evaluated more favorably *depends* on the type of outcome, success or failure. We discuss the statistical analysis of interactions in complex designs in the next section. For now, it is sufficient if you recognize that an interaction is likely to have occurred when the effect of one independent variable differs depending on the level of the second independent variable.

When one independent variable interacts with a second independent variable, the second independent variable must interact with the first one. For example, we described the interaction in Table 8.1 by stating that the effect of the race of the captain varies with the type of outcome. The reverse is also true; the effect of the type of outcome varies with the race of the captain. Black captains were evaluated more favorably than White captains in the success condition, but White captains were evaluated more favorably than Black captains in the failure condition. Haas et al. (1991) chose to describe the interaction by emphasizing that the evaluation of the Black captains was more extreme than was the evaluation of the White captains (the Black captains' evaluation was more positive with success and more negative with failure). How you choose to describe the results of an interaction depends on which aspect of the interaction you want to emphasize. For example, Haas et al. emphasized the more extreme ratings given to the Black captains because they were testing the hypothesis that cross-race evaluation leads to more polarized (more extreme) responses for

BOX 8.1

HERE AN INTERACTION, THERE AN INTERACTION, EVERYWHERE AN INTERACTION

In the spirit of practice makes perfect, let us now turn our attention to the exercise we have prepared to help you learn to identify interactions. Your task is to identify main effects and interactions in each of six complex design experiments (A through F). In each table or graph in this box, you are to determine whether the effect of each independent variable differs depending on the level of the other independent variable. In other words, is there an interaction? After checking for the interaction, you can also check to see whether each independent variable produced an effect when collapsed across the other independent variable. That is, is there a main effect of one or both independent variables? The exercise will be most useful if you also practice translating the data presented in a table (Figure 8.2) into a graph and those presented in graphs (Figures 8.3 and 8.4) into tables. The idea of the exercise is to become as comfortable as you can with the various ways of depicting the results of a complex design.[2]

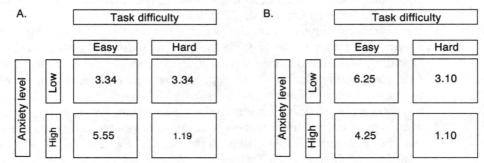

FIGURE 8.2   Mean number of correct responses as a function of task difficulty and anxiety level.

out-group members (White participants rating Black captains) than for in-group members (White participants rating White captains).

Mastering the concepts of main effects and interactions requires practice in identifying the various types of outcomes that can arise in a complex design. The exercise in Box 8.1 gives you an opportunity to practice identifying main effects and interactions in 2 × 2 designs using only descriptive statistics. Inferential statistics would be required to confirm the statistical significance of any obtained effects, but the effects themselves can best be seen in a table or graph of the means for the conditions of the experiment.

There are three common ways to report a summary of the descriptive statistics in a complex design: tables, bar graphs, and line graphs. The procedures

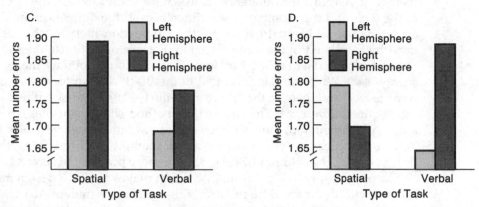

FIGURE 8.3   Mean number of errors as a function of type of task and brain hemisphere tested.

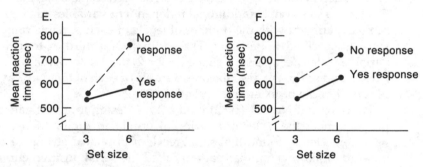

FIGURE 8.4   Mean reaction time as a function of set size and response type.

[2]Answer key for exercises in this box: An interaction occurs in A, D, and E.

for preparing such tables and figures and the criteria for deciding which type of presentation to use are described in Appendix C. In general, tables can be used for any complex design and are most useful when the exact values for each condition in the experiment need to be known. Bar graphs and line graphs, on the other hand, are especially good for showing patterns of results without dwelling on the exact values. Line graphs are a good choice for depicting the results of complex designs because an interaction can be seen so readily. *Nonparallel lines in the graph suggest an interaction; parallel lines suggest no interaction.*

When the results of a 2 × 2 design are summarized in a table, it is easiest to assess the presence or absence of an interaction by using the subtraction method. Determine the differences between the means in each row (or column) of the table and then compare these differences. If the differences are different, an interaction is likely. In applying the subtraction method, the differences must be calculated in the same direction. For example, to use the subtraction method for the data reported in Table 8.1, you could subtract the evaluation score for the White captain from that of the Black captain for the success outcome (+28.7) and then for the failure outcome (–40.8). Note carefully the sign of the obtained difference. The subtraction method shows you these differences are very different and, thus, an interaction between the two variables is likely. You can practice applying the subtraction method by determining the mean differences for the columns of Table 8.1. For more practice, see Box 8.1.

The opportunity to identify an interaction makes the 2 × 2 design more useful analytically than designs involving only one independent variable. Nonetheless, the 2 × 2 design barely scratches the surface when it comes to tapping the potential of complex designs. The 2 × 2 design can be extended in one of two ways. Additional levels of one or both of the independent variables can be included in the design, yielding designs such as the 3 × 2, the 3 × 3, the 4 × 2, the 4 × 3, and so on. Or additional independent variables can be studied in the same experiment with the number of levels of each variable ranging from 2 to some unspecified upper limit. The addition of a third or fourth independent variable yields designs such as the 2 × 2 × 2, the 3 × 3 × 3, the 2 × 2 × 4, the 2 × 3 × 3 × 2, and so on. We describe one example of each of the two ways that a complex design can be extended beyond the 2 × 2.

Hinrichs and Novick (1982) used a 2 × 4 design to investigate the way people remember the order of a string of unrelated digits. Memory researchers have consistently found that serial recall of unrelated strings of digits, letters, or words follows a familiar pattern called the serial position curve (Zechmeister & Nyberg, 1982). Recall of the first few items in a string is best (primacy effect) and recall of the last few items in the string is almost as good (recency effect), but recall of items from the middle of the string is much poorer. Although the serial position curve is one of the most reliable phenomena of human memory, Hinrichs and Novick wondered whether our memory for a sequence of numbers would always conform to this pattern.

Hinrichs and Novick (1982) distinguished between two different ways in which we use numbers. We sometimes use them as arbitrary strings, as is the case with telephone numbers. In this instance, Hinrichs and Novick argued, it would be reasonable to expect a person's memory for the number string to follow the serial position effect. Most of the time, however, we use numbers to reflect amounts or magnitudes, as when a number indicates the cost of a new car. In this case, Hinrichs and Novick expected the number to be remembered not as a string of unrelated digits but as an approximate amount. That is, the first digit should be remembered best, with each successive digit being less critical and thus less likely to be remembered. For example, the digit string 8,362 would need to be remembered exactly if it were a phone number, but remembering 8,300 would be close enough if the original number was intended to reflect the price of a car. When numbers reflected amounts, Hinrichs and Novick saw no reason why the serial recall of the digits should show a serial position curve.

The experiment Hinrichs and Novick did closely followed the logic described in the preceding paragraph. They manipulated two independent variables, using the repeated measures design for both. The first independent variable in their experiment was the type of list participants were asked to learn, which was manipulated using two levels. Half of the lists that participants were asked to learn consisted of 30 four-digit numbers, each paired with a person's name. Participants were told to consider the numbers as the four-digit extensions of campus phone numbers for a group of 30 students. For the other half of the lists, the four-digit numbers were paired with the names of cars, and participants were told to remember the numbers as the prices of new and used cars they might be interested in purchasing. In both lists, the pairs were shown for study for 5 seconds and a given pair was tested after varying numbers of other pairs had been presented. The test for both lists required participants to respond with the appropriate number when the name of the person or of the car was presented.

The second independent variable in the experiment was the serial position variable. The accuracy of participants' recall was determined for the digits at each of the four positions within the four-digit numbers. That is, the first digit of the four-digit number corresponded to the first serial position, the second number represented the second serial position, and so on. Thus, Hinrichs and Novick used a 2×4 design (two types of lists and four serial positions). They expected to find an interaction. That is, they expected the pattern of recall across serial positions to differ depending on the type of list the participant was trying to remember, phone numbers or car prices. The proportion of digits recalled correctly at each serial position for the two different lists is presented in Figure 8.5. As predicted by Hinrichs and Novick, recall was best for serial positions 1 and 4 when the list was "phone numbers"—the primacy and recency components of the serial position curve. For the "prices" list, however, recall systematically decreased across serial positions, at least across the first three positions. As we previously mentioned, the appearance of nonparallel lines in a line graph like that shown in Figure 8.5 suggests that an interaction has occurred. The different patterns of recall across serial positions for the two types of lists confirm that our memories for numbers differ depending on what those numbers represent.

The experiment by Hinrichs and Novick illustrates an intriguing fact about human memory. For our purposes, however, their experiment also shows that the concept of an interaction can be extended to complex designs beyond the 2 $\times$ 2, in this case to a 2×4 design. You should now be beginning to see how complex designs allow psychologists to test predictions that specify how two independent variables can work together to produce an interaction.

An even more powerful extension of complex designs arises when there are three independent variables in the experiment. Pingitore, Dugoni, Tindale, and

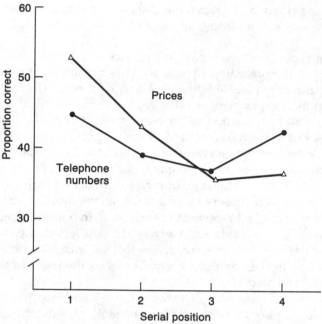

FIGURE 8.5   Illustration of an interaction in a complex design (2 × 4). (From Hinrichs & Novick, 1982.)

Spring (1994) examined three independent variables in their study of possible discrimination against moderately obese people in a mock job interview. Participants in the experiment viewed videotapes of job interviews. The role of the applicant for the job in the videotapes was played by professional actors who were of normal weight. In the moderately obese conditions, the actors wore makeup and prostheses so they appeared 20% heavier. Three of the independent variables in the experiment were the weight of the applicant (normal or overweight); the gender of the applicant (male or female); and the participants' concern about their own body (high or low). The degree of concern with one's own body was called the body-schema variable. It was based on the participants' satisfaction-dissatisfaction with their own bodies and the importance of body awareness to their self-concept. For this part of the study, then, Pingitore et al. used a 2 × 2 × 2 design. The dependent variable was the participants' rating on a 7-point scale of whether they would hire the applicant (1 = definitely not hire and 7 = definitely hire).

As a first step in describing the results of the Pingitore et al. study we examine an interaction of two independent variables, the applicant's weight and the applicant's gender. For normal weight applicants, male and female applicants were given very similar hiring ratings (means of 6.0 and 5.5 for males and females, respectively). For overweight applicants, however, mean hiring ratings were lower, especially the ratings of female applicants (means of 4.8 and 3.6 for males and females, respectively). The pattern of this interaction effect indicates that female applicants who are overweight may experience more job discrimination than male applicants who are overweight.

Pingitore et al. were able to refine their understanding of possible discrimination based on the applicant's weight even further when they included the independent variable of body schema in their analysis. The interaction of the applicant's weight and gender just described occurred only with participants who were high in concern about their own bodies. That is, those high on the body-schema variable gave overweight female applicants especially low ratings. Participants who were low on the body-schema variable, on the other hand, gave lower ratings to overweight applicants, but their ratings for male and female applicants were about the same.

One way to summarize the Pingitore et al. findings we have just described is to say that the interaction of the independent variables of the applicants' weight and the applicants' gender *depended on* the participants' body schema. We call this type of finding a three-way (or triple) interaction. As you can see, when we have a three-way interaction, all three independent variables must be taken into account when describing the results.

As way of summary, in general, when there are two independent variables, an interaction occurs when the effect of one of the independent variables differs depending on the level of the second independent variable. When there are three independent variables in a complex design, a three-way interaction occurs when the interaction of two of the independent variables differs depending on the level of the third independent variable.

The power and complexity of complex designs increase substantially when the number of independent variables in the experiment increases from two to three. In the two-factor design there can be only one interaction, but in the three-factor design each independent variable can interact with each of the other two independent variables and all three independent variables can interact together. Thus, the change from a two-factor to a three-factor design introduces the possibility of obtaining four different interactions. If the three independent variables are symbolized as A, B, and C, the three-factor design allows a test of the main effects of A, B, and C; the two-way interactions of A × B, A × C, B × C; and the three-way interaction of A × B × C. The efficiency of an experiment involving three independent variables is remarkable. Pingitore et al. would have had to perform three experiments involving two variables at a time (applicant's gender and applicant's weight; applicant's gender and participant's body schema; and applicant's weight and participant's body schema) in order to assess the three main effects and the three two-way interactions that they could examine in a single three-factor design. Furthermore, they could assess the simultaneous interaction of all three independent variables only by including all three variables in the same experiment. Complex designs are a very powerful tool in psychological research.

ANALYSIS OF COMPLEX DESIGNS

LOGIC OF ANALYSIS PLAN

The analysis of complex designs builds on the logic used in the analysis of experiments with only one independent variable (see Chapter 6). Briefly, the first step in analyzing such single-factor experiments is to perform an omnibus *F*-test to determine whether the independent variable has produced any systematic variation in the dependent variable. If the omnibus test is statistically significant, analytical comparisons can be used to pinpoint more precisely the source of the systematic variation.

The tracking of sources of systematic variation applies equally to the analysis of complex designs that involve more than one independent variable. The same basic tool—the analysis of variance—can be used for complex designs. In complex designs with two independent variables, however, there are three potential sources of systematic variation. Each independent variable can produce a main effect, and the two independent variables can combine to produce an interaction effect.

The experiment we use to illustrate the analysis plan for a complex design involved a 3×3 design with nine groups of participants. Children of three different ages (4, 5, and 6) were tested under one of three situations (alone, with a parent, and with another child). Thus, the first independent variable, age, is an individual differences variable with three levels, and the second independent variable, situations, is manipulated using three levels. The dependent variable in the experiment was the amount of time the child spent playing with novel (unfamiliar) toys. There were 10 children of each age tested under each of the

FIGURE 8.6   The experiment used to illustrate the analysis of a complex design involved a 3×3 design. One variable was an individual differences variable, age, and it had three levels: children were 4, 5, and 6 years of age. The other variable was a manipulated variable, and it also had three levels: children were tested with another child, alone, or with a parent. The dependent variable was time spent playing with new toys.

TABLE 8.2 TABLE OF MEAN TIMES (IN MINUTES) SPENT PLAYING WITH NOVEL TOYS IN A 3 × 3 DESIGN

Situation	Age			Means for main effect of condition
	4	5	6	
Alone	5	5	10	6.7
With a parent	15	25	35	25.0
With another child	10	15	15	13.3
Means for main effect of age	10.0	15.0	20.0	

three conditions, so there were 90 participants in the experiment, 10 participants in each of the 9 conditions.

Table 8.2 shows the mean times children in each group spent playing with novel toys. An analysis of variance summary table for this complex design is presented in Table 8.3.

Let's look first at the analysis of variance summary table. There are three potential sources of systematic variation in this experiment: the main effect of age, the main effect of situation, and the interaction between the age and situation variables. The summary table indicates the degrees of freedom (*df*) for each of these effects. For the main effects, the degrees of freedom are equal to the number of levels of the independent variable minus one. Since there are three levels for both age and situation, the degrees of freedom for both main effects are 2. The degrees of freedom for the interaction are obtained by multiplying the degrees of freedom for each independent variable entering into the interaction. Thus, there are 4 degrees of freedom for the Age × Situation interaction (2 × 2 = 4). The degrees of freedom for the Mean Square Within Groups (the estimate of error variation for all three effects in the complex design) are obtained by multiplying the degrees of freedom within each group times the number of groups. In our example, there are 10 participants in each group and therefore 9 degrees

TABLE 8.3 ANALYSIS OF VARIANCE SUMMARY TABLE FOR A 3 × 3 DESIGN

Source of variation	df	MS	F	p
Age (A)	2	35	3.5	.03
Situation (B)	2	92	9.2	.0005
Age × situation (A × B)	4	48	4.8	.002
Error variation within groups	81	10		
Total	89	—		

of freedom within each group. Because there are 9 groups in the experiment, there are 81 *df* within groups.

The three *F*-tests entered in the summary table were computed by dividing the mean square (MS) within groups into the mean square for age, for situation, and for the interaction. (The mean squares were computed using procedures for complex designs described in Appendix A.) The probabilities for each of the *F*-tests were determined using the value of *F* and the appropriate degrees of freedom for each effect (2 and 81 for each of the two main effects and 4 and 81 for the interaction). Using the criterion of $p < .05$ to determine statistical significance, we can see that the *F*-tests for each main effect and the interaction are statistically significant because the *p* value associated with each *F*-test is less than .05.

The information in the analysis of variance summary table is useful only in conjunction with the means reported in Table 8.2. The statistically significant *F*-test for the interaction indicates that the pattern of results across age differs for the three situations. As you can see in Table 8.2, the means reveal a larger increase across age in the time spent playing with a novel toy when the child is with a parent than when the child is either alone or with another child. The in-

FIGURE 8.7   This graph shows results of complex design involving three independent variables, each with three levels.

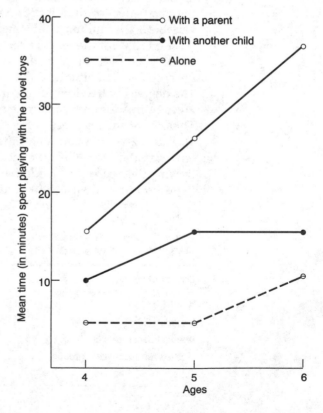

teraction can be seen clearly in the pattern of nonparallel lines shown in Figure 8.7. The means for the main effects of age and of situation on the outside of Table 8.2 also appear to differ, and these apparent differences are supported by the statistically significant *F*-test for each main effect.

The three *F*-tests in the summary table represent the counterpart of the omnibus *F*-tests we described when discussing the analysis of experiments with only one independent variable. In a complex design, just as in a single-factor design, follow-up analyses are needed to interpret the initial omnibus tests. The analysis plan for complex designs differs depending on whether a statistically significant interaction is present.

Table 8.4 provides guidelines for interpreting a complex design experiment when an interaction does occur and when one does not. We go through Table 8.4 twice, once describing an experiment in which there is an interaction and once describing a study in which there is no interaction.

ANALYSIS WITH AN INTERACTION

One of the many approaches psychologists have tried to use to understand depression is based on investigating the differences between the thought patterns of depressed and nondepressed people. You may remember that we touched briefly on this topic in Chapter 1. One aspect of this cognitive approach to depression deals with attributions, the causal explanations we use to try to account for our own behavior and the behavior of others. For example, nondepressed people tend to overestimate how much control they have over their lives; depressed people, more realistically, estimate they have less control (Bootzin, Acocella, & Alloy, 1993). According to the cognitive approach, this tendency toward less optimistic thinking on the part of depressed people may be critically involved in causing the onset of depression, maintaining depression once it occurs, and alleviating depression by changing depressive thinking

TABLE 8.4   GUIDELINES FOR THE ANALYSIS OF A TWO-FACTOR EXPERIMENT

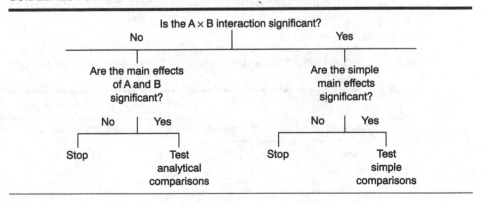

to be more optimistic. The study we are using to illustrate the interpretation of the results of a complex design with an interaction represents one of the many experiments investigating the cognitive bases of depression.

Rodman and Burger (1985) investigated a particular phenomenon called the defensive attribution effect. In previous experiments, nondepressed participants read a description of an accident in which a person suffered mild or severe consequences. These nondepressed individuals attributed more responsibility to the perpetrator in the severe than in the mild accident condition. One interpretation of this phenomenon is that people do not want to attribute the cause of a severe accident to chance. If they did attribute the accident to chance, they would be increasing the perceived possibility that they themselves could be involved in a severe accident. Their attribution of greater responsibility to the perpetrator in the severe accident is a defensive attribution, allowing them to perceive themselves as protected against a likelihood of future severe accidents. Rodman and Burger reasoned that depressed people might be less likely to show this type of defensive attribution effect because their negative thinking would lead them to be less self-protective. Stated more formally, they tested the hypothesis that the defensive-attribution effect would decrease as a person's level of depression increased.

Rodman and Burger tested 56 college students in a 2 × 3 design. The first independent variable was the severity of the described accident (severe and nonsevere), which was manipulated using the random groups design. The naturalgroups design was used for the second independent variable; students were selected on the basis of their scores on a paper-and-pencil test of depression to represent three groups: nondepressed, slightly depressed, and mildly depressed individuals. The dependent variable was a single item on a longer questionnaire that asked students to divide 100% among four potential sources of responsibility: each of the three drivers in the accident and uncontrollable "circumstances." The defensive-attribution effect would be reflected in a larger value assigned to uncontrollable circumstances for the nonsevere than for the severe accident. (Remember that it is protective to avoid making attributions to uncontrollable circumstances for severe accidents.) The mean percentage values for this uncontrollable factor for each of the six conditions are presented in Table 8.5.

TABLE 8.5   MEAN PERCENTAGE OF RESPONSIBILITY ATTRIBUTED TO UNCONTROLLABLE
CIRCUMSTANCES

	Level of depression		
Type of accident	Nondepressed	Slightly depressed	Mildly depressed
Severe	7.00 (9.2)	14.00 (16.1)	16.90 (16.0)
Nonsevere	30.50 (22.2)	16.50 (12.7)	3.75 (3.5)

Note: Standard deviations appear in parentheses. Adapted from Rodman and Burger (1985).

As Rodman and Burger had predicted, there was an interaction: As degree of depression increases, the differences between the percentage values for severe and nonsevere accidents change. (You may wish to use the subtraction method to see this.) Nondepressed students show the defensive-attribution effect and mildly depressed students do not. Analysis of these results using analysis of variance confirmed that the interaction was statistically significant.

Once we have confirmed there is an interaction of two independent variables, we must locate more precisely the source of that interaction. As outlined in Table 8.4, there are statistical tests specifically designed for tracing the source of a significant interaction. These tests are called simple main effects and simple comparisons (Keppel, 1991).

A **simple main effect** is the effect of one independent variable at one level of a second independent variable. In fact, one definition of an interaction is that the simple main effects across levels are different. We can illustrate the use of simple main effects by returning to the results of the Rodman and Burger experiment. There are five simple main effects in Table 8.5: the effect of the type of accident at each of the three levels of depression and the effect of the degree of depression at each of the two types of accident. Rodman and Burger predicted that the defensive-attribution effect (the difference between the means for severe and nonsevere accidents) would decrease as severity of depression increased. Therefore, they chose to test the simple main effects of type of accident at each of the three levels of depression. They found, as predicted, that the simple main effect of type of accident was statistically significant for nondepressed students, but the simple main effects of type of accident for the slightly depressed and for the mildly depressed students were not statistically significant.

Two of the simple main effects in the Rodman and Burger (1985) study each involve three means. One can also examine how nondepressed, slightly depressed, and mildly depressed students differed in their attributions for severe accidents and how these three groups differed in their attributions for nonsevere accidents. That is, if statistical analysis reveals a significant simple main effect, then one concludes that there is a difference among the means (e.g., among the three groups for severe accidents). The next step, then, is to conduct *simple comparisons*, which are analytical comparisons that can be used to analyze simple main effects more fully (Keppel, 1991). That is, once a simple main effect involving more than two levels of a variable has been shown to be statistically significant, simple comparisons can be done to determine the nature of the differences among the levels. In this procedure, means within the simple main effect are compared two at a time in order to identify the source of differences among levels. As you can see, simple comparisons only make sense when there is a simple main effect for an independent variable with three or more levels. With two levels, a simple main effect compares the difference between the two means and no additional comparisons are necessary.

Once an interaction has been thoroughly analyzed, researchers can also examine the main effects of each independent variable. As we mentioned earlier in this chapter, however, the main effects are of much less interest when we know an interaction is significant. For instance, once we know the effect of the type of accident varies depending on the level of depression, we have not added much when we learn that, overall, the nonsevere accident led to a higher mean percentage of responsibility attributed to uncontrollable circumstances than did the severe accident. Nonetheless, there are experiments in which the interaction and the main effects are all of interest. Rosnow and Rosenthal (1995) describe additional procedures that can help you gain further understanding in analyzing and interpreting interactions and main effects.

ANALYSIS WITH NO INTERACTION

Dittmar, Berch, and Warm (1982) used a 3×3 design to test whether people who are deaf perform better on a visual-vigilance task than people who can hear. A visual-vigilance task requires a person to detect intermittent visual signals such as blips on a radar screen for a long period of time. Dittmar et al. expected that deaf people would have an advantage on such a task because their deafness would keep them from being distracted. The deaf people who participated were offered a prize if their vigilance performance was the best in their group. To assess the possible effect of the prize as an incentive, two additional groups of hearing people were tested, one offered a prize and one not. These three groups represent the levels of the first independent variable in the experiment. The participants were all tested in a 45-minute session divided into three continuous 15-minute periods, and these three periods were the levels of the second independent variable. Note that the first independent variable is an independent groups variable, and the second is a repeated measures variable.

The mean percentage of correct detections across the three periods for the three different groups of participants is presented in Table 8.6. The same data are depicted graphically in Figure 8.8. The interaction, or more accurately the lack of an interaction, can best be seen in Figure 8.8. Although the three lines in the figure are not perfectly parallel, the mean percentage of correct detections appears to decrease in all three groups at approximately the same rate. That

TABLE 8.6   MEAN PERCENTAGE OF CORRECT DETECTIONS ACROSS THREE PERIODS OF A VIGILANCE TASK FOR DEAF AND HEARING PARTICIPANTS

| | Period | | |
Group	1	2	3
Deaf	95	85	78
Hearing—Prize	93	82	70
Hearing—No Prize	93	74	68

Adapted from Dittmar et al. (1982).

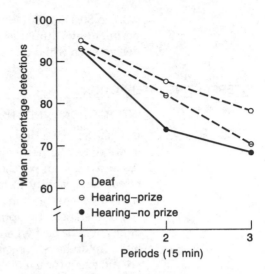

FIGURE 8.8   Results of a 3 × 3 complex design in which there was no interaction effect but there were two main effects. (Adapted from Dittmar et al., 1982.)

there was not a statistically significant interaction is confirmed by the results of the analysis of variance.

The guidelines for the analysis of a complex design listed in Table 8.4 suggest that, when the interaction effect is not significant, the next step is to examine the main effects of each independent variable. This can be done most easily by referring to the data in Table 8.6. By collapsing (averaging) across the three vigilance periods, we can obtain the mean detection rates for the main effect of the group variable. These means are 86.0, 81.7, and 78.3 for the Deaf, Hearing—Prize, and Hearing—No Prize groups, respectively. The overall analysis of the group main effect was statistically significant. As indicated in Table 8.4, the source of a statistically significant main effect can be specified more precisely by performing analytical comparisons (see Chapter 6 and Appendix A). For example, a comparison of performance in the Hearing—Prize and Hearing—No Prize groups (81.7 and 78.3) was not statistically significant, indicating that the presence of an incentive did not produce a difference between these two groups. However, the average performance of the two groups of hearing participants (80.0) was significantly lower than the performance of the deaf participants (86.0). These two analytical comparisons allow us to confirm that deaf participants were better at the vigilance task than hearing participants and that the offer of a prize did not affect the vigilance performance.

A similar approach would be followed in assessing the main effect of the period variable. By collapsing across the three groups of participants, we obtain the means 93.7 (first period), 80.3 (second period), and 72.0 (third period) for the main effect of the period variable. The main effect of this variable was statistically significant, and visual inspection of the means reveals that performance decreased, on the average, over time. Analytical comparisons could then be used to determine whether the decreases over each successive period

(93.7 to 80.3 and 80.3 to 72.0) were significant. The analysis of the vigilance experiment by Dittmar et al. illustrates that much can be learned from a complex design even when there is no interaction.

INTERPRETING INTERACTIONS

INTERACTIONS AND THEORY TESTING

In Chapter 1 we described the critical role that theories play in the scientific method. In Chapter 6 we described how experiments are used to test hypotheses derived from psychological theories. Complex designs greatly enhance the researcher's ability to test theories because of the possibility in complex designs to test for both main effects and interactions.

For instance, the optimal arousal theory of motivation predicts that performance will be best when our arousal level is moderate—neither too low nor too high. If you have ever had to perform in either a highly competitive athletic or artistic event (or even a class exam), you have some sense of what is meant by optimal arousal. Your performance is not likely to be at its best if your arousal level is too low (you don't care how well you do) or too high (you are scared out of your wits). The optimal arousal theory further predicts that the best level of arousal depends on the complexity of the task to be performed. Specifically, the theory predicts that higher arousal levels will lead to better performance on simple or well-learned tasks, but lower arousal levels will lead to better performance on complex tasks. For example, you would probably be able to do simple arithmetic problems at a high arousal level, but the same arousal level would probably be disastrous if you were solving differential equations. Our focus for now is not on the details of optimal arousal theory but on the use of complex designs to test predictions derived from such a theory.

If we were to test the prediction that optimal arousal varied with task complexity, we would need to manipulate two independent variables, each with at least two levels. For example, if our experiment included arousal level (high or low) and task complexity (simple or complex) we would have four conditions.

Task Complexity	Arousal Level	
	High	Low
Simple	50	35
Complex	10	25

The values of the dependent variable entered in the body of our table are the mean number of tasks completed correctly in each of the four conditions. As you can see, the effect of arousal level on performance depended on the level of task complexity—an interaction occurred. (You may want to use the subtraction method, or perhaps graph the results, in order to see the interaction.) For the simple task, high arousal led to better performance; however, for the complex task, low arousal led to better performance. This hypothetical but reasonable outcome supports the prediction derived from optimal arousal theory. The example also illustrates how interactions allow us to make more sophisticated tests of psychological theories.

INTERACTIONS AND CONTRADICTORY FINDINGS

When only one independent variable is manipulated in an experiment, all other potential independent variables must be controlled by holding them constant or by balancing them across conditions (see Chapter 6). A problem can arise, however, if two researchers choose to hold the same potential independent variable constant at different levels in their respective experiments. For example, two memory researchers might be studying the relative effectiveness of two different learning strategies (A and B). These two strategies would represent the levels of the manipulated independent variable in both experiments. One potential independent variable that would clearly need to be controlled in these experiments is the difficulty of the material to be learned. The first researcher might decide to control the level of difficulty of the material by giving students in both conditions relatively easy textbook passages to learn. The second researcher, who is equally concerned with the problem of controlling the difficulty of the material, might decide to give students in both conditions relatively hard textbook passages to learn. It would not be surprising if these two researchers obtained different results. One such possible outcome is illustrated in the following diagram:

	Learning Strategy	
Passage Difficulty	A	B
Easy (Researcher 1)	50	50
Hard (Researcher 2)	25	10

The first researcher found that the two learning strategies are equally effective; the second researcher found that strategy A is more effective than strategy B! Why couldn't these two researchers replicate each other's findings?

At first, we might try to account for the different outcomes in the two experiments by focusing on the difficulty of the textbook passages. We could argue that the two strategies are equally effective for learning easy textbook passages, but strategy A is better for learning hard passages. This argument would not be convincing, however, unless the two types of passages represented the only way the two experiments differed. This seems highly unlikely. For example, the passages may very well have been studied for different lengths of time in the two experiments, the passages were probably on different topics, and the experimenters and participants in the two experiments were undoubtedly different. Clearly, the difficulty of the passages is not the only factor that could be responsible for the different effects of the strategy variable in the two experiments.

The best way to identify which factor is responsible for the different findings in the two experiments is to use a complex design in which you manipulate the factor you think is responsible along with the strategy variable in the *same* experiment. The use of a complex design to resolve discrepant findings follows a logic similar to the logic of doing a partial replication to establish the external validity of a finding (see Chapter 6). In both cases, you are examining whether the effect of the independent variable of interest depends on a second independent variable; in this case, the variable of interest is the learning strategy (A or B), and the second independent variable is the difficulty of the passage. In an experiment in which the strategy variable and the passage-difficulty variable were both manipulated, there would be four conditions in a complex design: Strategy A—Easy Passage; Strategy A—Hard Passage; Strategy B—Easy Passage; and Strategy B—Hard Passage. By factorially combining the two independent variables, both easy and hard passages are tested using both learning strategies. Two possible outcomes of such an experiment are shown in the following diagram. The results outlined in Outcome 1 are the same as those observed for the two separate experiments when only the strategy variable was manipulated. That is, the strategies are equally effective for easy material, and strategy A is better than B for hard material. If you were to obtain this interaction, you could be confident that the difficulty of the text was responsible for the different effects of the strategy variable in the two original experiments.

Passage difficulty	Outcome 1 Strategy		Outcome 2 Strategy	
	A	B	A	B
Easy	50	50	50	50
Hard	25	10	15	15

The situation would be very different, however, if you were to obtain results in your new experiment like those displayed in Outcome 2. In Outcome 2, the strategy variable had no effect when tested using either the easy or the hard text material. Because the strategy variable has the same effect with both types of material, it would logically follow that differences in degree of difficulty between the materials in the two original experiments cannot be responsible for the different effects of strategy in those experiments. You must select another variable that you "suspect" and manipulate it along with the strategy variable. Both trial and error and the guidance of theory are involved in the selection of the variable. The process can be a painstaking one, but complex designs are extremely useful in tracking down the reasons for the seemingly contradictory finding that the same independent variable has had different effects in two different experiments.

INTERACTIONS AND EXTERNAL VALIDITY

In Chapter 6 we discussed at some length the procedures for establishing the external validity of a research finding when an experiment involves only one independent variable. We noted that partial replication was the primary means by which we establish external validity, that is, the extent to which our research findings may be generalized. We can now examine the role of complex designs in establishing the external validity of a finding. As you might have suspected, the presence or absence of an interaction is critical in determining the external validity of the findings in a complex design.

When no interaction occurs in a complex design, we know the effects of each independent variable can be generalized across the levels of the other independent variable. For instance, the Dittmar, Berch, and Warm (1982) study we just described showed that detection performance declined across three 15-minute vigilance periods, but the decline occurred at approximately the same rate for hearing and deaf participants. That is, there was no interaction of the hearing variable (hearing or deaf) and the period variable. Thus, declining performance in a vigilance task can be generalized to both hearing and deaf people.

Of course, we cannot generalize our findings beyond the boundaries or conditions that were included in the experiment. For example, the absence of an interaction between the hearing variable and periods in the vigilance task does not allow us to conclude that detection performance would decline at the same rate if young children or trained observers were tested. Similarly, we do not know whether the same decline across periods would occur if there were short breaks after each observation period. We must also remember that the absence of an interaction involves problems associated with the failure to reject the null hypothesis, such as the sensitivity of the experiment to detect any interaction that might be present (see Chapters 6 and 7).

As we have seen, the absence of an interaction increases the external validity of the effects of each independent variable in the experiment. Perhaps more important, the presence of an interaction identifies limits for the external validity of a finding. For example, when they tested young adults, May et al. (1993) found there was little effect of time of day on recognition memory performance. However, there was a substantial effect of time of day when older adults were tested. This interaction clearly sets limits on the external validity of the effect that time of day has on memory performance. Given this finding, the best way to respond to someone's query regarding the general effect that time of testing has on memory is to say "it depends." The presence of the interaction limits external validity but also specifies what those limits are.

INTERACTIONS AND RELEVANT INDEPENDENT VARIABLES

One of the primary tasks facing researchers who use the experimental method is identifying relevant and irrelevant independent variables. A **relevant independent variable** is one that has been shown to influence behavior; an irrelevant independent variable is one that has been shown not to influence behavior. Distinguishing between factors that affect behavior and those that do not is essential for developing adequate theories to explain behavior and for designing effective interventions to deal with problems in applied settings such as schools, hospitals, and factories (see Chapters 9 and 10).

If independent variables did not interact with one another, the task of identifying relevant independent variables would be a long one, but not a particularly challenging one. Each independent variable would simply be manipulated across a wide range of levels in separate single-factor experiments. The variables would be classified as either relevant or irrelevant depending on whether they produced a significant difference in the dependent variable. Independent variables do interact, however, and we must adjust our definition of relevant and irrelevant independent variables accordingly.

Consider the following example. Thousands of children in the United States receive drug treatment for hyperactivity every year. A reasonable question is whether dosage of the drugs is a relevant independent variable in determining the effectiveness of treatment. A hypothetical but typical experiment that could be done to address this question might include two dose levels (low and high) and three types of tasks (easy, moderate, and difficult). One possible outcome of such an experiment is summarized in the following table, with the dependent variable being the percentage correct performance in each condition.

| | Dose Level | | |
Type of Task	Low	High	Overall Mean
Easy	75	90	82.5
Moderate	70	70	70.0
Difficult	65	50	57.5
Overall Mean	70	70	

The overall means for the main effect of dose level are identical (70), and this information could mistakenly be used to argue that dose level was an irrelevant independent variable. By now you recognize, however, that the dose level produced different effects depending on the difficulty of the task. For difficult tasks a low dose is better, for moderate tasks there is no effect of dose level, and for easy tasks a high dose is better. Dose level is a relevant independent variable because it interacts with the difficulty variable. In general, *a relevant independent variable is one that influences behavior directly (results in a main effect) or produces an interaction when studied in combination with a second independent variable.*

In general, be cautious about declaring an independent variable irrelevant. First, if an independent variable is shown to have no effect in an experiment, you cannot assume this variable wouldn't have an effect if different levels of the independent variable had been tested. Second, if an independent variable has no effect in a single-factor experiment, this doesn't mean it won't interact with another independent variable when used in a complex design. Theories about the processes underlying behavior help us to deal effectively with interactions (Underwood & Shaughnessy, 1975). For now, it is best if you avoid being dogmatic about identifying any independent variable as irrelevant.

INTERACTIONS AND CEILING AND BASEMENT EFFECTS

Consider the results of a 3×2 experiment investigating the effects of increasing amounts of practice on performance during a physical fitness test. There were

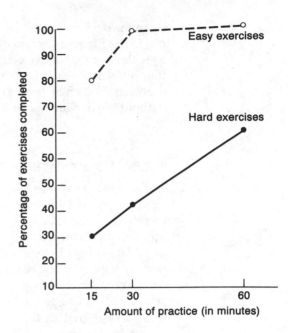

FIGURE 8.9   Illustration of a ceiling effect.

six groups of participants in this plausible but hypothetical experiment. Participants were first given 10, 30, or 60 minutes to practice, doing either easy or hard exercises. Then they took a fitness test using easy or hard exercises (the same they had practiced). The dependent variable was the percentage of exercises each participant was able to complete in a 15-minute test period. Results of the experiment are presented in Figure 8.9. The pattern of results in Figure 8.9 looks like a classic interaction; the effect of the practice time variable differed for the easy and hard exercises. Increasing practice time improved test performance for the hard exercises, but performance leveled off after 30 minutes of practice with the easy exercises. If a standard analysis of variance were applied to these data, the interaction effect would very likely be statistically significant. Unfortunately, this interaction would be essentially uninterpretable. For those groups given practice with the easy exercises, performance reached the maximum level after 30 minutes of practice, so no improvement beyond this point could be shown in the 60-minute group. Even if the participants given 60 minutes of practice had further benefited from the extra practice, the experimenter could not measure this improvement on the chosen dependent variable.

The preceding experiment illustrates the general measurement problem referred to as a **ceiling effect.** Whenever performance reaches a maximum in any condition of an experiment, there is danger of a ceiling effect. The corresponding name given to this problem when performance reaches a minimum (e.g., zero errors on a test) is a *basement effect* (or *floor effect*). In general, one can avoid ceiling and basement effects by selecting dependent variables that allow ample room for performance differences to be measured across conditions. For example, in the fitness experiment it would have been better to test participants with a greater number of exercises than anyone could be expected to complete in the time allotted for the test. The mean number of exercises completed in each condition could then be used to assess the effects of the two independent variables without the danger of a ceiling effect.

INTERACTIONS AND THE NATURAL-GROUPS DESIGN

The natural groups design, which we described briefly in Chapter 6, is one of the most popular research designs in psychology. Groups of people are formed by selecting individuals who differ on some characteristic such as gender, age, introversion-extraversion, or aggressiveness. Researchers then look for systematic relationships between these individual differences variables and other aspects of behavior. The natural groups design is an effective one for establishing correlations between individuals' characteristics and their performance. As we also noted in Chapter 6, however, the natural groups design is perhaps the most challenging design when it comes to drawing conclusions about the causes of behavior.

The difficulty in interpreting the natural groups design arises when we try to conclude that differences in performance are caused by the characteristics of the people we used to define the groups. For instance, consider an experiment in which participants are selected because of their musical training. One group of participants includes people with 10 or more years of formal musical training, and one group includes people with no formal training. Both groups are tested on their ability to remember the musical notation for simple 10-note melodies. Not surprisingly, the results of these tests show that those with musical training perform far better than those without such training.

We can conclude on the basis of these results that memory for simple melodies varies with (is correlated with) amount of musical training. But we cannot conclude that musical training *causes* superior memory performance. Why not? There are probably many additional ways in which people with 10 years of musical training differ from those without such training. The groups may differ in amount and type of general education, family background, socioeconomic status, and amount and type of experience they have had listening to music. Also, those with musical training may have generally better memories than those without such training, and their superior memory for simple melodies may reflect this general memory ability. Finally, those who sought out musical training may have done so because they had a special aptitude for music. Accordingly, they might have done better on the memory task even if they had not had any musical training. In short, there are many possible causes other than individual differences in musical training for the difference in memory performance that was observed.

There is a potential solution to the problem of drawing causal inferences based on the natural groups design (Underwood & Shaughnessy, 1975). The key to this solution is to develop a theory regarding the critical individual difference variable. For example, Halpern and Bower (1982) were interested in how memory for musical notation differs between musicians and nonmusicians. They developed a theory of how musical training would influence the cognitive processing of musical notation by those who had such training. Their theory was based on a memory concept called "chunking." You can get some sense of the memory advantage provided by chunking if you imagine trying to memorize the following string of 15 letters: IBMTWASOSUSANBA. Chunking helps memory by changing the same string of letters to a series of five more easily remembered chunks: IBM-TWA-SOS-USA-NBA.

Halpern and Bower theorized that musical training led musicians to "chunk" musical notation into meaningful musical units, thereby reducing the amount of information they needed to remember to reproduce the notation for a simple melody. Furthermore, if this process were responsible for the difference between the memory performance of musicians and nonmusicians, then the difference should be greater for melodies with good musical structure than for those with poor musical structure. Halpern and Bower manipulated the independent variable of musical structure to test their theory. To do this, they used three different types of melodies to test their groups of musicians and nonmusicians. They prepared sets of simple melodies whose notations had similar visual structures but that were either good, bad, or random in musical structure. The critical test was whether they would obtain an interaction of the two independent variables. Specifically, they expected that the difference in memory performance between musicians and nonmusicians would be largest for the melodies exhibiting good structure, next largest for the melodies exhibiting bad structure, and smallest for the random melodies. The results of Halpern and Bower's experiment conformed exactly to these expectations.

The obtained interaction allowed Halpern and Bower to rule out many alternative hypotheses for the difference in memory performance between musicians and nonmusicians. Such characteristics as amount and type of general education, socioeconomic status, and family background are not likely to explain why there is a systematic relationship between the structure of the melodies and the size of the difference in memory performance between musicians and nonmusicians. The interaction makes such simple correlational explanations much less plausible.

There are several steps the investigator must take in carrying out the general procedure for drawing causal inferences based on the natural groups design. The first step is to develop a theory explaining why a difference should occur in the performance of groups that have been differentiated on the basis of an individual differences variable. The second step is to select an independent variable that can be manipulated and is presumed to influence the likelihood this theoretical process will occur. This independent variable is then applied to both natural groups. The most critical aspect of the recommended approach is to strive to produce an interaction between the manipulated variable and the individual differences variable. The approach can be strengthened even further by testing predictions of interactions of three independent variables: two manipulated independent variables and the individual differences variable (Anderson & Revelle, 1982).

SUMMARY

A complex design is one in which two or more independent variables are studied in the same experiment. A complex design involving two independent variables allows one to determine the overall effect of each independent variable (the main effect of each variable). More important, complex designs can be used to reveal the interaction of two independent variables. Interactions occur when the effect of each independent variable depends on the level of the other independent variable.

The simplest possible complex design is the 2×2 design, in which two independent variables are both studied at two levels. The analytical power of complex designs increases when additional levels of one or both of the independent variables are included in the design, yielding designs such as the 3×2, the 3×3, the 4×2, the 4×3, and so on. Additional independent variables can also be included to yield designs such as the $2 \times 2 \times 2$, the $3 \times 3 \times 3$, and so on. Experiments involving three independent variables are remarkably efficient. They allow one to determine the main effects of each of the three variables, the three two-way interactions, and the simultaneous interaction of all three variables.

When two independent variables are studied in a complex design, three potential sources of systematic variation can be interpreted. Each independent variable can produce a significant main effect, and the two independent variables can combine to produce a significant interaction. Interactions can be initially identified by using the subtraction method when the descriptive statistics are reported in a table, or by the presence of nonparallel lines when the results appear in a line graph. If the interaction does prove to be statistically significant (using an analysis of variance), we can interpret the results further by examining simple main effects and simple comparisons. When no interaction arises, we interpret the main effects of each independent variable, using analytical comparisons when necessary.

Complex designs are essential to resolve contradictions that arise when two experiments involving the same independent variable result in different findings. Investigators can trace the source of the contradictory findings by using a complex design in which both the original independent variable and the independent variable presumed to be responsible for the discrepant findings are manipulated in the same experiment. Complex designs also play a critical role in the testing of predictions derived from psychological theories.

When a complex design is used and no interaction occurs, we know the effects of each independent variable can be generalized across the levels of the other independent variable(s). When an interaction does occur, however, limits on the external validity of a finding can be clearly specified. The possibility of interactions requires that we expand the definition of a relevant independent variable to include those that influence behavior directly (produce main effects) and those that produce an interaction when studied in combination with another independent variable.

Interactions that may arise because of measurement problems such as ceiling or basement effects must not be confused with interactions which reflect the true combined effect of two independent variables. Interactions can also be most helpful in solving the problem of drawing causal inferences based on the natural groups design.

KEY CONCEPTS

complex designs	simple main effect
interaction	relevant independent variable
main effect	ceiling (basement) effect

REVIEW QUESTIONS

1 Use the Haas et al. cross-racial evaluation experiment to illustrate there is one possible interaction in a 2×2 design but there are two possible ways to describe the interaction.

2 Describe the method you would use to decide whether an interaction was present in a table showing the results of a 2×2 complex design.

3 Describe the pattern in a line graph that indicates the presence of an interaction in a complex design.

4 Outline the steps in the analysis plan for a complex design with two independent variables when there is an interaction and when there is not an interaction.

5 Use an example to illustrate how a complex design can be used to test predictions derived from a psychological theory.

6 Explain how a complex design can be used to resolve contradictions that arise when two researchers obtain different results after manipulating the same independent variable in their respective single-factor experiments.

7 How is the external validity of the findings in a complex design influenced by the presence or absence of an interaction?

8 What expansion in the definition of a relevant independent variable is required by the use of complex designs?

9 What potential solution is there for the problem of drawing causal inferences on the basis of the natural-groups design?

CHALLENGE QUESTIONS

1 Consider an experiment in which two independent variables have been manipulated. Variable A has been manipulated at three levels, and Variable B has been manipulated at two levels.

   A Draw a graph showing an effect of Variable B, no effect of Variable A, and no interaction between the two variables.

   B Draw a graph showing no effect of Variable A, no effect of Variable B, but an interaction between the two variables.

   C Draw a graph showing an effect of Variable A, an effect of Variable B, and no interaction between the A and B variables.

2 A researcher has used a complex design to study the effects of training (untrained and trained) and problem difficulty (easy and hard) on participants' problem-solving ability. The researcher tested a total of 80 participants, with 20 randomly assigned to each of the four groups resulting from the factorial combination of the two independent variables. The data presented here represent the percentage of the problems that participants solved in each of the four conditions.

	Training	
Problem Difficulty	Untrained	Trained
Easy	90	95
Hxard	30	60

   A Is there evidence of a possible interaction in this experiment?

   B What aspect of the results of this experiment would lead you to be hesitant to interpret an interaction if one were present in this experiment?

   C How could the researcher modify the experiment so as to be able to interpret an interaction if it should occur?

3 A psychologist is interested in whether older people suffer a deficit with respect to their reaction time in processing complex visual patterns. He selects a random sample of 65-year-old people and another random sample of young adults (such as college students). He tests both groups of 50 people in the same reaction time task. He presents a simple figure to each participant, then a complex pattern, and asks the participant to indicate as quickly as possible whether the simple figure is present in the complex pattern. Participants are timed only for their reaction to the complex patterns. This test is called an embedded figures test. As he had expected, the mean reaction time for the older adults was markedly longer than that for the young adults. By any standard the results were statistically significant.

   A Explain what minimal set of conditions the psychologist would have to include in his experiment before he could conclude that older adults suffered a deficit in their processing of complex visual patterns. That is, state what additional reaction time test must be given to both groups. Finally, describe an outcome of the test you propose that would support his position and one which would lead you to question his conclusion.

   B Recognizing that this original study is flawed, the psychologist tries to use post hoc matching to try to equate his two groups. He decides to match on general health (i.e., the better your general health, the faster your reaction time). Although he cannot get an exact matching across groups, he does find that when he looks only at the 15 healthiest older adults, their reaction times are only slightly longer than the mean for the college students. Explain how this outcome would change the psychologist's conclusion concerning the effect of age on reaction time. Could the psychologist reach the general conclusion that older adults do not suffer a deficit in reaction time in this task? Why or why not?

ANSWER TO CHALLENGE QUESTION 1

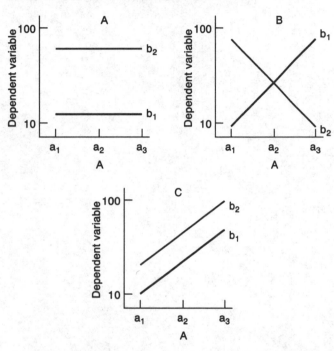

IV

Applied Research

Single-Case
Research Designs

What do Sigmund Freud and B. F. Skinner have in common? They are, of course, among the best-known psychologists of the twentieth century. However, having made this point, you may find it difficult to identify significant commonalities between these two psychologists. Freud introduced psychoanalysis. If we were to use the psychoanalyst's technique of free association, the mention of Freud would likely bring to mind concepts such as unconscious motives, defense mechanisms, and Freudian slips. Skinner developed the experimental analysis of behavior. Associations to Skinner's name are likely to include terms like behaviorism, reinforcement, and *Walden Two*. Interestingly, Freud and Skinner did have something in common: They based their research on the study of single subjects. And there the similarity ends!

Thus far in this book, we have emphasized *group methodology*, research designed to examine the average performance of one or more groups of subjects. This was particularly evident in the last few chapters, in which we examined experimental methods. The most common research design in psychological research is one involving many subjects, whose behavior is observed following one or more experimental treatments. A decision about the effectiveness of an independent variable is made when other potential independent variables have been controlled either within or between groups of subjects. Group methodology was emphasized when we discussed various kinds of independent groups designs in Chapter 6.

In this chapter we introduce an alternative methodology. The distinctive characteristic of this approach is its emphasis on a single subject or, at most, a few subjects (Kratochwill & Levin, 1992). The approach is sometimes called "small *n* research." We use the name *single-case research designs* to identify this kind of psychological research. Single-case designs have been used since scientific psychology began in the nineteenth century. Psychophysical methods had their origin in the work of Gustav Fechner and were described in his 1860 book, *Elemente der Psychophysik.* Fechner, and countless other psychophysicists since, have relied on data obtained through experiments with one or two individuals. You can find examples of single-case psychophysical experiments in journals such as *Perception & Psychophysics.*

Cognitive psychologists also have relied on single-case research designs. Most students of psychology know that Hermann Ebbinghaus initiated the scientific study of human memory with the publication, in 1885, of his monograph on memory. Ebbinghaus was both participant and experimenter; over a period of many months he learned and then attempted to relearn hundreds of series of nonsense syllables. His data provided psychologists with the first systematic evidence of forgetting over time (Zechmeister & Nyberg, 1982). Closer to the present, Linton (1978) examined the retention of everyday events over a 6-year period by testing a single participant, herself. The study of expert performance, whether it be that of a ballet dancer, chess player, or musician, also relies heavily on small *n* research (Ericsson & Charness, 1994). Ericsson, Chase, and Faloon (1980) studied the development of exceptional memory performance in a single undergraduate with average intelligence. The student practiced remembering sequences of random digits presented to him at the rate of one digit per second. Like most of us, he initially could remember only about seven digits, which is a typical adult "memory span" for digits. After more than 200 hours of practice, however, the student's memory span increased to nearly 80 digits! The *Journal of Cognitive Neuroscience* frequently publishes results of cognitive experiments based on only a few individuals.

In this chapter we discuss two specific single-case research methodologies. The first is the case study method. This approach, used by Freud and other psychoanalysts, is frequently associated with the field of clinical psychology, but as you will see, psychologists from other branches of psychology also make use of this important method. For example, Ruth Campbell's book *Mental Lives* (1992) is an interesting collection of case studies illustrating various aspects of human cognition. And the neurologist Oliver Sacks (1985, 1995) has captivated millions with his vivid descriptions of individuals with minds gone awry. Case studies are frequently the source of valuable hypotheses about behavior and can be an important complement to more rigorously controlled approaches to understanding behavior. We review both the advantages and the disadvantages of the case study method.

The second single-case methodology we discuss is derived from Skinner's experimental analysis of behavior. Techniques derived from laboratory studies of animal and human behavior have been found to be effective in managing behavior in numerous applied situations, including schools, the home, hospitals, and businesses. Single-case experimental designs, also frequently called "$N = 1$ experimental designs," are characteristic of the approach called *applied behavior analysis.* We examine the rationale behind this approach and provide specific illustrations of the more common $N = 1$ experimental design. These experimental designs represent a special case of the repeated measures design we introduced in Chapter 7.

THE CASE STUDY METHOD

CHARACTERISTICS

A **case study** is an intensive description and analysis of a single individual. The data for a case study may be obtained from several different sources, including naturalistic observation (Chapter 3), interviews and psychological tests (Chapter 4), and even archival records (Chapter 5). A case study occasionally describes the application and results of a particular treatment, as, for example, when a new therapeutic technique is used to treat an emotionally disabled person. However, in the context of a case study, treatment variables are rarely varied systematically in an effort to control extraneous variables, and several different treatments are often applied simultaneously. Thus, case studies differ from $N = 1$ experimental designs in the degree to which variables are controlled. The case study method has been used by child psychologists, memory researchers, and animal behaviorists, as well as by researchers in fields such as anthropology, criminology, neurology, and sociology.

In actual practice, the form and content of case studies are extremely varied. Published case studies may be only a few printed pages long or may fill a book. Kirsch (1978) described an attempt to implement "self-management training" with a woman experiencing low self-confidence and social inhibition. The case study, describing her treatment during nine therapy sessions and a 5-month follow-up, was presented in just four pages of one issue of the journal *Psychotherapy: Theory, Research and Practice.* In another case study, the personality psychologist Gordon W. Allport described the relationship between a mother and son as revealed in 301 letters that the mother wrote to friends. First reported in two consecutive issues of the *Journal of Abnormal and Social Psychology* (1946, Vol. 41, Nos. 3 and 4), this classic case study was published in 1965 as a 223-page book under the title *Letters from Jenny.*

Campbell's edited book, *Mental Lives* (1992), contains case studies of 15 individuals "with something 'abnormal' in the way they think, perceive, read, speak or remember" (p. 2). The focus of the book, however, is on what these cases reveal about *normal* cognitive functioning. In Chapter 10, Riddoch and Humphreys (1992) introduce us to Dennis, a 47-year-old man who experienced severe head trauma from a fall from a ladder. Dennis subsequently had difficulty recognizing familiar people (his own family) as well as common objects when he *saw* them (although his sight was good enough to watch TV); however, he could recognize people when he *heard* them speak and could identify common objects when he *touched* them. The authors of this case study use Dennis's experiences to teach us how visual recognition depends on stored knowledge. Emphasizing what we learn about normal behavior by examining unusual abnormal behaviors is, according to Campbell, what differentiates the case studies revealed in *Mental Lives* from those in other collections, such as those of Oliver Sacks. Sacks's collections of case studies focus mainly on detailed descriptions of individuals with peculiar, and rather fascinating, brain disorders. One of Sacks's best known books is *The Man Who Mistook His Wife for a Hat* (1985). In it, as the title indicates, we are introduced to a man who quite literally, when searching for his hat, seized his wife's head and tried to lift it off and put it on. These "clinical tales," as Sacks calls them, not only provide insights into the relationship between mind and brain, but also reveal how individuals adapt, cope, and succeed when faced with profound neurological deficits. As you can see, case studies serve many important purposes.

Many aspects of the case study method make it a unique means of studying behavior. It differs somewhat from more experimental approaches in terms of its goals, the methods used, and the types of information obtained (Kazdin, 1980b). For example, the case study method is often characterized as "exploratory" in nature and a source of hypotheses and ideas about behavior (Bolgar, 1965). Experimental approaches, on the other hand, are frequently viewed as opportunities to test specific hypotheses. The case study method has sometimes been viewed as antagonistic to more controlled methods of investigation. A more appropriate perspective is suggested by Kazdin (1980b), who sees the case study method as interrelated with and complementary to other research methods in psychology. For instance, *Mental Lives* shows how case studies of abnormal lives can complement nomothetic studies of "normal" lives.

The case study method offers both advantages and disadvantages to the research psychologist (Bolgar, 1965; Hersen & Barlow, 1976; Kazdin, 1980b). Before reviewing its advantages and disadvantages, however, let us illustrate the method with a summary of an actual case study reported by Kirsch (1978), which we mentioned earlier. It is important that you read this slightly abbreviated version of a case study carefully because we make reference to it when discussing the advantages and disadvantages of the methodology.

CAN CLIENTS BE THEIR OWN THERAPISTS?
A CASE STUDY ILLUSTRATION

This article reports on the use of Self-Management Training (SMT), a therapeutic strategy which capitalizes on the advantages of brief therapies, while at the same time reducing the danger of leaving too many tasks not fully accomplished. . . . The essence of this approach involves teaching the client how to be his or her own behavior therapist. The client is taught how to assess problems along behavioral dimensions and to develop specific tactics, based on existing treatment techniques, for overcoming problems. As this process occurs, the traditional client-therapist relationship is altered considerably. The client takes on the dual role of client and therapist, while the therapist takes on the role of supervisor.

The Case of Susan
Susan, a 28-year-old married woman, entered therapy complaining that she suffered from a deficient memory, low intelligence, and lack of self-confidence. The presumed

deficiencies "caused" her to be inhibited in a number of social situations. She was unable to engage in discussions about films, plays, books, or magazine articles "because" she could not remember them well enough. She often felt that she could not understand what was being said in a conversation and that this was due to her low intelligence. She attempted to hide her lack of comprehension by adopting a passive role in these interactions and was fearful lest she be discovered by being asked for more of a response. She did not trust her own opinions and, indeed, sometimes doubted whether she had any. She felt dependent on others to provide opinions for her to adopt.

Administering a Wechsler Adult Intelligence Scale (WAIS), I found her to have a verbal IQ of about 120, hardly a subnormal score. Her digit span (scale score = 12, raw score = 13) indicated that at least her short-term memory was not deficient. The test confirmed what I had already surmised from talking with her: that there was nothing wrong with her level of intelligence or her memory. After discussing this conclusion, I suggested that we investigate in greater detail what kinds of things she would be able to do if she felt that her memory, intelligence, and level of self-confidence were sufficiently high. In this way, we were able to agree upon a list of behavioral goals, which included such tasks as stating an opinion, asking for clarification, admitting ignorance of certain facts, etc. During therapy sessions, I guided Susan through overt and covert rehearsals of anxiety-arousing situations . . . structured homework assignments which constituted successive approximations of her behavioral goals, and had her keep records of her progress. In addition, we discussed negative statements which she was making to herself and which were not warranted by the available data (e.g., "I'm stupid"). I suggested that whenever she noticed herself making a statement of this sort, she counter it by intentionally saying more appropriate, positive statements to herself (e.g., "I'm not stupid—there is no logical reason to think that I am").

During the fifth session of therapy, Susan reported the successful completion of a presumably difficult homework assignment. Not only had she found it easy to accomplish, but, she reported, it had not aroused any anxiety, even on the first trial. . . . It was at this point that the nature of the therapeutic relationship was altered. During future sessions, Susan rated her progress during the week, determined what the next step should be, and devised her own homework assignments. My role became that of a supervisor of a student therapist, reinforcing her successes and drawing attention to factors which she might be overlooking.

After the ninth therapy session, direct treatment was discontinued. During the following month, I contacted Susan twice by phone. She reported feeling confident in her ability to achieve her goals. In particular, she reported feeling a new sense of control over her life. My own impressions are that she had successfully adopted a behavioral problem-solving method of assessment and had become fairly adept at devising strategies for accomplishing her goals.

Follow-up

Five months after termination of treatment, I contacted Susan and requested information on her progress. She reported that she talked more than she used to in social situations, was feeling more comfortable doing things on her own (i.e., without her husband), and that, in general, she no longer felt that she was stupid. She summarized by saying, "I feel that I'm a whole step or level above where I was."

I also asked her which, if any, of the techniques we had used in therapy she was continuing to use on her own. . . . Finally, she reported that on at least three separate occasions during the five-month period following termination of treatment, she had told another person: "I don't understand that—will you explain it to me?" This was a response which she had previously felt she was not capable of making, as it might expose her "stupidity" to the other person.

Three months after the follow-up interview, I received an unsolicited letter from Susan (I had moved out of state during that time), in which she reminded me that "one of [her] imaginary exercises was walking into a folk dancing class and feeling comfortable; well, it finally worked."*

ADVANTAGES OF THE CASE STUDY METHOD

Sources of Ideas About Behavior The "power" of the case study method, according to Bolgar (1965), "lies in its ability to open the way for discoveries" (p. 30). It acts as a breeding ground for hypotheses that may subsequently be pursued with more rigorous methodologies. This aspect of the case study method was acknowledged by Kirsch (1978) in discussing the successful psychotherapy with the woman named Susan (see case study here). He stated that the "conclusions [of this study] share the limitations of any inferences drawn from case study material. At this point they should be viewed as tentative. It is hoped that the utility of [this technique] will be established by more controlled research" (p. 305). The case study method is a natural starting point for a researcher who is entering an area of study about which relatively little is known. In psychology, the development of psychoanalytic theory stands as a classic example of hypothesis formation based on the case study method.

Opportunity for Clinical Innovation The case study method provides an opportunity to try out new therapeutic techniques or to attempt unique applications of existing techniques. In this way it offers an opportunity for clinical innovation. The use of self-management training (SMT) in psychotherapy changes the typical client-therapist relationship. The approach is based on teaching clients to be their own therapists—in other words, to identify problems and design behavioral techniques for dealing with them. The client is both client and therapist, while the therapist acts as supervisor. In a similar vein, Van Nuys (1975) used the case study method to call attention to the wording of hypnotic suggestions in helping a woman stop smoking. Information gained from this case study may provide guidance to other therapists who use hypnosis as a psychotherapeutic technique.

Method to Study Rare Phenomena Certain events appear so infrequently in nature that it is possible to describe them only through the intensive study of single cases. Many of the cases described in *Mental Lives* and in books by Oliver Sacks, for example, describe individuals with rare brain disorders. Other examples are found in the vivid case studies of so-called feral children. These are children abandoned at an early stage who developed without significant human contact while living in the wild. Among the most celebrated case stud-

*Source: Kirsch, I. (1978). Teaching clients to be their own therapists: A case-study illustration. *Psychotherapy: Theory, Research, and Practice, 15,* 302–305. (Reprinted by permission.)

FIGURE 9.1   Only surviving picture of the
"Wild Boy of Aveyron."

ies of a feral child is that of the "Wild Boy of Aveyron" (see, for example, *The Forbidden Experiment: The Story of the Wild Boy of Aveyron* [Shattuck, 1994]). Victor, as he came to be called, was captured in 1800 in the Aveyron district of France. Someone may have tried to kill him (as evidenced by the knife wound on his neck) and then abandoned him (perhaps had left him for dead) in the woods when he was about 5 years old. When he was captured, at about age 11 or 12, he was described as follows:

> He was human in bodily form and walked erect. Everything else about him suggested an animal. He was naked except for the tatters of a shirt and showed no modesty, no awareness of himself as a human person related in any way to the people who captured him. He could not speak and made only weird meaningless cries. (Shattuck, 1994, p. 5)

To many, Victor provided an opportunity to test what were then (and still are today) burning hypotheses about human nature. How are we different from animals? How do people learn language? What is "natural" and what is "cultural"? The story of Victor's reintroduction to society and his steps toward "humanity," under the tutelage of a devoted medical doctor and governess, in no way provides definitive answers to such abstract questions. Rather, in one author's view, this story "obliges us to reflect on how to live with those unsolved questions" (Shattuck, 1994, p. 182). Such can be the power of the case study.

Challenge to Theoretical Assumptions   A theory that all Martians have three heads would quickly collapse if a reliable observer spotted a Martian with only two heads. The case study method can often advance scientific thinking by providing a "counterinstance": a single case that violates a general proposition or universally accepted principle (Kazdin, 1980b). Consider, for example, the theory that human language development depends on exposure to normal language during a *critical period*, from about 2 years of age to puberty (suggested by Lenneberg, 1967). A human child deprived of language exposure during this period would, then, not be expected to acquire language. Of course, depriving a child of language experience for purposes of testing this hypothesis would be immoral. Yet, there are "nature's experiments." You see why Shattuck's story of the Wild Boy of Aveyron was titled "The Forbidden Experiment." What was Victor capable of learning after such deprivation? Interest in Victor was stimulated by age-old theories about language development similar to the critical period theory. So, too, was interest in "Genie," a child discovered more recently (in 1970). Genie had been cruelly isolated from most human contact and normal language from about the age of 2 to age 13 (Curtiss, 1977). The circumstances surrounding Genie's imprisonment and abuse, as well as the attempts by psychologists and linguists to rehabilitate her, have been chronicled by Rymer (1993). The scientists who surrounded her saw an opportunity to observe the results of a test (the forbidden one) of a critical period theory of language development:

> At best, Genie could have provided a flawed endorsement of Lenneberg's theory. But she was capable of a ringing refutation. If Genie could not learn language, her failure would be attributed ambiguously—either to the truth of the critical-period hypothesis or to her emotional problems. If Genie did learn language in spite of all that had happened to her, how much stronger the rebuttal! (Rymer, 1993, pp. 121–122)

According to the psychologist most closely associated with Genie's language training, Genie showed some language development but it was never completely normal. Thus, a "weak" version of Lenneberg's theory, namely, that *normal* language development would not appear after puberty without exposure during the critical period, "cannot be dismissed" by Genie's case study (Curtiss, 1977, p. 209).

Tentative Support for a Psychological Theory   Few researchers would accept the results of a case study as conclusive evidence for a particular hypothesis (see the discussion of disadvantages of the case study method that follows). The results of a case study generally must be viewed as tentative and must await investigation via more carefully controlled procedures before they are accepted by the scientific community. Nevertheless, the outcome of a case study can sometimes provide important evidence in support of a psychological theory, as we just saw occurred in the case of Genie and the weak version of

Lenneberg's critical period theory. As another illustration, we can take an example from the memory literature.

In 1968, Atkinson and Shiffrin proposed a model of human memory that was to have considerable influence on research in this field. The model, which was based on principles of information processing, described both a short-term memory (STM) system and a long-term memory (LTM) system. Human memory, in other words, should be thought of as containing at least two structures, each with different characteristics and functions. STM was identified with "working memory" and represented the locus of conscious rehearsal and elaboration of information. It was the kind of memory we might use when looking up a telephone number and "holding" it until we had dialed it correctly. Information in LTM did not have to be actively processed in order to be remembered; rather, information in this memory system was stored on a relatively permanent basis, from whence it could be retrieved and brought into conscious memory (into STM).

Although results of numerous experiments provided evidence for this dual nature of our memory, Atkinson and Shiffrin considered the results of several case studies as "perhaps the most convincing demonstrations of a dichotomy in the memory system" (p. 97). These case studies involved patients who had been treated for epilepsy via surgical removal of parts of the brain within the temporal lobes, including a subcortical structure known as the hippocampus. Of particular importance to Atkinson and Shiffrin's theory was the case study of a patient known as H. M. (Scoville & Milner, 1957). Following the brain operation, H. M. was found to have a disturbing memory deficit. Although he could carry on a normal conversation and remember events for a short period of time, H. M. apparently could not put new information into long-term memory. He could not remember day-to-day events. He was able to read the same magazine over and over again without finding its contents familiar. It looked as though H. M. had an intact short-term memory system but could not get information into a long-term memory system. Subsequent testing of H. M. and patients with similar memory deficits has shown that the nature of this memory problem is more complex than originally suggested (Zechmeister & Nyberg, 1982), but the case study of H. M. continues to be important whenever theories of human memory are discussed (Squire, Knowlton, & Musen, 1993).

Complement to the Nomothetic Study of Behavior   As we noted in Chapter 1, psychology is largely a nomothetic discipline. This means that psychology (like science in general) seeks to establish broad generalizations, "universal laws" that will apply to a wide population of organisms. As a consequence, psychological research is often characterized by studies that involve large numbers of subjects and seek to determine the "average" or typical performance of a group. This average may or may not represent the value of any one individual in the group. Rather, a researcher hopes to be able to predict, on the basis of this mean performance, what organisms will be like "in general."

Some psychologists, notably Allport (1961), argue that a nomothetic approach is inadequate—that the individual is more than what can be represented by the collection of average values on various dimensions. Allport argues that the individual is both unique and lawful (operates in accordance with internally consistent principles) and that the study of the individual, called **idiographic** research, is an important goal. The need for an idiographic approach can be illustrated by the task confronting the clinical psychologist. As Allport points out, the clinician's goal "is not to predict the aggregate, but to foretell 'what any one man [sic] will do.' In reaching this ideal, actuarial predictions may sometimes help, universal and group norms are useful, but they do not go the whole distance" (p. 21). Allport suggests that our approach to understanding human nature should be neither exclusively nomothetic nor exclusively idiographic but should represent an "equilibrium" between the two. At the very least the idiographic approach, as represented by the case study method, permits the kind of detailed observation that has the power to reveal various nuances and subtleties of behavior that a "group" approach may miss. And, as you have seen, case studies have the ability to teach us about typical or average behavior by studying what is not average and is atypical.

DISADVANTAGES OF THE CASE STUDY METHOD

Difficulty of Drawing Cause-Effect Conclusions   You are well aware by now that one of the goals of science is to discover the causes of phenomena—to reveal in an unambiguous manner the specific factors that produce a particular event. However, cause-effect conclusions can rarely be drawn on the basis of results obtained from the case study method. The major limitation of the case study method in this regard is its failure to control extraneous variables. Numerous plausible hypotheses are generally present to "explain" behavior change.

Consider, for instance, the treatment of Susan through SMT reported by Kirsch (1978). Although Susan apparently benefited from the SMT therapy, can we be sure this particular factor accounted for her improvement? Many illnesses and certainly numerous emotional disorders are known to subside spontaneously. That is, over the course of time a certain number of people generally report a decrease in symptoms and an overall improvement even without treatment. The case study method generally does not permit one to dismiss the hypothesis that improvement would have been observed even if the specific treatment had never been administered. In addition, numerous aspects of the situation may be responsible for Susan's improvement. Her care was in the hands of a "clinical psychologist" who assured her that she should not trust her own feelings and discussed with her the reasons for these feelings. The "insight" provided by a professional therapist may be sufficient to change Susan's attitudes toward herself. The therapist also asked Susan, as part of her therapy, to rehearse anxiety-arousing situations covertly and overtly. This technique is similar to rehearsal desensitization, which may be an effective therapeutic treatment in itself (Rimm & Masters, 1979).

The fact that several "treatments" were used simultaneously makes it difficult to argue conclusively that the SMT therapy "caused" Susan's improvement. As we have seen, Kirsch himself was sensitive to the limitations of his results and suggested that the inferences drawn from his study should be considered tentative until they were investigated more rigorously.

The case studies associated with feral children such as Victor, and abused and deprived children such as Genie, illustrate well the difficulty with isolating causal factors. We can only try to imagine the kinds of terror experienced by a child left alone in the woods year after year or of that experienced by a child who is isolated and physically abused by an emotionally disturbed parent. How much of the failure to acquire normal language is the result of such emotional disturbance? What else don't we know about these children? One story which circulated about Victor, for example, was that he had been abandoned by parents at about the age of 5 because he had not shown normal language development by that age (Shattuck, 1994). Did Victor have difficulty learning language *before* he was deprived of human contact? Genie had been severely ill at age 14 months and an attending physician had commented that she showed signs of retardation (Curtiss, 1977). Was Genie destined to be developmentally delayed even without the horrible isolation she experienced? The data from case studies frequently leave us wondering about causal events.

Sources of Bias in Interpretation   The "outcome" of a case study often depends on inferences drawn by a researcher who is both participant and observer (Bolgar, 1965). A therapist is an observer but is also certainly a participant in the therapeutic process. Problems of observer bias can arise in the context of the case study as they do in other types of observation (see Chapter 3). In the absence of independent measures, the outcome of a case study may be based mainly on the "impressions" of the observer (Hersen & Barlow, 1976). Kirsch (1978) described the patient Susan's "feelings" about her ability to achieve her goals and told how she reported a "sense of control" over her life. He stated that his "impressions are that she successfully adopted a behavioral problem-solving method of assessment and had become fairly adept at devising strategies for accomplishing her goals" (p. 304). Interpretation of an outcome solely on the basis of the subjective impressions of the observer can be seen as a serious weakness in the case study method.

Possible Biases in Data Collection   The material of a case study often includes several kinds of information, some of it obtained from personal documents and psychological tests. Each of these sources of information must be carefully examined for possible biases. Archival records, as we described in Chapter 5, are open to several sources of bias. Further, when information is based on self-reports, there is always the possibility of distortion or falsification. Such was a possibility (although not necessarily a significant one) in the case of Susan's treatment. We have no way of knowing whether the patient's self-reports of improvement were exaggerated or even false.

Reports of even the most intelligent and well-intentioned individuals are susceptible to biases and reconstructions, especially when memory for remote events is concerned. Consider the following excerpt from a self-analysis by the well-known personality psychologist Alfred Adler (1973, pp. 179–180):

> Shortly after I went to a board[ing] school. I remember that the path to the school led over a cemetery. I was frightened every time and was exceedingly put out at beholding the other children pass the cemetery without paying the least attention to it, while every step I took was accompanied by a feeling of fear and horror. Apart from the extreme discomfort occasioned by this fear I was also annoyed at the idea of being less courageous than the others. One day I made up my mind to put an end to this fear of death. Again (as on my first resolve), *I decided upon a treatment of hardening* (Proximity of death!). I stayed at some distance behind the others, placed my school-bag on the ground near the wall of the cemetery and ran across it a dozen times, until I felt that I had mastered the fear. After that, I believe, I passed along this path without any fear.
>
> Thirty years after that I met an old schoolmate and we exchanged childhood reminiscences of our school days. It happened to occur to me that the cemetery was no longer in existence and I asked him what had happened to it remembering the great uneasiness it had at one time caused me. Astonished, my former schoolmate who had lived longer in that neighborhood than I had, insisted that there never had been a cemetery on the way to our school. Then I realized that the story of the cemetery had been but a poetic dress for my longing to overcome the fear of death.

Problem of Generalizing from a Single Individual   As Bolgar (1965) stated, "Much of the criticism leveled against the case study method of research is based on the accepted canon that it is impossible to generalize from one case" (p. 30). As Kazdin (1980b) notes, however, the ability to generalize from a single case depends on the degree of variability in the population from which the case was selected. Psychologists who study visual perception are often able to make wide generalizations based on the study of one individual. The assumption is that visual systems in humans are very similar and are related to the biological makeup of all humans. Thus, as we mentioned earlier, many psychophysicists perform experiments with only a "small n." When significant variability exists among individuals, as would be the case when measures are made of learning and memory, emotionality, or personality, it becomes impossible to claim that what is observed in one individual will hold for all individuals. In this situation researchers often use the "average" performance of a large group for their interpretation.

Even if we accept the validity of Kirsch's (1978) conclusion regarding the effectiveness of the SMT technique of psychotherapy, we do not know whether this particular treatment would be as successful for other individuals who might differ from the patient Susan in any of numerous ways, including intelligence, age, family background, and gender.

THE CASE STUDY METHOD: FINAL COMMENTS

Case studies sometimes offer "dramatic" demonstrations of "new" or "unusual" findings or provide evidence for "success" of a particular treatment (Kazdin, 1980b). These reports are often highly persuasive. Everyday examples are found in the media and in advertisements for various products. How many people who worry about their weight can resist the example of a formerly overweight individual who is shown to have lost considerable weight through "Treatment X." The persuasive value of case study examples are both an asset and a liability to the scientific community. Demonstrations of new or unusual findings based on a case study may lead scientists to rethink their original theoretical assumptions or may lead them into new and fruitful avenues of research. Learning techniques used by the French scientist Itard, who worked with the feral child Victor, are used today in special education classes and in Montessori schools (Shattuck, 1994). Genie's case study stimulated other studies of language in atypical children (Rymer, 1993).

Nevertheless, the results of case studies are often accepted by nonscientists with little regard for the limitations of such evidence. This is particularly likely when individuals are in a position to identify with the subject of the case study. A person who suffers from a life-threatening illness may see more than a ray of hope in the results of a dramatic "new cure" based on treatment of an individual with the same illness. If this treatment worked for this person, why wouldn't it work for me? For people who have (or think they have) few alternatives, this grasping at straws may not be totally unreasonable. Nevertheless, too often people do not consider (perhaps they do not want to consider) the reasons why a particular treatment would *not* work for them. They fail, in other words, to recognize the limitations of the case study method. This may have unfortunate consequences. For example, during the early 1980s there was considerable controversy surrounding the supposed cancer-curing drug Laetrile (Sun, 1981). Few respectable scientists or medical researchers considered this drug, which was made from apricot pits, to be beneficial in the treatment of cancer. Positive results, however, based on individual "case studies," were presented as evidence by advocates of the drug. Largely because of public (not scientific) pressure, the government carried out systematic tests of the drug under controlled conditions. No beneficial effect of the drug was found. As others have commented, by using Laetrile instead of traditional therapies, many patients may have postponed or interrupted valid courses of treatment and thus contributed to the spread of their cancer.

A BRIEF INTRODUCTION TO EXPERIMENTAL ANALYSIS OF BEHAVIOR

Behaviorism, or behavior theory, was officially launched in 1913 with the publication of John B. Watson's article "Psychology as the Behaviorist Views It." Watson argued that psychology would be able to take its place among the natural sciences, such as chemistry and biology, only when it abandoned subjective methods of inquiry, such as introspection, and emphasized observable behavior instead. As the behaviorist viewed it, psychology's goal should be the prediction and control of behavior.

A particularly important form of behaviorism that emerged in the 1930s is that associated with B. F. Skinner. Skinner's approach is synonymous with what is called an *experimental analysis of behavior.* It presents a unique behavioral view of human nature that not only contains prescriptions for the way psychologists should do research but also has implications for the way society should be organized. Several of Skinner's books, including *Walden Two* and *Beyond Freedom and Dignity,* describe how the principles of behavior control that have been and will be derived from an experimental analysis of behavior can be put to work improving society.

In the experimental analysis of behavior, all behaviors can be classified as one of two types: respondent and operant (Reynolds, 1968). A response that is *elicited* naturally by an environmental event is a respondent. It is usually an innate reflex. Examples of respondents are the withdrawal of a hand from a hot stove, salivation in response to dry food placed in the mouth, the startle response made to a loud noise, and constriction of a pupil in response to a bright light. Respondents are clearly adaptive and help to ensure the safety and survival of an organism. That your eyelid closes "automatically" when a puff of air hits the eye serves to protect the eye from damage due to objects carried in the air. The Russian physiologist I. P. Pavlov carried out the first systematic experiments using respondent conditioning, which is also known as Pavlovian or (most frequently) classical conditioning.

Respondent behavior represents only a small part of all human behavior. Most human behaviors are classified as *operants.* These are responses that operate directly on the environment (Skinner, 1937). Operants have no identifiable eliciting stimulus; their "cause" is within the organism (Reynolds, 1968). Consequently, operants are said to be *emitted* by an organism rather than elicited by an environmental stimulus. Behaviors that we normally view as "voluntary" are operants. Walking, talking, sitting, jumping, standing, and hitting are good examples. Research methods employed in the experimental analysis of behavior are those associated with respondent and operant conditioning.

Operant conditioning is the process by which behavior is modified by its consequences. Changes in behavior are usually measured in terms of frequency of responding, although other measures (such as duration or latency) may be used. Thus, rate of responding is a major dependent variable in operant conditioning. The task of the operant researcher is to relate changes in rate of responding to changes in the environment. Generally, an increase in rate of responding is brought about by a procedure known as reinforcement. The giving of "rewards" (such as praise, candy, flowers, ribbons, or high grades) following a response is one way to increase the subject's rate of responding. Decreases in rate of responding are brought about by a procedure known as punishment. One way to punish an organism is to follow a response with an aversive (noxious) event. The laboratory rat that is shocked when it presses a bar will soon stop bar pressing. Another way to use punishment is, following a response, to remove something that an organism would normally want. The parent who takes away the keys to the family car after a teenager gets a traffic ticket and the teacher who denies recess privileges to students who misbehave are using this form of punishment.

In conducting the experimental analysis of behavior, experimenters frequently make observations on single subjects. As we said earlier, it is often the case in the experimental analysis of behavior (unlike the group methodologies discussed in previous chapters) that $N = 1$. Experimental control is demonstrated by arranging experimental conditions such that the individual's behavior changes systematically with the manipulation of an independent variable. As Skinner (1966, p. 21) commented,

> instead of studying a thousand rats for one hour each, or a hundred rats for ten hours each, the investigator is likely to study one rat for a thousand hours. The procedure is not only appropriate to an enterprise which recognizes individuality, it is at least equally efficient in its use of equipment and of the investigator's time and energy. The ultimate test of uniformity or reproducibility is not to be found in the methods used but in the degree of control achieved, a test which the experimental analysis of behavior usually passes easily.

There is a minimum of statistical analysis. Conclusions regarding the effect of an experimental variable are made by visually inspecting the behavioral record in order to observe whether behavior changes systematically with the introduction and withdrawal of the experimental treatment.

APPLIED BEHAVIOR ANALYSIS

In applied behavior analysis, the methods developed within an experimental analysis of behavior are applied to socially relevant problems. These applications are frequently referred to as **behavior modification,** but when applied to clinical populations the term **behavior therapy** is preferred (Wilson, 1978). Behavior therapy is seen by many as a more effective approach to clinical treatment than that based on a psychodynamic model of therapy. A psychodynamic model of therapy stresses "dynamics, or interaction, of forces lying deep within the mind" (Bootzin, Acocella, & Alloy, 1993). Therapies based on Freud's psychoanalytic theory are particularly representative of this approach. Behavior therapy focuses on observable behavior rather than hypothesized inner forces. For example, self-stimulatory behaviors (e.g., prolonged body rocking, gazing at lights, or spinning) that often characterize so-called autistic children may be conceptualized as operant behaviors. In this way, clinicians and teachers may be able to control their frequency of occurrence by using behavior modification techniques (Lovaas, Newsom, & Hickman, 1987). Numerous studies have been published showing how operant techniques can be employed successfully to change the behavior of psychotic individuals, normal and mentally impaired children and adults, individuals diagnosed as schizophrenic, stutterers, psychiatric patients, and many others. Behavior-analytic approaches have also been successfully used by school psychologists in educational settings (Kratochwill

& Martens, 1994). A primary source for these published studies is the *Journal of Applied Behavior Analysis.*

SINGLE-CASE (*N* = 1) EXPERIMENTAL DESIGNS

The use of a single subject, which we have seen is often characteristic of the experimental analysis of behavior, is also a hallmark of applied behavior analysis. The **single-case experiment,** as its name suggests, typically focuses on an examination of behavior change in one individual. This methodology can be extended, however, to treatments applied to single groups of individuals as well (Kazdin, 1980b). Single-case experiments differ from the traditional case study method in that they contrast conditions within an individual whose behavior is being continuously monitored. That is, the independent variable of interest is manipulated systematically for each individual. Consequently, single-case experimental designs are an important alternative to the relatively uncontrolled case study method (Kazdin, 1982).

For certain kinds of applied research, *N* = 1 experimental designs may be more appropriate than designs based on multiple-group methodology (Hersen & Barlow, 1976). This is likely to be true when research is directed toward changing the behavior of a specific individual. For example, the average response of a group of subjects will not necessarily be the same as the response of any one individual in the group. Therefore, the outcome of a group experiment may lead to recommendations about what treatments "in general" should be applied to modify behavior, but it is not possible to say what the effect of that treatment will be on any particular individual. As Kazdin (1982) commented, "Perhaps the most obvious advantage [of single-case experimental designs] is that the methodology allows investigation of the individual client and experimental evaluation of treatment for the client" (p. 482).

Another disadvantage of multiple-group methodology, particularly in the context of clinical research, is that ethical problems arise when a potentially beneficial treatment is withheld from individuals in order to provide a control group that satisfies the requirements of internal validity. Because single-case experimental designs contrast conditions of "No Treatment" and "Treatment" within the same individual, this problem can be avoided. Moreover, investigators doing clinical research often find it difficult to gain access to enough clients to do a group experiment. For instance, a clinician may be able to identify from a list of clients only a few individuals experiencing claustrophobia (excessive fear of enclosed spaces). The single-case experiment provides a practical solution to the problem of investigating cause-effect conclusions when only a few participants are available.

The first stage of a single-case experiment is usually an observation stage, or **baseline stage.** During this stage a record is made of the individual's behavior prior to any intervention. A typical measure is frequency of behavior per some unit of time, such as a day, an hour, or another recording interval. An applied researcher might record the number of times during a 10-minute interview that an excessively shy child makes eye contact, the number of headaches reported each week by a depressed migraine sufferer, or the number of verbal pauses per minute made by a chronic stutterer. The baseline record provides information about what behavior is like before treatment is provided (Kazdin, 1978).

Once behavior is shown to be relatively stable—that is, it exhibits little fluctuation between recording intervals—an intervention (treatment) is introduced. Behavior immediately following an intervention is contrasted with that seen during baseline performance. The effect of a behavioral intervention is typically evaluated by visual inspection of the behavioral record. How did behavior change, in other words, following the experimental treatment? Traditionally, tests of statistical significance have not been used, although there is some controversy surrounding this aspect of single-case methodology (Kratochwill & Brody, 1978). Later in this chapter we discuss some of the problems that arise when visual inspection is used to determine whether a treatment was effective.

Another approach to treatment evaluation is to assess the **clinical significance** of an experimental result. Information, for instance, about the strength of a treatment—how likely it is to improve the life of a client in a real-world setting—is often more important for the applied researcher than a treatment's statistical significance or even its "obvious" effect on behavior as contrasted with baseline performance (Yeaton & Sechrest, 1981). Two methods for determining clinical significance of a treatment are social comparison and subjective evaluation (Kazdin, 1977, 1982). In a **social comparison** approach to clinical significance, the researcher compares the behavior of a client after treatment with the behavior of a "normal" group of participants. For example, following treatment aimed at reducing the aggressive behavior of a child in a classroom, a researcher may compare the treated child's behavior with that of children who are not normally aggressive. A **subjective evaluation** approach uses the judgments of people who have contact with the client to help decide whether a treatment has been effective. Family members, teachers, friends, and staff members in a hospital might be asked, for example, whether the behavior of the individual after treatment is perceptibly different from the behavior before treatment.

Although there are numerous design possibilities for the researcher who uses a single-case experimental design (Hersen & Barlow, 1976; Kazdin, 1980a), the most commonly employed are the ABAB and multiple-baseline designs (Kazdin, 1978).

SPECIFIC EXPERIMENTAL DESIGNS

The ABAB Design   The ABAB design seeks to confirm a treatment effect by demonstrating that behavior changes systematically with alternating conditions of No Treatment and Treatment. An initial baseline stage (A) is followed by a treatment stage (B), next by a return to baseline (A), and then by another treatment stage (B). Because treatment is removed during the second A stage, and any improvement in behavior is likely to be reversed at this point, this design is also called a reversal design. The researcher using the ABAB design observes whether behavior changes immediately upon introduction of a treatment variable (first B), whether behavior reverses when treatment is withdrawn (second A), and whether behavior improves again when treatment is reintroduced (second B). When variations in behavior follow the introduction and withdrawal of treatment in this way, considerable evidence supports the conclusion that the treatment caused behavior change.

Horton (1987) used an ABAB design to assess the effects of facial screening on the maladaptive behavior of a severely mentally impaired 8-year-old girl. Facial screening is a mildly aversive technique involving the application of a face cover (for example, a soft cloth) when an undesirable behavior occurs. Previous research had shown this technique to be effective in reducing the frequency of self-injurious behaviors such as face slapping. Horton sought to determine whether it would reduce the frequency of spoon banging by a young child at mealtime. The spoon banging prevented the girl from dining with her classmates at the school for exceptional children that she attended. The banging was disruptive not only because of the noise but because it often led her to fling food on the floor or resulted in her dropping the spoon on the floor.

A clear definition of spoon banging was made to distinguish it from normal scooping motions. Then, a paraprofessional was trained to make observations and to administer the treatment. A frequency count was used to assess the magnitude of spoon banging within each 15-minute eating session. During the initial, or baseline, period the paraprofessional recorded frequency and, with each occurrence of the response, said "no bang," gently grasped the girl's wrist, and returned her hand to her dish. The procedure was videotaped, and an independent observer viewed the films and recorded frequency as a reliability check. Interobserver reliability was approximately 96%. The baseline stage was conducted for 16 days.

The first treatment period began on Day 17 and lasted for 16 days. Each time spoon banging was observed, the paraprofessional continued to give the corrective feedback of "no bang" and returned the girl's hand to her dish. However, the paraprofessional also pulled a terry-cloth bib over the girl's entire face for 5 seconds. Release from facial screening was contingent on the girl's not banging for 5 seconds. The first treatment phase was followed by a second baseline period and another treatment phase. Posttreatment observations were also made at 6, 10, 15, and 19 months.

Figure 9.2 shows changes in the frequency of the mentally impaired girl's spoon-banging behavior as a function of alternating baseline and treatment phases. Facial screening was not only effective in reducing this behavior during treatment phases, follow-up observations revealed that the target behavior was still absent months later. Following the final treatment phase, the girl no longer required direct supervision during mealtime at either school or home and was permitted to eat with her peers. The facial-screening technique was a successful procedure for controlling the maladaptive behavior of the young child when other, less intrusive procedures had failed. Because only one treatment was administered, and because visual inspection revealed that behavior changed systematically with the introduction and withdrawal of treatment, it can be concluded that application of the aversive stimulus was responsible for eliminating spoon banging.

Methodological Issues Associated with ABAB Designs   A major methodological problem that sometimes arises in the context of an ABAB procedure can be illustrated by looking again at the results of the Horton (1987) study shown in Figure 9.2. In the second baseline stage, when application of the facial screening was withdrawn, spoon banging increased in frequency. That is, the improvement observed under the preceding treatment stage was reversed. What if spoon-banging behavior remained low even when the treatment was withdrawn? What can be concluded? Behavior in a second baseline stage may not revert to what it was during the initial baseline period, and when that occurs it raises serious problems of interpretation.

One reason why improvement in behavior may not reverse is that the behavior that is the focus of treatment would not logically be expected to become worse once improvement was observed. This might be the case if treatment involved training an individual in a new skill, such as tying one's shoes or commuting successfully to a job. Once the skill is acquired, it cannot reasonably be expected to be unlearned. The solution to this problem is one of foresight. That is, the ABAB design should not be used when the target behavior could not logically be expected to show reversal when effective treatment is withdrawn.

Given that the experienced researcher is likely to avoid using an ABAB design in situations wherein behavior would not be expected to reverse, the fail-

FIGURE 9.2   Frequency of spoon-banging responses across baseline, treatment, and follow-up phases of study. (Adapted from Horton, 1987.)

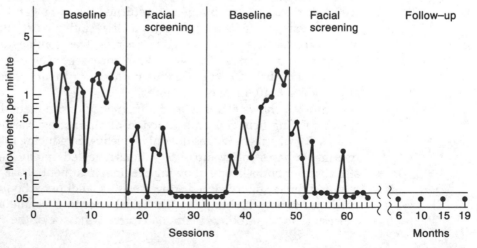

ure to observe a reversal of performance is probably due to one of two factors. One possibility is that a variable other than the treatment variable was responsible for the improvement in behavior in the first shift from baseline to treatment stages. For example, the individual may receive increased attention from staff or friends during treatment. This increased attention—rather than the treatment—may produce an improvement in behavior. If the attention persists even though the specific treatment is withdrawn, the behavior change is likely to persist as well. It is also possible that, although the treatment caused behavior to improve, other variables took over to control the new behavior. Again, we might consider attention as a variable having an effect on behavior. When family and friends witness a change in behavior, they may pay increased attention to the individual. Positive reinforcement in the form of attention may maintain the behavior change that was initiated by the treatment.

In either case, when improvement in behavior does not reverse, it is not clear whether the experimental treatment or some other factor led to the initial behavior change (Kazdin, 1980a). The solution to this set of circumstances is to examine the situation carefully in hopes of finding variables that might be confounding the treatment variable or to replicate the procedure with the same subject or with different subjects (Hersen & Barlow, 1976).

From an applied researcher's point of view, in some situations there is also an ethical problem in using the ABAB design. As you might imagine, the withdrawal of a beneficial treatment may not be justified in all cases. For example, although spoon-banging behavior would not be considered life threatening or exceptionally debilitating, other kinds of behavior might be, and it would not be ethical in these cases to remove or even suspend treatment once a positive effect was observed. Some autistic children exhibit self-injurious behaviors such as head banging or face slapping. If a clinical researcher succeeded in reducing the frequency of such behavior, it would be unethical to withdraw treatment to meet the requirements of the ABAB design. Fortunately, there are other single-case experimental designs that do not involve withdrawal of treatment and may be appropriate in such situations.

The Multiple-Baseline Design   The multiple-baseline design demonstrates the effect of a treatment by showing that behaviors in more than one baseline change following the introduction of a treatment. There are several variations on the multiple-baseline design, depending on whether multiple baselines are established for different individuals, for different behaviors in the same individual, or for the same individual in different situations. In each case, the conclusion that an experimental variable produced a reliable effect rests on the demonstration that behavior changed only when the experimental variable was introduced. Although they sound complex, multiple-baseline designs are frequently used and easily understood. Let us refer to a specific example of each type from the applied research literature.

A **multiple-baseline design across subjects** is a procedure wherein more than one individual is observed simultaneously. Specifically, baselines are first established for different individuals. When the behavior of each individual has stabilized, an intervention is introduced for one individual, then for another individual, later for another, and so on. That is, the experimental treatment is introduced at a different time for each subject. If the treatment is responsible for changing behavior, then an effect in the behavioral record will be seen immediately following the application of the treatment in each individual.

An interesting example of the use of a multiple-baseline design across subjects comes from the field of sports psychology. This subdiscipline involves the application of psychological principles to the improvement of recreation and sports (see, for example, Browne & Mahoney, 1984). Specifically, the researchers investigated the effect of a coaching method based on several behavioral techniques on the acquisition of specific football, tennis, and gymnastic skills (Allison & Ayllon, 1980). To evaluate this new behavioral coaching method, they used a multiple-baseline design. Although their investigation was successful in each sport, we examine the effects of behavioral coaching only as it was applied to the acquisition of a football skill.

The participants in this experiment were second-string members of a citywide football program chosen because they "completely lacked fundamental football skills" (Allison & Ayllon, 1980, p. 299). The skill to be acquired was blocking, which was defined operationally in terms of eight elements, ranging from the body's first being behind the line of scrimmage to maintaining body contact until the whistle was blown. Behavioral coaching involved specific procedures implemented by the team coach. The procedures included systematic verbal feedback, positive and negative reinforcement, and several other behavioral techniques. The experimenter first established baselines for several different members of the football team under "standard coaching" conditions. In this procedure, the coach used verbal instructions, provided occasional modeling or verbal approval, and, when execution was incorrect, "loudly informed the player and, at times, commented on the player's stupidity, lack of courage, awareness, or even worse" (p. 300), in short, an all-too-typical example of negative coaching behavior.

The experimenter and a second, reliability observer made observations of the frequency of correct blocks made in sets of 10 trials. Behavioral coaching was begun, in accordance with the multiple-baseline design, at different times for various football players. Results of this intervention are shown in Figure 9.3. Across four individuals, behavioral coaching was shown to be effective in increasing the frequency of correctly executed blocks. Observer agreement on blocking performance ranged from 84% to 94%, indicating that the observation of behavior change was reliable. The skill execution changed for each player at the point where behavioral coaching was introduced. Thus, it can be argued that this method caused the change in each player's performance.

When two or more baselines are established by observing different behaviors in the *same* individual, the design is called a **multiple-baseline design across behaviors.** A treatment is directed first at one behavior, then at another, and so on. A causal relationship between treatment and behavior is assumed if each behavior responds directly to treatment. For example, Bornstein, Bellack,

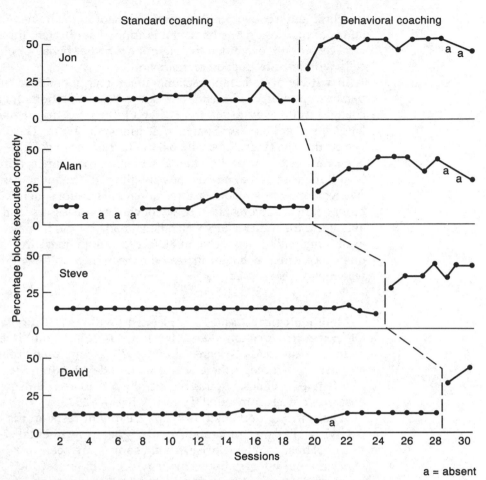

FIGURE 9.3   Multiple baselines showing percentage of football blocks executed correctly by four players as a function of standard coaching and behavioral coaching. (From Allison & Ayllon, 1980.)

and Hersen (1977) successfully treated an 8-year-old elementary school girl who was judged to be excessively shy, unassertive, and passive. Multiple baselines were established for behaviors of eye contact, number of requests, and loudness of speech. Intervention consisted of prompting, feedback, and modeling of behaviors and was instituted at different times for the three behaviors. An inspection of the behavioral record showed that the different behaviors changed immediately after introduction of the new intervention.

The third major variation on the multiple-baseline design is that across situations. In a **multiple-baseline design across situations**, baselines are established for an individual's behavior in different situations. For example, a researcher might establish baselines showing frequency of a target behavior in the clinic and frequency of this same behavior in the home. As with other variations of this design, the treatment is applied at different times and the behavioral records are examined to determine whether behavior changes systematically with the introduction of treatment.

In a study of verbal interaction among institutionalized mentally impaired persons, a multiple-baseline design across situations demonstrated that changes in the way meals were served influenced the frequency of mealtime language (VanBiervliet, Spangler, & Marshall, 1981). The investigators suggested that the typical institutional method of serving meals does not encourage peer interaction and that an alternative procedure, serving "family style," would increase verbal interactions. Baselines for frequency of verbalizations of five residents were made for three different situations (actually, three meals)—dinner, lunch, and breakfast. Behavior change was assessed in two ways: (1) by averaging the number of vocalizations made by the five residents, and (2) by examining individual behavioral records. Both measures showed that frequency of verbal behavior increased at each meal following the change in the way meals were served.

Methodological Issues Associated with Multiple-Baseline Designs

Often the first question to arise when one is doing a multiple-baseline experiment is "How many baselines do I need?" As with many other aspects of single-case methodology, there are no hard-and-fast rules. The bare minimum is clearly two baselines, but this is generally considered inadequate. Three to four baselines are recommended (Hersen & Barlow, 1976).

A convincing demonstration of a treatment rests on the observation that behavior changes immediately after the experimental variable is introduced. Thus, problems arise when changes are seen in a baseline *before* an experimental intervention. This may occur in any of the types of multiple-baseline designs we have considered, and the reasons are not always clear. When changes in baseline performance occur prior to an experimental intervention, it is often difficult to draw a conclusion about the efficacy of the experimental treatment. However, the multiple-baseline design can still be interpreted with some confidence when preintervention changes appear in only one of several baselines that are being recorded—so long as plausible explanations for the baseline change, explanations based on procedural or situational variables, are available. For instance, Kazdin and Erickson (1975) used a multiple-baseline design across subjects to help severely mentally impaired individuals respond to instructions. Participants who followed instructions were reinforced with candy-coated cereal and praise, and this intervention was introduced in each of four small groups at different points in time. Performance changed directly with the application of the positive reinforcement procedure in three groups, but not in the fourth. In this group, which had the longest baseline, behavior gradually improved prior to the intervention. The researchers reasonably suggested that this occurred because individuals in this group saw other patients comply with instructions and then imitated the treated participants' behavior.

Another problem sometimes seen in multiple-baseline designs occurs when changes in one behavior generalize to other behaviors or situations. For example, when researchers successfully increased the degree of verbal interaction of mentally impaired persons at a dinner meal, we might not have been totally surprised if the residents increased their amount of talking at other meals. Once behavior at dinner was changed, at other meals the sight of food being served or the act of sitting down beside an acquaintance might prompt an increased level of verbal interaction. Such generalization effects were not seen, however, so the effect of the mealtime intervention was clearly demonstrated (VanBiervliet et al., 1981).

To circumvent possible problems, we must again bring foresight to bear. If altering the behavior of one individual is likely to affect the behaviors of others, if behavior in one situation is likely to influence behavior in another situation, or if changing one type of behavior is likely to affect other behaviors, then multiple-baseline designs should not be used (Kazdin, 1980a). As we have noted, unless behavior improves directly following an experimental intervention, concluding that the treatment variable was effective is problematic. Unfortunately, anticipating when changes will occur simultaneously in more than one baseline is not always easy, but these problems appear to be relatively infrequent exceptions to the effects usually seen in a multiple-baseline design (Kazdin, 1980a).

PROBLEMS AND LIMITATIONS COMMON TO ALL
SINGLE-CASE DESIGNS

It is difficult to evaluate the effects of an intervention when there are increasing or decreasing baseline trends or excessive variability in behavioral records. An ideal baseline record and response to an intervention are shown in panel A of Figure 9.4. Behavior during baseline is very stable, and behavior changes immediately following the introduction of treatment. If this were the outcome of the first stages of either an ABAB or a multiple-baseline design, we would be headed in the direction of showing that our treatment is effective in modifying behavior. However, consider the baseline and treatment stages shown in panel B of Figure 9.4. The baseline shows extreme variability, and, although the desired behavior appears to increase in frequency following an intervention, it is difficult to know whether the treatment produced the change or behavior just happened to be on the upswing. In this case it would be hard to decide whether our intervention successfully increased behavior.

There are several approaches to the problem of excessive baseline variability. One approach is to look for variables in the situation that might be producing the variability and could be removed. The presence of a particular staff member, for instance, might be causing changes in the behavior of a psychiatric patient. Another approach is to "wait it out"—to continue taking baseline mea-

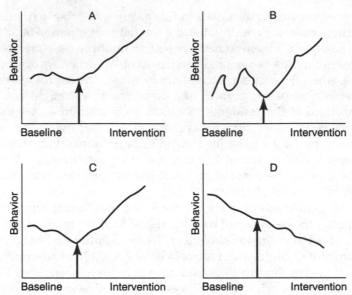

FIGURE 9.4   Examples of behavioral records showing possible relationships between baseline and intervention phases of a behavior modification program.

sures until behavior stabilizes. It is, of course, not possible to predict when and if this might occur, but introducing an intervention before behavior has stabilized would jeopardize a clear interpretation of the experimental outcome. Another approach is to average data points. By charting a behavioral record using averages of several points, we can sometimes reduce the "appearance" of variability (Kazdin, 1978).

Another problem arises when the baseline record shows an increasing or a decreasing trend. In panel C of Figure 9.4, we see how behavior might change following an intervention when the initial baseline stage was characterized by a reduction in frequency of behavior. If the goal of the intervention was to increase frequency of behavior, the change described in panel C offers little problem of interpretation. An intervention that reversed the decreasing trend can be taken as evidence that the treatment was effective. However, should the goal of intervention be to reduce frequency of behavior, it would be difficult to know whether the decrease in frequency of behavior following the intervention is due to the intervention or to continuation of the baseline trend. This situation is illustrated in panel D. Here we see a decreasing trend in the baseline stage and continued reduction of frequency in the treatment stage. It is difficult in this case to know whether the experimental treatment had an effect. Generally speaking, when an intervention is expected to have an effect in the same direction as a baseline trend, the effect must be very marked in order to conclude that behavior was modified by the application of a treatment (Kazdin, 1978). Moreover, because a treatment effect in a single-case design is usually judged by visually inspecting the behavioral record, it is often difficult to say what constitutes a "marked" change in the behavioral record (Parsonson & Baer, 1992). In such cases other means of evaluation, such as social comparison or subjective evaluation, should be employed.

When a treatment effect is demonstrated using an $N = 1$ design, a frequent criticism is that external validity is limited. In other words, the $N = 1$ experiment appears to have the same limitation as the traditional case study method. Because each person is unique, it can be argued that there is no way of knowing whether the effect of a particular intervention will generalize to other individuals. There are several reasons why this problem may not be as serious as it seems. First, the types of intervention used in single-case studies are often potent ones and frequently produce dramatic and sizable changes in behavior (Kazdin, 1978). Consequently, these types of treatments are often found to generalize to other individuals. Other evidence for the generality of effects based on single-case studies comes from the use of multiple-baseline designs. A multiple-baseline design across subjects, for example, is often able to show that a particular intervention was successful in modifying the behavior of *several* individuals. Similarly, multiple baselines across situations and behaviors attest to the external validity of a treatment effect.

A treatment effect can also be shown to generalize to other individuals when a "single group" of subjects is used in a single-case experiment. As we mentioned before, the procedures associated with single-case designs are sometimes used with small groups of individuals as well. We have already seen two examples of this. VanBiervliet et al. (1981) showed that changes in a mealtime procedure were effective in increasing the average frequency of verbalizations of five mentally impaired individuals who were treated simultaneously. Similarly, Kazdin and Erickson (1975) found that positive reinforcement improved responsiveness to instructions in small groups of mentally impaired individuals. In both these experiments, the researchers were able to demonstrate that an experimental treatment was, on average, effective for a small group of participants as well as for individuals in the group. In other words, an effect was replicated several times across members of a group each time an experimental manipulation was introduced. Such studies offer impressive evidence for both internal and external validity.

One limitation of the $N = 1$ methodology is no easily dismissed, and it illustrates again the lesson that no one research methodology is able to provide all the answers to questions that psychologists ask. The $N = 1$ experiment is usually not appropriate for examining the effect of interactions among variables. Although a single-case design can provide evidence of the effect of one variable (a main effect) by showing, for example, that behavior changes between conditions of No Treatment and Treatment, it is difficult to examine adequately the differential effect of combinations of various treatments. In this situation, a large group design is often most appropriate (see especially Chapter 8). The experienced research psychologist realizes there are problems and limitations associated with most methodologies. The methodology best suited to answering a particular question should be used. And, as we have stated previously, when possible, multimethod approaches to data collection are recommended.

SINGLE-CASE DESIGNS: ETHICAL ISSUES

Two particularly salient ethical issues associated with single-case research should be mentioned. One of these we have already discussed briefly, namely, the withholding of an effective treatment as is required in the ABAB design. Ethical issues arise when treatments aimed at reducing painful or harmful events are shown to improve behavior (for example, in the first, or treatment stage of an ABAB design) and then are withdrawn (in the second baseline stage) to provide more conclusive evidence of the treatment's efficacy. As you saw, one solution is to change research designs and use a multiple-baseline design in which treatments need not be withheld. This would obviously be an appropriate and obvious strategy in many situations, especially if previous research has demonstrated a treatment's worth and the behavior being modified is clearly harmful. In some situations, however, whether a treatment will be effective is clearly an unanswered question (after all, we do research to find out if a treatment *will* work!) and the benefits of the treatment may not be entirely clear.

Consider, for example, research aimed at increasing the use of designated drivers to reduce alcohol-related driving accidents (Brigham, Meier, & Goodner, 1995). Researchers used an ABAB design in which the treatment involved placing posters and table signs offering free nonalcoholic drinks to designated drivers at a bar frequented by college students. The dependent measure was the number of persons on a given weekend evening who registered with the bartender as designated drivers. Visual inspection of the graphed results revealed a clear effect of the prompts and free nonalcoholic drinks during the first treatment stage, then a reversal to baseline frequency when the prompts and drink offers were withdrawn, and finally, an increase in frequency again when the prompts and soft beverages were reinstated. Thus, we can suggest that drivers leaving the bar were "safer" when the signs were in evidence. Should an alternative design have been used to avoid the reversal during the second baseline stage?

Another ethical problem sometimes associated with single-case research concerns the nature of the treatment. Behavior modification using a noxious or aversive treatment is one example. Lovaas, for example, has used "aversives" such as mild electric shock with autistic and schizophrenic children in order to develop appropriate social responses (Lovaas, 1993; Lovaas, Schaeffer, & Simmons, 1965). This research has generated considerable controversy. The aversive treatments were used only when other methods had failed and the alternative appeared even more injurious. That is, the success of these treatments apparently saved some individuals from permanent institutionalization and little hope of successful therapeutic intervention. This type of research clearly illustrates the often difficult nature of ethical decision making. Is the risk to the

FIGURE 9.5   Research using an ABAB design revealed that offering free nonalcoholic drinks to designated drivers increased the frequency with which people registered with the bartender as designated drivers (Brigham, Meier, & Goodner, 1995).

participant outweighed by the benefit of the treatment? It is interesting to note that the French doctor Itard, who tried to rehabilitate the "wild boy" of Aveyron, faced a similar vexing ethical dilemma (Shattuck, 1994). At one point during training the boy became so frustrated and upset that he threw tantrums, biting the mantelpiece, tossing burning coals around the room, even losing consciousness. When this behavior was continually repeated the doctor had to decide whether to halt training or try somehow to control the tantrums. Itard decided on a most unconventional, but, as it turns out, highly effective treatment: He forcibly held the boy (who was afraid of heights) out the fifth-floor window. The boy was clearly scared and apparently cried for the first time, but training was able to proceed. Determining whether a treatment is justified requires careful consideration of all relevant factors and, as we noted in Chapter

2, consultation with knowledgeable others when the risk/benefit ratio is not easily calculated. Of course, these questions must be raised whenever research involves a potentially harmful treatment, and is not just associated with the use of single-case designs.

SUMMARY

Two important single-case research designs are the case study and the single-case experiment, or $N = 1$ design. The case study method can be an important source of hypotheses about behavior, can provide an opportunity for clinical innovation (for example, trying out new approaches to therapy), can permit the intensive study of rare phenomena, can challenge theoretical assumptions, and can provide tentative support for a psychological theory. The intensive study of individuals that is the hallmark of the case study method is called idiographic research, and it can be viewed as complementary to the nomothetic inquiry (seeking general laws or principles) that is also characteristic of psychology. Problems arise when the case study method is used to draw cause-effect conclusions, or when biases in the collection of, or interpretation of, data are not identified. The case study method also suffers from a lack of generalizability. How do we generalize on the basis of studying a single individual? Moreover, the dramatic results obtained from some case studies, although they may give scientific investigators important insights, are frequently accepted as valid by nonscientists who are not aware of the limitations of this method.

Behaviorism is an approach to the study of psychology that emphasizes the study of observable behavior under strictly controlled conditions. The behaviorism of B. F. Skinner is called the experimental analysis of behavior. Applied behavior analysis seeks to apply principles derived from an experimental analysis of behavior to socially relevant problems. The major methodology of this approach is the single-case experiment, or $N = 1$ design. Although there are many kinds of $N = 1$ designs, the most common are the ABAB design and the multiple-baseline design. An important consideration in applied behavior analysis is obtaining evidence for the clinical significance of a treatment—that is, how likely a treatment is to modify the behavior of a client in a real-world setting.

An ABAB design, or reversal design, allows a researcher to confirm a treatment effect by showing that behavior changes systematically with conditions of No Treatment (baseline) and Treatment. Methodological problems arise in this design when behavior that changed during the first treatment (B) stage does not reverse when treatment is withdrawn during the second baseline (A) stage. When this occurs, it is difficult to establish that the treatment variable, rather than some other variable, was responsible for the initial change. One may encounter ethical problems when using the ABAB design if a treatment that has been shown to be beneficial is withdrawn during the second baseline stage.

A multiple-baseline design demonstrates the effectiveness of a treatment by showing that behaviors across more than one baseline change as a consequence of the introduction of a treatment. Baselines are first established across different subjects, across behaviors in the same subject, or across situations. Methodological problems arise when behavior does not change immediately with the introduction of a treatment or when a treatment effect generalizes to other subjects, other behaviors, or other situations.

Problems of increasing or decreasing baselines, as well as excessive baseline variability, sometimes make it difficult to interpret the outcome of single-case designs. The problem of excessive baseline variability can be approached by seeking out and removing sources of variability, by extending the time during which baseline observations are made, or by averaging data points to remove the "appearance" of variability. Increasing or decreasing baselines may require the researcher to obtain other kinds of evidence for the effectiveness of a treatment—for example, measures of social comparison or subjective evaluation. Finally, the $N = 1$ design is often criticized for its lack of external validity. However, because treatments typically produce substantial changes in behavior, these changes can often be easily replicated in different individuals. The use of single "groups" of subjects can also provide immediate evidence of generality across subjects. Treatments that are clearly aversive to the participants should only be used after careful consideration of the ethical implications, including the risk/benefit ratio.

The fact that the $N = 1$ design usually is not appropriate for testing the possible interactions of variables highlights the importance of selecting the research methodology most relevant for answering the particular question under investigation.

KEY CONCEPTS

case study	clinical significance
nomothetic approach	social comparison
idiographic approach	subjective evaluation
behaviorism	ABAB design (reversal design)
behavior modification	multiple-baseline design (across
behavior therapy	subjects, across behaviors, across
single-case experiment	situations)
baseline stage	

REVIEW QUESTIONS

1 Cite and give an example of the advantages of the case study method.
2 Distinguish between a nomothetic and an idiographic approach to research.
3 Cite and give an example of the disadvantages of the case study method.
4 What is the major limitation of the case study method in drawing cause-effect conclusions?

5 Under what conditions might an $N = 1$ design be more appropriate than a multiple-group design?

6 Distinguish between baseline and intervention stages of an $N = 1$ experimental design.

7 How does clinical significance differ from statistical significance? Explain how clinical significance can be evaluated.

8 Why is an ABAB design also called a reversal design?

9 What major methodological problems are specifically associated with an ABAB design?

10 Outline the general rationale behind all the major forms of multiple-baseline designs.

11 What major methodological problems are specifically associated with multiple-baseline designs?

12 What major methodological problems are inherent in all $N = 1$ experimental designs?

13 How would you respond to the frequent criticism that $N = 1$ experimental designs lack external validity?

14 What types of research questions are not easily answered using single-case ($N = 1$) experimental designs?

CHALLENGE QUESTIONS

1 A case study showing how mud therapy was successful in treating an individual exhibiting excessive anxiety was reported in a popular magazine. The patient's symptoms included trouble sleeping, loss of appetite, extreme nervousness when in groups of people, and general feelings of arousal that led the individual always to feel on edge and fearful. The California therapist who administered the mud therapy was known for this treatment, having appeared on several TV talk shows. He first taught the patient a deep relaxation technique and a "secret word" to repeat over and over in order to block out all disturbing thoughts. Then the patient was asked to lie submerged for two hours each day in a special wooden "calm tub" filled with mud. During this time the patient was to practice the relaxation exercises and to concentrate on repeating the secret word whenever the least bit of anxiety was experienced. The therapy was very costly, but after six weeks the patient reported to the therapist that he no longer had the same feelings of anxiety he had had before. The therapist pronounced him cured and attributed the success of the treatment to immersion in the calming mud. The conclusion drawn by the author of the magazine article describing this therapy was that "it is a treatment that many people could benefit from." On the basis of your knowledge of the limitations of the case study method, answer the following questions:

A What possible sources of bias were there in the study?

B What alternative explanations can you suggest for the successful treatment?

C What problem arises from studying only one individual?

2 A 5-year-old child frequently gets skin rashes, and the mother has been told by her family doctor that the problem is due to "something" the child eats. The doctor suggests that she "watch carefully" what the child eats. The mother decides to approach this problem by recording each day whether the child has a rash and what the child has eaten the day before. She hopes to find some relationship between eating a particular food and the presence or absence of the rash. Although this approach might help discover a relationship between eating certain foods and the appearance of the rash, a

better approach might be one based on the logic and procedures associated with $N = 1$ designs. Explain how the mother might use such an alternative approach. Be specific and point to possible problems that may arise in this application of behavioral methodology.

3 During the summer months you find employment in a camp for mildly mentally impaired children. As a counselor you are asked to supervise a small group of children, as well as to look for ways to improve their attention to various camp activities that take place indoors (for example, craft making and sewing). You decide to explore the possibility of using a system of rewards (M & M candies) for "time on task." You realize that the camp director will want evidence of the effectiveness of your intervention strategy as well as some assurance it will work with other children in the camp. Therefore you are to do the following:

A Plan an intervention strategy based on operant principles that has as its goal an increase in the time children spend on a camp activity.

B Explain what behavioral records you will need to keep and how you will determine whether your intervention has produced a change in the children's behavior. You will need, for example, to specify exactly when and how you will measure behavior, as well as to justify your use of a particular design to carry out your "experiment."

C Describe the argument you will use to convince the director that your intervention strategy (assuming it works) will work with other, similar children.

4 A schoolteacher asks your help in planning a behavioral intervention that will help manage the behavior of a problem child in his classroom. The child does not stay at her desk when asked to do so, does not remain quiet during "quiet times," and exhibits other behaviors that disrupt the teaching environment. Explain specifically how a positive reinforcer, such as candy or small toys, might be used as part of a multiple-baseline across behaviors design to improve the child's behavior.

ANSWER TO CHALLENGE QUESTION 1

A One source of bias in this case study was that the same individual served as therapist and as researcher with the commensurate problems of observer bias. A second source of bias is that the therapist based his conclusion solely on the self-reports of the patient.

B The successful treatment may have resulted from the relaxation technique alone, the use of the "secret word" in the face of anxiety, attention the patient received from the therapist, or even the high cost of the treatment.

C The major problem that arises from studying one individual is a potential lack of external validity.

Chapter 10

Quasi-Experimental Designs and Program Evaluation

In the most general sense, an experiment is a test; it is a procedure used to find out something not presently known. In this sense we experiment when we add new ingredients to the chili in order to see whether they improve its taste. We experiment with new ways to catch fish by changing the lures we use. We experiment when we take a different route to our job in order to find a faster way to commute. As you have seen, however, in the conduct of psychological research, experiments are usually carried out in order to discover the causes of a phenomenon. Experimental methods, unlike other research techniques such as observation and surveys, are viewed as the most efficient way to determine causation. Indeed, in one way or another, discussions in Chapters 6 through 9 have emphasized experimental methods in psychological research.

By now you probably appreciate the complexity of the task facing the researcher who seeks to understand a phenomenon by discovering what caused it. In this chapter we continue our discussion of experimental methods, but we focus on experiments as they are often conducted in natural settings. You will see that the task of drawing cause-effect conclusions often becomes even more difficult, and new problems arise when an investigator leaves the confines of the laboratory to experiment in natural settings.

There are numerous reasons why experiments are carried out in natural settings. One important reason (mentioned in Chapter 6) is to test the external validity of a laboratory finding. Other reasons for doing field experiments are likely to be associated with attempts to improve conditions under which people live and work. The government may experiment with a new tax system or a new method of job training for the economically disadvantaged. Schools may experiment by changing lunch programs, after-school care, or curricula. A business may experiment with new product designs, methods of delivering employee benefits, or flexible work hours. In these cases, as is true in the laboratory, it is important to determine whether the "treatment" caused a change. Did a change in the way patients are admitted to a hospital emergency room cause patients to be treated more quickly and efficiently? Did a college energy conservation program cause a decrease in energy consumption? Knowing whether a treatment was effective permits us to make important decisions about continuing the treatment, about spending additional money, about investing more time and effort, or about changing the present situation on the basis of our knowledge of the results. Research that seeks to determine the effectiveness of changes made by institutions, government agencies, and other units of society is one goal of the discipline of *program evaluation*.

In this chapter we discuss the problems of conducting experiments in natural settings. We describe obstacles to doing true experiments in such settings, and we discuss ways of overcoming these obstacles so that true experiments are done whenever possible. Nevertheless, true experiments are sometimes not feasible outside the laboratory. In these cases, experimental procedures that only approximate the conditions of laboratory experiments must be considered. We discuss several of these quasi-experimental techniques. Problems with quasi-experimentation make us realize the value of true experiments, so we briefly consider alternatives to quasi-experiments in natural settings. One such alternative is the extension of single-case experimental designs (which we discussed in Chapter 9) to research in natural settings. We conclude the chapter by providing a brief introduction to the logic, procedures, and limitations of program evaluation.

DIFFERENCES BETWEEN LABORATORY EXPERIMENTS AND EXPERIMENTS IN NATURAL SETTINGS

There are some important considerations to keep in mind as we discuss experimentation in natural settings. Experimentation outside the confines of the psychology laboratory is likely to differ from laboratory research in a number of significant ways. Not every experiment in a natural setting differs from laboratory experiments in all of these ways, of course. But if you are thinking of doing research in a natural setting, we urge you to weigh the following points.

CONTROL

More than anything else, the scientist is concerned with control. Only by controlling those factors that are assumed to influence a phenomenon can one make a decision about causation. As you have seen in previous chapters, control takes several forms. The random assignment of participants to conditions of an experiment is a method of control used to balance participant characteristics in treatment and no-treatment conditions. Other factors likely to influence a phenomenon may be controlled by holding them constant. In a natural setting, a researcher may not always have the same degree of control over conditions of an experiment or over assignment of participants as in a laboratory. A field experiment may have to be conducted according to the availability of participants or at the discretion of an administrator or government official. Natural settings place various restrictions on an experiment that limit the researcher's control. It is even possible that an investigator may not directly participate in the planning and conduct of the "experiment" but may be asked afterward whether a treatment "worked." This kind of situation is clearly the most difficult because important factors may not have been considered in planning or executing the intervention.

As an illustration, consider the following situation. As you saw in Chapter 1, many people frequently are too willing to believe in paranormal phenomena, including ESP and the claims of so-called psychics. These beliefs may be due to deficiencies in human reasoning and in science education (Singer & Benassi, 1981). One response has been the creation of "critical thinking" and "science vs. pseudoscience" courses at the college level (Morier & Keeports, 1994). A reasonable question is, Do such courses work? That is, do students who take these courses acquire a more critical view of paranormal phenomena? The treatment in this case is exposure to the material and ideas presented in the course. The dependent variable might be responses to a questionnaire asking about belief in paranormal phenomena and the occult. We would like to know whether or not such courses "cause" a change in people's views of these ideas and events. However, you no doubt can see problems with this "experiment." Students are most likely not randomly assigned to take such a course. Are the students taking such a course already critical about paranormal claims, or did they take the course because of their interest and belief in paranormal phenomena? With whom do we compare the students in the course? Are there possible changes in students' views over time *that might occur independently of the course* and need to be taken into account? What other events are not controlled in such a situation that might influence people's attitudes toward paranormal phenomena? In order to find out whether the treatment worked, a researcher faces a host of problems that arise due to the lack of control over the situation. Later, we describe results of a published study that sought to answer this question: Can students be taught to be more critical of paranormal phenomena?

EXTERNAL VALIDITY

Field experiments are sometimes conducted with the goal of establishing the external validity of a laboratory finding. The artificial environment of the psychology laboratory, which increases the internal validity of research because of the high degree of control, often decreases the external validity of the findings. Experiments in natural settings may therefore need to be conducted in order to generalize results beyond the laboratory situation.

On the other hand, as you saw in Chapter 6, the external validity of a laboratory experiment may not be all that important (Mook, 1983). This may be particularly true when an experiment is done simply to test a specific psychological theory. In contrast, the external validity of research done in natural settings is often very important because the focus of such research is frequently on a treatment's general effectiveness. This is especially true when social experimentation serves as the basis for large-scale social changes, such as trying out new ways to curb drunk driving or new procedures for registering voters.

If the results of a field experiment are to be used to plan further interventions or to implement similar programs in other locations or different regions of the country, then it is vital to know to what extent the treatment and results can be generalized. For example, legislators may wish to generalize to a different state certain procedures that have been shown to produce an increase in voter registration in one state. A method to increase employee morale that succeeded in one branch of a company may be considered by company officials for all branches of the company. Will the results of a reading program that is judged to be beneficial at one grade level in one school generalize to other grade levels, other schools, or situations where it is implemented by different personnel? Does a course found to improve students' critical thinking skills at one college also "work" at other colleges? These are, of course, all questions of external validity.

GOALS

Experimentation in natural settings often has different goals from laboratory research. One major difference are the goals associated with basic and applied research. **Basic research** is often carried out with the single goal of understanding a phenomenon, of determining how "nature" works. It may be done to gain knowledge merely for knowledge's sake. **Applied research** is also directed toward discovering the reasons for a phenomenon, but it is likely to be done only when knowing the reasons for an event will lead to changes that will modify or improve the present situation. Experimentation in natural settings, therefore, is more likely to have practical goals. As you saw earlier, this is one reason why questions of external validity are more important for field experiments than they are for laboratory experiments.

CONSEQUENCES

Sometimes experiments are conducted that have a far-reaching impact on communities and society, affecting large numbers of people. For example, during the 1970s the U.S. government experimented with the "new town" concept. Thirteen new towns were created under government sponsorship. Beginning from scratch, designers tried to avoid all the problems of older unplanned urban communities. Towns such as Columbia, Maryland, and Reston, Virginia, are examples. Another example of an experiment by the U.S. government was a program designed to aid prisoners following release from incarceration

(Berk, Boruch, Chambers, Rossi, & Witte, 1987). Individuals released from prison often have little in the way of resources to help them begin a new life, and they frequently have difficulty finding jobs. This economic hardship can contribute to new crime. The program involved random assignment of ex-prisoners to groups that either received financial assistance on leaving prison or did not receive financial assistance. The program targeted as participants about 2,000 ex-prisoners in Texas and Georgia.

Clearly, these examples of society's "experiments," as well as those we might imagine being carried out on a smaller scale in natural settings (such as those conducted in schools or businesses), are likely to have consequences of greater immediate impact than those of laboratory research. Consider that the Head Start program for disadvantaged children and the *Sesame Street* television show were social experiments designed to improve the education of literally hundreds of thousands of children across the nation. Experiments in businesses may be carried out with the eventual goal of reducing the number of employees or in other ways affecting the quality of employees' lives. Moreover, as is true of all experiments, the consequences are not always those that were anticipated. Although a few planned communities worked, others did not, and planners and builders went bankrupt ("New Town Blues," 1978, p. 84). While the prison release program produced some identifiable positive results, it was also found to be responsible for an *increase* in crime, apparently due to the ex-prisoners' freedom from having to work (Berk et al., 1987).

In order to draw meaningful conclusions about the effects of these experiments, we must consider the design and implementation of these "treatments" and do the best we can to assess as clearly as possible whether the treatments worked. This is especially important because, as we have seen, the consequences of such experiments frequently are great in terms of money spent and the number of people whose lives are affected. By contrast, the consequences of a laboratory experiment are likely to be minimal. They may directly affect only the lives of a few researchers and of those relatively few participants recruited to participate.

TRUE EXPERIMENTS AND QUASI-EXPERIMENTS

CHARACTERISTICS OF TRUE EXPERIMENTS

Although many everyday activities (such as altering the ingredients of a recipe) might be called experiments, we would not consider them true experiments in the sense in which we have discussed experimentation in this textbook. Analogously, many so-called social experiments carried out by the government (such as the new town concept) and those conducted by company officials or educational administrators are also not true experiments. *A true experiment is one that leads to an unambiguous outcome regarding what caused an event.*

True experiments exhibit three important characteristics. First, in a true experiment some type of intervention or treatment is implemented. Second, true experiments are marked by the high degree of control an experimenter has over the arrangement of experimental conditions, assignment of participants, systematic manipulation of independent variables, and choice of dependent variables. The ability to assign participants randomly to experimental conditions is often seen as the most critical defining characteristic of the true experiment (Judd et al., 1991). Finally, true experiments are characterized by an appropriate comparison. Indeed, the experimenter exerts control over a situation principally in order to establish a proper comparison to evaluate the effectiveness of a treatment. In the simplest of experimental situations, this comparison is one between two groups that are treated exactly alike except for the variable of interest. Any differences in a dependent variable that arise can then logically be assigned to the differences between levels of the independent variable.

OBSTACLES TO CONDUCTING TRUE EXPERIMENTS IN NATURAL SETTINGS

Experimental research is an effective tool for solving problems and answering questions. Nevertheless, two major obstacles often arise when we try to carry out experiments in natural settings. The first problem is obtaining permission to do the research from individuals in positions of authority. Unless they believe the research will be useful, school board presidents and government and business leaders are unlikely to support research financially or otherwise.

The second, and often more pressing, obstacle to doing experiments in natural settings is the problem of access to participants. This problem can prove especially troublesome if participants are to be randomly assigned to either a treatment group or a control group.

Random assignment to conditions appears unfair at first—after all, random assignment requires that a potentially beneficial treatment be withheld from at least some participants. Suppose that a new approach to the teaching of foreign languages was to be tested at your college or university. Suppose further that, when you went to register for your next semester's classes, you were told you would be randomly assigned to one of two sections taught at the time you selected—one section involving the old method and one involving the new method. How would you react? Your knowledge of research methods tells you that the two methods must be administered to comparable groups of students and random assignment is the best way to ensure such comparability. Nonetheless, you might be tempted to feel that random assignment is not fair, especially if you are assigned to the section using the old (old-fashioned?) method. Let's take a closer look at the fairness of random assignment.

If those responsible for selecting the method of foreign language instruction already knew the new method was more effective than the old method, there would be little justification for testing the method again (unless, of course, the effectiveness of the new method had been demonstrated at schools very different from yours). Under such circumstances we would agree that withholding the new method from students in the control group would be unjust. If we do not know whether the new method is better, however, any approach other than conducting a true experiment will leave us in doubt about the new method's effectiveness. Random assignment to treatments—call it a "lottery" if you prefer—may be the fairest procedure for assigning students to sections. The old method of instruction, after all, was considered effective before the development of the new method. If the new method proves less effective, random assignment will have actually "protected" the control participants from receiving an ineffective treatment.

There are ways to offer a potentially effective treatment to all participants while still maintaining comparable groups. One way is to alternate treatments. For example, Atkinson (1968) randomly assigned students to receive computer-assisted instruction in either English or math (the "treatment") and then tested both groups in English and math. Each group served as a control for the other on the test for which its members had not received computer-assisted instruction. After completing the experiment, both groups could then be given computer-assisted instruction in the subject matter to which they had not been previously exposed. Thus, all participants received all potentially beneficial treatments.

Establishing a proper control group is also possible if there is more demand for a service than an agency can meet. People who are waiting to receive the service can become a "waiting list" control group. It is essential, however, that people be assigned to the waiting list randomly. People who are "first in line" are no doubt different on important dimensions from those who arrive last (e.g., more eager for treatment). Random assignment is necessary to distribute these characteristics in an unbiased way between treatment and comparison groups.

There will always be circumstances in which random assignment simply cannot be used. For example, in clinical trials involving tests of new medical treatments, it may be extremely difficult to get patients to agree to be randomly assigned to either the treatment group or the control group. As you will see, quasi-experimental designs can be used in these situations. We describe the logic and procedures for these quasi-experimental designs later in this chapter.

THREATS TO INTERNAL VALIDITY CONTROLLED BY TRUE EXPERIMENTS

One way to evaluate an experiment is to determine what kinds of alternative explanations for a phenomenon have been controlled. Prior to doing an experiment, we might look to see what major classes of possible explanations are ruled out by our experimental procedure. Only by eliminating all possible alternative explanations can we arrive at a definite conclusion about cause and effect. In previous chapters, we referred to various uncontrolled factors that threaten the internal validity of an experiment as confounding factors (they are also called confounds). Several types of confounds were identified in earlier chapters (see especially Chapter 6). We now list eight classes of confounds, using the terminology of Campbell and Stanley (1966; see also Cook & Campbell, 1979). You have already been introduced to some of these **threats to internal validity;** others will be new. After reviewing the major classes of confounds, we will be able to judge the extent to which various experimental procedures control for these kinds of alternative explanations of a treatment effect.

History   The occurrence of an event other than the treatment can threaten internal validity if it produces changes in the research participants' behavior. A true experiment requires that participants in the experimental group and in the control group be treated the same (have the same history of experiences) except for the treatment. In the laboratory, this is usually accomplished by balancing or holding conditions constant. For example, the same experimenter might be asked to test people in all conditions of an experiment. If different experimenters were to test experimental and control participants, we would confound the possible effect due to the experimenter and that of the treatment. When doing experiments in natural settings, the researcher may not always be able to exercise the degree of control associated with laboratory settings, so confounding due to history can be a threat to internal validity. For example, suppose you set out to test whether a college-level critical thinking course did, in fact, change students' thinking. And suppose further that your test was simply to examine students' performance on a critical thinking test at the beginning of the critical thinking course and then again at the end of the course. History would be a threat to internal validity if events other than the treatment (i.e., the critical thinking course) occurred that might improve the critical thinking abilities of the students. For example, suppose many students taking this course also took it upon themselves to view a video designed to teach critical thinking that wasn't required for the course, and also purchased extra books and pamphlets to help them think more critically. This particular history of experiences would confound the treatment.

Maturation   Participants in an experiment necessarily change as a function of time. They grow older, become more experienced, and so forth. Change associated with the passage of time per se is called maturation. For example, suppose a researcher is interested in assessing children's learning over a school year using a new teaching technique. Without a proper comparison a researcher might attribute the changes in performance between a pretest and a posttest of a group of schoolchildren to the effect of the teaching intervention when, in reality, the changes were simply due to the normal processes of maturation.

Testing   Taking a test generally has an effect on subsequent testing. Consider, for example, the fact that many students often improve from the initial test in a course to the second test. The familiarity with the testing procedure and with the instructor's expectations that they gain during the first test affects their performance on the second test. Likewise, in the context of a psychology experiment in which more than one test is given (e.g., in a pretest-posttest design), testing is a threat to internal validity if the effect of a treatment cannot be separated from the effect of testing. Can you see how an attempt to assess the effect of a critical thinking course would be problematic if the assessment is simply the same students' scores on a pretest and a posttest?

Instrumentation   It is possible that changes over time take place not only in the participants of an experiment (e.g., maturation or increased familiarity with testing), but also in the instruments used to measure the participants' performance. This is most clearly a possibility when human observers are used to assess behavior. As you learned in previous chapters (see especially Chapter 3), observer bias can result from fatigue, expectations, and other characteristics of observers. For example, as a researcher becomes more experienced in making observations, there is likely to be a change in the quality of the observations that she or he makes. Unless controlled for, these changes in instrumentation can threaten internal validity by providing alternative explanations for differences in behavior between one observation period and another. Mechanical instruments also may change with repeated use. A researcher known to the authors once found that a machine used to present material in a learning experiment was not working the same at the end of the experiment as it was at the beginning. Measures made near the end of the experiment differed from those made at the beginning of the experiment. Thus, what looked like a learning effect was really just a change in the instruments used to measure learning.

Regression   **Regression to the mean** (statistical regression) is always a problem when individuals have been selected to participate in an experiment because of their "extreme" scores. As summarized by Cook and Campbell (1979, pp. 52–53), regression to the mean

> (1) operates to increase obtained pretest-posttest gain scores among low pretest scores, since this group's pretest scores are more likely to have been depressed by error; (2) operates to decrease obtained change scores among persons with high pretest scores since their pretest scores are likely to have been inflated by error; and (3) does not affect obtained change scores among scorers at the center of the pretest distribution since the group is likely to contain as many units whose pretest scores are inflated by error as units whose pretest scores are deflated by it. Regression is always to the population mean of a group.

In other words, a very, very bad performance or a very, very good performance (both of which we have all experienced) is likely to be followed by a performance that is not quite so bad or not quite so good, respectively. Consider, for instance, your best ever performance on a classroom examination. What did it take to nail this test? It took no doubt a lot of hard work. But it is also likely that luck was involved. Everything has to work just right to produce an extremely good performance. If we are talking about an exam, then it is likely the material tested was what you just happened to study the hardest, or the test format was one you particularly like, or it came at a time when you were feeling particularly confident, and so forth (or all of these and more). Particularly good performances are, as Cook and Campbell (1979) stated, "extreme" because they are inflated (over our usual or typical performance) by chance (error). Similarly, an especially bad test performance is likely to have occurred because of some bad luck. When tested again (following either a very good or a very bad performance), it is just not likely that chance factors will gang up the same way to give us that super (inflated) score or that very poor (depressed) score. We will, as Cook and Campbell suggest, likely see a performance closer to the average of our overall scores.

Consider an attempt to raise the academic performance of a group of college students who have performed very poorly during their first semester of college (the "pretest"). Of course, participants are selected *because of their extreme performance* (in this case, extremely poor performance). Let us assume that a treatment (e.g., a 10-hour study skills workshop) is then applied. Statistical regression is a threat to internal validity, since we would expect these students to perform slightly better after the second semester (the "posttest") *without any treatment* simply due to statistical regression. An unknowing researcher may mistakenly confuse this "regression effect" with a "treatment effect."

Selection When, from the outset of a study, differences exist between the kinds of individuals in one group of an experiment and those in another, there is a confounding due to selection. That is, the people who are in the treatment group may differ from people in the comparison group in many ways *other* than their group assignment. In the laboratory, this threat to internal validity is generally handled by balancing participant characteristics through random assignment. When one is doing experiments in natural settings, there are often many obstacles to randomization of participants to treatment and comparison conditions. These obstacles prevent doing a true experiment and hence present a possible confound due to selection.

Subject Mortality When participants are lost from an experiment, there is a threat to internal validity. We discussed possible reasons for subject loss in Chapter 6. The threat to internal validity rests on the assumption that subject loss (attrition) changes the nature of a group from that established prior to the introduction of the treatment—for example by destroying the equivalence of groups that had been established through randomization. This might occur, for instance, if an experimental task is very difficult and causes some experimental participants to become frustrated and to drop out of the experiment. Participants who are left in the experimental group will differ from those who dropped out (and possibly from those in a control group) if for no other reason than that they were able to do the task (or at least stuck it out).

Interactions with Selection Several of the foregoing threats to internal validity can be a source of additional concern because they can interact with characteristics of groups of individuals selected for an experiment. Specifically, there are possible problems due to interactions between (1) selection and history, (2) selection and maturation, and (3) selection and instrumentation. Basically, this means that one or more groups of participants respond differently to effects associated with history, maturation, or instrumentation. For example, if groups of participants in an experiment mature at different rates, then differences between groups in the form of changes from pretest to posttest may be due to an interaction of selection and maturation rather than to any treatment. Such might be the case if first-year students in college who served as an experimental group were compared with sophomores who served as a control group. Changes in students that occur during their first year (as students gain familiarity with the college environment) might be presumed to be greater than such changes that occur during the second or sophomore year. These differences in maturation rates might explain any observed differences between the experimental and control groups, rather than any experimental intervention.

An interaction of selection and history results when events occurring in time have a different effect on one group of participants than on another. This is particularly a problem when intact groups are compared. Perhaps due to events that are peculiar to one group's situation, an event may have more of an impact on that group than on another. Consider, for example, research involving an investigation of the effectiveness of an AIDS awareness campaign involving two college campuses (one treatment and one control). Nationwide media attention to this problem might reasonably be assumed to affect students on both campuses equally. However, if a prominent student with AIDS died at one college during this period and the story was featured in the college newspaper, we would assume that students at this student's college would be affected differently than those at the other. In terms of assessing the effect of an AIDS awareness campaign, this situation would represent an interaction of selection and history.

Finally, an interaction of selection and instrumentation might occur if a test instrument is relatively more sensitive to changes in one group's performance than to changes in another's. This occurs, for instance, when ceiling or floor effects are present. Such is the case when a group scores initially so low on an instrument (*floor effect*) that any further drop in scores cannot be reliably measured, or so high (*ceiling effect*) that any more gain cannot be assessed. As you can imagine, a confound would be present if an experimental group showed relatively no change (due to floor or ceiling effects) while a control group changed reliably because its mean performance was initially near the middle of the measurement scale.

A true experiment controls all these threats to internal validity. Quasi-experiments can be viewed as compromises between the general aim of gaining valid knowledge regarding the effectiveness of a treatment and the realization that true experiments (and hence control of the major factors threatening internal validity) are not always possible. As Campbell (1969) emphasizes, so-called true experiments should be conducted when possible, but if they are not feasible, quasi-experiments should be conducted. "We must do the best we can with what is available to us" (p. 411).

PROBLEMS THAT EVEN TRUE EXPERIMENTS MAY NOT ELIMINATE

Before considering specific quasi-experimental procedures, we should point out that even true experiments may not control for all possible factors that might cloud the interpretation of an experimental result. Although major threats to internal validity are typically eliminated by the true experiment, there are some additional threats the investigator must guard against, particularly when working in natural settings. We use the term *contamination* to describe one general class of threats to internal validity. **Contamination** occurs when there is communication of information about the experiment between groups of participants. The result of this communication can be resentment on the part of individuals receiving less desirable treatments, rivalry among groups receiving different treatments, or a general diffusion of treatments across the groups (Cook & Campbell, 1979).

Consider a situation in which individuals have been randomly assigned to a control group. Further, assume that information is obtained by participants in this group indicating that "other" participants are receiving a treatment which appears to be beneficial. What do you think might be the reaction of the control participants? One possibility is resentment and demoralization. As Cook and Campbell explain, in an industrial setting the person receiving the less desirable treatment may retaliate by lowering productivity. In an educational setting teachers or students might lose heart or become angry. This effect of leaked information about a treatment may make a treatment look better than it ordinarily would because of the lowered performance of the control group that is demoralized.

Another possible effect that may occur when a control group learns about another group's good fortune is to generate a spirit of competition. That is, a control group might become motivated to reduce the expected difference between itself and the treatment group. As Cook and Campbell point out, this may be likely when intact groups (such as departments, work crews, branch offices, and the like) are assigned to various conditions. Realizing that another group will look better depending on how much it distinguishes itself from the control group, participants comprising the control group may be motivated to "try harder" so as not to look bad by comparison. Cook and Campbell call this problem compensatory rivalry. Like other contamination effects, it can potentially affect any experiment, but it can be of particular concern when experiments are done in natural settings.

Yet another possible effect of contamination is diffusion of treatments. According to Cook and Campbell, this occurs when participants in a control group use information given to others to help them change their own behavior. For example, control participants may use the information given to participants in the treatment group to imitate the behavior of individuals who were given the treatment. Of course, this reduces the differences between the treated and untreated groups and affects the internal validity of the experiment.

In addition to problems resulting from contamination, true experiments can be weakened by threats to external validity. As you have learned in previous chapters, the extent to which we can generalize across persons, settings, and times depends mainly on how representative our sample is of the persons, settings, and times to which we want to generalize. Representativeness is normally achieved through random sampling. However, because random sampling is used so infrequently, we can rarely say that our sample of participants, or the situation in which we are making observations, or the times during which we test individuals, are representative samples of all persons, settings, or times. Therefore, the investigator must be aware of possible interactions between the independent variable of an experiment and the type of individual, setting, or time of the experiment. Is a difference between an experimental group and a control group that is found when only volunteers are used, when the setting is an inner-city school, or when the experiment is conducted in the winter, also likely to be found when nonvolunteers are tested, when a suburban school is the setting, or when the experiment is performed in the spring of the year?

Cook and Campbell describe several approaches to evaluating threats to external validity, the foremost being determination of the representativeness of the sample. However, they point out that in the last analysis the best test of external validity is replication (see Chapter 6). External validity is an empirical question best answered through repetition of the experiment with different types of participants, in different settings, and at different times. Occasionally these replications can be built into an experiment—for example, by selecting more than one group to participate. Testing both schoolchildren from a lower socioeconomic group and a higher socioeconomic group in an experiment designed to determine the effectiveness of a new educational program would provide evidence of the generality of the treatment's effectiveness across these two socioeconomic groups.

Finally, true experiments do not always protect the experimenter from threats due to experimenter expectancy effects or to a Hawthorne effect. Effects due to experimenter expectancies were discussed in earlier chapters. They occur when the experimenter unintentionally influences the results. Systematic errors in interpretation or mistakes in recording data can be the result of experimenter expectancy effects. We outlined various ways to control experimenter or observer effects in Chapters 3 and 6 (e.g., using a double-blind procedure). The **Hawthorne effect** refers to changes in persons' behavior brought about by the interest that "significant others" show in them. The effect was named after events occurring at the Hawthorne plant of the Western Electric Company in Cicero, Illinois, near Chicago.

Between 1924 and 1932, officials at this plant conducted a series of studies aimed at examining the relationships among productivity, worker satisfaction, and worker motivation (Roethlisberger, 1977). One specific relationship of interest to the researchers was that between amount of lighting (illumination level) in the plant and productivity in simple, repetitive tasks, such as inspecting small parts and assembling relays and winding coils (Huse & Bowditch, 1977). Results of these early studies were difficult to interpret. According to a researcher involved with the project, the results were "not only inconclusive but also rather curious" (Roethlisberger, 1977, p. 46). Specifically, in one experiment workers were divided into two groups, one working under increasing levels of illumination and the other working under constant illumination. The result was increased productivity in *both* groups, with the rise in output being approximately the same magnitude. "Several further experiments of this character exhibited similar curious outcomes. It looked as if the workers were reacting more to the positive concern of the experimenters about their working conditions than to the actual physical changes in illumination. This response later came to be called the 'Hawthorne effect'" (Roethlisberger, 1977, p. 46). Although some controversy surrounds the exact factors responsible for this effect (Parsons, 1974), a Hawthorne effect generally refers to behavior change resulting from participants' awareness that someone is interested in them.

As one example of the Hawthorne effect, consider a study in which prisoners are chosen to participate in research examining the relationship between changes in prison cell conditions and attitudes toward prison life. If positive changes in prisoners' attitudes are obtained, the results could be due to the actual changes in cell conditions that were made, or they could be due to an increase in morale because prisoners saw the prison administration as expressing concern for them.

Hawthorne effects may be inextricably linked to the action of an independent variable intended to alter the participants' environment (Sommer, 1968). As Sommer points out, people naturally interpret changes in their environment according to various expectations that they have, according to their needs, and so forth. Just as prisoners may view changes in prison conditions as reflecting concern on the part of the prison staff, so factory workers, schoolchildren, college faculty members, and other groups may interpret changes made in their environment as reflecting interest in them by persons in authority. The psychology investigator must be conscious of the fact that changes in participants' behavior may be at least partially due to their awareness that others are interested in them. Thus, you can see that a Hawthorne effect represents a specific kind of reactivity (i.e., an awareness that one is being observed), which we discussed in previous chapters (especially Chapter 3).

QUASI-EXPERIMENTS

A dictionary will tell you that one definition of the prefix *quasi-* is "resembling." A quasi government, for example, is one resembling, but not actually the same as, a true government. Similarly, **quasi experiments** involve procedures that resemble those which are characteristic of true experiments. Generally speaking, quasi experiments include some type of intervention or treatment and they provide a comparison, but they lack the degree of control found in true experiments. Just as randomization is the hallmark of true experiments, so *lack of randomization* is the hallmark of quasi-experiments. As Campbell and Stanley (1966, p. 34) explain,

> there are many natural social settings in which the research person can introduce something like experimental design into [the] scheduling of data collection procedures (e.g., the when and to whom of measurement), even though [the researcher]

lacks the full control over the scheduling of experimental stimuli (the when and to whom of exposure and the ability to randomize exposures) which makes a true experiment possible. Collectively, such situations can be regarded as quasi-experimental designs.

Quasi-experiments are recommended when true experiments are not feasible. Some knowledge about the effectiveness of a treatment is more desirable than none. The list of possible confounds provided by Campbell and Stanley (1966; Cook & Campbell, 1979), which we reviewed earlier, can be used as a checklist in deciding just how good that knowledge is. Moreover, although a particular experimental procedure may not control for one or more possible types of confounds, the investigator must be prepared to look for additional kinds of evidence that might rule out a confound not specifically controlled by an experimental procedure. For example, suppose a quasi experiment explicitly controls for only six of the eight major classes of confounds that are eliminated by a true experiment. It may be possible, on the basis of supplementary data or through evidence offered by a logical analysis of the situation, to rule out the remaining two classes of explanations as plausible. In this case a strong argument can be made for the internal validity of the research design, even though a true experiment was not performed. The researcher must recognize the specific shortcomings of quasi-experimental procedures and be prepared to address these shortcomings through whatever evidence or logic is available.

With full knowledge of their limitations, then, we present the following information about specific quasi-experimental designs so you will understand the routes remaining open to an investigator when the path to a true experiment is hopelessly blocked. At the same time, this presentation should help you appreciate the clarity of inference provided by the true experiment. Following a discussion of specific quasi-experimental designs, we look at an alternative to quasi-experimentation—the extension of single-case experimentation to research in natural settings. You may also want to refer to the previous discussion of obstacles to true experiments in natural settings. *The difference between the power of the true experiment and that of the quasi-experiment is such that, before facing the problems of interpretation that result from quasi-experimental procedures, the researcher should make every effort possible to approximate the conditions of a true experiment.*

SPECIFIC QUASI-EXPERIMENTAL DESIGNS

THE NONEQUIVALENT CONTROL GROUP DESIGN

Perhaps the most serious limitation on experimentation in natural settings is that the experimenter is frequently unable to assign participants randomly to conditions. This occurs, for instance, when an intact group is singled out for treatment and when administrative decisions or practical considerations prevent random assignment of participants. Children in one classroom or school and workers at a particular plant are examples of groups that might be treated in the absence of any random assignment of individuals to conditions. If we assume that behavior of a group is measured both before and after treatment, such an "experiment" can be described as follows:

$$O_1 \times O_2$$

where O_1 refers to the first observation of a group, or pretest, $\times$ indicates a treatment, and O_2 refers to the second observation, or posttest.

Campbell and Stanley (1966) call this particular design the "one-group pretest-posttest design." Although it is sometimes used in psychological research, the design has very little internal validity. You should be able to see, for instance, that this design does not control for many factors that can threaten the internal validity of a study. For example, should a difference between pretest and posttest measures be found, how do we know this difference was not due to some event other than the treatment (*history threat*), that it was not due to the fact that participants benefited from initial testing (*testing threat*), or that it didn't occur simply because the group of participants changed over time (*maturation threat*)? This particular design has so little going for it in terms of allowing cause-and-effect inferences that it is sometimes referred to as a "preexperimental design," or one that serves as a "bad experiment" to illustrate possible confounds (Campbell & Stanley, 1966).

The one-group pretest-posttest design can be modified to create a quasi-experimental design with greatly superior internal validity if two conditions are met: (1) there exists a group "like" the treatment group that can serve as a comparison group, and (2) there is an opportunity to obtain pretest and posttest measures from individuals in *both* the treatment and the comparison groups. Because a comparison group is selected on bases other than random assignment, it cannot be assumed that individuals in the treatment and control groups are equivalent on all important characteristics (a selection threat arises). Therefore it is essential that a pretest be given to both groups to assess their similarity on the dependent measure. Campbell and Stanley (1966) call this quasi-experimental procedure a **nonequivalent control group design.** It can be outlined as follows:

$$\frac{O_1 \times O_2}{O_1 \quad O_2}$$

The dashed line indicates that the treatment and comparison groups were not formed by assigning participants randomly to conditions.

A nonequivalent control group design was used by Morier and Keeports (1994) to assess the effectiveness of a college course designed to introduce students to the scientific method and to the "faulty, and often fraudulent, methods of pseudosciences" (p. 443). We referred to this situation and experiment earlier when we discussed the problems of control often found in natural settings. The situation met the requirements for a nonequivalent control group design just outlined. There existed a group "like" the treatment group and it was possible to obtain both pretest and posttest measures from both groups. The investigators chose students enrolled in a course entitled "Psychology and Law" at the same college to serve as a comparison group. Both courses were seminars and enrolled primarily nonscience majors. Students completed a questionnaire designed to measure belief in paranormal phenomena at the beginning of their respective courses and at the end. Although the two groups of students did not differ in their beliefs at the beginning of the courses, at the end of the semester the students in the "Science and Pseudoscience" course (the treatment group) scored significantly lower in their beliefs about paranormal phenomena than did the students in the "Psychology and Law" course (the comparison group). The researchers suggested that the course worked to reduce belief in paranormal phenomena because it explicitly confronted claims of the pseudosciences in the classroom.

Let us examine in detail another study using a nonequivalent control group design. This will give us the opportunity to review both the specific strengths and weaknesses of this quasi-experimental procedure.

THE NONEQUIVALENT CONTROL GROUP DESIGN: THE LANGER AND RODIN STUDY

Langer and Rodin (1976) hypothesized that environmental changes associated with old age contribute, in part, to feelings of loss, inadequacy, and low self-esteem among the elderly. Of particular importance is the change that occurs when elderly persons move into a nursing home. Although they usually care for the elderly quite adequately in physical terms, nursing homes often provide what Langer and Rodin call a "virtually decision-free" environment. The elderly are no longer called on to make even the simplest decisions, such as what time to get up, whom to visit, what movie to watch, and the like. In a nursing home, many or most of these everyday decisions are made for the elderly, leaving them with little personal responsibility and choice.

To test the hypothesis that the lack of opportunity to make personal decisions contributes to the psychological and even the physical debilitation sometimes seen in the elderly, Langer and Rodin carried out a quasi experiment in a Connecticut nursing home. The independent variable was the type of communication given to two groups of nursing home residents. One group was given a communication stressing the many decisions that the patients needed to make regarding how their rooms were arranged, visiting, care of plants, movie selection, and so forth. These residents were also given a small plant as a gift (if they decided to accept it) and told to take care of it as they wished. This was the *responsibility-induced condition*. The second group of residents, the comparison group, was also called together for a meeting, but the communication given to

FIGURE 10.1   Langer and Rodin (1976) used a nonequivalent control group design to study the effect of two different types of communication on the behavior of nursing-home residents. A major difference in the two types of communication involved the offer, and subsequent care, of a small plant (see text).

this group stressed the staff's responsibility for them. These residents also received a plant as a gift (whether they chose to have one or not) and were told that the nurses would water and care for the plants for them.

Residents of the nursing home had been assigned to a particular floor and room on the basis of availability, and some residents had been there for a long time. As a consequence, randomly assigning residents to the two communications groups was impractical—and probably undesirable from the administration's point of view. Therefore the two communications were given to residents on two different floors of the nursing home. These floors were chosen, in the words of the authors, "because of similarity in the residents' physical and psychological health and prior socioeconomic status, as determined from evaluations made by the home's director, head nurses, and social worker" (Langer & Rodin, 1976, p. 193). The floors were randomly assigned to one of the two treatments. In addition, questionnaires were given to residents 1 week before and 3 weeks after the communications. The questionnaires contained items that related to "how much control they felt over general events in their lives and how happy and active they felt" (p. 194). Furthermore, staff members on each floor were asked to rate the residents, before and after the experimental communications, on such traits as alertness, sociability, and activity. The investigators also included a clever posttest measure of social interest by holding a competition that asked participants to guess the number of jelly beans in a large jar. Residents entered the contest if they wished by simply filling out a piece of paper giving their estimate and name. Thus, a number of dependent variables assessed the residents' perceptions of control, happiness, activity, interest level, and so forth.

The Langer and Rodin study nicely illustrates a nonequivalent control group procedure. Moreover, differences between pretest and posttest measures showed that the residents in the responsibility-induced group were generally happier, more active, and more alert following the treatment than were residents in the comparison group. Behavioral measures such as frequency of movie attendance also favored the responsibility-induced group, and, although 10 residents from this group entered the jelly bean contest, only 1 resident from the comparison group participated! The investigators point to possible practical implications of these findings. Specifically, they suggest that some of the negative consequences of aging can be reduced or reversed by giving the aged the opportunity to make personal decisions and to feel competent.

Before turning to the specific weaknesses associated with this design, let us call your attention to another feature of the Langer and Rodin study, one which characterizes many experiments in natural settings. The treatment in the Langer and Rodin study actually had several components. For example, residents were encouraged by the staff to make decisions about a number of different things (e.g., movies, rooms, etc.), and they were offered a plant to take care of. The experiment evaluated, however, the treatment "package." That is, the effectiveness of the overall treatment was assessed and not individual components of the treatment. We only know (or at least we assume based on the evidence) that the treatment with all its components worked; we don't necessarily know whether the treatment would work with fewer components or whether one component is more critical than another. In the same vein, consider the results of the course confronting the claims of pseudosciences we mentioned earlier (Morier & Keeports, 1994). There, too, investigators obtained evidence for the effectiveness of the treatment (the college course). Again, however, there were many components to the treatment: examples of legitimate scientific methods, introduction to logical fallacies and aspects of critical thinking, exposure to instructors skeptical of these claims, guest lecturers (including a magician posing as a psychic who then revealed himself as a fake). Again, the results of the experiment do not tell us about the effectiveness of these individual components.

Research in natural settings is often characterized by treatments with many components. Moreover, the initial goal of such research is often to assess the overall effect of the treatment "package." Finding evidence for an overall treatment effect, therefore, may be only the first stage in a research program if we want to identify the critical elements of a treatment. There may be practical as well as theoretical benefits to such identification. On practical grounds, should research reveal that only some of the treatment's features are critical to the effect, then perhaps the less critical features could be dropped. This may make the treatment more cost effective and more likely to be adopted and carried out. From a theoretical standpoint, it is important to determine whether components of the treatment specified by the theory as being critical are, indeed, the critical components. When you hear about research showing an overall treatment effect, you might think about how additional research could reveal what specific components are critical to the treatment's effect.

SOURCES OF INVALIDITY IN THE NONEQUIVALENT CONTROL GROUP DESIGN

According to Cook and Campbell (1979), the nonequivalent control group design generally controls for all major classes of potential threats to internal validity except those due to interactions of (1) selection and maturation, (2) selection and history, (3) selection and instrumentation, and (4) those due to differential statistical regression. We explore how each of these potential sources of invalidity might pose problems in an effort to interpret the results of the Langer and Rodin study. Then we explain what evidence or argument the authors offered in defense of their interpretation, which was that the differential responsibility-induced communication *caused* the differences in posttest behavior between the two groups of residents. We also examine how experimenter bias and problems of contamination were controlled, and we comment briefly on problems of external validity inherent in the nonequivalent control group design.

First, it should be mentioned that Langer and Rodin found that the residents in the two experimental groups did not differ significantly on the pretest measures. Because the residents were not randomly assigned to conditions, it might not have been surprising to find a difference between the two groups before the treatment was introduced. Moreover, it is important to recognize that, even when pretest scores show no difference between groups, as Langer and Rodin reported, one cannot assume the groups are "equivalent" (Campbell & Stanley, 1966). Why this is so will become apparent in the discussion that follows.

Interaction Between Selection and Maturation An interaction between selection and maturation occurs when individuals in one group grow more experienced, more tired, or more bored at a faster rate than individuals in another group (Cook & Campbell, 1979). Campbell and Stanley (1966) illustrate this problem by describing a nonequivalent control group design using psychotherapy patients as a treatment group and individuals not in therapy as a comparison group. The psychotherapy patients would normally be expected to show some improvement without the treatment (called spontaneous remission), a change that could be falsely interpreted (given no change in the comparison group) as a treatment effect. Whenever the treatment group consists of individuals who are brighter or more competent than those in the comparison group, differences in rate of maturation may be a confounding factor.

An interaction of selection and maturation is more likely to be an actual source of invalidity (as are other sources) when the treatment group is self-selected (the members deliberately sought out exposure to the treatment) and when the comparison group is from a different population from the treatment group (Campbell & Stanley, 1966). This occurs when a particular group is sin-

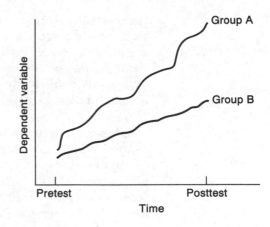

FIGURE 10.2   Possible differential growth rates for two groups (A and B) in the absence of a treatment.

gled out for treatment in order to determine whether behavior will improve as a function of the treatment. Psychotherapy patients who are compared with individuals not in therapy, which was mentioned earlier, is an example.

Before examining whether a selection and maturation interaction poses a problem for the Langer and Rodin study, we need to call your attention to another aspect of this issue: Even when *pretest* scores are the same on the average for the treatment and control groups, we cannot conclude the groups are equivalent (comparable). This is true for two reasons. First, the pretest is likely to measure respondents on only one measure, or at best on a few measures. The mere fact that individuals do not differ on one measure does not mean they don't differ on other measures relevant to their behavior in this situation. Second, the natural growth rate of two groups from different populations might be different, but the pretest may have been taken at a time when both groups happened to be about the same. This problem is illustrated in Figure 10.2. The normal rate of change is greater in Group A than in Group B, but the pretest is likely to show the groups do not differ. On the other hand, and again because of the differential growth rate, the groups would probably show a difference at the posttest that could be mistaken for a treatment effect. Langer and Rodin selected their groups (but not individuals) randomly from the same population of individuals. Consequently, their design more closely approaches a true experiment than it would if individuals in the two groups came from different populations (Campbell & Stanley, 1966), as would be the case if residents in a nursing home were compared with those attending a sheltered workshop program for the elderly.

Is there any reason to suspect an interaction of selection and maturation in the Langer and Rodin study? For instance, would residents on the treatment floor be expected to change naturally at a faster rate than patients on the no-treatment floor? Several kinds of evidence suggest this would not be the case. First, the procedure of assigning residents to floors was basically random, and floors were selected randomly for treatment and no treatment. The authors also point out that various measures showed that the residents of the two floors were, on the average, equivalent in socioeconomic status and length of time at the nursing home. Finally, although it is not sufficient evidence in itself, residents on the two floors did not differ on the pretest measures. Little in the Langer and Rodin study suggests a confound due to an interaction of selection and maturation.

Interaction Between Selection and History   Another type of confound not controlled in the nonequivalent control group design is the interaction between selection and history. Cook and Campbell (1979) refer to this problem as *local history effects.* This problem arises when an event other than the treatment affects one group and not the other. Local history, for example, could be a problem in the Langer and Rodin study if an event affecting the residents' happiness and alertness occurred on one floor of the nursing home but not on the other. You can probably imagine a number of possibilities. A change in nursing staff on one floor, for instance, might bring about either an increase or a decrease in residents' morale, depending on the nature of the change and the relationship between the behavior of a new nurse and that of an old one. Problems of local history become more problematic the more the locations or settings of the individuals in the treatment and comparison groups differ. Langer and Rodin do not specifically address the problem of local history.

Interaction Between Selection and Instrumentation   An interaction of selection and instrumentation occurs when changes in a measuring instrument are more likely to be detected in one group than they are in another. Floor or ceiling effects, for instance, could make it difficult to detect behavior change from pretest to posttest. If this is more of a problem in one group than in another, an interaction of selection and instrumentation is present. Cook and Campbell point out that this confound is likely to be more of a problem the greater the nonequivalence of the groups. Because Langer and Rodin's groups did not differ on the pretest, and because performance of the groups did not suggest floor or ceiling effects on the measurement scales used, this confound seems implausible in their study.

Differential Statistical Regression   Finally, the nonequivalent control group design does not control for differential statistical regression (Cook & Campbell, 1979). As we noted earlier, this is especially a problem when one group has been singled out for treatment because of its poor performance on some measure. Whenever individuals are selected on the basis of extreme scores (the poorest readers, the workers with the lowest productivity, the patients with the most severe problems), regression toward the mean is to be expected. Changes in behavior from pretest to posttest due to regression may be mistakenly interpreted as a treatment effect if regression is more likely in the treatment group than in the control group. Because the groups in the Langer and Rodin study came from the same population and no evidence indicates one group's scores were more extreme than another's, a problem of differential statistical regression is not plausible in their study.

Observer Bias and Contamination   It is worthwhile to consider how Langer and Rodin handled problems of observer bias and possible effects of contamination and to inquire whether a Hawthorne effect was present. If observers in their study had been aware of the experimental hypothesis, it is possible they might inadvertently have rated residents as being better after the experimental communication than before. However, all the observers were kept unaware of the experimental hypothesis. Thus, observer bias appears to have been controlled. Langer and Rodin were aware of possible contamination effects. Residents in the control group might have become demoralized if they learned that residents on another floor were given more opportunity to make decisions. In this case, the use of different floors of the nursing home was advantageous; Langer and Rodin indicate that "there was not a great deal of communication between floors" (1976, p. 193). Thus, if one accepts Langer and Rodin's argument, contamination effects do not seem to be present, at least on a scale that would destroy the internal validity of the study.

Hawthorne Effect   A Hawthorne effect would be present in the Langer and Rodin study if residents on the treatment floor interpreted the responsibility-inducing communication as a form of special attention. Such an interpretation might lead residents on the treated floor to feel better about themselves. The changes in behavior that Langer and Rodin observed could then be attributed to a change in morale due to a Hawthorne effect as easily as to the opportunity to make decisions and assume personal responsibility that was available to residents in the treatment group. It is difficult to rule out completely a Hawthorne effect in this study. According to the authors, however, "there was no difference in the amount of attention paid to the two groups" (p. 194). In fact, communications to both groups stressed that the staff cared for them and wanted them "to be happy." Thus, without additional evidence to the contrary, we can conclude that the changes in behavior Langer and Rodin observed were due to the effect of the independent variable and not to the effect of an extraneous variable that the investigators failed to control.

What should be apparent at this point is that for an investigator to decide, in the context of a particular experiment, whether an independent variable worked, he or she must be something of a detective. Evidence for and against the interpretation that the treatment actually caused behavior to change must be systematically (and sometimes ingeniously) collected and carefully weighed. As Cook and Campbell (1979, pp. 55–56) explain,

> Estimating the internal validity of a relationship is a deductive process in which the investigator has to systematically think through how each of the internal validity threats may have influenced the data. Then, the investigator has to examine the data to test which relevant threats can be ruled out. In all of this process, the researcher has to be his or her own best critic, trenchantly examining all of the threats he or she

can imagine. When all of the threats can plausibly be eliminated, it is possible to make confident conclusions about whether a relationship is probably causal. When all of them cannot, perhaps because the appropriate data are not available or because the data indicate that a particular threat may indeed have operated, then the investigator has to conclude that a demonstrated relationship between two variables may or may not be causal.

The Issue of External Validity   We must make the same systematic inquiry into the external validity of an experiment that we did into its internal validity. What evidence is there that the particular pattern of results is restricted to a particular group of participants, setting, or time? For example, although Langer and Rodin suggest certain changes be made in the way the elderly are cared for, we might question whether the effectiveness of the responsibility-inducing communication would hold for all elderly residents, for all types of nursing homes, and at different times. That the particular nursing home selected by Langer and Rodin was described as "rated by the state of Connecticut as being among the finest care units" (1976, p. 193) suggests that the residents, facilities, and staff there would be different from those found in other facilities. For instance, if residents at this particular nursing home were relatively more independent before coming to the home than residents at other homes (perhaps because of differences in socioeconomic status), then the changes experienced upon moving into a home might have had greater impact on them. Consequently, the opportunity to be more independent of staff might be more important to these residents relative to residents in other homes. Similarly, if staff members at this home were more competent than those at other homes, they might be more effective in communicating the experimental communications than would the staff members at other homes.

As we indicated earlier, in the last analysis, the investigator must be ready to replicate an experimental finding under different conditions in order to establish external validity. The deductive process applied to questions of internal validity must also be used to examine a study's external validity. Moreover, we must be ready to live with the fact that one experiment is very unlikely to answer all questions about an experimental hypothesis.

INTERRUPTED TIME-SERIES DESIGNS

In situations in which we can observe changes in a dependent variable for some time before and after a treatment is introduced, another quasi experiment is possible. It is called a **simple interrupted time-series design** (Cook & Campbell, 1979). The essence of this design is the availability of periodic measures before and after a treatment has been introduced. It can be outlined in the following way:

$$O_1 \; O_2 \; O_3 \; O_4 \; O_5 \times O_6 \; O_7 \; O_8 \; O_9 \; O_{10}$$

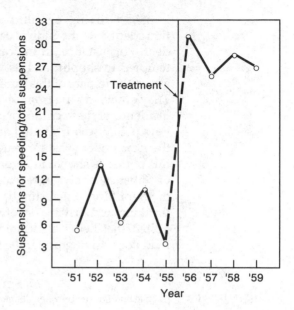

FIGURE 10.3   Suspensions of licenses for speeding, as a percentage of all suspensions. (From Campbell, 1969.)

Situations such as this may arise when a new product has been introduced, a new social reform instituted, or a special advertising campaign begun. Campbell's (1969) analysis of the effect on traffic fatalities of a crackdown on speeding ordered by the Connecticut governor made use of an interrupted time-series design. Because statistics related to traffic accidents are regularly kept by state agencies, a wealth of archival data was available to yield pretreatment and posttreatment measures. Besides number of fatalities, Campbell looked at number of speeding violations, number of drivers having their licenses suspended, and other measures related to driving behavior. Figure 10.3 shows the percentage of suspensions of licenses for speeding (as a percentage of all license suspensions) before and after the crackdown. A clear discontinuity in the time graph provides evidence for an effect of the treatment. Indeed, the discontinuity in the time series is the major evidence of an effect.

As Campbell points out, only abrupt changes in the time graph can be evaluated because gradual changes are indistinguishable from normal fluctuations over time. Unfortunately, changes often are not nearly so dramatic as those seen in Figure 10.3. In fact, Campbell's analysis of traffic fatalities over the same time period, while revealing evidence of an effect of the crackdown, did not show as abrupt a change as that associated with suspension of drivers' licenses (Campbell, 1969, Figure 2).

A typical outcome of an interrupted time-series design is illustrated by the findings of Ross and White (1987), who examined the effect of newspaper publicity on subsequent crime rates. In June 1984, a metropolitan newspaper instituted a policy of publishing the court results of people convicted of shoplifting, impaired driving, or failure to take a breathalyzer test. The published information identified the individual by name and also furnished details of the incident. For instance, in the case of shoplifting, the item that the individual attempted to shoplift and its value were also noted. Ross and White sought to assess the impact of this publication policy on the frequency of similar offenses. They obtained data from several police and government agencies detailing the incidence of these crimes over a time period beginning several years before the new policy was instituted and continuing for approximately 18 months after the new policy was implemented. The number of shoplifting offenses during this period is shown in Figure 10.4. Visual inspection, confirmed by the results of statistical analyses, revealed an effect of the publication policy on incidence of shoplifting. Interestingly, the policy showed no effect on the incidence of drinking and driving or refusing the breathalyzer test. The investigators suggested that being associated with shoplifting carries a greater social stigma than does driving under the influence of alcohol.

FIGURE 10.4   Shoplifting offenses between January 1980 and December 1985. (From Ross & White, 1987.)

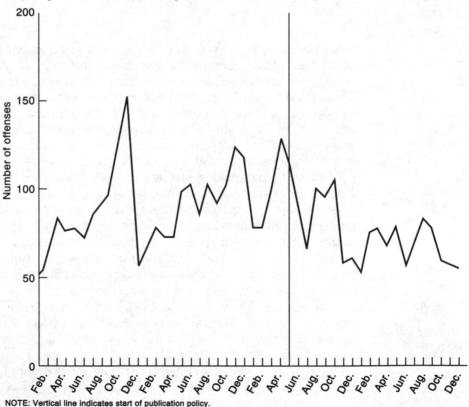

NOTE: Vertical line indicates start of publication policy.

Campbell and Stanley (1966) summarize the problem facing researchers using the simple interrupted time-series design: "The problem of internal validity boils down to the question of plausible competing hypotheses that offer likely alternate explanations of the shift in the time series other than the effect of X" (p. 39). An effect of history is the main threat to internal validity in this type of design (Cook & Campbell, 1979). For instance, considering the results in Figure 10.4, is it possible that some factor other than newspaper publicity was responsible for the reduction in the frequency of shoplifting offenses?

Particularly threatening to the internal validity of the time-series design are influences of a cyclical nature, including seasonal variation (Cook & Campbell, 1979). Thus, when Maki, Hoffman, and Berk (1978) assessed the effect of a water conservation program on water use in a California water district, they had to be sensitive to the possible influence of weather changes, including increased rainfall. Water use also would be expected to drop if the population decreased because residents fearful of water shortages left the area when the conservation program was announced. The time-series graph depicting water use revealed a slight dip in water use after the water conservation program was initiated. Only through a detailed and sophisticated analysis, taking into account other factors related to water use, were these researchers able to conclude that the reduction in water use could reasonably be attributed to the conservation program. Similarly, when analyzing the effect of the Connecticut governor's crackdown on speeding, Campbell (1969) gathered data from neighboring states in order to rule out possible regional trends due to weather or the introduction of automotive safety features in order to strengthen his case for the effect of this particular social policy change.

Instrumentation must also be considered a threat to internal validity in the simple interrupted time-series design (Cook & Campbell, 1979). When new programs or new social policies are instituted, for example, there are often accompanying changes in the way records are kept or in the procedures used to collect information. A program intended to reduce crime may lead authorities to modify their definitions of particular crimes or to become more careful when observing and reporting criminal activities. Nevertheless, for an instrumentation threat to be plausible, it must be shown how changes in instrumentation could occur at exactly the time of the intervention (Campbell & Stanley, 1966). Ross and White (1987) showed they were aware of possible influences due to instrumentation effects. They noted in their method section that data collected more than 18 months after the newspaper's new policy went into effect were not comparable to prior data because the laws defining a shoplifting offense had been changed. Hence, data were collected only during the 18-month period immediately after the policy change.

Most other threats to internal validity are controlled in the simple interrupted time-series design. Problems of maturation, testing, and regression are pretty much eliminated by the presence of multiple observations both before and after treatment. None of these threats can be ruled out when only a single pretest and posttest measure is available, as in the single-group pretest-posttest design mentioned earlier. For example, an effect of maturation would not normally be expected to show a sharp discontinuity in the time series, although this might be possible in some situations (Campbell & Stanley, 1966). When only one pretest and one posttest observation are available, it is not possible to decide whether performance changes from pretest to posttest reflect a treatment effect or are simply due to maturational processes. The simple time-series design usually permits this decision to be made.

Threats to external validity in the simple interrupted time-series design must be examined carefully. It should be obvious that, if pretreatment observations of behavior are based on multiple tests, then an effect of the treatment may be restricted to those individuals who have had multiple test experiences. Moreover, because only a single group is generally tested, one that was not randomly selected, it is always possible that the results are limited to people with characteristics similar to those who took part in the experiment.

TIME SERIES WITH NONEQUIVALENT CONTROL GROUP

The interrupted time-series design can be enhanced greatly by including a control group. This procedure is identical to that followed in constructing a nonequivalent control group design, which we discussed previously. In this case the researcher must find a group that is comparable to the treatment group and allows a similar opportunity for multiple observations before and after the time the treatment is administered to the experimental group. This **time series with nonequivalent control group design** is outlined as follows:

$$O_1 \; O_2 \; O_3 \; O_4 \; O_5 \; \times \; O_6 \; O_7 \; O_8 \; O_9 \; O_{10}$$
$$\overline{O_1 \; O_2 \; O_3 \; O_4 \; O_5 \qquad O_6 \; O_7 \; O_8 \; O_9 \; O_{10}}$$

As before, a dashed line indicates that participants were not randomly assigned to the control group and the experimental group. This interrupted time series with nonequivalent control group permits the investigator to control many threats due to history. As mentioned earlier, Campbell (1969) used traffic fatality data obtained from neighboring states to provide a comparison with traffic fatality data following the crackdown on speeding in Connecticut. Although traffic fatalities in Connecticut showed a decline immediately following the crackdown, data from comparable states did not exhibit any such decline. This fact tends to rule out changes that might have been due to favorable weather conditions, improved automobile design, or other potentially positive factors.

Archival data, rather than direct observation, frequently provide the basis for time-series designs. For example, the extensive archival data in various fields of sport have furnished social psychologists with an opportunity to test the real-life implications of laboratory-based theories. For example, in one study, researchers compiled statistics on baseball players who were traded in midseason to a new team (Jackson, Buglione, & Glenwick, 1988). A quasi-experimental analysis revealed that the batting average of these players was higher when playing for the new club than for the old club, confirming a prediction made from a drive theory of social facilitation. The possibility that baseball players, regardless of whether they are traded, increase their batting average over the full-year season was ruled out as an alternative explanation for these findings by demonstrating that averages of a random sample of non-traded players did not show a similar rise.

A particularly good illustration of the interrupted time-series design is provided by McSweeney (1978), who analyzed the frequency of telephone calls asking for directory assistance following initiation of a charge for such calls. Directory assistance calls requesting information about phone numbers listed in standard directories cost the telephone company money, and they pay these expenses by charging more for other services. As McSweeney pointed out, an intervention that would effectively reduce the frequency of these unnecessary calls would benefit both the telephone company and the consumer.

In 1974, officials at Cincinnati Bell Telephone Company initiated charges for local directory assistance calls in excess of three per month. Subscribers were charged 20 cents for each additional call. Because the telephone company keeps extensive archival records, the effect of this intervention could be assessed using a time-series analysis. Furthermore, a simple time series could be expanded by seeking a comparison group. McSweeney chose to use as a control measure the long-distance directory assistance calls that were made from outside the Cincinnati area, for which no charge was made. Although the exact number of "participants" could not be known, it was estimated the service charge for local directory assistance calls affected more than a million users. From data provided by Cincinnati Bell administrative records, McSweeney created the time-series graph shown in Figure 10.5. The frequency of local calls decreased dramatically after the charge was initiated; directory assistance calls from outside the area continued to increase gradually.

The time-series analysis revealed a small dip in frequency of local calls before the actual charges were levied. This was apparently in response to the announcement by telephone company officials of the upcoming cost to the user. McSweeney reasonably argued that this change was due to the fact that some individuals misunderstood the announcement in news reports and thought the charges were already being made. Others may simply have begun to change their calling habits in anticipation of the charges. The clear discontinuity in the time series associated with the treatment group, in conjunction with the absence of any decrease in calls by the comparison group, provides nearly incontrovertible evidence that the effect was due to the intervention made by the telephone company. A subsequent analysis showed that the decrease in local directory assistance calls resulted in an average savings of 65 cents on the telephone bill of each individual residential consumer.

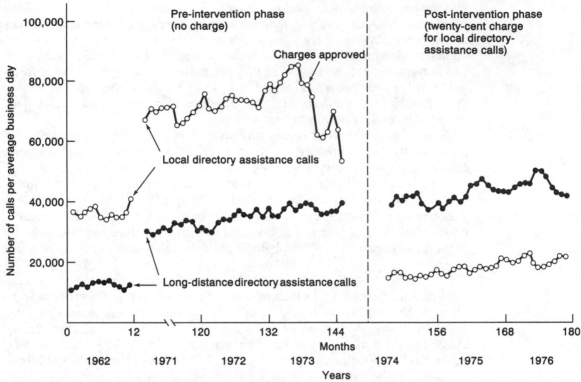

FIGURE 10.5   Number of local and long-distance directory assistance calls placed per average business day before and after charges were introduced. (From McSweeney, 1978.)

AN EXTENSION OF SINGLE-CASE EXPERIMENTAL DESIGNS TO RESEARCH IN NATURAL SETTINGS

RATIONALE

You may have noticed a similarity between the simple time-series design and the single-case experimental designs discussed in Chapter 9. In both situations, observations made prior to a treatment represent a baseline that is compared with observations obtained after the treatment. If there is a clear discontinuity in the behavioral record following the application of a treatment, it is evidence for the effect of the treatment. Furthermore, for both types of design the major threat to internal validity is history. It is possible that some factor affecting the participants' behavior, other than the independent variable, is responsible for the observed behavior change. However, the two types of design handle this threat differently.

When a simple time series is used, the investigator must search for historical factors (for example, seasonal variation) that might explain a change in the behavioral record. The addition of a nonequivalent control group greatly enhances the internal validity of the time-series design but does not completely rule out a possible interaction with history or other threats, such as an interaction with instrumentation. Moreover, unless the discontinuity in the time-series record is abrupt and obvious, the investigator must consider the possibility that one of numerous subtle factors produced a change, and he or she must rely on sophisticated mathematical models to determine whether an effect is present (McCain & McCleary, in Cook & Campbell, 1979). A single-case experimental design controls for effects due to history when changes in the behavioral record correspond systematically to the repeated introduction and withdrawal of an independent variable (as in an ABAB design) or to the staggered introduction of a treatment (as in a multiple-baseline design). Unless observed changes are very small, it may be possible to avoid using complex statistical procedures and to rely instead on visual inspection of the pattern of change associated with the sequential manipulation of a treatment.

Single-case experimental designs offer an alternative to quasi-experimental procedures when one is conducting research in natural settings (Horn & Heerboth, 1982). Although typically used to evaluate changes in a single participant, the single-case experimental design strategy can be used for a group of individuals, such as a classroom singled out for treatment. Examples of single-case experimental designs using groups of participants are found in Chapter 9 (see, for instance, VanBiervliet et al., 1981). In some situations a *multiple-baseline design* can be employed (Horn & Heerboth, 1982), as was done by Lyons and Ghezzi (1995) to evaluate the effect on the public's gambling behavior as a function of changes in state lottery games. Amount of dollars waged was measured in a multiple baseline "across states," Arizona and Oregon. To use an *ABAB design* the investigator must have control over the application and withdrawal of a treatment and an opportunity must be present for periodic observation both during no-treatment (baseline) stages and during treatment stages. Clearly this is not always possible in natural settings.

Treatments are often initiated under the assumption that they will work, and, unfortunately, their effects are often not evaluated. A water conservation program, for example, is not likely to be applied, withdrawn, and then applied again in an attempt to measure its effectiveness on water consumption. However, when control over the application and withdrawal of a treatment is feasible, a single-case ABAB design may be used to determine whether a treatment effect exists. The advantage to the researcher is a design whose internal validity is close to, if not the same as, that of a true experiment (Horn & Heerboth, 1982). The following example illustrates the possibilities of using an ABAB design in natural settings.

THE ABAB DESIGN

Schnelle and his associates used a single-case methodology to evaluate the effect of police procedures on reducing crime rate (Schnelle et al., 1978). In one study they sought evidence for the effect of a combined police car and helicopter patrol in reducing the frequency of home burglaries in a neighborhood of Nashville, Tennessee. The area was selected because police records showed it had a chronically high number of burglaries. (Even though this group was selected because it was extreme, do you see how the *chronic* nature of the burglaries neutralizes the problem of regression to the mean?) The plan was to increase surveillance of the area by adding a helicopter patrol to the usual police car patrol. When the helicopter was used, the pilots were told to fly low enough to observe suspicious activity. Pilots were in radio contact with the police in the patrol car. The helicopter was flown between 9 a.m. and 5 p.m. (weather permitting), a time that coincides with most home burglaries.

An ABAB procedure was used. Following a baseline observation of frequency of home burglaries in the experimental area, the helicopter was introduced for a period of time, then withdrawn, and then introduced again. The addition of the helicopter was an experimental program by the Nashville police, so the helicopter was again removed following the second treatment stage, providing an additional (and final) baseline period.

Figure 10.6 shows daily frequency of home burglaries during baseline and treatment periods. Visual inspection of the behavioral record clearly shows that the frequency of burglaries decreased when the helicopter was added to the police surveillance and increased when no helicopter was present. Interestingly, a check of police records showed no displacement of burglary activity to surrounding neighborhoods. That is, when the frequency of burglaries dropped in the experimental area, there was no corresponding rise in these types of crime in nearby neighborhoods, which served as a type of comparison group. Note that the dependent variable in this example is frequency based on a group of individuals—in this case, residents in an area of approximately six

FIGURE 10.6   Daily frequency of home burglaries. Arrows indicate the days the helicopter was prevented from flying. (From Schnelle et al., 1978.)

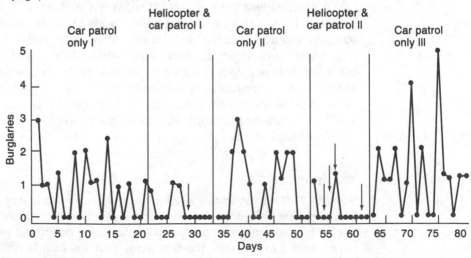

square miles. Except for this change in the way behavior is assessed, the design strategy is exactly the same as might be used with a single individual.

PROGRAM EVALUATION

Organizations that produce goods have a ready-made index of success. If a company is set up to make hammers, its success is ultimately determined by its profits from the sale of hammers. At least theoretically, the efficiency and effectiveness of the organization can be easily assessed by examining the company's financial ledgers. Increasingly, however, organizations of a different sort play a critical role in our society. Because these organizations typically provide services rather than goods, Posavac and Carey (1997) refer to them as *human service organizations*. For example, hospitals, schools, police departments, and government agencies provide a variety of services ranging from emergency room care to fire prevention inspections. Because profit making is not their goal, some other method must be found to distinguish between effective and ineffective agencies. One useful approach to assess the effectiveness of human service organizations is the discipline of program evaluation.

Posavac and Carey (1997, p. 1) define **program evaluation** as a "collection of methods, skills, and sensitivities necessary to determine whether a human service is needed and likely to be used, whether it is sufficiently intense to meet the unmet need identified, whether the service is offered as planned, and whether the human service actually does help people in need without undesirable side effects." These authors identify the basic goal of program evaluation as *providing feedback regarding human service activities.* Program evaluation represents a hybrid discipline that draws on political science, sociology, economics, education, and psychology. We discuss program evaluation at the end of this chapter on research in natural settings because it represents perhaps the most large-scale application of the principles and methods we have been describing throughout this book.

Program evaluations are designed to provide feedback to the administrators of human service organizations in order to help them decide what services to provide to whom and how to provide them most effectively and efficiently. Specifically, the questions asked by program evaluators are about needs, process, outcome, and efficiency (Posavac & Carey, 1997). An assessment of *needs* seeks to determine the unmet needs of the people for whom an agency might provide a service. If a city government were to consider instituting a program of recreational activities for senior citizens in the community, for example, it would first want to determine whether senior citizens actually need or want such a program and, if they do, what kind of program would be most attractive to them. The methods of survey research are used extensively in studies designed to assess needs. Information obtained in this type of program evaluation is also used to help program planning.

Once a program has been set up, program evaluators may ask about the process that has been established. Programs are not always implemented the way they were planned, and it is essential to know what actually *is* being done when a program is implemented. If the planned activities were not being used by the senior citizens in a recreational program designed specifically for them, it might suggest the program was inadequately implemented. An evaluation that provides answers to questions about *process,* that is, about how a program is actually being carried out, permits administrators to make adjustments in the delivery of services in order to strengthen the existing program (Posavac & Carey, 1997). Observational methods may be employed in such evaluations.

An evaluation of *outcome* is just that; it asks whether the program has been effective in meeting its stated goals. For example, do senior citizens now have access to more recreational activities, and are they pleased with these activities? Are these particular activities preferred over other activities? The outcome of a community-watch program designed to curb neighborhood crime might be evaluated by assessing whether there were actual decreases in burglaries and assaults following the implementation of the program.

Evaluators might also ask about the *efficiency* of the program, that is, about its cost. Choices often have to be made among possible services that a government or other institution is capable of delivering. Information about how successful a program is (outcome evaluation) and information about the program's cost (efficiency evaluation) are necessary if we want to make informed decisions about continuing the program, how to improve it, whether to try an alternative program, or to cut back on the program's services. These evaluations may use both experimental and quasi-experimental methods for research in natural settings. An evaluator may, for example, use a nonequivalent control group design to assess the effectiveness of a school reform program by comparing students' performance in two different school districts, one with the reform program and one without. It is also possible to use archival data like those described in Chapter 5 to carry out evaluations examining outcome and efficiency. For example, examining police records in order to document the frequency of various crimes is one way to assess the effectiveness of a community watch program.

Earlier in this chapter we described differences between basic and applied research. Program evaluation is perhaps the extreme case of applied research. The purpose of program evaluation is practical, not theoretical. Nevertheless, even in the context of blatantly practical goals, a case can be made for a reciprocal relationship between basic and applied research. Writing in the *International Journal of Psychology,* Salomon (1987) argues that each domain of research serves the other in an ongoing circular way. Specifically, basic research provides us with certain abstractions (for example, scientifically based principles) that express certain regularities in nature. When these principles are examined in the complex world where they supposedly apply, new complexities are recognized and new hypotheses are called for. These new complexities are then tested and evaluated before being tried out again in the real world. Salomon's model is illustrated in Figure 10.7:

Salomon points to the work of Ellen Langer as a concrete example of this circular relationship. She identified a decline in elderly people's health once they

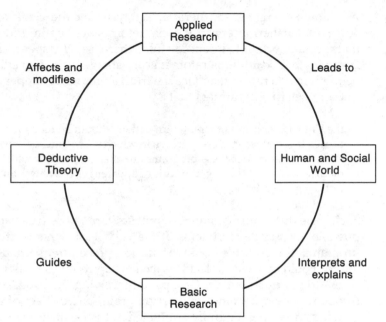

FIGURE 10.7   Model illustrating reciprocal relationship between basic and applied research. (From Salomon, 1987, p. 444.)

entered nursing homes (Langer, 1989; Langer & Rodin, 1976). This led her to develop a theory of mindfulness, which she has tested under controlled experimental conditions and has implications for more general theories of cognitive development (Langer & Piper, 1987). The theory provides a guide for her applied work—designing new models of nursing homes. Tests of the practical effects of changes in the care given by nursing homes on the residents' health and well-being will undoubtedly lead to modifications of her theory of mindfulness.

Perhaps the greatest difference between basic research and program evaluation lies in the political and social realities surrounding program evaluation. Governments at both local and national levels regularly propose, plan, and execute various types of social reforms. Tax relief programs, work incentive programs, educational reforms, police reforms, and medical care for senior citizens are just a few of the types of social reform programs that a government might initiate. Unfortunately, as Donald Campbell (1969), a past president of the American Psychological Association, pointed out, the outcome of these social reforms often cannot be meaningfully evaluated. Did a change in police techniques lead to greater crime stoppage? Are more elderly people gaining access to public transportation after a reduction in fares? Does a work incentive program take more people off the unemployment rolls? The answers to such questions often cannot be found, said Campbell, because most social reforms are instituted in a political climate that is not ready for hardheaded evaluation. What public official, for instance, wants to be associated with a program that failed?

As Campbell suggested, there is "safety under the cloak of ignorance" (pp. 409–410). Furthermore, many social reforms are begun under the assumption that they are certain to be successful. Otherwise why spend all that tax money? For many public administrators it is advantageous to leave that assumption in people's minds rather than face the truth about what happened.

Campbell (p. 409) argued that

> the United States and other modern nations should be ready for an experimental approach to social reform, an approach in which we try out new programs, in which we learn whether or not these programs are effective, and in which we retain, imitate, modify, or discard them on the basis of apparent effectiveness on the multiple imperfect criteria available.

Social scientists must convince administrators to use true experiments, if at all possible, or quasi-experiments at the very least, when instituting new social programs. For example, a randomization procedure, perhaps based on public lottery, could be used to decide which group receives a pilot program or gains access to scarce resources. Groups not receiving the program or the available resources would become comparison groups. The effect of a social treatment could then be meaningfully evaluated. At present, decisions regarding who gets what are often influenced by particular interest groups—as the result of intense lobbying, for example—or made on the basis of political favoritism.

According to Campbell, the most significant change needed is for public officials to emphasize the importance of the problem rather than the importance of the solution. Instead of pushing for one certain cure-all (which, in most cases, has little opportunity for success), officials must be ready to execute reform in a manner that permits the clearest evaluation and must be prepared to try different solutions if the first one fails. Public officials must, in other words, be ready to use the experimental method to identify society's problems and to determine effective solutions.

Campbell's (1969) idea that social reforms and experimental methods be routinely brought together has had some impact on social policymakers, but it is still underutilized (Berk et al., 1987). The reasons are some of the same ones initially identified by Campbell. Nevertheless, without social experimentation, especially that which makes use whenever possible of randomized field experiments, policymakers and the community at large may believe a treatment works when it doesn't or vice versa. Such incorrect decisions lead us to allocate money and resources to ineffective programs.

Not too many years ago, a show called "Scared Straight" was aired on national television. It described a juvenile education program implemented at Rahway State Prison in New Jersey. The program involved taking youthful offenders into a prison to meet with selected convicts from the inmate population. The goal was to inform juveniles about the reality of prison life and, thereby, the program leaders hoped, dissuade them from further illegal activity. Unsubstantiated claims were made for the effectiveness of the program, including some suggesting a success rate as high as 80% to 90% (Locke, Johnson, Kirigin-Ramp, Atwater, & Gerrard, 1986). The Rahway program is just one of several similar programs around the country. But do these programs really work?

Several evaluation studies of the exposure-to-prison programs have produced mixed results, including positive findings, findings of no difference between control and experimental participants, as well as results suggesting that the program may actually *increase* juvenile crime among some types of delinquents. There is a possibility that less hardened juvenile offenders may increase their criminal activity after meeting the prisoners. It has been suggested that because these less hardened offenders have recently begun a lifestyle wherein they are being recognized and reinforced by their peers for their toughness, this image is also reinforced by the tough image often projected by the prisoners. On the other hand, more frequent juvenile offenders, who have achieved a level of status among their peers for some period of time, may be more threatened by the prospects of prison life because it would mean loss of that status (Locke et al., 1986).

Attempts to evaluate the effectiveness of this significant social program provide good examples of the difficulties inherent in evaluation research: the difficulty of randomly assigning participants, of getting administrators to cooperate with experimental procedures, and of dealing with loss of participants during the evaluation. Nevertheless, program evaluation based on sound experimental methodology offers policymakers at all levels (institution, community, city, state, federal) the information that can help them make more rational choices among possible treatments for social problems. Since resources inevitably are in short supply, it is critical that those available to help society be put to the best possible use.

Our hope is that your knowledge of research methods will allow you to participate knowledgeably and perhaps contribute constructively to the ongoing debate concerning the role of experimentation in society.

SUMMARY

Experimentation in natural settings differs in many ways from experimentation in psychology laboratories. There are likely to be more problems in exerting experimental control in a natural setting, and establishing external validity or generalizing results is more often a key objective. The stated goals of the research and its possible consequences also differ when research is conducted in natural settings. Reasons for doing experiments in natural settings include testing the external validity of laboratory findings and assessing the effects of treatments aimed at improving conditions under which people work and live.

Campbell and others have argued that society must be willing to take an experimental approach to social reform—one that will allow the clearest evaluation of the effectiveness of new programs. In many situations (for instance, when available resources are scarce), true experiments involving randomization of individuals to treatment and no-treatment conditions are recommended. However, if a true experiment is not feasible, quasi-experimental procedures are the next best approach. Quasi-experiments differ from true experiments in that fewer plausible rival hypotheses for an experimental outcome are controlled. When specific threats to the internal validity of an experiment are not controlled, then the experimenter, by logically examining the situation and by collecting additional evidence, must seek to rule out these threats to internal validity.

A particularly strong quasi-experimental procedure is the nonequivalent control group design. This procedure generally controls for all major threats to internal validity except those associated with interactions of (1) selection and history, (2) selection and maturation, (3) selection and instrumentation, and (4) threats due to regression to the mean. In addition to the major threats to internal validity, an experimenter must be sensitive to possible contamination resulting from communication between groups of participants. Problems of observer or experimenter bias, questions of external validity, and Haw-thorne effects are potential problems in all experiments, whether conducted in the laboratory or in the field.

When it is possible to observe changes in a dependent measure before and after a treatment is administered, one can carry out a simple interrupted time-series design. The researcher using this design looks for an abrupt change in the time series that coincides with the introduction of treatment. The major threat to internal validity in this design is history—some event other than the treatment may have been responsible for the change in the time series. Instrumentation also can be a problem, especially when the treatment represents a type of social reform that may lead to changes in the way records are kept or data collected. By including a control group that is as similar as possible to the experimental group, one can strengthen the internal validity of a simple time-series design. A time series with nonequivalent control group, for example, controls for many possible history threats.

In this chapter we also discussed how the logic and methodology associated with single-case experimental designs (see Chapter 9) can be applied to experimentation in natural settings. For instance, an ABAB design may be used when a researcher can control the application and withdrawal of a treatment. In such cases the internal validity of the experiment can approach that of a true experiment.

A particularly important goal of research in natural settings is program evaluation. Persons other than psychologists (such as educators, political scientists, and sociologists) are often involved in this process. Types of program evaluation include assessment of needs, process, outcome, and efficiency. Perhaps the most serious constraints on program evaluation are the political and social realities that surround it. The reluctance of public officials to seek an evaluation of social reforms is often an obstacle to be overcome. Nevertheless, social scientists have called on individuals who are knowledgeable about the procedures of program evaluation to make themselves available to those responsible for the delivery of social services. By answering this call, we may help change society in a way that will bring the most effective services to those most in need.

KEY CONCEPTS

program evaluation
basic research
applied research
threats to internal validity
regression to the mean
contamination
Hawthorne effect
quasi experiments

nonequivalent control group
 design
simple interrupted time-series
 design
time series with nonequivalent
 control group design
program evaluation

REVIEW QUESTIONS

1 What special reasons are there for carrying out experiments in natural settings?
2 Explain how laboratory experiments and those in natural settings differ in control, external validity, goals, and consequences.
3 Distinguish between basic research and applied research.
4 Briefly explain what Donald Campbell meant when he called for an experimental approach to social reform.
5 What are the three distinguishing characteristics of true experiments?
6 What obstacles arise in trying to carry out experiments in natural settings?
7 Comment critically on the fairness of random assignment.
8 How can participants be randomly assigned to treatments while still giving all participants access to the experimental treatment?
9 How are participants in a control group likely to respond when contamination occurs?
10 What do Cook and Campbell (1979) consider the best test of external validity?
11 Why is the use of a pretest critical in the nonequivalent control group design?
12 Cite one example of a threat to internal validity that is controlled in the nonequivalent control group design and two examples of threats that are not controlled.
13 Explain why we cannot conclude that the treatment and control groups in a nonequivalent control group design are equivalent even when the pretest scores are the same for both groups.
14 What is meant by a "local history effect" in the nonequivalent control group design?
15 How did Langer and Rodin handle problems of observer bias and possible effects of contamination in their study of elderly residents of a nursing home?
16 What is the major evidence for an effect of the treatment in a simple interrupted time-series design?
17 Explain how the addition of a nonequivalent control group to a simple interrupted time-series design reduces the threat to the internal validity of the design.
18 How can single-case experimental designs be used to determine whether an effect is due to a treatment or to the threat to internal validity called *history*?
19 What are the four types of questions typically addressed in program evaluation?

CHALLENGE QUESTIONS

1 Because of your extensive background in research design, you have been appointed by a local school board committee to design a definitive study of the effect of a newly

developed nutritious breakfast as compared with the current, less nutritious, break-fast on the school performance of young children. The school board is trying to decide whether to establish a "nutritious breakfast program" at the school, and, because of the expense of this proposed program (and because of your persuasive arguments), they have decided to test the effectiveness of the breakfast before implementing the program. For this problem, pretend you are meeting with the principal of the school to work out the details of the study. You are to respond to each of the following sug-gestions made by the principal.

A   The principal first suggests that students be selected for the treatment during the test phase on the basis of their need. That is, the students who have the lowest nu-trition level now will be given the treatment. Explain to the principal why this is not an advisable procedure.

B   Having given up his suggestion in part A, the principal next suggests that the only fair procedure for the test is to give the treatment to all the students to see if there is any improvement in their performance. Explain to the principal what you would have to do under these circumstances to verify the effectiveness of the pro-gram, and explain why this could be a risky way to test the program.

C   Finally, the principal gives up and asks you to describe the design you would pro-pose for the study. Outline the essentials of your design. Be sure to use double-blind procedures and explain to the principal the how and why of these proce-dures.

2   A psychologist published a book describing the effects of divorce on men, women, and children. She was interested in the effects of divorce that occurred 10 years after the divorce. She found that even 10 years after a divorce half of the women and one-third of the men were still intensely angry. Although half the men and women de-scribed themselves as happy, 25% of the women and 20% of the men remained unable to "get their lives back on track." In only 10% of the divorced families did both the former husbands and wives have happy, satisfying lives a decade later. Finally, more than half of the children of divorce entered adulthood as underachieving and self-deprecating men and women. These findings were based on a 15-year study of 60 di-vorced couples and their 131 children living in Marin County, California (an affluent suburban area including mostly well-educated people). Explain how the use of a quasi-experimental design would have been helpful in order to specify which of the reported results are due to the effects of divorce.

3   The police force of a large city had to decide between two different approaches to keeping the officers on the force informed about the changes in laws. An enlightened administrator of this force decided to put the two approaches to test in a research study. She decided to use the random groups design and she assigned 30 officers ran-domly to each of the two programs for a period of 6 months. At the end of this time all the officers who successfully completed the training required under the two ap-proaches were given a final test on their knowledge of the law. The 20 officers who completed Program A showed a reliably higher mean score on this test than did the 28 officers who completed Program B. The administrator wisely chose not to accept these results as decisive evidence of the effectiveness of the two programs. Using only the data reported in this problem, explain why she made this decision. Next, explain how her decision would have been different if 20 officers completed both programs (from the original 30 assigned to each) and there was still a sizable difference favoring Program A. Be sure to mention any limitations on the conclusions she could reach concerning the overall effectiveness of these programs.

4 A small undergraduate college with a new physical fitness center decided to introduce a health enhancement program for faculty and staff. The program is designed to take one semester to complete with three 1-hour sessions per week. Comment critically on each of the following questions regarding the evaluation of this program.

   A How might an evaluation of needs have played a role in planning the program?

   B What obstacles generally exist in real-world settings, and probably apply in this situation, that prevent the conduct of a true experiment to evaluate the outcome of the program? (Be sure to define the three characteristics of a true experiment.)

   C As an alternative to a true experiment, a nonequivalent control group design is proposed in which a group of faculty who did not participate in the program agree to take the performance tests before the program begins and after the program has ended. Explain why this nonequivalent control group design is superior to a pretest-posttest design in which only the program participants would be tested. State one threat to internal validity that is controlled in the nonequivalent control group design.

ANSWER TO CHALLENGE QUESTION 1

1 A Selecting students on the basis of need may result in problems with regression to the mean, especially if the students are identified on the basis of an unreliable measure of need. If regression were to be a problem, the nutrition program could falsely appear to be effective.

   B Administering the program to all students would necessitate projecting what students' performance would have been without the program on the basis of their prior school performance, as is the case in a time-series design. Their prior performance would serve as a baseline, and the risks associated with variable baselines would apply to this situation. The test of the effectiveness of the program would also be potentially challenged by the threats to internal validity that apply to the time-series designs, such as history.

   C The most appropriate design for this problem would be a two-group experiment using the random groups design. Both groups should receive comparably packaged breakfast foods that had been previously coded by the manufacturer as containing the newly developed nutritious breakfast or the previously used (and presumably less nutritious) diet. Neither the students nor those responsible for assessing their school performance should know which diet a given student has received. This double-blind procedure avoids potential problems of demand characteristics (students working harder in school because they know they have received the "super" breakfast) and experimenter effects (teachers showing observer bias by varying their assessments of students in light of which treatment the student has received or influencing students' performance differentially by giving more individual attention and instruction to students whom the teachers know are receiving the new diet).

Statistical Methods

OVERVIEW

This appendix is intended primarily to assist students who have gathered data as part of a research project and who want to analyze their data. The first half of the appendix provides computational procedures for statistics that can be done relatively easily with a calculator. Before presenting the procedures for several statistical tests, we provide a review of some statistical notation with which students will need to be familiar to carry out the tests. Along with the computations for each test, we present a sample data set to illustrate the type of problem for which the statistical test is best suited.

In the second half of the appendix we present sample data sets for different experimental designs for which the analysis of variance is the appropriate inferential statistics test. For these analyses we do not provide computational procedures. Instead, we present the output from a software package that has been used to perform the computations. Our focus is on understanding the output and on interpreting the results of the F-tests appropriately. We hope this appendix will help students as they analyze the results of research projects they do in the context of their research methods course.

NOTES ON NOTATION

To learn the computational procedures for specific statistical tests, you need first to learn some general characteristics of statistical notation. A subject's score on a dependent variable is typically called "X." The scores of individual subjects are indicated by subscripts ($X_1 X_2 X_3$); thus, we refer to the score for the first subject as X_1, that for the second subject as X_2, and so on. If we have two scores for each subject on two different dependent variables, we typically refer to the first score as X and the second score as Y. For example, if we measured thefirst subject's height as 60 inches and weight as 120 pounds, then $X_1 = 60$ and $Y_1 = 120$.

The number of subjects in each group within a study is indicated using the symbol n. Once again, we use subscripts to differentiate the different groups. If there are 30 subjects in Group 1 and 25 subjects in Group 2, we indicate this in symbols as $n_1 = 30$; $n_2 = 25$. The subscripts need not be numbers; if there are 10 subjects in the control group and 12 subjects in the experimental group, we could write $n_c = 10$; $n_e = 12$. The total number of subjects across all the groups in the study is indicated by the symbol N. If there are three groups in an experiment and if $n_1 = 10$, $n_2 = 15$, and $n_3 = 5$, then $N = 30$.

The summation sign, Σ, indicates that you are to add all the values represented by the symbol(s) that appear to the right of the summation sign. If you had the three scores $X_1 = 4$, $X_2 = 5$, and $X_3 = 6$, the expression ΣX would indicate that you should do the following computation:

$$\Sigma X = X_1 + X_2 + X_3 = 4 + 5 + 6 = 15$$

Two other common expressions involving the summation sign appear in many statistical computations, ΣX^2 and $(\Sigma X)^2$. These two expressions look very similar, but they require very different computations. The expression ΣX^2 indicates that each individual score should first be squared and then the sum of these squared scores should be determined. The expression $(\Sigma X)^2$ requires the determination of the sum of the individual scores first and then the squaring of this sum. Using our sample of three scores ($X_1 = 4$, $X_2 = 5$, and $X_3 = 6$), the differences between the two calculations can be made clear.

$$\Sigma X^2 = X_1^2 + X_2^2 + X_3^2 = 4^2 + 5^2 + 6^2 = 16 + 25 + 36 = 77$$
$$(\Sigma X)^2 = (X_1 + X_2 + X_3)^2 = (4 + 5 + 6)^2 = (15)^2 = 225$$

DESCRIPTIVE STATISTICS

The scores representing performance of subjects in a particular group can be summarized most completely by constructing a frequency distribution. In a frequency distribution, the possible values of the dependent variable are listed from lowest to highest and the number of subjects obtaining each score is tabulated. While a frequency distribution provides the most complete summary of the results, reporting the frequency distributions for each of the six conditions in an experiment is too cumbersome. Most frequency distributions can be summarized by reporting one measure of central tendency and one measure of dispersion. We now describe each type of measure in turn.

MEASURES OF CENTRAL TENDENCY: MODE, MEDIAN, AND MEAN

Measures of central tendency indicate the score that identifies the center of the frequency distribution. The *mode* is the crudest measure of central tendency: It simply indicates the score in the frequency distribution that occurs most often. If two scores in the distribution occur with much higher frequency than do other scores in the distribution, and if these two scores occur at two different locations in the frequency distribution, this two-humped distribution is said to be *bimodal* (to have two modes).

The *median* is defined as the middle score in the frequency distribution. The median is calculated by ranking all the scores from lowest to highest. If there is an odd number of scores, then the middle score is equal to the median. If there is an even number of scores, then the median is the average of the two scores in the middle. For example, if a distribution of scores included the values 4, 7, 2, 1, 9, we would compute the median by first ranking the scores—1, 2, 4, 7, 9—and then selecting the third of the five scores (4) as the median. If a sixth score were included in the distribution (4, 7, 2, 1, 9, 5), we would again rank the scores (1, 2, 4, 5, 7, 9), but this time we would average the third and fourth scores to obtain the median

$$\left(\frac{4 + 5}{2} \right) = 4.5$$

The median is the best measure of central tendency when the distribution includes extreme scores because it is less influenced than is the mean by the extreme scores. For example, the median of the distribution of scores 1, 2, 3, 4, 5 is 3. The median would remain the same even if the distribution were changed to 1, 2, 3, 4, 50.

The *mean* is the most commonly reported measure of central tendency and it is determined by dividing the sum of the scores (ΣX) by the number of scores contributing to that sum (n). The mean of the five scores 4, 7, 2, 1, 9 would be calculated as follows:

$$\text{Mean} = \frac{\Sigma X}{n} = \frac{4 + 7 + 2 + 1 + 9}{5} = 4.6$$

The mean of a population is symbolized as μ (Greek letter mu); the mean of a sample of scores is usually indicated as $\overline{X}$ (read "X bar"), but it is sometimes symbolized as M. The mean should always be reported as a measure of central tendency unless there are extreme scores in the distribution.

The mean of several samples of the same size can be determined by averaging the means of the individual samples. For example, if each of the five groups included 10 subjects and the means for these five groups were as follows, $\overline{X}_1 = 4.6$, $\overline{X}_2 = 4.3$, $\overline{X}_3 = 6.2$, $\overline{X}_4 = 4.7$, and $\overline{X}_5 = 5.2$, then the mean across all five groups can be computed using the following equation in which K is the number of groups:

$$\text{Overall mean} = \frac{(\Sigma \overline{X})}{K} = \frac{4.6 + 4.3 + 6.2 + 4.7 + 5.2}{5}$$

$$= \frac{25}{5} = 5.00$$

When the overall mean for a group of samples of different sizes needs to be computed, the simple averaging of the sample means is not appropriate. Simple averaging would give undue weight to the scores for subjects in the smaller groups and would give too little weight to subjects' scores in the larger groups. The overall mean can be computed in a way that gives equal weight to the score for each individual subject. For example, if in Group 1 there are 20 subjects and $\overline{X}_1 = 4.45$, and in Group 2 there are 10 subjects and $\overline{X}_2 = 6.20$, and in Group 3 there are 20 subjects and $\overline{X}_3 = 4.95$, then the overall mean can be computed as follows:

$$\text{Overall mean} = \frac{\Sigma(n)(\overline{X})}{N} = \frac{(20)(4.45) + (10)(6.2) + (20)(4.95)}{50}$$

$$= \frac{89 + 62 + 99}{50}$$

$$= \frac{250}{50} = 5.00$$

MEASURES OF DISPERSION: RANGE AND STANDARD DEVIATION

Whenever you report a measure of central tendency, it should always be accompanied by an appropriate measure of dispersion. Measures of central tendency indicate the center of a frequency distribution; measures of dispersion indicate the breadth or variability of the distribution. The two distributions shown below have the same mean (13), but they clearly differ in how the scores are distributed about that mean. In Distribution A, the scores are tightly packed about the mean, indicating low dispersion. The scores in Distribution B, on the other hand, are more widely distributed about the mean, indicating greater dispersion.

Distribution A	Distribution B
13	9
13	11
13	13
13	15
13	17

The crudest measure of dispersion (the counterpart of the mode) is the range. The *range* is determined by subtracting the lowest score in the distribution from the highest score. In the small distribution made up of the scores 1, 3, 5, 7, the range would be equal to $7 - 1$, or 6.

The most commonly used measure of dispersion (the counterpart of the mean) is the standard deviation. The *standard deviation* tells you approximately how far on the average a score is from the mean. It is equal to the square root of the average squared deviations of the scores in the distribution about the mean. The definitional formula for the standard deviation is

$$\sqrt{\frac{\Sigma(X - \overline{X})^2}{n - 1}}$$

For reasons that need not concern us here the average of the squared deviations about the mean must involve division by $n - 1$ rather than n so as to provide an unbiased estimate of the population standard deviation based on the sample. The standard deviation of a population is symbolized as σ (Greek letter sigma); the standard deviation of a sample of scores is usually indicated as s, but it is sometimes symbolized as SD. The computational formula for the standard deviation is

$$s = \sqrt{\frac{\Sigma X^2 - \dfrac{(\Sigma X)^2}{n}}{n - 1}}$$

The use of this computational formula can be best illustrated by working through an example for a small distribution of scores: 2, 6, 10, 14, 18.

1 Compute $\Sigma X^2 = 2^2 + 6^2 + 10^2 + 14^2 + 18^2$
$\qquad\qquad\quad = 4 + 36 + 100 + 196 + 324$
$\qquad\qquad\quad = 660$

2 Compute $\Sigma X = 2 + 6 + 10 + 14 + 18$
$\qquad\qquad\quad = 50$

3 Compute $\dfrac{(\Sigma X)^2}{n} = \dfrac{(50)^2}{5} = \dfrac{2,500}{5} = 500$

4 Compute $\Sigma X^2 - \dfrac{(\Sigma X)^2}{n} = 660 - 500 = 160$

5 Compute $\dfrac{\Sigma X^2 - \dfrac{(\Sigma X)^2}{n}}{n - 1} = \dfrac{160}{4} = 40$

6 Compute $\sqrt{\dfrac{\Sigma X^2 - \dfrac{(\Sigma X)^2}{n}}{n - 1}} = \sqrt{40} = 6.32$

STANDARD ERROR OF THE MEAN

In doing inferential statistics, we use the sample mean as a point estimate of the population mean. That is, we use a single value ($\overline{X}$) to estimate (infer) the population mean (μ). It is often helpful to be able to determine how much error there is in estimating μ on the basis of $\overline{X}$. The central limit theorem in mathematics tells us that if we draw an infinite number of samples of the same size and we compute $\overline{X}$ for each of these samples, the mean of these sample means ($\mu_{\overline{X}}$) will be equal to the population mean (μ), and the standard deviation of the sample means ($\sigma_{\overline{X}}$) will be equal to the population standard deviation (σ) divided by the square root of the sample size ($\sqrt{n}$). The standard deviation of this theoretical sampling distribution of the mean is called the *standard error of the mean*.

Typically, we do not know the standard deviation of the population so we estimate it on the basis of a sample. Thus, the estimate of standard error of the mean ($s_{\overline{X}}$) is computed using the formula $s_{\overline{X}} = s/\sqrt{n}$. Small values of $s_{\overline{X}}$ suggest that we have a good estimate of the population mean, and large values of $s_{\overline{X}}$ suggest that we have only a rough estimate of the population mean. The formula for the standard error of the mean indicates that our ability to estimate the population mean on the basis of a sample depends on the size of the sample (large samples lead to better estimates) and on the variability in the population from which the sample was drawn, as estimated by the sample standard deviation (the less variable the scores in a population, the better our estimate of the population mean will be).

If the standard deviation of a sample of 25 scores (which can be computed from a set of scores following the procedures described in the previous section) is 5, then the standard error of the mean ($s_{\overline{X}}$) is equal to $s/\sqrt{n}$, which in this case is $5/\sqrt{25} = 5/5 = 1.00$.

CONFIDENCE INTERVALS

Imagine that you are having a physical examination at the campus health clinic. The technician reports that your pulse is 75 beats per minute. You are unlikely to be concerned that your heart is racing if you are also told the average pulse rate at rest for a person your age is 72 beats per minute. Your knowledge of the variability of pulse rates keeps you from being alarmed. In both physiological and psychological measurement we are often more interested in knowing a range of values that define a "normal" range than we are in specifying a single estimate of a population value. These normal ranges are based on the standard error of the mean and are called *confidence intervals*. In computing a confidence interval we specify a range of values within which we can have a certain degree of confidence that the population mean is included within the interval. As you may suspect, the larger the interval we specify, the greater our confidence that the mean will be included; but larger intervals give us less specific information about the exact value of the population mean. As a compromise, researchers have agreed that the 95% confidence interval and the 99%

confidence interval will be used when an interval estimate of the population. mean is desired. The confidence interval is centered about our point estimate of the mean ($\overline{X}$), and the boundaries of the 95% confidence interval can be calculated using the following formulas:

Upper limit of 95% confidence interval = $\overline{X} + [t(n-1)]_{\alpha = .05} [S_{\overline{X}}]$
Lower limit of 95% confidence interval = $\overline{X} - [t(n-1)]_{\alpha = .05} [S_{\overline{X}}]$

We have already described procedures for computing the sample mean ($\overline{X}$) and the standard error of the mean ($s_{\overline{X}}$). The unfamiliar symbols in the two equations for the limits of the 95% confidence interval are $[t(n-1)]$ and $\alpha = .05$. The level of significance ($\alpha = .05$) may be familiar to you if you have studied the procedures for inferential statistics tests described in Chapter 6. In the case of confidence intervals, $\alpha = (1 - $ level of confidence), expressed as a proportion. So, for the 95% confidence interval, $\alpha = 1 - .95 = .05$ and for the 99% confidence interval, $\alpha = 1 - .99 = .01$. The t statistic included in the equation is defined by the number of degrees of freedom ($n - 1$), and the t is determined by looking it up in Table A.5.

We are now ready to compute the 95% confidence interval for the mean of a sample in which $\overline{X} = 12$, $s = 4$, and $n = 25$.

1 Compute $s_{\overline{X}} = \dfrac{s}{\sqrt{n}} = \dfrac{4}{\sqrt{25}} = \dfrac{4}{5} = .8$

2 Determine degrees of freedom for t: $n - 1 = 25 - 1 = 24$

3 Determine $\alpha = 1 - .95 = .05$

4 Look up in Table A.5 the value for $t(24)_{\alpha = .05} = 2.06$

5 Compute upper limit of 95% confidence interval
$$= \overline{X} + [t(n-1)]_{\alpha = .05} [s_{\overline{X}}]$$
$$= 12 + [2.06][.8]$$
$$= 12 + 1.65 = 13.65$$

6 Compute lower limit of 95% confidence interval
$$= \overline{X} - [t(n-1)]_{\alpha = .05} [s_{\overline{X}}]$$
$$= 12 - [2.06][.8]$$
$$= 12 - 1.65 = 10.35$$

7 The 95% confidence interval for a sample mean of 12 from a sample size of 25 with a standard deviation of 4 is bounded by 10.35 and 13.65. We can thus be 95% confident that the specified interval captures the mean of the population from which the sample was drawn.

CORRELATIONAL ANALYSES

The degree of relationship between two dependent measures for the same sample of subjects is determined by calculating a correlation coefficient. If the two dependent measures both represent at least an interval scale of measurement (see Chapter 3), then the Pearson Product-Moment Correlation Coefficient r is used. If one or both dependent measures represent only an ordinal scale of measurement, however, then the appropriate correlation coefficient is Spearman's Rank-Order Correlation Coefficient r_s. We illustrate the computational procedures for both correlation coefficients. We also describe two important correlational analyses using the chi-square test.

PEARSON PRODUCT-MOMENT CORRELATION COEFFICIENT r

Each of 10 players agreed to keep track of how many hours were spent practicing the week before a Ping-Pong tournament. During the week of the tournament the number of games won by each of these 10 players was also determined. We refer to the number of hours of practice as X and to the number of games won as Y. The data for each of the 10 players on each of these two measures are listed in the following table, and these data were used to carry out the necessary computations for determining r.

Subject	Hours of practice (X)	Games won (Y)
1	40	10
2	20	3
3	10	1
4	15	2
5	18	4
6	35	6
7	27	9
8	16	8
9	4	5
10	33	7

1 Compute $\Sigma X = 40 + 20 + 10 + \ldots + 33 = 218$

2 Compute $\Sigma Y = 10 + 3 + 1 + \ldots + 7 = 55$

3 Compute $\Sigma X^2 = 40^2 + 20^2 + 10^2 + \ldots + 33^2 = 5{,}964$

4 Compute $\Sigma Y^2 = 10^2 + 3^2 + 1^2 + \ldots + 7^2 = 385$

5 Compute $\Sigma XY = (40)(10) + (20)(3) + \ldots (33)(7) = 1{,}404$

6 Compute $\Sigma XY - \dfrac{(\Sigma X)(\Sigma Y)}{n} = 1{,}404 - \dfrac{(218)(55)}{10} = 205$

7 Compute $\Sigma X^2 - \dfrac{(\Sigma X)^2}{n} = 5{,}964 - \dfrac{(218)^2}{10} = 1{,}211.60$

8 Compute $\Sigma Y^2 - \dfrac{(\Sigma Y)^2}{n} = 385 - \dfrac{(55)^2}{10} = 82.50$

9 Multiply step 7 by step 8 = $(1{,}211.60)(82.50) = 99{,}957$

10 Take the square root of step 9 = $\sqrt{99{,}957} = 316.16$

11 Divide step 6 by step 10 to obtain $r = \dfrac{205}{316.16} = .65$

The 11 steps we have just outlined have led you successfully through the computational formula for r. The computational formula in its complete form is as follows:

$$r = \frac{\Sigma XY - \dfrac{(\Sigma X)(\Sigma X)}{n}}{\sqrt{\left(\Sigma X^2 - \dfrac{(\Sigma X)^2}{n}\right)\left(\Sigma Y^2 - \dfrac{(\Sigma Y)^2}{n}\right)}}$$

To determine whether your obtained r is greater than zero, you can use Table A.2. The degrees of freedom (df) are $n - 2$, and Table A.2 lists the critical values of r for the .05 and .01 levels of significance. If your obtained r is *greater* than the tabled value, then the correlation you have obtained is statistically significant. In our example, the degrees of freedom for r would be 8 since n is 10. The obtained r of .65 is larger than the tabled r for a .05 level of significance (.632), so it would be considered statistically significantly larger than zero. Notice, however, if we had used a .01 level of significance, our obtained r of .65 would be *less* than the tabled value (.765) and thus judged to be *not* statistically significant. If we concluded that the correlation was statistically significant, then we would also conclude that the more hours a player practices Ping-Pong, the more games he or she is likely to win.

SPEARMAN'S RANK-ORDER CORRELATION COEFFICIENT r_s

The director of the admissions office at a very small college selected a random sample of 10 students from this year's incoming class to determine whether there was a correlation between the students' high school class ranks and their scores on a national college board test. The scores on the college board test represent an interval scale, with higher scores indicating better performance. The high school ranks, however, represent only an ordinal scale and so Spearman's rank-order correlation must be used.

Student	Class rank	Test score	Test rank	D	D²
1	2	675	1	1	1
2	4	525	6	−2	4
3	7	500	7.5	−.5	.25
4	9	450	9	0	0
5	6	650	2	4	16
6	1	600	3	−2	4
7	3	550	5	−2	4
8	8	500	7.5	.5	.25
9	10	425	10	0	0
10	5	575	4	1	1

Note: The students' actual high school class ranks would have ranged over ranks larger than 1 to 10. These are their converted class ranks within the sample of 10.

1 Rank the students from highest to lowest on their test scores. For students with the same test score, take the ranks these students would have received and average them. Then, assign the next rank to the next lowest student. For example, students 3 and 8 both have a score of 500. They are in ranks 7 and 8, so both receive a rank of 7.5 [(7 + 8)/2 = 7.5] and the next lowest student (student 4 with a score of 450) receives a rank of 9.

2 Compute D—the difference in the two ranks for each student. See column D in the table.

3 Compute D^2—square each difference score. See column D^2 in the table.

4 Compute $\Sigma D^2 = 1 + 4 + .25 + 0 + 16 + 4 + 4 + .25 + 0 + 1 = 30.5$

5 Multiply ΣD^2 by $6 = (6)(30.5) = 183$

6 Compute $n(n^2 - 1) = 10(10^2 - 1) = 10(100 - 1) = 10(99) = 990$

7 Divide step 5 by step 6: $\dfrac{183}{990} = .18$

8 Subtract step 7 from 1 to obtain $r_s = 1 - .18 = .82$

Once again, the steps we have just outlined have led you successfully through the computational formula for r_s. The computational formula in its complete form is

$$r_s = 1 - \frac{6(\Sigma D^2)}{n(n^2 - 1)}$$

To determine whether your obtained r_s is greater than zero, you can use Table A.3. The critical information you need in Table A.3 is n (in our example n = 10), and the level of significance you want to use. If the obtained r_s is *greater* than the tabled value, then the correlation you have obtained is statistically significant. In our example, the obtained r_s of .82 is larger than the tabled value for the .05 level of significance (.648), so it would be considered statistically significantly larger than zero. Thus, as you might expect, students' high school class ranks and college board test scores are correlated, although the actual correlation is usually less than .82.

CHI-SQUARE (χ^2) TEST: GOODNESS OF FIT

The chi-square (χ^2) goodness-of-fit test is used to determine whether the obtained freuencies in each of several nominal scale categories correspond to the expected frequencies in each category. The expected frequencies are often based on the laws of chance, but they can also represent expectations based on a formal psychological theory. It is essential that each individual observation be independent and that each observation be classified into one—and only one—category.

The example we will use to illustrate the computation of this test will involve testing the "fairness" of a six-sided die rolled 60 times. You could also consider these data to represent the responses of 60 students to a six-alternative multiple-choice test item on material the students have *not* studied. A fair die and a good test item should lead to equal frequencies across categories. The observed and expected frequencies on which the computations will be based are as follows:

	Outcome categories					
	1	2	3	4	5	6
Observed frequency	7	12	10	12	8	11
Expected frequency	10	10	10	10	10	10
(O – E)	–3	2	0	2	–2	1

1 Compute Observed (O) – Expected (E) frequencies in each category. (See last row of table.)

2 Compute $\chi^2 = \Sigma \dfrac{(O - E)^2}{E}$

$$= \frac{(-3)^2}{10} + \frac{(2)^2}{10} + \frac{(0)^2}{10} + \frac{(2)^2}{10} + \frac{(-2)^2}{10} + \frac{(1)^2}{10}$$

$$= \frac{9}{10} + \frac{4}{10} + 0 + \frac{4}{10} + \frac{4}{10} + \frac{1}{10}$$

$$= .9 + .4 + 0 + .4 + .4 + .1 = 2.20$$

3 Determine degrees of freedom for χ^2: (number of categories – 1) = 6 – 1 = 5

4 Use Table A.4 to determine critical χ^2 value for 5 degrees of freedom and α = .05

$$\chi^2(5)_{\alpha = .05} = 11.07$$

5 Compare obtained χ^2 with tabled χ^2 value.
   a If obtained χ^2 < tabled χ^2, then the expected frequencies provide a "good fit" for the obtained frequencies.
   b If obtained χ^2 > tabled χ^2, then the expected frequencies do *not* provide a good fit for the obtained frequencies.

6 Our result conforms to step 5a, and so we decide we have a fair die or a good test item.

CHI-SQUARE (χ^2) TEST: CONTINGENCY TABLE

The chi-square (χ^2) contingency test is used to determine whether there is a relationship between two nominal scale variables. This version of the chi-square test is used frequently in the analysis of cross tabulations in survey research. The observations entering into this analysis must be independent, and each observation must be classified into one and only one cell of the contingency table.

These assumptions are generally met by making only one observation of each subject, thereby ensuring that the total number of observations entering into the table equals the total number of subjects. In contingency tables having only one degree of freedom (2×2 tables), the computations we describe here should not be used if any expected values are less than 10. For chi-square contingency tests with two or more degrees of freedom, it is best if there are no expected frequencies less than 5.

In the following table, the category listed along the rows of the table is the number of hours that people reported they habitually slept each night, and the category listed across the columns of the table is the frequency with which these same people experienced headaches. The observed frequencies in the body of the table represent the numbers of people who experienced the particular combination of sleep and headache frequency.

Hours of sleep	Frequency of headaches			Row totals
	Never	Sometimes	Often	
≥ 8	38 [30.98]	17 [22.74]	3 [4.28]	58
7	37 [33.65]	21 [24.70]	5 [4.65]	63
≤ 6	19 [29.37]	31 [21.56]	5 [4.06]	55
Column totals	94	69	13	[176]

1 Compute row and column totals of observed frequencies. See table.

2 Compute overall total. Check to be sure both row and column totals sum to the same overall total. See boxed entry in lower right corner of the table.

3 Compute expected frequencies in each cell of the table by multiplying the row total by the column total for that cell and dividing by the overall total. For example, for the cell in the table for subjects getting more than 8 hours of sleep and never reporting headaches, the expected value is equal to

$$\frac{(58)(94)}{176} = \frac{5,452}{176} = 30.98$$

The expected values for each cell of the table are entered in the brackets below and to the right of each observed frequency.

4 Compute $\chi^2 = \Sigma \dfrac{(O - E)^2}{E} =$

$$\frac{(38 - 30.98)^2}{30.98} + \frac{(17 - 22.74)^2}{22.74} + \frac{(3 - 4.28)^2}{4.28} + \frac{(37 - 33.65)^2}{33.65}$$

$$+ \frac{(21 - 24.70)^2}{24.70} + \frac{(5 - 4.65)^2}{4.65} + \frac{(19 - 29.37)^2}{29.37}$$

$$+ \frac{(31 - 21.56)^2}{21.56} + \frac{(5 - 4.06)^2}{4.06}$$
$$= 1.59 + 1.45 + .38 + .33 + .55 + .03 + 3.66 + 4.13 + .22$$
$$= 12.34$$

5 Determine degrees of freedom for χ^2: (number of rows – 1) × (number of columns – 1)

$$= (3 - 1)(3 - 1)$$
$$= (2)(2)$$
$$= 4$$

6 Use Table A.4 to determine critical χ^2 value for 4 degrees of freedom and $\alpha = .05$

$$\chi^2(4)_{\alpha = .05} = 9.49$$

7 Compare obtained χ^2 with tabled χ^2 value.
  a If obtained χ^2 is greater than the tabled χ^2, then the two variables in the contingency table are significantly related.
  b If obtained χ^2 is less than the tabled χ^2, then the two variables in the contingency table are *not* significantly related.

8 Our result conforms to step 7a, so we conclude that habitual sleep duration and headache frequency are related.

INFERENTIAL STATISTICS FOR TWO-CONDITION EXPERIMENTS

INDEPENDENT SAMPLES *t*-TEST

The independent samples *t*-test is used to determine whether two sample means are sufficiently different so as to be unlikely to have been drawn from the same population. This test is applicable for the analysis of two-group designs involving either the random groups design or the natural groups design (see Chapter 6), although the assumptions underlying the test strictly apply only to the random groups design. If the independent variable has had no effect, then the two samples represent random samples drawn from the same population and they would therefore be expected to provide comparable estimates (within the bounds of sampling error) of the population mean. The independent samples *t*-test is based on the difference between the two sample means, so the expected value of *t* when the independent variable has had no effect is zero. If the independent variable has had an effect, however, the *t* will differ from zero. If the larger mean is subtracted from the smaller mean the *t* will become increasingly smaller than zero as the mean difference increases. If the smaller mean is subtracted from the larger mean, the *t* will become increasingly larger than zero. The difference may be taken in either direction, but you must be careful to note whether it is a positive or negative *t* value. Because sampling error can never be eliminated, the obtained *t* must be compared with a critical value from the appropriate t-distribution to determine if it is statistically significant.

The data presented in the following table represent the number of correct responses on a test given after subjects studied the material in one of two groups in a random groups design. Subjects were randomly assigned to either the experimental ($n_e = 4$) or to the control group ($n_c = 6$), and the hypothesis tested in the experiment was that the experimental group would do better on the test.[1] The subject numbers in each group are not in sequence, reflecting their random assignment.

Subject	Experimental group	Subject	Control group
2	20	1	16
5	14	3	15
8	17	4	12
9	21	6	12
		7	14
		10	15

1 Compute $\overline{X}_e = \dfrac{\Sigma X_e}{n_e} = \dfrac{20 + 14 + 17 + 21}{4} = \dfrac{72}{4} = 18$

2 Compute $\overline{X}_c = \dfrac{\Sigma X_c}{n_c} = \dfrac{16 + 15 + 12 + 12 + 14 + 15}{6}$

$\qquad = \dfrac{84}{6} = 14$

3 Compute $\Sigma X_e^2 = 20^2 + 14^2 + 17^2 + 21^2 = 400 + 196 + 289 + 441$
$\qquad = 1{,}326$

4 Compute $\Sigma X_c^2 = 16^2 + 15^2 + 12^2 + 12^2 + 14^2 + 15^2 = 256 + 225$
$\qquad + 144 + 144 + 196 + 225 = 1{,}190$

5 Compute $SS_e = \Sigma X_e^2 - \dfrac{(\Sigma X_e^2)}{n_e} = 1{,}326 - \dfrac{(72)^2}{4} = 1{,}326 - \dfrac{5{,}184}{4}$

$\qquad = 1{,}326 - 1{,}296 = 30$

6 Compute $SS_c = \Sigma X_c^2 - \dfrac{(\Sigma X_c)^2}{n_c} = 1{,}190 - \dfrac{(84)^2}{6} = 1{,}190 - \dfrac{7{,}056}{6}$

$\qquad = 1{,}190 - 1{,}176 = 14$

---

[1]Some investigators distinguish between directional statistical tests (also called "one-tailed" tests) and nondirectional tests (also called "two-tailed" tests). In a nondirectional test you are testing simply to see if the groups differ from each other; in a directional test you are testing to see if one group has done better (or worse). In this appendix we have tested all hypotheses as if they were nondirectional. Any introductory statistics textbook can be consulted if you need further information concerning the rationale and procedures for one-tailed tests. Table A.5 in this appendix is for nondirectional tests.

7 Compute pooled $s^2 = \dfrac{SS_e + SS_c}{n_e + n_c - 2} = \dfrac{30 + 14}{4 + 6 - 2} = \dfrac{44}{8} = 5.50$

8 Compute $s_{\bar{X}_e - \bar{X}_c} = \sqrt{\dfrac{s^2}{n_e} + \dfrac{s^2}{n_c}}$

$$= \sqrt{\dfrac{550}{4} + \dfrac{5.50}{6}} = \sqrt{1.38 + .92} = \sqrt{2.30} = 1.52$$

9 Compute t $\dfrac{\bar{X}_e - \bar{X}_c}{s_{\bar{X}_e - \bar{X}_c}} = \dfrac{18 - 14}{1.52} = \dfrac{4}{1.52} = 2.63$

10 Determine degrees of freedom for $t = n_e + n_c - 2 = 4 + 6 - 2 = 8$

11 Use Table A.5 to determine critical value for t with 8 degrees of freedom and $\alpha = .5$

$$t(8)_{\alpha = .05} = 2.31$$

12 Compare the *absolute value* of your obtained t value with the tabled value.
   a If the absolute value of your obtained t is larger than the tabled value, then the two sample means likely represent two different populations. That is, the mean difference is statistically significantly larger than zero.
   b If the absolute value of your obtained t is smaller than the tabled value, then the two sample means likely represent the same population. That is, the mean difference is *not* statistically significantly larger than zero.

13 Our outcome conforms to step 12a, so we would conclude that the experimental group likely did better.

EFFECT SIZE

An inferential test like the independent samples t-test we just described tells us whether there is a difference between the means for the experimental and control groups. What a statistically significant t-test does *not* tell us is how large of an effect the independent variable had. Measures of effect size are used to determine the strength of the relationship between the independent and dependent variables. That is, measures of effect size reflect how large the effect of an independent variable was. (See Chapter 6 for more information about interpreting effect sizes.) A common measure of effect size is d, which we now use to illustrate the computation of effect size. We use the data from the previous example involving the independent samples t-test.

1 Compute Mean for experimental group: $\dfrac{\Sigma X_e}{n_e}$

$$\dfrac{20 + 14 + 17 + 21}{4} = \dfrac{72}{4} = 18$$

2 Compute Mean for control group: $\dfrac{\Sigma X_c}{n_c}$

$$\frac{16 + 15 + 12 + 12 + 14 + 15}{6} = \frac{84}{6} = 14$$

3 Compute pooled $s^2 = 5.5$ (See step 7 of independent samples t-test computation.)

4 Compute $s = \sqrt{s^2}$
$\qquad\quad = 2.34$

5 Compute $d = \dfrac{\text{Mean Experimental} - \text{Mean Control}}{s}$

$$\qquad\quad = \frac{18 - 14}{2.34}$$

$$\qquad\quad = 1.71$$

6 To interpret our value of $d = 1.71$, we can use J. Cohen's (1992) classification of effect sizes of $d = .20$ for a small effect size, $d = .50$ for a medium effect size, and $d = .80$ for a large effect size. Because our value of d is larger than .80 we would conclude that this independent variable had a large effect on test performance.

DIRECT DIFFERENCE t-TEST

The direct difference t-test is used to determine the statistical significance of a mean difference in two-condition experiments in which each subject has participated in both conditions. The direct difference t-test is applicable, therefore, to the analysis of repeated measures design experiments involving two conditions.

The following data represent the scores for six subjects, each of whom was tested under the experimental and control conditions in a repeated measures design. The higher the score, the better the subject's performance.

Subject	Condition		D
	Experimental	Control	
1	80	60	20
2	90	75	15
3	65	75	−10
4	95	75	20
5	85	60	25
6	75	55	20

1 Compute a difference score (D) for each subject (see table). Be sure to compute the difference in the same direction for each subject and retain the sign of the difference score.

2 Compute $\Sigma D = 20 + 15 + (-10) + 20 + 25 + 20 = 90$

3 Compute $\overline{D} = \dfrac{\Sigma D}{n} = \dfrac{90}{6} = 15.0$

4 Compute $\Sigma D^2 = 20^2 + 15^2 + (-10)^2 + 20^2 + 25^2 + 20^2$
$$= 400 + 225 + 100 + 400 + 625 + 400$$
$$= 2{,}150$$

5 Compute $s_D = \sqrt{\dfrac{\Sigma D^2 - \dfrac{(\Sigma D)^2}{n}}{n-1}}$

$$= \sqrt{\dfrac{2{,}150 - \dfrac{(90)^2}{6}}{6-1}} = \sqrt{\dfrac{2{,}150 - \dfrac{8{,}100}{6}}{5}} = \sqrt{\dfrac{2{,}150 - 1{,}350}{5}}$$

$$= \sqrt{\dfrac{800}{5}} = \sqrt{160} = 12.65$$

6 Compute $s_{\overline{D}} = \dfrac{s_D}{\sqrt{n}} = \dfrac{12.65}{\sqrt{6}} = \dfrac{12.65}{2.45} = 5.16$

7 Compute $t = \dfrac{\overline{D}}{s_{\overline{D}}} = \dfrac{15.0}{5.16} = 2.91$

8 Determine degrees of freedom for t: $(n-1) = 6 - 1 = 5$

9 Use Table A.5 to determine critical value for t with 5 degrees of freedom and $\alpha = .05$

$$t(5)_{\alpha = .05} = 2.57$$

10 Compare the *absolute value* of your obtained t value with the tabled value.
   a If the absolute value of your obtained t is larger than the tabled value, then the mean difference ($\overline{D}$) is statistically significantly larger than zero.
   b If the absolute value of your obtained t is smaller than the tabled value, then the mean difference ($\overline{D}$) is *not* statistically significantly larger than zero.

11 Our result conforms to step 10a, and so we conclude that the experimental group did better.

COMPUTER-ASSISTED ANALYSES

Once an investigator moves beyond a simple correlational design or a two-group experiment, computational procedures become more cumbersome for describing data and for making statistical inferences from data. Fortunately, many researchers now have access to mainframe computers or microcomputers that include appropriate software to carry out the statistical analysis of large data sets. This access to computers has led to a change in the approach taken to introduce students to statistical analysis. Stated simply, the availability of computer-assisted analyses has made knowing step-by-step computational procedures for complex analyses less important. Being able to set up and carry out an analysis using a statistical software package and being able to interpret the "output" have become essential skills that need to be learned by researchers.

Carrying out statistical analyses using computer software requires two types of knowledge. First, the researcher must have a good knowledge of research design and statistics. Second, the researcher must be familiar with the requirements and capabilities of an appropriate statistical software package. Many software packages for statistical analysis are available for use both on mainframe computers and microcomputers. Some of the more popular ones are known by abbreviations like BMDP, SPSS, STATA, and SYSTAT. You may have access to one or more of these programs on the computers in your psychology department or at your campus computer center. Be sure to check with your instructor regarding the availability of these statistical packages on your campus. Should you decide to purchase a statistical software package for your personal computer, be sure to first obtain advice from an experienced researcher who is familiar with the brand of computer you have and with the kinds of statistical analyses you want to perform.

In Chapters 6, 7, and 8 of this text we introduced various experimental designs and the logic of null hypothesis testing and inferential statistics. This knowledge is essential if you wish to use computer-assisted analysis. A computer is not able to determine what research design you used or the rationale behind the use of that design (although some of the more user-friendly programs provide prompts to guide your thinking). To carry out an analysis, you must provide the computer with information such as: the type of design that was used (e.g., random groups or repeated measures); the number of independent variables (e.g., single factor or multifactor); the number of levels of each independent variable; and the number of dependent variables and the level of measurement employed for each. You must also be able to articulate your research hypotheses and to plan appropriate statistical tests of your research hypotheses. For example, you should know what analytical comparisons you plan to do after performing an omnibus F-test. A computer will quickly and efficiently perform the computations necessary for obtaining descriptive and inferential statistics. To use the computer effectively as a research tool, however, you must give it specific directions regarding which inferential test you want it to do and which data are to be used in computing the test. Finally, when the computer has carried out the computations, you must be able to interpret correctly the output showing the results of the analysis.

ANALYSIS OF VARIANCE

The most frequently used statistical procedure for analyzing results of psychology experiments is the analysis of variance (ANOVA). An introduction to

ANOVA, or the *F*-test, was presented in Chapter 6. In the following sections of this appendix we describe computer-assisted analyses using ANOVA. Our emphasis is on the interpretation of the output from a statistical software package that was used to compute the ANOVA. We first present the raw data in summary form. Then we provide an illustration of how the results of an ANOVA typically are displayed on a computer screen or on a printed page after the computer has performed the computations. Our examples are based on the SYSTAT program; however, the output can be expected to be similar to that of other software packages. The steps required to enter the data into the computer in accord with the particular requirements of the software package have been omitted. Procedures for data entry vary from one statistical package to another. Be assured, however, that knowing how to program a computer is *not* required to enter data into a statistical package. Step-by-step instructions are part of the written documentation that accompanies each software package. Through careful reading and a little practice, the procedures for handling data entry can typically be mastered in a relatively short period of time. Once you develop this skill you are freed forever from the chains of laborious statistical calculations!

We turn our attention now to the interpretation of the output for the ANOVA for four research designs: single-factor analysis for independent groups designs; single-factor analysis for repeated measures designs; two-factor analysis for independent groups designs; and two-factor analysis for mixed designs.

SINGLE-FACTOR ANALYSIS OF VARIANCE FOR INDEPENDENT GROUPS DESIGNS

The single-factor analysis of variance for independent groups designs is used to analyze the results of random groups and natural groups designs involving one independent variable with two or more levels. (The assumptions underlying the test strictly apply only to the random groups design.) The logic of this statistical test is described in Chapter 6. We first describe the procedures for computer-assisted analysis of an omnibus *F*-test. We then describe the procedures for developing the coefficients for analytical comparisons and for testing the statistical significance of the comparison. We consider only the case when all groups in the experiment are the same size.

The data in the following table represent the number of words correctly identified (out of a possible 20) on a vocabulary test. Five subjects were randomly assigned to each of four groups (defined by the method of study that subjects were instructed to use to learn the words in preparation for the vocabulary test). The control method involved no specific instructions, but in the three experimental methods subjects were instructed either to study a synonym of the to-be-learned word (synonym method), or a dictionary definition of the to-be-learned word (dictionary method), or a literary passage in which the to-be-learned word was used in context (passge method). The independent variable being manipulated is instruction, and it can be symbolized by the letter A. The levels of this independent variable can be differentiated by using the symbols a_1, a_2, a_3, and a_4 for the four respective groups. The number of subjects within each group is referred to as n; in this case, n = 5. The total number of subjects in the experiment is symbolized as N; in this case, N = 20. Finally, the number of groups is referred to as a; in this case, a = 4.

			Instruction (A)				
Subject	Control (a_1)	Subject	Synonym (a_2)	Subject	Definition (a_3)	Subject	Passage (a_4)
1	12	6	15	11	16	16	14
2	10	7	14	12	16	17	14
3	9	8	13	13	13	18	15
4	11	9	12	14	12	19	12
5	8	10	12	15	15	20	12
Mean	10.0		13.2		14.4		13.4
Standard deviation	1.6		1.3		1.8		1.3

The first step in the analysis of any experiment is to set up a data matrix like the one here. The number of correct responses is listed for each subject in each of the four groups with each subject identified with a unique subject number. Below the data matrix the mean and standard deviation are provided for each group. The mean and standard deviation can be computed with such a small data set using the procedures described earlier in this appendix. For most experiments, however, there will be more subjects in each group and the mean and standard deviation can be obtained using the same statistical program that is used to compute the omnibus F-test. As we have discussed, it is essential to have the means along with the outcome of the F-test to interpret the results of an experiment.

Screen A.1 represents the output of the SYSTAT statistical program after it has computed the omnibus F-test for the data in this experiment. The first line on the screen indicates that the program encountered four levels during processing that were identified as groups 1–4. The next line indicates that the dependent variable was called "words" and that the total number of subjects (N) was 20. On that same line the multiple R (.771) and the squared multiple R (.595) appear. These values pertain to the use of the correlational technique called regression analysis, which is related to the analysis of variance. But, these values are not critical in interpreting the statistical significance of an F-test. To interpret an F-test, the most critical information is the analysis of variance summary table that fills the remainder of the screen.

The first column of the table, labeled "Source," includes the two major sources of variation in the analysis of a single-factor analysis of variance: Variation due to the independent variable (GRP for group) and Error variation re-

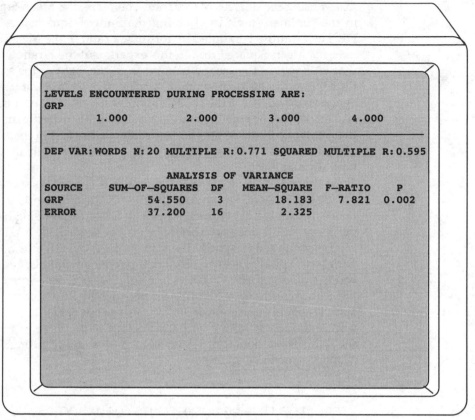

```
LEVELS ENCOUNTERED DURING PROCESSING ARE:
GRP
          1.000          2.000          3.000          4.000
_____

DEP VAR: WORDS  N: 20  MULTIPLE R: 0.771  SQUARED MULTIPLE R: 0.595

                       ANALYSIS OF VARIANCE
SOURCE     SUM-OF-SQUARES  DF    MEAN-SQUARE   F-RATIO     P
GRP             54.550      3        18.183     7.821    0.002
ERROR           37.200     16         2.325
```

SCREEN A.1

flecting variation within the groups. The second column presents the Sum-of-Squares for each of the two sources of variation. These values reflect the amount of variation produced in the experiment by each source of variation. The statistical program computes these values based on the data matrix, and it is these computations that would be cumbersome to compute with a calculator. The third column indicates the degrees of freedom (DF) for each source of variation. The DF for Group is equal to the number of groups minus 1 (in this case, $4 - 1 = 3$). The DF for Error is equal to the number of subjects in each group minus 1 times the number of groups. There were 5 subjects in each of the four groups so the DF for Error is: $(5 - 1) \, 4 = 16$.

The fourth column presents the Mean-Square for each source of variation. The mean square reflects somewhat of an average amount of variation for each source in the sense that it adjusts for the number of entries contributing to each source of variation. There is a potential bias in estimating a variance; so, instead of using the number of entries themselves, the sums of squares are adjusted using the degrees of freedom. Therefore, the Mean-Squares are obtained in the summary table by dividing the Sum-of-Squares by the corresponding DF. The F-ratio is computed by forming a ratio of the Mean-Square for Groups over the Mean-Square Error. In this experiment the F-ratio was 7.821, the value that is shown in the second column from the right of the summary table. The final piece of information that is provided by a computer-based statistical analysis of variance is the probability of the F-ratio assuming the null hypothesis is true. The probability for the F-ratio in this experiment of .002 appears in the far right column of the summary table. Since this probability is less than the conventional level of significance (.05), we can conclude that this F-ratio is statistically significant.

At this point we know that the omnibus F-test was statistically significant. So, we know there was an overall effect of the independent variable of type of instruction in the experiment. This tells us that something happened in the experiment, but it does not specify what has happened. Analytical comparisons can be computed to specify the source of the overall effect of the independent variable. Typically, a small set of comparisons would be required to locate the sources of systematic variation in a single-factor experiment. We illustrate the procedure for doing analytical comparisons by describing the computer-based analysis of only one comparison. We use as our example the analytical comparison of the control group with the average of the three experimental groups to see if this is one source of systematic variation contributing to the overall effect of the instructional variable.

STEPS IN DEVELOPING COEFFICIENTS FOR ANALYTICAL COMPARISON

1 State hypothesis in words: Compare control method with average of three experimental methods.

2 State null hypothesis for comparison: $\mu_{a_1} = \dfrac{\mu_{a_2} + \mu_{a_3} + \mu_{a_4}}{3}$

3 Set null hypothesis statement equal to zero:

$$\mu_{a_1} - \left[\frac{\mu_{a_2} + \mu_{a_3} + \mu_{a_4}}{3} \right] = 0$$

4 Expand expression by taking minus sign inside brackets and isolating terms over common denominator:

$$\mu_{a_1} - \frac{\mu_{a_2}}{3} - \frac{\mu_{a_3}}{3} - \frac{\mu_{a_4}}{3} = 0$$

5 Eliminate fractions by multiplying expression by common denominator:

$$3\mu_{a_1} - \mu_{a_2} - \mu_{a_3} - \mu_{a_4} = 0$$

6 The coefficients for each group are the multipliers for each mean in this equation.

$$C_1 = +3$$
$$C_2 = -1$$
$$C_3 = -1$$
$$C_4 = -1$$

7 Computation check: The coefficients for an analytical comparison must sum to zero.

8 If a group is not included in a comparison, its coefficient is 0.

F-TEST FOR ANALYTICAL COMPARISON

Once you have determined the coefficients for the analytical comparison you want to do, using the procedures described in the preceding section, you are ready to run the program to compute the *F*-test for your comparison. The output for the analysis of the comparison of the control group to the average of the three experimental groups appears in Screen A.2. The critical information among that appearing in the upper-left corner of the screen is the coefficients that were entered for the comparison. The format of the summary table is very similar to that for the single-factor analysis we described earlier. In fact, the Source of variation labeled "Error" is exactly the same as for the omnibus *F*-test for this experiment. In general, the error term for analytical comparisons is the same as the error term for the omnibus test.

The source of variation being tested in this analysis is labeled "Hypothesis." It reflects the potential systematic variation due to the analytical comparison being tested. Since analytical comparisons reflect the contrast between two sets of means, they always have only one degree of freedom. In this case, the contrast is between the mean for the control group and the mean of the three means in the experimental group. The *F*-ratio for testing the effect of the analytical comparison (called hypothesis in the summary table) is the ratio of the Mean-Square (MS) for Hypothesis over the MS Error. The resulting *F* shown in the summary table is 21.685. The probability of this *F* (with 1 and 16 degrees of freedom) under the null hypothesis is less than one in a thousand. This probability is less than the conventional level of significance (.05), and so we conclude that this analytical comparison is statistically significant.

The mean for the control group was 10.0, and the mean across the three experimental groups was 13.7. These means along with the statistically significant *F*-ratio lead to the conclusion that the three experimental groups recalled more vocabulary words than did the control group. This conclusion based on the test of an analytical comparison is much more specific than the conclusion based on the omnibus test that something happened in the experiment.

```
>output*
>hypothesis
>effect = grp
>contrast
>3 -1 -1 -1
>test

TEST FOR EFFECT CALLED:    GRP

TEST OF HYPOTHESIS

        SOURCE          SS        DF       MS        F        P
     HYPOTHESIS       50.417      1     50.417    21.685   0.000
         ERROR        37.200     16      2.325
```

SCREEN A.2

SINGLE-FACTOR ANALYSIS OF VARIANCE FOR REPEATED MEASURES (WITHIN-SUBJECTS) DESIGNS

The results of experiments which involve repeated measures designs (see Chapter 7) that include one independent variable manipulated at two or more levels are analyzed using a single-factor analysis of variance. The repeated measures designs are also called within-subjects designs. The underlying logic and the interpretation of the F-test are the same for the repeated measures designs and for the independent-groups designs. There are a few characteristics, however, that are sufficiently different to warrant a brief description of the analyses of the repeated measures designs.

The data from the time perception experiment outlined in Chapter 7 were analyzed with a single-factor analysis of variance for the repeated measures designs using the SYSTAT statistical software package. The purpose of the analysis was to determine if the subjects' estimates of the intervals changed with increasing interval length. The output of this analysis is shown on Screen A.3.

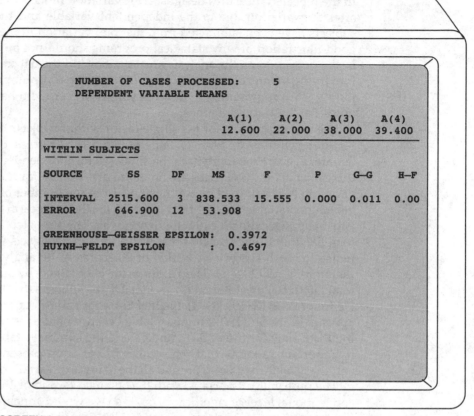

```
        NUMBER OF CASES PROCESSED:      5
        DEPENDENT VARIABLE MEANS

                                A(1)     A(2)     A(3)     A(4)
                              12.600   22.000   38.000   39.400

WITHIN SUBJECTS

SOURCE          SS      DF     MS        F        P      G-G     H-F

INTERVAL   2515.600      3  838.533  15.555   0.000   0.011   0.00
ERROR       646.900     12   53.908

GREENHOUSE-GEISSER EPSILON:     0.3972
HUYNH-FELDT EPSILON       :     0.4697
```

SCREEN A.3

As was the case for the single-factor analysis of the independent-groups designs, the results of the analysis of the repeated measures designs are summarized in an analysis of variance summary table. The output begins, however, by indicating that the number of cases (i.e., subjects) in the analysis was five. The output next displays the means for the four levels of the interval length variable. The program labels these levels with the generic indicators A(1), A(2), A(3), and A(4). It is important that these labels are correctly identified with the actual levels of the independent variable—in this case, A(1) is 12 sec, A(2) is 24 sec, A(3) is 36 sec, and A(4) is 48 sec.

The summary table begins with a clear label indicating that this is a within-subjects analysis. This label is important because the body of the summary table looks just like the one for the analysis of independent groups designs experiments. The F-ratio is still made up of a numerator reflecting potential systematic variation and a denominator reflecting only error variation. As we described in Chapter 7, however, the error variation in the repeated measures designs is different from the error variation in the independent groups designs.

In the repeated measures designs, error variation reflects the residual variation after the variation due to the independent variable and the variation due to subjects have been subtracted from the total variation in the analysis. This is a good illustration of why statistical programs should not be used "blind." That is, the person doing the analysis must understand the nature of the analysis before trying to interpret the computer output. The computer does well the computing it is programmed to do. It is you, however, who have to interpret the output of these computations.

The summary table for the single-factor within-subjects design includes the familiar columns of Source, Sum of Squares, Degrees of Freedom, Mean Square, F, and Probability (see the single-factor independent groups design in this appendix if these terms are not familiar). The DF for the Interval source of variation is determined by subtracting 1 from the number of levels of the interval length variable (i.e., $4 - 1 = 3$). The DF for the error term (residual variation) is usually determined in the following way. The first step is to determine the total DF. In this experiment there was a total of 5 subjects with four time estimates for each subject for a total of 20 scores to be analyzed. The Total DF, therefore, is 19 ($20 - 1$). The DF for error is obtained by subtracting from the total DF the DF for Interval (3) and the DF for Subjects ($5 - 1 = 4$). The resulting DF for error is 12 ($19 - 3 - 4$). Neither Subjects Variation nor the Total Variation appears in the SYSTAT summary table because neither is essential to computing the F-ratio for Interval. To understand the summary table well, however, it is important to know that the sources of variation presented in the SYSTAT summary table may not represent all the sources of variation in the experiment.

The probability associated with the obtained F-ratio of 15.555 is less than the conventional level of significance of .05 so we would conclude that the effect of the interval length variable as statistically significant. The subjects' time estimates did change with increasing interval length. The means of the median time estimates for the 12, 24, 36, and 48 sec intervals were 12.6, 22.0, 38.0, 39.4, respectively.

There are two additional columns in this output for the single-factor within-subjects analysis of variance. These columns are labeled "G–G" and "H–F." They reflect two corrections for evaluating the statistical significance of a within-subjects F-ratio that are called the Greenhouse-Geisser and Huynh-Feldt corrections (see Keppel, 1991). Because of certain characteristics of the repeated measures analysis of variance there is a greater likelihood of making a Type I error (rejecting the null hypothesis when it is true). The Greenhouse-Geisser and Huynh-Feldt corrections represent two ways of trying to compensate for the increased likelihood of a Type I error. As you can see, the corrections have led to larger probabilities in the last two columns than the one in column P. In this case, however, all three probabilities are less than the conventional level of significance of .05 so they lead to the same conclusion—the F-ratio is statistically significant.

Appropriate use of corrections for the Type I error rates in the analysis of repeated measures designs is a topic typically covered in graduate-level statistics classes. Their appearance on this SYSTAT summary table illustrates an important point about the use of statistical software packages. The statistical packages are designed to serve users with varying degrees of sophistication regarding methodological and statistical issues. It is likely that less sophisticated users will encounter information in the computer output that is unfamiliar. When this occurs, it is important to seek assistance and advice from someone who is an expert in the use of the statistical software package. When it comes to the analysis of data, it is definitely the case that what you don't know can hurt you.

The statistically significant F-test for the overall effect of interval length is an omnibus F-test. As was the case in the analysis of independent groups designs experiments, analytical comparisons can be used to identify the source of the effect of an independent variable more specifically. In the repeated measures designs the Residual Mean Square can be used as the error term for analytical comparisons (see Keppel, 1991, for more specific guidelines regarding appropriate error terms for analytical comparisons).

One common type of analytical comparison that is used for repeated measures within-subjects designs is called trend analysis. Trend analysis is used to determine whether the effect of an independent variable can best be described as linear or nonlinear. Trend analysis was used in the analysis of our time-perception experiment, and the trend analysis showed that the changes in subjects' time estimates with increasing interval lengths were best described as linear. The important point is that trend analysis represents a type of analytical comparison. As such, trend analysis allows a much more specific conclusion to be drawn than is possible based only on an omnibus F-test.

TWO-FACTOR ANALYSIS OF VARIANCE FOR INDEPENDENT GROUPS DESIGNS

The two-factor analysis of variance for independent groups designs is used for the analysis of experiments in which each of two independent variables has been manipulated at at least two levels. The logic of complex designs with two independent variables and the conceptual basis for the analysis of these experiments are described in Chapter 8. We focus in this appendix on the computer-assisted analysis of a complex design which involves an F-test for the main effect of A, the main effect of B, and the interaction effect, A × B. Our example involves a significant A × B interaction, and so we also illustrate the computations for a simple main effect. The two-factor analysis for independent groups is applicable to experiments in which both independent variables are manipulated using a random groups design, in which both independent variables represent the natural groups design, and in which one independent variable represents the natural groups design and the other represents the random groups design. In the last section of this appendix we describe the computations for a mixed design in which one independent variable represents an independent-groups design and the second independent variable represents a repeated measures design.

The data in the following table represent the number of correct responses on a simple motor learning task as a function of two independent variables. The first independent variable was the hand the subject used to perform the task, and the two levels of this variable were the dominant and the nondominant hand. The second independent variable was the delay (in seconds) between successive trials on the task, and it was manipulated at three levels (0, 30, and 60 seconds). The hand variable will be referred to as A, with the dominant hand being a_1, and the nondominant hand being a_2. The delay variable will be referred to as B with the 0-second delay as b_1, the 30-second delay as b_2, and the 60-second delay as b_3. Five subjects were randomly assigned to each of the six groups resulting from the factorial combination of the two independent variables.

Hand Dominance (Variable A) × Delay Interval (Variable B)

Dominant/0 sec		Dominant/30 sec		Dominant/60 sec	
Subject	a_1b_1	Subject	a_1b_2	Subject	a_1b_3
1	18	6	17	11	18
2	17	7	19	12	20
3	19	8	22	13	21
4	21	9	20	14	22
5	20	10	17	15	19

Nondominant/0 sec		Nondominant/30 sec		Nondominant/60 sec	
Subject	a_2b_1	Subject	a_2b_2	Subject	a_2b_3
16	9	21	15	26	16
17	11	22	17	27	19
18	10	23	16	28	18
19	11	24	17	29	20
20	12	25	14	30	18

The first step in carrying out a computer-assisted analysis of a two-factor analysis of variance is to enter the data matrix like the one in the preceding table into the computer. Typically the data for the three levels of the B variable (in this case, delay) are entered successively for each level of the A variable (in this case, hand dominance). That is, the Dominant/0 second group would be entered first, followed by the Dominant/30 second group, and ending with the Nondominant/60 second group. For this data matrix, therefore, the number of correct responses would be entered in the order of the subject numbers from 1 to 30. Once the data are entered into the computer, the next step is to examine the output for the descriptive statistics for a two-factor experiment.

Two screens are required to contain the output from SYSTAT. These screens show the descriptive statistics for a two-factor analysis of variance using the data for the experiment involving hand dominance and delay. The first set of results, displayed on Screen A.4, are the results for level 1 of hand and level 1 of delay. Once again, it is essential that the actual levels of the independent variables be identified. For this experiment, the first set of results corresponds to the group using their dominant hand with a 0-second delay. The corresponding groups for the results in the middle and at the bottom of Screen A.4 are dominant hand/30-second delay and dominant hand/60-second delay, respectively.

Screen A.4 displays the descriptive statistics for the dominant-hand groups across the three delay groups. Screen A.5 displays the descriptive statistics for the nondominant-hand groups across the three delay groups. Because the type of information provided for each of these six groups is the same, we will describe in detail only the data displayed for the first group on Screen A.4. The two columns headed Hand and Delay indicate the respective levels of these

SCREEN A.4

```
THE FOLLOWING RESULTS ARE FOR:
            HAND      =        1.000
            DELAY     =        1.000
TOTAL OBSERVATIONS:         5
                        RESPONSE      HAND        DELAY
    N OF CASES              5           5            5
       MINIMUM          17.000       1.000        1.000
       MAXIMUM          21.000       1.000        1.000
       MEAN             19.000       1.000        1.000
       STANDARD DEV      1.581       0.000        0.000

THE FOLLOWING RESULTS ARE FOR:
            HAND      =        1.000
            DELAY     =        2.000
TOTAL OBSERVATIONS:         5
                        RESPONSE      HAND        DELAY
    N OF CASES              5           5            5
       MINIMUM          17.000       1.000        2.000
       MAXIMUM          22.000       1.000        2.000
       MEAN             19.000       1.000        2.000
       STANDARD DEV      2.121       0.000        0.000

THE FOLLOWING RESULTS ARE FOR:
            HAND      =        1.000
            DELAY     =        3.000
TOTAL OBSERVATIONS:         5
                        RESPONSE      HAND        DELAY
    N OF CASES              5           5            5
       MINIMUM          18.000       1.000        3.000
       MAXIMUM          22.000       1.000        3.000
       MEAN             20.000       1.000        3.000
       STANDARD DEV      1.581       0.000        0.000
```

two independent variables in each group. The column headed Response is the most critical column. Entries in this column represent values on the dependent variable, in this case, number of correct responses (abbreviated as Response). The number of cases (5) is shown first, indicating that five subjects provided scores on the dependent variable in this group. The minimum and maximum scores in the group are shown in the next two rows; the minimum number correct in this group was 17 and the maximum was 21. The difference between these two indicates the range of scores in this group (see measures of dispersion earlier in this appendix). The minimum and maximum values can also be useful in identifying basement and ceiling effects (see Chapter 8) when the absolute minimum and maximum possible values in the experiment are known.

The most important descriptive statistic is the next one listed for the first group, the mean (19). It is the means for the six groups that are used to describe what happened in the experiment. These means should be summarized in a table or a figure (see Chapter 8 and Appendix C) before examining the analysis of variance summary table. It is also a good idea to use the raw data to check the computations of these means to be sure of their accuracy and to be sure the

SCREEN A.5

```
THE FOLLOWING RESULTS ARE FOR:
           HAND      =      2.000
           DELAY     =      1.000
TOTAL OBSERVATIONS:        5
                        RESPONSE      HAND        DELAY
      N OF CASES           5            5            5
        MINIMUM          9.000        2.000        1.000
        MAXIMUM         12.000        2.000        1.000
        MEAN            10.600        2.000        1.000
        STANDARD DEV     1.140        0.000        0.000

THE FOLLOWING RESULTS ARE FOR:
           HAND      =      2.000
           DELAY     =      2.000
TOTAL OBSERVATIONS:        5
                        RESPONSE      HAND        DELAY
      N OF CASES           5            5            5
        MINIMUM         14.000        2.000        2.000
        MAXIMUM         17.000        2.000        2.000
        MEAN            15.800        2.000        2.000
        STANDARD DEV     1.304        0.000        0.000

THE FOLLOWING RESULTS ARE FOR:
           HAND      =      2.000
           DELAY     =      3.000
TOTAL OBSERVATIONS:        5
                        RESPONSE      HAND        DELAY
      N OF CASES           5            5            5
        MINIMUM         16.000        2.000        3.000
        MAXIMUM         20.000        2.000        3.000
        MEAN            18.200        2.000        3.000
        STANDARD DEV     1.483        0.000        0.000
```

data have been entered into the computer properly. The table of means and the analysis-of-variance summary table are the essential tools needed to interpret the results of a factorial experiment.

The last descriptive statistic displayed for the first group is the standard deviation. The standard deviation provides helpful information about the variation in each group. Looking across the six groups displayed on the two screens, we can see that the largest standard deviation was in the dominant hand/30-second delay group (2.121) and the smallest standard deviation was in the non-dominant hand/0-second delay group (1.14). The small difference between these two values indicates that there was little difference in the amount of variation across the six groups in the experiment. The fact that the largest standard deviation in any group was just over two correct responses indicates that there was not much variation within any of the six groups. We are now ready to examine the analysis-of-variance summary table for our two-factor experiment to see if there were any statistically significant sources of variation.

Screen A.6 displays the output from the SYSTAT program for a two-factor analysis of variance for independent groups. At the top of the screen we have added a table of means for the experiment being analyzed. This table is based on the two screens of descriptive statistics with which we were just working, but it is not part of the output from SYSTAT. The actual output begins with the heading "LEVELS ENCOUNTERED DURING PROCESSING ARE:" near the middle of the screen. We included the table of means to make it easier to understand the interpretation of the summary table. The means indicate that there was little change in the number of correct responses as a function of delay for the dominant-hand groups. For the nondominant-hand groups, however, there was an apparent change across the three levels of delay. With this pattern of results in mind, we can turn to the analysis-of-variance summary table.

The output from SYSTAT near the middle of Screen A.6 begins by displaying that there were two levels of the independent variable of hand and three levels of the independent variable of delay encountered in the processing of the analysis. The presence of more than one independent variable marks this as a multifactor design, and the levels of the independent variables indicate that it is a 2×3 design. The next line of the output begins by indicating that the name of the dependent variable is Response (shorthand for number of correct responses). On that same line the total N of 30 is shown; the total N results from there being 5 subjects in each of the six groups of the experiment. The multiple R and the squared multiple R are indicated at the end of the same line. As we said in our description of the analysis of the single-factor analysis of variance for independent groups, the multiple Rs are related to regression analysis which is not directly related to the interpretation of the analysis of variance summary table.

The analysis of variance summary table for a two-factor design is shown in the lower third of the screen. In a single-factor experiment only one independent variable can be a potential source of systematic variation in an experiment. In a two-factor design, there are three sources of potential systematic variation: the main effect of each independent variable and the interaction of the two in-

```
TABLE OF MEANS
                              DELAY
HAND                 0          30          60
DOMINANT           19.0        19.0        20.0
NONDOMINANT        10.6        15.8        18.2


LEVELS ENCOUNTERED DURING PROCESSING ARE:

HAND      1.000      2.000
DELAY     1.000      2.000       3.000


DEP VAR:RESPONSE N:30 MULTIPLE R:0.915 SQUARED MULTIPLE R:0.838

                     ANALYSIS OF VARIANCE
SOURCE      SUM-OF-SQUARES   DF    MEAN-SQUARE   F-RATIO     P

HAND            149.633       1       149.633    61.075    0.000
DELAY            93.800       2        46.900    19.143    0.000
HAND * DELAY     60.467       2        30.233    12.340    0.000

ERROR            58.800      24         2.450
```

SCREEN A.6

dependent variables (see Chapter 8). These three sources of potential systematic variation are reflected in the summary table as the first three entries in the source column. The main effect of hand appears first, then the main effect of delay, and finally, the interaction of the two independent variables. The interaction of the two appears on the screen as HAND*DELAY; more typically interactions are written as Hand X Delay. Much more critical than the form of the notation for interactions is that interactions represent an important new dimension made possible by multifactor experiments. Interactions allow us to determine whether the effect of one independent variable differs depending on the level of a second independent variable. The final source of variation is a familiar one. The error variation that is used in the computation of the Fs for the two main effects and for the interaction is the variation within groups in the experiment.

The degrees of freedom for each independent variable are determined in the same way as in a single-factor experiment, namely, the number of levels of the variable minus 1. Since there were two levels of the hand variable and three levels of the delay variable, the corresponding DF for these variables are 1 and 2, respectively (as is indicated in the DF column of the summary table). The degrees of freedom for the interaction of the two variables are obtained by multiplying the DF for the two variables. The DF shown in the summary table for HAND*DELAY is 2 (1×2). The DF for the within-groups error is determined in the usual way by computing the DF within each group (number of subjects minus 1; in this case, $5 - 1 = 4$) and multiplying by the number of groups. Thus, the DF for error in the summary table is 24 (4×6).

The three F-ratios in a two-factor design have the same form as when the experiment involves only a single-factor in the independent groups designs. The Mean Square Error is used as the denominator for all three F-tests. The Mean Square for each main effect and for the interaction are used as the numerators for three independent F-ratios. The three F-ratios appear in the summary table in the F-RATIO column. It is best to evaluate the F-ratio for the interaction first (see Chapter 8). The obtained probability of less than one in a thousand for the F of 12.34 for the interaction is less than the conventional level of significance of .05. So, we can conclude that the interaction was statistically significant. A statistically significant interaction indicates that the effect of the delay variable was different as a function of which hand was used. The pattern in the table of means at the top of the screen indicates the nature of the interaction. The delay variable had less of an effect on the groups using their dominant hand than on those using their nondominant hand. In the next section we describe simple main effects, a type of analysis that can be used to specify the nature of an interaction even better.

After examining the interaction effect, the two main effects should be examined. The F-ratio for the main effect of hand was 61.075, with a probability of less than one in a thousand. Because the probability is less than the conventional level of significance of .05, the main effect of hand was statistically significant. The means for this main effect can be obtained by averaging across the columns of the table at the top of the screen, thereby computing a mean for the dominant hand of 19.3 and for the nondominant hand of 14.9. These means along with the statistically significant F-test indicate that those working with their dominant hand made more correct responses than those working with their nondominant hand. The F-ratio for the main effect of delay was 19.143, with a probability of less than one in a thousand. As was true for the main effect of hand, this probability is less than the conventional level of significance of .05, and thus the main effect of delay was statistically significant. The means for the main effect of delay are obtained by averaging across the rows of the table of means at the top of the screen. These three means for the main effect of delay are 14.8, 17.4, and 19.1 for the 0, 30, and 60 second delays, respectively. These means and the accompanying statistically significant F-test for the main effect of delay indicate that the number of correct responses increased with increasing delay. Analytical comparisons could be used to specify the nature of the changes as a function of delay more precisely.

ILLUSTRATION OF SIMPLE MAIN EFFECTS

Simple main effects are used in the analysis of two-factor designs to identify more specifically the nature of statistically significant interactions (see Chapter

8). A simple main effect involves the overall effect of one independent variable at one level of a second independent variable. Statistical software packages vary as to whether they include the computation of simple main effects. We illustrate the computation using calculations that can be done with a calculator. For these computations we use the data for the three delay groups who used their nondominant hand. These data are in the bottom half of the data matrix near the beginning of the section on the analysis of the two-factor design for independent groups. This simple main effect would be referred to as the effect of delay at the nondominant hand (or more generally, the effect of variable B at A2). We first present the computations and then briefly describe the interpretation of simple main effects.

Computing the simple main effect of B at a_2 (B/a_2).

1 Compute SS_{B/a_2}
$$= \frac{(\Sigma X_{a_2 b_1})^2 + (\Sigma X_{a_2 b_2})^2 + (\Sigma X_{a_2 b_3})^2}{n}$$
$$- \frac{(\Sigma X_{a_2 b_1} + \Sigma X_{a_2 b_2} + \Sigma X_{a_2 b_3})^2}{(b)(n)}$$

$$= \frac{(53)^2 + (79)^2 + (91)^2}{5} - \frac{(53 + 79 + 91)^2}{(3)(5)}$$

$$= \frac{2,809 + 6,241 + 8,281}{5} - \frac{(223)^2}{15}$$

$$= \frac{17,331}{5} - \frac{49,729}{15}$$

$$= 3,466.20 - 3,315.27 = 150.93$$

2 Compute $df_{B/a_2} = b - 1 = 3 - 1 = 2$

3 Compute $MS_{B/a_2} = \dfrac{SS_{B/a_2}}{df_{B/a_2}} = \dfrac{150.93}{2} + 75.47$

4 Compute $F (df_{B/a_2}, df_{WG}) = \dfrac{MS_{B/a_2}}{MS_{WG}} = \dfrac{75.47}{2.45} = 30.80$

The final computation of the F-ratio involved the use of the Mean Square Error (within groups) from the SYSTAT output for the two-factor design shown on Screen A.6. The computations of all the other values needed to compute a simple main effect are shown in the four steps we have outlined. As with any F-test, it is necessary to determine the probability of the F under the null hypothesis. The obtained $F (2, 24) = 30.8$ is associated with a probability of less than one in a thousand which is less than the conventional level of significance of .05. Thus, the simple main effect of delay at the level of nondominant hand was statistically significant. Although we will not illustrate the computations here, we did compute the simple main effect of delay for those subjects using their dominant hand. The resulting F (2, 24) was .68. An F-ratio less than 1 cannot be statistically significant so this nonsignificant simple main effect indicates that there was no effect of delay when subjects used their dominant hand.

Together, the two simple main effects help us to specify the source of the statistically significant interaction of delay and hand dominance. As described in Chapter 8, the source of an interaction can be specified even more exactly by using simple comparisons to follow up statistically significant simple main effects.

TWO-FACTOR ANALYSIS OF VARIANCE FOR A MIXED DESIGN

The two-factor analysis of variance for a mixed design is appropriate when one independent variable represents either the random groups or natural groups design and the second independent variable represents the repeated measures (within-subjects) design. The first independent variable is called the *between-subjects factor* and is symbolized as A. The second independent variable is typically called the *within-subjects factor* and is symbolized as B. The two-factor analysis for a mixed design is somewhat of a hybrid of the single-factor analysis for independent groups and the single-factor analysis for the repeated measures (within-subjects) designs.

The data presented in the following table represent the mean frequency judgments subjects gave to four brief segments of popular songs. The subjects listened to a tape including several songs; half the subjects did not expect the frequency judgment test (incidental group), and half did expect the test (intentional group). In addition, all subjects judged songs that had been presented either one, two, or three times. Thus, the experiment was a 2×3 design in which instructions were manipulated in a random groups design with five subjects assigned to each of two groups and in which the presented frequency variable was manipulated in a repeated measures design. The following data matrix shows the mean frequency judgments at three levels of presentation frequency for each subject in each group.

		Presentation Frequency (B)		
	Subject	1(b_1)	2(b_2)	3(b_3)
	1	1.2	2.2	3.0
	2	.8	2.0	3.2
Incidental	3	1.2	1.8	2.8
group (a_1)	4	1.5	2.0	2.5
	5	1.2	2.5	3.2
Group (A)				
	6	1.2	1.5	2.0
	7	1.0	2.0	2.5
Intentional	8	1.0	1.2	3.2
group (a_2)	9	1.2	2.2	2.8
	10	1.0	2.2	3.5

The 30 scores in the data matrix were entered into the SYSTAT program for a two-factor analysis of variance for a mixed design. The output from the program is presented in Screen A.7. The output begins by indicating that there were ten cases (i.e., 10 subjects) in the analysis. The next portion of the output presents the means for the three levels of the presentation (frequency) variable. These means describe the main effect of the presentation variable, and they are presented because this main effect was the only statistically significant effect in the analysis. Means for the main effect of group and for the interaction could be obtained by running the descriptive statistics program on SYSTAT or by computing the means directly from the data matrix. It is important to examine the means for both statistically significant and nonsignificant effects.

The summary table in Screen A.7 is divided into two parts. The Between Subjects section includes the *F*-test for the main effect of groups. The form of this part of the table is like that of a single-factor analysis for the independent groups design. The Error listed in this section is the within-groups variation.

SCREEN A.7

NUMBER OF CASES PROCESSED: 10
DEPENDENT VARIABLE MEANS

	PRESENT(1)	PRESENT(2)	PRESENT(3)
	1.130	1.960	2.870

BETWEEN SUBJECTS

SOURCE	SS	DF	MS	F	P
GROUP	0.225	1	0.225	1.718	0.226
ERROR	1.049	8	0.131		

WITHIN SUBJECTS

SOURCE	SS	DF	MS	F	P	G—G	H—F
PRESENT	15.149	2	7.574	58.640	0.000	0.000	0.00
PRESENT *GROUP	0.045	2	0.022	0.173	0.843	0.810	0.84
ERROR	2.067	16	0.129				

GREENHOUSE—GEISSER EPSILON: 0.8539
HUYNH—FELDT EPSILON   :   1.0000

The F-ratio for the effect of group was not statistically significant since the obtained probability of .226 was greater than the conventional level of statistical significance of .05.

The second part of the summary table in Screen A.7 is headed Within Subjects. It includes the main effect of the within-subjects variable of presentation frequency and the interaction of presentation frequency and group. In general, any effect including a repeated measures (within-subjects) variable (main effect or interaction) must be tested with the residual error term used in the repeated measures (within-subjects) design. The F-ratio for the interaction is less than 1 and so was not statistically significant. The main effect of presentation frequency, however, did result in a statistically significant F. As was true in the analysis of the single-factor repeated measures design, the SYSTAT output for the analysis of the mixed design provides corrected probability values for effects that include a repeated measures factor. The Greenhouse-Geisser and the Huynh-Feldt corrections attempt to adjust for the higher probability of a Type I error in the repeated measures design (see Keppel, 1991, for more details about these corrections).

The two-factor analysis for a mixed design follows the logic for any complex design (see Chapter 8). That is, the interaction is examined first, and if the interaction is statistically significant, then simple main effects and simple comparisons are used to identify the source of the interaction. The main effects are then examined, and analytical comparisons can be used to analyze further statistically significant main effects of independent variables with more than two levels. Care must be taken, however, when analyzing a mixed design to use the appropriate error term for analyses beyond those listed in the summary table (i.e., simple main effects, simple comparisons, and analytical comparisons). It is fitting that we end this appendix by encouraging you to seek expert advice when facing this or any other challenge in the analysis of your research findings.

STATISTICAL TABLES

TABLE A.1   TABLE OF RANDOM NUMBERS*

Col. Line	(1)	(2)	(3)	(4)	(5)	(6)	(7)	(8)	(9)	(10)	(11)	(12)	(13)	(14)
1	10480	15011	01536	02011	81647	91646	69179	14194	62590	36207	20969	99570	91291	90700
2	22368	46573	25595	85393	30995	89198	27982	53402	93965	34095	52666	19174	39615	99505
3	24130	48360	22527	97265	76393	64809	15179	24830	49340	32081	30680	19655	63348	58629
4	42167	93093	06243	61680	07856	16376	39440	53537	71341	57004	00849	74917	97758	16379
5	37570	39975	81837	16656	06121	91782	60468	81305	49684	60672	14110	06927	01263	54613
6	77921	06907	11008	42751	27756	53498	18602	70659	90655	15053	21916	81825	44394	42880
7	99562	72905	56420	69994	98872	31016	71194	18738	44013	48840	63213	21069	10634	12952
8	96301	91977	65463	07972	18876	20922	94595	56869	69014	60045	18425	84903	42508	32307
9	89579	14342	63661	10281	17453	18103	57740	84378	25331	12566	58678	44947	05585	56941
10	85475	36857	53342	53988	53060	59533	38867	62300	08158	17983	16439	11458	18593	64952

(continued)

TABLE A.1   TABLE OF RANDOM NUMBERS* (continued)

Col. Line	(1)	(2)	(3)	(4)	(5)	(6)	(7)	(8)	(9)	(10)	(11)	(12)	(13)	(14)
11	28918	69578	88231	33276	70997	79936	56865	05859	90106	31595	01547	85590	91610	78188
12	63553	40961	48235	03427	49626	69445	18663	72695	52180	20847	12234	90511	33703	90322
13	09429	93969	52636	92737	88974	33488	36320	17617	30015	08272	84115	27156	30613	74952
14	10365	61129	87529	85689	48237	52267	67689	93394	01511	26358	85104	20285	29975	89868
15	07119	97336	71048	08178	77233	13916	47564	81506	97735	85977	29372	74461	28551	90707
16	51085	12765	51821	51259	77452	16308	60756	92144	49442	53900	70960	63990	75601	40719
17	02368	21382	52404	60268	89368	19885	55322	44819	01188	65255	64835	44919	05944	55157
18	01011	54092	33362	94904	31273	04146	18594	29852	71585	85030	51132	01915	92747	64951
19	52162	53916	46369	58586	23216	14513	83149	98736	23495	64350	94738	17752	35156	35749
20	07056	97628	33787	09998	42698	06691	76988	13602	51851	46104	88916	19509	25625	58104
21	48663	91245	85828	14346	09172	30168	90229	04734	59193	22178	30421	61666	99904	32812
22	54164	58492	22421	74103	47070	25306	76468	26384	58151	06646	21524	15227	96909	44592
23	32639	32363	05597	24200	13363	38005	94342	28728	35806	06912	17012	64161	18296	22851
24	29334	27001	87637	87308	58731	00256	45834	15298	46557	41135	10367	07684	36188	18510
25	02488	33062	28834	07351	19731	92420	60952	61280	50001	67658	32586	86679	50720	94953
26	81525	72295	04839	96423	24878	82651	66566	14778	76797	14780	13300	87074	79666	95725
27	29676	20591	68086	26432	46901	20849	89768	81536	86645	12659	92259	57102	80428	25280
28	00742	57392	39064	66432	84673	40027	32832	61362	98947	96067	64760	64584	96096	98253
29	05366	04213	25669	26422	44407	44048	37937	63904	45766	66134	75470	66520	34693	90449
30	91921	26418	64117	94305	26766	25940	39972	22209	71500	64568	91402	42416	07844	69618
31	00582	04711	87917	77341	42206	35126	74087	99547	81817	42607	43808	76655	62028	76630
32	00725	69884	62797	56170	86324	88072	76222	36086	84637	93161	76038	65855	77919	88006
33	69011	65795	95876	55293	18988	27354	26575	08625	40801	59920	29841	80150	12777	48501
34	25976	57948	29888	88604	67917	48708	18912	82271	65424	69774	33611	54262	85963	03547
35	09763	83473	93577	12908	30883	18317	28290	35797	05998	41688	34952	37888	38917	88050
36	91567	42595	27958	30134	04024	86385	29880	99730	55536	84855	29080	09250	79656	73211
37	17955	56349	90999	49127	20044	59931	06115	20542	18059	02008	73708	83517	36103	42791
38	46503	18584	18845	49618	02304	51038	20655	58727	28168	15475	56942	53389	20562	87338
39	92157	89634	94824	78171	84610	82834	09922	25417	44137	48413	25555	21246	35509	20468
40	14577	62765	35605	81263	39667	47358	56873	56307	61607	49518	89696	20103	77490	18062
41	98427	07523	33362	64270	01638	92477	66969	98420	04880	45585	46565	04102	46880	45709
42	34914	63976	88720	82765	34476	17032	87589	40836	32427	70002	70663	88863	77775	69348
43	70060	28277	39475	46473	23219	53416	94970	25832	69975	94884	19661	72828	00102	66794
44	53976	54914	06990	67245	68350	82948	11398	42878	80287	88267	47363	46634	06541	97809
45	76072	29515	40980	07391	58745	25774	22987	80059	39911	96189	41151	14222	60697	59583
46	90725	52210	83974	29992	65831	38857	50490	83765	55657	14361	31720	57375	56228	41546
47	64364	67412	33339	31926	14883	24413	59744	92351	97473	89286	35931	04110	23726	51900
48	08962	00358	31662	25388	61642	34072	81249	35648	56891	69352	48373	45578	78547	81788
49	95012	68379	93526	70765	10592	04542	76463	54328	02349	17247	28865	14777	62730	92277
50	15664	10493	20492	38391	91132	21999	59516	81652	27195	48223	46751	22923	32261	85653

*Source: Table of 105,000 Random Decimal Digits, Starement no. 4914, File no. 261-A-1, Interstate Commerce Commission, Washington, D.C. May 1949.

TABLE A.2 VALUES OF *r* AT THE .05 AND .01 LEVELS OF SIGNIFICANCE*

df	.05	.01	df	.05	.01	df	.05	.01
1	.997	1.000	16	.468	.590	35	.325	.418
2	.950	.990	17	.456	.575	40	.304	.393
3	.878	.959	18	.444	.561	45	.288	.372
4	.811	.917	19	.433	.549	50	.273	.354
5	.754	.874	20	.423	.537	60	.250	.325
6	.707	.834	21	.413	.526	70	.232	.302
7	.666	.798	22	.404	.515	80	.217	.283
8	.632	.765	23	.396	.505	90	.205	.267
9	.602	.735	24	.388	.496	100	.195	.254
10	.576	.708	25	.381	.487			
11	.553	.684	26	.374	.478			
12	.532	.661	27	.367	.470			
13	.514	.641	28	.361	.463			
14	.497	.623	29	.355	.456			
15	.482	.606	30	.349	.449			

*Adapted from Table VII of Fisher and Yates, *Statistical Tables for Biological, Agricultural, and Medical Research,* 6th ed., 1974. Published by Oliver and Boyd, Limited, Publishers, Edinburgh, by permission of the authors and publishers. Published by Longman Group Ltd., London.

TABLE A.3 VALUES OF RANK-ORDER CORRELATION COEFFICIENT (r_s) AT THE .05 AND .01 LEVELS OF SIGNIFICANCE*

N	.05	.01
5	1.000	—
6	.886	1.000
7	.786	.929
8	.715	.881
9	.700	.834
10	.649	.794
12	.588	.735
14	.539	.680
16	.503	.636
18	.474	.600
20	.447	.570
22	.426	.544
24	.407	.521
26	.391	.501
28	.376	.484
30	.363	.467

*Adapted from Table 1 (p. 385) of McCall, R. B. (1980). *Fundamental Statistics for Psychology,* 3d ed., Harcourt, Brace, Jovanovich. Reproduced by permission of publisher.

TABLE A.4 CRITICAL VALUES OF THE CHI SQUARE (χ^2) DISTRIBUTION*

Instructions for use: To find the critical value of χ^2, locate the row in the left-hand column of the table corresponding to the number of degrees of freedom (df) associated with χ^2, and select the value of χ^2 listed for the desired level of significance (α).

df	$\alpha = .05$	$\alpha = .01$	df	$\alpha = .05$	$\alpha = .01$
1	3.84	6.63	16	26.30	32.00
2	5.99	9.21	17	27.59	33.41
3	7.81	11.34	18	28.87	34.81
4	9.49	13.28	19	30.14	36.19
5	11.07	15.09	20	31.41	37.57
6	12.59	16.81	21	32.67	38.93
7	14.07	18.48	22	33.92	40.29
8	15.51	20.09	23	35.17	41.64
9	16.92	21.67	24	36.42	42.98
10	18.31	23.21	25	37.65	44.31
11	19.68	24.72	26	38.89	45.64
12	21.03	26.22	27	40.11	46.96
13	22.36	27.69	28	41.34	48.28
14	23.68	29.14	29	42.56	49.59
15	25.00	30.58	30	43.77	50.89

*This table is abridged from Table 8 in *Biometrika tables for statisticians,* vol. 1 (3d ed.), New York: Cambridge University Press, 1970, edited by E. S. Pearson and H. O. Hartley, by permission of the *Biometrika* Trustees.

TABLE A.5 SELECTED VALUES FROM THE *t* DISTRIBUTION*

Instructions for use: To find a value of *t*, locate the row in the left-hand column of the table corresponding to the number of degrees of freedm (df) associated with the standard error of the mean, and select the value of *t* listed for your choice of α. The value given in the column labeled $\alpha = .05$ is used in the calculation of the 95 percent confidence interval, and the value given in the column labeled $\alpha = .01$ is used to calculate the 99 percent confidence interval.

df	$\alpha = .05$	$\alpha = .01$	df	$\alpha = .05$	$\alpha = .01$
1	12.71	63.66	18	2.10	2.88
2	4.30	9.92	19	2.09	2.86
3	3.18	5.84	20	2.09	2.84
4	2.78	4.60	21	2.08	2.83
5	2.57	4.03	22	2.07	2.82
6	2.45	3.71	23	2.07	2.81
7	2.36	3.50	24	2.06	2.80
8	2.31	3.36	25	2.06	2.79
9	2.26	3.25	26	2.06	2.78
10	2.23	3.17	27	2.05	2.77
11	2.20	3.11	28	2.05	2.76
12	2.18	3.06	29	2.04	2.76
13	2.16	3.01	30	2.04	2.75
14	2.14	2.98	40	2.02	2.70
15	2.13	2.95	60	2.00	2.66
16	2.12	2.92	120	1.98	2.62
17	2.11	2.90	Infinity	1.96	2.58

*This table is adapted from Table 12 in *Biometrika tables for statisticians,* vol. 1 (3d ed.), New York: Cambridge University Press, 1970, edited by E. S. Pearson and H. O. Hartley, by permission of the *Biometrika* Trustees.

TABLE A.6 CRITICAL VALUES OF THE *F*-DISTRIBUTION*

Instructions for use: To find the critical value of *F*, locate the cell in the table formed by the intersection of the row containing the degrees of freedom associated with the denominator of the *F*-ratio and the column containing the degrees of freedom associated with the numerator of the *F*-ratio. The numbers listed in boldface type are the critical values of *F* at α = .05; the numbers listed in Roman type are the critical values of *F* at α = .01. As an example, suppose we have adopted the 5 percent level of significance and wish to evaluate the significance of an *F* with df_{num} = 2 and df_{denom} = 12. From the table we find that the critical value of $F(2, 12)$ = 3.89 at α = .05. If the obtained value of *F* equals or exceeds this critical value, we will reject the null hypothesis; if the obtained value of *F* is smaller than this critical value, we will not reject the null hypothesis.

Degrees of freedom for numerator

	1	2	3	4	5	6	7	8	9	10	12	15	20	24	30	40	60	Infinity
1	**161**	**200**	**216**	**225**	**230**	**234**	**237**	**239**	**241**	**242**	**244**	**246**	**248**	**249**	**250**	**251**	**252**	**254**
	4052	4999	5403	5625	5764	5859	5928	5981	6022	6056	6106	6157	6209	6325	6261	6287	6313	6366
2	**18.5**	**19.0**	**19.2**	**19.2**	**19.3**	**19.3**	**19.4**	**19.4**	**19.4**	**19.4**	**19.4**	**19.4**	**19.4**	**19.4**	**19.5**	**19.5**	**19.5**	**19.5**
	98.5	99.0	99.2	99.2	99.3	99.3	99.4	99.4	99.4	99.4	99.4	99.4	99.4	99.5	99.5	99.5	99.5	99.5
3	**10.1**	**9.55**	**9.28**	**9.12**	**9.01**	**8.94**	**8.89**	**8.85**	**8.81**	**8.79**	**8.74**	**8.70**	**8.66**	**8.64**	**8.62**	**8.59**	**8.57**	**8.53**
	34.1	30.8	29.5	28.7	28.2	27.9	27.7	27.5	27.4	27.2	27.0	26.9	26.7	26.6	26.5	26.4	26.3	26.1
4	**7.71**	**6.94**	**6.59**	**6.39**	**6.26**	**6.16**	**6.09**	**6.04**	**6.00**	**5.96**	**5.91**	**5.86**	**5.80**	**5.77**	**5.75**	**5.72**	**5.69**	**5.63**
	21.2	18.0	16.7	16.0	15.5	15.2	15.0	14.8	14.7	14.6	14.4	14.2	14.0	13.9	13.8	13.8	13.6	13.5
5	**6.61**	**5.79**	**5.41**	**5.19**	**5.05**	**4.95**	**4.88**	**4.82**	**4.77**	**4.74**	**4.68**	**4.62**	**4.56**	**4.53**	**4.50**	**4.46**	**4.43**	**4.26**
	16.3	13.3	12.1	11.4	11.0	10.7	10.5	10.3	10.2	10.0	9.89	9.72	9.55	9.47	9.38	9.29	9.20	9.02
6	**5.99**	**5.14**	**4.76**	**4.53**	**4.39**	**4.28**	**4.21**	**4.15**	**4.10**	**4.06**	**4.00**	**3.94**	**3.87**	**3.84**	**3.81**	**3.77**	**3.74**	**3.67**
	13.8	10.9	9.78	9.15	8.75	8.47	8.26	8.10	7.98	7.87	7.72	7.56	7.40	7.31	7.23	7.14	7.06	6.88
7	**5.59**	**4.74**	**4.35**	**4.12**	**3.97**	**3.87**	**3.79**	**3.73**	**3.68**	**3.64**	**3.57**	**3.51**	**3.44**	**3.41**	**3.38**	**3.34**	**3.30**	**3.23**
	12.2	9.55	8.45	7.85	7.46	7.19	6.99	6.84	6.72	6.62	6.47	6.31	6.16	6.07	5.99	5.91	5.82	5.65
8	**5.32**	**4.46**	**4.07**	**3.84**	**3.69**	**3.58**	**3.50**	**3.44**	**3.39**	**3.35**	**3.28**	**3.22**	**3.15**	**3.12**	**3.08**	**3.04**	**3.01**	**2.93**
	11.3	8.65	7.59	7.01	6.63	6.37	6.18	6.03	5.91	5.81	5.67	5.52	5.36	5.28	5.20	5.12	5.03	4.86
9	**5.12**	**4.26**	**3.86**	**3.63**	**3.48**	**3.37**	**3.29**	**3.23**	**3.18**	**3.14**	**3.07**	**3.01**	**2.94**	**2.90**	**2.86**	**2.83**	**2.79**	**2.71**
	10.6	8.02	6.99	6.42	6.06	5.80	5.61	5.47	5.35	5.26	5.11	4.96	4.81	4.73	4.65	4.57	4.48	4.31
10	**4.96**	**4.10**	**3.71**	**3.48**	**3.33**	**3.22**	**3.14**	**3.07**	**3.02**	**2.98**	**2.91**	**2.85**	**2.77**	**2.74**	**2.70**	**2.66**	**2.62**	**2.54**
	10.0	7.56	6.55	5.99	5.64	5.39	5.20	5.06	4.94	4.85	4.71	4.56	4.41	4.33	4.25	4.17	4.08	3.91
11	**4.84**	**3.98**	**3.59**	**3.36**	**3.20**	**3.09**	**3.01**	**2.95**	**2.90**	**2.85**	**2.79**	**2.72**	**2.65**	**2.61**	**2.57**	**2.53**	**2.49**	**2.40**
	9.65	7.21	6.22	5.67	5.32	5.07	4.89	4.74	4.63	4.54	4.40	4.25	4.10	4.02	3.94	3.86	3.78	3.60
12	**4.75**	**3.89**	**3.49**	**3.26**	**3.11**	**3.00**	**2.91**	**2.85**	**2.80**	**2.75**	**2.69**	**2.62**	**2.54**	**2.51**	**2.47**	**2.43**	**2.38**	**2.30**
	9.33	6.93	5.95	5.41	5.06	4.82	4.64	4.50	4.39	4.30	4.16	4.01	3.86	3.78	3.70	3.62	3.54	3.36
13	**4.67**	**3.81**	**3.41**	**3.18**	**3.03**	**2.92**	**2.83**	**2.77**	**2.71**	**2.67**	**2.60**	**2.53**	**2.46**	**2.42**	**2.38**	**2.34**	**2.30**	**2.21**
	9.07	6.70	5.74	5.21	4.86	4.62	4.44	4.30	4.19	4.10	3.96	3.82	3.66	3.59	3.51	3.43	3.34	3.17
14	**4.60**	**3.74**	**3.34**	**3.11**	**2.96**	**2.85**	**2.76**	**2.70**	**2.65**	**2.60**	**2.53**	**2.46**	**2.39**	**2.35**	**2.31**	**2.27**	**2.22**	**2.13**
	8.86	6.51	5.56	5.04	4.69	4.46	4.28	4.14	4.03	3.94	3.80	3.66	3.51	3.43	3.35	3.27	3.18	3.00
15	**4.54**	**3.68**	**3.29**	**3.06**	**2.90**	**2.79**	**2.71**	**2.64**	**2.59**	**2.54**	**2.48**	**2.40**	**2.33**	**2.29**	**2.25**	**2.20**	**2.16**	**2.07**
	8.68	6.36	5.42	4.89	4.56	4.32	4.14	4.00	3.89	3.80	3.67	3.52	3.37	3.29	3.21	3.13	3.05	2.87
16	**4.49**	**3.63**	**3.24**	**3.01**	**2.85**	**2.74**	**2.66**	**2.59**	**2.54**	**2.49**	**2.42**	**2.35**	**2.28**	**2.24**	**2.19**	**2.15**	**2.11**	**2.01**
	8.53	6.23	5.29	4.77	4.44	4.20	4.03	3.89	3.78	3.69	3.55	3.41	3.26	3.18	3.10	3.02	2.93	2.75
17	**4.45**	**3.59**	**3.20**	**2.96**	**2.81**	**2.70**	**2.61**	**2.55**	**2.49**	**2.45**	**2.38**	**2.31**	**2.23**	**2.19**	**2.15**	**2.10**	**2.06**	**1.96**
	8.40	6.11	5.18	4.67	4.34	4.10	3.93	3.79	3.68	3.59	3.46	3.31	3.16	3.08	3.00	2.92	2.83	2.65
18	**4.41**	**3.55**	**3.16**	**2.93**	**2.77**	**2.66**	**2.58**	**2.51**	**2.46**	**2.41**	**2.34**	**2.27**	**2.19**	**2.15**	**2.11**	**2.06**	**2.02**	**1.92**
	8.29	6.01	5.09	4.58	4.25	4.01	3.84	3.71	3.60	3.51	3.37	3.23	3.08	3.00	2.92	2.84	2.75	2.57
19	**4.38**	**3.52**	**3.13**	**2.90**	**2.74**	**2.63**	**2.54**	**2.48**	**2.42**	**2.38**	**2.31**	**2.23**	**2.16**	**2.11**	**2.07**	**2.03**	**1.98**	**1.88**
	8.18	5.93	5.01	4.50	4.17	3.94	3.77	3.63	3.52	3.43	3.30	3.15	3.00	2.92	2.84	2.76	2.67	2.49
20	**4.35**	**3.49**	**3.10**	**2.87**	**2.71**	**2.60**	**2.51**	**2.45**	**2.39**	**2.35**	**2.28**	**2.20**	**2.12**	**2.08**	**2.04**	**1.99**	**1.95**	**1.84**
	8.10	5.85	4.94	4.43	4.10	3.87	3.70	3.56	3.46	3.37	3.23	3.09	2.94	2.86	2.78	2.69	2.61	2.42
22	**4.30**	**3.44**	**3.05**	**2.82**	**2.66**	**2.55**	**2.46**	**2.40**	**2.34**	**2.30**	**2.23**	**2.15**	**2.07**	**2.03**	**1.98**	**1.94**	**1.89**	**1.78**
	7.95	5.72	4.82	4.31	3.99	3.76	3.59	3.45	3.35	3.26	3.12	2.98	2.83	2.75	2.67	2.58	2.50	2.31
24	**4.26**	**3.40**	**3.01**	**2.78**	**2.62**	**2.51**	**2.42**	**2.36**	**2.30**	**2.25**	**2.18**	**2.11**	**2.03**	**1.98**	**1.94**	**1.89**	**1.84**	**1.73**
	7.82	5.61	4.72	4.22	3.90	3.67	3.50	3.36	3.26	3.17	3.03	2.89	2.74	2.66	2.58	2.49	2.40	2.21

Degrees of freedom for denominator

(continued)

TABLE A.6   CRITICAL VALUES OF THE *F*-DISTRIBUTION* (*continued*)

		1	2	3	4	5	6	7	8	9	10	12	15	20	24	30	40	60	Infinity
		\multicolumn{18}{Degrees of freedom for numerator}																	
Degrees of freedom for denominator	26	4.23	3.37	2.98	2.74	2.59	2.47	2.39	2.32	2.27	2.22	2.15	2.07	1.99	1.95	1.90	1.85	1.80	1.69
		7.72	5.53	4.64	4.14	3.82	3.59	3.42	3.29	3.18	3.09	2.96	2.81	2.66	2.58	2.50	2.42	2.33	2.13
	28	4.20	3.34	2.95	2.71	2.56	2.45	2.36	2.29	2.24	2.19	2.12	2.04	1.96	1.91	1.87	1.82	1.77	1.65
		7.64	5.45	4.57	4.07	3.75	3.53	3.36	3.23	3.12	3.03	2.90	2.75	2.60	2.52	2.44	2.35	2.26	2.06
	30	4.17	3.32	2.92	2.69	2.53	2.42	2.33	2.27	2.21	2.16	2.09	2.01	1.93	1.89	1.84	1.79	1.74	1.62
		7.56	5.39	4.51	4.02	3.70	3.47	3.30	3.17	3.07	2.98	2.84	2.70	2.55	2.47	2.39	2.30	2.21	2.01
	40	4.08	3.23	2.84	2.61	2.45	2.34	2.25	2.18	2.12	2.08	2.00	1.92	1.84	1.79	1.74	1.69	1.64	1.51
		7.31	5.18	4.31	3.83	3.51	3.29	3.12	2.99	2.89	2.80	2.66	2.52	2.37	2.29	2.20	2.11	2.02	1.80
	60	4.00	3.15	2.76	2.53	2.37	2.25	2.17	2.10	2.04	1.99	1.92	1.84	1.75	1.7	1.65	1.59	1.53	1.39
		7.08	4.98	4.13	3.65	3.34	3.12	2.95	2.82	2.72	2.63	2.50	2.35	2.20	2.12	2.03	1.94	1.84	1.60
	120	3.92	3.07	2.68	2.45	2.29	2.17	2.09	2.02	1.96	1.91	1.83	1.75	1.66	1.61	1.55	1.50	1.43	1.25
		6.85	4.79	3.95	3.48	3.17	2.96	2.79	2.66	2.56	2.47	2.34	2.19	2.03	1.95	1.86	1.76	1.66	1.38
	INFINITY	3.84	3.00	2.60	2.37	2.21	2.10	2.01	1.94	1.88	1.83	1.75	1.67	.57	1.52	1.46	1.39	1.32	1.00
		6.63	4.61	3.78	3.32	3.02	2.80	2.64	2.51	2.41	2.32	2.18	2.04	1.88	1.79	1.70	1.59	1.47	1.00

*This table is abridged from Table 18 in *Biometrika tables for statisticians*, vol. 1 (3d ed.), New York: Cambridge University Press, 1970, edited by E. S. Pearson and H. O. Hartley, by permission of the *Biometrika* Trustees.

Questionnaire Construction

INTRODUCTION

In Chapter 4 we discussed procedures for administering a survey without describing in detail the nature of the most common survey-research instrument, the questionnaire. Even if the sample used was perfectly representative, the response rate was 100%, and the research design was elegantly planned and perfectly executed, the results of a survey will be useless if the questionnaire was poorly constructed. Although nothing substitutes for experience when it comes to preparing a good questionnaire, there are a few general principles of sound questionnaire construction with which you should be familiar before you do your first survey. In this appendix we describe six basic steps in preparing a questionnaire and then offer some more specific guidelines for writing and administering individual questions. This material will be most useful should you decide to make use of a questionnaire as part of a research project you are doing.

STEPS IN PREPARING A QUESTIONNAIRE

Six basic steps in preparing a questionnaire are listed in Table B.1. The warning "Watch out for that first step!" is appropriate here. The first step in questionnaire construction, deciding what information is to be sought, should actually be the first step in planning the survey as a whole. This decision, of course, determines the nature of the questions to be included in the questionnaire. It is important to project the likely results of the survey if the proposed questionnaire is used and then to decide whether these findings will answer the questions the study is intended to address. Surveys are frequently done under con-

TABLE B.1   SIX BASIC STEPS IN PREPARING A QUESTIONNAIRE

1 Decide what information should be sought.
2 Decide what type of questionnaire should be used.
3 Write a first draft of the questionnaire.
4 Reexamine and revise the questionnaire.
5 Pretest the questionnaire.
6 Edit the questionnaire and specify the procedures for its use.

siderable time pressure, and inexperienced researchers are especially prone to impatience. Just remember that a poorly conceived questionnaire takes just as much time and effort to administer and analyze as a well-conceived one. The difference is that a well-constructed questionnaire leads to interpretable results. The best we can say for a poorly designed instrument is that it is a good way to learn how important careful deliberation is in the planning stages.

Once the information to be sought from respondents has been clearly specified, the next step is to decide on the type of questionnaire to be used. For example, will it be self-administered, or will trained interviewers be using it? This decision is determined primarily by the survey method you have selected. For instance, for a telephone survey, trained interviewers will be needed. In designing the questionnaire, also consider using items that have been prepared by other researchers. There is no reason to develop your own instrument to assess racial prejudice if a reliable and valid one is already available. Besides, if you use items from a questionnaire that has already been used, you can compare your results directly with those of earlier studies.

If you decide that no available instrument suits your needs, you will have to take the third step and write a first draft of your own questionnaire. We present guidelines concerning the format and ordering of questions, as well as suggestions for wording questions effectively, in later sections of this appendix.

The fourth step in questionnaire construction, reexamining and rewriting, is essential. Questions that appear objective and unambiguous to you may strike others as slanted and ambiguous. It is most helpful to have your questionnaire reviewed by experts, both those who have knowledge of survey-research methods and those with expertise in the area on which your study is focused. For example, if you are doing a survey of students' attitudes toward the campus food service, it would be advisable to have your questionnaire reviewed by the campus food service director. When you are dealing with a controversial topic, ask representatives of both sides of the issue to screen your questions for possible bias. Sometimes no one particular wording can be agreed on by all. In such cases, the *split-ballot technique* is helpful. In this technique, different wordings of the same questions are used for equivalent samples of respondents. The effect of the wording can be directly examined by comparing responses made in these two (or more) samples. For example, Schuman and Bobo (1988) used the split-ballot technique to embed randomized experiments within their survey design. Their overall objective was to examine the opposition of Whites to the rights of Blacks to open housing. They used the split-ballot technique to assign subgroups within their samples randomly to different versions of questions. Comparing the responses of these subgroups led to the identification of factors that affect attitudes toward open housing, factors such as people's general resistance to government coercion.

By far the most critical step in the development of a sound questionnaire is step 5, the pretest. A pretest involves actually administering the questionnaire to a small sample of respondents under conditions as much as possible like those to be used in the final administration of the survey. Pretest respondents must also be typical of those to be included in the final sample; it makes little sense to pretest a survey of nursing home residents by administering the questionnaire to college students. There is one way, however, in which a pretest does differ from the final administration of the survey. Respondents should be interviewed at length regarding their reactions to individual questions and to the questionnaire as a whole. This provides information about potentially ambiguous or offensive items.

The pretest should also serve as a dress rehearsal for interviewers, who should be closely supervised during this stage to ensure that they understand and adhere to the proper procedures for administering the questionnaire. If major changes have to be made as a result of problems arising during the pretest, a second pretest may be needed to determine whether these changes solved the problems originally encountered. After pretesting is completed, the final step is to edit the questionnaire and specify the procedures to be followed in its final administration.

In the next two sections, we return to two issues pertinent to the third step in preparing a questionnaire—writing a first draft. We consider two sets of guidelines: one for writing questions and one for the general format of a questionnaire.

GUIDELINES FOR THE EFFECTIVE WORDING OF QUESTIONS

Lawyers have long known that how a question is phrased has great impact on how that question is answered. Survey researchers need to be equally conscious of this principle. This point is illustrated in a survey Loftus (1979a) conducted for the manufacturer of a leading headache remedy. She found that people reported having more headaches when they were asked, "Do you get headaches frequently and, if so, how often?" than when they were asked, "Do you get headaches occasionally and, if so, how often?" Unfortunately, the extent of the influence of the wording of questions in a given survey can almost never be determined precisely. The problem is clearer than the solution. Schuman and Scott (1987) argue that investigators should realize the limitations on assessing, in an absolute sense, people's opinions or attitudes based on any one set of questions. They encourage researchers to emphasize participants' responses to the same set of questions over time. At a minimum, the exact wording of critical questions should always be reported along with the data describ-

APPENDIX B: QUESTIONNAIRE CONSTRUCTION

ing respondents' answers. The problem of the potential influence of the wording of questions is yet another illustration of why a multimethod approach is so essential in investigating behavior.

There are certain guidelines to follow to minimize problems arising from the phrasing of survey questions. These guidelines can be applied to *free-response* (open-ended) questions and to *closed* (multiple-choice) questions. Free-response questions, like the essay questions on a classroom test, merely specify the area to be addressed in a response. For example, the question "What are your views on the legalizing of abortion?" is a free-response question. By contrast, closed questions provide specific response alternatives. "Is police protection very good, fairly good, neither good nor bad, not very good, or not good at all?" is a closed question about the quality of police protection in a community.

The advantages of free-response questions are that they can be written more quickly and offer the respondent greater flexibility. However, these advantages are often more than offset by the difficulties that arise in recording and scoring responses to free-response questions. For example, extensive coding is frequently necessary before rambling responses to free-response questions can be summarized succinctly. Closed questions, on the other hand, are more difficult to write, but they can be answered more easily and quickly and fewer scoring problems arise. It is also much easier to summarize responses to closed questions because the answers are readily comparable across respondents. A major disadvantage of closed questions is that they reduce expressiveness and spontaneity. Further, the possibility exists that the respondent will have to choose a less than preferred response because no presented alternative really captures his or her views. Hence, the responses obtained may not accurately reflect the respondent's opinion.

Newcomb, Koenig, Flacks, and Warwick (1967) used both free-response and closed questions in a survey of students' attitudes. Their survey was done in two stages. In the first stage, student respondents were asked a series of free-response questions about how their lives had changed as a result of attending college. The trained interviewers used probes extensively and effectively in this stage. A self-administered questionnaire was then developed for the second stage of the survey. During this second stage, a different sample of students rated how much they had changed in each of a number of areas. The researchers wrote closed questions for the second stage of the survey using specific areas of change that had been indicated in the answers to the original set of free-response questions. This survey illustrates the complementary strengths of free-response and closed questions. The findings of the survey showed that one area in which change did occur was in the students' political views. What is more, these changes were shown to persist well after the students had left college.

Closed questions frequently include a scale that is used to measure the degree or amount of response to the question. A typical scale would include the categories "strongly agree," "agree," "neutral," "disagree," and "strongly disagree." Alternatively, degree of response can be measured by asking respondents to rank several alternatives from "most preferred" to "least preferred." The scale using strength of agreement is an illustration of category scaling. The scale ranking preferences is an illustration of rank-order scaling. Rank-order scaling has the advantage that it forces the respondent to make discriminations among alternatives. Rank-order scaling is thus more sensitive in measuring differences that respondents can detect.

But rank-order scaling is not informative about the absolute judgment of any one alternative. For example, respondents could rank the beauty of 15 photographs even if they judged all the photographs to be ugly; they could reliably identify the least ugly (most beautiful) of the group even if they judged them all to be ugly. If they were asked to use category scaling to rate the beauty of the photographs, it would be possible to measure the absolute level of rated beauty of each photograph. It would also be possible to interpret the relative distances between the ratings for different photographs, something not possible with rank-order scaling. (The winner and runner-up in a race can be decided in a photo finish or "by a mile," and the winner will still be first and the runner-up second.) The ability to obtain absolute judgments and to interpret distances between ratings are the primary advantages of category scaling. The major disadvantage is that respondents may fail to make discriminations they are capable of making. They may, for example, give the same rating of beauty to all the photographs. In general, rank-order scaling is preferred if the researcher is interested in relative preferences; category scaling is preferred if the researcher is interested in the absolute level of the respondents' reactions.

Several characteristics of good questionnaire items are listed in Table B.2. For instance, regardless of the type of question used, the vocabulary should be simple, direct, and familiar to all respondents. Questions should be as clear and specific as possible. Double-barreled questions should be avoided, for example, "Have you suffered from headaches and nausea recently?" A person may respond "no" if both symptoms have not occurred at exactly the same time or may respond "yes" if either symptom has occurred. The solution to the problem of double-barreled questions is a simple one—rewrite them as separate questions. Survey questions should be as short as possible without sacrificing the clarity of the questions' meaning. Twenty or fewer words should suffice for most survey questions. Each question should be carefully edited for readability and phrased in such a way that all conditional information precedes the key

TABLE B.2   GOOD QUESTIONNAIRE ITEMS SHOULD:

1 Include vocabularly that is simple, direct, and familiar to all respondents.
2 Be clear and specific.
3 *Not* involve leading, loaded, or double-barreled questions.
4 Be as short as possible (20 or fewer words).
5 Include all conditional information prior to the key idea.
6 Be edited for readability.

idea. For example, it would be better to ask, "If you were forced to leave your present job, what type of work would you seek?" than to ask, "What type of work would you seek if you were forced to leave your present job?"

Leading or loaded questions should also be avoided in a questionnaire. *Leading questions* take the form "Most people favor the use of nuclear energy. What do you think?" To avoid bias, it is better to mention all possible perspectives or to mention none. A survey question about attitudes toward nuclear energy could read either "Some people favor the use of nuclear energy, some people oppose the use of nuclear energy, and some people have no opinion one way or the other. What do you think?" or "What do you think about the use of nuclear energy?" *Loaded questions* are questions that contain emotion-laden words. For example, terms such as *radical* and *racist* should be avoided. To guard against loaded questions, ask individuals representing a range of social and political perspectives to review your questionnaire.

GUIDELINES FOR THE GENERAL FORMAT OF A QUESTIONNAIRE

Two aspects of the general format should be considered in constructing the final copy of a questionnaire: the design or layout of the questionnaire and the ordering of questions.

DESIGN

Try to make the design of the questionnaire attractive, but focus on making it as easy as possible to use.

A section of a questionnaire designed for personal or phone interviews is shown in Table B.3. This questionnaire was used by trained interviewers in a survey done by the Institute for Social Research at the University of Michigan. The aim of the survey was to examine the quality of American life (Campbell, Converse, & Rodgers, 1975). Several characteristics of this questionnaire are noteworthy. Each question is identified with a letter indicating the section of the questionnaire and a number specifying the individual question. This is done to facilitate later scoring and analysis of responses. The arrangement of the questions on each page is compact, but the structure is designed to make it easy to read the questions and to record responses. Whenever possible, questions with the same response format appear together. When closed questions are asked, a note is included to remind the interviewer to give the respondent a card listing the response alternatives so the respondent can concentrate on the question and not on remembering the alternatives. At the beginning of the first question, the respondent is given a brief rationale for the study as a whole, but this preamble is kept short so as to require as little of the respondent's time as possible.

The format of a questionnaire that is meant to be self-administered must be somewhat different. The first section of a self-administered questionnaire distributed to passengers on Amtrak trains is shown in Table B.4. The items are

TABLE B.3 SAMPLE QUESTIONNAIRE FORMAT FOR PERSONAL OR PHONE INTERVIEW

Section A: City and Neighborhood

A1 In this study we are interested in measuring the quality of life of people in this country—that is, the things people like and dislike about their homes, cities, neighborhoods, jobs, and so on. The first question is: How long have you lived in (INSERT NAME OF COMMUNITY, OR OF COUNTY IF RURAL)? _____. (IF *LESS* THAN TWO YEARS, GET NUMBER OF MONTHS.)

_____ YEARS _____ MONTHS, OR SINCE_____

A2 And how long have you lived here in this (house/apartment)? (IF *LESS* THAN TWO YEARS, GET NUMBER OF MONTHS.)

_____ YEARS _____ MONTHS, OR SINCE_____

A3 I'd like to ask how satisfied you are with some of the main public services you are supposed to receive. (Hand R CARD 1, YELLOW) Please tell me how you feel about each thing I mention, using one of the answers on this card. First, how about the way streets and roads are kept up around here. Would you say this service is *very good, fairly good, neither good nor bad, not very good,* or *not good at all?*

1. VERY GOOD	2. FAIRLY GOOD	3. NEITHER GOOD NOR BAD	4. NOT VERY GOOD	5. NOT GOOD AT ALL

A4 How do you feel about the quality of the *public* schools that the children from around here go to—would you say it is *very good, fairly good, neither good nor bad, not very good,* or *not good at all?* [DK is don't know.]

1. VERY GOOD	2. FAIRLY GOOD	3. NEITHER GOOD NOR BAD	4. NOT VERY GOOD	5. NOT GOOD AT ALL	8. DK

> IF R LIVES IN A CITY, TOWN, OR VILLAGE, ASK A5 AND A6: IF RURAL, TURN TO A7

A5 How good is garbage collection in this neighborhood? Is it *very good, fairly good, neither good nor bad, not very good,* or *not good at all?* [DK is don't know.]

1. VERY GOOD	2. FAIRLY GOOD	3. NEITHER GOOD NOR BAD	4. NOT VERY GOOD	5. NOT GOOD AT ALL	8. DK

A6 What about the parks and playgrounds for children in this neighborhood? Are they *very good, fairly good, neither good nor bad, not very good,* or *not good at all?* [DK is don't know.]

1. VERY GOOD	2. FAIRLY GOOD	3. NEITHER GOOD NOR BAD	4. NOT VERY GOOD	5. NOT GOOD AT ALL	8. DK

> ASK EVERYBODY:

A7 How about police protection around here. Is it *very good, fairly good, neither good nor bad, not very good,* or *not good at all?* [DK is don't know.]

1. VERY GOOD	2. FAIRLY GOOD	3. NEITHER GOOD NOR BAD	4. NOT VERY GOOD	5. NOT GOOD AT ALL	8. DK

TABLE B.4   SAMPLE FORMAT FOR SELF-ADMINISTERED QUESTIONNAIRE

Illinois Department of Transportation
Survey of Amtrak Passengers

> Dear Amtrak Passenger:
>
> The Illinois Department of Transportation is conducting a study of rail passenger service on the Chicago-St. Louis corridor to determine what improvements should be made to upgrade service on this route. This survey is designed to identify the preferences and travel needs of passengers on Amtrak trains. Your cooperation in filling out this questionnaire will be greatly appreciated.
>
> A Department representative will collect the survey when you have finished. If you leave your seat before the representative returns, kindly leave the questionnaire on your seat. If you have filled out this survey previously, please take a few minutes to answer questions 1 through 7 and 21 through 26.
>
> Have an enjoyable trip and thank you for your cooperation.

1 Please check the station where you boarded this train and the station where you will get off.

Station	Boarded	Will Get Off
Chicago	____ 01 (1–6)	____ 01(7–8)
Joliet	____ 02	____ 02
Pontiac	____ 03	____ 03
Bloomington	____ 04	____ 04
Lincoln	____ 05	____ 05
Springfield	____ 06	____ 06
Carlinville	____ 07	____ 07
Alton	____ 08	____ 08
St. Louis	____ 09	____ 09
Points in Missouri	____ 10	____ 10
Points in Arkansas	____ 11	____ 11
Points in Texas	____ 12	____ 12

2 Please indicate how you reached the station to board this train and how you will reach your next destination after you get off this train. (Check as many as apply.)

	To Station Where You Got On	From Station Where You Will Get off
Automobile	____ 01 (9–11)	____ 01(12–14)
Taxi	____ 02	____ 02
City Bus	____ 03	____ 03
Airline	____ 04	____ 04
Commuter Train	____ 05	____ 05
Amtrak Train	____ 06	____ 06
Amtrak Shuttle	____ 07	____ 07
Intercity Bus	____ 08	____ 08
Walker	____ 09	____ 09
Other	____ 10	____ 10

3 Is your car parked at or near an Amtrak Station during this trip?
Yes _____ 15.1   No _____ 15.2

4 What is the zip code of the place you left to get to this train? (If zip code is unknown, the city and a nearby major street intersection will be sufficient.)
Zip Code _____
$\overline{16}\ \overline{17}\ \overline{18}\ \overline{19}\ \overline{20}$
OR: City _____
Street
Intersection _____
_____

5 What is the zip code (or city and nearby street intersection) of the place where you will be going upon leaving this train?
Zip Code _____
$\overline{21}\ \overline{22}\ \overline{23}\ \overline{24}\ \overline{25}$
OR: City _____
Street
Intersection _____
_____

6 Which one of the following best describes the main purpose of this trip? (Mark only one)

26-1 _____ Business or work
  2 _____ Vacation or recreation
  3 _____ Travel to or from school
  4 _____ Personal business
  5 _____ Shopping
  6 _____ Visit family or friends
  7 _____ Entertainment/Spectator sport
  8 _____ Other (Please specify) _____

7 How long before the departure time of this train did you leave for the station?

27-1 _____ 10–15 minutes
  2 _____ 16–30 minutes
  3 _____ 31–45 minutes
  4 _____ 46–60 minutes
  5 _____ more than 1 hour

arranged in a clear and uncluttered manner, and the order of the questions is clearly indicated by the large boldface numbers. Each item is short and direct, and the instructions for each question are simple. The small numbers next to each blank are used to computer-code the responses. The numbers in parentheses indicate column numbers in a computer file, and the other numbers are the ones to be entered if the respondent checks that blank. Such prior coding saves time when the data are to be analyzed and helps reduce the number of errors in data entry. In designing a self-administered questionnaire, spare no effort to make it visually appealing; visual appeal increases the response rate. The questions should be self-explanatory and respondents must be able to complete the questionnaire quickly and correctly.

Certain procedures should be followed in a mail survey to enhance response rate. For instance, the initial mailing should include a letter summarizing the purpose of the survey, explaining the basis on which the respondents were selected, and assuring the respondents of confidentiality. A postage-paid return envelope should also be included along with the questionnaire. As questionnaires are returned, the researcher should plot a cumulative response rate graph. Numbering the returned questionnaires in the order received allows researchers to make comparisons such as that between early and late respondents. Plateaus in the cumulative response rate graph indicate that a follow-up mailing should be sent. To obtain a high response rate, it is often necessary to send three mailings. These should be spaced about 2 to 3 weeks apart or when a plateau appears on the cumulative response rate graph. Because the original copy is likely to have been lost, a new copy of the questionnaire should be sent with each mailing.

ORDERING OF QUESTIONS

A crucial issue in deciding the order of the questions in a survey is which question or questions to ask first. The first few questions set the tone for the rest of the questionnaire and determine how willingly and conscientiously respondents will work on subsequent questions. For example, it is best to begin self-administered questionnaires with the most interesting set of questions in order to capture the respondent's attention. Demographic data should be obtained at the end of a self-administered questionnaire. In surveys involving personal or telephone interviews, on the other hand, demographic questions are frequently asked at the beginning because they are easy for the respondent to answer and thus bolster the respondent's confidence. They also allow time for the interviewer to establish rapport before asking questions about more sensitive matters.

The order in which particular questions are asked can have dramatic effects, as illustrated in a study by Schuman, Presser, and Ludwig (1981). They found differential responding depending on the order of two questions concerning abortion, one general and one specific. The general question was "Do you think it should be possible for a pregnant woman to obtain a legal abortion if she is married and does not want any more children?" The more specific question was "Do you think it should be possible for a pregnant woman to obtain a legal abortion if there is a strong chance of a serious defect in the baby?" When the general question was asked first, 60.7% of respondents said "yes," but when the general question followed the specific question, only 48.1% of respondents said "yes." The corresponding values for the specific question were 84% and 83% agreement in the first and second positions, respectively. The generally accepted method for dealing with this problem is to use *funnel questions,* proceeding from the most general to the most specific when ordering the questions pertaining to a given topic.[1]

Problems resulting from the order of questions can also arise when several questions on the same topic are asked, all at the same level of specificity. For example, we might ask a series of questions regarding a person's views about several minority groups. Our interest might be in how the person's responses differ for the various minority groups. But responses could also be affected by the sequence in which the various questions were asked within each of the minority groups. A person's reaction to one question, for example, might influence how the next question is interpreted. Effects due to the order in which such questions are asked can be handled in one of two ways. The first technique is to use exactly the same order for all samples to be compared, thus holding the effect of order constant. This technique does not allow us to determine what the effects of order were. Alternatively, many different orders of the questions might be used within each of the samples to be compared, thus neutralizing the effect of order. We discuss this problem of dealing with order effects much more fully in Chapter 7.

The final aspect of the ordering of survey questions that we consider is the use of *filter questions,* general questions asked of respondents to find out whether they need to be asked more specific questions. For example, the question "Do you own a car?" might precede a series of questions about the costs of maintaining a car. In this instance, the respondents would answer the specific questions only if their response to the general question was "yes." If that answer was "no," the interviewer would not ask the specific questions (in a self-administered questionnaire, the respondent would be instructed to skip that section). When the filter questions involve objective information ("Are you over 65?"), their use is relatively straightforward. Caution must be exercised, however, in using behavioral or attitudinal questions as filter questions. Smith (1981) first asked respondents whether they approved of hitting another person in "any situations you can imagine." Logically, a negative response to this most general question should imply a negative response to any more specific

---

[1]Oppenheim (1966) describes in detail the question-wording plan developed by Gallup called the Quintamensional Plan of Question Design. The first step is to ask the respondent whether he or she has thought about the issue at all. This is followed by open-ended questions about general feelings and closed questions about specific aspects of the issue. The fourth step involves asking for the respondent's reasons for the views he or she holds. Finally, the interviewer inquires how strongly the respondent's views are held.

questions. Nonetheless, over 80% of the people who responded "no" to the general question then reported that they approved of hitting another person in specific situations, such as in self-defense. Although findings such as this suggest that filter questions should be used cautiously, the need to demand as little of the respondent's time as possible makes filter questions an essential tool in the design of effective questionnaires.

Communication in Psychology

Outline

Scientific research is a public activity. A clever hypothesis, an elegant research design, meticulous data collection procedures, reliable results, and an insightful theoretical interpretation of the findings are not useful to the scientific community unless they are made public. As one writer suggests most emphatically, "Until its results have gone through the painful process of publication, preferably in a refereed journal of high standards, scientific research is just play. Publication is an indispensable part of science" (Bartholemew, 1982, p. 233). Bartholemew expresses a preference for refereed journals because they involve the process of peer review. Submitted manuscripts are reviewed by other researchers who are experts in the specific field addressed in the paper. These peer reviewers decide whether the research is methodologically sound and makes a substantive contribution to the discipline of psychology. The reviews are then submitted to a senior researcher who serves as editor of the journal. It is the editor's job to decide which papers warrant publication. Peer review is the primary method of quality control for published psychological research.

There are many journals in which psychologists can publish their research. *Memory & Cognition, Child Development, Journal of Personality and Social Psychology,* and *Journal of Clinical and Consulting Psychology* are but a few of the many psychology journals. As we mentioned, editors of these journals make the final decisions about which manuscripts will be published. Their decisions are based on (1) the quality of the research, and (2) the effectiveness of its presentation in the written manuscript, as assessed by the editor and the peer reviewers. Thus, both content and style are important. Editors seek the best research, clearly described. The editors of the 24 primary journals of the American Psychological Association reviewed about 6,000 manuscript submissions per year in the early 1990s. Journal editors set rigorous standards; only about one of every four submitted manuscripts is accepted for publication (American Psychological Association, 1995).

Editorial review and the publication process take a long time. As long as a year or more can elapse between submission of a paper and publication. The review of the manuscript can take three to six months before a decision whether to accept the paper is made. Another seven to eight months is required for the production process between the time the paper is accepted and when it is actually published in the journal. To provide a more timely means of reporting research findings, professional societies such as the American Psychological Association, the American Psychological Society, the Psychonomic Society, the Society for Research in Child Development, and regional societies such as the Eastern, Midwestern, Southeastern, and Western Psychological Associations sponsor conferences at which researchers give brief oral presentations or present posters describing their recent work. Such conferences provide an opportunity for timely discussion and debate among investigators interested in the same research questions.

Researchers often must obtain financial support in the form of a grant from a government or private agency in order to carry out their research. These grants are typically awarded on the basis of a competitive review of research proposals. Because these proposals are written before the research is actually done, they require a slightly different style and format from a journal article that reports results of a completed study.

What do journal articles, oral presentations, and research proposals have to do with you? If you attend graduate school in psychology, you will probably have to describe your research using all three of these types of scientific communication. Even if you do not pursue a professional career in psychology, the principles of good written and oral research reports apply to a wide variety of employment situations. For example, a memo to your department manager describing the outcome of a recent sale may have much the same content and format as a short journal article. Of more immediate concern, you will likely have to write or deliver a research report in your research methods course. This appendix will help you do it well.

The primary source for scientific writing in psychology is the fourth edition of the *Publication Manual of the American Psychological Association* (1994). Editors and authors use this manual to ensure a consistent style across the many different journals in psychology. An APA journal style was first introduced in a manual published in 1952 as a 60-page supplement in the journal *Psychological Bulletin*. The present form of the publication manual is a book with approximately six times as many pages. It represents a style manual and much more, with chapters on the content and organization of a manuscript, the expression of ideas, APA editorial style, manuscript preparation, manuscript acceptance and production, and APA journals. The publication manual also includes information about ethical issues in scientific writing (see our discussion in Chapter 2) and instructions for submitting manuscripts in electronic form. The authors of the *Publication Manual* (1994) have given good advice regarding how best to use it:

> The *Publication Manual* presents explicit style requirements but acknowledges that alternatives are sometimes necessary; authors should balance the rules of the *Publication Manual* with good judgment. Because the written language of psychology changes more slowly than psychology itself, the *Publication Manual* does not offer solutions for all stylistic problems. In that sense, it is a transitional document: Its style requirements are based on existing scientific literature rather than imposed on the literature. (p. xxiii)

Throughout this appendix we have drawn heavily on the *Publication Manual* (1994).[1] This appendix will help you complete successfully the writing you are likely to be doing in your research methods course. It is not intended as a substitute for the *Publication Manual*. If advanced study in psychology is in your future, we recommend that you add the *Publication Manual* to your personal library. Another resource available from APA that you might find helpful is Gelfand, H., & Walker, C. J. (1994). *Mastering APA style: Student's workbook and training guide.* (You can order both from the American Psychological Association, 750 First Street, N.E., Washington, DC 20002-4242.)

Formal communication among researchers through journal articles and convention presentations is not sufficient to sustain the collaborative nature of science. Informal communication is vital to doing research. Research ideas are often formulated in research team meetings or in conversations with colleagues. Increasingly, researchers are collaborating at a distance using the Internet, one of today's most exciting developments in scientific communication. Researchers are using electronic mail to discuss their research and they are able to access databases on the Internet that make their research more efficient and more extensive. We describe some of the features of the Internet in the next section.

THE INTERNET AND RESEARCH

Are there more deaths from floods or from asthma? How likely are people to die from tornadoes? When people are asked to estimate the frequency of lethal events they often overestimate the true frequency of some type of events (Lichenstein, Slovic, Fischhoff, Layman, & Combs, 1978). Deaths from asthma, for example, are about nine times more likely than deaths from floods, but many people think that floods are more deadly.

A research psychologist set out to investigate the accuracy of people's decision making, following up on the interesting work by Lichenstein et al. However, she wished to update the death statistics to make sure that fre-

---

[1]Copyright © 1994 by the American Psychological Association. Reprinted by permission of the APA. Neither the original nor this reproduction can be republished, photocopied, reprinted, or distributed in any form, without the prior written permission of the APA.

quencies had not changed significantly since the work done in the 1970s. She used the Internet to access the database from the National Center for Health Statistics and obtain information regarding actual deaths from various lethal events in the United States during recent years.

What is the future of clinical psychology in a new managed health-care system? What does research reveal, for example, about the efficacy of short-term therapy approaches relative to more time-intensive (and more costly) approaches? Clinical psychologists participating in a discussion group on the Internet regularly discuss these and other issues pertinent to the field of psychology.

A junior undergraduate psychology major plans to apply to graduate programs in psychology that offer a Ph.D. in the field of cognitive science. She investigates various programs using standard printed sources, such as the American Psychological Association's *Graduate Study in Psychology* (available from APA, Order Dept., P.O. Box 2710, Hyattsville, MD 20784). However, she also searches the Internet via the World Wide Web (WWW) looking for home pages of particular universities in which she is interested. She clicks onto the home page of a school she is considering and finds a list of faculty names (with personal photographs) and their research interests.

A researcher looks over a recent issue of *Psychological Science* (a major printed journal published by the American Psychological Association) to see what's new. She comes across an article discussing a topic directly related to a research project on which her research team is working. The author's Internet address is found on the first page of the published article so she immediately e-mails the author asking for a copy ("reprint") of the article and inquiring about other research the author has done on this topic. In addition to sending the printed article by regular mail, the author of the article communicates via e-mail with the interested researcher. The psychologists begins a regular exchange of ideas about research in this area.

An undergraduate student is a member of a research team headed by an educational psychologist studying problems of illiteracy among high school dropouts. The team involves both undergraduate and graduate students in psychology and education. He is asked to help prepare a bibliography of pertinent research articles for the team to peruse and, perhaps, to be the basis of discussion at meetings of the research team. The student "Telnets" the Educational Research Information Center (ERIC) database and searches for citations related to the team's research topic.

Access to the Internet has already become an indispensable tool for research psychologists. Although mainly used for communication via electronic mail (e-mail), the Internet also serves students and professional psychologists in many other important ways (Azar, 1994b; Kardas & Milford, 1996; Kelley-Milburn &

Milburn, 1995). We describe here only a few of the many ways that the Internet is used by psychologists.

For many researchers, *e-mail* is now their primary means of communication with colleagues, journal editors, research collaborators, directors of granting agencies, and other professionals. In addition, many university faculty members publish their e-mail addresses on course syllabi so students can contact them in this manner. E-mailing is simple, efficient, and convenient. There is no danger of playing phone tag because an e-mail message is simply delivered within minutes to the mailbox of the recipient where it can be found when the recipient accesses it. Replying to an e-mail message is achieved with a few strokes on the computer keyboard. Many researchers regularly list their e-mail addresses along with the usual city and street addresses necessary for regular post office delivery (or what people sometimes call "snail mail"). The authors of your textbook, for example, can be reached via e-mail by sending a message via Internet to:

John J. Shaughnessy (Hope College) at shaughnessy@hope.edu
Eugene B. Zechmeister (Loyola University Chicago) at
ezechme@orion.it.luc.edu

There is also a home page on the WWW dedicated to this textbook, which can be accessed for information about the authors, changes in editions, additional resources for doing psychological research, errors or omissions in the current edition, publisher's address, ordering information, and so on. Visit our page at http://www.luc.edu/depts/psychology/research_methods.html

We are always glad to receive meaningful comments from users of our book. If you find something in the text to praise, please let us hear from you (we like positive reinforcers), but if something is not pleasing to you also let us know, and we'll consider making changes in a future edition. We'd very much like to learn how the Net has served you on a psychological research project.

Discussion groups, called "Listservs," allow interested individuals to communicate with each other about various psychological issues. The group consists of a "list" of "subscribers" who wish to contribute to an ongoing discussion. List members are immediately "served" any message posted by a subscriber. (If the Listserv is large, the number of messages accumulating in your mailbox can be rather daunting. As a consequence, unless regularly attended to and edited, you may find your abilities to keep up with new information seriously challenged.) Listservs on the Internet focus on a wide variety of topics, ranging from addiction to women's studies. The APA plans to create as many as 500 special-interest groups to link researchers around the world (Azar, 1994c). Some Listservs are open to anyone who wishes to take part in the discussion, or who even just want to "lurk" (only passively participate), as many people do who follow the discussion "threads" (a group of messages focusing on a special idea or issue). Other Listservs are open only to individuals with certain credentials (e.g., members of a particular APA division). Information about existing Listservs of interest to psychologists and ways to subscribe have been provided by Kelley-Milburn and Milburn (1995) and Kardas and Milford (1996).

Of particular interest to graduate students in psychology are two discussion groups set up by and for graduate students. These forums allow graduate students to share information about graduate programs, research projects, as well as about postdoctoral and career opportunities.

Discussion Group: APSSCNET, sponsored by the Student Caucus of APS (Fiore, 1994).
  Address: LISTSERV@GIBBS.OIT.UNC.EDU
Discussion group: PSYCGRAD, begun by a clinical psychology student at the University of Ottawa (Azar, 1994c).
  Address: PSYCGRAD@UOTTAWA

Databases on the Internet are just that: collections of information (data) available via an electronic hookup. Our colleague mentioned earlier accessed just one of many available databases when she obtained information from the National Center for Health Statistics. The ERIC database was also mentioned among our introductory examples. Databases related to medicine, alcoholism, and opinion polls are available, to mention but a few (Kelley-Milburn & Milburn, 1995). Many databases are reached by using a Telnet command. Telnetting allows you to connect your computer to a remote site, such as an information center like ERIC. By following the rules laid out for you when you access a site, you can carry out searches and even download information to your own computer. Kardas and Milford (1996) provide useful information about Telnetting.

Electronic journals are here, and more are on their way. Electronic journals such as *Psycholoquy* or *Psyche* can be subscribed to simply by sending the appropriate e-mail message to the host institution (Kelley-Milburn & Milburn, 1995). At that point, you will begin to receive articles in your mailbox to peruse and even to comment on should you have the expertise. Articles submitted to electronic journals for publication are professionally reviewed in the same manner as manuscripts submitted to print journals, but, of course, it is all done via the Internet.

Original research can also be done electronically (Kiesler, Walsh, & Sproull, 1992). Surveys, for example, can be conducted of individuals tied to a specific network or discussion group (Listserv). Respondents usually have the option of replying electronically or printing a copy of the questionnaire and mailing the completed form to the survey administrator. As more and more people become connected to the Internet through commercial systems such as CompuServe or America Online, there exists the potential for administering "treatments" electronically. Kiesler et al., for instance, describe a smoking cessation study carried out with CompuServe users.

WHERE TO BEGIN

How useful you find the Internet in planning and conducting research depends both on your specific needs and on your level of expertise at accessing the Internet. If you are already experienced at using psychology-related information on the Internet, then there isn't much we can tell you. You are already on the cutting edge of what will be the 21st century's main vehicle for information exchange.

If you are not yet "online," then you've got to obtain an Internet or Bitnet account where you can establish an e-mail address. Many universities and collegels provide free access to their full-time students who need only to apply for an account through the institutions's computer center. For those without this advantage, commercial services such as America Online, Delphi, or CompuServe offer access to the Internet for a fee. Once connected, you'll need some basic instruction in sending and receiving e-mail, using "gophers," and accessing WWW. When you have access to the WWW, you might try accessing the home page of either the American Psychological Society or American Psychological Association. You'll learn how to join these organizations if you are not already a member and find a wealth of psychology-related information.

> To access APA via the Web: http://www.apa.org (or http://gopher.apa.org)
> To access APS via the Web: http://psych.hanover.edu/APS

If you are already connected to the Internet and have had some experience using e-mail and searching the Web, then we suggest you broaden your horizons by identifying and searching databases of interest to psychologists. A good introduction is the article by Kelley-Milburn and Milburn (1995) that appeared in *Psychological Science*. Having identified a useful database, try telnetting and then retrieving information to your home computer. Many databases, as well as other sources of interest to psychologists, are listed in various sites on the Internet (Kardas & Milford, 1996). These sites are worth finding to see what's available. Information is expanding all the time, but many sources already exist on the Web to help keep you up to date on recent additions to the "infobahn" (Kardas & Milford, 1996).

GUIDELINES FOR EFFECTIVE WRITING

Learning to write well is like learning to swim, drive a car, or play the piano. Improvement is unlikely to result solely from reading about how the activity is done. A person learns to write well by writing and by getting critical feedback from writing "coaches" (teachers, friends, editors). Lee Cronbach (1992), author of several of the most widely cited articles in the *Psychological Bulletin*, writes:

> My advice must be like the legendary recipe for jugged hare, which begins, "First catch your hare." First, have a message worth delivering. Beyond that, it is care in writing that counts. . . . Rework any sentence that lacks flow or cadence, any sentence in which first-glance reading misplaces the emphasis, and any sentence in which comprehension comes less than instantly to that most knowledgeable of readers, the writer of the sentence. At best, technical writing can aspire to literary virtues—a change of pace from abstract thesis to memorable example, from brisk to easeful, from matter-of-fact to poetic. (p. 391)

Professional writer Jack Ridl provides the first maxim for effective writing: "Write, not assuming that you will be understood, but trying to avoid being misunderstood."

Good writing, like good driving, is best done defensively. Assume that whatever can be misunderstood will be! The first way to avoid being misunderstood is to know your audience. If you assume your readers know more than they actually do, you will leave them confused. If you underestimate your readers, you risk boring them with unnecessary details. Either risk increases the likelihood that what you have written will not be read. But if you must err, it is better to underestimate your readers. For example, when you prepare a research report you might reasonably assume that your intended audience is your instructor. Writing for your instructor might lead you to leave a lot out of your paper because, after all, you assume your instructor knows all that anyway. It would probably be better to consider students in another section of your research methods course as your audience. This might result in your including more detail than necessary, but it will be easier for your instructor to help you learn to edit out the nonessential material than to edit in essential material you have omitted. Whatever audience you choose, make the selection before you begin to write, and keep that audience in mind every step of the way.

A second task before you begin to write is to identify your purpose. The principal purposes of a journal article are to describe and to convince. You want first to describe what you have done and what you have found, and second to convince the reader that your interpretation of these results is an appropriate one. Journal articles fall within the general category of expository writing. Webster's dictionary defines exposition as "discourse designed to convey information or explain what is difficult to understand." The foundation of good expository writing is clarity of thought and expression. The *Publication Manual* (1994) clearly outlines the road to clarity:

> "You can achieve clear communication, which is the prime objective of scientific reporting, by presenting ideas in an orderly manner and by expressing yourself smoothly and precisely. By developing ideas clearly and logically and leading readers smoothly from thought to thought, you make the task of reading an agreeable one. (p. 23)

The *Publication Manual* cites three avenues to clarity:

1 economy of expression,
2 precision, and
3 adherence to grammatical rules.

Economy of expression can best be achieved by saying only what needs to be said. Short words and short sentences are easier for readers to understand. Wordiness can best be eliminated by editing your own writing across successive drafts and asking others to edit drafts of your paper. Another term for precision in using language is *diction,* choosing the right word for what you want to say. The *Publication Manual* contains sage advice regarding diction:

Make certain that every word means exactly what you intend it to mean. Sooner or later most authors discover a discrepancy between their accepted meaning of a term and its dictionary definition. In informal style, for example, *feel* broadly substitutes for *think* or *believe*, but such latitude is not acceptable in scientific style. (p. 28)

Failing to adhere to grammatical rules interferes with clear writing because it distracts the reader and can introduce ambiguity. Chapter 2 of the *Publication Manual* reviews solutions to several common grammatical problems. Economy of expression, precision, and adherence to grammatical rules do not guarantee effective writing. They do, however, greatly increase the likelihood that your writing will be effective.

As a writer you should also strive to choose words and use constructions that acknowledge people fairly and objectively. The American Psychological Association has developed guidelines (*Publication Manual*, 1994) regarding bias in the language authors use:

As a publisher, APA accepts authors' word choices unless those choices are inaccurate, unclear, or ungrammatical. As an organization, APA is committed both to science and to the fair treatment of individuals and groups, and policy requires authors of APA publications to avoid perpetuating demeaning attitudes and biased assumptions about people in their writing. Constructions that might imply bias against persons on the basis of gender, sexual orientation, racial or ethnic group, disability, or age should be avoided. Scientific writing should be free of implied or irrelevant evaluation of the group or groups being studied. (p. 46)

The *Publication Manual* (1994) describes several guidelines to achieve unbiased communication. One is to describe the person or persons at the appropriate level of specificity. For example, the phrase *men and women* is more accurate than the generic term *man* when referring to all human beings. "Chinese Americans" or "Mexican Americans" would be a more specific reference for participants in a study than would be Asian Americans or Hispanic Americans. Another guideline is to be sensitive to the labels we use to refer to people, for example, terms we use to refer to people's racial or ethnic identity. One of the best ways to follow this guideline is to avoid labeling people whenever possible. A label that is perceived by the labeled group as pejorative should never be used. In trying to follow this guideline, remember that preferences for labeling groups of individuals change with time and that people within a group disagree about what label is preferred. A third guideline for avoiding biased communication is to "Write about the people in your study in a way that acknowledges their participation" (p. 49). One way to accomplish this is to describe the people who participated in your study using more descriptive terms such as *college students* or *children* rather than the more impersonal term *subjects*. Active voice is better than passive voice in acknowledging participation: "The students completed the survey" is preferred over "The survey was administered to the students." The *Publication Manual* includes several good applications and illustrations of these guidelines to the labeling of persons based on their gender, sexual orientation, racial and ethnic identity, disabilities, and age.

Finally, the *Publication Manual* provides useful advice about the overall tone of scientific writing:

> Although scientific writing differs in form from literary writing, it need not and should not lack style or be dull. In describing your research, present the ideas and findings directly, but aim for an interesting and compelling manner that reflects your involvement with the problem. (p. 6)

One way to try to achieve an appropriate tone in writing your research reports is to strive to tell a good story about your research. Good research makes for good stories; and well-told stories are good for advancing research.

STRUCTURE OF A RESEARCH REPORT

The structure of a research report serves two major purposes. First, the structure provides an organization that helps the author present a clear description of the research and a convincing interpretation of the findings. In this sense, the structure of a research report parallels the structure of a Shakespearean play in which both the playwright and the audience share certain expectations about what should occur in each act as the play unfolds. For example, the stage is set in the first act, and the climax can be expected in the third act. Similarly, in a research report both author and reader share expectations about the content of each section of the report. Similar to a play, the reader of a research report can expect to find specific information in each section. If you want to know how an experiment was done, you would look in the Method section; if you want information about the statistics used in the study, you would refer to the Results section. The structure is not intended to shackle the playwright or the author. It simply provides a vehicle to make it easier for the audience to focus on the particular point being made in the play or the research report.

A research report consists of the following sections:

Title Page
Abstract
   Introduction
   Method
   Results
   Discussion
References
Footnotes
Appendixes

The body of the report is made up of four sections: introduction, method, results, and discussion (the four acts of the "play"). The title page and the abstract are like the playbill you see before the play itself begins, and the references, footnotes, and appendixes are analogous to the credits. In this appendix we provide descriptions of the content and format of each of these sections; more complete descriptions are provided in the *Publication Manual* (1994). Neither this appendix nor the *Publication Manual* will suffice for teaching you how to write a research report. The best preparation for that is to read journal articles reporting research in an area of psychology that interests you. Ultimately, you will develop the skills for writing research reports only by actually writing them.

TITLE PAGE

The first page of a research report is the title page. It includes the title of the research report, the name(s) of the author(s), the institutional affiliation(s) of the author(s), and a running head for publication. An illustration of a correctly typed title page and succeeding pages of a research report is presented in the sample paper at the end of this appendix. The sample paper includes notes to highlight several important aspects of the final typed draft of a research report. The sample paper should be helpful to you as you type your research reports in your research methods course.

The title page indicates what the research is about (i.e., the title), who did the research (i.e., the authors), where the research was done (i.e., authors' affiliation), and a brief heading to indicate to readers what the article is about (the "running head"). The title is perhaps the most critical aspect of your paper because it is the part most likely to be read! The title should clearly indicate what the central topic of your paper is. In the words of the *Publication Manual*,

> A title should summarize the main idea of the paper simply and, if possible, with style. It should be a concise statement of the main topic and should identify the actual variables or theoretical issues under investigation and the relation between them.
>
> Titles are commonly indexed and compiled in numerous reference works. Therefore, avoid words that serve no useful purpose; they increase length and can mislead indexers. For example, the word *method* and *results* do not normally appear in a title, nor should such redundancies as "A Study of" or "An Experimental Investigation of" begin a title. (p. 7)

A common format for the title of students' research reports is "[The Dependent Variable(s)] as a Function of [the Independent Variable(s)]." For example, "Anagram Solution Time as a Function of Problem Difficulty" would be a good title. The title must not only be informative, but it should also be brief; the recommended length is 10 to 12 words. Most important of all, be sure your title describes as specifically as possible the content of your research.

The byline for a research report includes the name(s) of the author(s) and the institution with which each author is affiliated. We discussed the criteria for authorship in Chapter 2; only those who meet these criteria should be listed as authors of a research report. Others who contributed to the research are acknowledged in an author note. The preferred form for an author's name is first name, middle initial, and last name.

The *Publication Manual* provides a succinct statement describing the last component of a title page, the running head: "The running head is an abbreviated title that is printed at the top of the pages of a published article to identify the article for readers" (p. 8). The running head should not exceed 50 characters, and it should appear on the title page typed in all uppercase letters one double-spaced line below the first line that includes the page 1 and the manuscript page heading (see sample paper). Note that the running head is *not* the same as the manuscript page heading that appears on every manuscript page. The running head appears once and only once in your manuscript, on the title page.

ABSTRACT

The second page of the report, the abstract, appears under that single word, which is typed as a centered heading (see sample paper). The abstract is a one-paragraph summary of the content and purpose of the research report and should be 100 to 120 words long (about ten double-spaced typewritten lines). It should include a statement of the problem under investigation; pertinent characteristics of the participants; the experimental method, including tests and apparatus that were used and data-gathering procedures; the findings; and the conclusions and implications of the findings. In other words, the abstract should highlight the critical points made in the introduction, method, results, and discussion sections of the research report.

A well-written abstract can have a big influence on whether the rest of a journal article will be read. Abstracts are used by information services to index and retrieve articles. The fate of an article based on a reader's reaction to its abstract is well described in the *Publication Manual:*

> Most people will have their first contact with an article by seeing just the abstract, usually on a computer screen with several other abstracts, as they are doing a literature search through an electronic abstract-retrieval system. Readers frequently decide on the basis of the abstract whether to read the entire article; this is true whether the reader is at a computer or is thumbing through a journal. The abstract needs to be dense with information but also readable, well organized, brief, and self-contained. Also, embedding many key words in your abstract will enhance the user's ability to find it. (p. 8)

Writing a good abstract is challenging. The best way to meet this challenge is to write it last. By writing the abstract after you have written the rest of the report you will be able to *abstract*, or paraphrase, your own words more easily.

INTRODUCTION

Objectives   The title of your report appears at the top of the third page as a centered heading, and then the first paragraph of the introduction section begins immediately (see sample paper). The introduction serves three primary objectives. The first is to introduce the problem being studied. The second is to summarize briefly the relevant background literature that led you to the present research problem and approach. Finally, the introduction states the purpose and rationale of the present study with a logical development of the predictions or hypotheses guiding the research. The order in which these objectives are met in any given report may vary, but the order in which we described them here is the most common one. All three of these objectives share a common purpose: to give the reader a firm sense of what you are doing and why you are doing it.

In order to meet these objectives, you might consider answering the following questions posed in the *Publication Manual*. Consider these questions before writing the introduction:

- What is the point of the study?
- How do the hypothesis and the experimental design relate to the problem?
- What are the theoretical implications of the study, and how does the study relate to previous work in the area?
- What are the theoretical propositions tested, and how were they derived? (p. 11)

The second objective, that of summarizing related research studies, is not to provide an exhaustive literature review. Instead, care should be taken to select the most pertinent studies to develop the rationale of your experiment. In summarizing these selected studies, emphasize whatever details of the earlier work will best help the reader understand what you have done and why. Acknowledge the contributions of other researchers to your understanding of the problem. Of course, if you quote directly from another person's work, you must use quotation marks (see Chapter 2 for advice about citing others' work).

More commonly, however, reference is made to the work of other researchers in one of two ways. Either you refer to the authors of the article you are citing by their last names, with the year in which the paper was published appearing in parentheses immediately after the names, or you make a general reference to their work and follow it with both the names and the year of publication in parentheses. For example, if you were citing a study by David G. Myers and Jane R. Dickie that was published in 1996, you would write either "Myers and Dickie (1996) have found . . ." or "Recent research (Myers & Dickie, 1996) has shown that . . ." Complete bibliographical information on Myers and Dickie's paper, including the journal title, volume number, and specific pages, would appear in the References section. Footnotes are not used to cite references in a research report in psychology.

You should include in your paper only those references that you have actually read. If you read a paper by Barney (1993) in which the research of Ludwig (1990) is described, you should not cite the Ludwig paper unless you have actually read that paper. Instead, you should use some form such as "Ludwig (1990), as reported by Barney (1993), found that . . ." You should use this approach for two reasons. The first and most obvious one is that you should accurately report what you have read. If this appeal to scholarly integrity does not suffice, you should recognize the risk you are taking. If Barney (1993) has misreported the work of Ludwig (1990) and you repeat this misrepresentation, you are equally subject to criticism. The general rule is simple: Cite only what you have read. (See also Chapter 2.)

Searching the Psychological Literature In the long run, the best way to develop ideas for research and to become familiar with the relevant literature is to read the journals in your area of interest regularly. Right now, though, while you are taking your research methods course, you may not have had a chance to read the research literature widely or to have settled on a principal area of interest in psychology. So when you are faced with the task of writing a research report, you may need help in searching the psychological literature. For example, you may have an idea for an experiment and you may wonder whether the experiment has already been done. Or you may have read an article describing an experiment on which you would like to base your experiment, and you may be interested in finding other studies related to this topic. Resources for searching the psychological literature are available to help you answer these types of questions.

Modern methods of searching the psychological literature are built on *Psychological Abstracts*, which the American Psychological Association has published since 1927. The abstracts, taken from over 1,000 national and international periodicals, are published monthly. These abstracts are organized under 16 general categories, such as "Physical and Psychological Disorders." In the printed version of *Psychological Abstracts*, abstracts are arranged alphabetically under each category by the first author's last name, and the abstracts are numbered consecutively in one or two volumes each year. Searching *Psychological Abstracts* was often a time consuming and cumbersome task before it became possible to use computers to search the psychological literature. Electronic databases have made the task of searching the psychological literature much less labor intensive.

PsycLIT is the CD-ROM version of *Psychological Abstracts*. As of 1995, PsycLIT included *Psychological Abstracts* going back to 1974 and it is updated quarterly. The inclusion of up-to-date research and the database spanning over 20 years of research makes PsycLIT an ideal resource for psychology students. One of the greatest advantages of PsycLIT is that it can be used so easily following brief instruction. PsychINFO is the online version of PsycLIT. Other online databases that permit electronic searching are *FirstSearch* and *InfoTrac 2000*. Check with your local library staff to find out what online services are available to you. Jostwick (1994) provides recommendations for electronic searches for those who want to move beyond the basics.

To illustrate the use of electronic databases to search the psychological literature, consider a computer-assisted search done by one of our undergraduate students. The student was interested in conducting a survey to determine the incidence of rapes and other sexual assaults on dates (i.e., date rape). She came across a few references to this topic in her general reading in the area of women's studies, and then wanted to make a more systematic search of the psychological literature. A reference librarian helped her make a search of PsycLIT and the electronic database that included the *Social Science Citation Index*, which records the reference history of an article. That is, once an article has been published, the citation index searches the reference sections of all articles which followed in that area and notes whenever the original article is cited. The citation index can be used to determine how many times a given article has been cited or to identify the specific articles in which the original article is cited.

The student used a keyword search on PsycLIT and she had a chapter on rape by Klemmack and Klemmack (1976) to serve as the basis of her search of the *Social Science Citation Index*. An electronic database makes it possible to scan the titles and abstracts of articles in the database and to identify all those that contain particular keywords. The most effective approach to this type of search is to have intersecting keywords both of which need to be present before the computer will "flag" an article. For example, the student used the keyword RAPE and the letter string DAT to guide her search. She chose the letter string DAT in order to catch such variants as DATE, DATES, and DATING. This intersection led to the identification of 75 references, 73 of which were written in English. The student also obtained 11 additional references that had cited the Klemmack and Klemmack (1976) paper when she did a computer search of the *Social Science Citation Index* database.

The major advantage of searching electronic databases is that they provide quick access to large amounts of information. The student completed both searches in less than half an hour. (Of course, she still had to locate the actual journal articles in the library's periodical stacks.) There are a few disadvantages. For example, the quality of the search greatly influences the likelihood that you will obtain all the relevant references. When it comes to electronic databases, what you search is what you get. Estimates are that 30% to 50% of all users miss pertinent information in their search (Jostwick, 1994). After searching such vast databases we may become unduly confident that we have identified "all there is on the subject." These two potential problems are not problems with the *use* of electronic databases but with their *users*. Another possible disadvantage is that many of the references the computer locates do not prove useful. For example, the student obtained one reference on rape among mallard ducks on specific chronological dates. Keywords can also prove tricky. The string DAT identified all studies using the word DATA, so a number of the student's references provided data about rape—but not solely in the context of dating. When they are used properly, the advantages of searching the psychological literature with electronic databases like PsycLIT and PsychINFO far outweigh their disadvantages.

METHOD

The second major part of the body of a research report is the Method section, usually identified by a centered heading ("Method") with a double space separating it from the preceding and following text (see sample paper). The introduction has provided a broad outline of the research you have done; the method fills in the details. The *Publication Manual* presents a straightforward description of the goals of the Method section: "The Method section describes in detail how the study was conducted. Such a description enables the reader to evaluate the appropriateness of your methods and the reliability and the validity of your results. It also permits experienced investigators to replicate the study if they so desire" (p. 12). Writing a good Method section can be difficult. It sounds easy because all you have to do is describe exactly what you have done. But if you want to get a sense of how challenging this can be, just try to write a clear and interesting paragraph describing how to tie your shoelaces.

The key to writing a good Method section is organization. Fortunately, the structure of this section is so consistent across research reports that a few basic subsections provide the pattern of organization you need. Before describing the content of these subsections, however, we must address the question that students writing their first research report ask most frequently: "How much detail should I include?" The quality of your paper will be adversely affected if you include either too much or too little detail. The rule stated in the *Publication Manual* seems simple enough: "Include in these subsections only the information essential to comprehend and replicate the study" (p. 13). As we have said before, the best way to learn how to follow this rule is to read the Method sections of journal articles and to write your own research reports. Be sure to get feedback from your instructor concerning the appropriate level of detail for your research reports.

The three most common subsections of the Method section are participants, materials (apparatus), and procedure. Each of these subsections is introduced by an underlined subheading that usually begins at the left margin (see sample paper). The *Publication Manual* (p. 13) aptly summarizes the purpose and the content of the participants subsection:

> Appropriate identification of research participants and clientele is critical to the science and practice of psychology, particularly for assessing the results (making comparisons across groups), generalizing the findings, and making comparisons in replications, literature reviews, or secondary data analyses.
>
> When humans are the participants, report the procedures for selecting and assigning them and the agreements and payments made. Report major demographic characteristics such as sex and age. When a particular demographic characteristic is an experimental variable or is important for the interpretation of results, describe the group specifically—for example, in terms of racial and ethnic designation, national origin, level of education, health status, and language preference and use.
>
> For nonhuman animal subjects, report the genus, species, and strain number or other specific identification, such as the name and location of the supplier and the stock designation.
>
> Give the total number of subjects and the number assigned to each experimental condition. If any did not complete the experiment, state how many and explain why they did not continue. (pp. 13–14)

The apparatus or materials subsection is not always included in a research report. If the only equipment you used is paper, pencils, and a stopwatch, it is better to include this information in the procedure subsection than in a separate apparatus section. On the other hand, if the apparatus or materials played a central role in the study, a separate subsection is useful. If complex or custom-made equipment has been used, a diagram or drawing is helpful for both the reader and the writer of an apparatus subsection. In general, the heading *Apparatus* is used when mechanical equipment is described. The heading *Materials* is used when less mechanical instruments, such as a paper-and-pencil questionnaire, have been constructed or used. If you use equipment or materials developed by another investigator, you should cite the work of that investigator, but you should also include the general characteristics of the materials in your own report.

The procedure subsection is the most critical component of the Method section. In this subsection you describe what happened from the beginning to the end of the sessions in which you tested your participants. As the previous sentence implies, the organization of the procedure subsection is usually chronological. You should begin writing this subsection by outlining the important steps in testing participants in each group of your study. Next you can either describe the procedure for each group in turn or describe the procedures common to all groups and then point out the distinguishing features of each group. Whichever organization you choose (you may not learn which works best until you have tried to write both), it is best to begin writing only after you have prepared a checklist of the important features of your procedure. The instructions given to participants should be presented in paraphrase form unless they define an experimental manipulation, in which case they should be reported verbatim. The *Publication Manual* recommends that the Method section, and especially the procedure subsection, "should tell the reader what you did and how you did it in sufficient detail so that a reader could reasonably replicate your study" (pp. 14–15).

RESULTS

The centered heading "Results" introduces this third major section of the body of a research report (see sample paper). Like the third act of a dramatic play, the Results section contains the climax of the research report—the actual findings of the study. For many students, though, the excitement of describing the climax is blunted by concern about the necessity of reporting statistical information in the Results section. The best way to alleviate this concern, of course, is to develop the same command of statistical concepts that you have of other concepts. While you are acquiring this mastery of statistics, however, you need a way to deal effectively with the problem of presenting statistical information. One solution is to adopt a simple organizational structure to guide your writing of the Results section.

You should use your Results section to answer the questions you raised in your introduction. However, the guiding principle in the Results section is to

TABLE C.1   STRUCTURE OF A TYPICAL PARAGRAPH IN THE RESULTS SECTION

1. State the purpose of the analysis.
2. Identify the descriptive statistic to be used to summarize results.
3. Present a summary of this descriptive statistic across conditions in the text itself, in a table, or in a figure.
4. If a table or figure is used, point out the major findings on which the reader should focus.
5. Present the reasons for, and the results of, inferential statistics tests.
6. State the conclusion that follows from each test, but do not discuss implications. These belong in the discussion section.

Sample paragraph

To examine retention as a function of instructions given at the time of study, the number of words recalled by each participant in each instruction condition was determined. Words were scored as correct only if they matched a word that had appeared on the target list. Thus, synonyms were not counted as correct; misspelled words were accepted if the spelling was sufficiently similar to a target item that it could be reasonably concluded that the intended word had actually appeared on the list. Mean numbers of words recalled were 15.6, 15.2, and 10.1 in the bizarre imagery condition, the standard imagery condition, and the control condition, respectively. Overall, mean recall differed significantly among the conditions, $F(2, 72) = 64.84$, $MS_e = 0.44$, $p = .0001$. Two analytical comparisons were performed to determine the source of this effect. These tests revealed that the two groups given imagery instructions when averaged together differed significantly from the control condition, $F(1, 72) = 44.62$, $p = .0001$; however, the two imagery conditions did not differ significantly from each other, $F(1, 72) = 1.66$, $p = .20$. In conclusion, retention by participants instructed to use imagery was higher than that by participants given no specific study instructions, but retention did not differ for the two types of imagery instructions.

"stick to the facts, just the facts." You will have the opportunity to move beyond just the facts when you get to the Discussion.

Reporting Statistics   The *Publication Manual* provides an excellent overview of the objectives of a Results section:

> The Results section summarizes the data collected and the statistical treatment of them. First, briefly state the main results or findings. Discussing the implications of the results is not appropriate here. Mention all relevant results, including those that run counter to the hypothesis. Do not include individual raw scores or raw data, with the exception, for example, of single-case designs or illustrative samples. (p. 15)

One way to meet these objectives is to use an organizational structure that is typical of paragraphs in the Results section. This structure is outlined in Table C.1, and an illustration of a paragraph from the Results section of a published article appears after the table. A Results section paragraph begins by stating the purpose of the analysis. The reason(s) for doing an analysis should be stated succinctly; often, no more than a phrase is necessary. In the sample paragraph, for example, the purpose of the analysis is "to examine retention as a function of the instructions given at the time of study." There are two reasons for making the purpose for each analysis explicit. It helps your reader follow the logic of your analysis plan. And, perhaps more importantly, it ensures that you will never try to report an analysis whose purpose you do not understand.

The second step in writing a Results section paragraph is to identify the descriptive statistic that will be used to summarize the results for a given dependent variable. For example, you might use the mean numbers of words recalled, as in the sample paragraph. Other possible descriptive statistics that could be used to summarize the results in each condition of your experiment are the median reaction time or the cumulative number of responses per minute.

The third step is to present a summary of this descriptive statistic across conditions. Whenever possible, measures of central tendency should be accompanied by corresponding measures of variability. If there are only two or three conditions in your experiment, this summary can be presented in the text itself. For instance, you could summarize the results of a two-group study by saying, "The mean number of correct responses for the experimental group was 10.5 ($s = 2.1$), whereas that for the control group was 5.2 ($s = 1.8$)." More commonly, however, you will have more data to summarize and you will need to present your findings in either a table or a figure (graph). We describe the procedures for constructing tables and figures later in this section. The *Publication Manual* gives good advice regarding the use of tables and figures:

> To report the data, choose the medium that presents them clearly and economically. Tables provide exact values and can efficiently illustrate main effects. Figures of professional quality attract the reader's eye and best illustrate interactions and general comparisons, but they are not quite as precise as tables.
>
> Summarizing the results and the analysis in tables or figures instead of text may be helpful; for example, a table may enhance the readability of complex sets of analysis of variance results. Avoid repeating the same data in several places and using tables for data that can be easily presented in a few sentences in the text. (p. 15)

Step 4 in Table C.1 reminds us that we should not expect a table or figure to be self-sufficient. Your reader will need help to gain as much information as possible from a table or figure. You are in the best position to offer this assistance because you are the person most familiar with your results. Direct your reader's attention to the highlights of the data in the table or figure, focusing especially on those aspects of the results that are consistent (or discrepant) with the hypotheses you proposed in the introduction. Usually the same data are not reported in both a table and a figure. Tables provide a more precise description of the results, but figures make it easier to see trends or patterns in the data. Whichever you choose, be sure to highlight in the text itself the critical results that the table or figure reveals.

The fifth step in writing a paragraph of the Results section is to present the results of inferential statistical tests. Three pieces of information should always be reported with any inferential statistics test: the name of the test (usually indicated by a symbol such as t, r, or F); the degrees of freedom for the test (presented in parentheses after the test is identified); and the value of the test statistic that you obtained. Two additional pieces of information are useful in reporting the results of an inferential test: the exact probability of the test under the assumption the null hypothesis is true and the estimate of error variation for that test. For instance, you might say, "The overall effect of the drug variable was statistically significant, $F(3, 64) = 7.15$, $p = .0005$, $MS_e = 2.4$." When you write the Results section, you should assume your reader has a basic knowledge of inferential statistics. Therefore, you do not need to refer to concepts such as the null hypothesis or mention whether your obtained probability is less than your chosen alpha level. All that is required is that you use the term *statistically significant* correctly. It is helpful to report measures of effect size along with the results of the inferential statistics tests (see Chapter 6).

The final step in writing a paragraph in the Results section is to state a brief conclusion that follows from each test you report. This is accomplished by referring to the descriptive statistics on which the inferential test is based. For example, if the mean number correct in the experimental group is 10, that in the control group is 5, and this difference is statistically significant, an appropriate concluding statement would be "The control group did worse than the experimental group." In this simple example the conclusion may seem obvious, but appropriate concluding statements are essential in more complex analyses. It is not enough to string together a series of inferential statistical tests with appropriate commentary on the statistical significance of each test, and then never report the descriptive statistics or any conclusion. It is almost useless for your readers to know that an independent variable has had a statistically significant effect if you have failed to describe the nature of that effect. Descriptive statistics are essential in providing such a description.

Each paragraph of the Results section follows the structure outlined in Table C.1. Do not overload your reader with statistics. The challenge is to select those findings that are most critical, being sure to report all the data pertinent to the questions raised in your introduction. Before concluding our discussion of the Results section, we briefly describe the basic procedures for constructing tables and figures, two key tools in reporting results effectively.

Presenting Data in Tables   Tables are an effective and efficient means for presenting large amounts of data in concise form. The table should supplement and not duplicate information in the text of the paper, but it should be well integrated into the text. The tables in your paper should be numbered consecutively (use arabic numerals) so they can be referred to easily in the text by their numbers. Each table should also have a brief explanatory title, and the columns and rows of the table should be labeled clearly. The data entries in the table should all be reported to the same degree of precision (that is, all values should have the same number of decimal places), and the values should be consistently aligned with the corresponding row and column headings. An appropriately constructed table appears in the sample manuscript at the end of this appendix.

When manuscripts are submitted for publication, each table is typed on a separate page and appears at the end of the paper after the references and footnotes sections. (Note: For class assignments, some instructors prefer to have their students type the table in the text itself at the point where reference to the table is made. A table number and title are required even when the table is placed directly in the text.)

Presenting Data in Figures   Figures, like tables, are a concise way to present large amounts of information. A figure has two principal axes: the horizontal axis, or X-axis, and the vertical axis, or Y-axis. Typically, the levels of the independent variable are plotted on the X-axis and those of the dependent variable are plotted on the Y-axis. When there are two or more independent variables, the levels of the second and succeeding independent variables serve as labels for the data within the figure or are indicated in a figure legend. Two illustrations of the format for figures are presented in Figures C.1 and C.2. In Figure C.1 the values of the dependent variable (mean number recalled) are plotted on the Y-axis; the levels of one independent variable (serial position) are indicated on the X-axis. The levels of the second independent variable (Cued [C] or NonCued [NC]) label the data within the figures, and the levels of the third independent variable (instructions) serve as the headings for each of the two separate panels of the figure. There are also three independent variables represented in Figure C.2: one on the X-axis (trials) and two differentiated by symbols that can be interpreted by using the legend at the top of the figure. For example, the "reversal" groups are represented by circles, and the "control" groups are represented by squares. The third variable is represented by

FIGURE C.1   Mean number of words recalled (of a possible ten) as a function of serial position within blocks, cuing (C = Cued; NC = Noncued), and instructional condition.

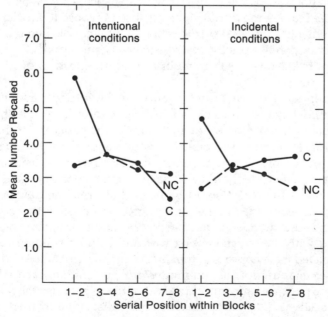

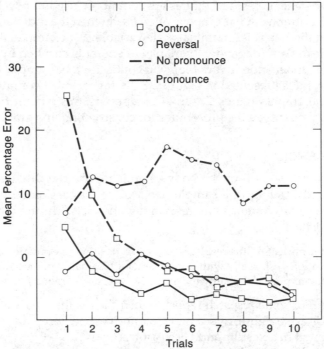

FIGURE C.2   Mean percentage error across trials for TCC transfer as a function of type of transfer task and pronunciation instructions.

the type of line: dashed lines represent the "No Pronounce" groups and solid lines represent the "Pronounce" groups. Here again, the Y-axis indicates values of the dependent variable (mean percentage error).

The two sample figures illustrate there are alternative ways to construct useful graphic presentations. All figures must include certain features, however. The X- and Y-axes must be clearly labeled, with each label printed next to the corresponding axis. Selected points (called grid points) on each axis must be identified with labeled grid marks, and the grid labels are always printed horizontally. Each figure is accompanied by a figure caption.

Figures are numbered consecutively in the paper with arabic numerals, and they are referred to by number. The numbering of figures is done separately from the numbering of tables. The grid scale for the X- and Y-axes should be chosen so the plotted data are legible and span the entire illustration. The captions of Figure C.1 and Figure C.2 appear at the bottom of the corresponding figures because this is a common format that instructors use for students' research reports. However, when a manuscript is submitted for publication, each figure appears on a separate page but the figure captions are presented on a separate page under the centered heading "Figure Captions." This page follows the tables at the end of the manuscript but precedes the figures, which are then presented in order.

Two general types of figures are commonly used in psychology: bar graphs and line graphs. A bar graph is often used when the independent variable plotted on the X-axis is a nominal-scale variable. For example, if you were plotting the mean GPA (dependent variable) of students enrolled in different academic majors (independent variable), you could use a bar graph. An illustration of a bar graph is presented in Figure C.3. By far the most common type of figure is the line graph. Figures C.1 and C.2 represent this type of figure, and we have already discussed the procedures for constructing line graphs.

DISCUSSION

The fourth section of the body of your report, the discussion, begins with a centered heading (see sample paper). The Discussion section, unlike the Results section, contains "more than just the facts." In the words of the *Publication Manual*:

> After presenting the results, you are in a position to evaluate and interpret their implications, especially with respect to your original hypothesis. You are free to examine, interpret, and qualify the results, as well as to draw inferences from them. (p. 18)

(Note: For some research reports, when the results are relatively brief and discussion is straightforward and also not very lengthy, the two sections can be combined in a Results and Discussion section.)

The discussion begins with a succinct statement of the essential findings. You should give particular attention to how your findings support or refute your original hypotheses. You do not repeat the descriptive statistics in this summary, nor do you necessarily refer to the statistical significance of the find-

FIGURE C.3   Proportion recognition errors made by two groups of college students after rating verbal items for either familiarity or meaning. The items were nonwords (NW) and words appearing less than one time, one through ten times and more than forty times per million in the Thorndike-Lorge count.

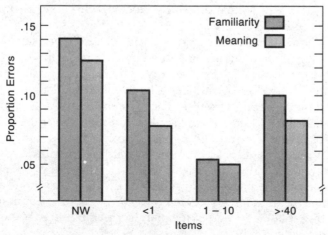

ings. The *Publication Manual* provides good advice about what to do and not to do after the succinct summary of the findings:

> Similarities and differences between your results and the work of others should clarify and confirm your conclusions. Do not, however, simply reformulate and repeat points already made; each new statement should contribute to your position and to the reader's understanding of the problem. You may remark on certain shortcomings of the study, but do not dwell on every flaw. Negative results should be accepted as such without an undue attempt to explain them away. (pp. 18–19)

The discussion is written in a tone and style consistent with the introduction. Be careful, however, to keep the statements you make in the discussion consistent with the data reported in the results. For instance, you should not report that one group did better than another if the comparison between these groups was not statistically significant—at least not without some qualification of what you mean by "better."

As we just noted from the *Publication Manual*, the discussion includes a description of how your findings relate to the relevant literature, most of which you will have cited in the introduction. If your results are not consistent with your original hypotheses, you should suggest an explanation for these discrepancies. Such post hoc (after-the-fact) explanations should be considered tentative at best. If the reasons for your results are unclear, do not hesitate to say so. In students' research reports, it is often necessary and helpful to include a paragraph describing limitations or problems in the research. As noted in the *Publication Manual*, however, "do not dwell compulsively on every flaw." Do try to anticipate criticisms of your study that others might make.

If appropriate, conclude the discussion by proposing additional research that should be done on the problem you are investigating. Avoid clichés such as "Additional research on this problem is needed before definitive conclusions can be reached." Instead, be specific about what research should be done and why it needs to be done. That is, be sure to explain what the new research should reveal that we do not already know. The reader will not learn much if you say "It would be interesting to do this experiment with younger participants." The reader can learn much more if you explain how you would expect the results to differ with younger participants and what you would conclude if the results of the proposed experiment were to turn out as expected. Remember, the watchword in proposing new research is to be specific. Your emphasis when writing your report should definitely be on quality, not quantity.

Again, the *Publication Manual* gives good advice for authors beginning to write their Discussion section:

> In general, be guided by the following questions:
>
> * What have I contributed here?
> * How has my study helped to resolve the original problem?
> * What conclusions and theoretical implications can I draw from my study?
>
> The responses to these questions are the core of your contribution, and readers have a right to clear, unambiguous, and direct answers. (p. 19)

REFERENCES

We have already described the procedure for citing references within the body of a research report by using the name(s) of the author(s) and the date of publication. The References section, which appears with a centered heading on a separate page after the discussion (see sample paper), includes the complete citation for each reference. "Just as data in the paper support interpretations and conclusions, so reference citations document statements made about the literature" (*Publication Manual*, p. 20).

Three types of references cover almost all those needed for students' research reports: journal articles, books, and chapters in edited books. The format for each of these reference types is illustrated in Table C.2. [Reference citations should be double-spaced.] As the table shows, the first line of each reference is indented. The journal article reference includes the authors, the year of publication, the title of the article, the name of the journal, the volume number, and the page numbers. The book citation includes the authors, the copyright date, the title, the city in which the book was published, and the publisher. The reference for a chapter in an edited volume includes the author of the chapter, the date, the chapter title, the editors of the book, the title of the book, the page numbers of the chapter, the city of publication, and the publisher. You can save your readers much aggravation if you follow the reference formats closely and proofread your reference list carefully. The references are listed in alphabetical order by the last name of the first author of each article. If there are two articles by the same author(s), they are arranged in ascending order by year of publication.

APPENDIXES

Appendixes are rare in published research articles, but they are a bit more common in students' research reports. When they are intended for a published arti-

TABLE C.2   ILLUSTRATION OF FORMAT OF REFERENCE CITATIONS

Journal article

Loftus, E. F., & Burns, T. E. (1982). Mental shock can produce retrograde amnesia. Memory & Cognition, 10, 318–323.

Book

Posavac, E. J., & Carey, R. G. (1992). Program evaluation (4th ed.). Englewood Cliffs, NJ: Prentice Hall.

Chapter in an edited book

Weiss, J. M. (1977). Psychological and behavioral influences on gastrointestinal lesions in animal models. In J.D. Maser & E. P. Seligman (Eds.), Psychopathology: Experimental models (pp. 232–269). San Francisco: W. H. Freeman.

cle, each appendix begins on a separate manuscript page and they appear at the end of the paper following the references. (Note: Instructors may require you to submit an appendix including your raw data, the worksheets for a statistical analysis, or the computer printout of the analyses. The appendix can also be used to provide a verbatim copy of the instructions to participants or a list of the specific materials used in an experiment.) Each appendix is identified by letter (A, B, C, and so on), and any reference to the appendix in the body of the text is made using this letter. For instance, "The complete instructions can be found in Appendix A."

AUTHOR NOTE

The *Publication Manual* provides a concise description of the contents of an author note:

> The author note (a) identifies the departmental affiliation of each author, (b) identifies sources of financial support, (c) provides a forum for authors to acknowledge colleagues' professional contributions to the study and personal assistance, and (d) tells whom the interested reader may contact for further information concerning the article. (p. 21)

The author note appears on a separate page under the centered heading "Author Note" immediately after the References section (or after the appendixes, if there are any).

FOOTNOTES

Because they are not used for citing references, footnotes are rare in journal articles and even more rare in students' research reports. When footnotes appear in the text they are of two types: content footnotes and copyright permission footnotes. Content footnotes supplement or expand on the text material. Copyright permission footnotes acknowledge the source of quotations. Footnotes (of both kinds) are numbered consecutively in the text. In the typed manuscript footnotes appear on a separate page following the References section under the centered heading "Footnotes."

ORDER OF MANUSCRIPT PAGES

The pages of your research report should be numbered consecutively in the following order:

> Title Page
> Abstract
> Text (introduction, method, results, discussion)
> References (start on a separate page)
> Appendixes (start each on a separate page)
> Author note (start on a separate page)

> Footnotes (list together, starting on a separate page)
> Tables (start each on a separate page)
> Figure Captions (list together, starting on a separate page)
> Figures (place each on a separate page).

ORAL PRESENTATIONS

Research psychologists regularly attend professional conventions at which they present brief oral descriptions of their research. Similarly, students may give oral presentations of their research either in class or at a department research symposium involving students from a number of different classes or at undergraduate research conferences (Palladino, Carsrud, Hulicka, & Benjamin, 1982). All of these settings share one characteristic—the time allowed for the presentation is usually no more than 10 to 15 minutes. In this length of time it is impossible to provide the detailed description that is included in a journal article. In general, as noted in the *Publication Manual,* "Material delivered verbally should differ from written material in its level of detail, organization, and presentation" (p. 339). To reach your audience the *Publication Manual* recommends the following:

> Omit most of the details of scientific procedures, because a listener cannot follow the same level of detail as a reader can. The audience wants to know (a) what you studied and why, (b) how you went about the research (give a general orientation), (c) what you discovered, and (d) the implications of your results. A verbal presentation should create awareness about a topic and stimulate interest in it; colleagues can retrieve the details from a written paper, copies of which you may want to have available. (p. 339)

A colleague of ours in the biology department has developed five principles that he distributes to his cell physiology students to help them prepare the oral presentation required in his class. These five principles are listed in Table C.3. Like all good maxims these five sound simple enough, but they are all too frequently ignored even by experienced researchers. The temptation described in the first principle can best be avoided by limiting your presentation to one or two main points. What are the important "take home messages"? The brief time available for an oral presentation is barely sufficient to allow you to present the evidence supporting these main points. There simply will not be time to discuss any side issues.

TABLE C.3   PRINCIPLES TO FOLLOW FOR AN EFFECTIVE ORAL PRESENTATION

1. Avoid the temptation to tell everything you know in 10 minutes.
2. Cultivate a good platform presence.
3. Accompany your talk with useful visual aids.
4. Leave at least 2 minutes of your allotted time for questions.
5. Practice your talk before a critical audience before you give it.

The second principle, cultivation of a good platform presence, can best be achieved by developing public speaking skills. Most people need a written copy of their presentation in front of them while they are presenting, but your presentation will be more effective if you can appear not to be reading. Many people speak too quickly in front of an audience, particularly if they are reading; it is best to use simple, direct sentences presented at a moderate rate. Most important, speak loudly and clearly.

The third principle, the use of effective visual aids, can help your listeners follow your presentation. Slides or material written on a transparency must be distinct enough to be seen clearly at a distance. The successful use of audiovisual aids is a skill that can be improved with practice. Be sure that whatever visual aids you use are as close to self-explanatory as you can make them.

You need to keep in mind the fourth principle, leaving time for questions, because most professional conferences and classroom presentations will require it. Although questions from the audience can be somewhat intimidating, the opportunity for questions gives your listeners a chance to become actively involved in your presentation.

The final principle is perhaps the most important one. Practicing your talk before an audience is more beneficial than simply rehearsing the talk over and over by yourself. Such private rehearsal is a good way to prepare for your dress rehearsal, but it is no substitute for practicing before others.

The five principles listed in Table C.3 provide a good coaching manual for oral presentations. The best way to develop this skill, however, is to deliver as many oral presentations as possible under game conditions. Practice may not make perfect, but it is the best route we know to improvement.

RESEARCH PROPOSALS

We discuss writing again here—but this time the writing of research proposals. As we mentioned earlier, researchers must often seek financial support for their work by submitting grant proposals to private or government agencies. Students in research methods classes are also sometimes required to submit proposals describing research they might do. Even if a written proposal is not required, only a foolhardy researcher would tackle a project without careful prior consideration of related literature, possible practical problems, workable statistical analyses of the data, and eventual interpretation of the expected results. Without a carefully constructed plan for the research, the unprepared investigator is likely to produce an unworkable, unanalyzable, or uninterpretable piece of research.

The purpose of a research proposal is to ensure a workable experimental design that, when implemented, will result in an interpretable empirical finding of significant scientific merit. No research proposal, no matter how carefully prepared, can guarantee important results. Researchers learn early in their careers about Murphy's law. In essence, Murphy's law states that "anything that can go wrong will go wrong." Nonetheless, it is worthwhile to develop a research proposal, if only to bypass the research problems that are avoidable.

A written research proposal follows the general format of a journal article, but the headings of the various sections are slightly different. The proposal should include the following main sections:

Introduction
Method
Expected Results and Statistical Treatment
References
Appendix
(Information for Institutional Review Board)

An abstract is not included in a research proposal. The introduction of a research proposal is likely to include a more extensive review of the relevant literature than is required for a journal article. The statement of the research problem and the logical development of hypotheses in a research proposal are the same as required in a journal article. Similarly, the Method section in the proposal should be as close as possible to the one that will accompany the finished research. Thus our remarks about the format and content of the Method section of a research report apply equally to the writing of a proposal.

The section of the proposal entitled "Expected Results and Statistical Treatment" should include a brief discussion of the anticipated results of the research. In most cases the exact nature of the results will not be known. Nevertheless, you will always have some idea (in the form of a hypothesis or prediction) of the outcome of the research. The Expected Results section may include tables or figures of the results as you expect (hope) they will come out. The results most important to the project should be highlighted. A statistical analysis plan for the proposed results should be in this section. For example, if you are proposing a complex design, you would need to indicate which effects you will be testing and what inferential test you will use for these tests. Reasonable alternatives to the expected results should also be mentioned, as well as possible problems of interpretation that will arise if the results deviate from the research hypothesis.

The References section should be in exactly the same form as the one you would summit with the final report. An appendix should complete the research proposal and include a list of all materials that will be used in doing the experiment. In most cases this will mean that a copy of the instructions to participants will be included, as well as the type of apparatus used, a list of stimulus materials or a description of the stimuli, and so on. To repeat, all materials should be listed. For example, if you are doing a study involving students' memory for lists of words, the following must be included in the appendix: actual lists with randomizations made, description of apparatus used for presentation, instructions to participants for all conditions, and randomizations of conditions.

Finally, a research proposal should include material to be submitted to an institutional review board (IRB) or similar committee designed to review the ethics of the proposed research (see Chapter 2).

A SAMPLE RESEARCH REPORT

First few words of title appear before page number.

5 spaces

Memory for Frequency   1

Type flush with margin.

Running Head: MEMORY FOR SONGS

Running head is typed in all caps (appears in journal article).

Number pages consecutively, beginning with title page.

Use upper and lower case for title, name and affiliation (centered)

Memory for Frequency of Hearing Popular Songs

Nancy A. Norton

Loyola University of Chicago

Note:
   Leave one-inch margins at the top, bottom, right and left of all pages.

Center, but do not underline.

Memory for Frequency   2

Abstract

No paragraph indentation for abstract

Memory for frequency of occurrences of popular songs was investigated. College students ($\underline{N}$ = 26) listened to a lengthy series of 10-s excerpts from popular songs, judged the number of times each song was heard, and tried to identify the title and artists of the songs. Each excerpt was presented 0, 1, 2, 3, or 4 times. All students were informed that their memory for the names of various popular songs would be tested, and that some songs would be repeated, but only half the students were also informed that a frequency test would be given. Mean frequency estimates corresponded closely to actual frequencies and did not differ as a function of instructions regarding a frequency judgment test. However, accuracy of frequency judgments was significantly correlated with degree of knowledge of the popular songs, suggesting that memory for frequency of songs may not be a strictly automatic process.

Abstract should be a single paragraph with no more than 960 characters, including punctuation and spaces (about 120 words).

Note:
Doublespace between all lines of the manuscript. There should be no more than 27 lines of text on each page.
When using a word processor, use left justification only (not full).

Title appears centered on page 3, with first letter of major words in caps.

Memory for Frequency   3

Memory for Frequency of Hearing Popular Songs

Memory for the number of times that an event has been experienced is often remarkably good. This is true whether the event to be remembered has been experienced in a particular situation, for example, as part of a laboratory experiment, or whether the event is one that an individual has experienced in many different situations as part of a lifetime of experiences (see Zechmeister & Nyberg, 1982, for a brief review of frequency judgment studies). This sensitivity to event frequency is assumed to play a role in many kinds of cognitive decisions. For example, frequency information is relevant when discriminating between old and new events as part of a recognition memory task (Underwood, 1971) or when assessing our degree of certainty about the truth or validity of statements (Hasher, Goldstein, & Toppino, 1977).

Hasher and Zacks (1979) have suggested that frequency information is encoded automatically. Automatic processes, in their view, are those that are completed without effort, are not affected by intention to learn, are not improved with practice, and are developmentally quite stable. Automatic encoding may, in fact, be something that humans are genetically "prepared" to do.

Hasher and Chromiak (1977) have provided empirical support for this theory of automatic encoding of frequency information. In one experiment, these

Leave one space at end of sentences and after all commas, colons and semi-colons.

Place comma before date.

Indent every paragraph five to seven spaces (consistently).

Memory for Frequency   4

investigators presented a list of 48 words to students
in the second, fourth, and sixth grades, and to college
students. The critical words were presented zero to four
times. Half the students at each grade level were warned
that a frequency judgment test would be forthcoming; the
other half were not told that memory for frequency would
be tested. Results revealed that students at all levels
judged frequency relatively accurately, that this
ability did not differ across grade levels, and that
students forewarned about a frequency test did not do
better than those not forewarned. In a second
experiment, Hasher and Chromiak investigated whether
memory for frequency improved with practice. It did not.

Studies investigating memory for event frequency
have generally examined retention of verbal stimuli,
such as words or parts of words (e.g., letters,
bigrams), or pictorial stimuli.   Nevertheless,
automatic encoding of frequency information is
assumed to extend potentially to all stimuli, whether
meaningful or not (Hasher & Chromiak, 1977). In the
present experiment, the generality of automatic encoding
of frequency was tested by examining memory for
frequency of hearing popular songs. College students
listened to a lengthy series of brief excerpts from
popular songs that were presented zero to four times.
After listening to the presentation series all students
were asked to judge the number of times that different
songs had been heard. Half of the students were informed
that a frequency test would be administered; half were

[Handwritten note left margin:] Use Latin abbreviations (such as e.g. and i.e.) only in parentheses.

[Handwritten note left margin:] Use ampersand for references within parentheses.

Memory for Frequency   5

not informed. If frequency of hearing popular songs is
encoded automatically, then students' estimates of
situational frequency should correspond closely to
actual frequency of occurrence and should not differ
between students told that a frequency test would be
given and those not told.

Method

Participants

Twenty-six students from a college psychology class
participated in the study. These students were randomly
assigned to either the informed or uninformed groups.
Thus, each group consisted of 13 students.

Materials

An audio cassette tape was prepared containing 52
10-s segments of popular songs. All of the song segments
were taken from rock songs that had been in the "top 20"
at some point in the past 3 years. The same song segment
was never repeated in successive positions on the tape;
there were always 4 to 10 intervening presentations
between the repetitions of any one song. Segments
contained no lyrics and were taken from the beginning of
the song. Each segment was separated from the next by
silent intervals of 5 to 7 s.

The 16 critical songs were presented either 1, 2,
3, or 4 times on the tape. The tape was divided into two
halves. In each half, different critical songs were
represented twice at each of the four levels of
frequency. Therefore, there were four songs presented at

Handwritten margin notes:

Note two types of headings for short manuscripts.

Always use words to express numbers that begin a sentence.

Use number for time or units of measure.

Use words to express numbers less than 10.

Center, no underline (→ Method)

Flush, underlined (→ Participants)

Note: Method, Results, and Discussion do not begin on new page (unless coincidentally).

Memory for Frequency   6

each of the frequency levels. To increase the apparent
range of frequencies on the tape, one song was recorded
six times and presented through both halves of the tape.
In addition, to avoid possible primacy or recency
effects, one filler song segment was presented twice and
two different segments were each played once at the
beginning of the tape (primacy) and two songs were each
played once at the end of the tape (recency).

The test tape was prepared in similar fashion. The
16 critical song segments, each of a 10-s duration, were
randomly ordered and recorded. In addition, four
additional song segments that had not been on the
presentation tape were included on the test. Thus, 20
song segments were on the test tape, four at each of
five frequency levels: 0, 1, 2, 3, or 4. Each segment
was separated by a 5-s silent interval to allow
participants time to record their frequency judgment for
each song.

Test booklets were prepared for all students. The
first page of these booklets contained instructions that
were to be read prior to listening to the tape. The
second page of the booklet was a questionnaire that was
not to be inspected until the presentation tape had
ended. The items on the questionnaire asked (a) how many
hours per day the student spent listening to music, (b)
which type of music the student preferred, and (c)
whether the student had ever played a musical
instrument. Additional items on the questionnaire asked

Handwritten margin note (left): "s" (with no period) is abbreviation for second.

Handwritten margin note (left): Within a paragraph or sentence use lowercase letters in parentheses to identify elements in a series (separate with commas when elements do not have internal commas).

students to use a 7-point rating scale to indicate (a)
how much they liked rock music, (b) how knowledgeable
they felt they were about contemporary music, and (c)
how good they felt their memory was for music heard
previously. The last page in the booklet was the answer
sheet for the frequency judgment test. Space was
provided for frequency judgments for each of the 20
songs. Space was also provided for identification of
each song title and of the artist or group.

Procedure

All students were assembled in a classroom and a
tape player was positioned at the front of the room so
that each student could hear the song segments. The
previously prepared booklets were distributed to the
students in a random order. Students were then told to
read the instructions on the first page of the booklet,
but to keep the booklet closed until after the tape had
been played. The booklets for students in the informed
group contained general memory instructions indicating
that the experiment involved a test of "your memory for
the names of various popular songs." Students in the
informed group were also asked to attend to the
frequency of each song segment so that they could later
make accurate frequency judgments. Students in the
uninformed group received similar instructions but they
were not told that their memory for the frequency of
occurrence of song segments would be tested. The
instructions also informed students in both groups about

Place periods or commas within quotation marks.

Do not use contractions such as weren't.

Memory for Frequency   8

the general nature of what would be played on the tape, and the fact that some songs would be repeated.

After the presentation tape was played, students were asked to fill out the brief questionnaire on the second page of the booklet. This took approximately 2 min. This questionnaire was used primarily as a filler activity to introduce a delay between hearing the tape and the frequency judgment test. The test tape, containing the 20 song segments, was then played and students were asked to estimate how many times each song was heard on the previous tape. Students were told to guess if they were not sure.

Finally, the test tape was played again, and students were asked to try to identify the title and the name of the artist for each song segment. The tape was stopped after each segment and approximately 30 s were allowed for the two identifications.

Results

Before carrying out the analysis of the frequency judgment test, the characteristics of the students tested in the experiment were examined using their responses to the questionnaire. The mean responses of the students in the informed and uninformed groups to four critical items on the questionnaire are summarized in Table 1. Although there were slight differences across groups, the mean responses indicated that the two groups of students were comparable in terms of the

"Min" (without period, except at end of sentence) is abbreviation for minute.

← Center

Table appears on separate page near end of manuscript. Do not refer to a table or figure by position (e.g., see Table 1 below).

Memory for Frequency   9

number of hours each day they spent listening to music, their liking of rock music, and their self-assessed memory ability for previously heard music.

Two dependent variables were considered in assessing the accuracy of students' frequency judgment performance. First, as a measure of what could be called absolute accuracy, the number of times each student correctly judged the actual frequency of presentation was recorded. The mean number of these "hits" was 9.46 (_SD_ = 3.04) for students in the informed group, and 9.00 (_SD_ = 2.89) for students in the uninformed group. The difference between these means was not statistically significant, _t_(24) = 0.40, _p_ > .05.

An alternative method for measuring the accuracy of frequency judgment performance is to assess the ability to discriminate among items of different presentation frequencies. This relative measure of frequency judgment accuracy was used as a second dependent variable in this study. The mean estimated frequency as a function of actual frequency was determined on the basis of the four frequency judgments made at each of five levels of frequency. Thus, for each student the mean estimated frequency for the four zero-presented songs, for the four once-presented songs, and so forth, was calculated. The means of these means for each frequency level and for both informed and uninformed students are shown in Figure 1. As can be seen in the figure, frequency estimates in both groups increased as actual frequency

Underline all statistical terms.

Degrees of freedom for t, F, or r are reported in parentheses (with no space after statistical term).

Do not abbreviate "Figure."

Names of conditions are not capitalized.

Figure caption and figure appear on separate pages at end of manuscript.

Memory for Frequency   10

of occurrence increased. Moreover, an inspection of the

data in Figure 1 reveals that there were only slight

differences in mean frequency judgments as a function of

being informed or not being informed about an upcoming

frequency judgment test.

— Can be abbreviated "ANOVA."

Put spaces between "x" and numbers indicating levels of design.

A 2 X 5 analysis of variance including the two

independent variables of instructions and frequency

level was carried out on the data summarized in Figure

1. Although there was some suggestion of an interaction

in the nonparallel lines in the figure, there was no

statistically significant interaction between

instructions and frequency level, $\underline{F}$(4, 96) = 1.82, $\underline{p}$ >

05. There was also no significant difference in the mean

judgments for students in the informed group (2.20) as

compared to those in the uniformed group (2.34), $\underline{F}$(1,24)

< 1. However, actual frequency was a statistically

significant variable, $\underline{F}$(4,96) = 129.40, $\underline{p}$ < .01. The

mean estimates for frequencies 0, 1, 2, 3, and 4, were

0.39, 1.38, 2.52, 3.31, and 3.76, respectively.

Therefore, there was evidence that accurate relative

frequency judgments for excerpts from popular songs can

be made. But there was no evidence that students

differed in their memory for frequency of hearing songs

as a function of the instructions given to them

regarding a frequency judgment test.

The number of titles and artists correctly

identified by each student was also determined. Among

Proofread! (Even spellcheckers miss some errors.)

Check to see that greater than or less than sign is correctly placed after $\underline{p}$.

M is abbreviation for arithmetic mean.

all 26 students the range of song titles (of 20 possible) identified correctly was 0 to 18, (M = 8.81). The range of correct identification of artists was the same (M = 8.27). The numbers of titles and artists correctly identified were highly correlated, r(24) = .90. Because of this close relationship, the number of titles correctly identified was chosen to indicate the degree of knowledge that a student had about the songs heard. The correlation was determined between students' knowledge of the songs and the accuracy of their frequency judgments as reflected by the number of "hits"

Footnote appears as raised numeral.

on the frequency judgement test.[1] The obtained correlation was r(24) = .70, which is reliably larger than zero, t(24) = 4.79, p < .01. The significant correlation suggests that frequency judgment accuracy varies with a person's knowledge of the to-be-judged stimuli.

Discussion   *←—— Center*

The present experiment investigated people's abilities to judge the frequency with which they heard a number of popular songs. Prior to listening to the songs, college students were either informed or not informed about the later frequency judgment task. In agreement with results of other published studies in this area (e.g., Hasher & Chromiak, 1977), no significant difference in frequency judgment performance was observed as a function of instructions to remember frequency. Moreover, in both the informed and uninformed conditions of the experiment, frequency estimates

increased as frequency of actual occurrence increased.
These findings support the notion that frequency
information for musical stimuli, like that for verbal or
pictorial stimuli, is encoded "automatically."

The finding, however, that accuracy of frequency
judgments correlated with students' knowledge of the
musical stimuli, poses a challenge for the strictly
automatic encoding process proposed by Hasher and Zacks
(1979). There are apparently individual differences in
frequency judgment performance that are linked to
knowledge of the stimuli to be judged. One possibility
is that memory for frequency is likely to be encoded
more easily when stimuli are meaningful than when they
are not meaningful. Although Hasher and Chromiak (1977)
have indicated that meaningfulness is not a critical
factor in determining automatic encoding of frequency
information, the present results suggest otherwise.

Although meaningful elaboration of the stimuli to
be judged may influence memory for frequency, this
suggestion must be made tentatively. The relationship
between knowledge (defined by number of song titles
identified) and memory for frequency (defined by number
of "hits") is only correlational. There are several
other possible factors that may be responsible for this
relationship. For example, students who know more song
titles are likely to be more familiar with music in
general than are students who do not know many titles.

Year of publication appears in parentheses even when reference has appeared previously in manuscript.

The correlation between knowledge of the songs and
accuracy of frequency judgments may be attributable to
this general expertise in music rather than to
meaningful elaboration. An "expert" might be able to
make finer discriminations among stimuli than can a
nonexpert. This alternative explanation could be tested
by administering a frequency judgment test for musical
stimuli to groups of people selected on the basis of
their musical expertise. If general musical expertise is
a critical factor, then frequency judgment accuracy
should be greater for groups with greater expertise. Of
course, in testing this possible explanation it would be
essential to demonstrate that frequency judgment
accuracy for nonmusical stimuli does not vary with
changes in musical expertise.

Because all students were advised that their memory
for song titles would be tested, it is possible that
students who knew many titles were less frustrated or
less anxious than those who knew only a few titles. Such
affective differences could account for the original
correlation if it were argued that frequency judgment
accuracy decreased with increasing anxiety or
frustration. An account based on differences in
frequency judgment performances as a function of mild
emotional changes would also provide evidence against
automatic encoding (see Hasher & Zacks, 1979).

In summary, the present results confirm that
accurate frequency judgments can be made for musical
stimuli, thereby extending the generality of frequency

Memory for Frequency   14

encoding beyond verbal and pictorial stimuli. The
absence of a difference in frequency judgment accuracy
for informed and uninformed groups supports the notion
that frequency information is encoded automatically. The
automatic encoding of frequency appears inconsistent,
however, with the obtained correlation between knowledge
of the musical stimuli and frequency judgment accuracy.
The basis for this correlation and the extent of the
challenge it poses to the automatic encoding theory are
unclear at this time.

Use initials for first names

Memory for Frequency   15

References   ← *Center*

Indent first line same as paragraph indentation for each reference.

Hasher, L., & Chromiak, W. (1977). The processing of frequency information: An automatic mechanism? Journal of Verbal Learning and Verbal Behavior, 16, 173-184.

Only first word of journal article or book title is in Caps.

Hasher, L., Goldstein, D., & Toppino, T. (1977). Frequency and the conference of referential validity. Journal of Verbal Learning and Verbal Behavior, 16, 107-112.

Hasher, L., & Zacks, R. T. (1979). Automatic and effortful processes in memory. Journal of Experimental Psychology: General, 108, 356-388.

Volume number of journal appears as Arabic numeral.

Underwood, B.J. (1971). Recognition memory. In H. H. Kendler & J.T. Spence (Eds.), Essays in neobehaviorism (pp. 313-335). New York: Appleton-Century Crofts.

Page numbers of book chapters are included.

Zechmeister, E. B., & Nyberg, S. E. (1982). Human memory: An introduction to research and theory. Monterey, CA: Brooks/Cole.

Underline titles of books.

Use ampersand to separate authors' names in title.

Journal titles are typed in lower and upper case, with major words in caps, underlined.

Word "data" is plural (i.e., takes plural verb).

Start each paragraph in author note with indentation.

Memory for Frequency   16

Author Note   ← Center

The data reported in this study are "real" and are based on an experiment performed as a classroom demonstration in an undergraduate course taught by E. B. Zechmeister. The author was asked, along with other members of the class, to participate in this experiment. Then, in order to pass the course the author was required to prepare a written manuscript, using strict American Psychological Association (APA) editorial style, which reported the results of this experiment. Subsequently, the instructor had the nerve to ask whether he might use the manuscript (after some "editing") in his book!

Both the author and the instructor wish to acknowledge the help of Jim Fidler in preparing the audio tapes used in this experiment.

Correspondence concerning this article should be addressed to Nancy A. Norton, Psychology Department, Loyola University of Chicago, 6525 N. Sheridan Road, Chicago, IL 60626.

Last paragraph in Author Note specifies author's address for correspondence. (Use this form exactly.)

Memory for Frequency   17

Footnote

[1] Typically a single correlation should not be computed across two or more groups of subjects who have been treated differently. Instead, the correlation of interest should be computed within each group of subjects and an average correlation across groups would then be used to describe the overall correlation. In the present study there were no significant differences between groups in either knowledge of the songs or accuracy of frequency judgments. Therefore, for the sake of simplicity, only one correlation was computed.

Note:
Use footnotes sparingly in manuscript.

Type word "Table" and Arabic numeral flush with margin →

Table 1

Mean Responses of Students in Informed and

Uninformed Groups to Questionnaire Items

← *Table title appears underlined with first letter of major words in Caps.*

Center column heads over appropriate columns.

Use horizontal rules (using underline function to separate headings from body of table.

Item	Condition	
	Informed	Uninformed
Hours listening to		
music	2.44	2.29
Liking of rock		
music	4.92	5.71
Knowledge of contemporary		
music	4.54	4.85
Memory for music		
previously heard	5.38	5.15

Note. Means for "hours listening" item are based on

students' judgments of number of hours; means for remaining

items are based on students' responses using a 7-point scale,

with 7 being the high end of the scale.

Table "notes" are typed flush with margin.

Do not.
abbreviate
"Figure."

Memory for Frequency   19

Figure Caption ⟵———— Center

⟶ <u>Figure 1.</u> Estimated frequency of occurrence as a function of
actual frequency of occurrence.

Note:

The figure itself appears on separate
page at end of manuscript.

Note:

More than one figure caption may
appear on figure caption page.

484   APPENDIX C: COMMUNICATION IN PSYCHOLOGY

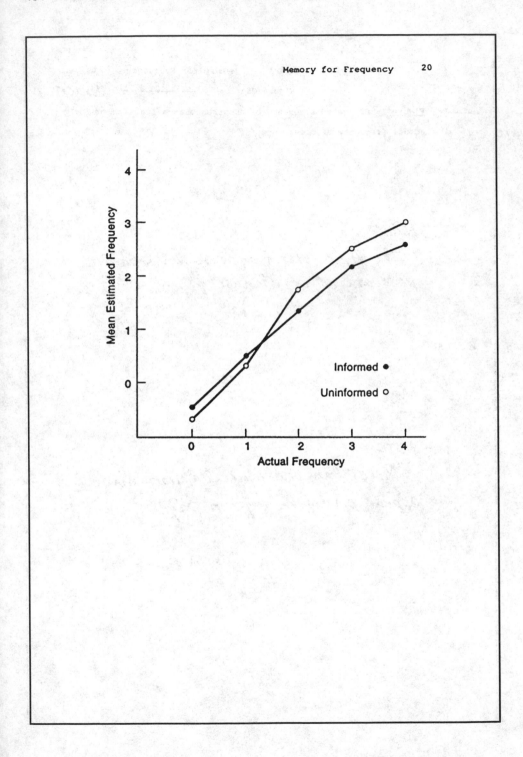

Glossary

ABAB design (reversal design)   Single-case experimental design in which an initial baseline stage (A) is followed by a treatment stage (B), a return to baseline (A), and then aother treatment stage (B); the researcher observes whether behavior changes on introduction of the treatment, reverses when the treatment is withdrawn, and improves again when the treatment is reintroduced.

ABBA counterbalancing   A technique for balancing practice effects in the complete repeated measures design that involves presenting the conditions in one sequence (e.g., AB) followed by the opposite of the same sequence (e.g., BA).

accidental sample   Type of nonprobability sample that results when availability and willingness to respond are the overriding factors used in selecting respondents; generally low in representativeness.

actuarial prediction   Prediction of people's typical or average behavior based on reliable correlations between variables (e.g., predicting students' college GPA based on SAT scores).

analytical comparison   A statistical technique that can be applied (usually after obtaining a significant omnibus *F*-test) to locate the specific source of systematic variation in an experiment.

applied research   See **basic versus applied research**.

archival data   Source of evidence based on records or documents relating the activities of individuals, institutions, governments, and other groups; used as an alternative to or in conjunction with other research methods.

baseline stage   First stage of a single-case experiment in which a record is made of the individual's behavior prior to any intervention.

basement effect   See **ceiling effect**.

basic versus applied research   Whereas basic research mainly seeks knowledge about nature simply for the sake of understanding it better, applied research seeks knowledge that will modify or improve the present situation; however, basic and applied research are considered to have a reciprocal relationship, for example, when basic research is used to identify abstract principles that can be applied in real-world settings and when applied research is used to reveal possible limitations or extensions of these principles.

behaviorism   Approach to the study of psychology that emphasizes observable behavior as the only legitimate source of scientific evidence and defines psychology's goal as the prediction and control of behavior.

behavior modification   Application of learning conditioning principles in order to change behavior; first used synonymously with behavior therapy.

behavior therapy   Application of learning conditioning principles to clinical populations; first used synonymously with behavior modification.

biased sample   Sample in which the distribution of characteristics is systematically different from that of the parent population.

block randomization   The most common technique for carrying out random assignment in the random groups design; each block includes a random order of the conditions, and there are as many blocks as there are subjects in each condition of the experiment.

case study   Intensive description and analysis of a single individual.

causal inference   Identification of the cause or causes of a phenomenon, by establishing covariation of cause and effect, a time-order relationship with cause preceding effect, and the elimination of plausible alternative causes.

ceiling (basement) effect   Measurement problem whereby the researcher cannot measure the effects of an independent variable or a possible interaction because performance has reached a maximum (minimum) in any condition of the experiment.

checklist   Instrument used to record the presence or absence of something in the situation under observation.

clinical significance   Measure of the strength of a treatment as indicated by the extent to which it has improved the life of a client in a real-world setting; usually assessed using either subjective evaluation or social comparison.

coding   Initial step in data reduction, especially with narrative records, in which units of behavior or particular events are identified and classified according to specific criteria.

complex design   Experiment in which two or more independent variables are studied simultaneously.

confederate   Someone in the service of a researcher who is instructed to behave in a certain way in order to help produce an experimental treatment.

confounding   Occurs when the independent variable of interest systematically covaries with a second, unintended independent variable.

contamination   Occurs when there is communication of information about the experiment between groups of participants.

content analysis   Any of a variety of techniques for making inferences by objectively identifying specific characteristics of messages, usually written communications but may be any form of message; used extensively in the analysis of archival data.

control   Key component of the scientific method whereby the effect of various factors possibly responsible for a phenomenon are isolated; three basic types of control are manipulation, holding conditions constant, and balancing.

correlation   Exists when two different measures of the same people, events, or things vary together; the presence of a correlation makes it possible to predict values on one variable by knowing the values on the second variable.

correlation coefficient   Statistic indicating how well two measures vary together; absolute size ranges from 0.0 (no correlation) to 1.00 (perfect correlation); direction of covariation is indicated by the sign of the coefficient, a plus (+) indicating that both measures covary in the same direction and a minus (–) indicating that the variables vary in opposite directions.

correlational research   Research whose goal is to identify predictive relationships among naturally occurring variables.

counterbalancing   Techniques for balancing practice effects across the conditions of an experiment.

cross-sectional design   Survey-research design in which one or more samples of the population are selected and information is collected from the samples at one time.

data reduction   Process in the analysis of behavioral data whereby results are meaningfully organized and statements summarizing important findings are prepared.

debriefing   Process following a research session through which participants are informed about the rationale for the research in which they participated, the need for any deception, and their specific contribution to the research. Important goals of debriefing are to clear up any misconceptions and to leave participants with a positive feeling toward psychological research.

deception   Intentionally withholding information about significant aspects of a research project from a participant or presenting misinformation about the research to participants.

demand characteristics   Cues and other information used by participants to guide their behavior in a psychological study, often leading participants to do what they believe the observer (experimenter) expects them to do.

dependent variable   Measure of behavior used by the researcher to assess the effect (if any) of the independent variables.

differential transfer   Potential problem in repeated measures designs when performance in one condition differs depending on which of two other conditions precedes it.

double-blind   Both the participant and the observer are kept unaware (blind) of what treatment is being administered.

ecological psychology   Has as its goal the comprehensive description of individuals in everyday contexts.

effect size   Index of the strength of the relationship between the independent variable and dependent variable that is independent of sample size.

element   Each member of the population of interest.

empirical approach   Approach to acquiring knowledge that emphasizes direct observation and experimentation as a way of answering questions.

ethogram   Complete catalog of all the behavior patterns of an organism, including information as to frequency, duration, and context of occurrence.

ethology   Study of the behavior of organisms in relation to their natural environment; generally considered a branch of biology.

event sampling   Procedure whereby the observer records each event that meets a predetermined definition; more efficient method than time sampling when event of interest occurs infrequently.

experimenter effects   Experimenters' expectations that may lead them to treat subjects differently in different groups or to record data in a biased manner.

external validity   Extent to which the results of a research study can be generalized to different populations, settings, and conditions.

extraneous variables   Potential independent variables that are not of direct interest to a researcher, but, in order to avoid confounding, must be controlled (e.g., nature of experimenters, size of group tested).

field experiment   Procedure in which one or more independent variables is manipulated by an observer in a natural setting to determine the effect on behavior.

field notes   Verbal records of a trained observer that provide a running description of participants, events, settings, and behaviors.

F-test   Statistical test based on the analysis of variance, specifically the ratio of systematic variation and error variation. Under the null hypothesis both sources of variation represent error variation only and the expected value of F is 1.00.

Hawthorne effect   Changes in a person's behavior brought about by the interest shown in that person by significant others.

hypothesis   Tentative explanation for a phenomenon.

idiographic approach   Intensive study of an individual, with an emphasis on both individual uniqueness and lawfulness.

independent groups design   Each separate group in the experiment represents a different condition as defined by the level of the independent variable.

independent variable   Factor for which the researcher either selects or manipulates at least two levels in order to determine its effect on behavior.

individual differences (subject) variable   Characteristic or trait that varies consistently across individuals (e.g., age, depression, gender, intelligence).

inferential statistics   Means to test whether the differences in a dependent variable associated with various conditions of an experiment are reliable, that is, larger than would be expected on the basis of error variation alone.

informed consent   Explicitly expressed willingness to participate in a research project based on clear understanding of the nature of the research, of the consequences of not participating, and of all factors that might be expected to influence willingness to participate.

interaction   What occurs when the effect of one independent variable differs depending on the level of a second independent variable.

internal validity   Degree to which differences in performance can be attributed unambiguously to an effect of an independent variable, as opposed to an effect of some other (uncontrolled) variable; an internally valid study is free of confounds.

interobserver reliability   Degree to which two independent observers are in agreement.

interrupted time-series design   See **simple interrupted time-series design** and **time series with nonequivalent control group**.

interviewer bias   Occurs when the interviewer tries to adjust the wording of a question to fit the respondent or records only selected portions of the respondent's answers.

Latin Square   Used in the incomplete repeated measures design to balance practice and order effects; a selection of orders in which each condition appears at each ordinal position once, and each condition precedes and follows each other condition exactly once.

longitudinal design   Survey research design in which the same sample of respondents is interviewed more than once.

main effect   Overall effect of an independent variable in a complex design.

margin of error   In survey research, an estimate of the difference between a result obtained from a sample (e.g., the sample mean) and the corresponding true population value (e.g., population mean).

matched groups design   Type of independent groups design in which the researcher forms comparable groups by matching participants on a pretest task and then randomly assigning the members of these matched sets of participants to the conditions of the experiment.

measurement scale   One of four levels of physical and psychological measurement: nominal (categorizing), ordinal (ranking), interval (specifying distance between stimuli), and ratio (having an absolute zero point).

mechanical subject loss   Occurs when a subject fails to complete the experiment because of equipment failure or because of experimenter error.

meta-analysis   Analysis of results of several (often, very many) independent experiments investigating the same research area; the measure used in a meta-analysis is typically effect size.

minimal risk   A research participant is said to experience minimal risk when probability and magnitude of harm or discomfort anticipated in the research are not greater than that ordinarily encountered in daily life or during the performance of routine tests.

multimethod approach   Approach to hypothesis testing that seeks evidence by collecting data using several different measures of behavior; a recognition of the fact that any single measure of behavior can result from some artifact of the measuring process.

multiple-baseline design (across subjects, across behaviors, across situations)   A single-case experimental design in which the effect of a treatment is demonstrated by showing that behaviors in more than one baseline change as a consequence of the introduction of a treatment; multiple baselines are established for different individuals, for different behaviors in the same individual, or for the same individual in different situations.

N = 1 designs   See **single-case experiment**.

narrative record   Record intended to provide a more or less faithful reproduction of behavior as it originally occurred.

natural groups design   Type of independent groups design in which the conditions represent the selected levels of a naturally occurring independent variable, for example, the individual differences variable age.

naturalistic observation   Observation of behavior in a more or less natural setting without any attempt by the observer to intervene.

nomothetic approach   Approach to research that seeks to establish broad generalizations or laws which apply to large groups (populations) of individuals; the average or typical performance of a group is emphasized.

nonequivalent control group design   Quasi-experimental procedure in which a comparison is made between control and treatment groups that have been established on some basis other than through random assignment of participants to groups.

nonprobability sampling   Sampling procedure in which there is no way to estimate the probability of each element's being included in the sample; two common types are accidental sampling and purposive sampling.

null hypothesis   Assumption used as the first step in statistical inference whereby the independent variable is said to have had no effect.

observer bias   Systematic errors in observation often resulting from the observer's expectancies regarding the outcome of a study (i.e., expectancy effects).

operational definition Procedure whereby a concept is defined solely in terms of the operations used to produce and measure it.

participant observation Observation of behavior by someone who also has an active and significant role in the situation or context in which behavior is recorded.

physical traces Source of evidence based on the remnants, fragments, and products of past behavior; used as an alternative to or in conjunction with other research methods.

placebo control Procedure by which a substance that resembles a drug or other active substance but is actually an inert, or inactive, substance is given to participants.

plagiarism Presentation of another's ideas or work without clearly identifying the source.

population Set of all the cases of interest.

power Probability in a statistical test that a false null hypothesis will be rejected; power is related to the level of significance selected, the size of the treatment effect, and the sample size.

practice effects Changes that participants undergo with repeated testing. Practice effects are the summation of both positive (e.g., familiarity with a task) and negative (e.g., boredom) factors associated with repeated measurement.

privacy Right of individuals to decide how information about them is to be communicated to others.

probability sampling Sampling procedure in which the probability that each element of the population will be included in the sample can be specified.

program evaluation Research that seeks to determine whether a change proposed by an institution, government agency, or other unit of society is needed and likely to have an effect as planned or, when implemented, to actually have an effect.

quasi-experiments Procedures that resemble those characteristics of true experiments, for example, that some type of intervention or treatment is used and a comparison is provided, but are lacking in the degree of control found in true experiments.

random assignment Most common technique for forming groups as part of an independent groups design; the goal is to establish equivalent groups by balancing individual differences.

random groups design Most common type of independent groups design in which subjects are randomly selected or randomly assigned to each group such that groups are considered comparable at the start of the experiment.

random sampling See **simple random sampling**.

reactivity Influence that an observer has on the behavior under observation; behavior influenced by an observer may not be representative of behavior when an observer is not present.

regression to the mean Because some component of a test score is due to error (as opposed to true score), extreme scores on one test are likely to be closer to the mean on a second test, thus posing a threat to the validity of an experiment in which extreme scores are selected; the amount of regression is greater for less reliable tests.

relevant independent variable Independent variable that has been shown to influence behavior, either directly, by producing a main effect, or indirectly, by resulting in an interaction in combination with a second independent variable.

reliability A measurement is reliable when it is consistent.

repeated measures designs Research designs in which each subject participates in all conditions of the experiment (i.e., measurement is repeated on the same subject).

replication Repeating the exact procedures used in an experiment to determine whether the same results are obtained.

representativeness   A sample is representative to the extent it has the same distribution of characteristics as the population from which it was selected; our ability to generalize from sample to population is critically dependent on representativeness.

response bias   Threat to the representativeness of a sample that occurs when some participants selected to respond to a survey systematically fail to complete the survey (e.g., due to failure to complete a lengthy questionnaire or to comply with a request to participate in a phone survey).

risk/benefit ratio   Subjective evaluation of the risk to a research participant relative to the benefit both to the individual and to society of the results of the proposed research.

sample   Something less than all the cases of interest; in survey research, a subset of the population actually drawn from the sampling frame.

sampling frame   Specific listing of all the members of the population of interest; an operational definition of the population.

scientific method   Approach to knowledge that emphasizes empirical rather than intuitive processes, testable hypotheses, systematic and controlled observation of operationally defined phenomena, data collection using accurate and precise instrumentation, valid and reliable measures, and objective reporting of results; scientists tend to be critical and, most importantly, skeptical.

selection bias   Threat to the representativeness of a sample that occurs when the procedures used to select a sample result in the over- or underrepresentation of a significant segment of the population.

selective deposit   Bias that results from the way physical traces are laid down and the way archival sources are produced, edited, or altered, as they are established; when present, the bias severely limits generality of research findings.

selective subject loss   Occurs when subjects are lost differentially across the conditions of the experiment as the result of some characteristic of each subject that is related to the outcome of the study.

selective survival   Bias that results from the way physical traces and archives survive over time; when present, the bias severely limits the external validity of research findings.

sensitivity   Refers to the likelihood in an experiment that the effect of an independent variable will be detected when that variable does, indeed, have an effect; sensitivity is increased to the extent that error variation is reduced (e.g., by holding variables constant rather than balancing them).

simple interrupted time-series design   Quasi-experimental procedure in which changes in a dependent variable are observed for some period of time both before and after a treatment is introduced.

simple main effect   Effect of one independent variable at one level of a second independent variable in a complex design.

simple random sampling (random selection)   Type of probability sampling in which each possible sample of a specified size in the population has an equal chance of being selected.

single-case experiment   Procedure that focuses on behavior change in one individual ($N = 1$) by systematically contrasting conditions within that individual while continuously monitoring behavior.

situation sampling   Random or systematic selection of situations in which observations are to be made with the goal of representativeness across circumstances, locations, and conditions.

social comparison Measure of clinical significance of a treatment in which the researcher compares the behavior of a client after treatment with the behavior of a "normal" group of people.

social desirability Pressures on survey respondents to answer as they think they should respond in accordance with what is most socially acceptable, and not in accordance with what they actually believe.

spurious relationship What exists when evidence falsely indicates that two or more variables are associated.

statistically significant When the probability of an obtained difference in an experiment is smaller than would be expected if error variation alone was assumed to be responsible for the difference, the difference is statistically significant.

stratified random sampling Type of probability sampling in which the population is divided into subpopulations called strata and random samples are drawn from each of these strata.

structured observation Variety of observational methods using intervention in which the degree of control is often less than in field experiments; frequently used by clinical and developmental psychologists when making behavioral assessments.

subjective evaluation Measure of clinical significance of a treatment in which the judgments of people who have contact with the client are used to assess whether the behavior of the client is perceptibly different after treatment from what it was before treatment.

successive independent samples design Survey research design in which a series of cross-sectional surveys is done and the same questions are asked of each succeeding sample of respondents.

theory Logically organized set of propositions that serves to define events, describe relationships among events, and explain the occurrence of these events; scientific theories guide research and organize empirical knowledge.

threats to internal validity Possible causes of a phenomenon that must be controlled so a clear cause-effect inference can be made.

time sampling Selection of observation intervals either systematically or randomly with the goal of obtaining a representative sample of behavior.

time series with nonequivalent control group (See also **simple interrupted time-series design**.) Quasi-experimental procedure that improves on the validity of a simple time-series design by including a nonequivalent control group; both treatment and comparison groups are observed for a period of time both before and after the treatment.

unobtrusive (nonreactive) measures Measures of behavior that eliminate the problem of reactivity because observations are made in such a way that the presence of the observer is not detected by those being observed.

validity The "truthfulness" of a measure; a valid measure is one that measures what it claims to measure.

References

Abelson, R. P. (1985). A variance paradox: When a little is a lot. *Psychological Bulletin, 97*, 129–133.

Adair, J. G., Dushenko, T. W., & Lindsay, R. C. L. (1985). Ethical regulations and their impact on research practice. *American Psychologist, 40*, 59–72.

Addison, W. E. (1986). Agonistic behavior in preschool children: A comparison of same-sex versus opposite-sex interactions. *Bulletin of the Psychonomic Society, 24*, 44–46.

Adjang, O. M. J. (1986). Exploring the social environment: A developmental study of teasing in chimpanzees. *Ethology, 73*, 136–160.

Adler, A. (1973). *Practice and theory of individual psychology* (P. Radin, Trans.). Totowa, NJ: Littlefield, Adams.

Adler, T. (1991, December). Outright fraud rare, but not poor science. *APA Monitor,* p. 11.

Albright, J. S., & Henderson, M. C. (1995). How real is depressive realism? A question of scales and standards. *Cognitive Therapy and Research, 19*, 589–609.

Allison, M. G., & Ayllon, T. (1980). Behavioral coaching in the development of skills in football, gymnastics, and tennis. *Journal of Applied Behavior Analysis, 13*, 297–314.

Allport, G. W. (1946). Letters from Jenny. *Journal of Abnormal and Social Psychology, 41* (3, 4).

Allport, G. W. (1961). *Pattern in growth and personality.* New York Holt, Rinehart and Winston.

Allport, G. W. (1965). *Letters from Jenny.* New York: Harcourt, Brace & World.

Altmann, J. (1974). Observational study of behavior: Sampling methods. *Behavior, 48*, 1–41.

American Psychiatric Association. (1994). *Diagnostic and statistical manual of mental disorders* (4th ed.). Washington, DC: Author.

American Psychological Association. (1991). Five-year report of the policy and planning board, 1990; Five years of turbulence, change, and growth within APA. *American Psychologist, 46,* 678–688.

American Psychological Association. (1992). Ethical principles of psychologists and code of conduct. *American Psychologist, 47,* 1597–1611.

American Psychological Association. (1994). *Publication Manual* (4th ed.). Washington, DC: Author.

American Psychological Association. (1995). Summary report of journal operations, 1994. *American Psychologist, 50,* 716–717.

Anderson, C. A. (1989). Temperature and aggression: Ubiquitous effects of heat on occurrence of human violence. *Psychological Bulletin, 106,* 74–96.

Anderson, C. R. (1976). Coping behaviors as intervening mechanisms in the inverted-U stress-performance relationship. *Journal of Applied Psychology, 61,* 30–34.

Anderson, J. R. (1990). *The adaptive character of thought.* Hillsdale, NJ: Erlbaum.

Anderson, J. R. (1993). *Rules of the mind.* Hillsdale, NJ: Erlbaum.

Anderson, J. R., & Milson, J. R. (1989). Human memory: An adaptive perspective. *Psychological Review, 96,* 703–719.

Anderson, K. J., & Revelle, W. (1982). Impulsivity, caffeine, and proofreading: A test of the Easterbrook hypothesis. *Journal of Experimental Psychology: Human Perception and Performance, 8,* 614–624.

Asch, S. E. (1951). Effects of group pressure upon the modification and distortion of judgments. In H. Guetzkow (Ed.), *Groups, leadership, and men* (pp. 177–190). Pittsburgh: Carnegie.

Asch, S. E. (1955). Opinions and social pressure. *Scientific American, 193,* 31–35.

Atkinson, R. C. (1968). Computerized instruction and the learning process. *American Psychologist, 23,* 225–239.

Atkinson, R. C., & Shiffrin, R. M. (1968). Human memory: A proposed system and its control processes. In K. W. Spence & J. T. Spence (Eds.), *The psychology of learning and motivation,* Vol. 2 (pp. 89–195). New York: Academic Press.

Azar, B. (1994a, December). Animal research threatened by activism. *APA Monitor,* p. 18.

Azar, B. (1994b, August). Computers create global research lab. *APA Monitor,* pp. 1, 16.

Azar, B. (1994c, August). Research made easier by computer networks. *APA Monitor,* p. 16.

Azar, B. (1995, May). Board approves ways to spend science funds. *APA Monitor,* p. 25.

Barash, D. P. (1977). Human ethology: Exchanging cheetahs for Chevrolets? *Environment and Behavior, 9,* 487–490.

Barker, R. G., Wright, H. F., Schoggen, M. F., & Barker, L. S. (1978). Day in the life of Mary Ennis. In R. G. Barker et al. (Eds.), *Habitats, environments, and human behavior* (pp. 51–98). San Francisco: Jossey-Bass.

Baron, J. N., & Reiss, P. C. (1985). Same time, next year: Aggregate analyses of the mass media and violent behavior. *American Sociological Review, 50,* 347–363.

Baron, R. M., & Kenny, D. A. (1986). The moderator-mediator variable distinction in social psychological research: Conceptual, strategic, and statistical considerations. *Journal of Personality and Social Psychology, 51,* 1173–1182.

Bartholomew, G. A. (1982). Scientific innovation and creativity: A zoologist's point of view. *American Zoologist, 22,* 227–335.

Bartlett, F. C. (1932). *Remembering: A study in experimental and social psychology.* Cambridge: Cambridge University Press.

Baumrind, D. (1985). Research using intentional deception: Ethical issues revisited. *American Psychologist, 40,* 165–174.

Berk, R. A., Boruch, R. F., Chambers, D. L., Rossi, P. H., & Witte, A. D. (1987). Social policy experimentation: A position paper. In D. S. Cordray & M. W. Lipsey (Eds.), *Evaluation Studies Review Annual,* Vol. 11 (pp. 630–672). Newbury Park, CA: Sage.

Bickman, L. (1976). Observational methods. In C. Selltiz, L. S. Wrightsman, & S. W. Cook (Eds.), *Research methods in social relations* (pp. 251–290). New York: Holt, Rinehart and Winston.

Blanchard, F. A., Crandall, C. S., Brigham, J. C., & Vaughn, L. A. (1994). Condemning and condoning racism: A social context approach to interracial settings. *Journal of Applied Psychology, 79,* 993–997.

Blank, P. D., Bellack, A. S., Rosnow, R. L., Rotheram-Borus, M. J., & Schooler, N. R. (1992). Scientific rewards and conflicts of ethical choices in human subjects research. *American Psychologist, 47,* 959–965.

Bloom, B. L., Asher, S. J., & White, S. W. (1978). Marital disruption as a stressor: A review and analysis. *Psychological Bulletin, 85,* 867–894.

Bolgar, H. (1965). The case study method. In B. B. Wolman (Ed.), *Handbook of clinical psychology* (pp. 28–39). New York: McGraw-Hill.

Bond, C. F., Jr., & Titus, L. J. (1983). Social facilitation: A meta-analysis of 241 studies. *Psychological Bulletin, 94,* 265–292.

Booth, W. (1988). Chimps and research: Endangered? *Science, 241,* 777–778.

Bootzin, R. R., Acocella, J. R., & Alloy, L. B. (1993). *Abnormal psychology: Current perspectives* (6th ed.). New York: McGraw-Hill.

Boring, E. G. (1950). *A history of experimental psychology.* New York: Appleton-Century-Crofts.

Boring, E. G. (1954). The nature and history of experimental control. *American Journal of Psychology, 67,* 573–589.

Bornstein, M. T., Bellack, A. S., & Hersen, M. (1977). Social-skills training for unassertive children: A multiple-baseline analysis. *Journal of Applied Behavior Analysis, 10,* 183–195.

Brainerd, C. J. (1978). *Piaget's theory of intelligence.* Englewood Cliffs, NJ: Prentice-Hall.

Brandt, R. M. (1972). *Studying behavior in natural settings.* New York: Holt, Rinehart and Winston: University Press of America, 1981.

Bridgewater, C. A., Bornstein, P. H., & Walkenbach, J. (1981). Ethical issues and the assignment of publication credit. *American Psychologist, 36,* 524–525.

Brigham, T. A., Meier, S. M., & Goodner, V. (1995). Increasing designated driving with a program of prompts and incentives. *Journal of Applied Behavior Analysis, 28,* 83–84.

Broach, D. (1992, June). *Non-cognitive predictions of performance in radar-based air traffic control training.* Paper presented at the Fourth Annual Convention of the American Psychological Society, San Diego, CA.

Brown, R., & Kulik, J. (1977). Flashbulb memories. *Cognition, 5,* 73–99.

Browne, M. A., & Mahoney, M. J. (1984). Sport psychology. *Annual Review of Psychology, 35,* 605–625.

Brush, S. G. (1991). Women in science and engineering. *American Scientist, 79,* 404–419.

Burns, M. S., Haywood, H. C., & Delclos, V. R. (1987). Young children's problem-solving strategies: An observational study. *Journal of Applied Developmental Psychology, 8,* 113–121.

Campbell, A. (1981). *The sense of well-being in America.* New York: McGraw-Hill.

Campbell, A., Converse, P. E., & Rodgers, W. L. (1975). *The quality of American life; July-August, 1971.* Ann Arbor: ISR Social Science Archive.

Campbell, D. T. (1969). Reforms as experiments. *American Psychologist, 24,* 409–429.

Campbell, D. T., & Stanley, J. C. (1966). *Experimental and quasi-experimental designs for research*. Chicago: Rand McNally.

Campbell, R. (Ed.). (1992). *Mental lives: Case studies in cognition*. Oxford: Blackwell.

Ceci, S. J. (1993, August). *Cognitive and social factors in children's testimony*. Master Lecture presented at the American Psychological Convention, Toronto, Ontario, Canada.

Chambers, J. H., & Ascione, F. R. (1987). The effects of prosocial and aggressive videogames on children's donating and helping. *Journal of Genetic Psychology, 148*, 499–505.

Cherlin, A. J., Furstenberg, F. F., Jr., Chase-Lansdale, P. L., Kiernan, K. E., Robins, P. K., Morrison, D. R., & Teitler, J. O. (1991). Longitudinal studies of effects of divorce on children in Great Britain and the United States. *Science, 252*, 1386–1389.

Chow, S. L. (1988). Significance test or effect size? *Psychological Bulletin, 103*, 105–110.

Christensen, L. (1988). Deception in psychological research: When is its use justified? *Personality and Social Psychology Bulletin, 14*, 664–675.

Cohen, D. (1979). *J. B. Watson: The founder of behaviorism*. London: Routledge & Kegan Paul.

Cohen, J. (1988). *Statistical power analysis for the behavioral sciences* (2nd ed.). Hillsdale, NJ: Erlbaum.

Cohen, J. (1992). A power primer. *Psychological Bulletin, 112*, 155–159.

Cohen, J. (1995). The earth is round ($p < .05$). *American Psychologist, 49*, 997–1003.

Cohen, N. J., McCloskey, M., & Wible, C. G. (1990). Flashbulb memories and underlying cognitive mechanisms: Reply to Pillemer. *Journal of Experimental Psychology: General, 119*, 97–100.

Cohen, S., Evans, G. W., Krantz, D. S., & Stokols, D. (1980). Physiological, motivational, and cognitive effects of aircraft noise on children: Moving from the laboratory to the field. *American Psychologist, 35*, 231–243.

Converse, P. E., & Traugott, M. W. (1986). Assessing the accuracy of polls and surveys. *Science, 234*, 1094–1097.

Cook, T. D., & Campbell, D. T. (1979). *Quasi-experimentation: Design and analysis issues for field settings*. Chicago: Rand McNally.

Cordaro, L., & Ison, J. R. (1963). Psychology of the scientist: X. Observer bias in classical conditioning of the planarian. *Psychological Reports, 13*, 787–789.

Coren, S., & Porac, C. (1977). Fifty centuries of right-handedness: The historical record. *Science, 198*, 631–632.

Coughlin, E. K. (1988). Scholar who submitted bogus articles to journals may be disciplined. *The Chronicle of Higher Education, 35*(1), A7.

Courneya, K. S., & Carron, A. V. (1992). The home advantage in sport competitions: A literature review. *Journal of Sport & Exercise Psychology, 14*, 13–27.

Cronbach, L. J. (1992). Four *Psychological Bulletin* articles in perspective. *Psychological Bulletin, 12*, 389–392.

Crossen, C. (1994). *Tainted truth: The manipulation of fact in America*. New York: Simon & Schuster.

Crusco, A. H., & Wetzel, C. G. (1984). The Midas touch: The effects of interpersonal touch on restaurant tipping. *Personality and Social Psychology Bulletin, 10*, 512–517.

Curtiss, S. R. (1977). *Genie: A psycholinguistic study of a modern-day "wild child."* New York Academic Press.

Dawes, R. M. (1988). *Rational choice in an uncertain world*. San Diego: Harcourt, Brace, Jovanovich.

Dawes, R. M. (1991, June). *Problems with a psychology of college sophomores.* Paper presented at the Third Annual Convention of the American Psychological Society, Washington, DC.

Dawes, R. M., Faust, D., & Meehl, P. E. (1993). Statistical prediction versus clinical prediction: Improving what works. In G. Keren & C. Lewis (Eds.), *A handbook for data analysis in the behavioral sciences: Methodological issues* (pp. 351–367). Hillsdale, NJ: Erlbaum.

Dickie, J. R. (1987). Interrelationships within the mother-father-infant triad. In P. W. Berman & F. A. Pedersen (Eds.), *Men's transitions to parenthood: Longitudinal studies of early family experience* (pp. 113–143). Hillsdale, NJ: Erlbaum.

Diener, E., & Crandall, R. (1978). *Ethics in social and behavioral research.* Chicago: University of Chicago Press.

Dittmar, M. L., Berch, D. B., & Warm, J. S. (1982). Sustained visual attention in deaf and hearing adults. *Bulletin of the Psychonomic Society, 19,* 339–342.

Divorce of the year. (1973, March 12). *Newsweek,* pp. 48–49.

Dolan, C. A., Sherwood, A., & Light, K. C. (1992). Cognitive coping strategies and blood pressure responses to real-life stress in healthy young men. *Health Psychology, 11,* 233–240.

Eibl-Eibesfeldt, I. (1975). *Ethology: The biology of behavior.* New York: Holt, Rinehart and Winston.

Entwisle, D. R., & Astone, N. M. (1994). Some practical guidelines for measuring youth's race/ethnicity and socioeconomic status. *Child Development, 65,* 1521–1540.

Epstein, S. (1979). The stability of behavior: On predicting most of the people much of the time. *Journal of Personality and Social Psychology, 37,* 1097–1126.

Erber, R. (1991). Affective and semantic priming: Effects of mood on category accessibility and inference. *Journal of Experimental Social Psychology, 27,* 480–498.

Ericsson, K. A., & Charness, N. (1994). Expert performance: Its structure and acquisition. *American Psychologist, 49,* 725–747.

Ericsson, K. A., Chase, W. G., & Faloon, S. (1980). Acquisition of a memory skill. *Science, 208,* 1181–1182.

Evans, R., & Donnerstein, E. (1974). Some implications for psychological research of early versus late term participation by college students. *Journal of Research in Personality, 8,* 102–109.

Fenney, D. M. (1987). Human rights and animal welfare. *American Psychologist, 42,* 593–599.

Festinger, L., Riecken, H., & Schachter, S. (1956). *When prophecy fails.* Minneapolis: University of Minnesota Press.

Fine, M. A., & Kurdek, L. A. (1993). Reflections on determining authorship credit and authorship order on faculty-student collaborations. *American Psychologist, 48,* 1141–1147.

Fiore, S. (1994, May/June). The student notebook. *APS Observer,* p. 28.

Fischer, K., Schoeneman, T. J., & Rubanowitz, D. E. (1987). Attributions in the advice columns: II. The dimensionality of actors' and observers' explanations for interpersonal problems. *Personality and Social Psychology Bulletin, 13,* 458–466.

Fisher, C. B., & Fryberg, D. (1994). Participant partners: College students weigh the costs and benefits of deceptive research. *American Psychologist, 49,* 417–427.

Fossey, D. (1981). Imperiled giants of the forest. *National Geographic, 159,* 501–523.

Fossey, D. (1983). *Gorillas in the mist.* Boston: Houghton-Mifflin.

Fowler, R. D. (1992). Report of the chief executive officer: A year of building for the future. *American Psychologist, 47,* 876–883.

Frame, C. L., & Strauss, C. C. (1987). Parental informed consent and sample bias in grade-school children. *Journal of Social and Clinical Psychology, 5,* 227–236.

Frank, M. G., & Gilovich, T. (1988). The dark side of self- and social perception: Black uniforms and aggression in professional sports. *Journal of Personality and Social Psychology, 54,* 74–85.

Frick, R. W. (1995). Accepting the null hypothesis. *Memory & Cognition, 23,* 132–138.

Friedman, M. P., & Wilson, R. W. (1975). Application of unobtrusive measures to the study of textbook usage by college students. *Journal of Applied Psychology, 60,* 659–662.

Gallup, G., Jr. (1988). *The Gallup poll: Public opinion 1987.* Wilmington, DE: Scholarly Resources.

Gannon, L., Luchetta, T., Rhodes, K., Pardie, L., & Segrist, D. (1992). Sex bias in psychological research. *American Psychologist, 47,* 389–396.

Geller, E. S., Russ, N. W., & Altomari, M. G. (1986). Naturalistic observations of beer drinking among college students. *Journal of Applied Behavior Analysis, 19,* 391–396.

Goldstein, R. S., Minkin, B. L., Minkin, N., & Baer, D. M. (1978). Finders, keepers?: An analysis and validation of a free-found-ad policy. *Journal of Applied Behavior Analysis, 11,* 465–473.

Goleman, D. (1981, January). The new competency tests: Matching the right people to the right jobs. *Psychology Today,* pp. 35–46.

Goodall, J. (1987). A plea for the chimpanzees. *American Scientist, 75,* 574–577.

Graham, S. (1992). "Most of the subjects were White and middle class": Trends in published research on African Americans in selected APA journals, 1970–1989. *American Psychologist, 47,* 629–639.

Grammer, K., Schiefenhovel, W., Schleidt, M., Lorenz, B., & Eibl-Eibesfeldt, I. (1988). Patterns on the face: The eyebrow flash in crosscultural comparison. *Ethology, 77,* 279–299.

Gray, J. N., & Melton, G. B. (1985). The law and ethics of psychosocial research on AIDS. *Nebraska Law Review, 64,* 637–688.

Griffin, J. H. (1960). *Black like me.* New York: New American Library.

Grisso, T., Baldwin, E., Blanck, P. D., Rotheram-Borus, M. J., Schooler, N. R., & Thompson, T. (1991). Standards in research: APA's mechanisms for monitoring the challenges. *American Psychologist, 46,* 758–766.

Guerin, B. (1986). Mere presence effects in humans: A review. *Journal of Experimental Social Psychology, 22,* 38–77.

Haber, L. R., & Haber, R. N. (1982). Does silent reading involve articulation? Evidence from tongue twisters. *American Journal of Psychology, 95,* 409–419.

Halpern, A. R., & Bower, G. H. (1982). Musical expertise and melodic structure in memory for musical notation. *American Journal of Psychology, 95,* 31–50.

Harlow, H. F., & Harlow, M. K. (1966). Learning to love. *American Scientist, 54,* 244–272.

Hart, B., & Risley, T. R. (1995). *Meaningful differences in the everyday experience of young American children.* Baltimore: Paul H. Brookes.

Hartup, W. W. (1974). Aggression in childhood: Development perspectives. *American Psychologist, 29,* 336–341.

Hass, R. G., Katz, I., Rizzo, N., Bailey, J., & Eisenstadt, D. (1991). Cross-racial appraisal as related to attitude ambivalence and cognitive complexity. *Personality and Social Psychology Bulletin, 17,* 83–92.

Hays, R. (1980). Honesty requiring a self-initiated response. *Psychological Reports, 46,* 87–90.

Heath, L., & Davidson, L. (1988). Dealing with the threat of rape: Reactance or learned helplessness? *Journal of Applied Social Psychology, 18,* 1334–1351.

Hersen, M., & Barlow, D. H. (1976). *Single-case experimental designs: Strategies for studying behavior change.* New York: Pergamon Press.

Hinrichs, J. V., & Novick, L. R. (1982). Memory for numbers: Nominal vs. magnitude information. *Memory & Cognition, 10,* 479–486.

Hirschberg, N., & Itkin, S. (1978). Graduate student success in psychology. *American Psychologist, 33,* 1083–1093.

Hite, S. (1987). *Women and love: A cultural revolution in progress.* New York: Knopf.

Holden, C. (1987). Animal regulations: So far, so good. *Science, 238,* 880–882.

Holsti, O. R. (1969). *Content analysis for the social sciences.* Reading, MA: Addison-Wesley.

Hops, J., Biglan, A., Sherman, L., Arthur, J., Friedman, L., & Osteen, V. (1987). Home observations of family interactions of depressed women. *Journal of Consulting and Clinical Psychology, 55,* 341–346.

Horn, W. F., & Heerboth, J. (1982). Single-case experimental designs and program evaluation. *Evaluation Review, 6,* 403–424.

Horton, S. V. (1987). Reduction of disruptive mealtime behavior by facial screening. *Behavior Modification, 11,* 53–64.

Hughes, H. M., & Haynes, S. N. (1978). Structured laboratory observation in the behavioral assessment of parent-child interactions: A methodological critique. *Behavior Therapy, 9,* 428–447.

Huse, E. F., & Bowditch, J. L. (1977). *Behavior in organizations: A systems approach to managing* (2nd ed.). Reading, MA: Addison-Wesley.

Jackson, J. M., Buglione, S. A., & Glenwick, D. S. (1988). Major league baseball performance as a function of being traded: A drive theory analysis. *Personality and Social Psychology Bulletin, 14,* 46–56.

Jenni, D. A., & Jenni, M. A. (1976). Carrying behavior in humans: Analysis of sex differences. *Science, 194,* 859–860.

Jenni, M. A. (1976). Sex differences in carrying behavior. *Perceptual and Motor Skills, 43,* 323–330.

Jessor, R., Chase, J. A., & Donovan, J. E. (1980). Psychosocial correlates of marijuana use and problem drinking in a national sample of adolescents. *American Journal of Public Health, 70,* 604–613.

Johnson, D. (1990). Animal rights and human lives: Time for scientists to right the balance. *Psychological Science, 1,* 213–214.

Joswick, K. E. (1994). Getting the most from PsycLIT: Recommendations for searching. *Teaching of Psychology, 21,* 49–53.

Judd, C. M., Smith, E. R., & Kidder, L. H. (1991). *Research methods in social relations* (6th ed.). Fort Worth, TX: Holt, Rinehart and Winston.

Kagan, J., Reznick, J. S., & Snidman, N. (1988). Biological bases of childhood shyness. *Science, 240,* 167–171.

Kahneman, D., Fredrickson, B. L., Schreiber, C. A., & Redelmeier, D. A. (1993). When more pain is preferred to less: Adding a better end. *Psychological Science, 4,* 401–405.

Kahneman, D., & Tversky, A. (1973). On the psychology of prediction. *Psychological Review, 80,* 237–251.

Kardas, E. P., & Milford, T. M. (1996). *Using the Internet for social science research and practice.* Belmont, CA: Wadsworth.

Kazdin, A. E. (1977). Assessing the clinical or applied significance of behavior change through social validation. *Behavior Modification, 1,* 427–452.

Kazdin, A. E. (1978). Methodological and interpretive problems of single-case experimental designs. *Journal of Consulting and Clinical Psychology, 46,* 629–642.

Kazdin, A. E. (1980a). *Behavior modification in applied settings* (rev. ed.). Homewood, IL: Dorsey Press.

Kazdin, A. E. (1980b). *Research design in clinical psychology.* New York: Harper & Row.

Kazdin, A. E. (1982). Single-case experimental designs. In P. C. Kendall & J. N. Butcher (Eds.), *Handbook of research methods in clinical psychology* (pp. 416–490). New York: Wiley.

Kazdin, A. E., & Erickson, L. M. (1975). Developing responsiveness to instructions in severely and profoundly retarded residents. *Journal of Behavior Therapy and Experimental Psychiatry, 6,* 17–21.

Keith, T. Z., Reimers, T. M., Fehrmann, P. G., Pottebaum, S. M., & Aubrey, L. W. (1986). Parental involvement, homework, and TV time: Direct and indirect effects on high school achievement. *Journal of Educational Psychology, 78,* 373–380.

Keith-Spiegel, P., & Koocher, G. P. (1985). *Ethics in psychology: Professional standards and cases.* New York: Random House.

Keller, F. S. (1937). *The definition of psychology.* New York: Appleton-Century-Crofts.

Kelley-Milburn, D., & Milburn, M. A. (1995). Cyberpsych: Resources for psychologists on the Internet. *Psychological Science, 6,* 203–211.

Kelly, J. A. (1986). Psychological research and the rights of animals: Disagreement with Miller. *American Psychologist, 41,* 839–841.

Kelman, H. C. (1967). Human use of human subjects: The problem of deception in social psychological experiments. *Psychological Bulletin, 67,* 1–11.

Kelman, H. C. (1972). The rights of the subject in social research: An analysis in terms of relative power and legitimacy. *American Psychologist, 27,* 989–1016.

Kenny, D. A. (1979). *Correlation and causality.* New York: Wiley.

Keppel, G. (1991). *Design and analysis: A researcher's handbook* (3rd ed.). Englewood Cliffs, NJ: Prentice Hall.

Kiesler, S., Walsh, J., & Sproull, L. (1992). Computer networks in field research. In F. B. Bryant, J. Edwards, F. S. Tindale, E. J. Posavac, L. Heath, E. Henderson, & Y. Suarez-Balcazar (Eds.), *Methodological issues in applied social psychology: Vol. 2. Social psychological applications to social issues* (pp. 239–267). New York: Plenum.

Kimble, G. A. (1989). Psychology from the standpoint of a generalist. *American Psychologist, 44,* 491–499.

Kirkham, G. L. (1975). Doc cop. *Human Behavior, 4,* 16–23.

Kirmeyer, S. L., & Biggers, K. (1988). Environmental demand and demand engendering behavior: An observational analysis of the Type A pattern. *Journal of Personality and Social Psychology, 54,* 997–1005.

Kirsch, I. (1978). Teaching clients to be their own therapists: A case-study illustration. *Psychotherapy: Theory, Research and Practice, 15,* 302–305.

Klemmack, S. H., & Klemmack, D. L. (1976). The social definition of rape. In M. J. Walker & S. L. Brodsky (Eds.), *Sexual assault.* Lexington, MA: Lexington Books.

Krantz, D. S. (1979). A naturalistic study of social influences on meal size among moderately obese and nonobese subjects. *Psychosomatic Medicine, 41,* 19–26.

Kratochwill, T. R., & Brody, G. H. (1978). Single subject designs: A perspective on the controversy over employing statistical inference and implications for research and training in behavioral modification. *Behavior Modification, 2,* 291–307.

Kratochwill, T. R., & Levin, J. R. (Eds.). (1992). *Single-case research design and analysis.* Hillsdale, NJ: Erlbaum.

Kratochwill, T. R., & Martens, B. K. (1994). Applied behavior analysis and school psychology. *Journal of Applied Behavior Analysis, 27,* 3–5.

LaFrance, M., & Mayo, C. (1976). Racial differences in gaze behavior during conversations: Two systematic observational studies. *Journal of Personality and Social Psychology, 33,* 547–552.

Lakatos, I. (1978). *The methodology of scientific research.* London: Cambridge University Press.

Landers, S. (1987a, September). CARE urges protection for animals and labs. . . . *APA Monitor,* pp. 28–29.

Landers, S. (1987b, December). Lab checks: Rigid or reciprocal? *APA Monitor,* pp. 6–7.

Landers, S. (1988, September). Adolescent study presents dilemma. *APA Monitor,* p. 6.

Langer, E. J. (1989). *Mindfulness.* Reading, MA: Addison-Wesley.

Langer, E. J., & Piper, A. I. (1987). The prevention of mindlessness. *Journal of Personality and Social Psychology, 53,* 280–287.

Lander, E. J., & Rodin, J. (1976). The effects of choice and enhanced personal responsibility for the aged: A field experiment in an institutional setting. *Journal of Personality and Social Psychology, 34,* 191–198.

Larose, S., & Roy, R. (1995). Test of reactions and adaptation in college (TRAC): A new measure of learning propensity for college students. *Journal of Educational Psychology, 87,* 293–306.

Latané, B., & Darley, J. M. (1970). *The unresponsive bystander: Why doesn't he help?* New York: Appleton-Century-Crofts.

Latané, B., Williams, K., & Harkin, S. (1979). Many hands make light the work: The causes and consequences of social loafing. *Journal of Personality and Social Psychology, 37,* 822–832.

Lau, R. R., & Russell, D. (1980). Attributions in the sports pages. *Journal of Personality and Social Psychology, 39,* 29–38.

Lenneberg, E. H. (1967). *Biological foundations of language.* New York: Wiley.

Lepore, S. J., & Sesco, B. (1994). Distorting children's reports and interpretations of events through suggestion. *Journal of Applied Psychology, 79,* 108–120.

Levine, R. V. (1990). The pace of life. *American Scientist, 78,* 450–459.

Levine, R. V., West, L. J., & Reis, H. T. (1980). Perceptions of time and punctuality in the United States and Brazil. *Journal of Personality and Social Psychology, 38,* 541–550.

Lichtenstein, S., Slovic, P., Fischhoff, B., Layman, M., & Combs, J. (1978). Judged frequency of lethal events. *Journal of Experimental Psychology: Human Learning and Memory, 4,* 551–578.

Linton, M. (1978). Real world memory after six years: An *in vivo* study of very long term memory. In M. M. Gruneberg, P. E. Morris, & R. N. Sykes (Eds.), *Practical aspects of memory* (pp. 69–76). New York: Academic Press.

Locke, T. P., Johnson, G. M., Kirigin-Ramp, K., Atwater, J. D., & Gerrard, M. (1986). An evaluation of a juvenile education program in a state penitentiary. *Evaluation Review, 10,* 281–298.

Loftus, E. F. (1979a). *Eyewitness testimony.* Cambridge, MA: Harvard University Press.

Loftus, E. F. (1979b). The malleability of human memory. *American Scientist, 67,* 312–320.

Loftus, E. F. (1993). The reality of repressed memories. *American Psychologist, 48,* 518–537.

Loftus, E. F., & Burns, T. E. (1982). Mental shock can produce retrograde amnesia. *Memory & Cognition, 10,* 318–323.

Loftus, G. R. (1993). A picture is worth a thousand *p* values: On the irrelevance of hypothesis testing in the microcomputer age. *Behavior Research Methods, Instruments, & Computers, 25,* 250–256.

Lovaas, O. I. (1993). The development of a treatment-research project for developmentally disabled and autistic children. *Journal of Applied Behavior Analysis, 26,* 617–630.

Lovaas, O. I., Newsom, C., & Hickman, C. (1987). Self-stimulatory behavior and perceptual reinforcement. *Journal of Applied Behavior Analysis, 20,* 45–68.

Lovaas, O. I., Schaeffer, B., & Simmons, J. Q. (1965). Building social behaviors in autistic children by use of electric shock. *Journal of Research in Personality, 1,* 99–109.

Lubin, B., Zuckerman, M., Breytspraak, L. M., Bull, N. C., Gumbhir, A. K., & Rinck, C. M. (1988). Affects, demographic variables, and health. *Journal of Clinical Psychology, 44,* 131–141.

Lyons, C. A., & Ghezzi, P. M. (1995). Wagering on a large scale: Relationships between public gambling and game manipulations in two state·lotteries. *Journal of Applied Behavior Analysis, 28,* 127–137.

Madigan, C. M. (1995, March 19). Hearing it right: Small turnout spoke. *Chicago Tribune,* pp. 1–2.

Maki, J. E., Hoffman, D. M., & Berk, R. A. (1978). A time series analysis of the impact of a water conservation campaign. *Evaluation Quarterly, 2,* 107–118.

Marx, M. H. (1963). The general nature of theory construction. In M. H. Marx (Ed.), *Theories in contemporary psychology* (pp. 4–46). New York: Macmillan.

Maser, J. D., & Seligman, M. E. P. (Eds.). (1977). *Psychopathology: Experimental models.* San Francisco: Freeman.

May, C. P., Hasher, L., & Stoltzfus, E. R. (1993). Optimal time of day and magnitude of age differences in memory. *Psychological Science, 4,* 326–330.

McCain, L. J., & McCleary, R. (1979). The statistical analysis of the simple interrupted time-series quasi-experiment. In T. D. Cook & D. T. Campbell (Eds.), *Quasi-Experimentation: Design & analysis issues for field settings* (pp. 233–293). Chicago: Rand McNally.

McCloskey, M., Wible, C. G., & Cohen, N. J. (1988). Is there a special flashbulb-memory mechanism? *Journal of Experimental Psychology: General, 117,* 171–181.

McGaugh, J. L. (1990, September). Happy birthday APA. *APS Observer,* p. 2.

McGrew, W. C. (1972). *An ethological study of children's behavior.* New York: Academic Press.

McKinney, J. D., Mason, J., Perkerson, K., & Clifford, M. (1975). Relationship between classroom behavior and academic achievement. *Journal of Educational Psychology, 67,* 198–203.

McSweeney, A. J. (1978). Effects of response cost on the behavior of a million persons: Charging for directory assistance in Cincinnati. *Journal of Applied Behavior Analysis, 11,* 47–51.

Meehl, P. E. (1954). *Clinical versus statistical prediction: A theoretical analysis and review of the literature.* Minneapolis: University of Minnesota Press.

Meehl, P. E. (1978). Theoretical risks and tabular asterisks: Sir Karl, Sir Ronald, and the slow progress of soft psychology. *Journal of Consulting and Clinical Psychology, 46,* 806–834.

Meehl, P. E. (1990a). Appraising and amending theories: The strategy of Lakatosian defense and two principles that warrant it. *Psychological Inquiry, 1,* 108–141.

Meehl, P. E. (1990b). Why summaries of research on psychological theories are often uninterpretable [Monograph Supplement 1-V66]. *Psychological Reports, 66,* 195–244.

Meehl, P. E. (1993). Philosophy of science: Help or hindrance? *Psychological Reports, 72,* 707–733.

Melton, G. B., & Gray, J. N. (1988). Ethical dilemmas in AIDS research: Individual privacy and public health. *American Psychologist, 43,* 60–64.

Melton, G. B., Levine, R. J., Koocher, G. P., Rosenthal, R., & Thompson, W. C. (1988). Community consultation in socially sensitive research. *American Psychologist, 43,* 573–581.

Merritt, C. B., & Fowler, R. G. (1948). The pecuniary honesty of the public at large. *Journal of Abnormal and Social Psychology, 43,* 90–93.

Miles, M. B., & Huberman, A. M. (1994). *Qualitative data analysis* (2nd ed.). Thousands Oaks, CA: Sage.

Milgram, S. (1974). *Obedience to authority.* New York: Harper & Row.

Milgram, S. (1977). Subject reaction: The neglected factor in the ethics of experimentation. *Hastings Center Report,* October.

Milgram, S., Liberty, H. J., Toledo, R., & Wackenhut, J. (1986). Response to intrusion into waiting lines. *Journal of Personality and Social Psychology, 51,* 683–689.

Miller, J. D. (1986, May). *Some new measures of scientific illiteracy.* Paper presented at the meeting of the American Association for the Advancement of Science, Philadelphia.

Miller, N. E. (1985). The value of behavioral research on animals. *American Psychologist, 40,* 423–440.

Miller, T. Q., Heath, L., Molcan, J. R., & Dugoni, B. L. (1991). Imitative violence in the real world: A reanalysis of homicide rates following championship prize fights. *Aggressive Behavior, 17,* 121–134.

Mook, D. G. (1983). In defense of external invalidity. *American Psychologist, 38,* 379–387.

Mooney, L. A., & Brabant, S. (1987). Deviance, deference, and demeanor: Birthday cards as ceremonial tokens. *Deviant Behavior, 8,* 377–388.

Moore, B. R., & Stuttard, S. (1979). Dr. Guthrie and *Felis domesticus* or: Tripping over the cat. *Science, 205,* 1031–1033.

Morier, D., & Keeports, D. (1994). Normal science and the paranormal: The effect of a scientific method course on students' beliefs. *Research in Higher Education, 35,* 443–453.

Myers, D. G., & Diener, E. (1995). Who is happy? *Psychological Science, 6,* 10–19.

Newcomb, T. M., Koenig, K. E., Flacks, R., & Warwick, D. P. (1967). *Persistence and change: Bennington College and its students after twenty-five years.* New York: Wiley.

New town blues: HUD abandons a disaster. (1978, October 16). *Time,* p. 84.

Novak, M. A. (1991, July). 'Psychologists care deeply' about animals. *APA Monitor,* p. 4.

Oppenheim, A. N. (1966). *Questionnaire design and attitude measurement.* New York: Basic Books.

Orne, M. T. (1962). On the social psychology of the psychological experiment: With particular reference to demand characteristics and their implications. *American Psychologist, 17,* 776–783.

Osgood, C. E., & Walker, E. G. (1959). Motivation and language behavior: A content analysis of suicide notes. *Journal of Abnormal and Social Psychology, 59,* 58–67.

Palladino, J. J., Carsrud, A. L., Hulicka, I. M., & Benjamin, L. T., Jr. (1982). Undergraduate research in psychology: Assessment and directions. *Teaching of Psychology, 9,* 71–74.

Parry, H. J., & Crossley, H. M. (1950). Validity of responses to survey questions. *Public Opinion Quarterly, 14,* 61–80.

Parsons, H. M. (1974). What happened at Hawthorne? *Science, 183,* 922–932.

Parsonson, B. S., & Baer, D. M. (1992). The visual analysis of data, and current research into the stimuli controlling it. In T. R. Kratochwill & J. R. Levin (Eds.), *Single-case research design and analysis* (pp. 15–40). Hillside, NJ: Erlbaum.

Patton, J. E., Routh, D. K., & Stinard, T. A. (1986). Where do children study? Behavioral observations. *Bulletin of the Psychonomic Society, 24*, 439–440.

Peterson, J. (1995). How are psychologists perceived by the public? *APA Monitor.*

Phillips, D. P. (1977). Motor vehicle fatalities increase just after publicized suicide stories. *Science, 196*, 1464–1465.

Phillips, D. P. (1978). Airplane accident fatalities increase just after newspaper stories about murder and suicide. *Science, 201*, 748–750.

Phillips, D. P. (1983). The impact of mass media violence on U.S. homicides. *American Sociological Review, 48*, 560–568.

Phillips, D. P., & Bollen, K. A. (1985). Same time, last year: Selective data dredging for negative findings. *American Sociological Review, 50*, 364–371.

Piaget, J. (1965). *The child's conception of number.* New York: Norton.

Pillemer, D. B. (1990). Clarifying the flashbulb memory concept: Comment on McCloskey, Wible, & Cohen (1988). *Journal of Experimental Psychology: General, 119*, 92–96.

Pingitore, R., Dugoni, B. L., Tindale, R. S., & Spring, B. (1994). Bias against overweight job applicants in a simulated employment interview. *Journal of Applied Psychology, 79*, 909–917.

Pishkin, V., & Shurley, J. T. (1983). Electrophysiological parameters in anxiety and failure: Evaluation of doxepin and hydroxyzine. *Bulletin of the Psychonomic Society, 21*, 21–23.

Pitman, R. K., Kolb, B., Orr, S. P., deJong, J., Yadati, S., & Singh, M. M. (1987). On the utility of ethological data in psychiatric research: The example of facial behavior in schizophrenia. *Ethology and Sociobiology, 8*, 111S–116S.

Popper, K. R. (1959). *The logic of scientific discovery.* New York: Basic Books.

Popper, K. R. (1976). *Unended quest.* Glasgow: Fontana/Collins.

Posavac, E. J., & Carey, R. G. (1997). *Program evaluation* (5th ed.). Englewood Cliffs, NJ: Prentice Hall.

Posner, M. I. (1973). *Cognition: An introduction.* Glenview, IL: Scott, Foresman.

Poulton, E. C. (1973). Unwanted range effects from using within-subject experimental designs. *Psychological Bulletin, 80*, 113–121.

Poulton, E. C. (1975). Range effects in experiments on people. *American Journal of Psychology, 88*, 3–32.

Poulton, E. C. (1982). Influential companions. Effects of one strategy on another in the within-subjects designs of cognitive psychology. *Psychological Bulletin, 91*, 673–690.

Poulton, E. C., & Freeman, P. R. (1966). Unwanted asymmetrical transfer effects with balanced experimental designs. *Psychological Bulletin, 66*, 1–8.

Powell, D. H., & Whitla, D. K. (1994). Normal cognitive aging: Toward empirical perspectives. *Current Directions in Psychological Science, 3*, 27–31.

Powell-Cope, G. M. (1995). The experience of gay couples affected by HIV infection. *Qualitative Health Research, 5*, 36–62.

Rachels, J. (1986). *The elements of moral philosophy.* New York: McGraw-Hill.

Reynolds, G. S. (1968). *A primer of operant conditioning.* Glenview, IL: Scott, Foresman.

Richardson, D. R., Pegalis, L., & Britton, B. (1992). A technique for enhancing the value of research participation. *Contemporary Social Psychology, 16*, 11–13.

Riddoch, M. J., & Humphreys, G. W. (1992). The smiling giraffe: An illustration of a visual memory disorder. In R. Campbell (Ed.), *Mental lives: Case studies in cognition* (pp. 161–177). Oxford: Blackwell.

Riley, D. A. (1962). Memory for form. In L. Postman (Ed.), *Psychology in the making* (pp. 402–465). New York: Knopf.

Rimm, D. C., & Masters, J. C. (1979). *Behavior therapy: Techniques and empirical findings* (2nd ed.). New York: Academic Press.

Rodman, J. L., & Burger, J. M. (1985). The influence of depression on the attribution of responsibility for an accident. *Cgnitive Therapy and Research, 9,* 651–657.

Roethlisberger, F. J. (1977). *The elusive phenomena: An autobiographical account of my work in the field of organized behavior at the Harvard Business School.* Cambridge, MA: Division of Research, Graduate School of Business Administration (distributed by Harvard University Press).

Rollin, B. E. (1985). The moral status of research animals in psychology. *American Psychologist, 40,* 920–926.

Rosenfeld, A. (1981). Animal rights vs. human health. *Science, 81,* 18, 22.

Rosenhan, D. L. (1973). On being sane in insane places. *Science, 179,* 250–258.

Rosenthal, R. (1963). On the social psychology of the psychological experiment: The experimenter's hypothesis as unintended determinant of experimental results. *American Scientist, 51,* 268–283.

Rosenthal, R. (1966). *Experimenter effects in behavioral research.* New York: Appleton-Century-Crofts.

Rosenthal, R. (1976). *Experimenter effects in behavioral research.* (Enlarged ed.). New York: Irvington.

Rosenthal, R. (1994a). Interpersonal expectancy effects: A 30-year perspective. *Current Directions in Psychological Science, 3,* 176–179.

Rosenthal, R. (1994b). Science and ethics in conducting, analyzing, and reporting psychological research. *Psychological Science, 5,* 127–134.

Rosnow, R. L., & Rosenthal, R. (1995). "Some things you learn aren't so": Cohen's paradox, Asch's paradigm, and the interpretation of interaction. *Psychological Science, 6,* 3–9.

Ross, A. S., & White, S. (1987). Shoplifting, impaired driving, and refusing the breathalyzer: On seeing one's name in a public place. *Evaluation Review, 11,* 254–260.

Rotter, J. B. (1966). Generalized expectancies for internal versus external control of reinforcement. *Psychological Monographs, 80* (1, Whole No. 609), 1–28.

Rymer, R. (1993). *Genie: A scientific tragedy.* New York: HarperCollins.

Sackheim, H. A., Gur, R. C., & Saucy, M. C. (1978). Emotions are expressed more intensely on the left side of the face. *Science, 202,* 434–436.

Sacks, O. (1985). *The man who mistook his wife for a hat and other clinical tales.* New York: Harper & Row.

Sacks, O. (1995). *An anthropologist on Mars.* New York: Knopf.

Salomon, G. (1987). Basic and applied research in psychology: Reciprocity between two worlds. *International Journal of Psychology, 22,* 441–446.

Satterfield, J. M., & Seligman, M. E. P. (1994). Military aggression and risk predicted by explanatory style. *Psychological science, 5,* 77–82.

Schaller, G. B. (1963). *The mountain gorilla.* Chicago: University of Chicago Press.

Schlosberg, H. (1965). Hints on presenting a paper at an APA convention. *American Psychologist, 20,* 606–607.

Schnelle, J. F., Kirchner, R. E., Macrae, J. W., McNees, M. P., Eck, R. H., Snodgrass, S., Casey, J. D., & Uselton, P. H., Jr. (1978). Police evaluation research: An experimental and cost-benefit analysis of a helicopter patrol in a high-crime area. *Journal of Applied Behavior Analysis, 11,* 11–21.

Schoeneman, T. J., & Rubanowitz, D. E. (1985). Attributions in the advice columns: Actors and observers, causes and reasons. *Personality and Social Psychology Bulletin, 11,* 315–325.

Schulman, P., Castellon, C., & Seligman, M. E. P. (1989). Assessing explanatory style: The content analysis of verbatim explanations and the Attributional Style Questionnaire. *Behavioral Research and Therapy, 27,* 505–512.

Schulz, R., & Bazerman, M. (1980). Ceremonial occasions and mortality: A second look. *American Psychologist, 35,* 253–261.

Schuman, H., & Bobo, L. (1988). Survey-based experiments on white racial attitudes toward residential integration. *American Journal of Sociology, 94,* 273–299.

Schuman, H., Presser, S., & Ludwig, J. (1981). Context effects of survey responses to questions about abortion. *Public Opinion Quarterly, 45,* 216–223.

Schuman, H., & Scott, J. (1987). Problems in the use of survey questions to measure public opinion. *Science, 236,* 957–959.

Scoville, W. B., & Milner, B. (1957). Loss of recent memory after bilateral hippocampal lesions. *Journal of Neurology, Neurosurgery, and Psychiatry, 20,* 11–19.

Seligman, M. E. P. (1988, August). *Why is there so much depression today? The waxing of the individual and the waning of the commons.* The G. Stanley Hall Lecture presented at the American Psychological Association, Atlanta.

Shapiro, K. J. (1991, July). Use mortality as basis for animal treatment. *APA Monitor,* p. 5.

Sharma, S., & Moskowitz, H. (1972). Effect of marijuana on the visual autokinetic phenomenon. *Perceptual and Motor Skills, 35,* 891–894.

Shattuck, R. (1994). *The forbidden experiment: The story of the Wild Boy of Averyon.* New York: Kodansha.

Simon, H. A. (1992). What is an "explanation" of behavior? *Psychological Science, 3,* 150–161.

Singer, B., & Benassi, V. A. (1981). Occult beliefs. *American Scientist, 69,* 49–55.

Singer, M. (1982). Comparing memory for natural and laboratory reading. *Journal of Experimental Psychology: General, 111,* 331–347.

Singer, P. (1990). The significance of animal suffering. *Behavioral and Brain Sciences, 13,* 9–12.

Skinner, B. F. (1937). Two types of conditioned reflex: A reply to Konorski and Miller. *Journal of General Psychology, 16,* 272–279.

Skinner, B. F. (1966). Operant behavior. In W. K. Honig (Ed.), *Operant behavior: Areas of research and application* (pp. 12–32). New York: Appleton-Century-Crofts.

Smith, P. K., & Lewis, K. (1985). Rough-and-tumble play, fighting, and chasing in nursery school children. *Ethology and Sociobiology, 6,* 175–181.

Smith, R. J. (1977). Electroshock experiment at Albany violates ethics guidelines. *Science, 198,* 383–386.

Smith, T. W. (1981). Qualifications to generalized absolutes: "Approval of hitting" questions on the GSS. *Public Opinion Quarterly, 45,* 224–230.

Sommer, R. (1968). Hawthorne dogma. *Psychological Bulletin, 70,* 592–595.

Spitz, R. A. (1965). *The first year of life.* New York: International Universities Press.

Squire, L. R., Knowlton, B., & Musen, G. (1993). The structure and organization of memory. *Annual Review of Psychology, 44,* 453–495.

Stern, G. S., McCants, T. R., & Pettine, P. W. (1982). Stress and illness: Controllable and uncontrollable life events' relative contributions. *Personality and Social Psychology Bulletin, 8,* 140–145.

Sternberg, R. J. (1986). A triangular theory of love. *Psychological Review, 93,* 119–135.

Strauss, A., & Corbin, J. (1990). *Basics of qualitative research.* Newbury Park, CA: Sage.

Sun, M. (1981). Laetrile brush fire is out, scientists hope. *Science, 212,* 758–759.

Tedeschi, J. T., Lindskold, S., & Rosenfeld, P. (1985). *Introduction to social psychology.* St. Paul, MN: West.

Thomas, L. (1992). *The fragile species.* New York: Charles Scribner's Sons.

Thompson, T. L. (1982). Gaze toward and avoidance of the handicapped: A field experiment. *Journal of Nonverbal Behavior, 6,* 188–196.

Tversky, A., & Kahneman, D. (1971). Belief in the law of small numbers. *Psychological Bulletin, 76,* 105–110.

Tversky, A., & Kahneman, D. (1974). Judgment under uncertainty: Heuristics and biases. *Science, 185,* 1124–1131.

Ulrich, R. E. (1991). Animal rights, animal wrongs and the question of balance. *Psychological Science, 2,* 197–201.

Ulrich, R. E. (1992). Animal research: A reflective analysis. *Psychological Science, 3,* 384–386.

Underwood, B. J. (1957). *Psychological research.* New York: Appleton-Century-Crofts.

Underwood, B. J. (1975). Individual differences as a crucible in theory construction. *American Psychologist, 30,* 128–134.

Underwood, B. J., & Shaughnessy, J. J. (1975). *Experimentation in psychology.* New York: Wiley: Robert E. Krieger, 1983.

VanBiervliet, A., Spangler, P. F., & Marshall, A. M. (1981). An ecobehavioral examination of a simple strategy for increasing mealtime language in residential facilities. *Journal of Applied Behavior Analysis, 14,* 295–305.

Van Meter, P., Yokoi, L., & Pressley, M. (1994). College students' theory of note-taking derived from their perceptions of note-taking. *Journal of Educational Psychology, 86,* 323–338.

Van Nuys, D. (1975). On the phrasing of hypnotic suggestions: A brief case report. *Psychotherapy: Theory, Research and Practice, 12,* 302–304.

Wallraff, H. G., & Sinsch, U. (1988). The role of "outward-journey information" in homing experiments with pigeons: New data on ontogeny of navigation and general survey. *Ethology, 77,* 10–27.

Ward, W. D., & Jenkins, H. M. (1965). The display of information and the judgment of contingency. *Canadian Journal of Psychology, 19,* 231–241.

Warwick, D. P., & Lininger, C. A. (1975). *The sample survey: Theory and practice.* New York: McGraw-Hill.

Watson, J. B. (1913). Psychology as the behaviorist views it. *Psychological Review, 20,* 158–177.

Watson, J. B. (1967). *Behavior: An introduction to comparative psychology.* New York: Holt, Rinehart and Winston. (Original work published 1914)

Webb, E. J., Campbell, D. T., Schwartz, R. D., Sechrest, L., & Grove, J. B. (1981). *Non-reactive measures in the social sciences* (2nd ed.). Boston: Houghton-Mifflin.

Weigel, R. H., Loomis, J. W., & Soja, M. J. (1980). Race relations on prime time television. *Journal of Personality and Social Psychology, 39,* 884–893.

Weiss, J. M. (1977). Psychological and behavioral influences on gastrointestinal lesions in animal models. In J. D. Maser and M. E. P. Seligman (Eds.), *Psychopathology: Experimental models* (pp. 232–269). San Francisco: Freeman.

Willems, E. P. (1969). Planning a rationale for naturalistic research. In E. P. Willems & H. L. Raush (Eds.), *Naturalistic viewpoints in psychological research* (pp. 44–71). New York: Holt, Rinehart and Winston.

Willems, E. P., & Raush, H. L. (Eds.). (1969). *Naturalistic viewpoints in psychological research*. New York: Holt, Rinehart and Winston.

Williams, K. D., Harkin, S., & Latané, B. (1981). Identifiability as a deterrent to social loafing: Two cheering experiments. *Journal of Personality and Social Psychology, 40,* 303–311.

Willingham, W. W. (1974). Predicting success in graduate education. *Science, 183,* 273–278.

Wilson, G. T. (1978). On the much discussed nature of the term "behavior therapy." *Behavior Therapy, 9,* 89–98.

Winer, B. J., Brown, D. R., & Michels, K. M. (1991). *Statistical principles in experimental design* (3rd ed.). New York: McGraw-Hill.

Yeaton, W. H., & Sechrest, L. (1981). Critical dimensions in the choice and maintenance of successful treatments: Strength, integrity, and effectiveness. *Journal of Consulting and Clinical Psychology, 49,* 156–167.

Yeaton, W. H., & Sechrest, L. (986). Use and misuse of no-difference findings in eliminating threats to validity. *Evaluation Review, 10,* 836–852.

Zechmeister, E. B., & Johnson, J. E. (1992). *Critical thinking: A functional approach.* Pacific Grove, CA: Brooks/Cole.

Zechmeister, E. B., & Nyberg, S. E. (1982). *Human memory: An introduction to research and theory.* Pacific Grove, CA: Brooks/Cole.

Acknowledgments

CHAPTER 1

Page 5. Photo courtesy of The Bettman Archive and Culver Pictures. Figure 1.1. Photos courtesy of the Research Center for Language and Semiotic Studies, Indiana University, Bloomington. Figure 1.2. Photo by Emil Posavac. Figure 1.3. From R. V. Levine, "The pace of life." *American Scientist* (1990), *78*, 450–459. Figure 3, page 453. Copyright 1990 by Sigma Xi, The Scientific Research Society, Inc. Used with permission of the publisher and author. Figure 1.4. Photo courtesy of UPI/Corbis-Bettmann. Used with permission.

CHAPTER 2

Figure 2.1. Photos by Eugene B. Zechmeister and John J. Shaughnessy. Special thanks go to Erica, Linda, and Hilary Bryant; Earron Henderson and members of his social psychology class; Candy Baguilat, Lynda Cafasso, and Peter Bergquist for being willing subjects for these photos; we thank Bill Shofner for helping us obtain animal pictures. And let us not forget to identify John's dog, Emma. We also wish to acknowledge the cooperation of the Parmly Institute of Loyola University of Chicago as well as Rich Bowen for providing experimental settings for some of these photos. Ethical principles 6.06–6.26 of the American Psychological Association, "Ethical principles of psychologists and code of conduct," *American Psychologist* (1992), *47*, 1597–1611. Copyright 1992 by the American Psychological Association. Reprinted by permission of the publisher. Neither the original nor this reproduction can be republished, photocopied,

lisher and author. Table 5.2. Adapted from material in R. M. Brandt, *Studying behavior in natural settings* (1972). New York: Holt, Rinehart & Winston. (Republished 1981 by University Press of America, Washington, D.C.). Pages 203–206. Used by permission of author. Figure 5.4. From C. A. Anderson, "Temperature and aggression: Ubiquitous effects of heat on occurrence of human violence." *Psychological Bulletin* (1989), *106*, 74–96. Adapted from: Figure 2, page 83; Figure 3, page 85. Copyright 1989 by the American Psychological Association. Reprinted with permission of publisher and author.

CHAPTER 6

Table 6.4. From R. Rosenthal, "Interpersonal expectancy effects: A 30-year perspective." *Current Directions in Psychological Science* (1994), *3*, 176–179. Adapted from Table 1, p. 177. Used with permission of author and publisher. Figure 6.1. Photo by Jonathan Hoffman, from D. G. Myers, *Social psychology* (1990). New York: McGraw-Hill. Used with permission of the publisher and photographer. Figure 6.2. From Loftus, E. F., & Burns, T. E., "Mental shock can produce retrograde amnesia." *Memory & Cognition* (1982), *10*, 318–323. Figure 1, page 319. Copyright 1982 by the Psychonomic Society, Inc. Used with permission of publisher and author. Figure 6.3. Photo by Jeanne S. Zechmeister. We wish to thank members of Jeanne S. Zechmeister's Spring 1996 research methods in psychology class for permission. Figure 6.4. From G. R. Loftus, "A picture is worth a thousand *p* values: On the irrelevance of hypothesis testing in the microcomputer age." *Behavior Research Methods, Instruments, & Computers* (1993), *25*, 250–256. Adapted from Figure 1, page 251. Copyright 1993 by the Psychonomic Society, Inc. Used with permission of the publisher and author.

CHAPTER 7

Figure 7.1. Reprinted with permission from H. A. Sackheim, R. C. Gur, and M. C. Saucy, *Science* (1978), *202*, 434–436. Figure 1, page 434. Copyright 1978 American Association for the Advancement of Science.

CHAPTER 8

Table 8.1. From R. G. Haas, I. Katz, N. Rizzo, J. Bailey, and D. Eisenstadt, "Cross-racial appraisal as related to attitude ambivalence and cognitive complexity." *Personality and Social Psychology Bulletin* (1991), *17*, 83–92. Based on Table 1, page 86. Copyright 1991 by Sage Publications, Inc. Adapted by permission of the publisher and author. Figure 8.5. From J. V. Hinrichs and L. R. Novick, "Memory for numbers: Nominal versus magnitude information." *Memory & Cognition* (1982), *10*, 479–486. Figure 1, page 484. Copyright 1982 by the Psychonomic Society. Reprinted by permission of publisher and author. Figure 8.6. Original drawing by Fran Hughes. Table 8.6 and Figure 8.8. From M. L. Dittmar, D. B. Berch, and J. S. Warm, "Sustained visual attention in deaf and hearing adults." *Bulletin of the Psychonomic Society* (1982), *19*, 339–342. Figure 1, page 341. Copy-

CHAPTER 9

CHAPTER 10

APPENDIX A

Computer-generated analyses and output shown on computer Screens A.1 through A.7 used with permission of SYSTAT, Inc. Permission to use statistical tables in Appendix A is acknowledged with tables in Appendix A.

APPENDIX B

Table B.3. Questionnaire used in a survey conducted by researchers at the Institute for Social Research (ISR), University of Michigan. Reprinted by permission of Willard Rodgers, ISR, Ann Arbor, MI 48106, and Sage Publications, Inc. Table B.4. Questionnaire given to authors, who were passengers on Amtrak's Chicago–St. Louis train, by representatives of the Illinois Department of Transportation.

APPENDIX C

Extensive quotations from *Publication Manual of the American Psychological Association*, 4th ed. (1994). Washington, DC. Copyright 1994 by the American Psychological Association. Reprinted by permission of the publisher. Neither the original nor this reproduction can be republished, photocopied, reprinted, or distributed in any form without the prior written permission of the APA.

Name Index

Subject Index